Dictionary of
Media Studies

Specialist dictionaries

Dictionary of Accounting	0 7475 6991 6
Dictionary of Aviation	0 7475 7219 4
Dictionary of Banking and Finance	0 7136 7739 2
Dictionary of Business	0 7475 6980 0
Dictionary of Computing	0 7475 6622 4
Dictionary of Economics	0 7475 6632 1
Dictionary of Environment and Ecology	0 7475 7201 1
Dictionary of Human Resources and Personnel Management	0 7475 6623 2
Dictionary of ICT	0 7475 6990 8
Dictionary of Information and Library Management	0 7136 7591 8
Dictionary of Law	0 7475 6636 4
Dictionary of Leisure, Travel and Tourism	0 7475 7222 4
Dictionary of Marketing	0 7475 6621 6
Dictionary of Medical Terms	0 7136 7603 5
Dictionary of Military Terms	0 7475 7477 4
Dictionary of Nursing	0 7475 6634 8
Dictionary of Politics and Government	0 7475 7220 8
Dictionary of Science and Technology	0 7475 6620 8

Easier English™ titles

Easier English Basic Dictionary	0 7475 6644 5
Easier English Basic Synonyms	0 7475 6979 7
Easier English Dictionary: Handy Pocket Edition	0 7475 6625 9
Easier English Intermediate Dictionary	0 7475 6989 4
Easier English Student Dictionary	0 7475 6624 0
English Thesaurus for Students	1 9016 5931 3

Check Your English Vocabulary workbooks

Academic English	0 7475 6691 7
Business	0 7475 6626 7
Computing	1 9016 5928 3
Human Resources	0 7475 6997 5
Law	0 7136 7592 6
Leisure, Travel and Tourism	0 7475 6996 7
FCE +	0 7475 6981 9
IELTS	0 7136 7604 3
PET	0 7475 6627 5
TOEFL®	0 7475 6984 3
TOEIC	0 7136 7508 X

Visit our website for full details of all our books: **www.acblack.com**

Dictionary of
Media Studies

A & C Black • London

www.acblack.com

First published in Great Britain in 2006

A & C Black Publishers Ltd
38 Soho Square, London W1D 3HB

A CIP record for this book is available from the British Library

ISBN-10: 0 7136 7593 4
ISBN-13: 978 0 7136 7593 1

1 3 5 7 9 8 6 4 2

Text Production and Proofreading
Sandra Anderson, Heather Bateman, Emma Harris, Katy McAdam

A & C Black uses paper produced with elemental chlorine-free pulp,
harvested from managed sustainable forests.

Text typeset by A & C Black
Printed in Italy by Legoprint

Preface

This dictionary provides a basic vocabulary of terms used in the media and entertainment industries. It is ideal for all students of Media Studies and related subjects, as well as those working for the first time in jobs such as journalism, radio and television production and advertising.

Each headword is explained in clear, straightforward English and quotations from newspapers and specialist magazines show how the words are used in context. There are also supplements including an overview of media law, details of major national publications and a list of media resources on the Web.

Thanks are due to Andrea Esser for her help and advice during the production of this book.

Pronunciation Guide

The following symbols have been used to show the pronunciation of the main words in the dictionary.

Stress is indicated by a main stress mark (') and a secondary stress mark (,). Note that these are only guides, as the stress of the word changes according to its position in the sentence.

Vowels		*Consonants*	
æ	back	b	buck
ɑː	harm	d	dead
ɒ	stop	ð	other
aɪ	type	dʒ	jump
aʊ	how	f	fare
aɪə	hire	g	gold
aʊə	hour	h	head
ɔː	course	j	yellow
ɔɪ	annoy	k	cab
e	head	l	leave
eə	fair	m	mix
eɪ	make	n	nil
eʊ	go	ŋ	sing
ɜː	word	p	print
iː	keep	r	rest
i	happy	s	save
ə	about	ʃ	shop
ɪ	fit	t	take
ɪə	near	tʃ	change
u	annual	θ	theft
uː	pool	v	value
ʊ	book	w	work
ʊə	tour	x	loch
ʌ	shut	ʒ	measure
		z	zone

A

A *abbreviation* **amp**

A&R /ˌeɪ ənd ˈɑː/ *noun* the section of a record company that tries to find new acts, works out contracts and copyright issues and generally protects their artists' interests. Full form **Artists and Repertoire**

AB /ˌeɪ ˈbiː/ *noun* the highest socioeconomic group, consisting of professionals with a high disposable income

abbreviate /əˈbriːvieɪt/ *verb* to make a piece of text shorter

ABC *abbreviation* **1.** Audit Bureau of Circulation **2.** Australian Broadcasting Corporation

AB deadline /ˌeɪ ˈbiː ˌdedlaɪn/ *abbreviation* **advance booking deadline**

aberrant decoding /æˌberənt diˈkəʊdɪŋ/ *noun* an understanding of a media product by an audience which is not the one intended by its maker

aberrant reading /æˌberənt ˈriːdɪŋ/ *noun* an interpretation of a text which was not the meaning which was intended when the text was written

aberration /ˌæbəˈreɪʃ(ə)n/ *noun* distortion of a television picture caused by a corrupt signal or incorrect adjustment

abjection /ˈæbdʒekʃ(ə)n/ *noun* the condition of, for example, a minority group, that has been cast out or expelled

above-the-fold /əˌbʌv ðə ˈfəʊld/ *adjective* **1.** E-COMMERCE referring to the most valuable area of a webpage which appears at the top of the screen so that the user does not have to scroll down to see it **2.** referring to the position of an important story or photograph on the front page of a newspaper so that it is visible when the newspaper is folded

above-the-line advertising /əˌbʌv ðə laɪn ˈædvətaɪzɪŋ/ *noun* advertising for which commission is paid to the advertising agency, for example an advertisement in a magazine or a stand at a trade fair

above-the-title /əˌbʌv ðə ˈtaɪt(ə)l/ *adjective* CINEMA relating to the credits that appear before the title of a film, listing the names of the starring actors, the directors and the producers

abridge /əˈbrɪdʒ/ *verb* to make a text shorter by reducing detail or cutting sections out

AB roll /ˌeɪ ˈbiː ˌrəʊl/ *noun* a sequence of two video or music segments that are synchronised so that one fades as the second starts

absolute cost /ˌæbsəluːt ˈkɒst/ *noun* the actual cost of placing an advertisement in a magazine or other advertising medium

absolute time /ˈæbsəluːt taɪm/ *noun* the length of time that an audio disc has been playing

abstract data type /ˌæbstrækt ˈdeɪtə ˌtaɪp/ *noun* a general data type that can store any kind of information

Academy Award /əˌkædəmi əˈwɔːd/ *noun* an award that the Academy of Motion Picture Arts and Sciences in the United States gives to particularly outstanding actors and many other workers in the film industry each year. Also called **Oscar**

acceleration factor /əkˌseləˈreɪʃ(ə)n ˌfæktə/ *noun* the idea that increased efficiency in communication and transport links speeds up the exchange of information, which has an immediate impact on the media

accent /ˈæksənt/ *noun* the way in which a language is pronounced, which is characteristic of a whole region, social group or other community

access /'ækses/ *noun* the ability of the public to question the actions and motives of major media companies. ◊ **right of reply**

access controller /'ækses kən,trəʊlə/ *noun* an electronic device that transfers image data to a video controller

accessed voices /,æksesd 'vɔɪsɪz/ *plural noun* those people in a society who are given exposure by the media, for example celebrities, politicians and experts in various fields, whose views are not necessarily representative of the views of society as a whole

access head /'ækses hed/ *noun* the part of a disk drive that moves to a particular part of the disk's surface and reads information stored on the disk

access number /'ækses ,nʌmbə/ *noun* ONLINE the telephone number that a computer uses to establish a dial-up connection to an Internet service provider or other network provider

accessory shoe /ək'sesəri ʃuː/ *noun* PHOTOGRAPHY a bracket on a camera to which an accessory such as a flash unit may be fitted

access panel /'ækses ,pæn(ə)l/ *noun* a group of people that allows their television watching habits to be monitored for research purposes. Also called **panel**

access provider /'ækses prə,vaɪdə/ *noun* same as **Internet service provider**

access television /,ækses 'telɪvɪʒ(ə)n/ *noun* television which is free of state control and broadcast independently, usually on a small budget and within a particular area

account /ə'kaʊnt/ *noun* an area of business such as design or publicity, that one company handles on behalf of another

account director /ə'kaʊnt daɪ,rektə/ *noun* a person who works in an advertising agency and who oversees various account managers who are each responsible for specific clients

account executive /ə'kaʊnt ɪg,zekjʊtɪv/ *noun* an employee, especially in an advertising or public relations company, who handles all of a client's business

account handler /ə'kaʊnt ,hændlə/, **account manager** /ə'kaʊnt ,mænɪdʒə/ *noun* a person who works in an advertising agency, and who is responsible for a particular client

acid house /,æsɪd 'haʊs/ *noun* electronic disco music that was popular in the late 1980s, and is associated with the use of the drug ecstasy

acid jazz /'æsɪd dʒæz/ *noun* a mixture of funk, jazz, and soul music that was developed in the 1980s

acid rock /,æsɪd 'rɒk/ *noun* a type of rock music that was popular in the late 1960s, with weird electronic instrumental effects suggestive of psychedelic experiences

ACORN /'eɪkɔːn/ *noun* MARKETING a classification of residential areas into categories, based on the type of people who live in them, the type of houses, etc., much used in consumer research. Full form **a classification of residential neighbourhoods**

acoustic /ə'kuːstɪk/ *adjective* **1.** referring to sound **2.** referring to a musical instrument or musical performance which is not amplified

acoustic coupler /ə,kuːstɪk 'kʌplə/ *noun* a device that connects to a telephone handset, converting binary computer data into sound signals to allow it to be transmitted down a telephone line

acoustic panel /ə,kuːstɪk 'pæn(ə)l/ *noun* a soundproof panel placed behind a device to reduce noise

acoustic rock /ə'kuːstɪk rɒk/ *noun* rock music that is mainly played on instruments without electronic amplification

acoustics /ə'kuːstɪks/ *noun* the study of sound and sound recording

acquiescent /,ækwi'es(ə)nt/ *noun* in advertising audience classifications, a person who has an easy-going attitude to advertising and is more likely to be impressed by adverts which are funny, clever or eye-catching. ◊ **ambivalent**, **cynic**, **enthusiast**

acquisition /,ækwɪ'zɪʃ(ə)n/ *noun* **1.** the accepting, capturing or collecting of information **2.** the act of or acquiring new customers for a company, brand or product, one possible aim of an advertising campaign. Compare **retention**

Acrobat /'ækrəʊbæt/ ♦ **Adobe Acrobat**

action /'ækʃən/ *interjection* the command a film director uses to tell actors to begin acting as filming begins ■ *noun, adjective* a genre of film featuring action sequences such as natural disasters, violence and acts of heroism

action code /'ækʃən kəʊd/ *noun* one of five codes used in the analysis of texts, describing events in a narrative. ◊ **enigma code**, **referential code**, **semantic code**, **symbolic code**

actioner /'ækʃənə/ *noun* a film that particularly features a large number of action sequences

ActionMedia /ˌækʃən'miːdiə/ a trade name for a digital video system developed by Intel that uses its i750 video processor chip to allow a computer to record, play back and manipulate digital video

action replay /ˌækʃən 'riːpleɪ/ *noun* the repeat of a brief part of a filmed event such as a sports match, often in slow motion

action shot /'ækʃən ʃɒt/ *noun* a scene with movement either in a film or on TV

active audience /ˌæktɪv 'ɔːdiəns/ *noun* the audience for a media product, seen not as accepting a product as it is presented to them, but as interpreting, interacting with and using it for their own agenda. ◊ **uses and gratifications theory**

active listening /ˌæktɪv 'lɪs(ə)nɪŋ/ *noun* the act of listening with the attitude of wanting to understand the speaker's point of view, thinking that it is worth considering. Compare **deliberative listening**

active participation /'æktɪv pɑːˌtɪsɪ'peɪʃ(ə)n/ the way in which media intrusion can influence the stories which they are supposed to be reporting impartially

active pixel region /ˌæktɪv 'pɪks(ə)l ˌriːdʒən/ *noun* an area of a computer screen that can display graphic image information

active video /ˌæktɪv 'vɪdiəʊ/, **active video signal** /ˌæktɪv 'vɪdiəʊ ˌsɪgn(ə)l/ *noun* a part of a video signal that contains picture information

actor /'æktə/ *noun* a person who acts in plays, films or television

ACTT /ˌeɪ siː tiː 'tiː/ *noun* formerly, the trade union representing workers in the film and television industries. Full form **Association of Cinematograph and Television Technicians**. ◊ **BECTU**

actuality /ˌæktʃu'ælɪti/ *noun* live or recorded sound of an event on location as it actually happens

ad /æd/ *abbreviation* **advertisement**

ADA *abbreviation* **audio distribution amplifier**

adaptive control model /əˌdæptɪv kən'trəʊl ˌmɒd(ə)l/ *noun* a model for planning advertising expenditure which takes into account changes in consumer responses to advertising

adaptor /ə'dæptə/ a device which converts a single plug socket into two, three or four sockets

add /æd/ *noun* additional material in the form of new paragraphs which updates or expands on an existing article

added value /ˌædɪd 'væljuː/ *noun*, *adjective* any extra promotion that a publication can offer its advertisers, such as press events, supplements or special sections ■ *noun* extra promotional items that are offered with publications as an enticement to buy, such as free gifts or offers

addendum /ə'dendəm/ *noun* an extra section of a book or magazine, such as an appendix

additive printing /'ædɪtɪv ˌprɪntɪŋ/ *noun* PHOTOGRAPHY a printing process in which all other colours are produced by mixing the three primary colours

addressee /ˌædre'siː/ *noun* in human interaction, the person who is receiving a piece of communication or at whom it is aimed. Compare **addresser**

addresser /ə'dresə/ *noun* in human interaction, the person who is trying to communicate with somebody. Compare **addressee**

ad impression /'æd ɪmˌpreʃ(ə)n/ *noun* the number of times an advertisement is downloaded from a webpage and assumed to have been seen by a potential customer. Also called **ad view**

adjacency /ə'dʒeɪs(ə)nsi/ *noun* a commercial which is run between two TV programmes

ad lib /'æd lɪb/ *noun* improvised speech ■ *verb* to improvise a speech

AdLib™ /'ædlɪb/ *noun* a type of sound card for a PC with basic sound playback and MIDI functions

adman /'ædmæn/ *noun* a man whose job is in advertising

admass /ˈædmæs/ *noun* MARKETING the part of society that advertising is aimed at

Adobe Acrobat /əˌdəʊbi ˈækrəbæt/ a trade name for a piece of software that converts documents and formatted pages into a file format that can be viewed on almost any computer platform or using a web browser on the Internet

adperson /ˈædˌpɜːsən/ *noun* a person whose job is in advertising

ADR *abbreviation* **Automatic Dialogue Replacement**

ADR editor /ˌeɪ diː ˈɑː ˌedɪtə/ *noun* in film and television production, the crew member who has responsibility for dubbing re-recorded sound (ADR) onto filmed pieces

adshel /ˈædʃel/ *noun* advertising space that is often illuminated and holds large posters in bus shelters

adspeak /ˈædspiːk/ *noun* jargon used in the advertising trade

'You obviously wouldn't bring in Stone to do a table-top (adspeak for static, studio-based commercial with endless close-ups of food products).' [Belinda Archer, *The Guardian*]

adspend /ˈædspend/ *noun* the amount of money that is spent on advertising a particular product

adult-oriented rock /ˌædʌlt ˌɔːrientɪd ˈrɒk/ *noun* classic rock music which appeals to an older audience. Abbreviation **AOR**

advance /ədˈvɑːns/ *noun* a statement offered in advance to the media, giving them time to cover it while it is still relevant news

advance booking deadline /əd ˌvɑːns ˌbʊkɪŋ ˈdedlaɪn/ *noun* the date by which an advertiser must book a particular media slot in order to guarantee the best rates and quality. Abbreviation **AB deadline**

advertise /ˈædvətaɪz/ *verb* to present information to the public, such as information about a product or service that is available

advertisement /ədˈvɜːtɪsmənt/, **advert** /ˈædvɜːt/ *noun* the public promotion of a product or service, in forms such as posters, short television or radio broadcasts and announcements in the press. Abbreviation **ad**

advertisement panel /ədˈvɜːtɪsmənt ˌpæn(ə)l/ *noun* a specially designed large advertising space in a newspaper

advertiser-financed programming /ˌædvətaɪzə ˌfaɪnænsd ˈprəʊɡræmɪŋ/ *noun* programmes whose making costs are paid by individual sponsors, rather than out of a larger budget for all programmes paid for by advertising, a licence fee or subscription. Abbreviation **AFP**

advertising /ˈædvətaɪzɪŋ/ *noun* the public promotion of something such as a product, service, business, or event in order to attract or increase interest in it

COMMENT: Advertising is a multi-billion pound industry worldwide and advertisers are forced to come up with new and innovative ways of catching the public eye. Techniques range from conventional television and radio slots, inserts in magazines and newspapers, maildrops and posters to less usual methods such as promotional weblog entries and e-mail spam, as well as product placement and subliminal advertising techniques.

advertising agency /ˈædvətaɪzɪŋ ˌeɪdʒənsi/ *noun* a company which creates advertising campaigns for products, from the advertisement concept and storyboard to its filming and production and finally its placement

advertising appropriation /ˈædvətaɪzɪŋ əˌprəʊprieɪʃ(ə)n/ *noun* money set aside by an organisation for its advertising

advertising boycotts /ˈædvətaɪzɪŋ ˌbɔɪkɒts/ the practice of advertising companies influencing media coverage by threatening to take their business elsewhere unless the newspaper publishes a particular story in their interests, or abandons one that they would prefer not to be published

advertising brief /ˈædvətaɪzɪŋ briːf/ *noun* basic objectives and instructions concerning an advertising campaign, given by an advertiser to an advertising agency

advertising budget /ˈædvətaɪzɪŋ ˌbʌdʒɪt/ *noun* money planned for spending on advertising

advertising campaign /ˈædvətaɪzɪŋ kæmˌpeɪn/ *noun* a coordinated publicity or advertising drive to sell a product

advertising control /'ædvətaɪzɪŋ kən,trəʊl/ *noun* legislative and other measures to prevent abuses in advertising

advertising department /'ædvətaɪzɪŋ dɪ,paːtmənt/ *noun* the department in a company that deals with the company's advertising

advertising expenditure /'ædvətaɪzɪŋ ɪk,spendɪtʃə/ *noun* the amount a company spends on its advertising

advertising hoarding /'ædvətaɪzɪŋ ,hɔːdɪŋ/ *noun* a billboard or wooden surface onto which advertising posters are stuck

advertising impression /'ædvətaɪzɪŋ ɪm,preʃ(ə)n/ *noun* the total number of times that an advertisement of any type reaches a person, including duplications. Also called **gross audience**. Compare **net audience**

advertising jingle /'ædvətaɪzɪŋ ,dʒɪŋg(ə)l/ *noun* a short and easily remembered tune or song used to advertise a product on television or the radio

advertising manager /'ædvətaɪzɪŋ ,mænɪdʒə/ *noun* the manager in charge of advertising a company's products

advertising medium /'ædvətaɪzɪŋ ,miːdiəm/ *noun* a type of advertisement such as a TV commercial

advertising rates /'ædvətaɪzɪŋ reɪts/ *noun* the amount of money charged for advertising space in a newspaper or advertising time on TV

advertising sales /'ædvətaɪzɪŋ seɪlz/ *noun* the work of selling advertising space in the media

advertising space /'ædvətaɪzɪŋ speɪs/ *noun* any available 'slot' in a media product, for example part of a newspaper page, 30 seconds of radio time, a banner on a webpage etc, which can be sold to companies for placing an advertisement

advertising specialities /,ædvətaɪzɪŋ ,speʃi'ælətiz/ *plural noun* special items given away as part of an advertising campaign, such as T-shirts, mugs or umbrellas

Advertising Standards Authority /,ædvətaɪzɪŋ 'stændədz ɔː,θɒrəti/ *noun* the body which regulates marketing and advertising in non-broadcast media, to make sure that it is 'legal, decent, honest and truthful'. Abbreviation **ASA**

advertising time /'ædvətaɪzɪŋ taɪm/ *noun* the time on television or radio set aside for advertising

'Clear Channel said the results reflected its strategy of cutting advertising time on radio stations to improve its product.' [Aline van Duyn, *The Financial Times*]

advertising weight /'ædvətaɪzɪŋ weɪt/ *noun* **1.** the amount of advertising given to a brand **2.** the amount of advertising of all types used in a particular campaign

advertorial /,ædvɜː'tɔːriəl/ *noun* a piece of text in a newspaper or magazine which is advertising a product or service

advice column /əd'vaɪs ,kɒləm/ *noun* the section of a newspaper or magazine where advice is given to readers who have sent in questions or problems

ad view /'æd vjuː/ *noun* same as **ad impression**

advocacy advertising /'ædvəkəsi ,ædvətaɪzɪŋ/ *noun* advertising by a business that expresses a particular point of view on an issue

advocacy journalism /'ædvəkəsi ,dʒɜːn(ə)lɪz(ə)m/ *noun* a type of journalism which seems neutral, but which in fact presents the facts in a persuasive way towards one point of view

adwoman /'ædwʊmən/ *noun* a woman whose job is in advertising

AE *abbreviation* **auto exposure**

aerial /'eəriəl/ *noun* a part of a radio or television system, often in the form of a metallic rod or wire, that transmits or receives radio waves. An aerial is attached to a radio or TV to improve the reception.

aerial advertising /,eəriəl 'ædvətaɪzɪŋ/ *noun* advertising displayed in the air from balloons or planes or in smoke designs

aerial perspective /,eəriəl pə'spektɪv/ *noun* ART the technique of making objects appear more distant by painting them less sharply and brightly

aerial shot /'eəriəl ʃɒt/ *noun* a shot taken from an extremely high angle, above the action. Also called **bird's-eye view**

aesthetic /iːs'θetɪk/ *noun* beauty, form, composition, as opposed to content

'…stylish sofas that compete with top end Conran in terms both of finger-on-the-pulse aesthetic and price...' [Victoria Stanley, *The Sunday Times*]

COMMENT: The adjective aesthetic means 'pleasing to the eye, exciting or arousing the senses', and refers to the guiding principles by which we judge that something is beautiful or striking.

aesthetics /i:s'θetɪks/ *noun* the study, pursuit and evaluation of beauty

aesthetic theory /i:,sθetɪk 'θɪəri/ *noun* a philosophical discipline in which art and media texts and products are evaluated in terms of their aesthetic qualities

AF *abbreviation* 1. PHOTOGRAPHY **autofocus** 2. **average frequency**

affective behaviour /ə'fektɪv bɪ,heɪvjə/ *noun* the category of human behaviour associated with feeling, believing and holding attitudes. Compare **cognitive behaviour**

affiliate /ə'fɪlieɪt/ *noun* a local TV station which is part of a national network

affiliate marketing /ə'fɪliət ,mɑːkɪtɪŋ/ *noun* the practice of marketing products for companies that pay to have their goods or services advertised on a centralised website

affiliate partner /ə'fɪliət ,pɑːtnə/ *noun* a company that puts advertising onto its website for other companies, who pay for this service

affiliate programme /ə'fɪliət ,prəʊgræm/ *noun* a form of advertising on the Internet, in which a business persuades other businesses to put banners and buttons advertising its products or services on their websites and pays them a commission on any purchases made by their customers

affordable method /ə'fɔːdəb(ə)l ,meθəd/ *noun* a method of budgeting how much can be spent on marketing and promotion, which is based on what you can afford, rather than what you want to achieve

AFM *abbreviation* **assistant floor manager**

AFP *abbreviation* **advertiser-financed programming**

Afropop /'æfrəʊpɒp/ *noun* contemporary music from Africa and African communities elsewhere in the world

afterpiece /'ɑːftəpiːs/ *noun* a short dramatic entertainment, usually comic, that follows the performance of a play

AFTRA /'æftrə/ *abbreviation* BROADCAST **American Federation of Television and Radio Artists**

agate line /'ægət laɪn/ *noun* a measure of publishing space on a page, for example in classified advertising, one column that is 1.8mm deep

ageism /'eɪdʒɪz(ə)m/ *noun* the highlighting of differences between older and younger people, especially when this leads to discrimination or prejudice

'The IT sector has a youthful image... however, the sector has a reputation for ageism and is often perceived as dealing unkindly or unfairly with older workers.' [Peter Skyte, *Computer Weekly magazine*]

agency /'eɪdʒənsi/ *noun* 1. an organisation, especially a company, that performs a particular type of service for its clients 2. the fact or condition of doing something, of being active

agency commission /'eɪdʒənsi kə,mɪʃ(ə)n/ *noun* the fee charged by an advertising agency for its services

agency mark-up /,eɪdʒənsi 'mɑːk ʌp/ *noun* an amount of money added by an advertising agency to purchases, which forms parts of the agency's commission

agency roster /'eɪdʒənsi ,rɒstə/ *noun* a group of different advertising agencies all which work for a large company

agenda /ə'dʒendə/ *noun* 1. a list of items to be dealt with by somebody, according to priority 2. the idea of a list of items, such as news items or issues, that should be considered important

agenda-setting /ə'dʒendə ,setɪŋ/ *noun* the power of the media to decide which issues are covered and to define the way in which they are covered, their order of importance and so on

'The paper continues to build on its reputation for breaking agenda-setting stories, not least the exclusive revelation of the ministerial rule breach that led to the resignation of David Blunkett.' [*The Independent on Sunday*]

COMMENT: McCombs and Shaw describe agenda-setting as a process of allowing the public to decide what is important, from a finite list of issues which the media have told them are worth thinking about.

agent /'eɪdʒənt/ *noun* 1. somebody who officially represents somebody else in business, especially in arranging work in entertainment **2.** the means by which an effect or result is produced **3.** a computer program that works automatically on routine tasks such as sorting e-mail or gathering information

age profile /ˈeɪdʒ ˌprəʊfaɪl/ *noun* the audience a particular media product is targeted at, defined by age group, such as teenagers or over-60s

aggregator /ˈægrɪgeɪtə/ *noun* a website which collects syndicated news from other websites, often using RSS technology

agit-prop /ˈædʒɪt prɒp/ *noun* the practice of using the media to distribute propaganda

agony aunt /ˈægəni ɑːnt/ *noun* a woman who gives personal advice to readers, viewers or listeners, in a newspaper or magazine, or on a radio or television programme

agony column /ˈægəni ˌkɒləm/ *noun* **1.** the section of a newspaper or magazine where advice is given to readers who have written in about their personal problems **2.** a newspaper column containing personal messages and advertisements, usually relating to missing relatives or friends

agony uncle /ˈægəni ˌʌŋk(ə)l/ *noun* a man who gives personal advice to readers, viewers or listeners, in a newspaper or magazine, or on a radio or television programme

agora /ˈægərə/ *noun* a marketplace on the Internet

agreed doorstep /ə,griːd ˈdɔːstep/ *noun* an interview which appears to be a doorstep, but which has been agreed to beforehand by the interviewee. ◊ **doorstep**

Agreement on Trade-Related Aspects of Intellectual Property Rights *noun* full form of **TRIPS agreement**

AI *abbreviation* **Audience Appreciation Index**

AIDA model /ˈeɪdə ˌmɒd(ə)l/ *noun* a model for what should be provoked by an advertisement for a product in its preliminary stages, that is: Awareness, Interest, Desire and Action

aided recall /,eɪdɪd ˈriːkɔːl/ *noun* an advertising research test to see how well someone remembers an advertisement by giving the respondent some help such as a picture which he or she might associate with it. Compare **unprompted recall**

aid-to-trade /,eɪd tə ˈtreɪd/ *noun* a service, such as banking or advertising, that supports trade

air /eə/ *verb* to broadcast a radio or television programme or to be broadcast

AIR *abbreviation* **Average Issue Readership**

airbrush /ˈeəˌbrʌʃ/ *noun* **1.** ART a device that uses compressed air to force a fine spray of paint onto a surface **2.** a tool in graphics and design software which allows flaws to be removed from images ■ *verb* to modify pictures in order to remove flaws etc using a computer airbrush tool

airdate /ˈeədeɪt/ *noun* the date of a radio or television broadcast

airing /ˈeərɪŋ/ *noun* the occasion of a radio or television broadcast

airplay /ˈeəpleɪ/ *noun* an occasion when a recording of music is broadcast on the radio, or the number of times a recording is broadcast on the radio

air time /ˈeə taɪm/, **airtime** *noun* **1.** the amount of time given to a programme or subject in radio or television broadcasting **2.** the time at which an item is scheduled to be broadcast

airwaves /ˈeəweɪvz/ *plural noun* the radio waves used in broadcasting, often used to refer to radio and television broadcasting in general

A law /ˈeɪ lɔː/ *noun* a method of encoding digital audio data so that an 8-bit data word can contain a 13-bit audio sample

album /ˈælbəm/ *noun* **1.** a recording of music that is issued and marketed as a single product **2.** the sleeves for several gramophone records, bound together like a book

ALC *abbreviation* **automatic level control**

Aldis lamp /ˈældɪs ˌlæmp/ *noun* a portable lamp used to flash messages in Morse code

Alexandra Palace /,æleksɑːndrə ˈpæləs/ *noun* the studios from which the United Kingdom first broadcast television in 1936, remaining in use until 1955

alienation effect /,eɪliəˈneɪʃ(ə)n ɪ,fekt/ *noun* in Marxist theory, the practice of using alienating techniques such as unsettling and unnatural lighting effects, or music to force an audience to develop a critical attitude to what they are seeing

alignment /ə'laɪnmənt/ *noun* the positioning of text and headlines within columns on a page

Al-Jazeera /ˌæl dʒə'zɪərə/ *noun* a satellite TV channel that is based in Qatar and broadcasts in Arabic

COMMENT: Al-Jazeera came to public notice with coverage of Taliban-controlled areas in Afghanistan and has long been the subject of international controversy because of its willingness to broadcast such footage as the interview with Osama Bin Laden which defended the September 11th attacks on New York City. Many claim that this supports the views of terrorists and helps spread their message to a wider audience, but the network says that such footage is news and should be broadcast uncensored.

all-age personals /ˌɔːl 'pɜːsən(ə)lz/ *plural noun* advertisements placed with Internet dating agencies by people of all ages who are looking for a romantic relationship

allegory /'æləg(ə)ri/ *noun* a story that is a metaphor for another situation, often carrying a moral message

alliteration /əˌlɪtə'reɪʃ(ə)n/ *noun* a poetic or literary effect achieved by using several words that begin with the same or similar consonants. Compare **assonance**

allness attitude /'ɑːlnəs ˌætɪtjuːd/ *noun* the attitude that it is possible to know everything there is to know about a person or issue. This shapes perceptions and therefore makes communication more difficult.

Alpha /'ælfə/ *noun* COMMUNICATION an internationally recognised code word for the letter A, used in radio communications

alt /ɔːlt/ *noun* a type of newsgroup on the Internet that contains discussions about alternative subjects

alterity /ɔːl'terɪti/ *noun* in the theories of structuralism and discourse, the state in which a person recognises that he or she is uniquely different from other people

alternate media /ɔːlˌtɜːnət 'miːdiə/ *plural noun* forms of advertising such as TV commercials or magazine inserts, which are not direct mailing

alternate route /ɔːlˌtɜːnət 'ruːt/ *noun* a backup path in a communications system, used in case of a fault or breakdown

alternative comedy /ɔːlˌtɜːnətɪv 'kɒmədi/ *noun* the presentation of comedy material that is deliberately different in style and subject matter from mainstream comedy

'I have infinite respect for Eric Morecambe. He exuded comedy, but he was also such an innovator. He was deconstructing humour way before alternative comedy came along.' [Simon Pegg, interview by Robert Colville, *The Daily Telegraph*]

alternative media /ɔːlˌtɜːnətɪv 'miːdiə/ *plural noun* **1.** media forms such as pamphlets and graffiti, which are not mainstream, and which challenge traditional controls over what is made public **2.** any media form which is used to transmit non-mainstream messages or is subject to more liberal controls, regulations over content etc

COMMENT: Alternative media is often cited as a method of avoiding the dangers of mainstream news presentation, which is subject to outside pressures and bias. However, the quality of reporting is often less reliable due to a lack of strong financial backing.

alternative press /ɔːlˌtɜːnətɪv 'pres/ *noun* non-mainstream news publications such as those with radical political standpoints or a narrow focus, usually with a small circulation

alt rock /'ɔːlt rɒk/ *noun* rock music that is considered alternative because it is not by well-known performers or promoted by large record companies

always on /ˌɔːlweɪz 'ɒn/ *adjective* **1.** referring to a feature of high-speed broadband communications devices such as cable modems and ADSL that link a computer to the Internet so that the computer appears to be permanently connected and there is no need to dial up a special number **2.** describes a home or business with several computers and mobile phones, in which Internet access is not restricted to specific times

am, AM *abbreviation* RADIO **amplitude modulation**

ambient advertising /ˌæmbiənt 'ædvətaɪzɪŋ/ *noun* advertising such as posters on the side of a bus or in a public toilet, to which people are exposed during their everyday activities

ambient media /ˌæmbiənt ˈmiːdiə/ *plural noun* advertising media outdoors, such as posters and advertisements on the sides of buses

ambient noise /ˌæmbiənt ˈnɔɪz/ *noun* background noise such as traffic noise or birdsong

ambisonics /ˌæmbiˈsɒnɪks/ *noun* the technique of using several separate channels to record and then reproduce sounds so that they seem to completely surround the listener. ◊ **surround sound**

ambivalent /æmˈbɪvələnt/ *noun* in advertising audience classifications, a person who is neither interested in nor opposed to advertising, but passively accepts its influence. ◊ **acquiescent, cynic, enthusiast**

ambush interview /ˈæmbʊʃ ˌɪntəvjuː/ *noun* a line of questioning that surprises an interviewee, perhaps by introducing a topic which was known to be unwelcome or contentious

American dream /əˌmerɪkən ˈdriːm/ *noun* the belief that anybody can succeed in America, regardless of their social background

American Federation of Television and Radio Artists /əˌmerɪkən ˌfedəreɪʃ(ə)n əv ˌtelɪvɪʒ(ə)n ən ˈreɪdiəʊ/ *noun* a trade union in the USA representing more than 70,000 artists, performers, actors and broadcast journalists. Abbreviation **AFTRA**

Americanisation /əˌmerɪkənaɪˈzeɪʃ(ə)n/ *noun* the process of globalisation by which American cultural forms become more widespread and eventually supplant others

American Sign Language /əˌmerɪkən ˈsaɪn ˌlæŋgwɪdʒ/ *noun* a dialect of sign language used primarily in the US. Abbreviation **ASL**

America Online /əˌmerɪkə ɒnˈlaɪn/ *noun* a company that is the largest Internet service provider in the world. Abbreviation **AOL**

amp /æmp/ *noun* a measure of current flow. Abbreviation **A**

ampersand /ˈæmpəsænd/ *noun* a symbol (&) that means 'and'

amplifier /ˈæmplɪfaɪə/ *noun* **1.** a device that makes sounds louder, especially one which increases the sound level of musical instruments **2.** an electronic device that increases the magnitude of a signal, voltage or current

amplify /ˈæmplɪfaɪ/ *verb* **1.** to become louder, or make a sound become louder, by electronic or other means **2.** to increase the magnitude of a signal using an amplifier, or undergo such an increase

amplitude /ˈæmplɪtjuːd/ *noun* a measurement of radio waves, describing the distance of the waves upwards or downwards from the centre point. ◊ **frequency, wavelength**

amplitude modulation /ˈæmplɪtjuːd ˌmɒdjuleɪʃ(ə)n/ *noun* a method of transmitting audio or visual information using radio waves, where the frequency remains constant but the amplitude varies according to the input signal. Abbreviation **am, AM**. Compare **frequency modulation**

anaglyph /ˈænəglɪf/ *noun* PHOTOGRAPHY the visual effect created by superimposing two images of the same object, taken from slightly different angles and each of a different colour, often red and green. The image appears three-dimensional when viewed through spectacles with one red and one green lens.

analogue /ˈæn(ə)lɒg/ *noun, adjective* a form of transmission in which a signal is sent in one continuously-varying stream. Compare **digital**

analogue channel /ˈæn(ə)lɒg ˌtʃæn(ə)l/ *noun* a communications line that carries analogue signals such as speech

analogue line /ˈæn(ə)lɒg laɪn/ *noun* a communications line such as a telephone line, that carries analogue signals

analogue recording /ˌæn(ə)lɒg rɪˈkɔːdɪŋ/ *noun* non-digital recording using magnetic tape

analytic editing /ˌænəlɪtɪk ˈedɪtɪŋ/ *noun* a type of editing in which a sequence of images is constructed to follow an argument, rather than to explain a narrative

anamorphic /ˌænəˈmɔːfɪk/ *adjective* a picture which is anamorphic has been stretched or distorted by changing the aspect ratio inefficiently

anamorphic lens /ˌænəˈmɔːfɪk lenz/ *noun* a lens which distorts the image in a particular way

anarchist cinema /ˌænəkɪst ˈsɪnɪmə/ *noun* a type of film-making which juxtaposes images to express the view that life is unfair and unequal

anchor /'æŋkə/ *verb* to present a news programme ■ *noun* a presenter who reads the news and introduces news reports and interviews from reporters located outside the studio. Also called **anchorperson**

anchorage /'æŋkərɪdʒ/ *noun* the ability of a piece of accompanying text or sound to focus the message of an image so that it is interpreted in the way that was intended

anchorman /'æŋkəmæn/ *noun* a man who presents a news programme

anchorperson /'æŋkə,pɜːsən/ *noun* same as **anchor**

anchorwoman /'æŋkə,wʊmən/ *noun* a woman who presents a news programme

ancillary-to-trade /æn,sɪləri tə 'treɪd/ *noun* a service such as banking or advertising, which supports trade

Andersch, Staats and Bostrom's model of communication 1969 /,ændɜːʃ stæts ənd 'bɒstrəm/ *noun* a model which stresses the transactional nature of any communication, in which meanings are constructed and interpreted by both the sender and the receiver and are also subject to outside influences

androcentric /,ændrəʊ'sentrɪk/ *adjective* referring first to men and male perspectives

'Rich also commends the emerging field of Women's Studies for offering a "woman-directed education" that transforms curricula and develops critical thinking about androcentric scholarship and society.' [*NWSA journal*]

androgyny /æn'drɒdʒɪni/ *noun* in feminism, the theoretical condition of being both male and female

anecdote /'ænɪkdəʊt/ *noun* a small personal story which helps to illustrate and stir up human interest in a more general issue

anechoic chamber /,ænekəʊɪk 'tʃeɪmbə/ *noun* a perfectly quiet room in which sound or radio waves do not reflect off the walls

angle /'æŋgəl/ *noun* the main point of focus when covering a story, usually stressed in the headline or introducing paragraph. Also called **hook**

animate /'ænɪmeɪt/ *verb* to make a series of drawings which, when filmed, will create moving images. ◊ **animation**

animatic /,ænɪ'mætɪk/ *noun* same as **storyboard**

animation /,ænɪ'meɪʃ(ə)n/ *noun* a moving image created from still objects such as drawings or models that are exposed on film for a few frames at a time, then moved slightly. The process is then repeated many times until an entire sequence has been completed.

animation cell /,ænɪ'meɪʃ(ə)n ,sel/ *noun* a single picture or part of a picture on a transparent sheet which can be overlaid with other sheets and backgrounds, used to create animations

animator /'ænɪmeɪtə/ *noun* a person who is involved in making animated films

animatronics /,ænɪmə'trɒnɪks/ *plural noun* puppets, models and prosthetics which are controlled electronically or mechanically to create movement

anime /'ænɪmeɪ/ *noun* manga animation. ◊ **manga**

annals /'æn(ə)lz/ *plural noun* the records that are published of events and developments in a particular field

Annan Commission Report on Broadcasting 1977 *noun* a report on the future of the broadcasting industry, which made recommendations for reforms for when the licences of various media companies expired in 1979. A change of government from Labour to Conservative led to most of the recommendations, such as the setting up of new, independent authorities, being rejected.

announce /ə'naʊns/ *verb* **1.** to read the news headlines or introduce programmes on the television or radio **2.** to present something such as a television or radio show

announcement /ə'naʊnsmənt/ *noun* a formal notice, making public the news of a birth, wedding, or other event

announcer /ə'naʊnsə/ *noun* a person who reads news headlines or gives programme information on the television or radio

annual /'ænjuəl/ *noun* a book or magazine, especially one for children, that is published every year and focuses on a particular subject or area of interest

anomie /'ænəmi/ *noun* the state in which there are either insufficient social norms governing behaviour in a particular society or for a particular individual or far too many, which is therefore confusing. This state is blamed for social breakdown and general malaise, and is believed by some to make people more susceptible to the effects of mass media.

anonym /'ænənɪm/ *noun* a publication by an unnamed or unknown author

answer /'ɑːnsə/ *verb* to reply to a signal and set up a communications link

answer/originate /ˌɑːnsə əˈrɪdʒɪneɪt dɪˌvaɪs/, **answer/originate device** *noun* a communications device such as a modem, that can receive or send data

answerprint /'ɑːnsəprɪnt/ *noun* the first print of a filmed piece for show, which is sent from the laboratory and checked for final changes

antenna /æn'tenə/ *noun* same as **aerial**

anthology /æn'θɒlədʒi/ *noun* **1.** a book that is made up of essays, stories or poems by different writers **2.** a collection of works from different musicians or artists

anthropology /ˌænθrə'pɒlədʒi/ *noun* the study of the human species, focusing on its cultural, historical and social development. Compare **sociology**

COMMENT: The study of anthropology draws together such diverse areas as archaeology, biology, linguistics, psychology and many more, to create a conception of a society's culture and its 'sense of self'.

anti-aliasing /ˌænti 'eɪliəsɪŋ/ *noun* a method of 'smoothing' digital picture or sound signals, by removing the parts of the signal which are too high-frequency to be represented correctly on the available technology and which may therefore create interference

anticlimax /ˌænti'klaɪmæks/ *noun* a sudden or disappointing change from the serious to the trivial or from compelling to dull

anti-climax order /ˌænti 'klaɪmæks ˌɔːdə/ *noun* a method of arranging the arguments or main points in a narrative so the most important point is presented first. Compare **climax order**

antics /'æntɪks/ *noun* the outrageous behaviour required of an actor or performer playing an exaggerated comic role

antifeminist /ˌænti'femɪnɪst/ *adjective* referring to the conscious rejection of feminist principles ■ *noun* a person who is hostile to feminist principles

antihero /'æntihɪərəʊ/ *noun* the central character in a story who is not a traditionally brave or good hero

anti-language /'ænti ˌlæŋgwɪdʒ/ *noun* a new dialectal form of a language which has been developed and designed to exclude outsiders from a group

anti-realism /ˌænti 'rɪəlɪz(ə)m/ *noun* a method of presenting narrative in a film or novel in which no attempt is made to represent a realistic situation

'In the new novel, Rooke seems to have outdone himself in wild, complex anti-realism. The narrative is steeped in parody, caricature… surrealism and general comic bumptiousness.' [*The Toronto Star*]

antisexist /ˌænti'seksɪst/ *adjective* GENDER ISSUES referring to somebody or something that challenges all discrimination on the grounds of sex, most particularly that against women

Anti-Terrorism, Crime and Security Act 2001 *noun* an act of Parliament that introduced the new offence of inciting racial hatred using the media. Rules on privacy were also relaxed, making personal information more freely available to the authorities when investigating crimes. It was introduced after the New York attacks of September 11th, 2001.

anti-trust laws /ˌænti 'trʌst ˌlɔːz/ *plural noun* legislation designed to prevent large corporations forming a monopoly to the detriment of smaller enterprises, for example by price-fixing. Companies found guilty of this practice can be fined up to 10% of their annual sales under EU law. ◊ **price-fixing**

AOL *abbreviation* **America Online**

AOR *abbreviation* MUSIC **adult-oriented rock**

AP *abbreviation* **1. Associated Press 2. assistant producer**

apache silence /ə.pætʃi 'saɪləns/ *noun* the use of silence as a form of non-verbal communication in situations in which words are difficult to find, such as when a person has been bereaved

aperture /'æpətʃə/ *noun* the hole at the centre of a lens which admits light, measured in f-stops. It may be increased or decreased in size to alter the exposure of the film.

aperture card /'æpətʃə kɑːd/ *noun* a piece of card that surrounds and supports microfilmed pages so that they can be handled easily

aperture priority /'æpətʃə praɪˌɒrɪti/ *noun* PHOTOGRAPHY an exposure system where the photographer decides on the aperture of the lens and the appropriate shutter speed is set automatically by the camera

apocryphal /ə'pɒkrəf(ə)l/ *adjective* referring to information or stories of false or doubtful origin

'And though the story of the judge who said: "What are the Beatles?" appears to be apocryphal, there are plenty of other stories which back up the commonly held view that judges live in a well-appointed cloud cuckoo land.' [Jennifer Selway, *The Express*]

apology /ə'pɒlədʒi/ *noun* a written retraction of something which was printed but has later been found to be inaccurate or to have caused offence

aporia /æ'pɔːriə/ *noun* in the theories of structuralism and discourse, a state in which there is doubt or uncertainty about how to proceed with an argument

appeal /ə'piːl/ *noun* a short radio or television programme or a charity campaign asking for donations, usually for a particular cause

appendix /ə'pendɪks/ *noun* extra material that appears at the end of a book or document

Apple /'æp(ə)l/ a trade name for computer technology company which has developed, among other products, the Apple Macintosh personal computer and the iPod

Apple Macintosh /ˌæp(ə)l 'mækɪntɒʃ/ *noun* a user-friendly personal computer developed by Apple with the Mac OS X operating system. Also called **Mac**

appreciation data /əˌpriːʃi'eɪʃ(ə)n ˌdeɪtə/ *noun* details of a viewer's or listener's reactions to a broadcast, used alongside audience numbers

appreciation index /əˌpriːʃi'eɪʃ(ə)n ˌɪndeks/ *noun* a measure of how much a person has enjoyed a programme that they

have watched, recorded as a score from 1 to 10

aquatint /'ækwətɪnt/ *noun* PRINTING a technique of etching with acid on a copper plate in order to produce prints that resemble watercolours

arbitrary /'ɑːbɪtrəri/ *adjective* referring to something that is chosen or determined at random. Human language described as arbitrary because the words or sounds that denote objects do not reflect their features in any meaningful way, but have been chosen as a name for convenience. Onomatopoeic words such as 'buzz' are an exception to this. Compare **representative**

arbitrary signifier /ˌɑːbɪtrəri 'sɪɡnɪfaɪə/ *noun* in semiology, a sign or symbol which bears no direct relation to the thing it signifies or refers to. Compare **icon**

arc /ɑːk/ *noun* a type of powerful light used for filming ■ *verb* to change the size or shape of a picture using an aspect ratio converter

ARC *abbreviation* aspect ratio converter

archaeology /ˌɑːki'ɒlədʒi/ *noun* in cultural theory, the study of ideas and theories, their history and how they interrelate

archive /'ɑːkaɪv/ *noun* a store of old material such as newspaper articles or pieces of film that can be used again later if needed

archive material /'ɑːkaɪv məˌtɪəriəl/ *noun* film or footage which has been stored in an archive and can be reused at a later date

archive site /'ɑːkaɪv saɪt/ *noun* a computer on the Internet that provides a vast collection of public-domain files and programs copied from other computers around the Internet, that a user can download

Areopagitica /ˌæriəʊ'pæɡɪsɪtə/ *noun* the title of a pamphlet distributed by John Milton in 1644, which defended the freedom of the press and the sanctity of books

COMMENT: Milton wrote the Areopagitica in protest at the Licensing Act 1643, in which Parliament banned printing without a licence and set up committees to monitor and censor all publications. The Areopagitica was addressed to Parliament and was writing in the style of a speech, imitating the original Areopagitica which was written by the Athenian Isocrates in 355 BC.

A roll /'eɪ rəʊl/ *noun* the primary footage used in an edited sequence, mainly interviews or pictures which are directly relevant to the issue. Compare **B roll**

array /ə'reɪ/ *noun* TELECOMS the spacing or arrangement of aerials so that their effectiveness is maximised

Arri /'æri/ a trade name for a German-made type of film camera

Arriflex /'ærifleks/ a trade name for a German-made type of film camera

art director /'ɑːt daɪˌrektə/ *noun* **1.** a person who coordinates creative work in advertising **2.** a crew member in television, film and theatre production, who is responsible for overseeing the look and feel of the set and instructing the set designer

artefacts /'ɑːtɪfækts/ *plural noun* items such as media products, that hold information about the culture that produced them

'Among the bones were those of the Mayan king Kan Maax and his wife, identified by their jewellery, headdresses and other precious artefacts.' [Andrew Gumbel, *The Independent*]

art film /'ɑːt fɪlm/ *noun* a film that is made not for commercial reasons, but as a work of art, usually on a low budget

art gallery /'ɑːt ˌgæləri/ *noun* a building or room where works of art can be seen by the public

art-house /'ɑːt haʊs/ *adjective* **1.** referring to films that are not mainstream and are more devoted to the art of film-making than to mass entertainment **2.** referring to cinemas that show art-house films

article /'ɑːtɪk(ə)l/ *noun* **1.** a text on a particular subject in a newspaper, magazine or reference book **2.** ONLINE a message or posting to an Internet newsgroup

Article 19 /ˌɑːtɪk(ə)l naɪn'tiːn/ *noun* a clause in the European Convention for the Protection of Human Rights and Fundamental Freedom. The Article defends both the right to freedom of expression and the need for legal conditions and restrictions to be placed upon expression in order to protect other rights such as the right to privacy.

articulation /ɑːˌtɪkjʊ'leɪʃ(ə)n/ *noun* the process of expressing something

artificial language /ˌɑːtɪfɪʃ(ə)l 'læŋgwɪdʒ/ *noun* a language that has been invented for a particular purpose, such as for use with computers. The best-known human artificial language, developed for international communication, is Esperanto.

artificial light /ˌɑːtɪfɪʃ(ə)l 'laɪt/ *noun* lighting used to enable filming where there is no natural light source, for example in a studio

artistic media /ɑːˌtɪstɪk 'miːdiə/ *noun* media such as paint, photography, sculpture, collage etc which are used to create works of art

arts /ɑːts/, **the arts** *plural noun* **1.** activities enjoyed for the beauty they create or the way they present ideas, for example painting, music, and literature **2.** nonscientific and nontechnical subjects at school or university

artwork /'ɑːtwɜːk/ *noun* **1.** graphics such as charts, diagrams or maps that accompany textual material **2.** in printing, any material which can be printed, whether illustrations or text

ASA *abbreviation* **Advertising Standards Authority**

ascender /ə'sendə/ *noun* PRINTING **1.** the part of a lowercase letter such as d, h or k, that extends above its lower half **2.** a letter with an ascender

ascription /æ'skrɪpʃ(ə)n/ *noun* the adjustment of statistics to reflect unexpected circumstances, for example a reduced circulation for a magazine caused by a delay at the printers

A-side /'eɪ saɪd/ *noun* the more important side of a pop, rock, or jazz single that usually contains the title track

ASL *abbreviation* **American Sign Language**

as-live /ˌæz 'laɪv/ *adjective* referring to film or sounds that are pre-recorded and then replayed as if live

aspect ratio /'æspekt ˌreɪʃiəʊ/ *noun* the ratio between the width and height of an image on-screen, such as 4:3, which is the usual television screen size, or 16:9, which is wide screen

aspect ratio converter /'æspekt ˌreɪʃiəʊ kənˌvɜːtə/ *noun* a device for converting pictures into a form that can be shown on a screen with a different aspect ratio. Abbreviation **ARC**

aspirational value /ˌæspɪˈreɪʃən(ə)l ˌvæljuː/ *noun* a quality in fiction that makes it appeal to an audience, in which it describes situations and objects which people aspire to or aspire to have, for example romance, money, prestige

aspirer /əˈspaɪrə/ *noun* in advertising audience classifications, a person who wants products which improve their image and are fashionable. ◊ **main-streamer, succeeder, reformer**

assertiveness /əˈsɜːtɪvnəs/ *noun* the ability to express needs, desires, values and opinions in a direct and confident manner. Assertiveness is not always considered a positive attribute since in many collectivist cultures it is considered more polite to consider the needs of others above your own.

assets /ˈæsets/ *plural noun* separate data elements such as video, audio and image that are used in a multimedia application

assimilate /əˈsɪmɪleɪt/ *noun* **1.** to integrate somebody into a larger group, so that differences are minimised or eliminated, or become integrated in this way **2.** to integrate new knowledge or information with what is already known

assistant floor manager /əˌsɪst(ə)nt ˈflɔː ˌmænɪdʒə/ *noun* an assistant to the floor or stage manager, who does such tasks as checking props and coordinating rehearsals. Abbreviation **AFM**

assistant producer /əˌsɪst(ə)nt prəˈdjuːsə/ *noun* in television production, the crew member who is responsible for directing the content and action, roughly equivalent to a director in film production. Abbreviation **AP**

Associated Press /əˌsəʊsieɪtɪd ˈpres/ *noun* a major international news agency founded in 1848. Abbreviation **AP**

associate producer /əˌsəʊsiət prəˈdjuːsə/ *noun* in television and film production, the producer's head assistant

Association of Cinematograph and Television Technicians /əˌsəʊsieɪʃ(æ)n əv ˌsɪnɪmətəgrɑːf ən ˌtelɪvɪʒ(ə)n tekˈnɪʃ(ə)nz/ *noun* full form of **ACTT**

assonance /ˈæsənəns/ *noun* a poetic or literary effect achieved by using several words that contain the same or similar vowel sounds. Compare **alliteration**

asterisk /ˈæstərɪsk/ *noun* a symbol (*) used to indicate that there is a footnote relating to the text after which the symbol appears. Asterisks are also used to replace letters of words which cannot be printed in full because they are considered obscene.

asterism /ˈæstɜːrɪz(ə)m/ *noun* PRINTING three asterisks that form a triangle and draw the reader's attention to the next piece of text

Aston /ˈæstən/ a trade name for a character generator which lays captions on an image

Aston operator /ˈæstən ˌɒpəreɪtə/ *noun* the member of a television production team who is responsible for on-screen graphics

Astra /ˈæstrə/ *noun* a satellite operator which broadcasts BSkyB and other European satellite channels, based in Luxembourg

atmosphere /ˈætməsfɪə/, **atmos** *noun* ambient noise, recorded and added to a radio recording to make it sound more realistic. Also called **wild track**

atmospherics /ˌætməsˈferɪks/ *noun* noises that interfere with radio reception, caused by natural electrical disturbances in the atmosphere

ATR /ˌeɪ tiː ˈɑː/ *noun* a model showing stages in the effects of advertising on the consumer. According to this model, the customer becomes aware of the product, buys it once to try it, and then buys it again when he or she finds it is satisfactory. Full form **awareness, trial, repeat**

attachment /əˈtætʃmənt/ *noun* same as **work experience**

attack /əˈtæk/ *noun* RADIO the shape of the start of a sound signal over time

attention economy /əˈtenʃən ɪˈkɒnəmi/ *noun* the view that people's attention, particularly their attention to websites, is a driving force in the economy

attention model of mass communication /əˌtenʃən ˌmɒd(ə)l əv ˌmæs kəˌmjuːnɪˈkeɪʃ(ə)n/ *noun* the idea that communication (especially in advertising) is a matter of attracting and holding the attention of the consumer or receiver

attention value /ə'tenʃən ˌvæljuː/ *noun* the likelihood of an advertisement attracting and holding attention

'Newspaper advertising is done at least twice a week, and David reports that the company is 'experimenting with TV and radio. The typical men's stores in Detroit don't do much advertising, so we get good attention value.'' [Stan Gellars, *DNR*]

attitude /'ætɪtjuːd/ *noun* the way in which a person approaches or receives something, formed by social norms, experience and personal taste. Attitudes can be shaped, refined and changed, for example by the presentation of stereotypes in the media.

attitude research /'ætɪtjuːd rɪˌsɜːtʃ/ *noun* research into the feelings, tastes and perceptions of an audience

attribution /ˌætrɪ'bjuːʃ(ə)n/ *noun* a credit for the original source of a piece of news, quote or photograph

attribution theory /ˌætrɪ'bjuːʃ(ə)n ˌθɪəri/ *noun* ♦ **dispositional attribution**, **situational attribution**

audience /'ɔːdiəns/ *noun* **1.** the group of people who are exposed to a media product. ♦ **target audience 2.** the people who receive a media product, or at whom a piece of advertising is aimed

COMMENT: Audience research plays an important role in dictating which media products are made and the way in which they are packaged. The more closely a product matches the needs and desires of its target audience, the more likely it is to be accepted and successful.

audience appreciation /ˌɔːdiəns ə ˌpriːʃi'eɪʃ(ə)n/ *noun* a measure of how an audience responded to a media product, used as a factor in ratings research alongside the bare statistics of how many people were watching

Audience Appreciation Index /ˌɔːdiəns əˌpriːʃi'eɪʃ(ə)n ˌɪndeks/ *noun* a study of audience opinions on programmes they have watched. Abbreviation **AI**

audience differentiation /ˌɔːdiəns ˌdɪfərenʃi'eɪʃ(ə)n/ the process of splitting an audience into groups according to age, social status and considering the needs of each group

audience duplication /ˌɔːdiəns ˌdjuːplɪ'keɪʃ(ə)n/ *noun* the percentage of audience for an advertisement that is reached by it more than once, or in more than one form

audience factor /'ɔːdiəns ˌfæktə/ *noun* the average number and constituency of viewers in each television-owning home

audience flow /'ɔːdiəns fləʊ/ *noun* the way in which the audience for a particular channel changes throughout the day, expressed by the percentage that changes the channel, turns the television on or off or leaves the room

audience measurement /'ɔːdiəns ˌmeʒəmənt/ *noun* research into how many people are receiving a particular media product and what they are like, their social status etc.

audience research /ˌɔːdiəns rɪ'sɜːtʃ/ *noun* research into the attitudes of an audience to an advertising campaign

audimeter /'ɔːdɪmiːtə/ *noun* an electronic device attached to a TV set, which records details of a viewer's viewing habits

audio /'ɔːdiəʊ/ *noun* recorded material

audiocassette /'ɔːdiəʊkəˌset/ *noun* an audiotape in a plastic box, for use in a tape recorder

audioconferencing /'ɔːdiəʊ ˌkɒnf(ə)rənsɪŋ/ *noun* BUSINESS the practice of holding a meeting between several people in different locations, whose discussions take place over the telephone

audio console /'ɔːdiəʊ ˌkɒnsəʊl/ *noun* a piece of furniture designed to house the separate components of an audio system such as a radio tuner, a compact disc player, a tape recorder and a record deck

audio description /'ɔːdiəʊ dɪ ˌskrɪpʃən/ *noun* a spoken description of what is happening onscreen for the visually impaired

audio distribution amplifier /ˌɔːdiəʊ ˌdɪstrɪ'bjuːʃ(ə)n ˌæmplɪfaɪə/ *abbreviation* ADA. ♦ **distribution amplifier**

audio EDL /ˌɔːdiəʊ ˌiː diː 'el/ *noun* ♦ **editing decision list**

audio feed /'ɔːdiəʊ fiːd/ *noun* recorded sound sent from one place to another where it can be used

audio insert /'ɔːdiəʊ ɪnˌsɜːt/ *noun* a feature on some video equipment which allows dubbing

audiophile /'ɔːdiəʊfaɪl/ *noun* somebody who has an enthusiasm for hi-fidelity sound reproduction, especially recordings of music

audiotape /'ɔːdiəʊteɪp/ *noun* **1.** a length of magnetic tape containing a sound recording for use in a tape recorder **2.** magnetic tape that is used for recording sound

audio-video support system /ˌɔːdiəʊ ˌvɪdiəʊ səˈpɔːt ˌsɪstəm/ *noun* full form of **AVSS**

audiovisual /ˌɔːdiəʊ ˈvɪʒuəl/ *noun* media that can be seen and also heard, for example a TV commercial. Abbreviation **AV**

Audit Bureau of Circulation /ˌɔːdɪt ˌbjʊərəʊ əv ˌsɜːkjʊˈleɪʃ(ə)n/ *noun* the body which provides official figures for newspaper circulation. Abbreviation **ABC**

audited circulation /ˌɔːdɪtəd ˌsɜːkjʊ ˈleɪʃ(ə)n/ *noun* circulation figures for newspapers or magazines that have been independently verified

aura /'ɔːrə/ *noun* in aesthetic theory, the idea that a piece of art retains its special unique qualities and mystical value even if it is mass-reproduced

aural signature /ˌɔːrəl ˈsɪɡnɪtʃə/ *noun* a set of musical sounds used to identify a product or service

Australian Broadcasting Corporation /ɒˌstreɪliən ˈbrɔːdkɑːstɪŋ ˌkɔːpəreɪʃ(ə)n/ the government-owned public service broadcaster of radio and television programmes in Australia. Abbreviation **ABC**

auteur /ɔːˈtɜː/ *noun* a film director who is known for their distinctive individual style

'But the talents of movie directors remain shrouded in mystery and ignorance. One of the complications is an ambiguous label – that of 'auteur', which attracts as much derision as it does respect and eulogy.' [Don Boyd, *Time Out*]

auteurism /ɔːˈtɜːrɪz(ə)m/ *noun* the principle that a director's influence on a film is its defining characteristic

auteur theory /ɔːˈtɜː ˌθɪəri/ *noun* the theory in film criticism that suggests that

a director may be regarded as a film's author

author /'ɔːθə/ *verb* to create a computer application such as a multimedia document, usually using special software

authoring software /ˌɔːθərɪŋ ˈsɒftweə/, **authoring system** /ˌɔːθərɪŋ ˈsɪstəm/ *noun* a special application for creating multimedia titles. Authoring software is for designing the pages of a multimedia book and placing video clips, images, text and sound on a page.

authorship /'ɔːθəʃɪp/ *noun* the idea that a particular person in a film's production (usually the director) is mainly responsible for the look and style of the film, rather than looking at the larger body of people who produced it as a whole

author's marks /'ɔːθəz mɑːks/ *plural noun* proofreading marks made by the author on a piece of text

auto-conforming /ˌɔːtəʊ kən ˈfɔːmɪŋ/ *noun* the process of conforming done by a special computer program, which automatically recreates the editing done during the off-line edit

autocracy /ɔːˈtɒkrəsi/ *noun* a system of government based on the principle of absolute power invested in one ruler, usually a monarch. Compare **democracy**

Autocue /'ɔːtəʊkjuː/ a trade name for a type of electronic scrolling script prompter, often used generically to mean any type of device like this

auto exposure /ˌɔːtəʊ ɪkˈspəʊʒə/ *noun* a feature on a camera to set the exposure level automatically. Abbreviation **AE**

autofocus /'ɔːtəʊfəʊkəs/ *noun* a camera system that allows the lens to be adjusted automatically so that the image is in focus. Abbreviation **AF**

auto-function /'ɔːtəʊ ˌfʌŋkʃən/ *noun* a feature in editing and playback equipment that performs functions such as focusing or tracking automatically. This can be helpful for amateur users but is usually set manually by the professional to give greater control over the output.

Automatic Dialogue Replacement /ˌɔːtəmætɪk ˈdaɪəlɒg rɪˌpleɪsmənt/ *noun* **1.** a device which allows actors to watch themselves on screen while re-recording their lines simultaneously, for greater clarity **2.** the practice of re-recording lines from a filmed piece, either because the sound was incorrectly recorded or just to make it louder and clearer, and dubbing them over the top so that they appear to be part of the original dialogue ▶ abbreviation **ADR**

automatic exposure /ˌɔːtəmætɪk ɪk 'spəʊʒə/ *noun* a camera system that automatically sets the lens aperture and shutter speed, after measuring how much light there is

automatic frequency control /ˌɔːtəmætɪk 'friːkwənsi kənˌtrəʊl/ *noun* a control system in a radio or television receiver that keeps it tuned to the incoming signal, even if its frequency varies slightly

automatic gain control /ˌɔːtəmætɪk 'ɡeɪn kənˌtrəʊl/ *noun* a control system in a radio receiver, that keeps the amplified volume constant in spite of variations in the volume of the signal

automatic level control /ˌɔːtəmætɪk 'lev(ə)l kənˌtrəʊl/ *noun* a device on recording machines that maintains a constant recording level. Abbreviation **ALC**

autonomy /ɔː'tɒnəmi/ *noun* in aesthetic theory, independence, without relying on any other idea, cultural form or value

autoscript /'ɔːtəʊskrɪpt/ *noun* a type of prompting system used by television presenters

auto white balance /ˌɔːtəʊ 'waɪt ˌbæləns/ *noun* a feature on a camera that sets the white balance automatically. Abbreviation **AWB**

AV *abbreviation* MEDIA **audiovisual**

availability /əˌveɪlə'bɪlɪti/ *noun* the time and number of advertising slots which are available to be used

avant-garde /ˌævɒŋ 'ɡɑːd/ *adjective* novel, experimental and outside the mainstream

'Braunstein… published an article called Stalking Kate in BlackBook, a progressive magazine that describes itself as 'clandestine and avant garde'.' [Tony Allen-Mills, *The Sunday Times*]

avatar /'ævətɑː/ *noun* a computer-generated icon or figure representing a character in a virtual world

average audience /ˌæv(ə)rɪdʒ 'ɔːdiəns/ *noun* the average of the minute-by-minute audience rating throughout the duration of a radio or television programme

average frequency /ˌæv(ə)rɪdʒ 'friːkwənsi/ *noun* **1.** the number of times on average that the same person is reached by advertising in the same campaign, either in the same or different media vehicles **2.** the average number of opportunities to see an advertisement. Abbreviation **AF**

average hours per head /ˌæv(ə)rɪdʒ ˌaʊəz pə 'hed/ *noun* the average number of television viewing hours across the whole population who did or could have watched

Average Issue Readership /ˌæv(ə)rɪdʒ ˌɪʃuː 'riːdəʃɪp/ *noun* an estimate of the number of people who have read or looked at a publication during its issue period. Abbreviation **AIR**

average quarter-hour figure /ˌæv(ə)rɪdʒ ˌkwɔːtər 'aʊə ˌfɪɡə/ *noun* the average number of people watching a TV programme during a 15-minute period

avi /ˌeɪ viː 'aɪ/ *noun* COMPUTING a file extension for a multimedia video format file

Avid technology /'ævɪd tekˌnɒlədʒi/ the market leader in software for non-linear editing

AVSS /ˌeɪ viː es 'es/ *noun* a digital video system, originally for MS-DOS, used to play back video and audio files on a computer

awareness /ə'weənəs/ *noun* same as **brand awareness**

awareness, trial, repeat /əˌweənəs ˌtraɪəl rɪ'piːt/ *noun* full form of **ATR**

AWB *abbreviation* **auto white balance**

AWM /ˌeɪ ˌdʌb(ə)l juː 'em/ *noun* a system developed by Yamaha to sample natural sounds and convert them to digital form

axe /æks/ *noun* a rock guitar or a brass instrument used in jazz, particularly a saxophone (*informal*)

axeman /'æksmən/ *noun* a rock guitarist, a jazz saxophonist or other horn player (*informal*)

B

B/A *abbreviation* **back-anno**

baby legs /ˈbeɪbi legz/ *noun* a camera tripod with especially short legs for low-angle shots

back /bæk/ *noun* the part of a book where the pages and the binding are joined together

back-anno /ˈbæk ˌænəʊ/ *noun* an announcement following an audio piece on the radio, explaining what has just been heard. Abbreviation **B/A**

backbench /ˈbækbentʃ/ *noun* a committee of senior journalists who decide the overall look, structure and focus of a particular newspaper

back catalogue /ˌbæk ˈkæt(ə)lɒg/ *noun* all the publications, recordings or films a particular artist or company has ever produced

back cover /ˌbæk ˈkʌvə/ *noun* the back of a magazine cover, which can be used for advertising

backfile /ˈbækfaɪl/ *noun* a collection of all the previous issues of a newspaper or magazine

background /ˈbækgraʊnd/ *noun* part of a feature that gives background details to the main part of a news story

backgrounder /ˈbækgraʊndə/ *noun* a feature that gives background details to another major news story

background music /ˈbækgraʊnd ˌmjuːzɪk/ *noun* music that accompanies action or dialogue in a film, or music played to create a pleasant environment and make people feel comfortable, for example in a shop or at a party

'When the BBC finally manages to give us a decent programme, why must they ruin it with irritating background music that runs right through the show? In many cases it completely drowns out the dialogue.' [*Letters Page, The Sun Newspaper*]

backing /ˈbækɪŋ/ *noun* the accompaniment for a solo musician or singer of popular music

backing track /ˈbækɪŋ træk/ *noun* a recording that is used as an accompaniment to a solo performance

back issue /ˈbæk ˌɪʃuː/ *noun* a previous edition of a paper or magazine

backlight /ˈbæklaɪt/ *noun* a light that illuminates the subject from behind on a film set, helping them to stand out against the background. Also called **rim light**

backlight correction /ˈbæklaɪt kə ˌrekʃ(ə)n/ *noun* an automatic function on some cameras to reduce the shadowing effect of lighting an object from behind. Abbreviation **BLC**

back projection /ˌbæk prə ˈdʒekʃ(ə)n/ *noun* the cinematic technique of creating a background for a scene by projecting other moving images onto a screen behind the action being filmed

back-story /ˈbæk ˌstɔːri/ *noun* CINEMA, TV same as **prequel**

back up /ˌbæk ˈʌp/ *verb* to print on the second side of a sheet of paper

backup /ˈbækʌp/ *noun* a copy of saved data that can be used if the original is lost, or a second source of energy or facilities that may be used if the first source fails

back-up /ˈbæk ʌp/ *noun* the accompaniment to the main performer of a piece of popular music or jazz

badged /bædʒd/ *adjective* referring to a distinctive branding that is given to a product to appeal to its target audience

bad language /ˌbæd ˈlæŋgwɪdʒ/ *noun* the use or misuse of language which is likely to cause offence to its audience, for example swearing, poor grammar or the use of certain accents or dialects

'Millions of pounds are spent researching whether television violence makes children more aggressive, but the mere price of a bus ticket will demonstrate conclusively that television swearing makes children use bad language more readily.' [Christopher Middleton, *The Daily Telegraph*]

bad taste /bæd teɪst/ ◇ **in bad taste** referring to a comment or joke that is considered unsuitable because it may offend a group or individual, particularly because of being ill-timed. An example of this would be light-hearted comments made about a person shortly after their death.

Bafta /ˈbæftə/ *noun* an award given in the UK every year by the British Academy of Film and Television Arts for outstanding work in films and television

BAFTA /ˈbæftə/ *abbreviation* **British Academy of Film and Television Arts**

balanced audio /ˌbælənst ˈɔːdiəʊ/ *noun* audio signals which are transmitted along the cable in inverted form, which eliminates any interference

balanced programming /ˌbælənst ˈprəʊɡræmɪŋ/ *noun* the practice of giving fair coverage to all subject matter, representing each view in an impartial manner and not marginalising any programming by, for example, always broadcasting it at off-peak times

ballad /ˈbæləd/ *noun* a slow romantic song in popular music, or an older song that tells a sentimental story

balloon /bəˈluːn/ *noun* the rounded space on a cartoon picture where the text of a character's speech or thoughts is printed. Also called **bubble**

ballyhoo /ˌbæliˈhuː/ *noun* sensational publicity for something such as a story or product

band /bænd/ *noun* a horizontal section of a reel-to-reel tape

bandpass filter /ˈbændpɑːs ˌfɪltə/ *noun* a device that filters out all sounds except those within a certain frequency

bandspreading /ˈbændˌspredɪŋ/ *noun* a tuning system on some radios that allows a narrow band of frequencies to be spread wider apart to enable more accurate tuning to a particular frequency

B & W *abbreviation* PHOTOGRAPHY **black-and-white**

bandwidth /ˈbændwɪdθ/ *noun* **1.** a range of frequencies that is used for radio or telecommunications transmission and reception **2.** ONLINE the amount of data, often measured in bits per second, that a communication channel such as an Internet connection, can transmit

bang /bæŋ/ *noun* PRINTING an exclamation mark (!)

bangtail /ˈbæŋteɪl/ *noun* a type of envelope with a piece that can be torn off and used as an order form or to collect marketing data

bank /bæŋk/ *noun* PRESS a secondary part of a headline running below the main headline in smaller type

banner /ˈbænə/ *noun* PRESS same as **banner headline**

banner ad /ˈbænə æd/, **banner advertisement** /ˌbænə ədˈvɜːtɪsmənt/, **banner advertising** /ˈbænə ˌædvətaɪzɪŋ/ *noun* an advertisement that stretches across the top or bottom of a printed page or a webpage. Also called **banner**

'…a mistake by the Lycos search engine resulted in the fledgling casino's banner advertising being flashed across the world. The surge in internet traffic was almost too big for the company's servers to cope with.' [Matthew Garrahan, *The Financial Times*]

banner exchange /ˈbænə ɪksˌtʃeɪndʒ/ *noun* an agreement between two or more businesses, in which each allows the others' advertising banners to be displayed on its website

banner headline /ˌbænə ˈhedlaɪn/ *noun* a large headline that stretches across the top of the page of a newspaper. Also called **banner**

bar /bɑː/ *noun* in music, a fundamental unit of time into which a musical work is divided, according to the number of beats

BARB *abbreviation* **Broadcasters' Audience Research Board**

barbershop /ˈbɑːbəʃɒp/ *noun* a style of arranging unaccompanied popular songs, originally for four male voices, that was developed in the US in the 1920s and 1930s. There are now many female barbershop groups and larger barbershop choirs.

bar counting /'bɑː ˌkaʊntɪŋ/ *noun* a method of timing camera shots by counting the bars of accompanying music

barn door /ˌbɑːn 'dɔː/ *noun* THEATRE, CINEMA one of four adjustable flaps on the front of a large industrial light used on film sets and in the theatre

baron /'bærən/ *noun* the main owner and controller of a newspaper or media empire. Examples include Rupert Murdoch, Robert Maxwell and Silvio Berlusconi. (*informal*) Also called **magnate**, **mogul**

barrier signals /'bæriə ˌsɪgn(ə)lz/ *plural noun* in human interaction, non-verbal communication such as crossing the arms or holding a hand in front of the face, which are seen as defensive signals

barter /'bɑːtə/ *noun* a system in which advertising space or time is exchanged for goods from the advertiser

base /beɪs/ *noun* **1.** RADIO the studio **2.** MARKETING the actual number of individuals that were asked questions in a survey

base and superstructure /ˌbeɪs ən 'suːpəstrʌktʃə/ *noun* a Marxist theory in which the economy is the 'base' of any society, around which is built the 'superstructure' of the law, religion, culture etc.

baseband /'beɪsbænd/ *noun* **1.** TELE-COMS the narrow range of frequencies necessary to transmit a single message **2.** the form of a satellite signal as it is transmitted, before it is received and converted into viewable pictures and sound

base station /'beɪs ˌsteɪʃ(ə)n/ *noun* a fixed radio transmitter/receiver that relays radio signals to and from data terminals or radios

basher /'bæʃə/ *noun* a small hand-held lamp used on a film shoot

basic service /ˌbeɪsɪk 'sɜːvɪs/ *noun* the basic package of television channels that are available on a cable or satellite subscription service. Extra channels can usually be paid for.

'Sky launched the service in October 2004, a month before the meeting, offering a set-top box and basic service for a flat £150.' [Jane Martinson and Rob Evans, *The Guardian*]

Basic **Telecommunications** **Agreement 1997** /ˌbeɪsɪk ˌtelikə ˌmjuːnɪ'keɪʃ(ə)nz əˌgriːmənt/ *noun* an agreement introduced by the World Trade Organisation to allow free trade for tele-communications services, signed by 69 countries

Baskerville /'bæskəvɪl/ *noun* PRINTING a typeface characterised by serifs and traditionally regarded suitable for books and periodicals

Bass's double action model of internal news flow 1969 /bæs/ *noun* a model which describes news as being processed in two stages before release – firstly by the newsgatherers, who are concerned only with factual reporting, then by the editors, who are more concerned with the values and norms of the news organisation

bastard title /'bɑːstəd ˌtaɪt(ə)l/ *noun* PRINTING same as **half title**

batter /'bætə/ *noun* PRINTING **1.** the impression produced by a damaged printing plate **2.** a damaged or worn area of printing type or a defective block

battery pack /'bæt(ə)ri pæk/ *noun* a powerful battery that can be recharged and used in portable machines such as laptop computers and video cameras

baud rate /'bɔːd reɪt/ *noun* the speed of data transfer within a network, measured in bits per second

BBC /ˌbiː biː 'siː/ *noun* the public service broadcaster in the UK that was established in 1922. As the BBC is non-commercial, it is funded by an annual licence fee paid by television owners. Full form **British Broadcasting Corporation**

COMMENT: The BBC has been subject to many reports since it was founded in 1922, primarily looking into the quality of its programming, its funding via the licence fee and the need for competition in the British broadcasting market. The most recent government white paper (called 'The Future of the BBC: Serving the Nation, Competing Worldwide') recommended that the BBC should continue to develop worldwide services, pay particular attention to matters of taste and decency and should provide programming dedicated to education, news and 'bringing the nation together'.

BBC digital /ˌbiː biː siː 'dɪdʒɪt(ə)l/ *noun* the six extra BBC channels available to digital viewers since 2002. These channels include a 24-hour news channel and round-the-clock children's programming.

BBC English /ˌbiː biː siː 'ɪŋglɪʃ/ *noun* the standard form of spoken English used by announcers on BBC television and radio

BBC World /ˌbiː biː siː ˈwɜːld/ noun the BBC's international 24-hours new service, which is commercially funded

BBC World Service /ˌbiː biː siː ˌwɜːld ˈsɜːvɪs/ noun the BBC's international radio news service, which is funded by the British government and broadcasts in 43 languages

BBC Worldwide /ˌbiː biː siː wɜːld ˈwaɪd/ noun a BBC company which makes consumer products relating to their television and radio broadcasts, such as audio books, magazines and book tie-ins

BBC written archives /ˌbiː biː siː ˌrɪt(ə)n ˈɑːkaɪvz/ noun a store of more than 200,000 files from the BBC's first 40 years of broadcasting, kept by the BBC Monitoring Service in Reading

BBFC abbreviation **British Board of Film Classification**

BBS abbreviation **1. Bulletin Board System 2. British Business Survey**

BCNZ abbreviation **Broadcasting Corporation of New Zealand**

BCU abbreviation **big close-up**

BDL /ˌbiː diː ˈel/ noun a company that makes autocue equipment. Full form **Broadcast Development Ltd**

BDS abbreviation **Broadcasting Data Services**

beach box /ˈbiːtʃ bɒks/ noun a device for connecting an external microphone to a hand-held digital video camera, to provide better sound recording quality

beam /biːm/ verb to broadcast radio or television signals to a particular place

beam aerial /ˈbiːm ˌeəriəl/ noun an aerial that sends or receives radio or television signals to or from a particular direction

beam splitter /ˈbiːm ˌsplɪtə/ noun a device that can split a beam such as a laser, into two beams of light that can be used to create a three-dimensional image such as a hologram

beatbox /ˈbiːtbɒks/ noun MUSIC a drum machine used in popular music to provide repetitive rhythm accompaniments

BECTU /ˈbektuː/ noun a trade union in the UK, representing employees in the film and television industries and also in theatre. Full form **Broadcasting, Enter-**tainment, Cinematograph and Theatre Union

bed /bed/ noun BROADCAST music or other background sounds that are played under an item such as the news

Beeb /biːb/ noun an informal way of referring to the BBC

beermat /ˈbɪəmæt/ noun MARKETING a cardboard mat for use under a beer glass in a pub, that often carries advertising for breweries or other drinks companies

behaviourism /bɪˈheɪvjərɪz(ə)m/ noun a psychological movement that focuses on what can be observed and measured about a person's behaviour, rather than what can only be inferred about their thought processes. Compare **cognitive psychology**

bellows /ˈbeləʊz/ noun the telescopic part of a camera or photographic enlarger, that houses its lenses

bells and whistles /ˌbelz ənd ˈwɪs(ə)lz/ plural noun every possible feature that could be included, for example, in an advertising campaign

below-the-fold /bɪˌləʊ ðə ˈfəʊld/ adjective relating to the parts of a webpage that can be seen only by scrolling down the page and that are therefore less commercially valuable for marketing purposes

below-the-line /bɪˌləʊ ðə ˈlaɪn/ adjective **1.** relating to advertising that is not mainstream, for example mailouts, beer mats, etc **2.** relating to advertising that is not paid for and for which no commission is paid to an advertising agency, for example work by staff who are manning an exhibition

belter /ˈbeltə/ noun a song that can be sung loudly and enthusiastically, especially by a group singing together (informal)

benchmark measure /ˈbentʃmɑːk ˌmeʒə/ noun the measure of a target audience's response at the beginning of an advertising campaign which is then compared to the response at the end of the campaign to test the efficiency of the campaign

benday /ˈbendeɪ/ adjective referring to a method of adding tone or shading to a line drawing by overlaying the image with a screen that bears a pattern of, for example, lines or dots, before a plate is made

Berliner /bɜːˈlɪnə/ *noun* a newspaper format slightly larger in size than tabloid, used by several European newspaper including France's Le Monde and The Guardian in the UK

Berlusconi phenomenon /ˌbɜːluˈskəʊni fəˌnɒmɪnən/ *noun* the way in which Silvio Berlusconi reached power as Italian prime minister due to his control of the country's media

best boy /ˌbest ˈbɔɪ/ *noun* **1.** the assistant to the chief lighting technician on a film or television set **2.** the chief assistant to the key grip on a film set

best-of-breed /ˌbest əv ˈbriːd/ *adjective* COMPUTING, MARKETING referring to a product that is the best in its class

'…consumers can mix and match components at will, without having to replace the entire system. They can buy individual components from specialised suppliers and then assemble these 'best-of-breed' components into a customised system.' [*The Financial Times*]

bestseller /bestˈselə/ *noun* a product such as a book or a CD that sells very well, often very quickly

Betacam /ˈbiːtəkæm/ a trade name for a videotape format, overtaken in the consumer market by VHS but still used for some professional productions

Beta SP /ˌbiːtə es ˈpiː/ a trade name for variant of the Betacam format for videotapes (the SP stands for 'superior performance')

Beta SX /ˌbiːtə es ˈeks/ a trade name for a digital version of the Beta SP videotape format

beta testing /ˈbiːtə ˌtestɪŋ/ *noun* the practice of asking consumers to test a product, after it has been officially tested, but before it is released to the general public

Beveridge Committee report on broadcasting 1950 /ˈbevərɪdʒ/ *noun* a report into the monopoly on broadcasting held by the BBC at the time. It recommended closer surveillance of governors' activities and output and some regional devolution of activities, but advised against greater competition, such as from commercial broadcasters, because it would reduce the overall quality of output.

bf *abbreviation* PRINTING **boldface**

BFI *abbreviation* CINEMA, UK **British Film Institute**

B-girl /ˈbiː gɜːl/ *noun* a young woman who is enthusiastic about hip-hop music and culture

'Another rising star in the British B-girl camp is Firefly – real name Andrea Parker. She's 26. She lives in Leeds. Now a full-time professional B-girl, she packed in her nine-to-five office job as an accounts director in a solicitors' firm six years ago.' [*The Independent*]

bhangra /ˈbʌŋgrə/ *noun* a style of popular music in British Asian communities that mixes elements of traditional Punjabi folk music and western pop music

bias /ˈbaɪəs/ *noun* **1.** the failure to report news in an impartial, factual manner, whether intentional or not **2.** a prejudiced or non-objective attitude, which may not fairly represent all sides of an issue

bibliography /ˌbɪbliˈɒgrəfi/ *noun* **1.** a list of books and articles consulted, appearing at the end of a book or other text **2.** a list of books and articles on a subject **3.** a list of the books and articles written by a specific author or issued by a specific publisher **4.** the history of books and other publications, and the work of classifying and describing them

big beat /ˈbɪg biːt/ *noun* a type of electronic music, later more usually called electronica, that incorporates elements of both dance and rock music and is characterised by its rock-style drum patterns

Big Brother *noun* a concept in George Orwell's novel 1984, describing an authoritarian government which 'watches' every move of its citizens, intercepts their communications etc and monitors them for any signs of unrest or non-conformity ■ a trade name for a reality television show format, in which a group of ordinary people are put together in a house and their behaviour monitored continuously by television cameras

big close-up /ˌbɪg ˈkləʊs ˌʌp/ *noun* PHOTOGRAPHY an extreme close-up shot of a person's face, in which the lower chin and top of the head are cut off. Abbreviation **BCU**

Bigfoot /ˈbɪgfʊt/ *noun* US a celebrity journalist employed by a large media organisation (*slang*)

big idea /ˌbɪg aɪˈdiə/ *noun* the main new idea behind an advertising campaign, the aim of which is to attract potential customers

bigotry /'bɪgətri/ *noun* unreasonable intolerance of other people's beliefs, values or opinions

big screen /ˌbɪg 'skriːn/ *noun* **1.** films that are made to be seen in a cinema rather than on a television **2.** a television report in which the presenter stands in front of a large screen, which is showing charts, graphs, short interviews etc

bill /bɪl/ *noun* MARKETING a piece of paper such as a poster or leaflet with an advertisement on it

billboard /'bɪlbɔːd/ *noun* **1.** a poster advertising a newspaper by displaying the main headline of the day, usually displayed outside newsagents on newspaper stands **2.** a sponsorship message shown before, after and in the breaks of a sponsored television programme

billing /'bɪlɪŋ/ *noun* **1.** the particular importance or prominence given to a performer or event in advertisements **2.** the details such as the cast list and length of a radio or television programme, as supplied to the Broadcasting Data Services **3.** the total amount of business done over a given period, especially in advertising **4.** the way in which a performance, event, or product is publicised

billing form /'bɪlɪŋ fɔːm/ *noun* one of the four forms which must be submitted when delivering a programme to the BBC, giving billing details for listings magazines. ◊ **transmission form**, **music reporting form**, **Programme as Completed form**

billposter /'bɪlpəʊstə/ *noun* a person whose job it is to put up advertisements in public places

bi-media /ˌbaɪ 'miːdiə/ *adjective* involving both radio and television

bi-media journalism /ˌbaɪ ˌmiːdiə 'dʒɜːn(ə)lɪz(ə)m/ *noun* a BBC scheme whereby journalists are trained for both television and radio at the same time

binary opposition /ˌbaɪnəri ˌɒpə 'zɪʃ(ə)n/ *noun* a pair of direct opposites such as good and evil, white and black or male and female

binaural /baɪn'ɔːrəl/ *adjective* referring to stereo sound that is recorded and then reproduced through two separate channels, one for each side of a pair of headphones

bind /baɪnd/ *verb* PRINTING to make pages into a book form by fastening them together inside a cover

binder /'baɪndə/ *noun* **1.** a machine that fastens pages together in the form of a book **2.** a firm cover that can hold separate items such as sheets of paper or magazines securely together

binding /'baɪndɪŋ/ *noun* the material that is used to fasten the pages of a book or booklet together

biodata /'baɪəʊdeɪtə/ *noun* details about an individual, relating for example, to his or her education or professional history

biographee /ˌbaɪɒgrə'fiː/ *noun* a person who is the subject of a biography

biography /baɪ'ɒgrəfi/ *noun* the story of a person's life, told by somebody else

biopic /'baɪəʊpɪk/ *noun* a biographical film

bird's-eye view /ˌbɜːdz aɪ 'vjuː/ *noun* same as **aerial shot**

biscuit /'bɪskɪt/ *noun* the connecting mechanism that allows the attachment of the plate on the bottom of a camera to the head of a tripod

bit /bɪt/ *noun* a binary digit, either '0' or '1'. More bits indicate more digits in a string, which means more possible combinations, so that a 24-bit palette of colours will have more shades and combinations available than a 16-bit palette.

BITC *abbreviation* **burned-in timecode**

bitmap /'bɪtmæp/ *noun* an image, the data for which is stored in the form of bits

bitmapped font /ˌbɪtmæpt 'fɒnt/ *noun* a typeface formed as a pattern of pixels or dots that are stored separately for each font size

biweekly /baɪ'wiːkli/ *noun* a magazine or paper that is published once every two weeks

black /blæk/ *noun* a back-up copy of a story, originally made using a carbon sheet when typing the story on a typewriter

black-and-white *adjective* **1.** referring to images shown only in black, white and shades of grey **2.** PHOTOGRAPHY, TV, CINEMA reproducing images in which colours have been converted to black, white, and shades of grey ■ *noun* PHOTOGRAPHY a visual medium without colours, and in hues of black, white, and shades of grey. Abbreviation **B & W**, **BW**

BlackBerry /'blækbəri/ a trade name for a hand-held wireless device which combines e-mail and Internet access, a phone and software applications

black comedy /ˌblæk 'kɒmədi/ *noun* comedy based on serious subjects that are not normally regarded as humorous, such as death or illness

black letter /ˌblæk 'letə/ *noun* same as gothic

black level /'blæk ˌlev(ə)l/ *noun* the level of a video signal that represents absolutely no light, i.e. total blackness

blacklist /'blæklɪst/ *noun* a list of people from whom e-mails are not welcome on a particular account

black out /'blæk aʊt/ *verb* **1.** to exclude all light from an area **2.** to stop news or information about a particular subject being made public **3.** to lose radio contact, for example with a vessel or aircraft **4.** to be unable to broadcast radio or television programmes, usually because of a strike ■ *noun* a period during which no news stories may be reported, imposed by a government or other organisation

black wrap /'blæk ræp/ *noun* black, reflective heat-resistant foil used to black out or direct light

blanket /'blæŋkɪt/ *noun* PRINTING a rubber or plastic sheet around the cylinder of a printing press, which transfers images in ink to the surface being printed on

blanket coverage /ˌblæŋkɪt 'kʌv(ə)rɪdʒ/ *noun* advertising to the general public with no particular target audience in mind

'More and more companies in the North-East are recognising the value of sending their message via taxis. It's a surprisingly cost-effective method of outdoor media advertising, achieving blanket coverage over a wide geographical area.' [*The Journal*]

blasphemous /'blæsfəməs/ *adjective* offensive because it defames the name of God

blasphemy /'blæsfəmi/ *noun* defamation of, or irreverence towards, God

blat /blæt/, **blatt** *noun* US a tabloid newspaper (*slang*)

blaxploitation /ˌblæksplɔɪ'teɪʃ(ə)n/ *noun* a style of film-making popular in the 1970s in which black people are represented as stereotypes

BLC *abbreviation* **backlight correction**

bleed /bliːd/ *verb* **1.** to print something or be printed so that the colours run into each or beyond the edge of an illustration **2.** to print something or be printed so that part of a text or graphic is missing when the page is trimmed ■ *noun* a graphic or piece of text, printed so that it runs off the edge of the page

bleep /bliːp/ *verb* to attract a person's attention by activating their bleeper – an electronic device that emits one or more short, high-pitched signals

bleep out /ˌbliːp 'aʊt/ *verb* to cover an offensive word on a radio or television programme with a high-pitched electronic sound

blimp /blɪmp/ *noun* a cover that was formerly used to muffle the sound of the camera whirring when recording sound

blind certificate /ˌblaɪnd sə'tɪfɪkət/ *noun* ONLINE a type of cookie that is used to track which websites a person visits by identifying their computer system, rather than their name

blind spot /'blaɪnd ˌspɒt/ *noun* a place where radio reception is poor, even though it is within the normal range of the transmitter

blink /blɪŋk/ *verb* to send a signal by flashing a light

blinker /'blɪŋkə/ *noun* a flashing light, used as a signalling device, for example, to indicate which way a vehicle is going to turn. Blinkers were used to send coded messages, especially between ships, to avoid interception of radio signals during World Wars I and II.

blitz /blɪts/ *noun* a marketing campaign which starts at full pressure, as opposed to a gradual build-up

blob paragraph /'blɒb ˌpærəɡrɑːf/ *noun* in newspaper terminology, a paragraph in a newspaper that is marked with a bullet point

block /blɒk/ *noun* a piece of hard material with a carved image in relief, that can be printed in ink ■ *verb* to use a block to print a design, especially a title on a book cover

block capital /ˌblɒk 'kæpɪt(ə)l/ *noun* a single capital letter

block letter /ˌblɒk ˈletə/ *noun* a compressed sans serif typeface or individual letter

block out /ˌblɒk ˈaʊt/ *verb* to mask part of a photographic negative during processing, to prevent light from passing through it

block printing /ˌblɒk ˈprɪntɪŋ/ *noun* the technique of printing from carved blocks

blog /blɒg/ *noun* same as **weblog**

'Blogging's conversational style and anti-establishment ethos have attracted a growing and loyal readership. Technorati, the internet search company, says the size of the known 'blogosphere' is about 20m blogs and counting.'
[Kevin Allison, *The Financial Times*]

blogger /ˈblɒgə/ *noun* a person who creates or runs a weblog

blogging /ˈblɒgɪŋ/ *noun* the act of creating or maintaining a weblog

COMMENT: Blogging provides an easy way of maintaining an online diary or news site, as new content can be easily uploaded and also filtered and archived. It also makes it simple for outside contributors (visitors to the site) to submit content without prior programming knowledge.

blogosphere /ˈblɒgəˌsfɪə/ *noun* the parts of the World Wide Web where bloggers communicate with each other

blogware /ˈblɒgweə/ *noun* computer software that is designed to help people create weblogs

blonde /blɒnd/ *noun* TV a 2,000 watt halogen spotlight

blow-in /ˈbləʊ ɪn/ *noun* a postcard-size advertising card inserted in a magazine

blow up /ˌbləʊ ˈʌp/ *verb* **1.** to enlarge all or part of a photograph **2.** to make the images of a motion picture fit a larger gauge of film

blowup /ˈbləʊʌp/ *noun* **1.** an enlargement of all or part of a photograph or picture **2.** a motion picture that has been enlarged from a smaller gauge of film, for example from 16mm to 35mm

blue-eyed soul /ˌbluː aɪd ˈsəʊl/ *noun* soul music that is performed by white musicians

blue-pencil /ˌbluː ˈpensɪl/ *verb* to edit a piece of writing or a film, especially in order to censor it

blues /bluːz/ *noun* **1.** a style of music that developed from African American folk songs early in the 20th century. The structure and harmony of the blues is usually uncomplicated and the music is often slow and sad. **2.** a piece of music in the style of the blues

blue-screen director /ˌbluː skriːn daɪˈrektə/ *noun* the member of a film or television production team who is responsible for managing effects using chromakey, or blue-screen, technology

blue-screen effect /ˌbluː skriːn ɪ ˈfekt/ *noun* same as **chromakey**

bluesman /ˈbluːzmən/ *noun* a man who plays or sings the blues

blueswoman /ˈbluːzwʊmən/ *noun* a woman who plays or sings the blues

bluesy /ˈbluːzi/ *adjective* reminiscent of a blues style

Bluetooth /ˈbluːtuːθ/ a trade name for a technology that enables portable electronic devices such as mobile phones, to connect with each other and the Internet

blurb /blɜːb/ *noun* a short piece of complimentary text about a product, often written about a book on its cover

BMIG *abbreviation* **British Media Industry Group**

bodkin /ˈbɒdkɪn/ *noun* a long pointed tool used for making corrections in typesetting

Bodoni /bɒ ˈdəʊni/ *noun* PRINTING a font or style of typeface

body /ˈbɒdi/ *noun* the main part of a piece of text after the introductory paragraph

body double /ˈbɒdi ˌdʌb(ə)l/ *noun* a person whose job is to substitute for a starring actor when body, rather than facial shots are being filmed

body language /ˈbɒdi ˌlæŋgwɪdʒ/ *noun* gestures, expressions, and movements which show what somebody's response is to a situation

'Body language is a strong factor. If someone isn't making eye contact or paying attention to what I'm saying, perhaps it's because they don't understand, so now I'll go over it again or deliver it in a different way.' [*The Times*]

boil down /ˌbɔɪl ˈdaʊn/ *noun* to shorten a piece of text

bold /bəʊld/ *noun* lettering with darker thicker lines than usual ■ *adjective* referring to lettering with darker and thicker lines than usual. Also called **boldfaced** ■ *verb* to set, print, or display text in bold type ▶ also called (all senses) **boldface**

boldface /'bəʊldfeɪs/ *verb* to make letters darker and thicker for emphasis. Abbreviation **bf** ■ *adjective* PRINTING same as **bold**

Bollywood /'bɒliwʊd/ *noun* a humorous name for India's prolific film industry, based in Bombay. Typical Bollywood films are colourful epics with big musical numbers.

bongs /bɒŋz/ *noun* the clock chimes that are heard before a news broadcast

bonk journalism /'bɒŋk ˌdʒɜːn(ə)lɪz(ə)m/ *noun* journalism which is frivolous and more concerned with reporting sex scandals and titillating gossip than serious events (*informal*)

bonus spot /'bəʊnəs spɒt/ *noun* a free television or radio slot offered to an advertiser as part of an advertising package

book /bʊk/ *noun* a publication in book form, such as a magazine or brochure

bookbinding /'bʊkˌbaɪndɪŋ/ *noun* the process of creating a bound book with a spine and cover from separate sheets of paper and other materials

bookmaker /'bʊkmeɪkə/ *noun* a person whose job it is to design, print or bind books

bookmark /'bʊkmɑːk/ *noun* **1.** the address of a website that is stored on a computer so that it can be revisited easily **2.** an electronic marker that enables the user to return quickly to a particular place in a document ■ *verb* to list a website on a computer for future reference

book palette /'bʊk ˌpælət/ *noun* a set of colours that is used in a particular multimedia application

bookstall /'bʊkstɔːl/ *noun* a stand or stall where it is possible to buy newspapers, magazines or books

boom /buːm/ *noun* a long, adjustable pole, used during filming to suspend a microphone above what is being filmed without getting in shot

boom box /'buːm bɒks/ *noun* a portable machine that contains a radio and cassette or CD player with built-in

speakers at each end and a carrying handle on top

boomerang response /'buːməræŋ rɪˌspɒns/ *noun* a response by an audience to a media text which is the opposite of the one intended

boom shadow /'buːm ˌʃædəʊ/ *noun* the accidental shadow of a boom microphone cast on set

boom swinger /'buːm ˌswɪŋə/ *noun* the person who controls a boom

boost /buːst/ *noun* a promotion or advertising campaign

boosted sample /ˌbuːstɪd 'sɑːmp(ə)l/ *noun* a sample of a particular sub-section of the population, rather than the whole

booster /'buːstə/ *noun* a radio-frequency amplifier that strengthens weak television or radio signals

booth /buːð/ *noun* a soundproof room used in sound recordings or for broadcasting

borderless world /ˌbɔːdələs 'wɜːld/ *noun* the global economy in the age of the Internet, which is thought to have removed all the previous barriers to international trade

bounce /baʊns/ *verb* to reflect light from a source onto a subject to make it less harsh

bowdlerise /'baʊdləraɪz/ *verb* to censor something by removing all possibly offensive or contentious material from it

COMMENT: The word **bowdlerise** comes from Thomas Bowdler, an Englishman who in 1818 published an edition of Shakespeare called *Family Shakespeare* in which he omitted scenes that he considered unsuitable.

box camera /'bɒks ˌkæm(ə)rə/ *noun* a camera shaped like a box, with a simple lens, a single shutter speed and an elementary viewfinder

box number /'bɒks ˌnʌmbə/ *noun* a reference number used instead of an address for mail that is delivered to a post office or in answer to a newspaper advertisement

box office /'bɒks ˌɒfɪs/ *noun* **1.** the office in a cinema, theatre or concert-hall where the public can buy tickets **2.** the income generated from ticket sales for an entertainment event

boy band /'bɔɪ bænd/ *noun* a young, all-male pop group that uses backing tracks to accompany their singing and dancing

'They were the biggest-selling boy band since the Beatles – five likely lads who churned out a seemingly endless stream of hits, while pushing all the right buttons for a generation of young females' [Nicola Methvyn, *The Mirror*]

B picture /'biː ˌpɪktʃə/ *noun* **1.** in a cinema double bill, the first-shown, less important film **2.** a general, old-fashioned term for any less successful film with poor production values and usually a small budget

brace /breɪs/ *noun* either of a pair of brackets, { }, used singly to group lines of text together or as a pair in mathematical formulae where parentheses and square brackets have already been used. Also called **curly bracket**

bracket /'brækɪt/ *noun* **1.** an informal word for parenthesis, square bracket or brace **2.** one of a pair of shallow, curved signs, ( ), used to separate words from the surrounding text. Also called **round bracket**, **parenthesis**

Braille /breɪl/ *noun* a writing system for visually impaired people, consisting of patterns of raised dots that are read by touch

Brailler /'breɪlə/ *noun* a machine that can be used to type documents in Braille

brains trust /'breɪnz trʌst/ *noun* a panel of knowledgeable or respected people who discuss topics in public, especially on television or radio

brainwash /'breɪnwɒʃ/ *verb* to make a person believe or do something such as buy a new product, as a result of constantly repeated advertising

brainwashing /'breɪnwɒʃɪŋ/ *noun* the process of changing a person's attitude, usually by isolating them and subjecting them to intense coercion, replacing previously-held beliefs with new ones

brand awareness /'brænd əˌweənəs/ *noun* a measure of how many people are aware of a brand, and how aware they are. Also called **awareness**

brand image /ˌbrænd 'ɪmɪdʒ/ *noun* the associations and feelings that an audience has of a particular brand

'Indeed, Mr. Maradona, 44, is re-emerging as the hottest ad pitchman in Argentina. "He now personifies resilience and social responsibility," values advertisers are keen to associate with their brands, said Horacio Castelli, a brand image consultant.' [Charles Newbery, *Advertising Age*]

branding /'brændɪŋ/ *noun* the practice of attaching distinctive associations and meanings to a product, which identify it and assure consumers of its quality and the reputation of the company producing it

COMMENT: The branding of a product makes an important contribution to its public perception and the future success of other products in that line. For example, a particular manufacturer of cars may wish their products to be seen as safe, comfortable, reliable and good for a family, so when that future models are designed and released they will already have these associations.

brand loyalty /ˌbrænd 'lɔɪəlti/ *noun* the tendency of consumers to buy the same brands they have bought before

brand X /ˌbrænd 'eks/ *noun* the anonymous brand used in television commercials to compare with the named brand being advertised

Bravo /'brɑːvəʊ/ *noun* an internationally recognised code word for the letter B, used in radio communications

bray /breɪ/ *verb* PRINTING to spread ink over a printing block or type

break /breɪk/ *noun* the point at which a word is hyphenated at the end of a line of text

breakbeat /'breɪkbiːt/ *noun* a type of electronic music characterised by its electronically produced drum patterns, used mostly in jungle, drum and bass, and breakbeat hard-core music

break bumper /'breɪk ˌbʌmpə/ *noun* the technique of announcing a competition or quiz during a programme, the answer to which is contained in the commercial break. The aim is to get viewers to pay attention to the advertisements.

breakdancing /'breɪkˌdɑːnsɪŋ/ *noun* an acrobatic style of solo dancing to rap music, typically involving spinning of the body on the ground

breaker /'breɪkə/ *noun* any device such as a subtitle, which breaks up a solid piece of text to make it more accessible

breakfast paper /'brekfəst ˌpeɪpə/ *noun* an early edition of a daily newspaper

breakfast television /ˌbrekfəst 'telɪvɪʒ(ə)n/ *noun* informal, magazine-style television programmes that are broadcast early in the morning

break in /ˌbreɪk 'ɪn/ *verb* to interrupt another programme to broadcast something such as a news flash

breaking news /ˌbreɪkɪŋ 'njuːz/ *noun* same as **spot news**

break up /ˌbreɪk 'ʌp/ *verb* to start to lose clear communication when using a mobile phone

bribery /'braɪb(ə)ri/ *noun* the practice of offering money or other incentives to persuade somebody to do something, especially something dishonest or illegal

bricolage /'brɪkəlɑːʒ/ *noun* the technique, frequently used in postmodern art, of putting together different articles that are already available, to create something new

bricoleur /'brɪkəlɜː/ *noun* a person who uses bricolage

bridge /brɪdʒ/ *noun* **1.** a passage in a song or other musical work which links two sections **2.** ONLINE a connection between two local area networks

brief /briːf/ *noun* a short news article, anything from a few lines to a couple of paragraphs long. Also called **nib, filler**

Bristol board /'brɪst(ə)l bɔːd/ *noun* fine quality lightweight cardboard that is used in design and drawing

British Academy of Film and Television Arts /ˌbrɪtɪʃ əˌkædəmi əv ˌfɪlm ən 'telɪvɪʒ(ə)n ˌɑːts/ *noun* an organisation in the UK that gives annual awards for achievements in film and television. Abbreviation **BAFTA**

British Board of Film Censors /ˌbrɪtɪʃ bɔːd əv 'fɪlm ˌsensəz/ *noun* the name for the British Board of Film Classification before the 1984 Video Recording Act

British Board of Film Classification /ˌbrɪtɪʃ ˌbɔːd əv 'fɪlm ˌklæsɪfɪkeɪʃ(ə)n/ *noun* the Soho-based organisation that gives certificates to films in the UK based on how suitable they are

for particular audiences. Abbreviation **BBFC**

British Broadcasting Corporation /ˌbrɪtɪʃ 'brɔːdkɑːstɪŋ ˌkɔːpəreɪʃ(ə)n/ *noun* full form of **BBC**

British Business Survey /ˌbrɪtɪʃ 'bɪznəs ˌsɜːveɪ/ *noun* a wide-ranging survey into the readership of business magazines and the lifestyle of their readers, used for advertising strategies. Abbreviation **BBS**

British Code of Advertising Practice /ˌbrɪtɪʃ kəʊd əv 'ædvəˌtaɪzɪŋ ˌpræktɪs/ *noun* same as **Code of Advertising Standards and Practice**

British Film Institute /ˌbrɪtɪʃ 'fɪlm ˌɪnstɪtjuːt/ *noun* a body in the UK that promotes the cultural heritage of film. It also produces a range of educational books, sponsors British film projects and runs festivals and the National Film Theatre. Abbreviation **BFI**

British Media Industry Group /ˌbrɪtɪʃ ˌmiːdiə 'ɪndəstri ˌgruːp/ *noun* a pressure group comprising several large media groups in the UK, which lobbies against restrictions on cross-media ownership. Abbreviation **BMIG**

British Rate and Data /ˌbrɪtɪʃ ˌreɪt ən 'deɪtə/ *noun* a regular publication which lists British newspapers and magazines, giving information about their circulation, rates, frequency and other advertising services offered

British Sign Language /ˌbrɪtɪʃ 'saɪn ˌlæŋgwɪdʒ/ *noun* a dialect of sign language used primarily in the UK. Abbreviation **BSL**

British Sky Broadcasting /ˌbrɪtɪʃ skaɪ 'brɔːdkɑːstɪŋ/ *noun* full form of **BSkyB**

broadband access /'brɔːdbænd ˌækses/ *noun* a connection to the Internet that allows it to remain connected while still using phone and fax facilities on the same line, as many signals can be transmitted simultaneously. Compare **dial-up access**

broadband cable /'brɔːdbænd ˌkeɪb(ə)l/ *noun* a cable which allows broadband communications

broadband communications /ˌbrɔːdbænd kəˌmjuːnɪ'keɪʃ(ə)nz/ *plural noun* the number of different communications channels which are available using broadband cable

broadcast /'brɔːdkɑːst/ noun **1.** a television or radio programme **2.** the transmission of a radio or television programme ■ verb **1.** to take part in a radio or television programme **2.** to transmit information or a television or radio programme

Broadcast Development Ltd /ˌbrɔːdkɑːst dɪ'veləpmənt ˌlɪmɪtɪd/ noun full form of **BDL**

Broadcasters' Audience Research Board /ˌbrɔːdkɑːstəz ˌɔːdiəns rɪ'sɜːtʃ ˌbɔːd/ noun a body that provides official viewing figures for broadcasters, based on a panel of approximately 5,000 homes in the UK. Abbreviation **BARB**

broadcasting /'brɔːdkɑːstɪŋ/ noun the practice of making and transmitting television and radio programmes

Broadcasting, Entertainment, Cinematograph and Theatre Union noun full form of **BECTU**

Broadcasting Act 1980 /'brɔːdkɑːstɪŋ ækt/ noun the act of Parliament that set up provisions for the new Channel 4 in the UK and S4C in Wales, administered by the Independent Broadcasting Authority

Broadcasting Act 1990 /'brɔːdkɑːstɪŋ ækt/ noun the act of Parliament that proposed Channel 5 in the UK, and recommended a devolution of power from the BBC by creating more satellite radio and television channels and by allocating television franchises

Broadcasting Act 1996 noun the act of Parliament that removed regulations on licensing for media groups in the UK and also paved the way for a greater number of digital channels

Broadcasting Complaints Commission /ˌbrɔːdkɑːstɪŋ kəm'pleɪnts kə,mɪʃ(ə)n/ noun the body that formerly investigated complaints about decency and unjust treatment in broadcasting. It was merged with the Broadcasting Standards Council in 1994 to form the Broadcasting Standards Commission.

Broadcasting Corporation of New Zealand /ˌbrɔːdkɑːstɪŋ ˌkɔːpəreɪʃ(ə)n əv ˌnjuː 'ziːlənd/ noun until 1988, the company that had the monopoly on television and radio broadcasting in New Zealand. It was dissolved to allow freer competition. Abbreviation **BCNZ**

Broadcasting Data Services /ˌbrɔːdkɑːstɪŋ 'deɪtə ˌsɜːvɪsɪz/ noun a company that supplies television schedule information to listings programmes and magazines. Abbreviation **BDS**

broadcasting media /'brɔːdkɑːstɪŋ ˌmiːdiə/ plural noun media such as radio or television

Broadcasting Standards Commission /ˌbrɔːdkɑːstɪŋ 'stændənz kə,mɪʃ(ə)n/ noun the body formerly responsible for regulating broadcasting standards in the UK, adjudicating on complaints and undertaking research into standards and fairness. It was formed in 1994 by the merger of the Broadcasting Standards Council and the Broadcasting Complaints Commission, and was itself replaced by OFCOM under the 2003 Communications Act. ◊ **OFCOM**

Broadcasting Standards Council /ˌbrɔːdkɑːstɪŋ 'stændənz ˌkaʊns(ə)l/ noun a body formerly responsible for monitoring broadcasting standards in the UK, particularly in relation to the amount or sex, drugs and violence broadcast. It was merged with the Broadcasting Complaints Commission in 1994 to form the Broadcasting Standards Commission.

broadcast quality /ˌbrɔːdkɑːst 'kwɒlɪti/ noun a quality of video image or signal that is the same as that used by professional television stations

'In what they describe as the first ever interactive and broadband election, they will beam broadcast quality video footage directly to people's computers.' [Richard Alleyne, *The Daily Telegraph*]

broadsheet /'brɔːdʃiːt/ noun a large-size newspaper such as the Daily Telegraph, with the added implication that it covers the news in a serious, informative way. Compare **tabloid**

COMMENT: *The Guardian, The Times* and *The Independent* have recently changed from the broadsheet format to smaller formats, leaving *The Daily Telegraph* and *The Financial Times* as the only national broadsheets in the UK In most cases the new format adopted by these newspapers was the tabloid format – blurring the alleged quality distinction between the two formats – but *The Guardian* instead adopted the Berliner format. The main reason for the change in format was to make the newspapers more portable, and this seems to have had the effect of increasing sales.

brochure /'brəʊʃə/ *noun* a booklet or pamphlet that contains advertising and descriptive details of products or services

brochure site /'brəʊʃə saɪt/ *noun* a simple website that advertises a company's products and gives contact details

B roll /'biː rəʊl/ *noun* the secondary footage used in an edited sequence, such as scene-setting background shots, footage of the interviewer etc., used for cutaways. Compare **A roll**

bromide paper /'brəʊmaɪd ˌpeɪpə/ *noun* a type of light-sensitive photographic paper that is coated with a layer of silver bromide emulsion

Bronze Lion /ˌbrɒnz 'laɪən/ *noun* an award given at the Cannes International Advertising Festival

browse /braʊz/ *noun* a leisurely look through something such as a magazine or newspaper, or around a shop ■ *verb* to look up and view websites, particularly on the Internet

browser /'braʊzə/ *noun* a software program that allows a user to browse the World Wide Web

browsing /'braʊzɪŋ/ *noun* the activity of moving through sites on the Internet, a list of files or a multimedia title in no particular order

brute /bruːt/ *noun* TV a large arc lamp

B-side /'biː saɪd/ *noun* the less important side of a pop, rock, or jazz single, which does not usually contain the title track

BSkyB /ˌbiː skaɪ 'biː/ *noun* a company operating the most popular subscription satellite television service in the UK. Full form **British Sky Broadcasting**

BSL *abbreviation* **British Sign Language**

bubble /'bʌb(ə)l/ *noun* PRESS same as **balloon**

bubblegum /'bʌb(ə)lgʌm/ *noun* a type of commercial pop music that is aimed at young teenagers and usually considered to be unoriginal and banal

bucket /'bʌkɪt/ *noun* the bottom bar in a colour bar test pattern, which is usually red

buddy movie /'bʌdi ˌmuːvi/ *noun* a film that focuses on the adventures and relationship of two friends

buffo /'bʊfəʊ/ *noun* a male opera singer, especially a bass in a comic role

bulk eraser /ˌbʌlk ɪ'reɪzə/ *noun* a device for wiping the contents from magnetic tape

bulk mail /'bʌlk meɪl/ *noun* mail, usually advertising, that is sent by post at reduced rates because there is a lot of it

bulk rate /'bʌlk reɪt/ *noun* a cheap rate offered to advertisers who take large amounts of advertising space

bullet /'bʊlɪt/ *noun* a printed dot placed before a line of text to highlight it, for example, at the beginning of a paragraph or to introduce an item in a list. Also called **bullet point**

bulleted /'bʊlɪtɪd/ *adjective* referring to a line of text such as the beginning of a paragraph, or an item in a list, that is marked by a bullet

bulletin /'bʊlɪtɪn/ *noun* a radio report with information on for example the weather or the traffic

bulletin board /'bʊlɪtɪn bɔːd/ *noun* a website that allows members of an interest group to exchange e-mails, chat online and access software

Bulletin Board System /'bʊlɪtɪn bɔːd ˌsɪstəm/ *noun* a precursor to the Internet, using software that could dial up a connection and upload and download information. Abbreviation **BBS**

bullet point /'bʊlɪt pɔɪnt/ *noun* same as **bullet**

bumper /'bʌmpə/ *noun* a short separating device such as a piece of music, after and before a commercial break in a radio or television programme

bumper sticker /'bʌmpə ˌstɪkə/ *noun* an sticker put onto the bumper of a car to advertise a product or convey a message

burden of representation /ˌbɜːd(ə)n əv ˌreprɪzen'teɪʃ(ə)n/ *noun* the difficulties faced by the media when they use a single character to represent an entire social group, wishing to avoid creating stereotypes or unwelcome associations

bureau /'bjʊərəʊ/ *noun* an office attached to a newspaper but in a different country

burn /bɜːn/ *verb* to copy data onto a CD

burned-in timecode /ˌbɜːnd ɪn 'taɪmkəʊd/ *noun* a timecode which is included in a video signal as an image that is visible on any television or monitor. Abbreviation **BITC**

burn in /ˌbɜːn ˈɪn/ *verb* to expose to light part of an image on photographic paper, while protecting other areas so that they do not darken any further

burst campaign /ˈbɜːst kæmˌpeɪn/ *noun* a concentrated period of advertising for a product, such as before the launch of a new product line. Compare **drip campaign**

bury /ˈberi/ *verb* **1.** to release news at a time at which it will be given less coverage, for example when a another large important story is breaking **2.** to place important information within the body of the text so that it is less noticeable and loses its impact

bush telegraph /ˌbʊʃ ˈtelɪɡrɑːf/ *noun* **1.** a primitive method of communicating over long distances, such as by beating a drum **2.** a method of communicating information or rumours swiftly and unofficially by word of mouth or other means

business /ˈbɪznɪs/ *noun* an action or series of actions that an actor includes for dramatic or comic effect or to fill in a pause when nothing of interest is happening on stage

business-to-business advertising /ˌbɪznɪs tə ˈbɪznɪs ˌædvətaɪzɪŋ/ *noun* advertising aimed at businesses and not at households or private consumers

bust /bʌst/ *noun* the situation when an article or headline is larger than the space allotted to it. Compare **fit**

button apathy /ˈbʌt(ə)n ˌæpəθi/ *noun* the condition of a television viewer who watches a programme purely because they were watching the previous programme on that channel and they cannot be bothered to change channels

buying service /ˈbaɪɪŋ ˌsɜːvɪs/ *noun* an agency that buys advertising space or time for its clients

buy-up /ˈbaɪ ʌp/ *noun* MEDIA same as **chequebook journalism**

buzz track /ˈbʌz træk/ *noun* BROADCAST same as **atmosphere**

BW *abbreviation* PHOTOGRAPHY **black-and-white**

byline /ˈbaɪlaɪn/ *noun* a credit for the journalist who has written an article, sometimes with a photograph. Also called **sign-off**

byte /baɪt/ *noun* the basic unit of electronic data storage. The size of files and of a computer's memory are measured in bytes, kilobytes, megabytes or gigabytes.

C

cabaret /ˈkæbəreɪ/ *noun* live entertainment in a restaurant, club or bar, consisting of singing, dancing or comic acts

cable /ˈkeɪb(ə)l/ *verb* **1.** to send a telegram **2.** to supply a place with a link to a cable telecommunications network ■ *noun* **1.** a telegram, nowadays sent abroad by telephone, radio or satellite, and formerly sent by submarine cable **2.** TV same as **cable television**

cable-access /ˈkeɪb(ə)l ˌækses/ *adjective* relating to television programming that is made for and by a particular community, as opposed to commercially produced material

cablecast /ˈkeɪb(ə)lkɑːst/ *noun* a broadcast that is transmitted on a cable television network

cable duct /ˈkeɪb(ə)l dʌkt/ *noun* a permanent channel under some sort of obstacle such as a road, through which cables for broadcast equipment can be run

cable modem /ˈkeɪb(ə)l ˌməʊdem/ *noun* a modem that enables a computer to connect to the Internet via a cable television network

Cable News Network /ˌkeɪb(ə)l njuːz ˈnetwɜːk/ *noun* full form of **CNN**

cable penetration /ˌkeɪb(ə)l ˌpenɪˈtreɪʃ(ə)n/ *noun* the number of homes in the UK that have cable television subscriptions

cable reel extension /ˌkeɪb(ə)l riːl ɪkˈstenʃən/ an extension lead that can be wound up on a reel and stored away

cable release /ˈkeɪb(ə)l rɪˌliːs/ *noun* an extension cable on the shutter release system of a camera that is used to take photographs without shaking the camera, for example on long exposures

cable run /ˈkeɪb(ə)l rʌn/ *noun* the route of a cable for broadcast equipment

cable television /ˌkeɪb(ə)l ˌtelɪˈvɪʒ(ə)n/, **cable TV** /ˌkeɪb(ə)l ˌtiːˈviː/ *noun* a television service that a viewer receives via a cable from a particular station and pays for by subscription. Also called **cable**

cache /kæʃ/ *noun* a system of storing data from visited websites in a temporary file on a person's computer, speeding up access to related pages

café society /ˈkæfeɪ səˌsaɪəti/ *noun* the people, particularly working in the media, who attend fashionable events and visit fashionable restaurants, clubs and bars

'But after a few weeks I began to tire of the constant round of promotional parties that fuel this bright, shiny and, of course, ultimately false world. It was the worst excesses of café society and my boyfriend hated it.' [Julia Stephenson, *The Daily Mail*]

Cahiers du Cinéma /ˌkaɪeɪ duː ˈsɪnemɑː/ *noun* a French film magazine of the 1950s, concerned with New Wave cinema

Calcutt Committee Report on Privacy and Related Matters 1990 /ˈkælkʌt/ *noun* a report which investigated privacy issues and the press, recommending the formation of the Broadcasting Complaints Commission

call /kɔːl/ *verb* **1.** to contact a person by telephone or radio **2.** to give a running commentary on a sports event, especially a horse race

callback /ˈkɔːlbæk/ *noun* the practice of making a second or further attempt to contact a person for interview, random sampling etc., after the first attempt has failed

caller /'kɔːlə/ *noun* a person who gives a running commentary on a sports event, especially a horse race

call-in /'kɔːl ɪn/ *noun* a telephone call from a radio listener or a television viewer to a talk show

call letters /'kɔːl ˌletəz/ *plural noun* a particular sequence of letters that a radio station uses to identify itself when broadcasting

call sheet /'kɔːl ʃiːt/ *noun* a schedule of the times that each actor in a film should arrive on set for a day's shooting

calotype /'kæləʊtaɪp/ *noun* **1.** an early photographic process in which a negative was produced on paper coated with silver iodide **2.** a photograph produced by the calotype process

calypso /kə'lɪpsəʊ/ *noun* Caribbean dance music that has syncopated rhythms, is usually improvised, and is often played by a steel band

camcorder /'kæmkɔːdə/ *noun* a camera that both films and records video pictures

cameo /'kæmiəʊ/ *noun* a short appearance by a famous actor in a film or play

camera /'kæm(ə)rə/ *noun* **1.** a device for taking photographs by letting light from an image fall briefly onto sensitized film, usually by means of a lens-and-shutter mechanism **2.** a device that converts images into electrical signals for television transmission, video recording or digital storage

camera angle /'kæm(ə)rə ˌæŋɡəl/ *noun* the relation between the position of the camera and the action being filmed, for example higher, lower, closer or further away

camera card /'kæm(ə)rə kɑːd/ *noun* the directions for an individual camera, attached to the camera for constant reference throughout a film shoot

camera control unit /ˌkæm(ə)rə kən'trəʊl ˌjuːnɪt/ *noun* a console in a television production control room that allows cameras on the studio floor to be controlled remotely. Abbreviation **CCU**

camera lucida /ˌkæm(ə)rə 'luːsɪdə/ *noun* an instrument that allows an image to be projected onto a surface such as a piece of paper, so that it can be traced

camera obscura /ˌkæm(ə)rə ɒb'skjʊərə/ *noun* the precursor of a modern camera that uses a dark chamber with a small aperture allowing light in, which brings an image of an object outside into focus on a facing surface

cameraperson /'kæm(ə)rəˌpɜːsən/ *noun* the operator of a video, film or television camera

camera-ready /'kæm(ə)rə ˌredi/ *adjective* referring to material that is of good enough quality to be photographed for the purpose of creating printing plates

camera script /'kæm(ə)rə skrɪpt/ *noun* a script which includes camera directions

camera-shy /'kæm(ə)rə ʃaɪ/ *adjective* referring to a subject who dislikes being photographed or filmed

'No Direction Home is the first-ever film biography of this notoriously camera-shy figure and sees Dylan granting Scorsese his first full-length interview in 20 years.' [Fiona Sturges, *The Independent*]

camerawoman /'kæm(ə)rəˌwʊmən/ *noun* a woman who operates a video, film or television camera

camerawork /'kæm(ə)rəwɜːk/ *noun* the camera techniques used in making films or television programmes

cam L /ˌkæm 'el/ *noun* the left-hand side of a stage or set from the camera's point of view, facing towards the actors. Compare **stage left**

camp /kæmp/ *adjective* referring to the intentionally theatrical, often effeminate behaviour supposedly characteristic of homosexual men

campaign /kæm'peɪn/ *noun* a coordinated attempt to persuade an audience of something. ◊ **advertising campaign**

Campaign for Press and Broadcasting Freedom /kæmˌpeɪn fə ˌpres ən 'brɔːdkɑːstɪŋ ˌfriːdəm/ *noun* a pressure group in the UK that campaigns for greater accountability of the media, particularly for the right to reply

Campaign for Quality Television /kæmˌpeɪn fə ˌ'kwɒləti 'telɪvɪʒ(ə)n/ *noun* a campaign relaunched in 1995 that maintains that the quality of television programming is being compromised as a result of deregulation, independent production and the increasing number of channels available

campaigning journalism /ˌkæm ˈpeɪnɪŋ ˈdʒɜːnəlɪz(ə)m/ *noun* the practice of reporting a story from a particular viewpoint or promoting a cause

cam R /ˌkæm ˈɑː/ *noun* the right-hand side of a stage or set from the camera's point of view, facing towards the actors. Compare **stage right**

Canadian Broadcasting Corporation /kəˌneɪdiən ˈbrɔːdkɑːstɪŋ ˌkɔːpəreɪʃ(ə)n/ *noun* the government-owned public service broadcaster of radio and television programmes in Canada. Abbreviation **CBC**

Canadian Press /kəˈneɪdiən pres/ *noun* the major multimedia news and information service for Canada. Abbreviation **CP**

cancel /ˈkæns(ə)l/ *noun* **1.** a page or section of a book that needs to be replaced because it contains an error **2.** a page or section of a book that is inserted to replace one that was missing or one that was faulty

candid /ˈkændɪd/ *noun* an unposed and informal photograph of a person or group ■ *adjective* referring to a photograph or film that was taken without the subject knowing or having the opportunity to prepare or pose

'…this book, with its candid photographs of Lennon, like this one with Yoko Ono and baby son Sean, is something different from the usual look at the boys with their haircuts and guitars.' [*The Express*]

candid camera /ˌkændɪd ˈkæm(ə)rə/ *noun* the practice of secretly filming subjects who are likely to do something amusing in situations that are often stage-managed for the sake of viewers' entertainment

canned /kænd/ *adjective* **1.** referring to audience laughter on a television programme which is dubbed in later, rather than provided by a live audience reacting to the jokes in the show **2.** referring to a website that is designed according to a standard template rather than to particular specifications

Cannes Film Festival /ˌkæn ˈfɪlm ˌfestɪvəl/ *noun* a prestigious film festival held annually in May in Cannes, south-

east France and attended by stars and the media

Cannes International Advertising Festival /ˌkæn ˌɪntənæʃ(ə)nəl ˈædvətaɪzɪŋ ˌfestɪvəl/ *noun* an annual festival held to honour the best in advertising, which awards the prestigious Palme d'Or to the best production company and Gold, Silver and Bronze Lion awards to advertising agencies

canon /ˈkænən/ *noun* **1.** in aesthetic theory, the collection of literature from classical to modern times, which forms the backbone of literary culture and embodies all human and moral values **2.** the accepted 'history' of a fictional character, which provides background for their current actions

cans /kænz/ *plural noun* a set of headphones

cap /kæp/ *abbreviation* **capital letter**

CAP *abbreviation* **Committee of Advertising Practice**

CAP codes /ˌsiː eɪ ˈpiː ˌkəʊdz/ *plural noun* the codes of advertising standards and practice which are written by the Committee of Advertising Practice and enforced by the ASA

capi *abbreviation* **computer-assisted personal interview**

capital /ˈkæpɪt(ə)l/ *adjective* referring to the form of letters used at the beginning of sentences and names, for example A, B and C as distinct from a, b and c ■ *noun* same as **capital letter**

capitalise /ˈkæpɪtəlaɪz/ *verb* to write or print something with an initial capital letter or entirely in capital letters

capitalism /ˈkæpɪt(ə)lɪz(ə)m/ *noun* an economic system in which goods are owned and controlled by private individuals and their movements dictated by the free market

capitalist /ˈkæpɪt(ə)lɪst/ *adjective* relating to capitalism in terms of outlook or policy

capital letter /ˌkæpɪt(ə)l ˈletə/ *noun* an alphabetical letter in the larger form used to begin sentences and names, for example A, B or C. Also called **capital**. Abbreviation **cap**

caps /kæps/ *plural noun* capital letters

capstan /ˈkæpstən/ *noun* a spindle of a tape player that keeps the tape pressed against the magnetic read/write head or pinch roller

caption /'kæpʃən/ *noun* **1.** a few words accompanying a picture or piece of artwork **2.** a short piece of on-screen writing which explains something that is happening, for example the name of a person that is talking **3.** same as **subtitle**

capture card /'kæptʃə kɑːd/ *noun* a removable device on video equipment which receives analogue signals, which the computer converts to digital

carabiner /ˌkærə'biːnə/ *noun* a steel coupling link for connecting equipment securely

carbon process /'kɑːbən ˌprəʊses/ *noun* a method of making photographic print by soaking carbon tissue in a sensitising solution to produce positive prints

card deck /'kɑːd dek/ *noun* a series of small cards, advertising different products or services, that are posted to prospective customers as a pack in a plastic envelope

cardioid microphone /ˌkɑːdiɔɪd 'maɪkrəfəʊn/ *noun* a microphone with a pick-up pattern which captures most sounds in the vicinity

card rate /'kɑːd reɪt/ *noun* an advertising charge which is based on the charges listed in a rate card, i.e. without any discounts

caret /'kærət/ *noun* a symbol written on a piece of text to show where something such as a letter or word should be inserted

caricature /'kærɪkətjʊə/ *noun* a drawing, description or performance that exaggerates somebody's or something's characteristics for humorous or satirical effect

'Wright is not only something of a genius as a writer, he is also clearly a good sport who has no objection to being portrayed as a hilariously camp and po-faced caricature gay.' [Rebecca Tyrell, *The Daily Telegraph*]

carnival /'kɑːnɪv(ə)l/ *noun* the idea of an 'escape from reality', in which people temporarily ignore the restrictions society normally imposes on them and enjoy excess in all its forms for a short period

carousel /ˌkærə'sel/ *noun* a circular holder for photographic slides that turns through the projector so that the pictures can be viewed one after the other

carrier /'kæriə/ *noun* **1.** a company that conveys telecommunications messages **2.** a high-frequency electromagnetic wave that is modulated to carry a signal in radio or television transmission

carrier wave /'kæriə weɪv/ *noun* BROADCAST, TELECOMS same as **carrier**

carry /'kæri/ *verb* to publish or broadcast an article, picture, item of news or piece of information

cartel /kɑː'tel/ *noun* a group of companies who illegally and secretly agree to fix the price of their products in order to destroy the competition

cartoon /kɑː'tuːn/ *noun* **1.** a humorous or satirical drawing relating to a topical event and published in a newspaper or magazine **2.** a strip of drawings, sometimes with captions, that tell a short story and are published in a newspaper or magazine **3.** an animated film, especially a humorous one intended primarily for children. Also called **toon** **4.** a full-size drawing, often including a large amount of detail, that is done as preparation for a painting or other work of art

cartoonish /kɑː'tuːnɪʃ/ *adjective* relating to or reminiscent of an animated cartoon

cartridge /'kɑːtrɪdʒ/ *noun* **1.** the end section of the arm of a record player that holds the needle over the record **2. cartidge, cart** a plastic box containing a length of magnetic tape for recording

cascading style sheet /kæˌskeɪdɪŋ 'staɪl ˌʃiːt/ *noun* a method of describing the font, spacing and colour of text within a webpage and storing this information in a style sheet that can be applied to any text within the page. Abbreviation **CSS**

case /keɪs/ *noun* **1.** PRINTING a compartmentalised tray in which loose metal type is kept before being combined for printing **2.** one of the two kinds of printed letters of the alphabet, either a capital or small letter

cassette /kə'set/ *noun* a sealed plastic box containing a length of audiotape or videotape for playing or recording

cassette recorder /kə'set rɪˌkɔːdə/ *noun* a machine for transferring audio signals onto magnetic tape

cast /kɑːst/ *noun* **1.** the actors or other performers in a drama, dance or other production **2.** each individual part of a multimedia presentation or animation. The members of a cast can be individual images, sound clips or text. ■ *verb* to choose somebody for a particular role in a drama, dance, or other performance, or choose people for all the roles in a production

casting agency /'kɑːstɪŋ ˌeɪdʒənsi/ *noun* a company which will audition and hire actors for a particular production

Casting Society of America /ˌkɑːstɪŋ səˌsaɪəti əv əˈmerɪkə/ *noun* an association of film, television and theatre casting directors in the USA. Abbreviation **CSA**

cast off /ˌkɑːst ˈɒf/ *verb* to estimate the potential length of a story

castoff /'kɑːstɒf/ *noun* an estimate of how much space a piece of text will occupy when it is printed in a particular font and size

casual /'kæʒuəl/ *noun* a journalist employed on a temporary rather than a permanent basis by a newspaper

casualisation /ˌkæʒuəlaɪˈzeɪʃ(ə)n/ *noun* the process whereby jobs in the media industry are shifting from generally full-time, long-term contracts to more part-time or project-based appointments. This is seen as a double-edged sword, opening up the field to free competition based on talent, but raising concerns about training and specialisation of employees.

catalyst effect /'kætəlɪst ɪˌfekt/ *noun* the process whereby coverage of an issue in the media can draw attention to it or present it in a particular way, which can lead to knock-on effects for the issue itself, such as increased funding for a charity

catch /kætʃ/ *verb* to manage to capture somebody or something on film or tape

catchline /'kætʃlaɪn/ *noun* a word at the top of a script that identifies an item on a radio programme. Also called **slug**

catchword /'kætʃwɜːd/ *noun* the first word on a page of printed text, that also appears in the bottom right-hand corner of the previous page, originally placed there to draw the binder's attention to it

catharsis /kəˈθɑːsɪs/ *noun* the idea that exposure to emotive media products such as violence on television, or a tragic play in a theatre, is therapeutic for the audience and releases emotions in a harmless way

cathode ray tube /ˌkæθəʊd ˈreɪ ˌtjuːb/ *noun* a display device for television and computer screens which uses electron beams fired at the screen's phosphorescent coating to display video pictures

Catholic Legion of Decency /ˌkæθlɪk ˌliːdʒ(ə)n əv ˈdiːs(ə)nsi/ *noun* a US pressure group advocating severe film censorship from the 1930s, made up of religious leaders from all Catholic denominations

CATV *abbreviation* TV **community antenna television**

CBC *abbreviation* BROADCAST **Canadian Broadcasting Corporation**

cc /ˌsiː ˈsiː/ *noun* a copy of an e-mail message sent to another recipient ■ *verb* to copy a message to another recipient, either by using the cc line on an e-mail or by sending a photocopy

CC *abbreviation* **closed captioning**

CCIR 601 /ˌsiː siː aɪ ɑː ˌsɪks əʊ ˈwʌn/ *noun* a recommended standard for defining digital video

c-clamp /'siː klæmp/ *noun* the standard clamp used to attach lights to a studio's lighting rig

CCTV *abbreviation* BROADCAST, TV **closed-circuit television**

CCU *abbreviation* **camera control unit**

CD /ˌsiː ˈdiː/ *noun* a small disk on which data can be stored and read by a computer or other device

CD+G /ˌsiː diː plʌs ˈdʒiː/, **CD+Graphics** /ˌsiː diː plʌs ˈgræfɪks/ *noun* a CD format that adds graphics data to an audio disc and so can be used to store song title information or display the lyrics of the song for use in karaoke

CD-ROM /ˌsiː diː ˈrɒm/ *noun* a disc which has computer-readable data on it

CDV *abbreviation* RECORDING, VIDEO **CD-video**

CD-video /ˌsiː diː ˈvɪdiəʊ/ *noun* **1.** a machine that plays compact discs that store and play back video images **2.** a compact disc that can store video images. Abbreviation **CDV**

CE *abbreviation* ONLINE **creative editing**

Ceefax /'siːfæks/ a trade name for the teletext service of the BBC

celebrity /sɪˈlebrəti/ *noun* a person in the public eye, who audiences are interested in finding out more about. Compare **star**

'So if Mr and Mrs Joe Public forget to pay for stuff they get the book thrown at them. But if you're a millionaire C-list celebrity who might help sell their clothes and give them a bit of free publicity – then, hey, take what you want.'

[Carole Malone, *The Sunday Mirror*]

COMMENT: A celebrity may be famous for a particular talent or skill that they have, but the fact that the are famous is often for other reasons such as a relationship with another famous person or the ability to 'sell' their personality and to appear interesting, attractive and entertaining.

celebrity journalism /sɪˈlebrəti ˌdʒɜːn(ə)lɪz(ə)m/ *noun* journalism which is concerned with the private lives of the rich and famous

cell /sel/ *noun* 1. the local area covered by one of the transmitters in a mobile telephone network 2. same as **animation cell**

cell phone /ˈsel fəʊn/ *noun* a mobile telephone

cellular /ˈseljʊlə/ *adjective* relating to a system of cells, such as in a mobile telephone network

cellular radio /ˌseljʊlə ˈreɪdiəʊ/ *noun* radio frequencies which operate in cells according to position, so that if a person is using a radio communications system in a car, they will be swapped to the right frequency as they move through cell areas

celluloid /ˈseljʊlɔɪd/ *noun* 1. the photographic film used for making films 2. the cinema as a medium or art form

censor /ˈsensə/ *verb* to remove or change any part of a play, film or publication because the content is considered offensive or a threat to security ■ *noun* an official who examines plays, films or publications with a view to removing or banning content considered to be offensive or a threat to security

censorship /ˈsensəʃɪp/ *noun* 1. the practice of deciding that something or part of something may not be broadcast, published, distributed etc., because of its content. ◊ **pre-emptive censorship**, **punitive censorship** 2. the suppression or attempted suppression of anything regarded as objectionable

centralised organisational structure /ˌsentrəlaɪzd ˌɔːɡənaɪzeɪʃ(ə)n(ə)l ˈstrʌktʃə/ *noun* a method of organising international advertising and promotion where all decisions are made in a company's central office

centralised system /ˌsentrəlaɪzd ˈsɪstəm/ *noun* a system where advertising and other marketing activities are run from one central marketing department

centrality /senˈtræliti/ *noun* the idea that a person is more influential because they communicate with a greater number and wider range of people

central machine room /ˌsentrəl mə ˈʃiːn ˌruːm/ *noun* in a broadcasting studio, a separate room in which heavy machinery is kept so that it does not produce excessive heat

centrefold /ˈsentəfəʊld/ *noun* 1. an illustration, advertisement or feature that stretches across the two facing pages in the middle of a magazine or newspaper 2. the subject of a centrefold photograph, especially a naked or nearly-naked model 3. PRESS same as **centre spread**

centre spread /ˌsentə ˈspred/ *noun* 1. the single piece of paper that forms the central two pages of a magazine or newspaper 2. an article that appears in the middle of a newspaper or magazine to give it prominence

cert. *abbreviation* CINEMA **certificate**

certificate /səˈtɪfɪkeɪt/ *noun* the rating given to films which dictates how old a person must be to see it, based on its content. Abbreviation **cert.**

COMMENT: In the United Kingdom, the ratings designated by the British Board of Film Certification are: Uc and U (suitable for children), PG (parents may not want extremely young children to see it), 12 (or 12A for films which children under the age of 12 can see if accompanied by an adult), 15 and 18 (suitable for viewers older than the specified age), and R18 (extremely explicit content). In the United States, the ratings designated by the Motion Picture Association of America are: G (suitable for all), PG, PG-13 (as PG but with some content not suitable for children under 13), R (not suitable for viewers under the age of 17 unless accompanied by an adult), NC-17 (suitable for viewers over the age of 17 only).

CGI /ˌsiː dʒiː ˈaɪ/ *noun* special visual effects created by a computer. Full form **Computer Generated Imagery**

channel /ˈtʃæn(ə)l/ *noun* 1. a television or radio station which broadcasts on a particular band of radio frequencies 2. a band of frequencies set aside for a particular purpose, such as broadcasting for a television or radio station

Channel 4 /ˌtʃæn(ə)l ˈfɔː/ *noun* a commercial television channel in the UK which was started in 1982 with a commitment to quality wide-ranging programming

Channel 5 /ˌtʃæn(ə)l ˈfaɪv/ *noun* a commercial television channel in the UK which started broadcasting in 1997

channel capacity /ˈtʃæn(ə)l kəˌpæsɪti/ *noun* the amount of information that a communication system can carry

channel-hop /ˈtʃæn(ə)l hɒp/ *verb* to browse through different television channels, especially using a remote control device

'...if you are a pop kid, it will be your kind of station. [My daughter] watches it occasionally. She channel hops and shows no loyalty to the channels. I think she is representative of her age.' [Jo Whiley, *The Independent*]

channel mapping /ˈtʃæn(ə)l ˌmæpɪŋ/ *noun* a function inside a television or digital set-top box that allows the device to find channels on the best frequency without the need for retuning

channel of communication /ˌtʃæn(ə)l əv kəˌmjuːnɪˈkeɪʃ(ə)n/ *noun* something such as a cable or a satellite system which is capable of transmitting signals

channel share /ˈtʃæn(ə)l ʃeə/ *noun* the percentage of all viewers who are watching a particular channel

channel-surf /ˈtʃæn(ə)l sɜːf/ *verb* same as **channel-hop**

chaos theory /ˈkeɪɒs ˌθɪəri/ *noun* the idea that although many natural systems are apparently based on rules and laws, they are prone to wild, seemingly random, changes in response to the tiniest change in conditions

chapel /ˈtʃæp(ə)l/ *noun* the National Union of Journalists' newspaper division

character /ˈkærɪktə/ *noun* a person in a book, play, or film

character actor /ˈkærɪktə ˌæktə/ *noun* an actor who does not generally play the lead role in productions but smaller, usually humorous roles such as the hero's best friend

character generator /ˈkærɪktə ˌdʒenəreɪtə/ *noun* a device for generating text on a screen

charge artist /ˈtʃɑːdʒ ˌɑːtɪst/ *noun* the member of a theatre production team who is responsible for overseeing the painting of stage scenery according to the set designer's plans

charge-coupled device /ˌtʃɑːdʒ ˌkʌp(ə)ld dɪˈvaɪs/ *noun* a high-speed semiconductor that processes the light patterns of images into digital signals for a computer, especially in digital cameras and optical scanners

Charlie /ˈtʃɑːli/ *noun* an internationally recognised code word for the letter C, used in radio communications

chart /tʃɑːt/ *verb* to appear in the charts of best-selling recordings

charts /tʃɑːts/ *plural noun* a list of the best-selling musical recordings of the last week or month, etc.

chart-topping /ˈtʃɑːt ˌtɒpɪŋ/ *adjective* referring to a musical number or performer at the top of the charts of best-selling musical recordings

chase /tʃeɪs/ *noun* PRINTING a rectangular metal frame into which metal type or blocks are placed as on a page, before it is printed

chat group /ˈtʃæt gruːp/ *noun* a group of people who share a common interest and exchange messages about it online

chat room /ˈtʃæt ruːm/ *noun* a website where computer users can exchange messages in real time

chat show /ˈtʃæt ʃəʊ/ *noun* a television or radio show on which the host interviews celebrities

chauvinism /ˈʃəʊvɪnɪz(ə)m/ *noun* extreme pride in belonging to a group, such as ones gender or nationality, especially when expressing disdain or hatred for a rival group

check call /ˈtʃek kɔːl/ *noun* a call made or visit paid by a journalist to a place such as a police station to see whether any news is breaking

chequebook journalism /ˈtʃekbʊk ˌdʒɜːn(ə)lɪz(ə)m/ *noun* the practice of paying somebody for an exclusive story, usually a dramatic one which will sell many copies of the newspaper and be prestigious for the journalist reporting it. Also called **buy-up**

cherry-picker /'tʃeri ˌpɪkə/ *noun* a hoist used to raise lights high above the action when making a film at night on location

chiaroscuro /ˌtʃærə'skjʊərəʊ/ *noun* a term originally from art appreciation that refers to a style of lighting which creates deep shadows and contrasts

chick flick /'tʃɪk flɪk/ *noun* a film that is aimed at or intended to appeal primarily to women

'This enjoyable but meandering picture... is a chick flick about the relationship between two sisters and how a crisis between them precipitates the discovery of some family secrets.'
[Henry Fizherbert, *The Sunday Express*]

chick lit /'tʃɪk lɪt/ *noun* a genre of book which is aimed at or intended to appeal primarily to women, on the same basis as chick flicks

Chief Income Earner /ˌtʃiːf 'ɪnkʌm ˌɜːnə/ *noun* a term used by advertisers to describe the individual in a household who earns the highest income

Chief Shopper /ˌtʃiːf 'ʃɒpə/ *noun* a term used by advertisers to describe the individual in a household who does the shopping for that household

chillout /'tʃɪlaʊt/ *noun* MUSIC same as **downtempo**

chimera /kaɪ'mɪərə/ *noun* a box that is put over a harsh light to soften the effect

chopsocky /'tʃɒpsɒki/ *noun* a genre of excessively violent films in which martial arts such as kung fu feature prominently

chora /'kɔːrə/ *noun* the link between two worlds, such as between mind and body, or between thoughts and feelings. This link is often described in feminist theory as the bridge between mother and child.

chorus /'kɔːrəs/ *noun* **1.** a set of lines that are sung at least twice in the course of a song, usually being repeated after each verse **2.** a group of people who appear, sing, and sometimes dance together as a unit in a performance, usually providing backing for the principal performers **3.** a group of actors in ancient Greek drama who sing or speak in unison, generally commenting on the significance of the events that take place in the play

chroma /'krəʊmə/ *noun* the parts of an image or video signal which control the colour of the image, represented by the symbol 'C'. Compare **luma**

chromakey /'krəʊməkiː/ *noun* a filming technique in which a particular colour in a shot is 'keyed out' and replaced by another background. An example of this on television is in weather reporting, where the presenter stands in front of a chromakey screen and the weather map is superimposed over it. Also called **blue-screen effect, colour separation overlay**

chrome tape /'krəʊm teɪp/ *noun* magnetic recording tape coated with chromium dioxide

chrominance /'krəʊmɪnəns/ *noun* the part of a video signal or image which contains colour hue and saturation information. Compare **luminance**

chronology /krə'nɒlədʒi/ *noun* the order in which events occur, or their arrangement according to this order

chronotope /'krɒnətəʊp/ *noun* a combination form from the Greek words for 'time' and 'place', describing the historical setting of a work such as a novel

churn /tʃɜːn/ *noun* the rate of turnover of a company's customers

'The operator has managed to reduce churn with its tempting discount packages in the first half of this year, and will be looking to keep defections low.'
[Jessica Ramakrishnan, *World Markets Analysis*]

chutney /'tʃʌtni/ *noun* a popular up-tempo style of East Indian song, usually written in Hindi or English and much influenced by calypso rhythms and subjects

cicero /'sɪsərəʊ/ *noun* a size of type slightly larger than the pica

cine- /sɪni/ *prefix* relating to film or motion pictures

cineaste /'sɪneɪæst/ *noun* **1.** a film-maker. Also called **cinephile 2.** a film enthusiast

cine camera /'sɪni ˌkæm(ə)rə/ *noun* a camera with a moving film in it for taking moving pictures

cine-club /'sɪni klʌb/ *noun* an independent rival to conventional cinemas showing less mainstream and often non-fictional films

cine film /'sɪni fɪlm/ *noun* photographic film used in a cine camera, for taking moving pictures

cinema /'sɪnɪmə/ *noun* **1.** a building or room designed for people to watch films in **2.** the art or business of making films **3.** films considered collectively **4.** cinemas considered collectively

cinema advertising /'sɪnɪmə ˌædvətaɪzɪŋ/ *noun* advertising using short films or still messages on cinema screens

cinemagoer /'sɪnɪmə,gəʊə/ *noun* a person who regularly goes to the cinema

CinemaScope /'sɪnɪməskəʊp/ *noun* the brand name for the anamorphic process which resulted in widescreen pictures developed by 20th Century Fox in the 1950s

cinematheque /'sɪnɪmətek/ *noun* a small cinema with an intimate atmosphere

cinematic /ˌsɪnɪ'mætɪk/ *adjective* **1.** relating to films or film-making **2.** referring to or reminiscent of the style in which films are made

'What Minghella has done… is to marry his genius for arresting cinematic images with the language of traditional Japanese theatre to create a truly spectacular production.' [Barry Millington, *Evening Standard*]

cinematise /'sɪnɪmətaɪz/ *verb* to make a play, novel or other work into a film for the cinema

cinematograph /ˌsɪnɪ'mætəgrɑːf/ *noun* a combined cine camera, printer and projector now rarely used

cinematographer /ˌsɪnɪmə'tɒgrəfə/ *noun* the person who is responsible for lighting and cameras on a film shoot

cinematographie /ˌsɪnɪmætɒgræ'fiː/ *noun* a brand of French camera for filming

cinematography /ˌsɪnɪmə'tɒgrəfi/ *noun* the lighting and photography in a film

cinephile /'sɪnɪfaɪl/ *noun* same as **cineaste**

Cinerama /ˌsɪnɪ'rɑːmə/ a trade name for a method of producing widescreen pictures developed in the 1950s, in which 3 separate projectors are used

ciné-verité /ˌsɪneɪ 'verɪteɪ/ *noun* a genre of film in which the film-maker tries to shoot documentary-style footage while interfering as little as possible in the scenes being filmed, usually with a small hand-held camera. Also called **direct cinema**

circular /'sɜːkjʊlə/ *noun* a message such as an advertisement or announcement, that is distributed to a large number of people

circulation /ˌsɜːkjʊ'leɪʃ(ə)n/ *noun* the number of copies sold of each issue of a publication. Compare **readership**

citizenship /'sɪtɪz(ə)nʃɪp/ *noun* the idea of being a participating, aware member of a community such as a state

city desk /'sɪti desk/ *noun* the section of a newspaper devoted to financial reporting

city editor /'sɪti ˌedɪtə/ *noun* **1.** the newspaper editor who deals with financial and commercial news **2.** the newspaper editor in charge of local news

city room /'sɪti ruːm/ *noun* the department of a newspaper that deals with local news

cityscape /'sɪtiskeɪp/ *noun* a picture of all or part of a city or town

civil inattention /ˌsɪv(ə)l ˌɪnə'tentʃ(ə)n/ *noun* a typical way that strangers behave, for example in the street, in which they may make brief eye contact, but quickly retract it to remove the need for recognition or further contact

civil society /ˌsɪv(ə)l sə'saɪəti/ *noun* the institutions, social relationships and organisations that function under the rule of the state but are not necessarily aligned with it

clapper board /'klæpə bɔːd/ *noun* a pair of hinged boards filmed at the start of each take in a film to identify it, and clapped together to help to synchronise the soundtrack with the film. Also called **slate**

clapper/loader /'klæpə ˌləʊdə/ *noun* an assistant on the camera crew whose job it is to reload the cameras with film and to operate the clapper board at the start of each shot

Clarendon /'klærəndən/ *noun* a style of boldface roman type

class /klɑːs/ *noun* **1.** a social classification loosely based on the comparative level of wealth and opportunity into which a person is born **2.** ♦ **JICNARS scale**

classification /ˌklæsɪfɪ'keɪʃ(ə)n/ *noun* the process of putting people or things into categories such as grouping people according to their economic status or classifying films according to the minimum age that a person must be to watch it

classified ads /'klæsɪfaɪd ædz/, **classifieds** *plural noun* advertisements that are grouped together in a newspaper or magazine according to their subject matter, usually without illustrations. Compare **display ads**

classified display advertising /ˌklæsɪfaɪd dɪs'pleɪ ˌædvətaɪzɪŋ/ *noun* advertising that, although it is classified, may also have individual features such as its own box border or the company logo

Claymation /ˌkleɪ'meɪʃ(ə)n/ a trade name for the process of creating animated films from sequences of images of clay figures. The figures are moved slightly between each shot so that they appear to move when the sequence is run at the correct speed.

clean /kliːn/ *adjective* referring to text that contains relatively few mistakes or corrections

clean feed /'kliːn fiːd/ *noun* **1.** a video recording without any added captions **2.** a sound recording without added commentary **3.** an earpiece that a television or radio presenter uses to hear all sound apart from their own commentary. Also called **clean FX, mix minus**

clean FX /ˌkliːn ˌef 'eks/ *noun* same as **clean feed**

Clean Up TV Movement /ˌkliːn ʌp ˌtiː 'viː 'muːvmənt/ *noun* formerly, a movement dedicated to clean, moral and wholesome programming, formed in 1963 by Mary Whitehouse

clear /klɪə/ *verb* to release a communications link when transmissions have finished

clearing house /'klɪərɪŋ haʊs/ *noun* an central agency that collects and distributes information

clear scan /'klɪə skæn/ *noun* a function that reduces the flicker seen when filming a computer monitor or television screen, by adjusting the scan rate of the recording device

cliché /'kliːʃeɪ/ *noun* a phrase or word that is overused and has therefore lost its original effectiveness or power

click /klɪk/ *verb* to press and release a key or a button on a keyboard or the mouse ■ *noun* the act of pressing a mouse button or a key on a keyboard

clicker /'klɪkə/ *noun* a foreman or forewoman in a printing press

clickstream /'klɪkstriːm/ *noun* a record of how a user navigates around a website, sometimes used in marketing research

click through /'klɪk θruː/ *noun* an act of clicking on a banner ad or other on-screen advertising that takes the user through to the advertiser's website

click through rate /'klɪk θruː ˌreɪt/ *noun* a method of charging an advertiser for the display of a banner advertisement on a website. Each time a visitor clicks on a displayed advertisement which links to the advertiser's main site, the advertiser is charged a fee.

'The interactive banners could be downloaded and include hilarious, cartoonish ads… the ad campaign boasted a click-through rate 12% higher than the average.' [*Advertising Age*]

client list /'klaɪənt lɪst/ *noun* a list of clients of an advertising agency

cliffhanger /'klɪfhæŋə/ *noun* an unresolved ending in a part of a serialised drama or book that leaves the audience or reader eager to know what will happen next

climax order /'klaɪmæks ˌɔːdə/ *noun* a method of arranging arguments or main points in a narrative so that the most important point is presented at the end. Compare **anti-climax order**

Clio /'kliːəʊ/ *noun* an annual award for excellence in package design and advertising in print, on television and on radio

clip /klɪp/ *noun* an extract from a recording. Also called **cut**

clipart /'klɪpɑːt/ *noun* commercially produced artwork that is available freely at low cost. Many computers contain free clipart.

clipper chip /'klɪpə tʃɪp/ *noun* a data-encryption chip proposed in the mid-1990s allowing communication by computer that it was implanted in to be recorded and >'spied on'. It was thought invasive and potentially insecure and was never developed.

clippings /ˈklɪpɪŋz/ *plural noun* PRESS same as **cuttings**

clipsheet /ˈklɪpʃiːt/ *noun* text from a newspaper or magazine reprinted on one side of plain paper and used for distribution to interested parties

clone /kləʊn/ *noun* an exact copy of a digital recording, taken as back-up

closed /kləʊzd/ *adjective* referring to a narrative that is brought to a conclusion at the end. Compare **open**

closed-captioned /ˌkləʊzd ˈkæpʃənd/ *adjective* referring to a broadcast that has captions, for example for the hard of hearing, that can be seen if the television set is fitted with the correct decoder

closed captioning /ˌkləʊzd ˈkæpʃənɪŋ/ *noun* a system that transfers text information with a video signal so that the text data can be decoded and displayed at the bottom of the television screen. Abbreviation **CC**

closed-circuit television /ˌkləʊzd ˌsɜːkɪt ˈtelɪvɪʒ(ə)n/ *noun* a television transmission system in which cameras transmit pictures by cable to connected monitors. Surveillance systems are based on this type of transmission.

closed-face lamp /ˌkləʊzd feɪs ˈlæmp/ *noun* same as **spot**

close down /ˌkləʊz ˈdaʊn/ *verb* to stop broadcasting for the day

closedown /ˈkləʊzdaʊn/ *noun* the end of a period of broadcasting

closed text /ˌkləʊzd ˈtekst/ *noun* a text which leaves very little room for free interpretation of meaning. Compare **open text**

close-up /ˈkləʊs ʌp/ *noun* a shot which shows the whole of a person's face, but no other part of their body. Abbreviation **CU**

closing sentence /ˌkləʊzɪŋ ˈsentəns/ *noun* the last sentence in a marketing e-mail which pushes the customer to take action

closure /ˈkləʊʒə/ *noun* a situation in which somebody receiving a piece of communication 'closes down' and refuses to accept any more of it, usually because it conflicts with the receiver's already-held beliefs or values

clown /klaʊn/ *noun* **1.** a person who behaves comically **2.** a comic performer, usually in a circus, who often wears an outlandish costume and heavy makeup

cluster group /ˈklʌstə gruːp/ *noun* in audience analysis, a group of people with similar traits, lifestyle, social background etc

clutter /ˈklʌtə/ *noun* **1.** a mass of advertising units shown together, so that any single advertisement or commercial tends to get lost **2.** visual stimuli which distract a viewer or reader from the main message, such as flashy advertisements on a webpage

CMA *abbreviation* **Community Media Association**

CMCCR *abbreviation* **combined mobile central control room**

CMCR *abbreviation* **colour mobile control room**

CMYK /ˌsiː em waɪ ˈkeɪ/ *noun* the standard colour model for printing in which all colours are described in terms of cyan, magenta, yellow and black

CNN /ˌsiː en ˈen/ *noun* an international news and broadcasting company which was founded in 1980 and which was the first to introduce 24-hour news coverage. Full form **Cable News Network**

coanchor /kəʊˈæŋkə/ *verb* to present a television or radio programme jointly with another presenter

co-anchor /ˌkəʊ ˈæŋkə/ *noun* either of two presenters who jointly present a television programme, especially a news programme

cobranding /kəʊˈbrændɪŋ/ *noun* the practice of displaying two or more corporate logos on a product or website to show that it is a joint enterprise

cobweb site /ˈkɒbweb saɪt/ *noun* a website that has not been updated for a long period of time

co-channel /ˌkəʊ ˈtʃænəl/ *adjective* relating to a radio transmission that occupies the same frequency band as another

cock /kɒk/ *verb* to set a device or mechanism such as a camera shutter release, so that it will work when it is triggered

code /kəʊd/ *noun* a set of rules governing some form of behaviour, either rigidly enforced or used for guidance only

Code of Advertising Standards and Practice /ˌkəʊd əv ˌædvətaɪzɪŋ ˌstændədz ənd ˈpræktɪs/ *noun* a code formerly administered by the Independent

Broadcasting Authority, which stated that advertisements should not be misleading, immoral or underhanded, but that they should be 'legal, decent, honest and truthful'

COMMENT: The Code is mandatory and is enforced by OFCOM. Failure to meet standards may result in an advertisement being dropped, whereas failure to properly vet an advertisement before transmission can lead to financial penalties or even the loss of the transmitter's broadcasting licence.

Code of Programme Sponsorship /ˌkəʊd əv ˈprəʊɡræm ˌspɒnsəʃɪp/ *noun* a rule imposed by the Independent Television Commission (now administered by OFCOM) stating that any programme may be sponsored apart from news and current affairs programmes, but that product placement must not occur as a result

COMMENT: Organisations which may not sponsor programmes or are restricted in their sponsorship include: political bodies, tobacco companies, manufacturers of drugs available only on prescription, and betting or gaming companies.

codes of narrative /ˌkəʊdz əv ˈnærətɪv/ *plural noun* a set of five codes used in the analysis and deconstruction of texts. ◊ **action code**, **semantic code**, **enigma code**, **referential code**, **symbolic code**

coffin /ˈkɒfɪn/ *noun* a frame that holds electrotype or stereotype printing plates

co-financing /ˌkəʊ ˈfaɪnænsɪŋ/ *noun* a situation in which two or more film studios share production costs of a film in return for sharing the profits, rights etc

cognitive behaviour /ˈkɒɡnɪtɪv bɪ ˌheɪvjə/ *noun* the category of human behaviour associated with knowing, reasoning and understanding. Compare **affective behaviour**

cognitive dissonance /ˌkɒɡnətɪv ˈdɪsənəns/ *noun* the feeling of dissatisfaction experienced by a person who cannot deal with apparently contradictory information, for example when making buying decisions or comparing purchases with the claims made for them in advertising

cognitive mapping /ˌkɒɡnɪtɪv ˈmæpɪŋ/ *noun* the process of creating a mental 'map' of one's environment

(cultural, social, physical, etc.) and using this to make decisions

cognitive processing /ˌkɒɡnɪtɪv ˈprəʊsesɪŋ/ *noun* the way in which a person changes external information into patterns of thought and how these are used to form judgments or choices

cognitive psychology /ˌkɒɡnɪtɪv saɪˈkɒlədʒi/ *noun* a psychological movement which infers people's thought processes from their behaviour, and believes that these thought processes can be affected by behaviour and/or changed to affect behaviour. Compare **behaviourism**

col. *abbreviation* PRINTING **column**

cold media /ˌkəʊld ˈmiːdiə/ *plural noun* media which demand a greater degree of interaction and interpretation from the audience, for example television. Compare **hot media**

cold type /ˈkəʊld taɪp/ *noun* PRINTING typesetting that is done without casting metal

collate /kəˈleɪt/ *verb* to make sure that the pages in a book are sequenced correctly and completely

collateral services /kəˌlæt(ə)rəl ˈsɜːvɪsɪz/ *plural noun* agencies which provide specialised services such as package design, production of advertising material or marketing research

collation /kəˈleɪʃ(ə)n/ *noun* **1.** the technical description of a book that includes its bibliographical details and information about its physical construction **2.** the process of assembling sheets of paper in the right order, particularly the sections of a book before it is bound

collective representation /kə ˌlektɪv ˌreprɪzenˈteɪʃ(ə)n/ *noun* the creation of media texts by a community which reveal or represent something about its culture, history, beliefs etc.

collectivist /kəˈlektɪvɪst/ *adjective* referring to a culture that places an emphasis on the needs and achievements of the group rather than of the individual. Personal achievement and assertiveness is considered less important than conformity to society and an 'unselfish attitude'. Such communities have a strong sense of family and community. Compare **individualist**

collodian process /kəˈləʊdiən ˌprəʊses/ *noun* an early process of photography development, using collodian solution to fix light-sensitive iodide to the photography plate

colonialism /kə'ləʊniəlɪz(ə)m/ *noun* in Marxist theory, a situation in which one powerful country has taken control of the economic and political systems of others, which has a far-reaching impact on its cultural forms

colonisation /ˌkɒlənaɪ'zeɪʃ(ə)n/ *noun* the process of using cultural signifiers from one community to appeal to another in order to sell a product

colorcast /'kʌləkɑːst/ *noun* a colour television broadcast

colour /'kʌlə/ *noun* the type and amount of inks used in a printing job ■ *adjective* referring to an article or section of an article, focusing more on descriptions, impressions and subjective reporting rather than impartial reporting of the facts

colour bar /'kʌlə bɑː/ *noun* a type of test pattern on paper or a screen, consisting of vertical coloured bars

colour correction filter /ˌkʌlə kə'rekʃ(ə)n ˌfɪltə/ *noun* same as **gel**

colour grading /'kʌlə ˌgreɪdɪŋ/ *noun* the process of preparing film so that colours and lighting effects are uniform throughout the feature, these days most often done digitally

colourise /'kʌləraɪz/ *verb* to add colour to a black-and-white film

colourist /'kʌlərɪst/ *noun* the person who does the primary and secondary grading to a piece of film

colour mobile control room /ˌkʌlə ˌməʊbaɪl kən'trəʊl ˌruːm/ *noun* a mobile control room used for coordination on small outside broadcasts. Abbreviation **CMCR**

colour separation overlay /ˌkʌlə ˌsepə'reɪʃ(ə)n ˌəʊvəleɪ/ *abbreviation* CSO. Same as **chromakey**

colour standard /'kʌlə ˌstændəd/ *noun* one of three international standards, NTSC, PAL and SECAM, used to describe how colour TV and video images are displayed and transmitted

colour subcarrier /ˌkʌlə 'sʌbkæriə/ *noun* the component of an analogue television signal that transmits colour information to the receiver

colour supplement /'kʌlə ˌsʌplɪmənt/ *noun* a magazine that is distributed with a newspaper, usually with a weekend issue, printed in colour and containing a lot of advertising

colour temperature /'kʌlə ˌtemprɪtʃə/ *noun* the 'warmth' of any colour, as measured on the Kelvin scale

colour temperature blue /ˌkʌlə ˌtemprɪtʃə 'bluː/ *noun* a gel that is placed over an artificial light source to make it appear more like natural light (blue-toned). Abbreviation **CTB**

colour temperature orange /ˌkʌlə ˌtemprɪtʃə 'ɒrɪndʒ/ *noun* a gel which is placed over a natural light source to make it appear more like artificial light (orange-toned). Abbreviation **CTO**

colour TV /ˌkʌlə ˌtiː 'viː/ *noun* a television set showing pictures in colour, which was first available in the US in 1954

Columbia Pictures /kəˌlʌmbiə 'pɪktʃəz/ *noun* a major film studio based in Hollywood and formed in 1914. It has produced many popular family films including Karate Kid (1984), Men in Black (1997), Stuart Little (1999), Charlie's Angels (2000) and the Spiderman films (from 2002).

column /'kɒləm/ *noun* the arrangement of newspaper copy on a page in a vertical strip. Abbreviation **col.**

column inch /'kɒləm ɪntʃ/ *noun* the amount of printed type that would fill an area on a page one column wide and one inch deep

'Posters of several of the Ashes heroes can be found in cricket magazines, the England players' thoughts fill endless column inches in the newspapers, and every aspect of the forthcoming Test series is being dissected.' [Jonathon Dyson, *The Observer*]

columnist /'kɒləmnɪst/ *noun* a journalist who writes a regular feature for a newspaper or magazine, usually based on personal comment

column rule /'kɒləm ruːl/ *noun* the blank line between columns of text

comb filter /'kəʊm ˌfɪltə/ *noun* an electronic device used to separate the luma (Y) and chroma (C) signals from a composite video signal

combination commercial /ˌkɒmbɪ'neɪʃ(ə)n kəˌmɜːʃ(ə)l/ *noun* a television advertisement which combines still pictures with action shots

combination rate /ˌkɒmbɪ'neɪʃ(ə)n ˌreɪt/ *noun* a special rate or discount for advertising in two or more magazines

combined mobile central control room /kəmˌbaɪnd ˌməʊbaɪl ˌsentrəl kən'trəʊl ˌruːm/ *noun* a mobile control room used for coordination on large outside broadcasts. Abbreviation **CMCCR**

comedian /kə'miːdiən/ *noun* an entertainer who specialises in comedy

comedienne /kəˌmiːdi'en/ *noun* a female entertainer who specialises in comedy

comedy /'kɒmədi/ *noun* **1.** comic entertainment, especially plays, considered as a literary genre **2.** a genre of film that focuses on comic characters in humorous situations

come in /ˌkʌm 'ɪn/ *verb* to enter a discussion or reply to a radio signal

come on /ˌkʌm 'ɒn/ *verb* to appear on a television programme, or to begin to speak on the telephone

comic-book movie /ˌkɒmɪk bʊk 'muːvi/ *noun* a genre of film that is based on a comic strip and tries to recreate that style, with strong images and cartoonish characters

comic opera /ˌkɒmɪk 'ɒp(ə)rə/ *noun* a genre of opera that involves humorous situations and characters and often, a lot of dialogue

comic relief /ˌkɒmɪk rɪ'liːf/ *noun* a comic scene or passage in an otherwise serious work, that provides a contrast and therefore some relaxation for a short time

comics /'kɒmɪks/ *plural noun* the part of a newspaper where the comic strips appear

comic strip /'kɒmɪk strɪp/ *noun* a sequence of drawings that tell a story or a joke. Also called **strip cartoon**

comic-strip oriented /ˌkɒmɪk strɪp 'ɔːrientɪd/ *adjective* referring to a film image that is oriented at right angles to the outer edge of the film

comix /'kɒmɪks/ *plural noun* comics and comic strips that are designed for adults, especially those containing nudity and obscenity

commentariat /ˌkɒmən'teəriət/ *noun* the print and broadcast journalists who comment on current affairs

commentary /'kɒmənt(ə)ri/ *noun* a report broadcast live from an event which comments on what is happening, for example at a sports match

commentary box /'kɒmənt(ə)ri bɒks/ *noun* a room from which a television or radio commentator broadcasts while watching an event such as a football match

commentary position /'kɒmənt(ə)ri pəˌzɪʃ(ə)n/ *noun* the vantage point from which a commentator can watch the action

commentate /'kɒmənteɪt/ *verb* to provide personal and professional comments and opinions, either in radio or television broadcasting or on texts

commentator /'kɒmənteɪtə/ *noun* **1.** a journalist who analyses the news for radio, television or a newspaper **2.** a radio or television broadcaster who describes and comments on events, especially sporting events, as they happen

commercial /kə'mɜːʃ(ə)l/ *noun* a radio or television advertisement ■ *adjective* referring to enterprises that use money raised from advertising

commercial art /kəˌmɜːʃ(ə)l 'ɑːt/ *noun* graphic art that is created for commercial reasons such as advertising and packaging

commercial break /kəˌmɜːʃ(ə)l 'breɪk/ *noun* a slot during a radio or television programme when advertisements are broadcast

commercial confidentiality /kəˌmɜːʃ(ə)l ˌkɒnfɪdenʃi'ælɪti/ *noun* grounds for not allowing information to be published because it may damage commercial interests

'Ofwat refused to be drawn on its plans, saying its ability to provide more information on individual investment decisions was limited by commercial confidentiality, as MPs had recognised.' [Andrew Taylor, *The Financial Times*]

commercial Internet exchange /kəˌmɜːʃ(ə)l 'ɪntənet ɪksˌtʃeɪndʒ/ *noun* a multilateral agreement between Internet service providers to allow commercial traffic on the Internet

commercial laissez-faire model of media communication /kəˌmɜːʃ(ə)l ˌleseɪ ˌfeə ˌmɒd(ə)l əv ˌmiːdiə kəˌmjuːnɪ'keɪʃ(ə)n/ *noun* a model which states that there is free trade in the market for media texts, with each producer having to compete against others for the consumer's attention, and so the audience are unlikely to be swayed by any one communication. Compare **mass manipulative model of media communication**

commercial minutage /kə,mɜːʃ(ə)l 'mɪnɪtɪdʒ/ *noun* the number of minutes over the course of a day which are used for broadcasting adverts on a particular channel

commercial radio /kə,mɜːʃ(ə)l 'reɪdiəʊ/ *noun* a radio station which broadcasts advertisements, which help to pay for its programming costs

commercial services /kə,mɜːʃ(ə)l 'sɜːvɪsɪz/ *plural noun* services which support trade, for example banking and advertising

commercial television /kə,mɜːʃ(ə)l ,telɪ'vɪʒ(ə)n/, **commercial TV** /kə ,mɜːʃ(ə)l tiː'viː/ *noun* a television station which broadcasts advertisements, which help to pay for its programming costs

commercial time /kə,mɜːʃ(ə)l taɪm/ *noun* the amount of time that a television or radio station devotes to advertising

commère /'kɒmeə/ *noun* a woman who introduces people as they appear on a television, radio or stage show

commissionaire /kə,mɪʃə'neə/ *noun* a uniformed doorman at a cinema, hotel or theatre

commission rebating /kə'mɪʃ(ə)n ,riːbeɪtɪŋ/ *noun* the practice by which an advertising agency may discount invoices for media costs sent to clients, in effect taking them out of its own commission or profit margin

Committee of Advertising Practice /kə,mɪti əv 'ædvətaɪzɪŋ ,præktɪs/ *noun* the body which produces the codes of advertising practice which are independently administered by OFCOM (broadcast advertising) and ASA (non-broadcast advertising). Abbreviation **CAP**

commoditisation of information /kə,mɒdɪtaɪzeɪʃ(ə)n əv ,ɪnfə'meɪʃ(ə)n/ *noun* the idea that information is a commodity that can be bought and sold, not something which should be freely available

commodity fetishism /kə'mɒdɪti ,fetɪʃɪz(ə)m/ *noun* a Marxist theory which suggests that objects produced,

sold and exchanged under a capitalist system take on the characteristics of a fetish, replacing some other desire or form of social interaction

commonality /kɒmə'næləti/ *noun* all the things that a community have in common, in terms of beliefs, ideas, cultural heritage etc.

common carrier /,kɒmən 'kæriə/ *noun* a company, such as a telephone company, that provides telecommunications services to the general public

common culture /,kɒmən 'kʌltʃə/ *noun* cultural forms that are shared between all members of a community, and are one of the things which define them as such

common intermediate format /,kɒmən ,ɪntəmiːdiət 'fɔːmæt/ *noun* a standard for video images that displays an image 352 pixels wide and 288 pixels high

common sense /,kɒmən 'sens/ *noun* the idea that most of the sets of meanings attached to things can be easily understood and do not need to be studied or analysed

communicate /kə'mjuːnɪkeɪt/ *verb* **1.** to reveal or express a feeling, thought or idea by words or gesture so that it is clearly understood **2.** to give or exchange ideas or information by words or gestures

communication /kə,mjuːnɪ 'keɪʃ(ə)n/ *noun* **1.** the exchange of information between people, for example by means of speaking, writing, or using a common system of signs or behaviour **2.** a spoken or written piece of information

communication network /kə ,mjuːnɪ'keɪʃ(ə)n ,netwɜːk/ *noun* any method of communicating multiple messages between multiple people, such as the Internet

communication objectives /kə ,mjuːnɪ'keɪʃ(ə)n əb,dʒektɪvz/ *plural noun* objectives that a company tries to achieve through its advertising, for example creating awareness, knowledge, images, attitudes, preferences or purchase intentions

communications /kə,mjuːnɪ 'keɪʃ(ə)nz/ *plural noun* the systems used for sending and receiving information, for example postal, computer and telephone networks ■ *noun* the study of the way people communicate with each other

Communications Act 2003 /kə
‚mjuːnɪˈkeɪʃ(ə)nz ‚ækt/ *noun* the Act
which created the 'super-regulator'
OFCOM, which replaced 5 former regulatory bodies covering radio, television and
telecommunications in the UK. ◊ **OFCOM**

COMMENT: The former regulatory bodies
which were replaced were: the
Broadcasting Standards Commission,
the Office of Telecommunications, the
Radio Authority, the
Radiocommunications Agency and the
Independent Television Commission.

**Communications Decency Act
1996** /kə‚mjuːnɪkeɪʃ(ə)nz ˈdiːsənsi
‚ækt/ *noun* the Act in the US designed to
prevent the transmission of pornography
on the Internet. The Act has been criticised for being almost impossible to
enforce and also on the grounds that it
goes against the principle of freedom of
speech.

communications gap /kə‚mjuːnɪ
ˈkeɪʃ(ə)nz ‚gæp/ *noun* a lack of understanding because of some failure in
communication, such as between different
cultural groups without a common reference point

communications management /kə
‚mjuːnɪˈkeɪʃ(ə)nz ‚mænɪdʒmənt/ *noun*
the process of managing communications,
so that advertising messages are sent efficiently to people who need to receive
them

communications satellite /kə
‚mjuːnɪˈkeɪʃ(ə)nz ‚sætəlaɪt/ *noun* a
satellite used to relay radio, telephone and
television signals around the world

communication task /kə‚mjuːnɪ
ˈkeɪʃ(ə)n tɑːsk/ *noun* things that can be
attributed to advertising, for example
awareness, comprehension, conviction
and action, following the DAGMAR
approach to setting advertising goals and
objectives

communication theory /kə‚mjuːnɪ
ˈkeɪʃ(ə)n ˈθɪəri/ *noun* the study of the
principles and methods of communication

communicative /kəˈmjuːnɪkətɪv/
adjective relating to the transfer of information or ideas

communicology /kə‚mnjuːnɪ
ˈkɒlədʒi/ *noun* the study of forms of
communication

communiqué /kəˈmjuːnɪkeɪ/ *noun* an
official announcement or statement, especially to the press or public

communisuasion /kə‚mjuːnɪ
ˈsweɪʒ(ə)n/ *noun* communication that is
intended to persuade

Community Action Programmes
/kə‚mjuːnɪti ˈækʃən ‚prəʊɡræmz/ *noun*
a programme which centres on some
social issue such as crime or health care

community antenna television /kə
‚mjuːnɪti æn‚tenə ˈtelɪvɪʒ(ə)n/ *noun* TV
same as **cable television**

Community Media Association
/kə‚mjuːnɪti ˈmiːdiə ə‚səʊsieɪʃ(ə)n/
noun a not-for-profit organisation in the
UK which promotes access to the media
for all. Abbreviation **CMA**

commutation test /‚kɒmjʊˈteɪʃ(ə)n
‚test/ *noun* **1.** a test used in semiotics in
which one symbol in a set is replaced to
see how it affects the 'reading' of the
others **2.** a method of analysing meaning
in a text, by taking elements of meaning
and substituting them for alternatives to
see what effect this has on the whole

compact camera /ˈkɒmpækt
ˈkæm(ə)rə/, **compact** /ˈkɒmpækt/ *noun*
a small camera with a built-in lens

comparative advertising /kəm
‚pærətɪv ˈædvətaɪzɪŋ/ *noun* advertising
that compares a company's product with
competing brands to its own advantage

comparative analysis /kəm
‚pærətɪv əˈnæləsɪs/ *noun* the practice of
carrying out analysis of the different
media available to an advertiser in order to
decide which should be used during an
advertising campaign

compassion fatigue /kəmˈpæʃ(ə)n
fə‚tiːɡ/ *noun* a loss or lessening of
sympathy for the suffering of others,
experienced by an audience that has been
over-exposed to media images of
suffering

'The charity Oxfam said less than 30 per
cent of the UN's original target had been
pledged. There are concerns that
compassion fatigue has set in after a
series of natural disasters, including the
tsunami and Hurricane Katrina.' [Justin
Huggler, *The Independent*]

compere /ˈkɒmpeə/ *noun* a person who
introduces people as they appear on a television, radio or stage show

competence /ˈkɒmpɪt(ə)ns/ *noun* **1.**
the ability to carry out a task safely and
efficiently **2.** a person's ability to use a

language because they understand its rules, structures etc

competitive analysis /kəm,petɪtɪv ə'næləsɪs/ *noun* the practice of carrying out analysis of an industry, and the customers and competitors within that industry, in order to discover how competitive an organisation, project or product is, especially by evaluating the capabilities of key competitors

competitive check /kəm,petɪtɪv 'tʃek/ *noun* the analysis of rival advertising levels and patterns, often conducted on the basis of data supplied by monitoring organisations

compilation film /,kɒmpɪ'leɪʃ(ə)n ,fɪlm/ *noun* a film which is put together from previously shot footage

complementary /,kɒmplɪ'ment(ə)ri/ *noun* referring to colours which are 'opposite' and produce a shade of grey when mixed, such as green and orange or blue and yellow

complicity of users /kəm,plɪsɪti əv 'juːzəz/ *noun* the idea that the audience does not want to be given the full truth in news reports about difficult situations, crises etc., which reinforces the journalist's tendency to censor coverage

component video /kəm'pəʊnənt ,vɪdiəʊ/ *noun* **1.** a video signal in which the colour and the light/dark portions of the signal are kept separate, allowing for easier editing without distortion. Compare **composite video 2.** a method of transmitting video information, used in professional video systems, that has separate signals for the luminance and two chrominance channels to avoid interference

composer /kəm'pəʊzə/ *noun* a creator or writer of music for a film score

composite monitor /,kɒmpəzɪt 'mɒnɪtə/ *noun* a colour monitor that receives one video signal from a graphics display adapter, which is then electronically separated inside the monitor into the red, green and blue colour signals

composite photograph /,kɒmpəzɪt 'fəʊtəɡrɑːf/ *noun* an image that is made up of two or more images, for example overlapping or superimposed on each other

composite video /,kɒmpəzɪt 'vɪdiəʊ/ *noun* a method of transmitting a video signal in which the colour signals

and the monochrome signal are combined into one single signal

composition /,kɒmpə'zɪʃ(ə)n/ *noun* **1.** the way in which objects are arranged in a space, their shape, size, colour and relation to each other **2.** the different target groups which make up the readership of a publication or the audience of a broadcast

compositor /kəm'pɒzɪtə/ *noun* a person whose job is to assemble text for printing

compressed video /,kɒmprest 'vɪdiəʊ/ *noun* video signals that have been compressed to reduce the data rate required to transmit the information. Whereas a normal television picture is transmitted at around 5090 Mbits/second, a compressed video signal can be transmitted at around one tenth of the data rate.

compulsory heterosexuality /kəm ,pʌlsəri ,hetərəʊsekʃu'ælɪti/ *noun* in feminism, the idea that homosexuality is repressed by the prevailing ideology that says that heterosexual behaviour is the norm

computer-assisted personal interview /kəm,pjuːtə ə,sɪstɪd ,pɜːs(ə)nəl 'ɪntəvjuː/ *noun* a face-to-face interview for research purposes in which the interviewer reads the questions from a computer and directly inputs the answers. Abbreviation **capi**

computer conferencing /kəm ,pjuːtə 'kɒnf(ə)rənsɪŋ/ *noun* the practice of people at distant sites, each with a computer, exchanging text and graphic messages and participating in meetings together

Computer Generated Imagery /kəm,pjuːtə ,dʒenəreɪtɪd 'ɪmɪdʒəri/ *noun* full form of **CGI**

computer illiterate /kəm,pjuːtə ɪ 'lɪtərət/ *adjective* unable to understand computer-related expressions or operations

computer literacy /kəm,pjuːtə 'lɪt(ə)rəsi/ *noun* the understanding of the basic principles of computers, related expressions and concepts, and the ability to use computers for programming or applications

computer-literate /kəm,pjuːtə 'lɪt(ə)rət/ *adjective* able to understand expressions relating to computers and how to use a computer

'As internet chat and instant messaging increasingly become a part of life for China's computer-literate youth, the use of internet slang has grown and adoption of the terms has permeated all areas of Chinese life.' [Robert Hughes, *The Independent*]

computer-telephone integration /kəm,pjuːtə ˌtelɪfəʊn ˌɪntɪˈgreɪʃ(ə)n/ *noun* the integration of telephone and computer systems so that the same networks can be shared by voice and data traffic

Comstockery /ˈkɒmstɒkəri/ *noun* the practice of censoring anything that could be seen as immoral or obscene in published material

COMMENT: The word **comstockery** comes from Anthony Comstock, a US reformer who campaigned in the late 1800s for stronger obscenity laws and was behind the Comstock Law which prohibited the delivery of 'obscene, lewd or lascivious material'.

conative /ˈkəʊnətɪv/ *adjective* of a message or piece of communication, having the function of instilling feelings in the listener covertly. ◊ **emotive, metalingual, phatic, poetic**

conceal /kənˈsiːl/ *verb* to hide information or graphics from a user, or not to display them

concentrated marketing /ˌkɒnsəntreɪtɪd ˈmɑːkətɪŋ/, **concentrated segmentation** /ˌkɒnsəntreɪtɪd ˌsegmənˈteɪʃ(ə)n/ *noun* the promotion of a product aimed at one particular area of the market

conceptual art /kən,septʃuəl ˈɑːt/ *noun* art in which the ideas expressed by the work are more important to the piece than the means used to put them across

concrete music /ˌkɒŋkriːt ˈmjuːzɪk/ *noun* a type of electronic music created by editing together recordings of live sounds, usually including natural and mechanical sources, and combining them with previously-composed musical tracks

concurrence-seeking tendency /kənˈkʊrəns ˌsiːkɪŋ ˌtendənsi/ *noun* the tendency of people in a group to agree with each other

condensation /ˌkɒnden'seɪʃ(ə)n/ *noun* one of the two main mechanisms by which dreams express the subconscious, by 'condensing' a number of fears into a small yet complex sign. ◊ **displacement**

conditional access /kən,dɪʃ(ə)n(ə)l ˈækses/ *noun* the practice of encrypting signals such as digital television channels so that they can be decoded only by people who have paid for the privilege

conference /ˈkɒnf(ə)rəns/ *noun* a meeting to discuss the previous edition of a newspaper or magazine and to plan the forthcoming one

confidence limits /ˌkɒnfɪd(ə)ns ˈlɪmɪts/ *plural noun* the likelihood that the results of a survey are true and trustworthy, taking into account such things as survey methods, size of sample etc

confirmation /ˌkɒnfəˈmeɪʃən/ *noun* an expression of agreement from somebody which reinforces the opinion, beliefs, values etc. that you already hold. Compare **disconfirmation**

conforming /kənˈfɔːmɪŋ/ *noun* the practice of using the off-line edit of a television film to make the final piece, using the actual shots rather than the low-quality copies

conglomerate /kənˈglɒmərət/ *noun* a large business organisation that consists of a number of companies that deal with a variety of different business, manufacturing, or commercial activities

congruence theory /ˈkɒngruːəns ˌθɪəri/ *noun* the relationship between people who either like or dislike each other, based on whether they are in agreement ('in congruence') on other issues and the imbalance this creates

conjuncture /kənˈdʒʌŋktʃə/ *noun* in Marxist theory, the interrelation of all social factors which bring about a change or new movement. The factors can include the political climate, economic system or technological advances.

connect /kəˈnekt/ *verb* to enable people and organisations in different places to contact each other, for example by computer or telephone

connection /kəˈnekʃən/ *noun* a link such as between telephones

connectivity /ˌkɒnekˈtɪvɪti/ the ability to communicate with another system or piece of hardware or software, or with an Internet site

connotation /ˌkɒnəˈteɪʃ(ə)n/ *noun* the meanings implied or suggested by a word, image, phrase etc., as opposed to the literal meaning. Compare **denotation**

consciousness /'kɒnʃəsnəs/ *noun* in Marxist theory, the attitudes, values and beliefs that characterise a person's self-awareness

consensus /kən'sensəs/ *noun* a shared acceptance of values, norms and beliefs, a similar outlook. Compare **dissensus**

consent form /kən'sent fɔːm/ *noun* a form giving the official consent of any person appearing on film for that footage to be broadcast, usually featuring their name and signature

consistency /kən'sɪstənsi/ *noun* the practice of ensuring that media coverage is uniform and does not contradict itself. The aim of this is to make the audience more likely to believe the coverage.

console /'kɒnsəʊl/ *noun* a desk, table, display, or keyboard onto which the controls of an electronic system or some other machine are fixed

consolidated viewing /kən‚sɒlɪdeɪtɪd 'vjuːɪŋ/ *noun* all viewing, including video recording and playback within 7 days of the original transmission

conspiracy of silence /kən‚spɪrəsi əv 'saɪləns/ *noun* an agreement not to broadcast a certain piece of sensitive information between those who have access to it

'The parents of Leo Blockley, the Oxford University rower who died during a training trip to Spain, have spoken of their fight to… expose a conspiracy of silence surrounding allegations that the head coach was drunk.' [Russell Jenkins, *The Times*]

conspiracy theory /kən'spɪrəsi ‚θɪəri/ *noun* a suspicion that there is a conspiracy among people in power to cover up or suppress sensitive information

constellation /‚kɒnstə'leɪʃ(ə)n/ *noun* the 'pattern' caused by events of the present combined with events of history

constituency /kən'stɪtjʊənsi/ *noun* the readership of a newspaper. The suggestion from this term is that the political views of a readership are shaped by the newspaper they read.

construct /kən'strʌkt/ *verb* to create something such as a theory, concept, image or media text by putting parts together systematically ■ *noun* the idea that media products are 'made' artificially and not taken directly from nature

construction /kən'strʌkʃən/ *noun* a visual work of art that is a combination of a variety of abstract materials, and is usually three-dimensional

constructivism /kən'strʌktɪvɪz(ə)m/ *noun* the theory that a person's perception of reality is dependent on the language that is used to construct and interpret that reality

consumer /kən'sjuːmə/ *noun* **1.** the person who buys a product advertised, at whom the advertising is aimed **2.** a person who is exposed to a media product, i.e. the audience

consumer advertising /kən'sjuːmə ‚ædvətaɪzɪŋ/ *noun* advertising direct to individual consumers, as opposed to businesses

consumer culture /kən'sjuːmə ‚kʌltʃə/ *noun* a view of society as dominated by consumerism

'…the rise of the 'new puritans': young people who have reacted against consumer culture by refusing to drink, smoke, buy big brands, take cheap flights, drive a fancy car or get fat.' [Jemima Lewis, *The Independent*]

consumerisation /kən‚sjuːmərai'zeɪʃ(ə)n/ *noun* the process by which a society becomes dominated by consumerism, caused by globalisation resulting in a much greater range and availability of competing products

consumerism /kən'sjuːmərɪz(ə)m/ *noun* a view of society which is overly concerned with material goods

consumer panel /kən'sjuːmə ‚pæn(ə)l/ *noun* a group of consumers who report on products they have used so that the manufacturers can improve them or use what the panel says about them in advertising

Consumer Protection Act 1987 /kən‚sjuːmə prə'tekʃən ‚ækt/ *noun* an act of Parliament that bans the use of misleading information to encourage potential purchasers to buy

consumer sovereignty /kən‚sjuːmə 'sɒvrɪnti/ *noun* the view that the consumer of a media product should dictate through their tastes and opinions what is broadcast

consumer survey /kən‚sjuːmə 'sɜːveɪ/ *noun* a questionnaire into the lifestyle, habits and behaviour of a particular group of established or potential consumers

cont.   *abbreviation*   BROADCAST continued

contact /'kɒntækt/ *noun* a person who provides information for a journalist

contact print /'kɒntækt prɪnt/ *noun* a photographic print made by exposing a negative to light directly on top of photo-sensitive paper

contacts book /'kɒntækts bʊk/ *noun* a small book containing contact details of sources, carried by a journalist

contagion effect /kən'teɪdʒən ɪˌfekt/ *noun* a situation in which media coverage of something creates a craze or fad, for example copycat crimes based on coverage of an original crime

contd   *abbreviation*   BROADCAST continued

content analysis /'kɒntent əˌnæləsɪs/ *noun* research into what is broadcast by the media in order to identify and assess trends

content management /'kɒntent ˌmænɪdʒmənt/ *noun* the management of the textual and graphical material contained on a website

content provider /'kɒntent prəˌvaɪdə/ *noun* **1.** a media company that produces material for broadcast on a particular network, for example cable or satellite distribution **2.** any organisation or individual which provides content to be broadcast or published elsewhere, such as contributors to a website

content-rich /ˌkɒntent 'rɪtʃ/ *adjective* containing a lot of useful information

'As the broadband juggernaut finally gathers momentum, a few content-rich sites are coming into their own. Leading the pack is Shockwave's interactive feast of games, films, sounds and pictures.'
[James Knight, *The Sunday Times*]

contents /'kɒntents/ *plural noun* a list at the beginning of a publication such as a book, that shows how it is divided up and gives the number of the first page of each chapter, article or part

context /'kɒntekst/ *noun* **1.** the words, phrases, or passages that come before and after a particular word or passage in a speech or piece of writing and help to explain its full meaning **2.** the circum-

stances or events that form the environment within which something exists or takes place **3.** additional information about a product that is considered to be helpful to customers and is shown on a website, for example, reviews by other customers displayed on the site for a particular book

continuity /ˌkɒntɪ'njuːɪti/ *noun* **1.** a comprehensive script that details each shot or scene of a film or broadcast, including such items as cast movements, props and camera positions and costume features **2.** the announcements that link television or radio programmes **3.** the maintenance of smoothness in the narrative flow in a film or broadcast **4.** the job of making sure that the costumes, lighting, make-up etc. used in consecutive scenes are the same even if the scenes are not shot continuously **5.** commentary by a television or radio broadcaster that fills the time between the end of one programme or programme segment and the beginning of the next **6.** the process of making sure that details of time, place, costume etc. are kept consistent from one part of a film or broadcast to another

continuity editing /ˌkɒntɪ'njuːɪti ˌedɪtɪŋ/ *noun* the job of editing a film to make sure that the details of time, place, costume etc. are kept consistent throughout the entire sequence

continuity person /ˌkɒntɪ'njuːɪti ˌpɜːs(ə)n/ *noun* the member of a film or television production team who is responsible for continuity of costume, lighting, make-up etc.

continuity programme /ˌkɒntɪ 'njuːɪti ˌprəʊgræm/ *noun* a marketing programme that offers a series of products that are sent to customers at regular intervals

contracting company /kənˌtræktɪŋ 'kʌmp(ə)ni/ *noun* an independent broadcasting company that sells advertising time

contrast /'kɒntrɑːst/ *noun* **1.** the effect created when very different things such as colours, shades or textures are placed near or next to each other **2.** the different levels of brightness and darkness in a single image or moving image

contrastive /kən'trɑːstɪv/ *adjective* referring to the effect of a contrast, or using contrasting colours, tones or textures

contrasty /'kɒntrɑːsti/ *adjective* referring to a sharp contrast between the lightest and darkest areas in a photograph or television or movie image

contributed content website /kən,trɪbjuːtd ,kɒntent 'websaɪt/ *noun* a website that allows visitors to add their contributions to its content, for example, to write reviews of books that are advertised on the site

contribution /,kɒntrɪ'bjuːʃ(ə)n/ *noun* an article or other material that is submitted for use in a publication or broadcast

control group /kən'trəʊl gruːp/ *noun* in research, the 'average' or unaffected group against which an experimental group is measured. Compare **experimental group**

controlled circulation /kən,trəʊld ,sɜːkjʊ'leɪʃ(ə)n/ *noun* the circulation of a publication only to the people on a particular mailing list

controlled circulation magazine /kən,trəʊld ,sɜːkjʊleɪʃ(ə)n ,mægə'ziːn/ *noun* a magazine which is sent free to a limited number of readers, and is paid for by the advertising it contains

conventions /kən'venʃ(ə)nz/ *plural noun* the 'rules' that are generally understood and accepted when producing a media work in a particular genre. For example, the conventions of a soap opera include the setting in a small community of place of work, the fact that there is generally one episode broadcast per day, often with an omnibus at the weekend, the cliff-hanger ending to encourage the audience to watch again tomorrow, and many more. Observing these conventions makes a media product more 'mainstream'.

convergence /kən'vɜːdʒəns/ *noun* the ability of a single device to receive two or more different media inputs, such as a television which has interactive digital access and can also receive radio channels

conversion rate /kən'vɜːʃ(ə)n reɪt/ *noun* the proportion of people contacted, by mailing, advertising or e-mail marketing, who actually end up purchasing a particular product or service

cooperative /kəʊ'ɒp(ə)rətɪv/ *noun* a business that organises cooperative

mailing or advertising for different companies

cooperative advertising /kəʊ,ɒp(ə)rətɪv 'ædvətaɪzɪŋ/ *noun* **1.** the practice of mailing advertising material from different companies in the same mailing pack **2.** the practice in which two companies, often a producer and a distributor, share advertising costs

co-ordinating producer /,kəʊ,ɔːdɪneɪtɪŋ prə'djuːsə/ *noun* the member of a television or film production team who is responsible for coordinating two or more producers working on related projects

copperplate /'kɒpəpleɪt/ *noun* **1.** a polished copper printing plate with an etched or engraved design on it **2.** a print made from a copperplate

co-producer /,kəʊ prə'djuːsə/ *noun* in television and film production, a producer who works in tandem with other producers on the same project

co-production /,kəʊ prə'dʌkʃ(ə)n/ *noun* a film or television production which has more than one producers, financers etc

copy /'kɒpi/ *noun* **1.** written information designed to be read out on the radio **2.** text that will be laid out and printed on a page

copy approval /'kɒpi ə,pruːv(ə)l/ *noun* the right to check and approve copy before it is published

'The tabloids may strike deals with publicists that hand over control to the star – a practice exposed by Piers Morgan, the former editor of the Daily Mirror, when he announced that he would no longer give copy approval to celebrities.'
[Alan Ruddock, *The Guardian*]

copyboy /'kɒpibɔɪ/ *noun* a person whose job is to run errands in a newspaper office

copy brief /'kɒpi briːf/ *noun* the instructions from an advertiser to a copywriter explaining the objectives of an advertising campaign

copy-cat crime /'kɒpi kæt ,kraɪm/ *noun* a crime which mimics another criminal's 'style', after this has been reported in the media

copy date /'kɒpi deɪt/ *noun* the date by which an advertisement must be delivered to the media concerned

copy desk /ˈkɒpi desk/ *noun* a desk at which copy is edited for publication, especially in a newspaper office

copy-edit /ˈkɒpi ˌedɪt/ *verb* to read written text and correct it for publication

copy editor /ˈkɒpi ˌedɪtə/ *noun* a person whose job is to read and correct written texts for publication

copy fitting /ˈkɒpi ˌfɪtɪŋ/ *noun* the arrangement of advertising text so it fits the space allowed for it

copy protection /ˈkɒpi prəˌtekʃən/ *noun* a way of preventing copying from a copyrighted CD or DVD, such as by encoding it or downgrading the quality dramatically when copied

copyright /ˈkɒpiraɪt/ *noun* legal ownership of a piece of intellectual property, protection by law against its theft or exploitation

copy tasting /ˈkɒpi ˌteɪstɪŋ/ *noun* checking copy to select which pieces will be published. Also called **tasting**

cor. *abbreviation* PRESS **correspondent**

core audience /ˌkɔː ˈɔːdiəns/ *noun* the percentage of viewers of a radio or television programme who watch or listen to the entire show from beginning to end

core nations /ˌkɔː ˈneɪʃ(ə)nz/ *plural noun* those nations with greater access to information, generally those thought of as industrial or 'developed' such as the USA, the UK, Japan etc. Compare **peripheral nations**

corporate advertising /ˌkɔːp(ə)rət ˈædvətaɪzɪŋ/ *noun* the advertising of an organisation rather than a product

corporate discount /ˌkɔːp(ə)rət ˈdɪskaʊnt/ *noun* a reduction in advertising charges calculated on the basis of the total advertising revenue from all the brands of a company

corporate media /ˌkɔːp(ə)rət ˈmiːdiə/ *noun* the mass media, with the suggestion that such forms of media are controlled by large corporations

corporate portal /ˌkɔːp(ə)rət ˈpɔːt(ə)l/ *noun* a main website that allows access to all the information and software applications held by an organisation and provides links to information from outside it

corporate speech /ˈkɔːp(ə)rət spiːtʃ/ *noun* the way in which large businesses 'speak' to an audience, primarily through advertising

Corporation for Public Broadcasting /ˌkɔːpəreɪʃ(ə)n fə ˌpʌblɪk ˈbrɔːdkɑːstɪŋ/ *noun* an organisation in the USA which funds local broadcasters to produce educationally- or culturally-valuable programming. Abbreviation **CPB**

corpse /kɔːps/ *verb* to mess up spoken lines in a script by laughing or becoming distracted

corr. *abbreviation* PRESS **correspondent**

correlation /ˌkɒrəˈleɪʃ(ə)n/ *noun* a relationship in which two or more things are mutual or complementary, or one thing is caused by another

correspondence /ˌkɒrɪˈspɒndəns/ *noun* the process of communicating by writing letters or messages such as e-mails

correspondence column /ˌkɒrɪˈspɒndəns ˌkɒləm/ *noun* a section of a newspaper or magazine where readers' letters are published

correspondent /ˌkɒrɪˈspɒndənt/ *noun* a journalist who regularly reports from a particular geographical area or on a particular topic. Abbreviation **cor., corr.**

cosmeceutical /ˌkɒsməˈsjuːtɪk(ə)l/ *noun* a product such as an antiperspirant or anti-wrinkle cream that is marketed as a cosmetic, but which contains biologically active ingredients and should therefore possibly be designated as a pharmaceutical

'…the seaweed extracts help give the skin a toned appearance, while the caffeine penetrates it, enters the fat cells and helps them release their fatty content – a real 'cosmeceutical' double act if ever there was one.' [Amanda Ursell, *The Sunday Times*]

cosmopolitanism /ˌkɒzmə ˈpɒlɪtəniz(ə)m/ *noun* **1.** a situation in which a place or culture is composed of or influenced by people from different countries or cultures **2.** in cultural theory, the condition of belonging less to one state than to many, being 'multi-lingual' in various cultural forms

cosmopoliteness /ˌkɒzməpə ˈlaɪtnəs/ *noun* the degree to which a person has contact with others outside their own social structure and is aware of and involved in other social situations

cost efficiency /ˌkɒst ɪ'fɪʃənsi/ *noun* the 'value' of an advertisement (the number of consumers it reaches, the amount of revenue it attracts etc.) in relation to the cost of placing it

cost per click-through /ˌkɒst pə 'klɪk θruː/ *noun* a method of pricing online advertising, based on the principle that the seller gets paid whenever a visitor clicks on an advertisement

cost per thousand /kɒst pɜː 'θauz(ə)nd/, **cost per mille** *noun* the cost of an advertisement, calculated as the cost for every thousand people reached or the cost of a thousand impressions for a website

cost rank /'kɒst ræŋk/ *noun* the cost efficiency of a particular section of the media in relation to others

costume /'kɒstjuːm/ *noun* clothes worn to make a person look like somebody or something else, especially in a dramatic performance

costume designer /'kɒstjuːm dɪ ˌzaɪnə/ *noun* the member of a television or film production team who is responsible for designing, sourcing and maintaining the actors' costumes

costume drama /'kɒstjuːm ˌdrɑːmə/ *noun* a drama which is set in a particular historical period, requiring elaborate costumes and sets to create the right effect. Also called **period drama**

couch potato /ˌkautʃ pə'teɪtəu/ *noun* a person who watches a lot of television (*informal*)

counter /'kauntə/ *noun* PRINTING the hollow part of a piece of type that is not filled with ink, for example the inside of the letter 'D'

counteradvertising /ˌkauntər 'ædvətaɪzɪŋ/ *noun* advertising which is aimed as a reply to a competitor's advertisements

counter-argument /'kauntər ˌɑːgjumənt/ *noun* a response that is opposed to the suggestion of an advertising message

counterculture /'kauntəˌkʌltʃə/ *noun* the cultural networks such as the music scene, drug use, communal mentality etc. which sprang up in opposition to post-Vietnam War America

counterleak /'kauntəliːk/ *noun* the process of anonymously revealing to a reporter the fact that somebody else has leaked information, which then leads to the reporter suspecting a conspiracy

counter-programming /'kauntə ˌprəugræmɪŋ/ *noun* the technique of presenting television programmes that are designed to appeal to the audience of competing programmes run during at the same time

counterproof /'kauntəpruːf/ *noun* a second print of an engraving, taken as an impression of the first, while it was still wet

coupon ad /'kuːpɒn æd/ *noun* an advertisement with a form attached, which the consumer cuts out and returns to the advertiser with their name and address for further information

coups and earthquakes syndrome /ˌkuːz ənd 'ɜːθkwaɪks ˌsɪndrəum/ *noun* the supposed Western attitude to events in less-developed nations, namely that unless they involve major political turmoil or a natural disaster they are not newsworthy

court circular /ˌkɔːt 'sɜːkjulə/ *noun* a report of the official duties of a country's monarch and other members of the royal family, published in a national newspaper

cover /'kʌvə/ *verb* to have the job of reporting on an event or a particular class of events for a newspaper or a broadcasting company ■ *noun* **1.** the outer binding of a book or magazine **2.** MUSIC same as **cover version**

coverage /'kʌv(ə)rɪdʒ/ *noun* **1.** the attention that the media give to an event or topic **2.** the percentage of the public who are reached by a newspaper or radio or television station **3.** same as **reach**

cover boy /'kʌvə bɔɪ/ *noun* a young man whose picture is on the cover of a newspaper or magazine

cover girl /'kʌvə gɜːl/ *noun* a young woman, especially a glamorous model, whose picture is on the cover of a newspaper or magazine

cover lines /'kʌvə laɪnz/ *plural noun* short phrases on the cover of a magazine describing major articles inside. Also called **teasers**

covermount /'kʌvəmaunt/ *noun* an item fixed to the cover of a magazine as a gift to the reader, for example a diary or a lipstick

cover story /'kʌvə ˌstɔːri/ *noun* the most important article in a magazine, that is featured on the front cover

cover version /'kʌvə ˌvɜːʃ(ə)n/ *noun* a new recording of a song by a different artist from the one that originally recorded it. Also called **cover**

cowboy /'kaʊbɔɪ/ *noun* a typical male character in stories and films about the western United States in the late 1800s, who is usually a cattle herder, but who is often shown fighting Native Americans or outlaws

cowgirl /'kaʊgɜːl/ *noun* a typical female character in stories and films about the western United States in the late 1800s, who is often involved in the same adventures as cowboys

CP *abbreviation* PRESS **Canadian Press**

CPB *abbreviation* BROADCAST **Corporation for Public Broadcasting**

CPT *abbreviation* **cost per thousand**

crab /kræb/ *noun* a sideways movement of a camera using a moveable mounting while filming

crane /kreɪn/ *noun* **1.** a large movable arm for a camera on which the cameraman and assistants can stand when filming **2.** a moving platform with a long support for a film or television camera

crane shot /'kreɪn ʃɒt/ *noun* a film shot taken from a crane, creating a high angle

crash /kræʃ/ *verb* to carry on broadcasting a live event for longer than intended because of overruns etc.

Crawford Committee /'krɔːfəd kəˌmɪti/ *noun* the committee whose 1925 recommendations for an independent, public-service broadcasting body led to the inauguration of the BBC

crawl /krɔːl/ *noun* the process of scrolling text across a television or motion picture screen to convey information, for example programming credits or news updates

crawler /'krɔːlə/ *noun* a line of text which scrolls along the screen from right to left

creative /kri'eɪtɪv/ *adjective* relating to the conceptual or artistic side of advertising

creative director /kriˌeɪtɪv daɪ'rektə/ *noun* an employee of an advertising agency who is in overall charge of finding the right words and images to promote the product during an advertising campaign

creative editing /kriˌeɪtɪv 'edɪtɪŋ/ *noun* the process of editing pieces together to create a sequence, effect etc., rather than to tidy up or shorten an existing piece. Abbreviation **CE**

creative shop /kriˌeɪtɪv 'ʃɒp/, **creative boutique** /kriˌeɪtɪv buː'tiːk/ *noun* a highly specialised business offering creative customer advertising services

credit /'kredɪt/ *noun* text that names the photographer or illustrator when their work is used

credit line /'kredɪt laɪn/ *noun* a published acknowledgment of who wrote something or where it was sourced from

credit roller /'kredɪt ˌrəʊlə/ *noun* a series of credits which roll from the bottom to the top of a television or cinema screen

credits /'kredɪts/ *plural noun* text at the end of a broadcast programme or film giving details of the people that worked on it

crew /kruː/ *noun* the group of people who do technical work for a television programme or film production

crisis definition /'kraɪsɪs ˌdefɪnɪʃ(ə)n/ *noun* the theory that a crisis is only defined as such in its media coverage, forcing those in authority to react accordingly. ◊ **agenda-setting**

critic /'krɪtɪk/ *noun* a person, especially a journalist, who expresses opinions about the quality of literary works, drama productions, art exhibitions and society as a whole

'His first Whitney show in 1975 caused a furore, with the public and many critics unable to appreciate his radical vision. 'One critic raged that it was a disgrace: pathetic, boring rubbish.'' [Claire Henry, *The Financial Times*]

critical news analysis /ˌkrɪtɪk(ə)l njuːz ə'næləsɪs/ *noun* an approach to analysing news coverage, its content, presentation, effects and degree of neutrality

critical pluralism /ˌkrɪtɪk(ə)l 'plʊərəlɪz(ə)m/ *noun* the theory that while there are many different ideas and value systems within society, some of them are powerful and some suppressed, and that there is a struggle for dominance

critical theory /ˌkrɪtɪk(ə)l ˈθɪəri/ *noun* in Marxist theory, a form of social theorising aimed at discovering, and suggesting answers to, social problems, rather than merely understanding them

criticise /ˈkrɪtɪsaɪz/ *verb* to judge and express an opinion on the qualities of something, especially a creative work

criticism /ˈkrɪtɪsɪz(ə)m/ *noun* the process of judging and expressing opinions on the qualities of something, especially a creative work. Also called **critique**

critique /krɪˈtiːk/ *verb* in Marxist theory, to analyse and explain the valid features, weaknesses and strengths of a piece of work ∎ *noun* same as **criticism**

crop /krɒp/ *noun* to cut down a picture to make it the correct size for use or to cut out unwanted parts of it

cross-border /ˌkrɒs ˈbɔːdə/ *adjective* referring to programmes broadcast in several different countries

crosscut /ˈkrɒskʌt/ *noun* same as **cross-cutting** ∎ *verb* to alternate short sections of two or more scenes of a film to give the impression that the events they show are happening at the same time

cross-cutting /ˌkrɒs ˈkʌtɪŋ/ *noun* **1.** repeated alternation between brief filmed sequences to give the impression that the events they show are happening at the same time **2.** the technique of running several different narratives simultaneously and cutting between scenes from each

cross fade /ˈkrɒs feɪd/ *verb* **1.** a way of mixing from one image to another in which one image gradually fades in as another fades out. Also called **dissolve**. Compare **wipe 2.** in film or television editing, to gradually introduce a new sound or picture while causing another one to disappear

cross-generic /ˌkrɒs dʒəˈnerɪk/ *adjective* referring to the blending of conventions from different genres

crosshead /ˈkrɒshed/ *noun* a subtitle of one or two words, used to break up chunks of text in news articles

crossing the line /ˌkrɒsɪŋ ðə ˈlaɪn/ *noun* ♦ **180º rule**

cross-media advertising /ˌkrɒs ˌmiːdiə ˈædvətaɪzɪŋ/ *noun* advertising the same product or service in several different types of media which are offered by a single-company media provider

cross-media ownership /ˌkrɒs ˌmiːdiə ˈəʊnəʃɪp/ *noun* the situation in which one company owns different media outlets in press, television, radio etc.

cross-over /ˈkrɒs ˌəʊvə/ *noun* a media product which was made for one genre, but gains popularity in another

cross-promotion /ˌkrɒs prəˈməʊʃ(ə)n/ *noun* a process in which two or more advertisers of a product or service associate themselves with each other to increase their profile, reach more people etc.

cross ref /ˈkrɒs ref/ *noun* a note referring the reader to another page to continue the story or find a related story

cross-reference /ˌkrɒs ˈref(ə)rəns/ *noun* a note to the reader of a text, that tells him or her to look in another specified place for information

crosstalk /ˈkrɒstɑːk/ *noun* the unwanted noises or sounds that may come through on, for example telephones or loudspeakers, when signals are transferred from one channel to another

crossword /ˈkrɒswɜːd/ *noun* a word game in which words that are the answers to numbered clues, are entered horizontally or vertically into a correspondingly numbered grid of squares

cryptography /ˌkrɪpˈtɒgrəfi/ *noun* the act of transferring messages into code so that the information can only be accessed by the appropriate people

crystal set /ˈkrɪstəl set/ *noun* a simple early form of radio receiver that used a quartz crystal as a detector and had no amplifier or loudspeaker speaker, therefore requiring an ear phone

CSA *abbreviation* **Casting Society of America**

CSO *abbreviation* **colour separation overlay**

C-SPAN /ˈsiː spæn/ *noun* a US cable television channel that covers politics and current affairs such as cultural and social issues

CSS *abbreviation* **cascading style sheet**

CTB *abbreviation* **colour temperature blue**

CTO *abbreviation* **colour temperature orange**

CU *abbreviation* **close-up**

cub reporter /ˌkʌb rɪˈpɔːtə/ *noun* a trainee reporter

cue /kjuː/ *noun* **1.** a written introduction to a piece of audio **2.** a signal given for the next item to begin **3.** a signal given through headphones to someone to begin broadcasting ■ *verb* to get a piece of pre-recorded audio or video ready to play at the correct time during a live broadcast

cue card /ˈkjuː kɑːd/ *noun* a card near a television camera that a presenter reads, while appearing to look straight at the audience

cue light /ˈkjuː laɪt/ *noun* **1.** a light that comes on to tell a television or radio presenter that they should begin to speak **2.** the red light on top of a television camera that tells the cameraman or presenter that the camera is recording. Also called **tally light**

cue sound /ˈkjuː saʊnd/ *noun* a sound feed of what is being broadcast, that outside broadcast staff can hear, so that they are aware of what is going on

cue vision /ˈkjuː ˌvɪʒ(ə)n/ *noun* a monitor showing pictures that are being broadcast, so that outside broadcast staff are aware of what is going on

cult /kʌlt/ *adjective* relating to a media product that is not mainstream, but gathers a devoted group of enthusiastic followers by word of mouth

cultivation /ˌkʌltɪˈveɪʃ(ə)n/ *noun* the slow process by which an audience is 'persuaded' to hold values, ideas, beliefs etc. that are presented to them by media coverage over a period of time

cultivation differential /ˌkʌltɪˈveɪʃ(ə)n ˌdɪfərenʃəl/ the degree to which a person has been exposed to culti-vation and the effect that it has had on their views and beliefs

cultivation theory /ˌkʌltɪˈveɪʃ(ə)n ˌθɪəri/ *noun* the theory that the mass media 'cultivates' ideas, attitudes, values etc which are already present but have not been reinforced or widely disseminated

cultural apparatus /ˌkʌltʃər(ə)l ˌæpə ˈreɪtəs/ *noun* the means by which a domi-nant institution such as a government uses

culture to impose values, definitions, opinions etc. on the general public

cultural capital /ˌkʌltʃər(ə)l ˈkæpɪt(ə)l/ *noun* the accumulated knowl-edge, accomplishments and qualifications that a person has, which would allow them to enter a given social circle

cultural identity /ˌkʌltʃ(ə)rəl aɪ ˈdentɪti/ *noun* the way in which an indi-vidual defines themselves in terms of their cultural background and heritage

cultural imperialism /ˌkʌltʃər(ə)l ɪm ˈpɪəriəlɪz(ə)m/ *noun* the belief that the globalisation of communication has been driven entirely by Western technological advances, and as such constitutes a form of rule by the West over other countries. Also called **media imperialism**

cultural intermediaries /ˌkʌltʃər(ə)l ˌɪntəˈmiːdɪəriz/ *plural noun* people working in advertising, design and other industries, who try to tailor products to the consumer according to cultural values

culturalism /ˈkʌltʃərəlɪz(ə)m/ *noun* the idea that a society can be understood through analysis of their cultural prod-ucts, such as literature, throughout history

cultural materialism /ˌkʌltʃər(ə)l məˈtɪəriəlɪz(ə)m/ *noun* the view of culture as being embedded in and inextri-cable from its material products

cultural memory /ˌkʌltʃər(ə)l ˈmem(ə)ri/ *noun* the knowledge and experience which is accumulated from being immersed in a culture and which defines an individual or group

cultural metaphor /ˌkʌltʃər(ə)l ˈmetəfə/ *noun* an object or image which is seen as representative of a culture, for example a bonsai tree or geisha costume for Japan

cultural mode /ˈkʌltʃər(ə)l məʊd/ *noun* the way in which cultural works are transmitted, either orally or through liter-ature

cultural politics /ˌkʌltʃər(ə)l ˈpɒlɪtɪks/ *noun* the view of culture through the filter of politics, for example, the effect of governmental funding on the Arts

cultural theory /ˈkʌltʃ(ə)rəl ˌθɪəri/ *noun* analysis of the mass media and its relationship with and effect on people's identities, sexuality and behaviour

culture /ˈkʌltʃə/ *noun* the beliefs, customs, practices, characteristics and social behaviour of a particular nation or people

COMMENT: The notion of culture has been variously defined as: a common view on the world; the shared products of civilisation within a community; the codes of behaviour by which people within the community abide; the artefacts, texts, symbols or activities produced by a society; and a mechanism by which a community is unified and stabilised.

culture industries /ˈkʌltʃə ˌɪndəstriz/ *plural noun* organisations in media and the arts, which produce and distribute cultural goods and services

culture of deference /ˌkʌltʃə əv ˈdef(ə)rəns/ *noun* the idea that news reporters may unconsciously censor themselves, because they know that their coverage may not be acceptable to the larger organisation for which they work

cumulative audience /ˌkjuːmjʊlətɪv ˈɔːdiəns/ *noun* **1.** the proportion of a target audience for a broadcast who have had the opportunity to see it after a given number of advertisements have been shown **2.** same as **net audience**

cumulative readership /ˌkjuːmjʊlətɪv ˈriːdəʃɪp/ *noun* the proportion of a target audience for a publication who have had opportunity to see it after a given number of advertisements have been published

curly bracket /ˌkɜːli ˈbrækɪt/ *noun* PRINTING same as **brace**

cursive /ˈkɜːsɪv/ *noun* a typeface which resembles handwriting in that the letters are joined together

curtain raiser /ˈkɜːtɪn ˌreɪzə/ *noun* a story that goes before, and provides the background to, another event

custom audience research /ˌkʌstəm ˌɔːdiəns rɪˈsɜːtʃ/ *noun* audience research undertaken by a company with particular focus on their own products or services, which is often seen as less objective

cut /kʌt/ *noun* same as **clip** ■ *verb* to remove unwanted text ■ *interjection* an instruction from a director to stop filming

cutaway /ˈkʌtəˌweɪ/ *noun* a short scene inserted in between two scenes to avoid a clumsy edit. ◊ **jump cut**

cut-in /ˈkʌt ɪn/ *noun* in a filmed sequence, a scene that is inserted into another shot or scene

cutline /ˈkʌtlaɪn/ *noun* a caption to a photograph or illustration

cut-off /ˈkʌt ɒf/ *noun* a stance or gesture which avoids interpersonal communication, for example avoiding a person's gaze

cutout /ˈkʌtaʊt/ *noun* the subject of an illustration or photograph which has been removed from its original background so that it appears against a plain white background

cut-out /ˈkʌt aʊt/ *noun* a recording sold at a discount because it is out-of-date and supply exceeds demand

cut spot /ˈkʌt spɒt/ *noun* an edited television report

cut throat /ˈkʌt θrəʊt/ *noun* a signal given by a floor manager to a television presenter, telling them to finish immediately, indicated by drawing a flat hand across the throat in a 'cutting' motion

cutting /ˈkʌtɪŋ/ *noun* **1.** the technique of moving from one shot to another when editing a film **2.** the process of editing a text, film or recording **3.** an article, photograph or other piece that has been cut out of a newspaper or other publication

cutting copy /ˈkʌtɪŋ ˌkɒpi/ *noun* a copy of a film which is physically cut and joined with leader tape by an editor, then copied and printed as a whole when complete

cutting room /ˈkʌtɪŋ ruːm/ *noun* the room in which film editing is done

'Sadly, most of Paul's scenes ended up on the cutting-room floor – though he does appear on the two-disc DVD.' [Nick Webster, *The Mirror*]

cuttings /ˈkʌtɪŋz/ *plural noun* published stories taken from newspapers, usually filed. Also called **clippings**

cyan /ˈsaɪən/ *noun* a deep greenish-blue colour that, with yellow and magenta, is one of the three primary subtractive colours

cybercafé /ˈsaɪbəˌkæfeɪ/ *noun* a café where people can pay to browse the Internet

cyberfeminism /ˈsaɪbəˌfemɪnɪz(ə)m/ *noun* the study of new technology and its effect on women's issues

cyber mall /ˈsaɪbə mɑːl/ *noun* a shopping centre on the Internet that links a homepage with a large number of online businesses, allowing customers to collect purchases in a shopping cart and pay for them all at once, for example by credit card

cybermarketing /'saɪbə,mɑːkɪtɪŋ/ noun the use of any kind of Internet-based marketing promotion, for example targeted e-mails, bulletin boards, websites or sites from which the customer can download files

cybernetics /,saɪbə'netɪks/ noun the organisational and control systems in networks using computers

cyberporn /'saɪbəpɔːn/ noun material that is sexually explicit and available on the Internet or using virtual reality

cyberpunk /'saɪbəpʌŋk/ noun a movement associated with the technological breakthroughs of the early 80s and their effect on the underground pop culture of the time

cybersales /'saɪbəseɪlz/ plural noun the activity of trading over the Internet or the total amount sold

cybersex /'saɪbəseks/ noun sexual activity involving virtual reality or the Internet

'The remainder of the resource pack comprises worksheets and games, such as the Face Exploitation Game, a board game with questions and scenario cards that prompt specific discussions, such as What is cybersex and is it legal?'

[Su Clark, *The Times Educational Supplement*]

cybershopping /'saɪbə,ʃɒpɪŋ/ noun the activity of buying goods and services over the Internet

cyberspace /'saɪbəspeɪs/ noun the notional space where Internet activity takes place, by analogy to a real, physical space

cybersurfer /'saɪbə,sɜːfə/ noun a person who spends a lot of time browsing on the Internet

cyberwar /'saɪbəwɔː/ noun the use of electronic communications and the Internet to damage an adversary's computer-based information systems

cyborg /'saɪbɔːg/ noun a living organism which has been 'enhanced' by the use of robotic technology, such as with a prosthetic limb

cyc /saɪk/ abbreviation cyclorama

cyclorama /,saɪkləʊ'rɑːmə/ noun a curved wall or stretched cloth backdrop in a television studio, used for projecting lighting

cyclostyle /'saɪkləʊ,staɪl/ noun a duplication method, now obsolete, in which ink is forced through the tiny holes of a waxed paper stencil to produce multiple copies of the original design or text

cyc track /'saɪk træk/ noun the curtain rail on which a cyc cloth is hung

cylinder /'sɪlɪndə/ noun a rotating metal drum of a printing press

cylinder press /'sɪlɪndə pres/ noun a printing press in which the type is carried on a flat bed that moves under a revolving cylinder carrying the paper

cynic /'sɪnɪk/ noun in advertising audience classifications, a person who does not welcome advertising and regards it as intrusive and insidious. ◊ **acquiescent**, **ambivalent**, **enthusiast**

D

D3 /ˌdiː ˈθriː/ *noun* a digital tape format that records composite video signals

DA *abbreviation* **distribution amplifier**

DAB *abbreviation* **Digital Audio Broadcasting**

dabber /ˈdæbə/ *noun* a pad used by printers to apply ink or colour to a surface by hand

dagger /ˈdægə/ *noun* a sign (†) that is used in printed texts to indicate a reference, especially to a footnote. Also called **obelisk**, **obelus** ■ *verb* to mark text with a dagger sign

DAGMAR /ˈdægmɑː/ *noun* a model showing stages in the effect of advertising on a consumer, for example awareness, comprehension, conviction and action. Full form **defining advertising goals for measured advertising results**

daguerreotype /dəˈgɜːriəʊˌtaɪp/ *noun* an early forerunner of the photograph, which fixed images onto a silver-coated plate treated with mercury iodide

dailies /ˈdeɪliz/ *plural noun* US same as **rushes**

daily /ˈdeɪli/ *noun* a newspaper that is published every day except Sunday

Dalek /ˈdɑːlek/ *noun* a fictional robot-like alien in a metal casing and with a harsh monotonous voice, from the British science-fiction television series *Dr Who*

dance hall /ˈdɑːns hɔːl/ *noun* a type of electronically produced dance music with a disc jockey talking or rapping over reggae-style music

dance music /ˈdɑːns ˌmjuːzɪk/ *noun* electronic music that people dance to in nightclubs

DAR *abbreviation* **day-after-recall**

darkroom /ˈdɑːkruːm/ *noun* a room for developing photographs and handling light-sensitive photographic materials, from which natural light is excluded

DAT *abbreviation* **digital audio tape**

data /ˈdeɪtə/ *noun* information available on computer, for example letters or figures

data acquisition /ˈdeɪtə ˌækwɪzɪʃ(ə)n/ *noun* the act of gathering information about a subject

data analysis /ˈdeɪtə əˌnæləsɪs/ *noun* the process of extracting information and results from data

database /ˈdeɪtəbeɪs/ *noun* an archive of data stored electronically, that can be accessed and manipulated

database management system /ˌdeɪtəbeɪs ˈmænɪdʒmənt ˌsɪstəm/ *noun* a computer program that is specially designed to organise and process the information contained in a database

database modelling /ˈdeɪtəbeɪs ˌmɒd(ə)lɪŋ/ *noun* the technique of using the information from a database to create a website or to forecast trends in a market

database publishing /ˈdeɪtəbeɪs ˌpʌblɪʃɪŋ/ *noun* the practice of publishing of information selected from a database, either on-line where the user pays for it on a per-page inspection basis or as a CD-ROM

data capture /ˈdeɪtə ˌkæptʃə/, **data entry** /ˌdeɪtə ˈentri/ *noun* the act of putting information onto a computer by keyboarding or by scanning

data mining /ˈdeɪtə ˌmaɪnɪŋ/ *noun* the act of searching through large quantities of data to find hidden patterns, for example analysing the shopping habits of a product's customers to determine its advertising strategy

dataport /ˈdeɪtəpɔːt/ *noun* COMPUTING a socket, such as an infrared, parallel or serial port, that is used for data communications

data protection /ˈdeɪtə prəˌtekʃən/ *noun* technology, legislation etc. used to prevent data being used by unauthorised people and thereby protecting people's privacy

Data Protection Act 1984 /ˌdeɪtə prəˈtekʃ(ə)n ˌækt/ *noun* an act of Parliament which regulates the way in which personal data can be used, stored and passed on by companies, and allows individuals access to their own data records

datasheet /ˈdeɪtəʃiːt/ *noun* a document available online that gives a detailed description of a product

data word /ˈdeɪtə wɜːd/ *noun* a unit of data storage in an electronic processing device, measured in bits

dateline /ˈdeɪtlaɪn/ *noun* the day on which a story coming in from abroad was filed

DATV *abbreviation* TV **digitally assisted television**

Da Vinci /ˌdæ ˈvɪntʃi/ a trade name for a grading system for use in post-production

day-after-recall /ˌdeɪ ˌɑːftə ˈriːkɔːl/ *noun* the ability of a television viewer to remember what programmes, channels etc. they were watching the day before. Abbreviation **DAR**

day after recall test /ˌdeɪ ˌɑːftə ˈriːkɔːl ˌtest/ *noun* an advertising research test to see how much someone can remember of an advertisement the day after it appeared or was broadcast

'day in the life' feature /ˌdeɪ ɪn ðə ˈlaɪf ˌfiːtʃə/ *noun* a feature that describes the events of one day in the life of a subject. Compare **'life in the day' feature**

daypart /ˈdeɪpɑːt/ *noun* a division of the day for programming and advertising purposes

day player /ˈdeɪ ˌpleɪə/ *noun* an extra who is only involved in the production of a film for one day

DBS *abbreviation* **direct broadcasting by satellite**

DCC *abbreviation* RECORDING **digital compact cassette**

DCD *abbreviation* RECORDING **digital compact disc**

dead air /ˈded eə/ *noun* a period when the feed of audio and video signals unexpectedly stops during a broadcast, causing silence and a blank or frozen television screen

deadline /ˈdedlaɪn/ *noun* the time by which copy must be submitted

dead spot /ˈded spɒt/ *noun* a place where radio reception is poor, even though it is within the normal range of the transmitter

Dead White European Male /ˌded waɪt ˌjʊərəpiːən ˈmeɪl/ *noun* a man such as a writer or philosopher, who is conventionally regarded as important, but whose significance may have been exaggerated simply because he came from Europe or North America

dead zone /ˈded zəʊn/ *noun* an area where mobile phone networks do not operate

'Rural England hasn't quite caught up with the technological revolution. Vast tracts have no access to broadband Internet, are in mobile phone dead zones and receive few, if any, digital radio stations.'
[Rory Clements, *The Mail on Sunday*]

dealer aids /ˈdiːlər eɪdz/ *plural noun* types of advertising material used by shops to stimulate sales

dealer tie-in /ˌdiːlə ˈtaɪ ˌɪn/ *noun* advertising that advertises the names of local dealers that stock the product

death knock /ˈdeθ nɒk/ *noun* the practice of breaking the news of somebody's death to the public through news coverage

death metal /ˈdeθ ˌmet(ə)l/ *noun* a type of heavy metal music characterised by brutality and speed, growling vocals and horror film iconography

decentralised system /diːˌsentrəlaɪzd ˈsɪstəm/ *noun* a system where responsibility for marketing, advertising and promotion lies with a product manager rather than a centralised department

decipher /dɪˈsaɪfə/ *verb* to succeed in establishing what a word or piece of writing says when it is difficult or almost impossible to read

decisive moment /dɪˌsaɪsɪv ˈməʊmənt/ *noun* the exact moment when a photographer presses the shutter release button and captures a shot

deck /dek/ *noun* a part of a newspaper headline that summarises the story

decks /deks/ *noun* same as **turntables**

decode /diːˈkəʊd/ *verb* to receive an encoded signal and understand (or appear to understand) the message it is carrying

decoder /diːˈkəʊdə/ *noun* **1.** a device for unscrambling satellite signals using a decoder card, obtained by paying a subscription **2.** same as **receiver**

decoding /diˈkəʊdɪŋ/ *noun* the process of interpreting the meanings in a text or other media product

deconstruction /ˌdiːkənˈstrʌkʃ(ə)n/ *noun* the act of analysing a media text to find its component signifiers and how they affect the meaning of one other

décor /ˈdeɪkɔː/ *noun* the scenery of a stage

dedicate /ˈdedɪkeɪt/ *verb* to play a piece of music on the radio as a greeting or tribute to someone

dedication /ˌdedɪˈkeɪʃ(ə)n/ *noun* a piece of music that is played or requested as a greeting or tribute, especially on the radio

dedolights /ˈdeɪdəʊˌlaɪts/ *plural noun* small, highly-directional set lights for filming, designed by German Dedo Weigert

deductive reasoning /dɪˌdʌktɪv ˈriːz(ə)nɪŋ/ *noun* the use of an already-established principle to make a decision about what to do in an individual relevant situation. Compare **inductive reasoning**

deejay /ˈdiːdʒeɪ/ *noun* a disc jockey

deep-focus /ˌdiːp ˈfəʊkəs/ *noun* a situation in which the depth of field in a camera shot is very large, meaning that everything in the scene is in focus

deep structure /ˌdiːp ˈstrʌktʃə/ *noun* in linguistics, the idea that there is an underlying organisational structure to language, which is expressed through grammar and word order, forming surface structure

Deep Throat /ˈdiːp θrəʊt/ *noun* **1.** the anonymous informant to the press during the Watergate scandal, eventually revealed as W. Mark Felt, the second most important official with the FBI at the time. **2.** any anonymous informant on a major scandal

'Sir Christopher says that Jack Straw, the foreign secretary, blocked the book personally and that it will not be published 'until another foreign secretary occupies that chair'. 'Deep throats inside the Foreign Office tell me so,' he adds.' [Julian Glover and Ewen MacAskill, *The Guardian*]

defamation /ˌdefəˈmeɪʃ(ə)n/ *noun* a statement made about a person which is untrue and is harmful to their reputation in some way. ◊ **libel, slander**

defamiliarisation /ˌdiːfəmɪliəraɪˈzeɪʃ(ə)n/ *noun* same as **estrangement**

defensive communication /dɪˌfensɪv kəˌmjuːnɪˈkeɪʃ(ə)n/ *noun* communication in which the recipient deliberately misreads or rejects the intended message because of its dissonance with their own values, beliefs etc.

definition /ˌdefɪˈnɪʃ(ə)n/ *noun* the degree of clarity an image in a photograph or on a screen has

defocus /diːˈfəʊkəs/ *verb* to soften or blur an image by deliberately allowing it to go out of focus ■ *noun* the condition of being defocused, for example the blurring of a photographic image

defog /diːˈfɒg/ *verb* to clear a lens of condensation, especially by allowing it to warm up, or to lose condensation in this way

del *abbreviation* COMPUTING, PRINTING **delete**

DEL /del/ *noun* a telephone line. Full form **direct exchange line**

delay line /dɪˈleɪ laɪn/ *noun* a device that delays the transmission of an electronic signal by a given interval

delay system /dɪˈleɪ ˌsɪstəm/ *noun* a device that delays transmission of something being broadcast live by a few seconds so that, for example, any profanities can be bleeped out

dele /ˈdeli/ *verb* to mark part of a printed text for deletion ■ *noun* a mark in the margin of a printed page indicating that something that has been highlighted should be deleted

delegitimation /ˌdiːlədʒɪtɪˈmeɪʃ(ə)n/ *noun* the process by which certain values, ideas and beliefs etc. are rejected and deemed to be almost or totally unacceptable by the society in which they are found. Compare **legitimation**

delete /dɪˈliːt/ *verb* to remove something printed or written from the surrounding text, or to mark it for removal. Abbreviation **del**

deliberative listening /də‚lɪbərətɪv 'lɪs(ə)nɪŋ/ *noun* the act of listening with the sole intention of deciphering the message being sent. Compare **active listening**

delineate /dɪ'lɪnieɪt/ *verb* to sketch or draw the outline of something

delivery system /dɪ'lɪv(ə)ri ‚sɪstəm/ *noun* the combination of hardware and software required to play a particular multimedia title

Delta /'deltə/ *noun* an internationally recognised code word for the letter D, used in radio communications

dematerialisation /‚diːmətɪəriəlaɪ'zeɪ(ə)n/ *noun* a process in conceptual art in which the thing represented (the object) becomes less important and more detached from the way it is represented

demo /'deməʊ/ *noun* a demonstration recording of music produced for audition or promotional purposes

democracy /dɪ'mɒkrəsi/ *noun* a system of government based on the principle of majority decision-making, representing the rights of each and every citizen in a society. Compare **autocracy**

demodulate /diː'mɒdjʊleɪt/ *verb* to decode an analogue signal into digital data

demographic analysis /‚deməgræfɪk ə'næləsɪs/ *noun* the research and interpretation of data according to demographic principles

demographics /‚demə'græfɪks/ *plural noun* the practice of grouping people according to their social characteristics, for example gender, age, social class, wealth, occupation etc.

demonisation /‚diːmənaɪ'zeɪ(ə)n/ *noun* the act by the media of undermining a public figure such as a politician who is speaking out on issues which are considered dangerous or unacceptable, usually by attacking them on a personal level

'He is the Republican paymaster, one of the authors of the K Street Project and the driving force behind a vicious, organised demonisation and attempted marginalisation of Democrats…' [Will Hutton, *The Observer*]

demonstration effect /‚demən'streɪʃ(ə)n ɪ‚fekt/ *noun* the theory that people buy products to impress or stay on the same level as their neighbours

demy /'demi/ *adjective* referring to printing paper that is 444.5 mm/17.5 in by 571.5 mm/22.5 in or writing paper that is 393.7 mm/15.5 in by 508 mm/20 in

denotation /‚diːnə'teɪʃ(ə)n/ *noun* the literal meaning of a word, image or phrase etc., as opposed to the meanings which are merely suggested or implied. Compare **connotation**

departmental system /‚diːpɑːt 'ment(ə)l ‚sɪstəm/ *noun* a way of organising an advertising agency into departments such as creative, media, administration etc.

dependency theory /dɪ'pendənsi ‚θɪəri/ *noun* the idea that audiences are dependent upon the mass media to feed them ideas, interpretations and values

depth interview /'depθ ‚ɪntəvjuː/ *noun* an interview with no preset questions and following no fixed pattern, but which can last a long time and allows the respondent time to express personal views and tastes

depth of field /‚depθ əv 'fiːld/ *noun* the distance in front of a camera within which subjects are shown in focus, which can be adjusted by changing the lens aperture

depth of focus /‚depθ əv 'fəʊkəs/ *noun* the distance that a camera lens can be moved closer to or further from the film, without the image being focused on becoming unclear

deregulation /diː‚regjʊ'leɪʃ(ə)n/ *noun* the relaxation of government restrictions on what the media can and cannot report

desaturated colour /diː‚sætʃəreɪtɪd 'kʌlə/ *noun* colour that is watery and less vivid than is usual. Compare **saturated colour**

descender /dɪ'sendə/ *noun* the lower part of a lowercase letter that extends below its upper half, for example on a y or g

desensitisation /diː‚sensɪtaɪ 'zeɪʃ(ə)n/ *noun* the theory that repeated exposure to something shocking such as violence will lead an audience to be less affected by it. ◊ **compassion fatigue**

'Yet, no matter how well-intentioned, the frequent broadcasting of the brutal images of war may bring about a progressive desensitisation and brutalisation of those viewing them.' [John Peacock, *The Independent*]

desexualise /diːˈseksjuəlaɪz/ *verb US* to remove sexist features from something

design audit /dɪˈzaɪn ˌɔːdɪt/ *noun* the process of checking and evaluating design, especially in advertising materials or on a website

design department /dɪˈzaɪn dɪ ˌpɑːtmənt/ *noun* the department in a large company that designs the company's products or its advertising

design factor /dɪˈzaɪn ˌfæktə/ *noun* the margin of possible error in a survey, caused by not having used a 100% random sample of the population

design grid /dɪˈzaɪn ɡrɪd/ *noun* the basic form used for designing the page layout of a magazine

desire /dɪˈzaɪə/ *noun* in psychoanalysis, a conscious or unconscious longing for something or somebody

desk /desk/ *noun* a control panel in a radio broadcasting studio where different audio feeds can be mixed for transmission

desk editor /ˈdesk ˌedɪtə/ *noun* a person whose job is to prepare text for publishing

deskman /ˈdeskmən/ *noun* a man who works at a desk and edits news copy

deskperson /ˈdeskpɜːsən/ *noun* a worker at a desk, especially one who edits copy for a newspaper

desk research /ˈdesk rɪˌsɜːtʃ/ *noun* the process of looking for information which is in printed sources such as directories

desks /desks/ *noun* departments within a newspaper, for example the sports desk, the City desk

desktop /ˈdesktɒp/ *noun* the way that a computer screen has been designed to simulate the traditional desk layout, with tools for writing, drawing, making calculations etc.

desktop media /ˌdesktɒp ˈmiːdiə/ *plural noun* a combination of presentation graphics, desktop publishing and multimedia

desktop publishing /ˌdesktɒp ˈpʌblɪʃɪŋ/ *noun* the use of a personal computer and specialist software to lay out and produce typeset-quality documents for printing

despatch rider /dɪˈspætʃ ˌraɪdə/ *noun* a reporter who is sent off on a motorbike to the scene when a piece of news breaks, to capture the first pictures. Abbreviation **DR**

detection /dɪˈtekʃən/ *noun* the act or process of extracting information, especially audio or video signals, from an electromagnetic wave

detector /dɪˈtektə/ *noun* a piece of equipment which extracts information such as audio or video signals from an electromagnetic wave

determination /dɪˌtɜːmɪˈneɪʃ(ə)n/ *noun* a Marxist theory that the economy determines or shapes the society's 'superstructure'

determiner deletion /dɪˈtɜːmɪnə dɪ ˌliːʃ(ə)n/ *noun* the journalistic practice of omitting a determiner ('a' or 'the') when mentioning a person, instead using their defining, news-worthy characteristic to 'label' them ○ *'LOVE cheat Jude Law has desperately been pulling out all the stops to salvage his rocky romance with blonde beauty Sienna Miller.'* (Suzanne Kerins, *Sunday Mirror*, 14 August 2005)

develop /dɪˈveləp/ *verb* to use chemical treatments to produce visible images from photographic film that has previously been exposed to light

developer /dɪˈveləpə/ *noun* **1.** a person who works in an industry such as software production, creating new and innovative products and making more advanced technology available to users **2.** a chemical solution used to treat photographic film and produce visible images. Also called **developing agent**

developing agent /dɪˈveləpɪŋ ˌeɪdʒənt/ *noun* PHOTOGRAPHY same as **developer**

development media /dɪˈveləpmənt ˌmiːdiə/ *noun* media companies that are concerned with aid programmes

'National development is a matter for the media in its entirety. Development media ought to include economic programmes, interviews, and cultural and social information directed by the official authorities to the society.' [*BBC Monitoring International Reports*]

deviance /ˈdiːviəns/ *noun* social behaviour which is considered to be unacceptable within a particular society

deviancy amplification spiral /ˌdiːviənsi ˌæmplɪfɪˈkeɪʃ(ə)n ˌspaɪrəl/ *noun* a situation in which coverage of a deviant event in the media makes it appear more common and more of a social problem than is actually the case, causing more attention to be paid to it and more people to engage in the behaviour

device control /dɪˈvaɪs kənˌtrəʊl/ *noun* a tool that allows another device to be controlled remotely, such as a video editing package from which it is possible to control the recording camera

devil /ˈdev(ə)l/ *noun* a printer's apprentice

DG *abbreviation* BROADCAST **director-general**

diachronic /ˌdaɪəˈkrɒnɪk/ *adjective* referring to the study of something as it has changed through history. Compare **synchronic**

diachronic linguistics /ˌdaɪəkrɒnɪk lɪŋˈgwɪstɪks/ the study of language focusing on the changes that have taken place over its history. Compare **synchronic linguistics**

diagonal /daɪˈægən(ə)l/ *noun* PRINTING same as **slash**

diagram /ˈdaɪəgræm/ *verb* to show or demonstrate something by making a diagram of it ■ *noun* a chart, graph or simplified drawing that illustrates or explains a point or argument

dial /ˈdaɪəl/ *noun* **1.** a round control disc that is turned with the fingers to adjust a piece of electrical or mechanical equipment such as a radio **2.** a panel on a radio with a movable pointer that shows the frequency and waveband of the station it is tuned to ■ *verb* to tune to a radio or television station or programme using a dial

dialect /ˈdaɪəlekt/ *noun* a regional form of a language, usually involving small variations in vocabulary, grammar and pronunciation to those of other regions

dialectical montage /ˌdaɪəlektɪk(ə)l ˈmɒntɑːʒ/ *noun* a sequence which juxtaposes different scenes to highlight the struggle described in the theory of dialectics

dialectics /ˌdaɪəˈlektɪks/ *noun* in Marxist theory, the idea that change comes about through the constant struggle of opposing ideas, producing eventual synthesis

dialogics /ˌdaɪəˈlɒdʒɪks/ *plural noun* in theories of structuralism and discourse, a model in which verbal utterances in a dialogue is seen as being both opinionated and ideological, caught and implicated in a power struggle

dialogist /ˈdaɪəlɒgɪst/ *noun* a person who writes dialogue for films, television or radio

dialogue /ˈdaɪəlɒg/ *noun* conversation that takes place between characters in fiction, such as in a film or play

dialogue coach /ˈdaɪəlɒg kəʊtʃ/ *noun* the member of a film or television production team who is responsible for helping the actors to master accents and dialects for a role

dial-up access /ˌdaɪəl ʌp ˈækses/ *noun* a connection to the Internet that is not permanent but requires a modem or ISDN adapter to dial a telephone access number to connect to the Internet, as in making a normal telephone call. Compare **broadband access**

diaphragm /ˈdaɪəfræm/ *noun* **1.** a curved muscular membrane separates the abdomen from the area around the lungs and is used in singing to control the breathing **2.** a disc with an opening to control the amount of light that is allowed to enter a camera or other optical instrument

diary column /ˈdaɪəri ˌkɒləm/ *noun* a column written by a journalist about their life and including pieces of gossip that people have told them

diary method /ˈdaɪəri ˌmeθəd/ *noun* a market research method in which respondents keep a regular written account of the advertising they have noticed, purchases they have made and products they have used

diary piece /ˈdaɪəri piːs/ *noun* an article which has been scheduled to be covered, for example an event which has happened and needs to be written up, or a follow-up to a previous article. Compare **off-diary piece**

diaspora /diːˈæspərə/ *noun* the dispersal of communities that once lived together in a single location, for example because of war, persecution or natural disaster

diazo /daɪˈæzəʊ/ *noun* a photograph or photocopy made using the diazotype process. Also called **dyeline**

diazotype /ˈdaɪˌæzəʊtaɪp/ *noun* a reproductive printing or photographic process that makes use of the way diazo compounds, formed from nitrogen, decompose when exposed to ultraviolet light

dicroic filter /daɪˌkrəʊik ˈfiltə/ *noun* a glass filter placed over a light that only allows light of a certain colour to pass through

Dictaphone /ˈdɪktəfəʊn/ a trade name for a small tape recorder used for dictating letters or documents which can then be typed by someone playing the recording back

diegetic sound /ˌdaɪədʒetɪk ˈsaʊnd/ *noun* sound from a recognisable source in a piece of film, for example dialogue from a character. Compare **non-diegetic sound**

diesis /ˈdaɪiːsɪs/ *noun* PRINTING same as **double dagger**

différance /ˈdiːferɑːns/ *noun* the view of the concept of difference with the consideration that terms and meanings are constantly shifting, and therefore affecting and reconstructing each other

difference /ˈdɪf(ə)rəns/ *noun* the idea that meaning can be defined by what it does not represent. So the verb 'to drink' can be defined using the differences between it and the verb 'to eat', or between it and any other verb or noun.

differend /ˈdɪfərend/ *noun* the idea that conflicts between cultural forms can not always be resolved, because of insurmountable differences between the two

differential pricing /ˌdɪfərenʃəl ˈpraɪsɪŋ/ *noun* the practice of adjusting the pricing of products according to how much each market can afford to pay for it

'Companies like Priceline and E-Bay and major hotels and airlines are already… offering the same product at different prices to different customers. While differential pricing had been prevalent in the traditional economy also, the degree of differentiation was not so acute and also not so personalized.' [Dipayan Biswas, *Journal of Business Research*]

diffuse /dɪˈfjuːz/ *verb* to make something, especially light, less bright or intense, or become less bright or intense

diffuser /dɪˈfjuːzə/ *noun* tracing paper or some other transparent material, fixed over a light to make it less bright and harsh

diffusion /dɪˈfjuːʒ(ə)n/ *noun* the channels through which the idea of an innovation reaches all members of a social community

dig /dɪɡ/ *verb* to do deep research for a journalistic piece

digerati /ˌdɪdʒəˈrɑːti/ *plural noun* people with expertise or professional involvement in computers, the Internet or the World Wide Web

'…plonk the digital camera into its 'dock', and then plug in the A/V cables that came with the camera. Stick those into the back of the TV, and voila, instant photo slideshow. The real digerati will go one better, and load their photos onto an iPod Photo or other digital media player.' [Charles Arthur, *The Independent*]

digest /ˈdaɪdʒest/ *noun* a compilation of articles or stories, originally from different sources, edited and brought together in a magazine, book or broadcast

digibeta /ˈdɪdʒibiːtə/ *noun* a type of videotape format

digicam /ˈdɪdʒikæm/ *noun* PHOTOGRAPHY, COMPUTING same as **digital camera**

digilink /ˈdɪdʒilɪŋk/ *noun* a camera that transmits a digital signal to a nearby receiver

digital /ˈdɪdʒɪt(ə)l/ *adjective* referring to a form of transmission in which a signal is sent in small, separate packages. Compare **analogue**

Digital Audio Broadcasting /ˌdɪdʒɪt(ə)l ˌɔːdiəʊ ˈbrɔːdkɑːstɪŋ/ *noun* the process of broadcasting using digital recordings which give clearer sound than analogue recordings. Abbreviation **DAB**

digital audio tape /ˌdɪdʒɪt(ə)l ˈɔːdiəʊ ˌteɪp/ *noun* a magnetic tape used in the digital recording of music. Abbreviation **DAT**

digital camera /ˌdɪdʒɪt(ə)l ˈkæm(ə)rə/ *noun* a camera that takes pictures that are stored in digital form and so can be viewed, manipulated and printed using a computer. Also called **digicam**

digital colour proof /ˌdɪdʒɪt(ə)l ˌkʌlə ˈpruːf/ *noun* a colour proof taken from digital files prior to film output at high or low resolution

digital compact cassette /ˌdɪdʒɪt(ə)l ˌkɒmpækt kə'set/ *noun* magnetic tape in a compact cassette box that is used to store computer data or audio signals in a digital format. Abbreviation **DCC**

digital compact disc /ˌdɪdʒɪt(ə)l ˌkɒmpækt 'dɪsk/ *noun* a form of compact disc which offers a greater storage capacity

digital divide /ˌdɪdʒɪt(ə)l dɪ'vaɪd/ *noun* the state of inequality that exists between people who have access to modern information technology and those who do not, since the former have many more opportunities open to them than the latter

digital imaging /ˌdɪdʒɪt(ə)l 'ɪmɪdʒɪŋ/ *noun* photography using digital equipment, instead of the traditional exposure of an image onto light-sensitive film

digitally assisted television /ˌdɪdʒɪt(ə)li ə,sɪstɪd 'telɪvɪʒ(ə)n/ *noun* a system for reducing the bandwidth needed for sending a television signal by sending part of it through digital means. Abbreviation **DATV**

digitally originated graphic /ˌdɪdʒɪt(ə)li ə,rɪdʒɪneɪtɪd 'ɡræfɪk/ *noun* a small stationary logo, usually used to identify a channel, shown in one corner of a screen. Abbreviation **DOG**

digital radio /ˌdɪdʒɪt(ə)l 'reɪdiəʊ/ *noun* radio broadcasting that is transmitted in digital form, is received on a digital receiver, provides a greater choice of stations and does not suffer from interference

digital recording /ˌdɪdʒɪt(ə)l rɪ'kɔːdɪŋ/ *noun* sound recorded using a computerised system (as opposed to analogue), which can therefore be copied without loss of quality

digital retouching /ˌdɪdʒɪt(ə)l riː'tʌtʃɪŋ/ *noun* the process of using digital technology to alter a photograph, either to remove imperfections or to subtly change what appears to be happening in the picture, while still giving the impression that the photograph has not been altered

digital television /ˌdɪdʒɪt(ə)l 'telɪvɪʒ(ə)n/ *noun* **1.** television broadcasting in which the picture is transmitted in digital form and decoded at the televi-sion receiver. Abbreviation **DTV 2.** a television set specially constructed or adapted for receiving digital signals

digital terrestrial broadcasting /ˌdɪdʒɪt(ə)l tə,restriəl 'brɔːdkɑːstɪŋ/ *noun* the policy of making all of a country's terrestrial television and radio broadcasting digital, which offers greater choice and quality of sound and picture, but requires special receiving equipment

digital transmission area /ˌdʒɪt(ə)l trænz'mɪʃ(ə)n ,eəriə/ *noun* the control suite used to transmit the BBC digital channels. Abbreviation **DTA**

digital TV /ˌdɪdʒɪt(ə)l tiː'viː/ *noun* a television that can receive and decode television images and audio sent as digital data, then displayed on a standard screen

digital video /ˌdɪdʒɪt(ə)l 'vɪdiəʊ/ *noun* the format used by small, hand-held video recorders which record digitally. Abbreviation **DV**

digital video camera /ˌdɪdʒɪt(ə)l 'vɪdiəʊ ,kæm(ə)rə/ *noun* a video camera which records digital files. Abbreviation **DVC**

digital video edit /ˌdɪdʒɪt(ə)l 'vɪdiəʊ ,edɪt/ *noun* the editing of a piece of video using digital technology

digital video effects /ˌdɪdʒɪt(ə)l 'vɪdiəʊ ɪ,fekts/ *noun* any program which can be used to create complex video effects. Abbreviation **DVE**

digital video recorder /ˌdɪdʒɪt(ə)l 'vɪdiəʊ rɪ,kɔːdə/ *noun* a video recorder which records on an internal data storage system, without the need for removable videotapes. Abbreviation **DVR**

digital zoom /ˌdɪdʒɪt(ə)l 'zuːm/ *noun* a zoom facility on a camera which crops and enlarges an already-captured image, losing some quality. Compare **optical zoom**

digitisable /'dɪdʒɪtaɪzəb(ə)l/ *adjective* referring to conversion into digital form for distribution via the Internet or other networks

digitisation /ˌdɪdʒɪtaɪ'zeɪʃ(ə)n/ *noun* **1.** the process of converting analogue signals to digital **2.** the process by which most media forms are becoming digitised so that they can be more readily accessed, reproduced with no loss of quality and stored in a permanent, non-perishable form

'...digitisation of content – which has made it very easy for internet pirates to steal, copy and share movies via cyberspace – has put pressure on movie studios to make changes to the way they distribute movies.' [Scott Morrison, *The Financial Times*]

digitise /'dɪdʒɪtaɪz/ *verb* **1.** to convert analogue signals to digital, for example so that they can be edited using digital equipment **2.** to put data into a digital form so that it can be stored, accessed and reproduced more effectively

digitising /'dɪdʒɪtaɪzɪŋ/ *noun* the process of burning the rushes of a film onto the hard disk of a computer, ready for editing

digizine /'dɪdʒiːn/ *noun* a magazine that can be accessed by computer, either on the Internet or on a CD-ROM

dimmer /'dɪmə/ *noun* a device that allows you to make a light brighter or dimmer

DIN /,diː aɪ 'en/ *noun* a system of numbers used to indicate the speed of a photographic film

dingbat /'dɪŋbæt/ *noun* PRINTING a typographical symbol or character other than a letter or numeral, for example a star or pointing hand

DIN number /,diː aɪ 'en ,nʌmbə/ *noun* a number that indicates the speed of a photographic film

diorama /,daɪə'rɑːmə/ *noun* a scene that appears to be three-dimensional, for example one that is painted on layers of translucent material which the viewer looks at through a small hole

dip into /,dɪp 'ɪntə/ *verb* to browse through a text such as a book or magazine rather than read it all

Diploma in Journalism /dɪ,pləʊmə ɪn 'dʒɜːnə,lɪz(ə)m/ needs def

dipstick survey /'dɪpstɪk ,sɜːveɪ/ *noun* a survey which only reveals one aspect of the true picture, such as the number of viewing hours but not the programme watched

direct-action advertising /daɪ,rekt ,ækʃən 'ædvətaɪzɪŋ/ *noun* advertising that aims to get a quick response

direct broadcast by satellite /daɪ,rekt ,brɔːdkɑːst baɪ 'sætəlaɪt/ *noun* the process of broadcasting radio and television signals over a wide area from an earth station via a satellite, that are received with a dish aerial

direct broadcasting by satellite /daɪ,rekt ,brɔːdkɑːstɪŋ baɪ 'sætəlaɪt/ *noun* broadcasting in which the television signal is sent directly from the satellite to individual receiver dishes. Abbreviation **DBS**

direct cinema /daɪ,rekt 'sɪnɪmə/ *noun* same as **ciné-verité**

direct democracy /daɪ,rekt dɪ 'mɒkrəsi/ *noun* a proposed form of democratic government in which all citizens have direct input into the legislative process

direct entry /daɪ,rekt 'entri/ *noun* the process of entering journalism through a training course run by the publication offering the job

direct exchange line /daɪ,rekt ɪks 'tʃeɪndʒ ,laɪn/ *noun* full form of **DEL**

direct input /daɪ,rekt 'ɪnpʊt/ *noun* the process by which copy can be transferred directly from the reporter's computer to the computer on which typesetting is done, rather than the layout being assembled by hand using printouts of the text

directional /daɪ'rekʃən(ə)l/ *adjective* able to transmit or receive sound waves, nuclear particles, light or radio waves more efficiently if they travel in a particular direction

directional antenna /daɪ,rekʃən(ə)l æn'tenə/ *noun* an antenna which sends and receives signals more effectively in one particular direction. Compare **omnidirectional antenna**

directional medium /daɪ,rekʃən(ə)l 'miːdiəm/ *noun* an advertising medium that gives potential customers information on where to find products or services, for example a directory

directional microphone /daɪ ,rekʃən(ə)l 'maɪkrəfəʊn/ *noun* a microphone which picks up audio signals only from a particular direction or within a narrow range, cutting out extra background noise

direct-mail advertising /daɪ,rekt 'meɪl ,ædvətaɪzɪŋ/ *noun* the practice of advertising by sending leaflets to people through the post

direct marketing /daɪ,rekt 'mɑːkɪtɪŋ/ *noun* methods of marketing that bypass retailers, such as mail order, direct-mail advertising, telephone sales, Internet shopping etc.

direct-marketing media /daɪˌrekt 'mɑːkɪtɪŋ ˌmiːdiə/ *plural noun* media that are used for direct marketing, for example direct mail, telemarketing, and television

director /daɪ'rektə/ *noun* **1.** the member of a film production team who is responsible for directing the actors, the camera crew and other staff **2.** the member of a television production team who is responsible for deciding which shots will be used

director-general /daɪˌrektə 'dʒen(ə)rəl/ *noun* the chief of a governmental agency or other organisation which is headed by several directors. Abbreviation **DG**

directorial /ˌdaɪrek'tɔːriəl/ *adjective* relating to, belonging to, or suitable for a director

director's chair /daɪˌrektəz 'tʃeə/ *noun* the chair used by the director on a film set

director's cut /daɪ'rektəz kʌt/ *noun* a version of a film that its director has complete artistic control over, often not the version that is released commercially

direct response advertising /daɪ ˌrekt rɪ'spɒns ˌædvətaɪzɪŋ/ *noun* the practice of advertising in such a way as to get customers to send in inquiries or orders directly by mail

direct response television /daɪ ˌrekt rɪ'spɒns ˌtelɪvɪʒ(ə)n/ *noun* advertising which seeks an immediate response from the audience, such as calling an on-screen number. Abbreviation **DRTV**

disaster movie /dɪ'zɑːstə ˌmuːvi/ *noun* a genre of film in which the plot centres on a natural disaster such as an earthquake, or a human-made crisis such as a train crash or the collapse of a building etc.

disavowal /ˌdɪsə'vaʊəl/ *noun* the ability of a person to both admit to and deny their own desires, a concept of particular interest in feminist study of sexuality

disc camera /'dɪsk ˌkæm(ə)rə/ *noun* a camera that uses film on a disc rather than on a roll or a cartridge

disc jockey /'dɪsk ˌdʒɒki/ *noun* MUSIC, RADIO full form of **DJ**

disclosure of information /dɪs ˌkləʊʒər əv ˌɪnfə'meɪʃ(ə)n/ *noun* the act of or process of passing on information that was intended to be kept secret or private to someone else

disco /'dɪskəʊ/ *noun* **1.** a place such as a club, or an event such as a party, where people dance to recorded pop music, often introduced by a DJ. Full form **disco-theque 2.** a style of up-tempo pop music originating in the early 1970s for dancing. It developed from soul music, in response to the growing popularity of discos. **3.** the equipment used to play recordings for people to dance to at a disco, usually comprising amplifiers, speakers, and a record, tape or CD deck, often with lighting equipment

discography /ˌdɪsk'ɒɡrəfi/ *noun* the full list of the recordings of a particular type, for example by one performer or group, or of a particular category of music

disconfirmation /ˌdɪskɒnfɜː 'meɪʃ(ə)n/ *noun* an expression of disagreement from somebody which challenges already-held opinions, values, beliefs etc. Compare **confirmation**

discotheque /'dɪskətek/ *noun* MUSIC, DANCE full form of **disco**

discourse /'dɪskɔːs/ *noun* the form of language used in a given situation, including such things as choice of appropriate vocabulary, tone, grammar, level of formality etc.

discourse analysis /'dɪskɔːs ə ˌnæləsɪs/ *noun* the analysis of a media text such as a news bulletin, focusing on the discourse used in its presentation

discretionary income /dɪ ˌskreʃ(ə)n(ə)ri 'ɪnkʌm/ *noun* the income left after fixed payments have been made and the spending of which is therefore subject to advertising influence

discursive contestation /dɪsˌkɜːsɪv ˌkɒntes'teɪʃ(ə)n/ *noun* the potential for the audience of a news broadcast to challenge or disagree with its presentation

discursive gap /dɪˌskɜːsɪv 'ɡæp/ *noun* the distinction between formal, written language used in a text such as a news article, and the less formal, more personal internal language of the reader. The popular press try to mimic this language in a way which engages the reader more.

discussion group /dɪˈskʌʃ(ə)n gruːp/ *noun* a feature of a website that lets any visitor write and post a message on a particular subject, which is displayed to any other visitors, who can then add their comments in reply to the message

discussion list /dɪˈskʌʃ(ə)n lɪst/ *noun* a subscription e-mail service

disempowerment /ˌdɪsemˈpaʊəmənt/ *noun* the reduction of the power which individuals have to make their own choices and shape their own lives

dish /dɪʃ/ *noun* **1.** same as **dish aerial 2.** a satellite dish, or a vehicle transporting one on an outside broadcast

dish aerial /ˈdɪʃ ˌeəriəl/ *noun* ELEC-TRONICS a transmitting and receiving aerial in the form of a dish-shaped reflector, as used in satellite broadcasting

disinformation /ˌdɪsɪnfəˈmeɪʃ(ə)n/ *noun* forged information presented as real as a form of propaganda, to discredit a person in power such as a politician

disk /dɪsk/ *noun* a storage facility for data on a computer, either built-in and permanent (hard disk) or removable and rewritable (floppy disk)

Disneyesque /ˌdɪzniˈesk/ *adjective* resembling or reminiscent of the style of the films and cartoons created by Walt Disney or the Disney studios

disparaging copy /dɪˌspærɪdʒɪŋ ˈkɒpi/ *noun* advertising copy which is critical of another company's products

dispatch /dɪˈspætʃ/ *noun* **1.** a news item or report sent by a news correspondent or agency **2.** an official message or report, especially from a diplomat or an officer in the armed forces

displacement /dɪsˈpleɪsmənt/ *noun* one of the two main mechanisms by which dreams express the subconscious, by using other signs to represent a fear which we feel unable to face head-on. ◊ **condensation**

displacement effect /dɪsˈpleɪsmənt ɪˌfekt/ *noun* the way in which new media, such as the World Wide Web, have pushed other older media such as television and books into a different, smaller role

display /dɪˈspleɪ/ *adjective* referring to typefaces that are designed for prominent use in advertising ■ *noun* printed advertising that uses attractive pictures, typography or other features

display ads /dɪsˈpleɪ ædz/ *plural noun* large advertisements, usually containing illustrations, appearing in a newspaper. Compare **classified ads**

display advertising /dɪˈspleɪ ˌædvətaɪzɪŋ/ *noun* advertising that has individual features such as photographs, its own box border, or the company logo in addition to text

display colour /dɪsˈpleɪ ˌkʌlə/ *noun* the colour of characters in a videotext display system

display memory /dɪsˈpleɪ ˌmem(ə)ri/ *noun* memory on a graphics card or held separate from the main processing memory in a computer, which is used to store image display information

dispositif /dɪsˌpɒziˈtiːf/ *noun* in French philosophy, an agent of power and control over the general population

dispositional attribution /ˌdɪspəzɪʃən(ə)l ˌætrɪˈbjuːʃ(ə)n/ *noun* the tendency to analyse a person's actions in light of their personality traits, rather than the situation that they are in. Compare **situational attribution**

disqualifying communication /ˌdɪskwɒlɪfaɪɪŋ kəmˌjuːnɪˈkeɪʃ(ə)n/ *noun* a type of defensive communication in which the recipient steers the subject to a less challenging one or avoids facing the issue head-on in some other way

disseminate /dɪˈsemɪneɪt/ *verb* to distribute or spread something, especially information, widely, or become widespread

dissemination /dɪˌsemɪˈneɪʃ(ə)n/ *noun* the distribution of something throughout an area or medium

dissensus /dɪˈsensəs/ *noun* a situation in which two or more people fail to agree on values, norms, ideas, beliefs, etc. Compare **consensus**

dissolve /dɪˈzɒlv/ *verb* same as **cross fade**

dissonance /ˈdɪsənəns/ *noun* conflict between the ideas, values, beliefs, etc. that a person already holds and those directed at them in some form of communication, the effect being that of some discomfort

dissonance/attribution model /ˌdɪsənəns ˌætrɪˈbjuːʃ(ə)n ˌmɒd(ə)l/ *noun* a response model which follows the opposite sequence from normal: consumers first act in a specific way, then develop feelings as a result of their behaviour, and then look for information that supports their attitude and behaviour

Distagon /'dɪstəgɒn/ a trade name for a type of prime lens

distantiation /ˌdɪstænsi'eɪʃ(ə)n/ *noun* the idea that a media product or piece of art has an 'internal distance' from the ideology in which it was created

distinction /dɪ'stɪŋkʃən/ *noun* the power conferred upon somebody with cultural capital, as distinguished from the masses

distort /dɪ'stɔːt/ *verb* to process something such as a radio or television signal inaccurately to the extent that it becomes unclear or unrecognisable, for example in amplification

distortion /dɪ'stɔːʃ(ə)n/ *noun* the way in which images are stretched, squashed or twisted by a lens which bends the light ineffectively. For example, a fisheye lens produces extreme distortion around the edges of the image.

distribution /ˌdɪstrɪ'bjuːʃ(ə)n/ *noun* **1.** the act of sending information out, especially via a network **2.** the selling and delivery of goods to retailers, such as films to cinemas or magazines to shops

distribution amplifier /ˌdɪstrɪ'bjuːʃ(ə)n ˌæmplɪfaɪə/ *noun* a piece of equipment which takes one feed, either video or audio, and splits it to multiple destinations on different lines without loss of quality. Abbreviation **DA**

distribution rights /ˌdɪstrɪ'bjuːʃ(ə)n ˌraɪts/ *noun* the right to copy and distribute a piece of work such as a film within a certain market area

distributor /dɪ'strɪbjʊtə/ *noun* a company that advertises films and supplies them to cinemas

district office /ˌdɪstrɪkt 'ɒfɪs/ any newspaper office which is not the main base of the operation

diversification /daɪˌvɜːsɪfɪ'keɪʃ(ə)n/ *noun* a major media company's spread into ownership of other related and unrelated products. For example, Virgin started as a music distributor, expanded into a record label, radio empire, mobile phone provider, book publishing and then into cosmetics, soft drinks, personal finance, an airline and many more products and services.

diversity /daɪ'vɜːsɪti/ *noun* the range of different programmes broadcast on a single network

division of labour /dɪˌvɪʒ(ə)n əv 'leɪbə/ *noun* the process of dividing work into specific sections to be completed by experts in that field, traditional in the media

DJ /'diːdʒeɪ/ *noun* **1.** a person who plays recordings of music, for example at a dance or on the radio **2.** a person who uses various electronic techniques to manipulate samples of recorded music, often to the point where a new composition has been created. Full form **disc jockey**

D-notice /'diː ˌnəʊtɪs/ *noun* an official communication from the UK government, advising newspapers that they should not publish specific information for security reasons

doco /'dɒkəʊ/ *noun* TV same as **documentary**

Doctrine of Misappropriation /ˌdɒktrɪn əv ˌmɪsəˌprəʊpri'eɪʃ(ə)n/ *noun* a principle introduced by a 1918 Supreme Court judgment that news gathered by a press agency be considered intellectual property and protected from exploitation by rivals. ◊ **International News Service**

docudrama /'dɒkjuːˌdrɑːmə/ *noun* a film or television drama that is based on true events

document /'dɒkjʊmənt/ *noun* a paper, especially an official paper, with written information on it

documentary /ˌdɒkjʊ'ment(ə)ri/ *noun* a television programme or film that depicts facts and real-world events. Also called **doco**

document reader /'dɒkjʊmənt ˌriːdə/ *noun* a device that converts written or typed information to a form that a computer can understand and process

docusoap /'dɒkjuːsəʊp/ *noun* a serial that follows the lives of real people, for example in a place of work or a family home, creating a 'real-life' soap opera

docutainment /ˌdɒkjuː'teɪnmənt/ *noun* TV same as **infotainment**

dodge /dɒdʒ/ *verb* to manipulate a photographic print during exposure to allow more or less light to reach particular parts of it

dodger /ˈdɒdʒə/ *noun* a small leaflet or handout

DOG *abbreviation* **digitally originated graphic**

dog-eat-dog /ˌdɒg iːt ˈdɒg/ *noun* marketing activity where everyone fights for their own product and attacks competitors mercilessly

Dolby /ˈdɒlbi/ a research laboratory that provides ways to improve the quality of recorded sound

dolly /ˈdɒli/ *noun* a mobile apparatus for mounting a camera, allowing it to be easily moved

dolly shot /ˈdɒli ʃɒt/ *noun* a tracking shot using a dolly rather than a guiding rail

dolphin arm /ˈdɒlfɪn ɑːm/ *noun* a short arm on which a camera is mounted

domain name /dəʊˈmeɪn neɪm/ *noun* the Internet address of a computer or network

dominant /ˈdɒmɪnənt/ *adjective* more powerful than the others in its field

dominant discourse /ˌdɒmɪnənt ˈdɪskɔːs/ *noun* that form of discourse which is most socially accepted and has precedence over others

dominant response /ˌdɒmɪnənt rɪ ˈspɒns/ *noun* one of three supposed responses to receiving a message, a dominant response involves whole-hearted acceptance of whatever messages, values, ideas etc. are being received. ◊ **subordinate response**, **radical response**

donut /ˈdəʊnʌt/ *noun* a piece in which a reporter on an outside broadcast introduces a guest or piece of pre-recorded video

doorstep /ˈdɔːstep/ *verb* to try to obtain a photograph of, or interview with someone by waiting for them outside their home or workplace ■ *noun* an interview achieved by waiting outside a celebrity's house or place of work until they come out

doorstepping /ˈdɔːˌstepɪŋ/ *noun* the practice of putting pressure on an unwilling source for a story by standing outside their house or place of work to ask them questions as they walk by

doo-wop /ˈduː wɒp/ *noun* a type of harmonised singing in a rhythm-and-blues style, which became popular in the US in the late 1950s

dot-com /ˌdɒt ˈkɒm/ *noun* a company that conducts its business on the Internet or that provides Internet services

dot-com bubble /ˌdɒt kɒm ˈbʌb(ə)l/ *noun* the unsustainable situation that was the result of multiple dot-com businesses becoming successful in the late 1990s, leading to many more being started up and also enjoying success, but later failing

dot-com crash /ˌdɒt kɒm ˈkræʃ/ *noun* a phrase to describe how the dot-com bubble eventually burst, as starting businesses invested far more capital than they could make back and were forced to retreat

'Lastminute, which survived the dot-com crash that claimed expensive UK start ups such as Boo.com and Letsbuyit.com, saw its shares surge…' [Nic Hopkins, *The Times*]

dot-comer /ˌdɒt ˈkʌmə/ *noun* a person who owns or works for a dot-com

dots per inch /ˌdɒts pɜːr ˈɪntʃ/ *noun* an expression of the resolution of a printer or image based on the number of dots of ink or toner it can print in a linear inch. The higher the number, the better quality of the printing. Abbreviation **dpi**

double /ˈdʌb(ə)l/ *verb* to substitute for an actor in a film in scenes such as those that include danger, special skill or nudity ■ *noun* **1.** a substitute who resembles a film actor and takes their place, for example in scenes that involve danger, special skill or nudity **2.** PRINTING same as **doublet**

double bill /ˌdʌb(ə)l ˈbɪl/ *noun* a cinema or television programme that shows two feature films consecutively

double dagger /ˌdʌb(ə)l ˈdægə/ *noun* a sign (‡) that is used in printed texts to indicate a reference, especially to a footnote. Also called **diesis**, **double obelisk**

double-decker /ˌdʌb(ə)l ˈdekə/ *noun* two advertising panels, one on top of the other

double exposure /ˌdʌb(ə)l ɪk ˈspəʊʒə/ *noun* the exposure of two images onto a single piece of film, so that they appear as though they have been photographed at a single time

double feature /ˌdʌb(ə)l ˈfiːtʃə/ *noun* a cinema programme of two full-length films shown consecutively. Also called **twin bill**

double-header /ˌdʌb(ə)l ˈhedə/ *noun* a radio programme with two presenters

double obelisk /ˌdʌb(ə)l ˈɒbəlɪsk/ *noun* PRINTING same as **double dagger**

double opt-in /ˌdʌb(ə)l ˈɒpt ˌɪn/ *noun* a method by which users who want to receive information or services from a website can register themselves as subscribers

double-page spread /ˌdʌb(ə)l peɪdʒ ˈspred/ *noun* a feature or article that runs across the middle folding page of a newspaper or magazine. Also called **double spread**

double quote /ˌdʌb(ə)l ˈkwəʊt/ *noun* a quotation mark that consists of two marks ("), not one

double-space /ˌdʌb(ə)l ˈspeɪs/ *verb* to arrange printed text with one blank line between each typed or printed line

double-spotting /ˌdʌb(ə)l ˈspɒtɪŋ/ *noun* the practice of running an advertising spot twice

double spread /ˌdʌb(ə)l ˈspred/ *noun* PUBLISHING same as **double-page spread**

doublet /ˈdʌblət/ *noun* a letter, word or line that is printed a second time in error. Also called **double**

doughnut /ˈdəʊnʌt/ *verb* **1.** to make sure that a speaker in frame on a television broadcast is closely surrounded by people, to give viewers the impression that there is a large crowd present when there is not **2.** to surround a Member of Parliament who is speaking and being filmed for television in order to give the impression that the chamber is fuller than it really is

downbeat /ˈdaʊnbiːt/ *noun* electronic music that is for listening to instead of dancing to

downlink /ˈdaʊnlɪŋk/ *noun* the transmission of data from a satellite downwards to receivers within its footprint. Compare **uplink**

download /ˌdaʊnˈləʊd/ *verb* to transfer data from the Internet to a computer, or from one computer to another ■ *noun* a file which has been transferred from the Internet to a personal computer

downpage /ˈdaʊnpeɪdʒ/ *noun* the lower half of a newspaper page. Stories are said to 'appear downpage'.

downtable /ˈdaʊnteɪb(ə)l/ *noun* all the subeditors of a newspaper other than the chief and deputy chief

downtempo /daʊnˈtempəʊ/ *noun* electronic music in a variety of styles that is usually for listening to instead of dancing to. Also called **chillout**

down-the-line /ˌdaʊn ðə ˈlaɪn/ *adjective* referring to an interview carried out over the phone. Abbreviation **DTL**

downtime /ˈdaʊntaɪm/ *noun* a period of time that a communications network is not functioning, because of breakdown or maintenance

dpi /ˌdiː piː ˈaɪ/ *noun* a measure of the density of the image on a computer screen

DR *abbreviation* **despatch rider**

drabble /ˈdræb(ə)l/ *noun* a short piece of fiction, often fan fiction, usually 100 words in length. Also called **ficlet**

drag /dræg/ *noun* the clothing of the opposite sex used as a costume for performances, most usually used to refer to glamorous and ostentatious female clothing worn by males

drag king /ˈdræg kɪŋ/ *noun* a woman who dresses in men's clothes and attempts to appear 'male' with facial hair, a male body shape etc, especially as a performer

drag queen /ˈdræg kwiːn/ *noun* a man who dresses in women's clothes, especially a performer affecting exaggerated feminine mannerisms for comic effect

drama /ˈdrɑːmə/ *noun* **1.** the genre of literary works written for performance on the stage, radio or television **2.** a play written to be performed on the stage, television or radio **3.** exciting, tense, and gripping events and actions, or an exciting, tense, and gripping quality, either in a work of art or in a real-life situation

drama documentary /ˈdrɑːmə ˌdɒkjʊment(ə)ri/ *noun* a television or radio programme based on real events which are dramatised, or in which real events and characters are mingled with fictional ones

drama series /ˈdrɑːmə ˌsɪəriːz/ *noun* a television or radio drama shown in several episodes, as a series

dramatic /drəˈmætɪk/ *adjective* **1.** involving exciting, tense or gripping events and actions **2.** referring to a medium that involves movement and performance such as dance. Compare **static**

dramatic irony /drəˌmætɪk ˈaɪrəni/ *noun* an effect created in a dramatic performance by the difference between what a character is seen to understand about their situation and what the audience knows to actually be the case, having been party to extra information

dramatisation /ˌdræmətaɪˈzeɪʃ(ə)n/ *noun* **1.** an adaptation of a work of fiction or a presentation of a real event that is intended for performance on the stage, television or radio **2.** the act, art, or process of turning a literary work or a real event into a drama for performance on the stage, television, or radio

dramatise /ˈdræmətaɪz/ *verb* to present a real event as a dramatic presentation for the stage, television or radio

dramatist /ˈdræmətɪst/ *noun* somebody who writes drama for the stage, television or radio

drawing /ˈdrɔːɪŋ/ *noun* **1.** the art, activity, or practice of making pictures using lines of pencil, crayon or pen, rather than colours **2.** a picture of something made with lines, often with shading, but generally without colour

dream-work /ˈdriːm wɜːk/ *noun* the mechanisms by which unconscious thoughts are transformed into dreams, including condensation and displacement

DreamWorks SKG /ˌdriːmwɜːks ˌes keɪ ˈdʒiː/ *noun* a major film studio formed by Steven Spielberg and David Geffen along with Jeffery Katzenberg (former head of the Walt Disney Company) in 1997. It is best-known for its co-production and co-distribution deals with other studios such as Universal.

dress /dres/ *noun* the clothes that a person wears and the way in which they visually present themselves, an important factor in non-verbal communication

dresser /ˈdresə/ *noun* **1.** a person from the wardrobe department who fits actors for their clothes **2.** the member of a television, film or theatre production team who is responsible for helping the actors into and out of their costumes

dress rehearsal /ˈdres rɪˌhɜːs(ə)l/ *noun* **1.** the final rehearsal of something such as a play, opera, or ballet in full costume and with lights, music, and effects, before it is given its first public performance **2.** a full-scale practice before any important event

drip campaign /drɪp/, **drip method** /ˈdrɪp kæmˌpeɪn/, **drip** /ˈdrɪp ˌmeθəd/ *noun* a steady low-level stream of advertising for a product, to maintain awareness of the brand in general. Compare **burst campaign**

'The Meat and Livestock Commission is taking a £10m gamble with its new umbrella campaign... The idea is to encourage all consumers to eat meat more often, with a drip campaign running for 35 weeks of the year.' [Alex Benady, *Marketing*]

drive /draɪv/ *verb* 'to drive the desk' – to operate an editing or mixing desk

drive-time /ˈdraɪv taɪm/ *noun* a peak period in the late afternoon when there are lots of radio listeners in their cars on the way home

drop /drɒp/ *noun* a short branch line from a cable television trunk line, that feeds signals to an individual house or flat

drop cap /ˈdrɒp kæp/ *noun* a larger-size capital letter appearing at the start of an article or paragraph, which drops below the line on which it appears

drop out /ˈdrɒp aʊt/ *noun* a broadcasting situation in which a video feed is lost or distorted because of poor reception, faulty tape or a faulty playback machine

dropped call /ˌdrɒpt ˈkɔːl/ *noun* a call on a mobile phone which is terminated because of loss of signal

'For the moment, a number of problems at 3 have meant that competitors have been able to dismiss its pricing challenge. Dropped calls, patchy customer service and bulky, unattractive handsets with low battery life are still putting off many customers.' [Maija Pesola, *The Financial Times*]

DRTV *abbreviation* **direct response television**

drum and bass /ˌdrʌm ən ˈbeɪs/ *noun* electronic music originating in the UK in the 1990s that is very fast, has reggae bass lines and complex percussion

dry hire /ˌdraɪ ˈhaɪə/ *noun* the hire of equipment, facilities etc. without operators, so it must be self-staffed

dry run /ˌdraɪ ˈrʌn/ *noun* a rehearsal which does not use any recording equipment

DSL /ˌdiː es ˈel/ *noun* a high-speed telephone line that can be used for telephony, television and Internet access and has a much greater digital capacity than an ordinary telephone line

D-SUB connector /ˌdiː sʌb kəˈnektə/ *noun* a video connector commonly used on PC monitors to carry all the video signals in one cable

DTA *abbreviation* **digital transmission area**

DTL *abbreviation* **down-the-line**

DTV *abbreviation* BROADCAST **digital television**

dual path /ˈdjuːəl pɑːθ/ *noun* the ability to broadcast two separate feeds from a single source, as for different channels

dub /dʌb/ *verb* to make a copy of something recorded, usually from one source to another, for example from cassette to disc

dubbing /ˈdʌbɪŋ/ *noun* the work of adding extra sound to film, such as music and sound effects

dumbing-down /ˌdʌmɪŋ ˈdaʊn/ *noun* the process of making popular media texts such as newspapers less intellectually challenging

dummy /ˈdʌmi/ *noun* a rough version of the layout of a newspaper page, showing placement of advertisements

dump bin /ˈdʌmp bɪn/ *noun* a basket or tub situated in a shop in which products can be prominently placed and brought to consumers' attention

duodecimo /ˌdjuəʊˈdekɪməʊ/ *noun* a book size traditionally created by folding one sheet of standard-sized printing paper to make 12 leaves or 24 pages. Also called **twelvemo**

duopoly /djuːˈɒpəli/ *noun* a situation in which two organisations have control of their field, as opposed to a monopoly, in which only one has total control

duplicator /ˈdjuːplɪkeɪtə/ *noun* a machine or device that makes copies, especially a machine for copying printed matter

duration /djʊˈreɪʃ(ə)n/ *noun* **1.** the length of time of a broadcast item, to the nearest second **2.** the amount of time that an advertising poster is visible to the average passer-by

DV *abbreviation* **digital video**

DVC *abbreviation* **digital video camera**

DVC-Pro /ˌdiː viː siː ˈprəʊ/ a trade name for a type of videotape format

DVD /ˌdiː viː ˈdiː/ *noun* a CD on which can be stored large amounts of data, most usually a compressed .mpeg file of a feature film. They have largely replaced video cassettes as the most popular format for watching (although not recording) films at home, as they are less prone to distortion and damage. Full form **Digital Versatile Disc**

DVD-video /ˌdiː viː ˌdiː ˈvɪdiəʊ/ *noun* a standard that defines how full-length films can be compressed and stored on a DVD and played back on a dedicated player attached to a television set or viewed on a computer fitted with a DVD drive

DVE *abbreviation* **1.** digital video edit **2.** digital video effects

DVR *abbreviation* TV **digital video recorder**

dyad /ˈdaɪæd/ *noun* a unit of two people

dyeline /ˈdaɪlaɪn/ *noun* PRINTING same as **diazo**

dynamic microphone /daɪˌnæmɪk ˈmaɪkrəfəʊn/ *noun* a microphone that uses electromagnetic principles to convert audio signals to an electrical current without using external power

dysequilibrium /ˌdɪsekwɪˈlɪbriəm/ *noun* the appearance of tensions within a narrative. The end is usually reached by resolving these tensions and achieving equilibrium once more. Compare **equilibrium**

dystopia /dɪsˈtəʊpiə/ *noun* a representation of a society in which everything is flawed and much has gone wrong, especially when intended as a condemnation of modern society's values. Examples of dystopian works are 1984 (George Orwell, 1949) and Brave New World (Aldous Huxley, 1932). Compare **utopia**

E

Ealing comedy /ˌiːlɪŋ ˈkɒmədi/ *noun* one of the characteristically British comedy films that were made at Ealing Studios between 1945 and 1955

Ealing Studios /ˌiːlɪŋ ˈstjuːdiəʊz/ *noun* the film studios in Ealing, West London, where the 'Ealing comedies' were made

ear /ɪə/ *noun* a box in the top corner of the front page of a newspaper, used for advertising or a weather forecast

earned rate /ˌɜːnd ˈreɪt/ *noun* **1.** the actual rate for a printed advertising space after taking discounts into account **2.** a discounted rate for advertising space earned by repeated or loyal custom by an advertiser

earpiece /ˈɪəpiːs/ *noun* the part of a listening device such as headphones that is placed on the ear and converts signals into sound

earth /ɜːθ/ *verb* to equip an electrical circuit or appliance with a connection to the ground so that current is carried safely away in the event of a fault

earth hum /ˈɜːθ hʌm/ *noun* audio or visual interference caused by the equipment being inefficiently earthed

easy listening /ˌiːzi ˈlɪs(ə)nɪŋ/ *noun* a style of popular music that usually incorporates simple melodies, sometimes with lyrics, simple harmonies nearly always orchestrated, and gentle rhythms, often suitable for dancing to

e-blocker /ˈiː ˌblɒkə/ *noun* an employer who uses special software to prevent employees from visiting particular websites while at work

e-book /ˈiː bʊk/ *noun* a hand-held reading device for displaying electronic text such as a complete book, on a high-resolution screen. E-books can be updated either from a book shop or a website that sells digital texts.

e-business /ˈiː ˌbɪznɪs/ *noun* **1.** a company that operates through the Internet **2.** the practice of conducting business using Internet technology

ECCA *abbreviation* European Cable Communications Association

echelon /ˈeʃəlɒn/ *noun* a global computer surveillance system used by UK and US security services, which intercepts and analyses communications

echo plate /ˈekəʊ pleɪt/ *noun* an electromechanical device used in broadcasting or recording to create reverberation or echo effects

ecology /ɪˈkɒlədʒi/ *noun* in sociology, the study of the relationships between living organisms and their environments, especially in political arguments against capitalism and industrialisation

e-commerce /ˌiː ˈkɒmɜːs/ *noun* transactions that are carried out over the Internet, either between consumers and businesses or between businesses themselves

economic determinism /ˌiːkənɒmɪk dɪˈtɜːmɪnɪz(ə)m/ *noun* the theory that economic inequalities can explain most social and cultural phenomena

economies of scale /ɪˌkɒnəmiz əv ˈskeɪl/ *plural noun* the savings that can be made per unit by producing larger quantities of a product, for example by reducing wastage

e-consulting /ˈiː kən,sʌltɪŋ/ *noun* the business of providing services such as webpage design and marketing advice to companies doing business on the Internet

écriture /'ektrɪtjʊə/ *noun* in the theories of structuralism and discourse, 'writing' as a critical concept

écriture feminine /ˌektrɪtjʊə ˌfemɪ'næn/ *noun* writing seen as a feminist concept, in which the author uses female constructions of identity to analyse and challenge symbolic representation

ECS *abbreviation* TELECOMS **European Communications Satellite**

e-democracy /'iː dɪˌmɒkrəsi/, **eDemocracy** *noun* the use of Internet technology to freely distribute information on politics and hold discussions, think tanks, polls, mock elections etc

edge numbers /'edʒ ˌnʌmbəz/ *plural noun* the numbers that appear beside each frame on a piece of film, helping to identify shots

edit /'edɪt/ *verb* **1.** to alter text to make it clearer or more concise, or simply to make it shorter **2.** to be in overall charge of the publication of a newspaper, magazine or broadcast **3.** to trim an audio recording down to make it ready for transmission, for example to make it more concise or flow better

edit caravelle /'edɪt ˌkærəvel/ *noun* a van on an outside broadcast containing an entire editing suite for on-the-spot editing

editing decision list /ˌedɪtɪŋ dɪ'sɪʒ(ə)n ˌlɪst/ *noun* **1.** a list of all the shots, audio pieces etc. available to edit together for a filmed sequence **2.** a list of instructions to a computer, telling it which frames (by edge number) should begin and end a particular shot, so that it can automatically create an edited sequence ▶ *abbreviation* **EDL**

edition /ɪ'dɪʃ(ə)n/ *noun* **1.** all the copies of a publication such as a newspaper or book that were printed at the same time **2.** one version of a publication that may be reissued at other times or in other formats **3.** a particular version or instalment of a regular broadcast

editio princeps /ɪˌdɪtiəʊ 'prɪnseps/ *noun* the first printed edition of a book

editor /'edɪtə/ *noun* **1.** the person in charge of the style, direction and editorial content of a newspaper, magazine or book **2.** somebody who edits written text, scripts, radio programmes, etc to make it clearer or more concise

editorial /ˌedɪ'tɔːriəl/ *noun* **1.** all copy in a newspaper or magazine with no advertising content **2.** a column in a newspaper giving opinion on news items covered elsewhere in that issue. Also called **leader**

editorialise /ˌedɪ'tɔːriəlaɪz/ *verb* **1.** to express an opinion or view in an editorial in a newspaper or magazine **2.** to introduce personal comments or opinions, especially in inappropriate contexts

'Cooper's interview with Patrick Bennett, a victim of the paedophile cleric Sean Fortune, was not just a powerfully moving piece of radio. It was exemplary in its approach to the subject: Cooper drew out Bennett's testimony with subtlety and gentleness, without trying to editorialise.' [Gerry McCarthy, *The Sunday Times*]

editor in chief /ˌedɪtə ɪn 'tʃiːf/ *noun* the controlling editor of a publication or publishing house

edit out /ˌedɪt 'aʊt/ *verb* to delete unwanted parts from a text, film or recording

e-division /'iː dɪˌvɪʒ(ə)n/ *noun* a part of an organisation that deals with its Internet business

EDL *abbreviation* **editing decision list**

EDTV /ˌiː diː tiː 'viː/ *noun* an enhancement to the NTSC standard for television transmission that offers higher definition and a wider aspect ratio. EDTV normally has an aspect ratio of 4:3, if the broadcaster provides a greater aspect ratio than this, the standard is EDTV-wide. Full form **extended-definition television**

educational advertising /ˌedjʊ 'keɪʃ(ə)nəl ˌædvətaɪzɪŋ/ *noun* advertising that informs consumers about a product, particularly important when the product has only recently been introduced

edutainment /ˌedjʊ'teɪnmənt/ *noun* any media which both educates and entertains, such as an interactive CD-ROM

effective frequency /ɪˌfektɪv 'friːkwənsi/ *noun* the exposure to an advertisement thought to be 'optimum', i.e. enough to make the consumer aware of your product without being tiresome or wasting money

effective reach /ɪˌfektɪv 'riːtʃ/ *noun* the percentage of an audience which has had effective exposure to an advertisement

'John Sintras, chief executive of Starcom and head of the Media

Federation of Australia, said the campaign and "the staggering" number of ads had been a significant talking point in the industry. "There is a fine line between effective reach and overkill and they have crossed it".' [Simon Canning, *The Australian*]

effective sample size /ɪˌfektɪv 'saːmpəl ˌsaɪz/ *noun* the size of a survey sample after weighting

effects /ɪ'fekts/ *plural noun* ♦ **visual effects, special effects**

effects co-ordinator /ɪ'fekts kəʊ ˌɔːdɪneɪtə/ *noun* the member of a film or television production team who is responsible for planning and directing special effects

effects model /ɪ'fekts ˌmɒd(ə)l/ *noun* a model of communications that attempts to explain the effect that a media product has on its audience

EFJ *abbreviation* **European Federation of Journalists**

e-fraud /'iː frɔːd/ *noun* criminal deception for financial gain, that takes place over the Internet

18 /ˌeɪ'tiːn/ *noun* in the United Kingdom, a rating given by the British Board of Film Classification to films and videos that are considered unsuitable for people under the age of 18

eighteenmo /ˌeɪtiːn'məʊ/ *noun* PRINTING same as **octodecimo**

eightvo /'eɪtvəʊ/ *noun* PRINTING same as **octavo**

EJC *abbreviation* **European Journalism Centre**

elaborated code /ɪˌlæbəreɪtɪd 'kəʊd/ *noun* speech patterns that are thought to be more common among middle-class, educated people, using a large vocabulary, full grammatical structures, without the assumption of mutual understanding based on shared information or background. Compare **restricted code**

elasticity /ˌɪlæ'stɪsɪti/ *noun* the sensitivity of an economic variable, for example demand, in response to changes in other variables, for example price or income

e-learning /'iː ˌlɜːnɪŋ/ *noun* education that is based on electronic technologies such as computer networks and Internet-based courseware

electrician /ɪˌlek'trɪʃ(ə)n/ *noun* the member of a film or television production team who is responsible for operating and maintaining electrical equipment

electro /ɪ'lektrəʊ/ *noun* **1.** MUSIC same as **electronic music 2.** a style of electronic dance music that became popular in the 1980s, making use of drumming machines, synthesisers and many other artificial sounds

electro-funk /ɪ'lektrəʊ fʌŋk/ *noun* same as **electronic music**

electrograph /ɪ'lektrəgrɑːf/ *noun* **1.** a picture transmitted by an electrograph **2.** an machine that transmits pictures by electrical means, for example by fax

electron beam /ɪ'lektrɒn biːm/ *noun* part of a television's internal display mechanism, which fires charged particles over a light-responsive screen to create a picture

electronic /ˌelek'trɒnɪk/ *adjective* relating to, using, or accessed through a computer or computer network, for example the Internet

electronica /ɪˌlek'trɒnɪkə/ *noun* popular dance music that includes a range of styles, all characterised by electronic production

electronic bookmark /ˌelektrɒnɪk 'bʊkmɑːk/ *noun* a function on an Internet browser that allows you to return to a particular webpage easily

electronic church /ˌelektrɒnɪk 'tʃɜːtʃ/ *noun* US the use of electronic media such as radio, television and the Internet, to broadcast religious subject matter and involve people in religious activities

electronic flash /ˌelektrɒnɪk 'flæʃ/ *noun* a device used in still photography to produce a very bright flash of light, caused by passing an electric charge through a gas-filled tube

electronic journalism /ˌelektrɒnɪk 'dʒɜːn(ə)lɪz(ə)m/ *noun* the practice of transmitting news coverage electronically, for example by television or over the Internet

electronic magazine /ˌelektrɒnɪk 'mægəziːn/ *noun* a magazine that readers access online using a computer network

electronic media /ˌelektrɒnɪk 'miːdiə/ *plural noun* electronic-based media, for example television and radio

electronic music /ˌelektrɒnɪk ˈmjuːzɪk/ *noun* music that is created by being processed through electronic machines, either directly or including previously-recorded material, especially with the aid of a computer. Also called **electro**

electronic news gathering /ˌelektrɒnɪk ˈnjuːz ˌgæðərɪŋ/ *noun* the practice of using small video cameras and minimal crew to record footage for the news. Abbreviation **ENG**

"'The speed of electronic news-gathering has turned newspapers into magazines", says Peter Ibbotson, former editor of Panorama and now a media consultant. "Being unable to compete on news, they put their resources into features".'
[Bob Woffinden, *The Guardian*]

Electronic News Production System /ˌelektrɒnɪk njuːz prə ˈdʌkʃ(ə)n ˌsɪstəm/ *noun* a desktop computer program that allows newsroom production on a personal computer. Abbreviation **ENPS**

Electronic News Provision Service /ˌelektrɒnɪk njuːz prəˈvɪʒ(ə)n ˌsɜːvɪs/ *noun* the electronic system used by the BBC to organise their audio and text items. Abbreviation **ENPS**

electronic payment system /ˌelektrɒnɪk ˈpeɪmənt ˌsɪstəm/ *noun* a means of making payments over an electronic network such as the Internet

Electronic Programme Guide /ˌelektrɒnɪk ˈprəʊgræm ˌgaɪd/ *noun* an on-screen guide with cable and satellite systems that identifies and gives information about programmes and channels. Abbreviation **EPG**

electronic publishing /ˌelektrɒnɪk ˈpʌblɪʃɪŋ/ *noun* the production of material in forms such as CD-ROMs that can be accessed by readers using computers

electronic shopping /ˌelektrɒnɪk ˈʃɒpɪŋ/ *noun* the practice of buying goods and services over a computer network, especially the Internet

electronic smog /ˌelektrɒnɪk ˈsmɒg/ *noun* the electromagnetic fields produced in the atmosphere by the overflow of non-ionising radiation from radar, radio and television broadcasting and electrical appliances such as microwave ovens and mobile phones, considered by some people to pose a general health risk

electronic town hall /ˌelektrɒnɪk taʊn ˈhɔːl/ *noun* the use of electronic communication such as television and the Internet, between members of the public and public institutions for the purposes of feedback, comments, suggestions and discussion

electrophotography /ɪˌlektrəʊfəˈtɒgrəfi/ *noun* any form of photography such as laser printing and photocopying, that uses electricity rather than chemicals to transfer an image onto paper

electrostatic printing /ɪˌlektrəʊstætɪk ˈprɪntɪŋ/ *noun* the process of photocopying or printing images on a surface using electrostatic charges

electrotactile illusion /ɪˌlektrəʊtæktaɪl ɪˈluːʒ(ə)n/ *noun* the use of virtual reality technology to recreate 'touch' sensations such as texture, temperature etc.

electrotype /ɪˈlektrəʊtaɪp/ *noun* **1.** a copy of a block of type or engraving made by depositing copper on a wax, lead or plastic mould of the original by electrolysis **2.** an item printed from an electrotype ■ *verb* to print something using an electrotype

elephant folio /ˈelɪfənt ˌfəʊliəʊ/ *noun* a book size from 61 to 63.5 cm/24 to 25 in in height

elephant trunking /ˈelɪfənt ˌtrʌŋkɪŋ/ *noun* a raised platform, with sloped edges and grooves in it to carry cables so that vehicles can drive safely over

eligibility criteria /ˌelɪdʒɪˈbɪlɪti kraɪ ˌtɪəriə/ *noun* requirements for a person to be able to take part in a survey, such as being in the right age range

elite /eɪˈliːt/ *adjective* the small subsection of people within a society who conform to its most serious and important values – for example intellectual, moral, financial, artistic, etc.

ellipsis /ɪˈlɪps/, **ellipse** *noun* a printed mark, either three dots (…) or asterisks (***), indicating that something has been omitted from a text

Ellul's theory of technique /ˈeləl/ *noun* the idea that technological advances contribute to a world which is increasingly ruled by efficiency and conformity, and are beyond the control of governments which must conform to them

em /em/ *noun* **1.** a unit for measuring print size, equal to the height of the typeface being used **2.** PRINTING same as **pica**

e-mail /'i: meɪl/, **email** /'i:meɪl/ *noun* **1.** a system that allows the electronic transmission of text-based messages, for example between computers or mobile phones **2.** a message sent by e-mail ∎ *verb* to send somebody an e-mail

e-mail address /'i: meɪl ə,dres/ *noun* a string of characters that identifies where an e-mail should be delivered or where it has originated

e-mail campaign /'i: meɪl kæm,peɪn/ *noun* a series of e-mails which deliver marketing messages to individuals

embargo /ɪm'bɑːgəʊ/ *noun* a request not to release material until a particular time or date

'International critics were fuming last week over their treatment at the hands of The War of the Worlds people. Germany's official critics' body urged its members to boycott the film entirely after it was asked to sign embargos promising not to publish any reviews before its global release date of 29 June.' [Jason Solomons, *The Observer*]

embed /ɪm'bed/ *noun* a war reporter who officially accompanies an active military unit and is able to report any information that does not endanger national security ∎ *verb* to officially assign a reporter to accompany a military unit during a war

embedded audio /ɪm,bedɪd 'ɔ:diəʊ/ *noun* audio which is included as part of the digital video signal

embedded journalist /ɪm,bedɪd 'dʒɜːn(ə)lɪst/ *noun* same as **embed**

em dash /'em dæʃ/ *noun* PRINTING a printed dash that measures one em long. Abbreviation **m**, **M**

emergent culture /ɪ,mɜːdʒənt 'kʌltʃə/ *noun* the idea that radical cultural forms will always emerge from the general population to challenge the established 'order of things'

Emmy /'emi/ a trade name for an award in the form of a small statue, that is given annually by the American Academy of Television Arts and Sciences for outstanding television programming, production or performance

emo /ɪ məʊ/ *noun* a type of punk rock music that began in the mid-1980s in Washington, D.C., is noted for its thoughtful lyrics and the tendency of its performers to become emotionally affected by them on stage

emotional appeal /ɪ,məʊʃ(ə)n(ə)l ə 'pi:l/ *noun* an attempt by advertising to persuade through an emotional rather than a rational message

emotive /ɪ'məʊtɪv/ *adjective* **1.** causing or intended to cause emotion **2.** of a message or piece of communication, having the function of revealing the speaker's feelings covertly. ◊ **conative**, **metalingual**, **phatic**, **poetic**

emotive language /ɪ,məʊtɪv 'læŋgwɪdʒ/ *noun* words that carry certain connotations, designed to make the reader reach a particular conclusion or feel a particular emotion

empathy /'empəθi/ *noun* the ability to identify with and understand another person's feelings or difficulties

'...Sigal's unhistrionic prose makes the chaos and sadness in his novel seem manageable, and he renders the schizophrenic characters that people it with a rare empathy and dignity.' [Laurance Phelan, *The Independent on Sunday*]

empirical /ɪm'pɪrɪk(ə)l/ *adjective* referring to research that is based on direct observation and experience, rather than on theory

empirical data /ɪm,pɪrɪk(ə)l 'deɪtə/ *noun* data or information that comes from actual observation or that can be proved

empowerment /ɪm'paʊəmənt/ *noun* the process or policy of giving people the ability to make their own choices and control their own lives

emulsion /ɪ'mʌlʃən/ *noun* the chemical coating on film that is light-sensitive and records the image, available in different speeds and altitudes

en /en/ *noun* a unit for measuring print width, being half that of an em. Also called **nut**

encode /ɪn'kəʊd/ *verb* to transmit a message in such a form that the recipient can decode it easily and fully

encoder /ɪn'kəʊdə/ *noun* same as **sender**

encompassing situation /ɪn
ˌkʌmpəsɪŋ ˌsɪtjuˈeɪʃ(ə)n/ *noun* the
social context in which an action or piece
of communication takes place

encrypt /ɪnˈkrɪpt/ *verb* to encode or
scramble a signal such as for pay-per-
view television, so that only those with the
correct decoder can receive them

encrypted service /ɪnˌkrɪptɪd
ˈsɜːvɪs/ *noun* same as **pay-per-view**

encryption technology /ɪnˈkrɪpʃən
tekˌnɒlədʒi/ *noun* software etc. that
encrypts information so that it cannot be
accessed easily

enculturation /ɪnˌkʌltʃəˈreɪʃ(ə)n/
noun the process by which a person is
exposed to and acquires cultural values,
ideas, beliefs etc.

en dash /ˈem dæʃ/ *noun* PRINTING a
printed dash that is one en in length.
Abbreviation **n**, **N**

end board /ˈend bɔːd/ *noun* a clapper
board that is used at the end of a film
shoot, rather than at the beginning, and is
always shown upside down

endnote /ˈendnəʊt/ *noun* a comment or
reference that appears at the very end of a
chapter, book or essay, rather than at the
bottom of a page

endorse /ɪnˈdɔːs/ *verb* to publicly
approve of a product for advertising
purposes

endorsement /ɪnˈdɔːsmənt/ *noun* the
act of giving or instance of having given
public support for a product for advertising purposes

ENG *abbreviation* electronic news
gathering

engr. *abbreviation* PRINTING **1.**
engraving **2.** engrave

engrave /ɪnˈgreɪv/ *verb* **1.** to cut a
design into a hard surface for decoration
or printing **2.** to carve or etch a design or
lettering into a hard surface for decoration
or printing **3.** to print a design or image
from an engraved printing plate

engraving /ɪnˈgreɪvɪŋ/ *noun* **1.** the art
or process of carving images or lettering
into a hard surface **2.** a design engraved
for decoration or printing **3.** an image that
was printed from an engraved block **4.** a
plate or block on which an image has been
engraved for printing

enigma code /ɪˈnɪgmə kəʊd/ *noun*
one of five codes used in the analysis and

deconstruction of texts, describing secrets
and how they are alluded to and disclosed
in a narrative. ◊ **action code**, **referential
code**, **semantic code**, **symbolic code**

enlarge /ɪnˈlɑːdʒ/ *verb* to make a copy
of a photographic print or image that is
larger than the original

enlargement /ɪnˈlɑːdʒmənt/ *noun* a
copy of a photographic print or image that
is larger than the original from which it
was made

enlightenment /ɪnˈlaɪt(ə)nmənt/
noun an 18th-century movement in
philosophy which stressed the power and
beauty of reason

ennage /ˈenɪdʒ/ *noun* a calculation of
the number of ens contained in a piece of
text for typesetting

énoncé /eɪˈnɒnseɪ/ *noun* in cultural
theory, the content of that which is said, a
statement or proposition. Compare **énonciation**

énonciation /eɪˌnɒnsiˈeɪʃ(ə)n/ *noun*
in cultural theory, the form of that which
is said, an utterance. Compare **énoncé**

enprint /enˈprɪnt/ *noun* a photographic
print in standard size, usually 15 cm x 10
cm/6 in x 4 in, enlarged from a negative

ENPS *abbreviation* **1.** Electronic News
Production System **2.** Electronic
News Provision Service

enterprise fiction /ˈentəpraɪz
ˌfɪkʃən/ *noun* fiction written by women,
on the theme of triumphing in a male-
dominated society through hard work and
determination

enthusiast /ɪnˈθjuːziæst/ *noun* in
advertising audience classifications, a
person who is interested in advertisements
and watches them keenly. ◊ **acquiescent**,
ambivalent, **cynic**

entropy /ˈentrəpi/ *noun* the proportion
of words in a piece of communication
which are meaningful. Compare **redundancy**

envelope stuffer /ˈenvələʊp ˌstʌfə/
noun advertising material that is mailed in
an envelope

environment /ɪnˈvaɪrənmənt/ *noun* a
framework within which a computer,
program, or user operates

EPG *abbreviation* Electronic
Programme Guide

epic /ˈepɪk/ *noun* **1.** a work of literature,
cinema, television, or theatre that is large-

scale and expensively produced and often deals with a historical theme **2.** a lengthy narrative poem in elevated language celebrating the adventures and achievements of a legendary or traditional hero, for example Homer's *Odyssey* ■ *adjective* impressive by virtue of greatness of size, scope or heroism

epilogue /'epɪlɒg/ *noun* **1.** a short chapter or section at the end of a literary work, sometimes detailing the fate of its characters **2.** a short programme broadcast at the end of the day, often having religious content

episode /'epɪsəʊd/ *noun* one of the separate instalments of a serialised story or programme

épistème /ˌepɪˈstem/ *noun* in the theories of structuralism and discourse, the ways of thinking, knowing and analysing that are characteristic of an intellectual era

.eps *noun* a computer image format that allows the image to be placed in a text document. Full form **Encapsulated PostScript**

equal time /'iːkwəl taɪm/ *noun* a broadcasting policy in the US that allows exactly the same amount of radio and television air time to opposing political candidates

equilibrium /ˌiːkwɪˈlɪbriəm/ *noun* **1.** a state or situation in which opposing forces or factors balance each other out and stability is attained **2.** within a narrative, the absence of tensions in need of resolution. Compare **dysequilibrium**

errata /eˈrɑːtəm/ *plural noun* a list of errors that were noticed after a book was printed and inserted in the book as a separate sheet

escapism /ɪˈskeɪpɪz(ə)m/ *noun* the act of 'escaping' from reality, daily routine, drudgery etc. by using fantasy, daydreams or other absorbing entertainment

escapist /ɪˈskeɪpɪst/ *adjective* referring to a novel or film that is purely entertaining, allowing the viewer a 'break from reality'

essentialism /ɪˈsenʃ(ə)lɪz(ə)m/ *noun* in feminist theory, the idea that every object or text possesses an underlying 'essence' which defines it and all others of its genre

establishing shot /ɪˈstæblɪʃɪŋ ʃɒt/ *noun* an extended panning shot at the beginning of a filmed scene to set the mood, establish location, characters present etc.

establishment survey /ɪˈstæblɪʃmənt ˌsɜːveɪ/ *noun* a quarterly survey to try to determine the television-owning population of the UK

estrangement /ɪˈstreɪndʒmənt/ *noun* in aesthetic theory, the process of becoming detached or alienated, either from one's sense of self or from the world and situation in which you exist

e-system /'iː ˌsɪstəm/ *noun* multiple electronic communications or information systems or networks, viewed as one for operational purposes

etch /etʃ/ *verb* **1.** to create a design or drawing on the surface of something, especially a printing plate, by the action of an acid **2.** to cut a design or mark into the surface of something using a sharp point or laser beam

etching /'etʃɪŋ/ *noun* **1.** a print made from an etched plate **2.** the art or process of creating etched designs or making prints from etched surfaces **3.** a printing plate with an etched design

ethics /'eθɪks/ *noun* **1.** the study of the notion of right and wrong, morally speaking, in thought, feelings, beliefs etc. **2.** the internal set of rules and guidelines which a person has regarding these notions of right and wrong

ethnicity /eθˈnɪsɪti/ *noun* **1.** the social and cultural characteristics of a person which form part of their definition of self, alongside considerations such as race, gender, political standpoint etc. **2.** ethnic affiliation or distinctiveness

"'A highly effective team is a rare thing", [chief Executive Andy] Green says. "It has to be diverse in all sorts of ways, in terms of gender, ethnicity, nationality even".' [Claire Dight, *The Times*]

ethnic media /ˌeθnɪk ˈmiːdiə/ *plural noun* magazines or TV stations that appeal to ethnic audiences

ethnocentric /ˌeθnəʊˈsentrɪk/ *adjective* **1.** referring to study that is based on ethnic considerations and differences **2.** having a tendency to view things through the filter of one's own ethnicity

ethnocentric stage /ˌeθnəʊsentrɪk ˈsteɪdʒ/ *noun* an early stage in a company's marketing when goods are sent overseas with no concessions to local needs or tastes

ethnography /eθ'nɒgrəfi/ *noun* the anthropological study of a particular society or section of society, using a long period of personal research of and exposure to the group

euphemism /'juːfəmɪz(ə)m/ *noun* a word or phrase used in place of a term that might be considered too direct, harsh, unpleasant or offensive

eurocentric /ˌjʊərəʊ'sentrɪk/ *adjective* focussed or based primarily on Europe, sometimes to the detriment of other nations and cultural groups

Euronet /'jʊərəʊnet/ *noun* a collection of computer companies aiming to create a Europe-wide database, keeping control of information in European hands

European Cable Communications Association /ˌjʊərəpiən ˈkeɪb(ə)l kəˌmjuːnɪ'keɪʃ(ə)nz əˌsəʊsieɪʃ(ə)n/ *noun* a trade association representing cable companies. Abbreviation **ECCA**

European Communications Satellite /ˌjʊərəpiən kəˌmjuːnɪ'keɪʃ(ə)nz ˌsætəlaɪt/ *noun* a telecommunications satellite that primarily serves Europe. Abbreviation **ECS**

European Federation of Journalists /ˌjʊərəpiːən ˌfedəreɪʃ(ə)n əv 'dʒɜːnəlɪsts/ *noun* the European arm of the International Federation of Journalists. Abbreviation **EFJ**

European Journalism Centre /ˌjʊərəpiːən 'dʒɜːnəlɪz(ə)m ˌsentə/ *noun* a not-for-profit training centre for established journalists, based in the Netherlands. Abbreviation **EJC**

Eurovision song contest /ˌjʊərəvɪʒ(ə)n 'sɒŋ ˌkɒntest/ *noun* an competition held annually and broadcast on television, in which singers from many European countries perform a specially composed song and judges from each participating nation vote for their favourite. The contest has been criticised for the blandness of the winning entries and the political nature of the voting.

Eutelsat /'juːtelsæt/ *noun* a major international satellite services provider for broadcasters

evaluation /ɪˌvælju'eɪʃ(ə)n/ *noun* an analysis of how well a media product has

met its original aims, often requested by those that have funded the product

event /ɪ'vent/ *noun* in news coverage, something that takes place which has news value

event television /ɪ'vent ˌtelɪvɪʒ(ə)n/ *noun* programming which reports live or as-live on a particular event, such as a sports match, concert, state funeral etc

everyday life /ˌevrideɪ 'laɪf/ *noun* the routine practices of daily existence, as followed by reality television shows

excess /ɪk'ses/ *noun* in feminist theory, the unrestricted, enjoyable expenditure of resources such as energy, money, time etc.

exclusive /ɪk'skluːsɪv/ *noun* a story which has only been covered in one newspaper in advance of its rivals

excorporation /eksˌkɔːpə'reɪʃ(ə)n/ *noun* the act of using objects from a society's dominant culture to express a person's affiliation with a subculture, for example safety pins as worn by punks

executive producer /ɪgˌzekjʊtɪv prə'djuːsə/ *noun* **1.** the member of a television production team who is responsible for finding money to finance a project, as well as being involved in creative and business matters **2.** the member of a film production team who is responsible for supervising other producers and sometimes for financing

existential /ˌegzɪ'stenʃ(ə)l/ *adjective* concerned with or relating to existence, especially human existence

exnomination /eksˌnɒmɪ'neɪʃ(ə)n/ *noun* the assumption that certain values are so widely held that they cannot be challenged and need not be expressed

exotica /ɪg'zɒtɪkə/ *noun* items, trends, ideas etc. from a different ethnic group

expanded /ɪk'spændɪd/ *adjective* referring to type or printed characters that are wider than usual in relation to their height. Also called **extended**

expansion card /ɪk'spænʃ(ə)n kɑːd/ *noun* a small device that can be inserted into a computer to improve its memory or other capabilities, such as a sound card

expectations /ˌekspek'teɪʃ(ə)nz/ *plural noun* ideas that a person has about what other people expect them to do, how to behave etc.

experiential advertising /ek ˌspɪərienʃəl 'ædvətaɪzɪŋ/ *noun* advertising which gives the customer the real sensation of using the product

experimental group /ɪkˌsperɪ'ment(ə)l ˌgruːp/ *noun* in research, the group which is being experimented upon, measured against the control group. Compare **control group**

experimental method /ɪkˌsperɪ'ment(ə)l ˌmeθəd/ *noun* the use of controlled experiments to discover the influence of variables in marketing such as types of promotion and sales training

expose /ɪk'spəʊz/ *verb* to allow light to contact photographic film, usually by opening a camera shutter

exposé /ek'spəʊzeɪ/ *noun* a report, usually in a newspaper, that reveals details of a scandal or crime ■ *verb* to publish or broadcast new information about a scandal or crime

exposure /ɪk'spəʊʒə/ *noun* the amount of light that a film is exposed to, controlled by the size of the lens aperture

exposure meter /ɪk'spəʊʒə ˌmiːtə/ *noun* an instrument that measures the strength of light for photography, so that the correct combination of shutter speed and lens aperture can be set. Also called **light meter**

expressionism /ɪk'spreʃənɪz(ə)m/ *noun* **1.** the technique of exaggerating elements such as lighting, sound etc. in order to show ideas and feelings **2.** an artistic movement that flourished in Germany between 1905 and 1925 whose adherents sought to represent feelings and moods rather than objective reality, often distorting colour and form **3.** a literary movement of the early 20th century, especially in the theatre, that represented external reality in a highly stylised and subjective manner, attempting to convey a psychological or spiritual reality rather than a record of actual events

extended /ɪk'stendɪd/ *adjective* PRINTING same as **expanded**

extended-definition television /ɪkˌstendɪd ˌdefɪnɪʃ(ə)n 'telɪvɪʒ(ə)n/ *noun* full form of **EDTV**

extended-play /ɪkˌstendɪd 'pleɪ/ *adjective* **1.** referring to the format of a vinyl record of the same size as a single but with two tracks on each side **2.** referring to a videotape format that can store four or six hours of material on a two-hour tape

extender /ɪk'stendə/ *noun* the part of a lower-case letter such as p or h that extends above or below the rounded body of the letter

extension lead /ɪk'stenʃən led/ *noun* a long cable has a plug at one end and a socket at the other so that it can be used to plug in a piece of electrical equipment a long way away from the socket

exterior /ɪk'stɪəriə/ *adjective* referring to an outdoor setting for a photograph or film scene

external analysis /ɪkˌstɜːn(ə)l ə'næləsɪs/ *noun* the analysis of an organisation's customers, market segments, competitors and marketing environment

external search /ɪkˌstɜːn(ə)l 'sɜːtʃ/ *noun* a method of finding information from external sources such as advertising, or from the World Wide Web using a search engine

external search engine /ɪkˌstɜːn(ə)l 'sɜːtʃ ˌendʒɪn/ *noun* a search engine that allows the user to search millions of Internet pages rapidly

extra /'ekstrə/ *noun* **1.** a special issue of a newspaper or magazine, often reporting more recent developments in the news or concentrating on a particular subject **2.** a person who is temporarily employed in a minor, usually non-speaking part in a film, for example in a crowd scene. Also called **supporting artist**

extremely high frequency /ɪk ˌstriːmli haɪ 'friːkwənsi/ *noun* a radio frequency in the range between 30,000 and 300,000 megahertz

extremely low frequency /ɪk ˌstriːmli ləʊ 'friːkwənsi/ *noun* a radio frequency below 30 hertz

eyeballs /'aɪbɔːlz/ *plural noun* users of the Internet who visit a particular website or use a particular product

eye candy /'aɪ ˌkændi/ *noun* ONLINE, COMPUTING decorative, but non-essential features on a webpage

'We want access to your corporate information, to your plans and strategies, your best thinking, your genuine knowledge. We won't settle for the four-color brochure, for websites stuffed with eye candy but lacking any

substance.'
[Stephen Pizzo, *Mortgage Technology*]

eye contact /'aɪ ˌkɒntækt/ *noun* a feature of interpersonal communication which is non-verbal, which helps to express meaning and attitude

eyeline /'aɪlaɪn/ *noun* the direction in which a performer is looking

eye-movement test /'aɪ ˌmuːvmənt ˌtest/, **eye tracking** /'aɪ ˌtrækɪŋ/ *noun* an advertising research test which involves recording the movement of a person's eyes as they look at an advertise-ment to see which parts are of special interest

eye-witness account /ˌaɪ ˌwɪtnəs ə'kaʊnt/ *noun* a story given about something that has happened by somebody who was there to observe it

eye-witness reporting /ˌaɪ ˌwɪtnəs rɪ'pɔːtɪŋ/ *noun* a story filed by a reporter who was actually present at an event, rather than gathering details from a desk

e-zine /'iː ziːn/ *noun* a magazine composed of webpages, available on the World Wide Web

F

fable /ˈfeɪb(ə)l/ *noun* **1.** a short story with a moral, especially one in which the characters are animals **2.** a story about supernatural, mythological, or legendary characters and events

fabliau /ˈfæbliəʊ/ *noun* a comic story in verse, usually bawdy and popular in 12th- and 13th-century France

fabula /ˈfæbjʊlə/ *noun* a Russian term meaning 'story' – the narrative

face /feɪs/ *noun* **1.** somebody who is well-known or important and who represents a company, brand or product in its advertising **2.** a typeface, or the printing surface of a type character

facial expression /ˈfeɪʃ(ə)l ɪk ˌspreʃ(ə)n/ *noun* the way in which the face can reveal emotions, attitudes etc., in addition to those expressed by what the person is saying

fact book /ˈfækt bʊk/ *noun* data put together about a product on the market that can be used for reference by the producers or by an advertising agency

fact file /fækt faɪl/ *noun* a list of short, snappy facts relating to a story, often boxed

fact-finding mission /ˈfækt faɪndɪŋ ˌmɪʃ(ə)n/ *noun* a visit by a person or group of people, usually to another country, to obtain information about a specific issue

fact sheet /ˈfækt ʃiːt/ *noun* an information sheet or booklet giving further details about a subject, especially one covered in a broadcast programme

fad /fæd/ *noun* something that is very popular but only for a short time, for example an image, joke or game on the Internet

fadeaway /ˈfeɪdəˌweɪ/ *noun* the process of gradually decreasing light or sound until it disappears completely

fade down /ˌfaɪd ˈdaʊn/ *verb* same as **fade out**

fade-down /ˈfaɪd daʊn/ *noun* same as **fade-out**

fade in /ˌfeɪd ˈɪn/ *verb* to increase the volume of a sound from nothing or allow an image to become visible, or gradually to become audible or visible. Also called **fade up**

fade-in /ˈfeɪd ɪn/ *noun* the process of gradually introducing light or sound until it is visible or audible. Also called **fade-up**

fade out /ˌfeɪd ˈaʊt/ *verb* to gradually disappear

fade-out /ˈfeɪd aʊt/ *noun* **1.** a gradual loss of reception of a television or radio broadcast signal **2.** a gradual decrease in brightness or sound until an image or sound completely disappears

fader /ˈfeɪdə/ *noun* a mechanism in a radio studio that controls the volume of an audio channel

fade up /ˌfeɪd ˈʌp/ *verb* BROADCAST, CINEMA, TV same as **fade in**

fade-up /ˈfeɪd ʌp/ *noun* BROADCAST, CINEMA, TV same as **fade-in**

fairness doctrine /ˈfeənəs ˌdɒktrɪn/ *noun* the principle in the US that broadcasters should allow equal air time to opposing points of view on controversial issues

false claim /ˌfɔːls ˈkleɪm/ *noun* an untrue or exaggerated claim made in the advertising of a product

'…have been barred from marketing "HGH Revolution" and "Natural Rejuvenator HGH-R" – which don't actually contain human growth hormone, or HGH. Among the other false claims, the FTC said, were that the products could... increase strength and energy, restore the size of "bodily organs that shrink with age" and improve memory.' [Rebecca Carroll, *Associated Press*]

fan /fæn/ *noun* a person who is passionately interested in and attached to a performer

fandom /ˈfændəm/ *noun* the state of being a fan of something or somebody

fan fiction /ˈfæn ˌfɪk(ə)n/, **fanfic** /ˈfænfɪk/ *noun* a piece of fiction written by the fan of a famous person, which uses the celebrity as a character in the story, often posted and shared on websites

fantasy /ˈfæntəsi/ *noun, adjective* a genre of film that creates an alternative, imaginative 'reality' that is escapist

fanzine /ˈfænziːn/ *noun* a magazine, usually produced by amateurs for other fans of a pastime or celebrity

FAQ /fæk, ˌef eɪ ˈkjuː/ *noun* a section on many websites which answers basic questions which visitors may have about the site, or the product or service offered on the site. Full form **frequently asked questions**

farce /fɑːs/ *noun* 1. a comic drama in which ordinary people are caught up in extraordinary, usually ludicrous events 2. farce as a genre

farceur /fɑːˈsɜː/ *noun* a comedian or writer of comedy

fare /feə/ *noun* the type of material usually found in a magazine, television show or other form of entertainment

fascicle /ˈfæskɪk(ə)l/ *noun* one part of a book that is published in instalments

fashion photography /ˈfæʃ(ə)n fə ˌtɒɡrəfi/ *noun* the art or practice of photographing models wearing new fashions or clothing accessories, especially for newspapers or fashion magazines

fashion plate /ˈfæʃ(ə)n pleɪt/ *noun* an picture showing a style of clothing, especially a new fashion

fashion shoot /ˈfæʃ(ə)n ʃuːt/ *noun* a session for photographing models wearing new fashions

fast /fɑːst/ *adjective* referring to photographic equipment that requires or permits a short exposure time

fast-forward *noun* 1. a function on a tape machine causes the tape to wind forwards quickly 2. a button or switch that controls the fast-forward function on an electronic recording device ■ *verb* to wind a tape forwards quickly on an tape machine

fast motion /ˌfɑːst ˈməʊʃ(ə)n/ *noun* action on film that appears faster than is naturally possible because it was shot at a slower rate than it is projected at. It is often used for comic effect.

fast stock /ˈfɑːst stɒk/ *noun* film that has high-speed emulsion on it which responds quickly to the light it is exposed to

fatalistic /ˌfeɪtəˈlɪstɪk/ *adjective* showing resignation in the face of events regarded as controlled by fate

fat face /ˈfæt feɪs/ *noun* PRINTING a typeface with wide main strokes and prominent serifs that produces a relatively heavy dark image when set as text

father of the chapel /ˌfɑːðə əv ðə ˈtʃæp(ə)l/ *noun* a shop steward representing members of a publishing or printing trade union. Abbreviation **FoC**

fat suit /ˈfæt suːt/ *noun* a costume designed to make an actor appear naturally overweight

fatwa /ˈfætwə/ *noun* a pronouncement according to Muslim religious law. The most famous fatwa was that issued in 1989 declaring that author Salman Rushdie should be killed for the blasphemous views expressed in his book *The Satanic Verses*.

fax /fæks/ *noun* a method of sending and receiving images in digital form over a telephone or radio link

FCC *abbreviation* **Federal Communications Commission**

fear appeal /ˈfɪə əˌpiːl/ *noun* an advertising message that makes the reader anxious about something, especially about not doing something

'...a long-term health fear appeal may have little or no effect on the attitudes and behaviour of adolescents towards smoking. Short-term cosmetic fear appeals, on the other hand, discuss negative social consequences of smoking, such as bad breath, smelly hair or yellow teeth. These risks are both immediate   and   important   to

adolescents.'
[*Journal of Consumer Behaviour*]

feathering /'feðərɪŋ/ *noun* **1.** the way that printing ink spreads in lines on paper that is too absorbent **2.** the process of putting extra leading between the lines of typeset text, in order to make the type area of the page longer

feature /'fiːtʃə/ *noun* **1.** an newspaper article that is longer and more descriptive than a news story, containing more background and colour **2.** an item for a radio or television programme, usually consisting of interviews, actuality and links edited together

feature creature /'fiːtʃə ˌkriːtʃə/ *noun* a designer who adds excessive unnecessary features to a design, especially a software program or website, often at the expense of coherence or utility

feature film /'fiːtʃə fɪlm/ *noun* a full-length film made for the cinema

feature-length /'fiːtʃə leŋθ/ *adjective* referring to a film that is full-length

feature programme /'fiːtʃə ˌprəʊɡræm/ *noun* a television or radio programme devoted to a special issue or topic

Federal Communications Commission /ˌfed(ə)rəl kəˌmjuːnɪ'keɪʃ(ə)nz kəˌmɪʃən/ *noun* a regulatory body in the US whose job is to monitor all non-government communications and broadcasts. Abbreviation **FCC**

Fédération Internationale des Editeurs de Journaux et Publications *abbreviation* FIEJ. ◊ **World Association of Newspapers**

feed /fiːd/ *noun* **1.** the signal a network sends to local radio or television stations for broadcast **2.** audio or video material which is sent from one place to another, such as instructions into a presenter's earpiece

feedback /'fiːdbæk/ *noun* **1.** response to a publication from readers or colleagues **2.** a high-pitched howling sound caused by the signal from a microphone being transmitted through speakers, which is then picked up by the microphone, for example when a radio listener phones in and has the radio playing in the background. Also called **howl**, **howlround**

feeder /'fiːdə/ *noun* a line connecting an aerial to a receiver or transmitter

feed point /'fiːd pɔɪnt/ *noun* permanent feed equipment in outside broadcast locations that are often used, such as the High Court

feint /feɪnt/ *adjective* referring to paper printed with faint horizontal lines across it as a guide for writing

Felliniesque /fəˌliːnɪ'esk/ *adjective* referring to or reminiscent of the blend of reality and fantasy that Federico Fellini creates in his films

female /'fiːmeɪl/ *adjective* **1.** relating or belonging to women or girls **2.** describes a component or part of a component such as an electric socket that has a recess designed to receive a corresponding projecting part

female suffrage /ˌfiːmeɪl 'sʌfrɪdʒ/ *noun* GENDER ISSUES same as **women's suffrage**

feminise /'femɪnaɪz/ *verb* **1.** to cause somebody to behave in ways conventionally associated with women **2.** to give somebody or something characteristics conventionally considered suitable for women

'Sarah Sands, the editor of The Sunday Telegraph launches her new magazine today. She is keen to emphasise the "incredibly pretty design" of the section, which is unarguably a central plank in her plan to feminise the newspaper.'
[Jane Thynne, *The Independent on Sunday*]

feminism /'femɪnɪz(ə)m/ *noun* a movement which advocates the same rights and opportunities for women as are enjoyed by men

feminist theory /ˌfemɪnɪst 'θɪəri/ *noun* the study of concepts and symbols in such fields as literature which create and perpetuate an image of women

fetish /'fetɪʃ/ *noun* an object, idea, or activity that somebody 'worships', is irrationally obsessed with or attached to and which may have sexual associations

fetishism /'fetɪʃɪz(ə)m/ *noun* in psychoanalysis, the desire to invest new, usually sexual meanings in objects not usually associated or so deeply associated with them

feuilleton /'fɜːɪətɒn/ *noun* **1.** a section of a European newspaper containing fiction, reviews and articles of general interest **2.** an article published in a feuilleton

fibre /'faɪbə/ *noun* a fibreoptic cable

fibreoptic cable /ˌfaɪbərɒptɪk 'keɪb(ə)l/ *noun* a glass or plastic tube the width of a hair, through which signals can be sent in the form of light pulses

fibreoptics /'faɪbər 'ɒptɪks/ *noun* the transmission of data using light pulses that are sent through hair-thin glass fibres. It is possible to send more data this way with less risk of corruption or interference.

ficlet /'fɪklət/ *noun* same as **drabble**

fiction /'fɪkʃən/ *noun* novels and stories that describe imaginary people and events

fiction values /'fɪkʃən ˌvæljuːz/ *plural noun* the criteria that an issue must supposedly fulfil to be 'fiction-worthy', such as being relevant to the reader and having aspirational value

FIEJ *abbreviation* **Fédération Internationale des Editeurs de Journaux et Publications**

field /fiːld/ *noun* in sociology, an area in which a person has multiple interpersonal relationships and experiences conflict and struggle

field of view /ˌfiːld əv 'vjuː/ *noun* the amount of a scene which can be captured by a lens, measured as an angle. For example, a fisheye lens may capture as much as 180° (but with distortion), whereas a telephoto lens may have a field of view of as little as 5°.

field research /'fiːld rɪˌsɜːtʃ/ *noun* the process of looking for information that is not yet published and must be obtained in surveys

15 /fɪf'tiːn/ *noun* in the United Kingdom, a rating given by the British Board of Film Classification to films and videos that are considered unsuitable for people under the age of 15

figure /'fɪgə/ *noun* an illustration or diagram in a book or article

file /faɪl/ *verb* to send in a story to a newspaper's offices from abroad

file header /'faɪl ˌhedə/ *noun* the part of a file description that describes what format it is in

filler /'fɪlə/ *noun* same as **brief**

fillet /'fɪlɪt/ *noun* a thin line impressed around the edge of the cover of a book, or the wheel-like tool used to make it

fill light /'fɪl laɪt/ *noun* a light source used when filming, which eliminates shadows caused by the key light

film /fɪlm/ *noun* **1.** a series images recorded by a camera and projected onto a screen as a sequence of moving pictures, usually with an accompanying soundtrack **2.** films collectively, considered as an art form **3.** a thin strip of cellulose coated with a light-sensitive emulsion, fed through a camera to take still or moving pictures ■ *verb* **1.** to record images on film **2.** to record a story or event on film **3.** to make or be involved in making a film **4.** to be a suitable subject for being filmed

filmgoer /'fɪlmɡəʊə/ *noun* a person who goes to the cinema to see films, especially regularly

filmi /'fɪlmi/ *noun* a famous actor in the Indian film industry ■ *adjective* relating to the Indian film industry

filming stage /'fɪlmɪŋ steɪdʒ/ *noun* the period during a film's production during which all material is filmed

filmless camera /ˌfɪlmləs 'kæm(ə)rə/ *noun* same as **digital camera**

filmmaker /'fɪlmˌmeɪkə/ *noun* a producer or director of films for the cinema. Also called **moviemaker**

film noir /ˌfɪlm 'nwɑː/ *noun* dark crime thrillers as a genre, highly stylised and characterised by fatalistic, existential themes

'Double Indemnity… The textbook film noir, with a classic 'let's kill my husband and get the insurance' plot. It's beautifully designed and delectably moody, and despite the rapid-fire dialogue, the leads manage to play it totally cool.' [*The Guardian*]

filmography /fɪlm'ɒgrəfi/ *noun* **1.** writing about films and the cinema **2.** a complete list of the films made by a particular actor or director or on a particular subject

filmsetting /'fɪlmˌsetɪŋ/ *noun* a typesetting process in which the text to be printed is projected onto photographic film and then printing plates are made from the film

film star /'fɪlm stɑː/ *noun* a famous film actor or actress

filter /'fɪltə/ *noun* a cover which is put over a light or camera lens to give a particular effect, for example a colour cast

filter wipe /'fɪltə waɪp/ *noun* a soft cleaning cloth that can be used on camera lenses and lens filters

final cut /,faɪn(ə)l 'kʌt/ *noun* the final edited version of a film, which is released for viewing by the public

financial advertising /faɪ,nænʃ(ə)l 'ædvətaɪzɪŋ/ *noun* advertising by companies in the field of financial investment

financial audit /faɪ,nænʃ(ə)l 'ɔːdɪt/ *noun* an examination of the books and accounts of an advertising agency

Financial Times /faɪ,nænʃ(ə)l 'taɪmz/ *noun* a global business news organisation that publishes a daily newspaper in 23 cities internationally and also has a news website. Abbreviation **FT**

fine cut /'faɪn kʌt/ *noun* the final version of a programme, with no edits left to be made

finial /'faɪnɪəl/ *noun* a curve that ends a main stroke in some italic typefaces

fireman /'faɪəmən/ *noun* a journalist sent out from the office to cover a major story

fireside chat /,faɪəsaɪd 'tʃæt/ *noun* a broadcast in which the president of the United States talks in an informal manner to the people of the nation. During the Great Depression Franklin D. Roosevelt gave fireside chats over the radio as a way of raising national morale and explaining his policies.

first /fɜːst/ *abbreviation* first assistant director

first assistant director /,fɜːst ə ,sɪst(ə)nt daɪ'rektə/ *noun* the person in a television production team who is responsible for making sure that each person is in the right place at the right time, and that shooting stays on schedule. Also called **first**

first edition /,fɜːst ɪ'dɪʃ(ə)n/ *noun* **1.** the first printed copy or batch of a daily newspaper **2.** the first batch of copies of a book issued by the original publisher

firsthand information /,fɜːsthænd ,ɪnfə'meɪʃ(ə)n/ *noun* information from an original source

first impressions /,fɜːst ɪm'preʃ(ə)nz/ *noun* the initial information received about and impressions formed of an individual, which can be difficult to forget, even when they are contradicted later

'From first impressions, Davydenko appears to be gawky and slightly lightweight. But he is an awkward opponent who hits the ball much harder than should be possible from his skinny frame, and he has electric speed around the court.' [Mark Hodgekinson, *The Daily Telegraph*]

fisher boom /'fɪʃə buːm/ *noun* a type of boom microphone used in television studios

fisheye lens /,fɪʃaɪ 'lenz/ *noun* a wide-angle lens with a field of view of up to 180°, but producing extreme distortion at the edges of the image

fishpole boom /'fɪʃpəʊl buːm/ *noun* a boom which is small and light enough to be moved and adjusted by one person (the boom swinger)

fist /fɪst/ *noun* PRINTING same as **index**

fit /fɪt/ *noun* the situation when an article or headline is the right size for the space allotted to it. Compare **bust**

fix /fɪks/ *verb* to make an image such as a photograph, permanent, by treating it with chemicals

fixed break /,fɪkst 'breɪk/ *noun* the practice of placing a television or radio advertisement in a specific commercial break on a specific day, at the advertiser's insistence

fixed point /,fɪkst 'pɔɪnt/ *noun* a non-movable camera

fixed spot /,fɪkst 'spɒt/ *noun* an item that is regularly broadcast in a programme at a particular time, for example news on the hour

fixer /'fɪksə/ *noun* a chemical that is used to treat a photographic image on film or paper in order to make it permanent

flack /'flæk/ *noun* a publicity agent ■ *verb* to act as a publicity agent for somebody

flag /flæg/ *noun* **1.** a piece of flat wood, cardboard or other material used to shield the camera lens from unwanted light sources **2.** PRESS same as **masthead**

flak /flæk/ *noun* criticism of something broadcast, received as a 'storm' of complaints, letters, phone calls etc.

flâneur /flæ'nɜː/ *noun* in sociology, an aimless wanderer, a man-about-town, used as an allegory for the writer or poet who can 'stroll along' in a society observing it while pursuing their own agenda

flare /fleə/ *noun* the undesirable effect of light reflecting off a camera lens, or being reflected off a shiny surface into the camera lens

flash /flæʃ/ *noun* **1.** a device used in photography to produce a short bright flash of light **2.** the brief moment when a subject is brightly lit for photographic to be taken **3.** an important news story that is broadcast immediately. Also called **news flash** ■ *verb* to broadcast a newsflash, often interrupting a scheduled programme

flash back /ˈflæʃ bæk/ *verb* to go back to an earlier time in a narrative, to fill in information or explain something that is happening in the present

flashback /ˈflæʃbæk/ *noun* a narrative device showing an event that happened earlier that has a bearing on the plot

flashbulb /ˈflæʃbʌlb/ *noun* a small glass bulb that can produce a very bright flash of light for taking photographs. Also called **photoflash**

flash forward /ˌflæʃ ˈfɔːwəd/ *verb* to jump forward to a later point of time in a narrative, usually for dramatic effect or irony ■ *noun* a scene or event from the future that appears in a narrative out of chronological order

flashgun /ˈflæʃgʌn/ *noun* a camera attachment with a flashtube or flashbulb in it that produces a bright flash of light as the camera's shutter opens

flashlight /ˈflæʃlaɪt/ *noun* a brief intense flash of light produced by a flashtube or flashbulb

flash-mobbing /ˈflæʃ ˌmɒbɪŋ/ *noun* the practice of people being alerted by e-mail to appear together in a predetermined public place and perform harmless attention-seeking activities before quickly dispersing

'Details of the venues are kept secret until the last minute and are revealed only to those who register at the Flash Fusion Concerts website. It turns out that the concerts are being staged by Ford Motor with Sony Pictures Digital to promote the launch of the new Ford Fusion car… Trust big business to turn flash mobbing to its advantage.' [Richard Tomkins, *The Financial Times*]

flash photography /ˌflæʃ fəˈtɒgrəfi/ *noun* photography that makes use of a brief flash of artificial light on its subject

flash prank /ˈflæʃ præŋk/ *noun* a website designed to shock the viewer by presenting a normal picture, game or video that then pops up with a sudden scary image and often a loud noise. Also called **screamer**

flashtube /ˈflæʃtjuːb/ *noun* a glass or quartz tube filled with gas that emits a short burst of light when electric current is passed through it for flash photography

flash unit /ˈflæʃ ˌjuːnɪt/ *noun* **1.** a flashtube and its power supply **2.** a flashgun, or a flashgun and a reflector in one unit

flat /flæt/ *noun* a wooden screen used as part of a stage set, painted to look like a door or a wall etc.

flatbed /ˈflætˌbed/ *adjective* refers to any piece of equipment such as a scanner or editing table which has a large flat surface to hold paper, film etc

flatbed press /ˈflætbed pres/ *noun* a printing press in which the type lies on a flat surface and moves under a rotating cylinder to which the paper is fixed

flat-screen technology /ˌflæt skriːn tekˈnɒlədʒi/ *noun* ♦ **Malvern screen**

fleapit /ˈfliːpɪt/ *noun* a shabby run-down cinema or theatre

Fleet Street /ˈfliːt striːt/ *noun* a street in London where many major newspaper offices used to be situated, near to St Paul's Cathedral

flick /flɪk/ *noun* CINEMA same as **film**

flicker /ˈflɪkə/ *noun* the effect of wavering or unsteady light on a television screen, caused by differences in update rates as the image is being created on the screen and perceived by the eye

flicks /flɪks/ *plural noun* the cinema

flick through /ˈflɪk θruː/ *verb* to glance at the opened pages of a book or magazine in quick succession

flier /ˈflaɪə/ *noun* a leaflet, usually advertising a product or event

flip /flɪp/ *verb* to glance at the pages of a magazine or book quickly

flog /flɒg/ *verb* to publicise something very aggressively

flong /flɒŋ/ *noun* a sheet of papier-mâché or cardboard used to make a mould for a metal plate for printing a page of newspaper

flood /flʌd/, **floodlight** /'flʌdlaɪt/ *noun* a lamp with a wide angle that spreads the beam of light broadly. Also called **open-face lamp**. Compare **spot**

floor manager /'flɔː ˌmænɪdʒə/ *noun* the person who is responsible for safety and general organisation during a rehearsal or shoot in a television studio. Abbreviation **FM**

floor plan /'flɔː plæn/ *noun* a map of the studio floor showing positions of the audience, cameras etc.

floppy disk /ˌflɒpi 'dɪsk/ *noun* ♦ **disk**

flow /fləʊ/ *noun* **1.** the movement of something such as information from one place to another **2.** an evening's scheduled programming

fluorescent light /ˌfluəres(ə)nt 'laɪt/ *noun* light from a tube with an internal coating which glows when electricity is passed through it

flush /flʌʃ/ *adjective* referring to a printed page with an even margin, without any indentations

flutter /'flʌtə/ *noun* a slow variation in pitch of recorded sound, occurring at higher frequencies than wow

flyaway /'flaɪəˌweɪ/ *noun* satellite equipment which can be disassembled and packed away enough to be flown as cargo to an outside broadcast location, then reassembled

flying erase head /ˌflaɪɪŋ ɪ'reɪz ˌhed/ *noun* a head on a video recorder which erases old material on the tape as new material is being recorded

fly-on-the-wall /ˌflaɪ ɒn ðə 'wɔːl/ *noun* a genre of documentary-making similar to ciné-verité, in which the cameras used are small, unobtrusive and often numerous and the subjects are filmed continuously as they go about their everyday lives. ◊ **reality TV**

'James McCaskill clearly cares very much about his parish… More controversial is the use of a slick marketing campaign and the latest concept in reality TV. For the past year cameras have been recording James's every move for a Channel 4 fly-on-the-wall documentary comically called Priest Idol.' [Yvonne Illsey, *The Express*]

flyposting /'flaɪpəʊstɪŋ/ *noun* the practice of displaying posters wherever possible, often illegally

flysheet /'flaɪʃiːt/ *noun* a leaflet or pamphlet, usually containing advertising

FM *abbreviation* **1.** RADIO **frequency modulation 2. floor manager**

FoC *abbreviation* PRINTING, UK **father of the chapel**

focal length /'fəʊk(ə)l leŋθ/ *noun* the distance away from the camera at which objects are in focus. Different lenses and lens apertures produce different focal lengths.

focus /'fəʊkəs/ *noun* a device on a camera for adjusting the lens so that the image is clear

focus group /'fəʊkəs gruːp/ *noun* a small group who discuss a topic such as their viewing preferences. Their discussions are taped and later analysed by audience researchers.

focus puller /'fəʊkəs ˌpʊlə/ *noun* **1.** a member of a camera crew whose job it is to keep moving objects in focus throughout a shot by constantly adjusting the lens **2.** an assistant to the camera operator, who control the focus during complex camera movements

fog /fɒg/ *verb* to produce a cloudy image on a negative, print or transparency by allowing too much light to reach it in the developing process ■ *noun* a cloudy area on a photographic image, caused by too much light

foldback /'fəʊldbæk/ *noun* sound played from the control room down into a studio, for example music to which a performer can mime

foldout /'fəʊldaʊt/ *noun* PRINTING same as **gatefold**

foley artist /'fəʊli ˌɑːtɪst/ *noun* a person whose job is to produce sound effects for a film, that can be dubbed onto a soundtrack in postproduction

folio /'fəʊliəʊ/ *noun* a single sheet of hard copy

folk /fəʊk/, **folk music** /'fəʊk ˌmjuːzɪk/ *noun* **1.** traditional songs and music, passed from one generation to the next **2.** modern music composed in imitation of traditional music

folk devil /'fəʊk ˌdev(ə)l/ *noun* an individual or group that is the subject of a moral panic, caused by media demonisation

folk-rock /'fəʊk rɒk/ *noun* a type of popular music combining folk melodies with the rhythms of rock music

follow shot /'fɒləʊ ʃɒt/ *noun* a camera shot in which a moving subject is filmed as the camera moves alongside or behind

follow-up /'fɒləʊ ʌp/ *noun* a news story that has been spotted in another newspaper or in other media and investigated further

font /fɒnt/ *noun* a typeface. Newspapers generally use a house font which forms part of their characteristic style and appearance. Also called **fount**

footage /'fʊtɪdʒ/ *noun* recorded material on film or tape

footer /'fʊtə/ *noun* a section at the bottom of a webpage, which usually contains any essential links and information on how to contact the organisation that owns the page and on its copyright and privacy policy

footnote /'fʊtnəʊt/ *noun* further information, usually printed at the bottom of a page, about something mentioned in the text above. A reference number or symbol is usually printed after the relevant word in the text and before the corresponding footnote.

footprint /'fʊtprɪnt/ *noun* **1.** the area affected or covered by something such as a device, phenomenon, service provider etc **2.** the area supplied by a signal from a particular broadcasting satellite

Fordism /'fɔːdɪz(ə)m/ *noun* the idea in mass production that the product should be accessible and affordable to the workers producing it and that they should be paid a fair wage based on the value of what they are producing

forecast /'fɔːkɑːst/ *noun* a prediction of what the weather will be like in the near future, usually broadcast on television or radio or printed in a newspaper

fore-edge /'fɔː edʒ/ *noun* the outer edge of a page of a book

foreground /'fɔːɡraʊnd/ *noun* the area of a picture or scene that appears to be nearest to the viewer

foreign correspondent /ˌfɒrɪn ˌkɒrɪ'spɒndənt/ *noun* a journalist who lives in or visits another country and writes news reports or features for broadcast or publication in his or her own country

form /fɔːm/ *noun* the general structure of a piece of text or a film

formal /'fɔːm(ə)l/ *adjective* **1.** done or carried out in accordance with established or prescribed rules **2.** used in serious, official or public communication but not appropriate in everyday contexts **3.** referring to the form and appearance of a media product, for example its layout, rather than the content

formalist /'fɔːməlɪst/ *adjective* relating to the principle that form is more important than content

format /'fɔːmæt/ *noun* **1.** the presentation of a television show which makes it different from others of the same genre, for example on a game show, the set, the number of contestants, the way in which they are eliminated, the prize offered etc. **2.** the type and quality of recording equipment used **3.** the structure of a radio programme according to an agreed style, for example timings, fixed spots etc. **4.** the different size, shape and appearance of competing media products, for example the page size of a tabloid vs. broadsheet.

formation /fɔː'meɪʃ(ə)n/ *noun* the association between artists in a particular movement or cultural group

format radio /'fɔːmæt ˌreɪdiəʊ/ *noun* a station which only plays one type of music, for example country music

Format Recognition and Protection Association /ˌfɔːmæt ˌrekəɡnɪʃ(ə)n ən prə'tekʃ(ə)n ə ˌsəʊsieɪʃ(ə)n/ *noun* an organisation in the UK which seeks to protect the formats of television shows as intellectual property. Abbreviation **FRAPA**

forme /'fɔːm/ *noun* blocks of type, assembled in a metal frame in preparation for printing

form letter /'fɔːm ˌletə/ *noun* a standard printed letter that is sent to many people for the same reason, for example one dealing with a common customer complaint

fort-da game /ˌfɔːt dæ 'ɡeɪm/ *noun* a concept from Freud, in which an infant learns to differentiate itself as a person from other objects and experiences loss

fortnightly /'fɔːtnaɪtli/ *noun* a publication that is published once every two weeks

forum /ˈfɔːrəm/ *noun* **1.** a medium in which debate, discussion and argument can take place, for example a magazine or newspaper **2.** a website on which people can post opinions and read what others have to say about the subjects they are all interested in

forward slash /ˌfɔːwəd ˈslæʃ/ *noun* COMPUTING, PRINTING same as **slash**

foundationalism /faʊn ˈdeɪʃ(ə)nəlɪz(ə)m/ *noun* the study of arguments as being reducible to a set of commonly-held 'basic beliefs', which are so ingrained as to be considered not in need of justification

fount /fɒnt/ *noun* PRINTING another spelling of **font**

four-by-three /ˌfɔː baɪ ˈθriː/ *adjective* referring to the normal aspect ratio of non-widescreen broadcasts (often written 4:3). ◊ **sixteen nine**

four-colour /ˌfɔː ˈkʌlə/ *adjective* PRINTING referring to the process of full-colour printing by combining the primary colours cyan, magenta, yellow and black

four O's /ˌfɔːr ˈəʊz/ *plural noun* a simple way of summarising the essentials of a marketing operation, which are Objects, Objectives, Organisation and Operations

four P's /ˌfɔː ˈpiːz/ *plural noun* a simple way of summarising the essentials of the marketing mix, which are Product, Price, Promotion and Place

Fourteen Day Rule /ˌfɔːtiːn ˈdeɪ ˌruːl/ *noun* in the period following the World War II, a restriction placed on the BBC by the government forbidding them to broadcast on any issue debated in Parliament until 14 days after the debate had taken place

Fourth Estate /ˌfɔːθ ɪˈsteɪt/ *noun* the press, supposedly the fourth most important institution in the UK (after Lords (spiritual), Lords (temporal) and the Commons)

Foxtrot /ˈfɒkstrɒt/ *noun* an internationally recognised code word for the letter F, used in radio communications

fps *abbreviation* PHOTOGRAPHY **frames per second**

fractal compression /ˌfrækt(ə)l kəmˈpreʃ(ə)n/ *noun* a technique used to compress images

fragmentation /ˌfrægmənˈteɪʃ(ə)n/ *noun* the use of a variety of media for a publicity campaign

fragmentation of audience /ˌfrægmənteɪʃ(ə)n əv ˈɔːdiəns/ *noun* the idea that with so much choice over which television channels to watch, there is no such thing as a 'shared public experience' of a broadcast as there was in the early days of television (with everybody watching the same thing)

fragrance strip /ˈfreɪgrəns strɪp/ *noun* a fold of paper on an advertisement, that is impregnated with a fragrance that is released when the fold is opened

Fraktur /frækˈtɜː/ *noun* a thick ornate style of printed letter, the standard typeface for all printing in German until the mid-20th century

frame /freɪm/ *noun* **1.** a single exposure on a film **2.** the borders of a film shot or scene

frame rate /ˈfreɪm reɪt/ *noun* the speed at which frames in a video sequence are displayed, measured in frames per second

frames per second /ˌfreɪmz pə ˈsekənd/ *noun* the numbers of frames shown in a second, usually 24 during normal playback. Abbreviation **fps**

framing /ˈfreɪmɪŋ/ *noun* **1.** the adjustment of the positioning of a film in a projector so that the image on the screen is shown in the correct position **2.** the way a scene in a film is composed within the visual field of the camera

franchise /ˈfræntʃaɪz/ *noun* **1.** a successful media product such as a film which can be developed into sequels, spin-offs and merchandising **2.** a licence to use a successful brand name **3.** a licence granted by the ITC, allowing a television company to broadcast within a specific area and/or for a particular length of time only

Franchises for Independent Television /ˌfræntʃaɪzəz fɔː ˌɪndɪpendənt ˈtelɪvɪʒ(ə)n/ *noun* licences granted by the ITA in 1955 allowing independent companies to produce regional programming for broadcast on non-BBC Channel 3

Frankfurt School /ˈfræŋkfɜːt skuːl/ *noun* a group of critical theorists of social and mass culture, active in Germany from 1923

FRAPA /'fræpə/ *abbreviation* **Format Recognition and Protection Association**

free /friː/, **freesheet** /'friːʃiːt/ *noun* same as **freesheet**

freebie /'friːbi/ *noun* a free service or product offered to journalists, for example meals, flights, tickets for events etc.

freedom of information /ˌfriːdəm əv ɪnfəˈmeɪʃ(ə)n/ *noun* the idea that citizens of a country should have free access to any information that is in the public interest

Freedom of Information Act 2000 /'friːdəm əv ˌɪnfəˈmeɪʃ(ə)n ˌækt/ *noun* an act of Parliament which states that any person has the right to apply for information held by public bodies that is of public interest. It must usually be disclosed within 20 days of the request.

freedom of the press /ˌfriːdəm əv ðə ˈpres/ *noun* liberty to print or disseminate information in the press or in the media generally, without censorship before or after the event and without incurring penalties

Freefone /'friːfəʊn/ a trade name for a phone system in which the holder of the phone number pays the cost of the call, not the caller

freelance /'friːlɑːns/ *adjective* working or earning a living as a freelancer in any profession

freelancer /'friːlɑːnsə/ *noun* **1.** a reporter who contributes copy on an ad-hoc basis to several different news outlets but is not on the permanent staff of any. Also called **stringer 2.** any person who works on an ad-hoc basis for several different companies for a limited time each

freenet /'friːnet/ *noun* an online information network, often run by volunteers and charging no access fees

free paper /ˌfriː ˈpeɪpə/ *noun* a newspaper which is given away free, and which relies for its income on its advertising

freephone /'friːfəʊn/, **freefone** *noun* a system where a person can telephone to reply to an advertisement, to place an order or to ask for information and the seller pays for the call

freepost /'friːpəʊst/ *noun* a system where someone can write to an advertiser to place an order or to ask for information to be sent, without paying for a stamp. The company pays for the postage on receipt of the envelope.

freesheet /'friːʃiːt/ *noun* a free newspaper or news leaflet that is funded by advertising and often delivered to all the households in a particular area. Also called **free**, **giveaway**

free space /ˌfriː ˈspeɪs/ *noun* space that can be used as an absolute standard because it contains no matter and no gravitational or electromagnetic fields

free-standing insert /ˌfriː ˌstændɪŋ ɪnˈsɜːt/ *noun* advertising material on one or more pages that is inserted into a newspaper

free-to-air /ˌfriː tə ˈeə/ *adjective* referring to television programmes that are available to all customers without charge

Freeview /'friːvjuː/ *noun* a box which connects to a television and, for a one-off charge, allows free access to up to 30 digital channels without subscription to a cable or satellite service. Also called **set-top box**

freeware /'friːweə/ *noun* software which can be downloaded free of charge from the Internet with no usage restrictions

'Corona makes his music on a PC he built himself. "I have favourite programs, but I'm always trying new stuff to look for new ways of working. I use brand software but also a lot of freeware and dodgy plug-ins".' [John L Walters, *The Guardian*]

freeze /friːz/ *verb* **1.** to take a still photograph of somebody or something in motion **2.** to show a single frame of a moving film so that it appears to be a still image

freeze frame /'friːz freɪm/ *noun* **1.** the act of stopping a moving piece of video or film on a single, still frame **2.** a device on a video recorder that enables a single static image to be viewed **3.** a single frame of a film or video recording viewed as a static image ■ *verb* to present something contained in a single frame from a film or video recording as a static image

freq. *abbreviation* **frequency**

frequency /'friːkwənsi/ *noun* **1.** a measurement of radio waves, describing how quickly the waves are being transmitted. It determines where a station is found on a radio dial. Abbreviation **freq.** ◊ **amplitude**, **wavelength 2.** the amount of exposure a topic is given in the media. A high frequency means that it appears often and prominently.

frequency discount /'fri:kwənsi ˌdɪskaʊnt/ *noun* reduced rates offered for frequent use of an advertising medium

frequency modulation /'fri:kwənsi ˌmɒdjuleɪʃ(ə)n/ *noun* a method of transmitting audio or visual information using radio waves, where the amplitude remains constant but the frequency varies according to the input signal. Abbreviation **FM**. Compare **amplitude modulation**

frequency response /'fri:kwənsi rɪˌspɒns/ *noun* the sensitivity of a microphone to a particular range of sound frequencies

frequently asked questions /ˌfri:kwənt(ə)li ˌɑ:skd 'kwestʃənz/ *noun* full form of **FAQ**

fresnel lens /'freɪnel lenz/ *noun* an adjustable lens for a light source that allows the beam to be changed easily from spot to flood

fringe area /'frɪndʒ ˌeəriə/ *noun* an area near the edge of a radio or television transmitter's range, where reception may sometimes be weak or disrupted

fringe time /'frɪndʒ taɪm/ *noun* television air time around prime time where there is usually more availability

frisket /'frɪskɪt/ *noun* a thin frame that holds the paper on a hand-operated printing press, and masks any parts, such as the margins, that are not to be printed

front /frʌnt/ *verb* to present a television or radio programme ■ *noun* the first pages of a book or magazine

front of house /ˌfrʌnt əv 'haʊs/ *noun* the areas of a theatre, cinema or concert hall used by members of the audience

front-page /ˌfrʌnt 'peɪdʒ/ *adjective* referring to news that is important or interesting enough to appear on the front page of a newspaper ■ *verb* to publish something on the front page of a newspaper

f-stop /'ef stɒp/ *noun* an increment used in measuring the size of a lens aperture

FT *abbreviation* PRESS, UK **Financial Times**

full duplex /ˌfʊl 'dju:pleks/ *noun* a communications network connection that allows signals to be sent in opposite directions at the same time

full-motion video adapter /ˌfʊl ˌməʊʃ(ə)n 'vɪdiəʊ əˌdæptə/ *noun* a computer fitted with a digitising card that is fast enough to capture and display moving video images, at a rate of 25 or 30 frames per second

full nester /ˌfʊl 'nestə/ *noun* in marketing, an older customer who has their own home and who is interested in a good quality of life, eats in restaurants, buys new gadgets and is not influenced by advertising

full-page /'fʊl peɪdʒ/ *adjective* referring to a printed item such as an advertisement, that takes up a complete page

full scene anti-aliasing /ˌfʊl si:n ˌænti 'eɪliəsɪŋ/ *noun* a method of anti-aliasing a complete frame of a video or animation rather than just one object, which requires powerful graphics hardware

full-service advertising agency /ˌfʊl ˌsɜ:vɪs 'ædvətaɪzɪŋ ˌeɪdʒənsi/, **full-service agency** /fʊl ˌsɜ:vɪs 'eɪdʒənsi/ *noun* an advertising agency offering a full range of services such as sales promotion, design of house style, advice on public relations and market research and creating stands for exhibitions

full-wave rectifier /ˌfʊl weɪv 'rektɪfaɪə/ *noun* an electronic circuit in which both polarities of the input alternating current are converted to the direct current output

fully connected world /ˌfʊli kə ˌnektɪd 'wɜ:ld/ *noun* a world where most people and organisations are linked by the Internet or similar networks

functionalist mode /'fʌŋkʃ(ə)nəlɪst məʊd/ *noun* a mode of media analysis that treats all behaviours as either contributing to or detracting from the general equilibrium of society. Compare **Marxist mode**

fundamentalism /ˌfʌndə 'ment(ə)lɪz(ə)m/ *noun* a return to the founding or guiding principles of something, for example a religion, without consideration for modern thought or advances

funk /fʌŋk/ *noun* a style of popular music that derives from jazz, blues and soul and is characterised by a heavy rhythmic bass, syncopated rhythms, African tones and danceability

funky /'fʌŋki/ *adjective* **1.** with the backbeat and rhythmic bass typical of funk music **2.** referring to or resembling of blues music

funnies /'fʌni/ *plural noun US* the part of a newspaper where comic strips are published

furniture /'fɜːnɪtʃə/ *noun* strips of hard material such as wood, metal or plastic that fill the spaces between and around metal type that has been set up to be printed

fuse /fjuːz/ *noun* part of a plug or other electrical circuit that breaks and cuts off the flow of electricity if there is a fault with the current

fuzzbox /'fʌzbɒks/ *noun* an electronic device that distorts the sound that passes through it, especially one wired to an electric guitar and operated by foot

FX *abbreviation* **effects**

G

G /dʒiː/ *noun* in the United States, Canada, Australia, and New Zealand, a film rating that means that a film or video is suitable for anyone to watch

gaffer /'gæfə/ *noun* the senior lighting electrician on a film shoot

gaffer tape /'gæfə teɪp/ *noun* strong adhesive tape used to secure equipment, wires etc. on a film shoot

gag /gæg/ *noun* a joke or comic story told by a comedian

gagging order /'gægɪŋ ˌɔːdə/ *noun* an order preventing a piece of information from being published if it is against the law, particularly human rights laws

'…a spokeswoman said: "I would be grateful if you did not report Mrs Blair's trip in your newspaper tomorrow"… The request follows a similar gagging order from No 10 in the summer when the British media were told not to reveal that the Blairs were holidaying in Cliff Richard's villa in Barbados.' [Jonathon Oliver, *The Mail on Sunday*]

gallery /'gæləri/ *noun* the main production control room in a television studio, where the production assistant, director and vision mixer sit. Also called **production gallery**

galley /'gæli/ *noun* a long metal tray, open at one end, used for holding type that is ready for printing

galley proof /'gæli pruːf/, **galley** /'gæli/ *noun* a proof which contains just columns of text (rather than the layout of the entire page) to be read and corrected by hand

Galtung and Ruge's model of selective gatekeeping 1965 /ˌgæltʊŋ ən 'ruːʒ/ *noun* a model of the way in which events are selected as being newsworthy and their importance relative to each other, first passing through the media gatekeeping filter (essentially personal opinion based on experience), then the analysis of their news value

gambling /'gæmblɪŋ/ *noun* betting money or other valuables on the outcome of a game, either involving chance or skill, for entertainment

game console /'geɪm ˌkɒnsəʊl/ *noun* a dedicated computer that is used primarily to play games, designed to connect to a television set rather than a monitor and usually used with a game controller rather than a keyboard and mouse

game controller /'geɪm kənˌtrəʊlə/ *noun* any hand-held device used to control a video game, such as a joystick or gamepad

gamepad /'geɪmpæd/ *noun* a game controller used to interact with a video game, which can be held with both hands and typically consisting of buttons for directions and actions. Also called **joypad**

game show /'geɪm ʃəʊ/ *noun* a television programme in which a game is played by members of the public and a prize is awarded to the winner

gaming /'geɪmɪŋ/ *noun* the playing of video games for entertainment

gamma /'gæmə/ *noun* a measure of the contrast in a developed photograph or a television image

gangsta /'gæŋstə/ *noun* a performer of gangsta rap

gangsta rap /'gæŋstə ræp/ *noun* a style of hip-hop music in which the lyrics tend to deal with gangs and gangsters

gantry /'gæntri/ *noun* a high platform around the wall of a television studio giving access to the lighting rig

garage /'gærɪdʒ, 'gærɑːʒ/ *noun* a style of electronic dance music inspired by disco and house music and associated with the urban styles of hip-hop, rap and R&B

Garamond /'gærəmɒnd/ *noun* PRINTING a Roman typeface often used in books

garble /'gɑːb(ə)l/ *noun* 1. the act of distorting a message, piece of information or signal so that it is misleading or unintelligible 2. a jumbled or distorted message, piece of information or signal that is confusing to listen to

gate /geɪt/ *noun* the part of a camera through which film passes to be exposed

gatefold /'geɪtfəʊld/ *noun* a page in a book or magazine that is larger than the others, but folded in to be the same size. Also called **foldout**

gatekeeper /'geɪt,kiːpə/ *noun* the person on a newspaper who undertakes the gatekeeping role

gatekeeping /'geɪt,kiːpɪŋ/ *noun* the job of deciding which news stories will and will not be covered, usually undertaken by the editor

'The BBC's Nik Gowing [said] "The challenge is how to gate-keep, to discriminate and to know how good that information is. It's not just the press, radio, TV, but every form of transmission by whoever has the means… You watch us because you expect us to do the gatekeeping".'
[Richard Doughty, *The Guardian*]

gateway page /'geɪtweɪ peɪdʒ/ *noun* the opening page of a website, that contains key words and phrases that enable a search engine to find it

gather /'gæðə/ *verb* to put the printed sections of a book together ready for binding

gay, bisexual, lesbian, transgender /,geɪ baɪ,seksjuəl ,lezbiən trænz'dʒendə/ *adjective* referring to minority gender and sexuality issues, particularly their representation in the mass media. Abbreviation **GBLT**

gaz. *abbreviation* PRESS **gazette**

gaze /geɪz/ *noun* in feminist theory, a term to describe the act of seeing something, and how this defines the power structure between the 'watcher' and the 'watched'

gazette /gə'zet/ *verb* to report or announce something in a gazette ■ *noun* 1. an official publication in the UK in which government appointments, public notices etc. appear. Abbreviation **gaz.** 2. a newspaper, especially a local one or the official journal of an organisation or institution

GBLT *abbreviation* GENDER ISSUES **gay, bisexual, lesbian, transgender**

gel /dʒel/ *noun* a sheet of coloured acetate placed over a light in the theatre or on a film set to create different lighting effects. Also called **colour correction filter**

gelatin /'dʒelətɪn/ *noun* thin translucent gel used to bind the light-sensitive chemicals to photographic paper

gelatinise /dʒə'lætɪnaɪz/ *verb* to coat a photographic medium with gelatin

gels /dʒelz/ *plural noun* coloured transparencies used to alter the colour and quality of light from a light source, or of natural light through a window

gender /'dʒendə/ *noun* the notion of sexual identity

COMMENT: Gender is based on social, cultural and historical considerations and more describes the 'feeling' of sexuality that a person has than the pure biological differences between men and women. According to Money (1955), "…the term 'gender role' is used to signify all those things that a person says or does to disclose himself or herself as having the status of boy or man, girl or woman, respectively. It includes, but is not restricted to, sexuality in the sense of eroticism".

gender awareness /'dʒendə ə,weənəs/ *noun* sensitivity to how communities differentiate between male and female roles, especially in particular environments, such as the workplace

gender bias /'dʒendə ,baɪəs/ *noun* a situation in which men or women are treated differently because of their sex

gendered genre /,dʒendəd 'ʒɒnrə/ *noun* a genre of television programme or film which appeals to and is pitched at one gender in particular, for example soap operas which are more watched by women

gender gap /'dʒendə gæp/ *noun* a difference in the way males and females behave or think about things

'The rise of "female late adopters" has profound implications on a purchase decision traditionally reserved for men. Women favour mainstream retail outlets over specialist camera stores, and are more pragmatic… according to a recent IDC report on the technology "gender gap".'
[Geoff Nairn, *The Financial Times*]

gender identity disorder /ˌdʒendə aɪˈdentɪti dɪsˌɔːdə/ *noun* a condition in which a person is unable to accept his or her birth gender

genderlect /ˈdʒendəlekt/ *noun* the idea that each gender makes different language choices, the female being more focused on bonding, intimacy and encouragement while the male concentrates on asserting independence and power

gender-neutral /ˌdʒendə ˈnjuːtrəl/ *adjective* without reference to masculinity or femininity

gender-specific /ˌdʒendə spəˈsɪfɪk/ *adjective* referring to or affecting only males or only females

genealogy /ˌdʒiːniˈælədʒi/ *noun* the study of genre constructions and their cultural basis, history, formation etc.

General MIDI /ˌdʒen(ə)rəl ˈmɪdi/ *noun* a set of standards for a synthesiser that set out the first 128 different instrument sounds in a synthesiser and the number that refers to it. For example, 40 is always a violin.

General National Vocational Qualification /ˌdʒen(ə)rəl ˌnæʃ(ə)nəl vəʊˌkeɪʃ(ə)nəl ˌkwɒlɪfɪˈkeɪʃ(ə)n/ *noun* a vocational qualification which measures standards of competence in a general area of work such as performing arts. Abbreviation **GNVQ**

general packet radio system /ˌdʒen(ə)rəl ˌpækɪt ˈreɪdiəʊ ˌsɪstəm/ *noun* full form of **GPRS**

general preplanning input /ˌdʒen(ə)rəl priːˈplænɪŋ ˌɪnpʊt/ *noun* market research which can be used to prepare the initial stages of an advertising campaign

general view /ˈdʒen(ə)rəl vjuː/ *noun* film footage or a shot that provides background or that is used when more detailed pictures are not available, for example, the outside of a building. Abbreviation **GV**

generator /ˈdʒenəreɪtə/ *noun* a mobile source of electricity for use when filming on location

genre /ˈʒɒnrə/ *noun* the category or type into which a film or text falls

COMMENT: Examples of film genre are: comedy, horror, documentary, musical, Western, science fiction, action, adventure, crime, historical, war, and many more. The notion of genre also applies to books (for example non-fiction, mystery, chick lit, comic book) and to television programmes (for example soap opera, documentary, drama, news programme) as well as many other products.

geocentric stage /ˌdʒiːəʊsentrɪk ˈsteɪdʒ/ *noun* an advanced stage in a company's international marketing when there is great co-ordination of overseas marketing activities

geotargeting /ˌdʒiːəʊˈtɑːgɪtɪŋ/ *noun* a method of analysing what a visitor to a website is viewing or doing and deducing his or her location, then displaying custom content or advertisements accordingly

Gerbner's model of communication 1956 /ˈdʒɜːbnə/ *noun* a model of the different stages in the communicative process, emphasising the perception of both sender and receiver, the context in which the communication takes place and the form in which the message is transmitted

gestural dance /ˌdʒestʃərəl ˈdɑːns/ *noun* the way in which two people speaking will coordinate their body language, gestures, eye contact etc. with each other

gesture /ˈdʒestʃə/ *noun* a movement of the body, either made deliberately to signify something or unconsciously, but which reveals something about what the person making the gesture is thinking

get /get/ *verb* to be able to receive a broadcast signal such as a radio or television broadcast

get out /ˌget ˈaʊt/ *verb* to publish something, especially a newspaper or magazine

ghetto blaster /ˈgetəʊ ˌblɑːstə/ *noun* a large portable machine that combines a radio receiver and a cassette or CD player, having a built-in speaker at each end and a carrying handle on top

ghost /gəʊst/ *noun* a fuzzy or weak television picture

ghost site /ˈgəʊst saɪt/ *noun* a website that is no longer being updated, but is still available for viewing

ghost-writer /ˈgəʊst ˌraɪtə/ *noun* a writer whose work is credited to another person, usually a celebrity

.gif *noun* a computer image format, the one most commonly used for non-photographic images on webpages. Full form **Graphic Interchange Format**

giveaway /ˈgɪvəweɪ/ *noun* **1.** a radio or television programme involving games or competitions and the chance for contestants to win prizes, especially cash prizes **2.** PRESS same as **freesheet**

giveaway paper /ˈgɪvəweɪ ˌpeɪpə/ *noun* a newspaper which is given away free, and which relies for its income on its advertising

glam rock /ˈglæm rɒk/ *noun* a style of popular music of the 1970s, characterised more by the extravagant clothes, makeup and hairstyles of its performers, than the music itself. Its most famous exponents were the singers Gary Glitter and Marc Bolan and the band Sweet.

Glasgow University Media Group /ˌglɑːzgəʊ ˌjuːnɪvɜːsɪti ˈmiːdiə ˌgruːp/ *noun* a research group that has published three scathing reports on the objectivity and reliability of television news reporting

glasnost /ˈglæznɒst/ *noun* a Russian term meaning 'openness, publicity, freedom of speech', one of Mikhail Gorbachev's policies for reforming the Soviet Union in 1985 by lifting restrictions on what could be published in the press

'Ali Reza Sami-Azar, who recently resigned as the head of the Teheran Museum of Contemporary Art [in Iran], said the cultural glasnost of the past five years had come to an end. "We are in very grave danger of reverting back to the post-revolutionary days, when only those artists who were deemed as expressing so-called Islamic values were displayed",' he said.' [Lilian Swift, *The Daily Telegraph*]

global advertising /ˌgləʊb(ə)l ˈædvətaɪzɪŋ/ *noun* the use of a common advertising message to advertise the same product internationally

globalisation /ˌgləʊbəlaɪˈzeɪʃ(ə)n/ *noun* the process of making things (access to technology, cultural and media products etc.) available on a global scale

COMMENT: Some believe that globalisation allows developing countries access to advances and information which are valuable to them, which they would otherwise be unable to use for their own development and quality of life. Others believe that it amounts to cultural imperialism and poses a distinct threat to the beliefs and values of the receiving countries.

globalisation of culture /ˌgləʊbəlaɪzeɪʃ(ə)n əv ˈkʌltʃə/ *noun* the spread of a dominant society's culture into a different society using communication networks, either damaging or improving (depending on your attitude) the culture that it already has

globalisation of news /ˌgləʊbəlaɪzeɪʃ(ə)n əv ˈnjuːz/ *noun* the spread of information technology across the world, so that 'local' news can be accessed wherever you are

global marketing /ˌgləʊb(ə)l ˈmɑːkɪtɪŋ/ *noun* the use of a common marketing plan to sell a product or service everywhere in the world

global media system /ˌgləʊb(ə)l ˈmiːdiə ˌsɪstəm/ *noun* a large multinational media corporation, such as AOL, Disney, Sony etc.

global positioning system /ˌgləʊb(ə)l pəˈzɪʃ(ə)nɪŋ ˌsɪstəm/ *noun* full form of **GPS**

global scrutiny /ˌgləʊb(ə)l ˈskruːtɪni/ *noun* the fact of being more 'visible' to others on a global scale due to increased communication networks

global village /ˌgləʊb(ə)l ˈvɪlɪdʒ/ *noun* the idea that the whole world can be considered as a compact community because of electronic communications and information technology

glorify /ˈglɔːrɪfaɪ/ *verb* to make something seem exciting and interesting, particularly something which is generally thought to be morally dubious such as violence

gloss /glɒs/ *noun* a short definition of a word or phrase on a page that may be unfamiliar to the reader ■ *adjective* of a photographic print, made on shiny paper. Compare **matte**

glossy /ˈglɒsi/ *noun* **1.** a photograph printed on shiny paper **2.** PUBLISHING same as **glossy magazine**

glossy magazine /'glɒsi ˌmægə'ziːn/ *noun* a magazine containing many high-quality colour photographs. Also called **glossy**

GMT *abbreviation* **Greenwich Mean Time**

GNVQ *abbreviation* **General National Vocational Qualification**

go /gəʊ/ *verb* to take part in a television or radio programme

gobo /'gəʊbəʊ/ *noun* a metal cut-out that is used to project a shape or lighting effect against a wall using a bright studio light

God slot /'gɒd slɒt/ *noun* a time in a radio or television schedule when religious programmes are broadcast

go-go /'gəʊ gəʊ/ *noun* a style of popular music originating in Washington D.C. in the 1970s, having a strong funk beat and often involving crowd call-and-response breaks

gold disc /ˌgəʊld 'dɪsk/ *noun* an award in the form of a golden replica of a recording that has sold in exceptionally high numbers, given to an artist by the recording company

'Golden Age of Cinema' /ˌgəʊldən ˌeɪdʒ əv 'sɪnɪmə/ *noun* the period in the late 1920s and throughout the 1930s when Hollywood studios were enjoying an unprecedented boom in the quality and quantity of output

golden oldie /ˌgəʊld(ə)n 'əʊldi/ *noun* a popular music recording that was popular in the past

Golden Pen of Freedom /ˌgəʊld(ə)n pen əv 'friːdəm/ *noun* a journalistic award, formerly presented annually by the International Federation of Newspaper Publishers

goldfishing /'gəʊldfɪʃɪŋ/ *noun* a broadcast that shows a person talking, but without the relevant sound

Gold Lion /ˌgəʊld 'laɪən/ *noun* an award given at the Cannes International Advertising Festival

gold record /ˌgəʊld 'rekɔːd/ *noun* a golden replica of a recording that has achieved a particular exceptionally high number of sales

Golf /gɒlf/ *noun* an internationally recognised code word for the letter G, used in radio communications

gonzo journalism /'gɒnzəʊ ˌdʒɜːn(ə)lɪz(ə)m/ *noun* a type of reporting which is more concerned with recreating a mood, the pursuit of the story, the journalist's own involvement in the situation etc. than with straight factual reporting

COMMENT: The term **gonzo journalism** is usually used to describe the work of US author Hunter S Thompson, who would become heavily involved in the events that he was documenting and record his own actions and the reactions of others. It is also sometimes used to describe the rambling, stream-of-consciousness writing style that Thompson was notorious for.

Google /'guːg(ə)l/ *noun* the largest Internet search engine, which can search from an index of more than 8 billion webpages ■ *verb* to search for something on the Internet using Google

go out /ˌgəʊ 'aʊt/ *verb* to be broadcast on television or the radio

gopher /'gəʊfə/ *noun* a computer program that searches for file names and resources on the Internet, organising them into menus containing links to text files, graphic images, databases and further menus

gospel /'gɒspəl/ *noun* highly emotional evangelical vocal music that originated among African American Christians in the southern United States and was a strong influence in the development of soul music

gossip /'gɒsɪp/ *noun* a form of (generally female) talk that is more focused on intimacy and bonding than on exchange of information

'…there's no doubt that the trickiest people I've ever worked with have also been female. But they haven't been bad, so much as barking mad… such diversions helped fuel the gossip that is such an essential part of a female-dominated office.' [*The Mail on Sunday*]

gossip column /'gɒsɪp ˌkɒləm/ *noun* a regular column in a magazine or newspaper where rumours and personal details about well-known personalities are printed

gossip network /'gɒsɪp ˌnetwɜːk/ *noun* a seemingly-trivial, but emotionally important bonding group, usually of women, based on non-confrontational intimate conversation

goth /gɒθ/ *noun* a style of popular music that became popular during the early 1980s, combining features of heavy metal and punk

gothic /'gɒθɪk/ *adjective* part of a subculture in art, architecture, film and dress, which is characterised by a dark aesthetic which challenges accepted norms ■ *noun* a simple sans serif typeface with strokes of uniform width. Also called **black letter**

Gouraud shading /'guːrəʊ ˌʃeɪdɪŋ/ *noun* shading within a three-dimensional scene created by a mathematical equation that is applied to each side of each object and produces a gradual change in colour to give the impression of light and shade

governmentality /ˌgʌvəmən'tælɪti/ *noun* the theory behind government, its construction and its approach to the institutions it presides over

GPMU *abbreviation* RADIO, TV **Graphical, Paper and Media Union**

GPRS /ˌdʒiː piː ɑː 'es/ *noun* the technology that allows a mobile phone to make calls while maintaining a connection to the Internet. Full form **general packet radio system**

GPS /ˌdʒiː piː 'es/ *noun* the use of satellite technology to identify the location of something such as a mobile phone anywhere within the world, often to within a few metres. Full form **global positioning system**

grab /græb/ *noun* **1.** same as **sound bite 2.** a still picture taken from a video

grading /'greɪdɪŋ/ *noun* the process or act of matching different shots intended for an edited sequence for quality and colour in a laboratory

graffiti /grə'fiːti/ *noun* drawings or words that are scratched, painted or sprayed on walls or other surfaces in public places

grain /greɪn/ *noun* **1.** the rough effect on a television image caused by electrical noise **2.** a particle in a photographic emulsion, on whose size the extent of possible enlargement depends

grainy /'greɪni/ *adjective* referring to a photograph that is unclear because it has been enlarged too much

Grammy /'græmi/ a trade name for an award given annually for outstanding work in the recorded music industry

gramophone /'græməfəʊn/ *noun* a machine formerly used for playing recorded sound using records and speakers

grapevine /'greɪpvaɪn/ *noun* an informal and unofficial communications network within an organisation that passes on information by word of mouth

graphic /'græfɪk/ *adjective* including a number of vivid descriptive details, especially unpleasant and disturbing ones ■ *noun* **1.** a part of a film that consists of text and illustrations, for example the title and credits **2.** a printed picture, drawing or diagram

'James Caviezel plays Christ in the powerful movie, which features graphic violence in the torture and beatings scenes.' [Sandro Monetti, *The Sun*]

Graphical, Paper and Media Union /ˌgræfɪk(ə)l ˌpeɪpə ənd 'miːdiə ˌjuːniən/ *noun* a trade union that once represented workers in the paper and printing industries. It merged in 2004 with general manufacturing trade union Amicus. Abbreviation **GPMU**

graphic design /ˌgræfɪk dɪ'zaɪn/ *noun* the art or skill of combining text and illustrations in the production of advertising, books and magazines

graphic display /ˌgræfɪk dɪs'pleɪ/ *noun* a computer screen able to present graphical information

graphic equaliser /ˌgræfɪk 'iːkwəlaɪzə/ *noun* a facility on an electronic machine for playing back recorded music, that allows separate adjustments to be made to the strength of sounds on different frequency bands

graphic novel /ˌgræfɪk 'nɒv(ə)l/ *noun* a work of fiction for adults, published as a comic strip

graphics /'græfɪks/ *plural noun* **1.** illustrations and drawings (not photographs) used in the layout of a printed page **2.** images created by computer or by hand, rather than by filming something 'real'

graphics display adapter /ˌgræfɪks dɪs'pleɪ əˌdæptə/ *noun* a cable that allows a computer to be connected to a television or video screen to give a larger display while still retaining digital image quality

gravure /grə'vjʊə/ *noun* PRINTING same as **intaglio**

graze /greɪz/ *verb* to switch between television channels without watching much of any programme

green room /'griːn ruːm/ *noun* a room where actors or guests on a television show can rest backstage

greenwash /'griːnwɒʃ/ *noun* a show of concern on behalf of an organisation or business for the environmental impact of its activities

Greenwich Mean Time /,grenɪtʃ 'miːn ,taɪm/ *noun* the exact solar time on the prime meridian (at 0° latitude, found in Greenwich, UK) from which the local time in all time zones is calculated. Abbreviation **GMT**

Greenwich Time Signal /,grenɪtʃ 'taɪm ,sɪgn(ə)l/ *noun* six pips broadcast from Greenwich to mark the hour, often broadcast on radio shows

grey card /'greɪ kɑːd/ *noun* a predictably-reflective, grey-coloured card which is used to calibrate equipment

grey scale /'greɪ skeɪl/ *noun* **1.** the shades that are produced from displaying what should be colour information on a monochrome monitor **2.** a series of shades from white to black used in displaying or printing text and graphics

grip /grɪp/ *noun* a member of a filming crew responsible for moving and setting up heavy equipment such as camera dollies

groove /gruːv/ *verb* to play jazz or dance music well, with the full support of the audience (*informal*)

gross /grəʊs/ *verb* to multiply a survey group by a particular factor in order to estimate results for a larger population

gross audience /,grəʊs 'ɔːdiəns/ *noun* same as **advertising impression**

gross cover /,grəʊs 'kʌvə/ *noun* the number of times a television or radio spot has been seen, based on television ratings

gross opportunity to see /,grəʊs ,ɒpətjuːnɪti tə 'siː/ *noun* the number of opportunities that an average member of the target audience will have to see the advertisements in an advertising campaign

gross rating point /,grəʊs 'reɪtɪŋ ,pɔɪnt/ *noun* a way of calculating the effectiveness of outdoor advertising, where each point represents one per cent of the population in a specific market

group /gruːp/ *noun* the social networks that a person is involved in, either primary such as the family, or secondary such as friendship groups, work colleagues, etc.

group system /'gruːp ,sɪstəm/ *noun* a system of organising an advertising agency into groups, each group having specialists in creative, media, marketing services and other areas, and each group dealing with particular accounts

Grub Street /'grʌb striːt/ *noun* any sort of journalistic work which is dull and usually given to lower-ranking newspaper staff

COMMENT: The term comes from the former **Grub Street** near Moorfields in London, which was famous for its population of low-paid writers and literary reviewers.

grunge /grʌndʒ/ *noun* a type of rock music that grew in the US in the 1980s and is influenced by punk and heavy metal

GSM /,dʒiː es 'em/ a trade name for an international wireless communications network for mobile phones

GTS *abbreviation* **Greenwich Time Signal**

guaranteed circulation /,gærəntiːd ,sɜːkjʊ'leɪʃ(ə)n/ *noun* the audited circulation of a magazine that is used as a basis for calculating advertising rates

guaranteed homes impressions, guaranteed homes ratings *plural noun* an advertising package offered by television companies that guarantees the advertisers that their advertising will reach a specified number of people, but leaves it to the broadcaster to choose the number and timing of the spots

guard band /'gɑːd bænd/ *noun* a narrow band between adjacent frequency bands (channels), which protects them from overlapping or interference

guard book /'gɑːd bʊk/ *noun* a hardcover album which allows pages to be inserted into it, for example for showing samples or advertising material

guard dog metaphor /'gɑːd dɒg ,metəfə/ *noun* the idea of the media as a sentry that sounds a warning whenever the 'family' (the structure and stability of society) is threatened

guerrilla marketing /gə,rɪlə 'mɑːkɪtɪŋ/ *noun* a form of unconventional flexible marketing, adapted to the products or services sold, or to the type of customer targeted

'Jack's official description is an "ambient marketing agency". The company uses projectors, works online and offers street stunts – such as an open-air acrobatic performance for Ikea where the tumblers landed on mattresses; events; and a broad set of viral, in-store and guerrilla marketing techniques.'
[Stephen Armstrong, *The Guardian*]

guest /gest/ *noun* a person who is invited to appear on a radio or television programme ■ *verb* to appear on a radio or television programme as a guest

guest star /'gest stɑː/ *noun* a well-known performer who agrees to appear in a television or radio programme

guest viewer /'gest ˌvjuːə/ *noun* a guest in a television access panel who is asked to register their presence and give basic demographic information for the survey

guide /gaɪd/ *noun* a publication that gives basic information or instructions on a subject

guide sign /'gaɪd saɪn/ *noun* any gesture which indicates direction, usually some form of pointing

guide track /'gaɪd træk/ *noun* a commentary recorded by a member of the production team to be used in editing the accompanying video (it is re-recorded later by a professional voiceover artist)

gum print /'gʌm prɪnt/ *noun* formerly, a mode of printing photographs producing an 'oil painting' effect

gun mike /'gʌn maɪk/ *noun* a directional microphone designed to pick up sound within a narrow area without picking up sound from other areas. Also called **rifle mike**, **super-cardioid microphone**. Compare **omnidirectional microphone**

gutter /'gʌtə/ *noun* the fold between the two pages in the centre spread of a magazine or newspaper

gutter press /'gʌtə pres/ *noun* a disapproving term for tabloid newspapers in general

GV *abbreviation* **general view**

gynesis /gaɪ'niːsɪs/ *noun* the feminist theory that female connotations and readings can invade and disrupt the male narrative of texts

gynocriticism /ˌgaɪnəʊ'krɪtɪsɪz(ə)m/ *noun* in feminist theory, the study of female writing, its history and creativity and how it describes the common 'female experience'

H

H/A *abbreviation* **high-angle**

habitus /ˈhæbɪtəs/ *noun* the set of values, beliefs and ideas that a person acquires through their exposure to home life, schooling, social groups and so on

hack /hæk/ *noun* a disapproving term for a journalist

hacker /ˈhækə/ *noun* a person with knowledge of information systems, encryption codes etc. who breaks into systems and networks to which they should not have access

hacktivist /ˈhæktɪvɪst/ *noun* a hacker with a political or social agenda

hair in gate /ˌheə ɪn ˈɡeɪt/ *noun* a hair or other piece of debris that is trapped in the gate of the camera and causes problems with the picture being filmed

hairline /ˈheəlaɪn/ *noun* a very thin line on a typeface, or a typeface consisting of very thin lines

hair space /ˈheə speɪs/ *noun* the thinnest possible space between printed words or letters

hair stroke /ˈheə strəʊk/ *noun* a very thin line in writing or printing

halation /həˈleɪʃ(ə)n/ *noun* a patch of blurring around a light source on a photographic image, caused by light being reflected from the back of the film

half binding /ˈhɑːf ˌbaɪndɪŋ/ *noun* a type of bookbinding in which the spine and sometimes the corners of a book are bound in a different material from the sides

half-bound /ˈhɑːf baʊnd/ *adjective* referring to a book that is bound on the back and sometimes the corners, in a different material from the sides

half-length /ˈhɑːf leŋθ/ *adjective* referring to a portrait showing a person from the waist up

half title /ˈhɑːf ˌtaɪt(ə)l/ *noun* **1.** a title printed on the right-hand page before the beginning of a section of a book **2.** the title of a book printed separately on the right-hand page before the main title page ▶ also called **bastard title**

halftone /ˈhɑːftəʊn/ *noun* a process by which shading is produced on an image by photographing it through a screen, then etching a plate so that the shading appears as dots

halo effect /ˈheɪləʊ ɪˌfekt/ *noun* the way in which a person's appearance or demeanour can lead an observer to make other assumptions about them – for example, that an unshaven, scruffily-dressed person would not be a conscientious worker and so would not be suitable for a job

halogen lamp /ˈhælədʒən læmp/ *noun* a type of light source popular in lighting rigs, which uses quartz. It is more long-lasting than tungsten but can give off intense heat. Compare **tungsten lamp**

ham /hæm/ *noun* **1.** someone, especially an actor, who performs in an exaggerated showy style **2.** an amateur radio operator ■ *verb* **ham it up** to behave, overact, or perform a role in an exaggerated showy style

hammocking /ˈhæməkɪŋ/ *noun* the technique of scheduling a programme between two other highly-rated programmes to boost its viewing figures

hamper /ˈhæmpə/ *noun* PRESS a story which is laid out in a strip across the whole width of the page, usually at the top

hand /hænd/ *noun* PRINTING same as **index**

hand-held /ˌhænd ˈheld/ *adjective* **1.** referring to a camera that is steadied on the shoulder of the operator rather than on a dolly or other apparatus. Abbreviation **H-H 2.** filmed with a camera that is carried by the operator rather than mounted on a support

handouts /'hændaʊts/ *plural noun* stories given out by public relations departments to the media

hand over /ˌhænd 'əʊvə/ *verb* to allow another person to take over a commentary during a broadcast

handover /'hændəʊvə/ *noun* the act or process of transferring control of the commentary during a broadcast to another person

hand press /'hænd pres/ *noun* a hand-operated printing press

hands-free /ˌhændz 'friː/ *adjective* referring to a device that allows a person to use portable communications equipment such as mobile phones without having to hold them

hanging indent /ˌhæŋɪŋ 'ɪndent/ *noun* a style of paragraph where all but the first line is indented on the left-hand side

hang time /'hæŋ taɪm/ *noun* the amount of time a person spends visiting a website. Longer viewing times are considered to be commercially more valuable, on the assumption that the message is holding the viewer's interest.

Hankey Committee Report on Television /'hæŋki/ *noun* a report commissioned after World War II to explore the usefulness of bringing back television broadcasting, which stated that it would provide 'a great service'

happy hard core /ˌhæpi 'hɑːd ˌkɔː/ *noun* a type of popular dance music that evolved from rave music in the early 1990s, often achieving its emotional effect by the use of piano samples and simplistic female vocals over straightforward rhythms

happy talk /'hæpi tɔːk/ *noun* informal conversation between broadcasters during a television news programme

hardback /'hɑːdbæk/ *noun* a book with a solid inflexible cover, usually more expensive and in a larger format than a paperback. Also called **hard cover**

hard copy /ˌhɑːd 'kɒpi/ *noun* printed copy on A4 sheets

hard core /'hɑːd kɔː/ *noun* **1.** an extreme version of a type of popular music such as punk, techno and hip-hop **2.** films, photographs or publications which depict sexual acts in an explicit way

hard-core /'hɑːd kɔː/ *adjective* **1.** referring to rock music with repetitive rhythmic synthesised sounds and a fast tempo **2.** depicting sexual acts in an explicit way

hardcover /'hɑːdkʌvə/ *noun* same as **hardback**

hard disk /'hɑːd dɪsk/ *noun* a permanent storage disk in a computer, which is not removable

hard news /ˌhɑːd 'njuːz/ *noun* news reported using merely facts and quotes with little description or opinion. Compare **soft news**

hard rock /ˌhɑːd 'rɒk/ *noun* a form of rock music, usually written in a major key, that has simple lyrics, bright, distorted guitar effects and a strong insistent beat

hard sell /ˌhɑːd 'sel/ *noun* an aggressive insistent way of trying to sell or advertise something

hardware /'hɑːdweə/ *noun* in computer science, the physical objects such as the monitor, disc drives, keyboard etc. needed to construct a computer. Compare **software**

Harlequin /'hɑːləkwɪn/ *noun* a traditional pantomime character who usually wears multicoloured diamond-patterned tights and a black mask

harmonious interaction /hɑːˌməʊniəs ˌɪntər'ækʃən/ *noun* the way in which advertising and editorial styles reflect each other in a publication to produce a coherent message

hate speech /'heɪt spiːtʃ/ *noun* any speech or written work which is intended to offend or degrade a person on the grounds of their ethnicity, sexuality, disability etc

'A Protestant evangelical pressure group has warned that it will try to use the government's racial and religious hatred law to prosecute bookshops selling the Qur'an for inciting religious hatred. "If the Qur'an is not hate speech, I don't know what is. We will report staff who sell it. Nowhere in the Bible does it say that unbelievers must be killed".' [Stephen Bates and Julian Glover, *The Guardian*]

Hays code /'heɪz kəʊd/ *noun* a set of censorship guidelines for US films, issued by the Hays office in 1934. Also called **Production Code**

Hays office /'heɪz ˌɒfɪs/ *noun* the board of censors in the USA from 1922 to 1966

H-certificate /'eɪtʃ səˌtɪfɪkət/ *noun* formerly, a film classification certificate that meant that the film dealt with horror themes and was unsuitable for children (now included in the X certification)

HDTV *abbreviation* **high-definition television**

head /hed/ *noun* a heading at the top of a text, for example a newspaper headline or a title ■ *verb* to be or supply a heading on a printed page

headcam /'hedkæm/ *noun* a video camera that a person fixed to a person's head or headgear

header label /'hedə ˌleɪb(ə)l/ *noun* a section of data at the beginning of a magnetic tape, that contains identification, format and control information

heading /'hedɪŋ/ *noun* a title for a paragraph, section, chapter or page

headline /'hedlaɪn/ *noun* **1.** a title printed across a page or before a newspaper article, usually in larger heavier letters and indicating what follows it **2.** the printed line at the top of a page of a book showing the page number and sometimes other information such as the title or the author's name ■ *verb* to provide a page or story with a title

headlines /'hedlaɪnz/ *plural noun* a brief summary of one of the most important items of news covered by a newspaper or a news broadcast

head nods /'hed nɒdz/ *plural noun* a form of body language which indicates agreement with the speaker and a desire to take a turn at speaking

headnote /'hednəʊt/ *noun* a summary at the top of a chapter or a page that summarises what follows

head of programming /ˌhed əv 'prəʊɡræmɪŋ/ *noun* the person whose job is to be responsible for what television or radio programmes are broadcast

headphones /'hedfəʊnz/ *plural noun* a pair of earphones joined across the top of the listener's head

headpiece /'hedpiːs/ *noun* a decorative design printed at the beginning of a chapter in a book

headroom /'hedruːm/ *noun* the amount of space in a photographic image between the top of the subject's head and the top of the frame

heads /hedz/ *plural noun* **1.** news headlines **2.** the parts of a tape recorder that read the magnetic tape

headset /'hedset/ *noun* headphones, often with a small microphone to enable two-way communication

headshot /'hedʃɒt/ *noun* a photographic image of a head, especially a person's head

head wheel /'hed wiːl/ *noun* a wheel that keeps video tape in contact with the playing head

Health and Safety at Work Act 1974 /ˌhelθ ən ˌseɪfti ət 'wɜːk ˌækt/ *noun* an act of Parliament that lays out which steps employers have to take to make sure that people are not injured at work

heavy /'hevi/ *noun* same as **broadsheet**

heavy metal /ˌhevi 'met(ə)l/ *noun* an aggressive style of loud rock music that was most popular in the 1980s. Also called **metal**

heavy user /ˌhevi 'juːzə/ *noun* a person who buys or uses a larger than average amount of a product or service

heavy viewer /ˌhevi 'vjuːə/ *noun* a person who watches a lot of television, and is part of the target audience for commercials

hedge /hedʒ/ *noun* a mostly redundant phrase used in speech, such as 'I think' or 'you know', whose purpose is to make a statement less blunt

hegemony /hɪ'ɡeməni/ *noun* the prominence given to the dominant class's ideas, values, belief systems etc., which labels those of other classes as 'minority', and so further controls production of future ideas, values etc.

helical scan /ˈhelɪk(ə)l skæn/ *noun* a method of storing data on magnetic tape in which the write head stores data in diagonal strips rather than parallel with the tape edge so using the tape area more efficiently and allowing more data to be recorded. It is used most often in videotape recorders.

Heliochrome /'hiːliəʊkrəʊm/ *noun* a trade name for a photograph that reproduces the colours of the original subject very accurately

help screen /'help skri:n/ *noun* the part of computer program that contains help and advice about using the application

he/man language /ˌhi: 'mæn ˌlæŋgwɪdʒ/ *noun* language that supposedly helps to reinforce the perspective of male as the superior gender, for example the use of 'man' to mean 'human being'

heritage /'herɪtɪdʒ/ *noun* the status, conditions, or character acquired by being born into a particular family or social class

Herman and Chomsky's propaganda model /ˌhɜːmən ənd 'tʃɒmski/ *noun* a model of news selection in which the overriding consideration is not threatening the values, norms etc. of the power elite, in essence producing a form of propaganda

hermeneutics /ˌhɜːməˈnjuːtɪks/ *noun* in aesthetic theory, the theory, practice and methodology of interpretation

hero /'hɪərəʊ/ *noun* in a narrative, the main character who represents 'good', who has to defeat the forces of 'evil' represented by the villain

heroine /'herəʊɪn/ *noun* in a narrative, a female hero

herstory /'hɜːstəri/ *noun* GENDER ISSUES **1.** the biography or study of a particular woman or group of women **2.** history as it affects women or looked at from a female perspective, especially in contrast to conventional approaches to history, which feminists see as having favoured men

Hertzian wave /ˌhɜːtsiən 'weɪv/ *noun* a radio wave

heterodyne /'hetərədaɪn/ *verb* to combine two signals of different frequencies to produce two new frequencies, one equal to the sum of and one equal to the difference between the original two signals

heteroglossia /ˌhetərəˈglɒsiə/ *noun* in the theories of structuralism and discourse, another 'language' that is unfamiliar to a person, for example a new perspective, voice, situation, meaning etc.

heterophily /ˌhetəˈrɒfɪli/ *noun* the state in which a person has differing values, beliefs etc. to the person with whom they are interacting. Compare **homophily**

heterotopia /ˌhetərəʊˈtəʊpiə/ *noun* in the theories of structuralism and discourse, a single location in which several 'social spaces' co-exist without interrelating

H-H *abbreviation* **hand-held**

hiatus /haɪˈeɪtəs/ *noun* a space or break where something is missing, especially in a manuscript

hickey /'hɪki/ *noun* an imperfection in print, especially one caused by dirt on the printing plate

HICT project /ˌaɪtʃ aɪ siː 'tiː ˌprɒdʒekt/ *noun* a research project into families to determine their domestic use of televisions, radios, computers etc. Full form **Household Uses of Information and Communication Technology project**

hidden agenda /ˌhɪd(ə)n əˈdʒendə/ *noun* a plan, motive, or aim underlying a person's actions that is kept secret from others

hidden needs /ˌhɪd(ə)n 'niːdz/ *plural noun* secret but powerful desires which an advertiser can appeal to, such as the desire to be thought attractive or worthwhile

COMMENT: Other hidden needs include: the need for ego gratification or power; the need to feel competent and worthwhile, the need for good health; the need for love and familial security, and many others.

hierarchy of effects /ˌhaɪərɑːki əv ɪ 'fekts/ *noun* a model showing the stages in the effect of advertising on a consumer such as awareness, knowledge, liking, preference, conviction and purchase

hi-fi /'haɪ faɪ/ *abbreviation* MUSIC, RECORDING **high fidelity**

high-angle /ˌhaɪ 'æŋgəl/ *adjective* referring to a camera shot that is taken from above the action being filmed. Abbreviation **H/A**

high concept /ˌhaɪ 'kɒnsept/ *noun* an important and persuasive idea expressed clearly and in few words

high-concept /ˌhaɪ 'kɒnsept/ *adjective* referring to a film that has popular appeal, for example big stars, fast action and glamour

high-definition television /ˌhaɪ ˌdefɪnɪʃ(ə)n 'telɪvɪʒ(ə)n/ *noun* a television system with a higher resolution than normal television systems, allowing for a clearer picture and less flickering. Abbreviation **HDTV**

high fidelity /ˌhaɪ fɪˈdelətɪ/ *noun* the near-perfect reproduction of sound, with little or no distortion, that can be achieved with electronic equipment. Abbreviation **hi-fi**

high frequency /ˌhaɪ ˈfriːkwənsɪ/ *noun* a radio frequency in the range 3–30 MHz or of wavelength 10–100 metres

high-key /ˌhaɪ ˈkiː/ *adjective* referring to a style of lighting in which there are few deep shadows or contrasts, giving a bright effect. Compare **low-key**

highlight /ˈhaɪlaɪt/ *noun* **1.** an area in a light tone in a picture that provides contrast or the appearance of illumination **2.** the reflection of a light source in a photograph, for example the reflection of a studio light in somebody's eye ■ *verb* to pick out parts of a picture with highlights to provide the appearance of illumination or prominence

high-speed /ˈhaɪ spiːd/ *adjective* **1.** PHOTOGRAPHY referring to a very fast exposure rate, between 50 and several million frames per second **2.** referring to a film that needs a very short exposure time

high-speed photography /ˌhaɪ spiːd fəˈtɒɡrəfɪ/ *noun* a technique in which multiple shots are taken at extremely short intervals to capture a process or action too fast to see with the naked eye

hip-hop /ˈhɪp hɒp/ *noun* a form of popular culture that started in African American areas of New York City in the 1970s, characterised by rap music, graffiti art and breakdancing

historical allusion /hɪˌstɒrɪk(ə)l əˈluːʒ(ə)n/ *noun* the act of comparing some current news event with a well-known one from the past in order to increase its news value – for example, to compare a politician involved in a cover-up scandal with Richard Nixon

historicism /hɪˈstɒrɪsɪz(ə)m/ *noun* in Marxist theory, an approach that places a text in its historical setting

hit /hɪt/ *noun* something such as a play, musical or single which is a success with critics and audiences. ■ *verb* to open a particular webpage

HMI /ˌaɪtʃ em ˈaɪ/ *noun* an artificial light that reproduces the effect of daylight. Full form **hydragyrum medium iodide**

hoarding /ˈhɔːdɪŋ/ *noun* same as **billboard**

hoist /hɔɪst/ *noun* a crane used to raise a camera for a high-angle shot

hoke /həʊk/ *verb* to perform in an excessively theatrical, possibly ludicrous way in order to captivate an audience

hold /həʊld/ *noun* copy which is prepared and set aside for later publication (for example, an obituary of a person in the public eye). Also called **set and hold**

Hollywood /ˈhɒliwʊd/ *noun* the centre of the film industry in the US, based in California

HOLMES 2 /ˌhəʊlmz ˈtuː/ *noun* a computer database system used by police to hold large quantities of searchable personal data for use in emergencies, such as data about missing persons after a disaster. Full form **Home Office Large Major Enquiry System**

holography /hɒˈlɒɡrəfɪ/ *noun* the art of producing three-dimensional images which are viewable from different angles, used as a security device on items such as credit cards because they are very difficult to fake

homepage /ˈhəʊmpeɪdʒ/ *noun* the first page that is loaded when a person opens up their browser to use the Internet

Home Service /ˌhəʊm ˈsɜːvɪs/ *noun* the first BBC talk radio station founded in 1939, now called Radio 4

home shopping /ˌhəʊm ˈʃɒpɪŋ/ *noun* shopping done from home by mail order, over the Internet or a television shopping channel

homes passed /ˌhəmz ˈpɑːst/ *noun* the number of homes that do not, but could have a cable connection easily as there is a cable to a home nearby

home video /ˌhəʊm ˈvɪdiəʊ/ *noun* a video recording made at home, often a recording of family events

homology /həˈmɒlədʒi/ *noun* in Marxist theory, the way in which the structure of a media text and the structure of the social context in which it is viewed correspond

homophily /həˈmɒfɪli/ *noun* the state in which a person shares the same values, ideas, beliefs etc. as the person with whom they are interacting. Compare **heterophily**

homophobia /ˌhəʊməʊˈfəʊbiə/ *noun* fear of homosexuality, expressed in a range of ways from discrimination in the workplace to using demeaning language and hostile behaviour

honeywagon /ˈhʌniˌwægən/ *noun* a portable toilet used at location film shoots and outside broadcasts

hood /hʊd/ *noun* a cover for an appliance, or part of one, such as a camera lens

hook /hʊk/ *noun* **1.** a device to attract the attention of a viewer and keep them interested **2.** same as **angle 3.** a pleasing and easily remembered refrain in a pop song **4.** in writing or printing, a short curve of a letter that extends above or below the line

horizontal cooperative advertising /ˌhɒrɪzɒnt(ə)l kəʊˌɒp(ə)rətɪv ˈædvətaɪzɪŋ/ *noun* cooperative advertising where the advertising is sponsored by a group of retailers

horizontal integration /ˌhɒrɪzɒnt(ə)l ˌɪntɪˈgreɪʃ(ə)n/ *noun* the acquisition of a company at the same level of production in the same market sector as another company already owned. An example of horizontal integration is a newspaper magnate taking over a rival newspaper. Compare **vertical integration**

horror /ˈhɒrə/ *adjective* referring to a genre of motion picture or literature intended to provoke feelings of fear, revulsion or shock

horse-race story /ˈhɔːs reɪs ˌstɔːri/ *noun* a report of a story such as a political race with analogy to a horse race, with statements such as 'neck-and-neck' and 'falling behind'

host /həʊst/ *noun* **1.** a person who welcomes and speaks to invited guests on a radio or television programme such as a chat or game show **2.** the main computer that controls specific functions or files in a network ■ *verb* to be the host of a television or radio programme

hostess /ˈhəʊstɪs/ *noun* a woman who welcomes and speaks to invited guests on a radio or television programme such as a chat or game show

hosting /ˈhəʊstɪŋ/ *noun* the business of putting websites onto the Internet so that people can visit them

hosting centre /ˈhəʊstɪŋ ˌsentə/ *noun* a business that makes the pages of other businesses available in the Internet and guarantees maintenance of Internet links to clients housing their own processors

host service /ˈhəʊst ˌsɜːvɪs/, **hosting service provider** /ˈhəʊstɪŋ ˌsɜːvɪs prəˌvaɪdə/ *noun* a company that provides connections to the Internet and storage space on its computers, which can store the files for a user's website

Hotel /həʊˈtel/ *noun* an internationally recognised code word for the letter H, used in radio communications

hot media /ˌhɒt ˈmiːdiə/ *plural noun* media which require little interaction and interpretation by the audience, for example film, radio. Compare **cold media**

hot metal /ˌhɒt ˈmet(ə)l/ *noun* **1.** printing type that is cast from molten metal **2.** a typesetting technique using hot metal type

hot shoe /ˈhɒt ʃuː/ *noun* a socket on a camera to which an electronic flash can be fitted

hot spot /ˈhɒt spɒt/ *noun* a building or area where wireless Internet users can access a high-speed Internet connection

house /haʊz/ *noun* **1.** a style of dance music first developed by adding electronic beats to disco records, and later characterized by the addition of repetitive vocals, extracts from other recordings, or synthesized sounds **2.** a media organisation

house agency /ˈhaʊs ˌeɪdʒənsi/ *noun* an advertising agency owned and used by a large company, and which other companies may also use

households using television /ˌhaʊshəʊldz ˌjuːzɪŋ ˌtelɪˈvɪʒ(ə)n/ *noun* the percentage of homes watching television during a specific time period and within a specific area. Abbreviation **HUT**

Household Uses of Information and Communication Technology project /ˌhaʊshəʊld ˌjuːsɪz əv ˌɪnfəmeɪʃ(ə)n ənd kəˌmjuːnɪˈkeɪʃ(ə)n tekˌnɒlədʒi/ *noun* full form of **HICT project**

house music /ˈhaʊs ˌmjuːzɪk/ *noun* MUSIC same as **house**

house organ /ˈhaʊs ˌɔːgən/ *noun* a magazine published by a company for its employees and clients, containing details about the company, its products and its workers

house style /ˌhaʊs ˈstaɪl/ *noun* in the style that is characteristic of a particular organisation, for example a newspaper article written in the house style will use the particular language, structure, layout etc usually used by that publication

House Un-American Activities Committee /ˌhaʊs ʌnəˌmerɪkən æk ˈtɪvɪtiz kəˌmɪti/ *noun* a witch-hunt committee in the US that ran from 1938–69, which was formed to hunt for subversives and Communists and 'root them out'. Abbreviation **HUAC**

howl /haʊl/, **howlround** *noun* same as **feedback**

HTML /ˌeɪtʃ ti: em ˈel/ *noun* a set of codes used for writing and displaying webpages. Full form **hypertext mark-up language**

HUAC *abbreviation* **House Un-American Activities Committee**

hub /hʌb/ *noun* a control room in a television studio that is dealing with a very large number of outside feeds, for example for a special event

huckster /ˈhʌkstə/ *noun* a publicity agent or writer of advertising copy, especially for broadcasting

hue /hjuː/ *noun* **1.** a colour or shade of a colour **2.** a property of a colour that enables it to be perceived, determined by its dominant wavelength

human interest story /ˌhjuːmən ˈɪntrəst ˌstɔːri/ *noun* an emotive piece of reporting that touches on issues that are important to all people, usually telling the story of one or a few people's experiences

humanism /ˈhjuːmənɪz(ə)m/ *noun* the philosophical view that the 'person' or individual is of more importance than any religious or spiritual power

Human Rights Act 2000 /ˌhjuːmən ˈraɪts ˌækt/ *noun* the act of Parliament which incorporated the European Convention on Human Rights into British law, protecting the right to freedom of thought and expression without persecution

Human Rights Watch /ˌhjuːmən ˈraɪts ˌwɒtʃ/ *noun* an independent organisation that monitors human rights infringements across the globe

humorist /ˈhjuːmərɪst/ *noun* a performer or writer of comic material

hunch marketing /ˈhʌntʃ ˌmɑːkɪtɪŋ/ *noun* the process of making marketing decisions following a hunch, rather than relying on market research

Hunt Committee Report on Cable Expansion and Broadcasting Policy /hʌnt/ *noun* a 1982 report on the available market for and proposed regulations on cable and satellite broadcasting in the UK

HUT *abbreviation* **households using television**

hybrid /ˈhaɪbrɪd/ *noun* a combination of cultural forms (styles of music, genres of film etc.) resulting in a new form, or one that is popular with the audiences of both the original forms. ◊ **masala**, **cross-over**

hybridity /haɪˈbrɪdɪti/ *noun* in cultural theory, a term which describes the cross-breeding and intertwining of different identities

hype /haɪp/ *noun* **1.** greatly exaggerated publicity intended to excite public interest in something such as a film or theatrical production **2.** a widely publicised person or thing ■ *verb* **1.** to promote someone or something with intense publicity **2.** to artificially boost sales of a pop music recording by paying people to buy it in large quantities

hyperbole /haɪˈpɜːbəli/ *noun* exaggeration or over-statement for literary effect, not intended to be taken literally

'Meyer's book, DC Confidential, the first insider's account of the decision making that led to war, is described with questionable hyperbole by his publisher as "one of the most important political memoirs of the decade".' [*The Sunday Times*]

hyperfocal distance /ˌhaɪpəfəʊk(ə)l ˈdɪstəns/ *noun* the distance between a camera lens and the point beyond which everything appears in focus when the lens is focused at infinity

hyperlink /ˈhaɪpəlɪŋk/ *noun* a word, image or button on a webpage or multimedia title that moves the user to another page when it is clicked

hypermedia /ˈhaɪpəmiːdiə/ *noun* computer software and hardware that supports the linking of graphics, audio and video elements, and text and allows interaction between any of them

hyperreality /ˌhaɪpəriˈælɪti/ *noun* in postmodernist theory, the suggestion that the way in which a copy (of an event, object, media text etc.) selects and imitates reality makes it 'more real than real', a preferred form of reality to the original

hypersensitise /ˌhaɪpəˈsensɪtaɪz/ *verb* to treat a photographic emulsion to increase its speed

hypertext /ˈhaɪpətekst/ *noun* **1.** a piece of highlighted text on a webpage that can be clicked on to link to another page **2.** the way in which technology makes it more possible to produce, access and interact with texts than before

hypertext mark-up language /ˌhaɪpətekst ˈmɑːkʌp ˌlæŋgwɪdʒ/ *noun* full form of **HTML**

hypodermic model /ˌhaɪpəˈdɜːmɪk ˌmɒd(ə)l/ *noun* a model of communications that holds that an intended message in a media product will be accepted wholly and without question or interpretation by the receiver. Also called **magic bullet**

hypoing /ˈhaɪpəʊɪŋ/ *noun* using special promotions to increase the audience of a television station during the sweep periods and so affect the ratings

hypothesis /haɪˈpɒθəsɪs/ *noun* a tentative explanation for a phenomenon, used as a basis for further investigation

IBA *abbreviation* **Independent Broadcasting Authority**

iceberg principle /'aɪsbɜːg ˌprɪnsɪp(ə)l/ *noun* the principle that strong needs and desires lie deep in the human personality and that advertising must work at this level if it is to be effective

icon /'aɪkɒn/ *noun* **1.** a film or music superstar, seen as a good role model **2.** in semiology, a sign or symbol that represents a real object. Compare **arbitrary signifier**

iconography /ˌaɪkə'nɒgrəfi/ *noun* the study of iconic symbols

iconoscope /aɪ'kɒnəskəʊp/ *noun* an early form of television camera tube in which a beam of high-velocity electrons converts an image into electrical impulses to produce a picture signal

IDD /ˌaɪ diː 'diː/ *noun* a telephone line which allows international calls to be made directly. Full form **international direct dial**

idealism /aɪ'dɪəlɪz(ə)m/ *noun* the philosophical view that reality is only a creation of the mind based on perceptions of and ideas about it

ideational function of language /ˌaɪdieɪʃən(ə)l ˌfʌnkʃ(ə)n əv 'læŋgwɪdʒ/ *noun* the use of language to express ideas and feelings, or to interpret and construct viewpoints etc. Compare **interpersonal function of language**

ident /'aɪdent/ *noun* a visual image that appears briefly between television programmes to identify a television channel

ident clock /'aɪdent klɒk/ *noun* a black and white graphic screen on a video just before the start of a programme, which contains production details and a clock that counts down to the start

identification /aɪˌdentɪfɪ'keɪʃ(ə)n/ *noun* the ability of people to identify and sympathise with a fictional character

identity /aɪ'dentɪti/ *noun* the individual characteristics of a person that most define them

'I never use the word racist easily. But I do think he is part of a new wave that has been building up since The Satanic Verses … a feeling that too much diversity unravels the core identity and the values of this country.' [James Silver, *The Guardian*]

idents /'aɪdents/ *plural noun* a jingle or announcement that identifies a radio station

ideological criticism /ˌaɪdiəlɒdʒɪk(ə)l 'krɪtɪsɪz(ə)m/ *noun* critical reading of a text which makes a deliberate effort to go 'against the grain', reject norms and preferred readings etc

ideological presumption /ˌaɪdiəlɒdʒɪk(ə)l prɪ'zʌmpʃən/ *noun* the idea that the media are ideologically implicated in the messages that they shape and transmit

ideological state apparatus /ˌaɪdiəlɒdʒɪk(ə)l ˌsteɪt ˌæpə'reɪtəs/ *noun* in Marxist theory, the ways in which a society imposes its ideology on its citizens, either by coercion through such mechanisms as the law, or by persuasion by religious beliefs or the family

ideology /ˌaɪdi'ɒlədʒi/ *noun* the system of values and beliefs which an individual, group or society holds to be true or important. The media is one agent that perpetuates these within a society, as are the government, the church, the education system and others.

ideology critique /ˌaɪdi'ɒlədʒi krɪˌtiːk/ *noun* in Marxist theory, the study and analysis of ideology, its mechanisms and structures

ideology of romance /ˌaɪdiɒlədʒi əv 'rəʊmæns/ *noun* the way in which the mass media impose romantic, subordinate, patriarchal ideals onto women

idiolect /'ɪdiəlekt/ *noun* a person's individual dialect, the exact way that they choose to use language to express themselves

idiot board /'ɪdiət bɔːd/ *noun* a hand-held board with a presenter's or actor's lines written on it, in case they forget what to say. Also called **idiot card**

idiot box /'ɪdiət bɒks/ *noun* television, or a television set (*informal*)

idiot card /'ɪdiət kɑːd/ *noun* TV same as **idiot board**

idiot tape /'ɪdiət teɪp/ *noun* a continuous tape for a typesetting machine, containing text but no formatting except markers for new paragraphs

IFB *abbreviation* **interruptible fold back**

IFG *abbreviation* **International Federation of Journalists**

illuminate /ɪ'luːmɪneɪt/ *verb* to decorate a letter or a page with colour, gold or silver ornamentation

illumination /ɪˌluːmɪ'neɪʃ(ə)n/ *noun* a decorated letter, design or illustration on a manuscript or page, or the art or act of decorating written texts

illusionism /ɪ'luːʒ(ə)nɪz(ə)m/ *noun* the techniques used to make artistic representations resemble reality

illustration /ˌɪlə'streɪʃ(ə)n/ *noun* the art or process of producing or providing pictorial matter to accompany a text

image /'ɪmɪdʒ/ *noun* **1.** a picture, photograph or diagram **2.** how something is represented to the outside world, the reputation or general understanding of something or somebody

COMMENT: The public image of a figure such as a celebrity or politician is something in which the media are heavily implicated. By judiciously reporting and emphasising certain events over others, a person can be made to appear untrustworthy, reliable, wild, family-oriented, good at their job, crazy, dynamic, or attributed any other characteristics.

image advertising /'ɪmɪdʒ ˌædvətaɪzɪŋ/ *noun* advertising with the aim of making a brand or company name easily remembered

'Of all major drug marketers, GlaxoSmithKline has done the most to restore consumers' faith… running a campaign reminding people that the business is mostly about researching cures for Parkinson's and Alzheimer's. GSK is not alone. Through August, corporate image advertising by all drug companies was up 33%, to $270 million, according to Nielsen Monitor-Plus.' [Jim Edwards, *Brandweek*]

image area /'ɪmɪdʒ ˌeəriə/ *noun* a region of microfilm or display screen on which characters or designs can be displayed

image compression /'ɪmɪdʒ kəmˌpreʃ(ə)n/ *noun* the process of compressing the data that forms an image

image degradation /'ɪmɪdʒ ˌdegrədeɪʃ(ə)n/ *noun* the loss of picture contrast and quality due to signal distortion or bad copying of a video signal

imagemap /'ɪmɪdʒmæp/ *noun* a graphic image on a website that has areas of the image defined as hyperlink hotspots that link to another webpage

image processing /'ɪmɪdʒ ˌprəʊsesɪŋ/ *noun* the analysis of information contained in an image, usually by electronic means or using a computer which provides the analysis or recognition of objects in the image

image processor /'ɪmɪdʒ ˌprəʊsesə/ *noun* an electronic or computer system used for image processing, and to extract information from the image

image resolution /'ɪmɪdʒ ˌrezəluːʃ(ə)n/ *noun* the number of pixels in an image. The higher the number, the clearer the image will be.

image retention /'ɪmɪdʒ rɪˌtenʃən/ *noun* the time taken for a television image to disappear after it has been displayed, caused by long persistence phosphor

imaginary /ɪ'mædʒɪn(ə)ri/ *noun* existing only in the mind, not in reality

imagined community /ɪˌmædʒɪnd ˌkɒntɪ'njuːɪti/ *noun* the idea that people do not bond and form a community according to territorial boundaries, but according to shared ideas

imaging system /'ɪmɪdʒɪŋ ˌsɪstəm/ *noun* equipment and software used to capture, digitise and compress video or still images

IMAX /'aɪmæks/ a trade name for a large-format film projection system that uses a cinema screen that is ten times larger than a conventional screen and compatible with 3-D technology

immediacy /ɪ'miːdiəsi/ *noun* how recently a news story being reported actually happened, a key news value

immersion /ɪ'mɜːʃ(ə)n/ *noun* the state of being totally surrounded by something such as a culture or language by being in the country from which it originates

impact /'ɪmpækt/ *noun* **1.** the powerful or dramatic effect that something or someone has **2.** one person viewing one 30-second advertisement, once only. Used in measurements of advertising exposure and reach.

impactaplan /ɪm'pæktəplæn/ *noun* an extensive poster advertising campaign

impact printer /ɪm'pækt ˌprɪntə/ *noun* any printing device such as a traditional typewriter, in which ink is pressed onto the paper by the printing element

impact scheduling /'ɪmpækt ˌʃedjuːlɪŋ/ *noun* the practice of running advertisements for the same product close together so as to make a strong impression on the target audience

impartiality /ɪmˌpɑːʃi'ælɪti/ *noun* the idea of being completely objective and uninvolved in reporting news

'Sir Christopher Meyer was resisting fresh demands to step down as head of the Press Complaints Commission yesterday… In his letter, leaked to The Observer, Mr Prescott [wrote]: "How can I or others criticised in your book come to the PCC in future and expect impartiality when you have made it clear you are anything but?"' [George Jones, *The Daily Telegraph*]

imperfect competition /ɪmˌpɜːfɪkt ˌkɒmpə'tɪʃ(ə)n/ *noun* a situation in which market forces are dependent on those buying and selling, and can be easily influenced by them. Compare **perfect competition**

imperial /ɪm'pɪəriəl/ *noun* the largest of the traditional UK and US paper sizes. The UK imperial measures 559 x 762

mm/22 x 30 in. The US imperial measures 584 x 838 mm/23 x 33 in.

imperialism /ɪm'pɪəriəlɪz(ə)m/ *noun* the policy or practice of one country ruling over one or more others by means of physical occupation and the assumption of governmental powers

implication /ˌɪmplɪ'keɪʃ(ə)n/ *noun* something which is not said but is assumed to already be known

impose /ɪm'pəʊz/ *verb* to order the pages of a book or magazine correctly for printing and folding

imposition /ˌɪmpə'zɪʃ(ə)n/ *noun* the skill or act of setting up and ordering pages for printing

impression /ɪm'preʃ(ə)n/ *noun* **1.** a particular version of a printed book **2.** the total number of copies of a book printed at one time, or the printing of these

impression cover /ɪm'preʃ(ə)n ˌkʌvə/ *noun* the amount of advertising necessary to ensure the required number of advertising impressions

impressionist /ɪm'preʃ(ə)nɪst/ *noun* **1.** a performer who impersonates well-known people in a humorous exaggerated way **2.** an painter, writer or composer whose work is in the style of Impressionism, especially one active in France at the end of the 19th century

impressionistic /ɪmˌpreʃ(ə)'nɪstɪk/ *adjective* relating to or reminiscent of the style of the impressionists in painting or music

impression management /ɪm'preʃ(ə)n ˌmænɪdʒmənt/ *noun* the art of presenting yourself to others, highlighting your most attractive features and hiding others

imprimatur /ˌɪmprɪ'meɪtə/ *noun* permission for a book or other work to be published, now usually confined to religious works sanctioned by the Roman Catholic Church

imprint /'ɪmprɪnt/ *noun* the name and address of the printer and publisher of a newspaper, printed on every newspaper as a legal requirement

impro, improv *noun* same as **improvisation**

improvisation /ˌɪmprəvaɪ'zeɪʃ(ə)n/ *noun* **1.** something performed or done without any preparation or set text to follow **2.** the skill or creative process of creating and performing something without any preparation or set text to follow

improvise /'ɪmprəvaɪz/ *verb* to perform or compose something, especially a sketch, play, song, or piece of music, without any preparation or set text to follow

Impulse Pay-Per-View /ˌɪmpʌls peɪ pə 'vjuː/ *noun* a form of pay-per-view television that does not have to be ordered in advance, but can be purchased on the spot. Abbreviation **IPPV**

incentive-based system /ɪn'sentɪv beɪst ˌsɪstəm/ *noun* a payment system by which an advertising agency's commission depends on how well it performs

incentive marketing /ɪn'sentɪv ˌmɑːkɪtɪŋ/ *noun* any additional incentives to buy apart from advertising, for example free gifts

inch rate /'ɪnʃ reɪt/ *noun* an advertising rate for periodicals, calculated on a normal column width, one inch deep

incidental music /ˌɪnsɪ'dent(ə)l ˌmjuːzɪk/ *noun* music specifically written to be played at the same time as the action of a film, play or television programme

incorporation /ɪnˌkɔːpə'reɪʃ(ə)n/ *noun* the way in which underground cultural forms are absorbed and 'softened' by popular culture, as happened with punk

incunabulum, incunable *noun* a book printed before 1501

COMMENT: The word derives from the Latin *incunabula*, meaning 'swaddling clothes worn in the cradle', to refer to the fact that the books represent the infancy (the first 50 years) of printing

indent /'ɪndent/ *noun* the amount of white space at the beginning and end of lines of text

indentation /ˌɪnden'teɪʃ(ə)n/ *noun* the practice or act of leaving space between the margin and the beginning of a line of text, or the blank space left

independent /ˌɪndɪ'pendənt/ *noun* any media company that is not a major

Independent Broadcasting Authority /ˌɪndɪpendənt 'brɔːdkɑːstɪŋ ɔːˌθɒrɪti/ *noun* the regulatory body that controlled television and radio broadcasting from 1974 until 1990, when it was replaced by the Broadcasting Standards Commission, the Independent Television Commission and the Radio Authority. Abbreviation **IBA**

Independent Television /ˌɪndɪpendənt 'telɪvɪʒ(ə)n/ *noun* a British commercial television station. Abbreviation **ITV**

Independent Television Association /ˌɪndɪpendənt 'telɪvɪʒ(ə)n əˌsəʊsieɪʃ(ə)n/ *noun* a council made up of representatives from each of the independent companies which form the ITN. Abbreviation **ITVA**

Independent Television Authority /ˌɪndɪpendənt 'telɪvɪʒ(ə)n ɔːˌθɒrəti/ *noun* the body which regulated the independent television companies prior to 1974. Abbreviation **ITA**. ◊ **Independent Broadcasting Authority**

Independent Television Commission /ˌɪndɪpendənt 'telɪvɪʒ(ə)n kəˌmɪʃ(ə)n/ *noun* the regulatory authority for television in the UK before it was replaced by OFCOM under the 2003 Communications Act. Abbreviation **ITC**. ◊ **OFCOM**

independent television company /ˌɪndɪpendənt ˌtelɪ'vɪʒ(ə)n ˌkʌmp(ə)ni/ *noun* a company with a franchise to broadcast as part of the ITV network

Independent Television Network /ˌɪndɪpendənt 'telɪvɪʒ(ə)n ˌnetwɜːk/ *noun* the group of independent television companies who share the single ITV channel

in-depth reporting /ˌɪn depθ rɪ'pɔːtɪŋ/ *noun* coverage that goes into a lot of detail and has been well researched

index /'ɪndeks/ *noun* **1.** a front-page list of the contents of a newspaper **2.** a symbol that calls attention to a particular section or paragraph in a piece of text. Also called **fist**, **hand 3.** a list of books which must not be read, especially on religious grounds **4.** a measurement used in statistics in relation to a norm of 100 – so that an index of 140 would mean that the measurement was 40% higher than the norm

indexical /ɪn'deksɪk(ə)l/ *adjective* in semiotics, relating to something which shows the value of something else, such as a thermometer displaying heat on an rising scale of numbers

India /'ɪndjə/ *noun* an internationally recognised code word for the letter I, used in radio communications

indicators /'ındıkeıtəz/ *plural noun* non-verbal cues used in interpersonal communication, such as nodding, folding the arms, frowning etc.

indie /'ındi/ *adjective* referring to music produced by small independent record companies, or artists who play the type of music recorded by such companies ■ *noun* a small independent record or film company

indirect channel /,ındaırekt 'tʃæn(ə)l/ *noun* a sales method where wholesalers and retailers are used to sell a product, as opposed to using a direct sales force

individualist /,ındı'vıdjuəlıst/ *adjective* referring to a culture in which an emphasis is placed on the rights and desires of an individual rather than of the larger community. In these cultures, personal achievement and assertiveness is prized and there is a strong sense of competition. Independence is also seen as more important than conformity. Compare **collectivist**

indoctrination /ın,dɒktrı'neıʃ(ə)n/ *noun* a negative and controversial term meaning to be forcibly educated and 'fed' with values and ideas without being given a chance to properly analyse them or make free choices

'If the business community is the "old boys' network" in the west, the Communist party is the "old boys' network" in China. Bright young officials are selected for ideological indoctrination and management training, and moved through increasingly responsible positions.' [James McGregor, *The Observer*]

inductive reasoning /ın,dʌktıv 'ri:z(ə)nıŋ/ *noun* the use of observations of a single event to draw more general conclusions. Compare **deductive reasoning**

industrial advertising /ın,dʌstriəl 'ædvətaızıŋ/ *noun* advertising to businesses, not to private individuals

industrialisation /ın,dʌstriəlaı 'zeıʃ(ə)n/ *noun* the adoption of industrial methods of production and manufacturing by a country or group, with all the associated changes in lifestyle, transport, and other aspects of society

inferior /ın'fıəriə/ *adjective* referring to characters written slightly lower than the

rest of the line, for example the '2' in 'CO₂' ■ *noun* a character written below the line

infinity /ın'fınıti/ *noun* a point sufficiently far from a lens or mirror that the light emitted from it falls in parallel rays on the surface

inflight advertising /,ınflaıt 'ædvətaızıŋ/ *noun* advertising on television screens inside a plane

inflight magazine /,ınflaıt ,mægə 'zi:n/ *noun* a magazine which is provided free for each passenger on a flight

infoholic /,ınfəʊ'hɒlık/ *noun* a person who is obsessed with obtaining information, especially on the Internet

infomediary /'ınfəʊ,mi:diəri/ *noun* a website where specialist information is gathered for a target audience

infomercial /,ınfəʊ'mɜːʃ(ə)l/ *noun* an extended advertisement that is presented in the form of a television show

infonesia /,ınfəʊ'ni:ziə/ *noun* the inability to remember a piece of information or its location on the Internet

informant /ın'fɔːmənt/ *noun* same as **respondent**

information and communications technologies /,ınfəmeıʃ(ə)n ən kə ,mju:nı'keıʃ(ə)nz tek,nɒlədʒiz/ *plural noun* computer and telecommunications technologies considered together. Abbreviation **ICT**

information architecture /,ınfə 'meıʃ(ə)n ,ɑːkıtektʃə/ *noun* the methods used in designing the navigation, search and content layout for a website

information blizzards /,ınfə 'meıʃ(ə)n ,blızədz/ *noun* the overload of information that the media exposes people to, which is difficult to take in and make sense of

information gap /,ınfə'meıʃ(ə)n ,gæp/ *noun* the divide between those with access to information and those with none

information line /,ınfə'meıʃ(ə)n ,laın/ *noun* a line running across a computer screen that gives the user information about the program being executed or the file being edited

information management /,ınfə 'meıʃ(ə)n ,mænıdʒmənt/ *noun* the task of controlling information and the flow of information within an organisation, which involves acquiring, recording, organising, storing, distributing and retrieving it

information overload /ˌɪnfə ˈmeɪʃ(ə)n ˌəʊvələʊd/ *noun* having too much information to process

'DAVID AYLWIN, founder and managing director [of the Training Association], said: "With the huge explosion in emails and web pages, the average number of hours people spend having to read in a day is between four and seven. People are suffering from information overload. They need to update the reading skills they were taught when they were five".' [Mary Morgan, *The Daily Mail*]

information processing model /ˌɪnfəmeɪʃ(ə)n ˈprəʊsesɪŋ ˌmɒd(ə)l/ *noun* a way of evaluating the effect of advertising in which the receiver of the message is regarded as somebody who processes information and deals with problems

information rate /ˌɪnfəˈmeɪʃ(ə)n ˌreɪt/ *noun* the amount of information content per character multiplied by the number of characters transmitted per second

information retrieval /ˌɪnfə ˈmeɪʃ(ə)n rɪˌtriːv(ə)l/ *noun* the process of locating quantities of data stored in a database and producing useful information from the data

information retrieval centre /ˌɪnfə ˈmeɪʃ(ə)n rɪˈtriːv(ə)l ˌsentə/ *noun* a research system providing specific information from a database for a user

information science /ˌɪnfəˈmeɪʃ(ə)n ˌsaɪəns/ *noun* the study of the processes involved in the collection, categorisation and distribution of information

information society /ˌɪnfəˈmeɪʃ(ə)n səˌsaɪəti/ *noun* a society in which everybody has full and free access to information for the sake of personal and community development

information storage and retrieval /ˌɪnfəmeɪʃ(ə)n ˌstɔːrɪdʒ ən rɪˈtriːv(ə)l/ *noun* the techniques involved in storing information and retrieving data from a store

information superhighway /ˌɪnfəmeɪʃ(ə)n ˌsuːpəˈhaɪweɪ/ *noun* the worldwide computer network that includes the Internet, which permits the high-speed transfer of many different forms of data, including voice, video and text

information technology /ˌɪnfəmeɪʃ(ə)n tekˈnɒlədʒi/ *noun* the whole range of communications technologies, including those used in television, radio, print media and the Internet

infotainment /ˌɪnfəʊˈteɪnmənt/ *noun* information presented in an entertaining and engaging way. This term is often used pejoratively. Also called **docutainment**

infrared photography /ˌɪnfrəred fə ˈtɒɡrəfi/ *noun* photography with film that is sensitive to infrared light and can be used for taking pictures at night, in misty conditions or to detect camouflaged objects

ingénue /ˈænʒənjuː/ *noun* a naive inexperienced young woman

ingredient sponsored cooperative advertising /ɪnˌɡriːdiənt ˌspɒnsəd kəʊˌɒp(ə)rətɪv ˈædvətaɪzɪŋ/ *noun* advertising sponsored by the producers of raw materials, that aims to encourage the production of products that use these raw materials

inherent drama /ɪnˌhɪərənt ˈdrɑːmə/ *noun* advertising that emphasises the benefits of purchasing a product or service, such as the speed of a car, the nutritional value of cereals, etc.

inheritance factor /ɪnˈherɪt(ə)ns ˌfæktə/ *noun* a situation in which the programme's ratings rise if it is aired after a popular programme, resulting from button apathy

in-home viewing /ˌɪn həʊm ˈvjuːɪŋ/ *noun* television viewers who are watching in private homes only. Compare **out-of-home viewing**

in-house /ˌɪn ˈhaʊs/ *adjective* within the same company

in-house agency /ˌɪn haʊs ˈeɪdʒənsi/ *noun* an advertising agency which is owned and operated by a company and is responsible for the company's advertising programme

initial /ɪˈnɪʃ(ə)l/ *noun* the large and often decorative first letter of a verse, paragraph, page, chapter or work

inject box /ɪnˈdʒekt bɒks/, **inject point** /ɪnˈdʒekt pɔɪnt/ *noun* BROADCAST same as **feed point**

ink /ɪŋk/ *noun* publicity, especially in the print media ■ *verb* to cover with ink, usually in preparation for printing

ink in /ˌɪŋk 'ɪn/ *verb* to apply ink to a surface before printing from it

in-line /ˌɪn 'laɪn/ *noun* a graphic image that is part of a webpage

inoculation effect /ɪˌnɒkjʊ'leɪʃ(ə)n ɪˌfekt/ *noun* the ability of an audience to resist being persuaded of something if they are warned beforehand that an attempt to persuade them is about to take place

in-point /'ɪn pɔɪnt/ *noun* the point at which a piece in an edited sequence should start

input /'ɪnpʊt/ *verb* to type something into a computer ■ *noun* a contribution to something, especially comments or suggestions made to a group

inquiry test /ɪŋ'kwaɪəri test/ *noun* a method of measuring the effectiveness of advertising based on responses following the advertisement such as requests for information, phone calls or the number of coupons redeemed

INS *abbreviation* PRESS **International News Service**

insert /'ɪnsɜːt/ *noun* 1. a piece of extra text added into text that has already been written 2. same as **loose insert**

insert shot /ɪn'sɜːt ʃɒt/ *noun* a close-up shot of an item, headline, etc., inserted into a filmed scene to show the audience what the character in the scene can see

inside back cover /ˌɪnsaɪd bæk 'kʌvə/ *noun* the page on the inside of the back cover used for advertising

inside story /ˌɪnsaɪd 'stɔːri/ *noun* a piece of reporting based on the first-hand experiences of those inside a company or organisation in the news – either the reporter or his or her sources

'Vatican sources said that, as the Foreign Minister from 1990 until November 2003, the cardinal knew "the inside story" of the Vatican's troubled relations with China. In his current post as the head of the Secret Archives, he remained "one of the Pope's confidants".'

[Richard Owen, *The Times*]

instant messaging /ˌɪnstənt 'mesɪdʒɪŋ/ *noun* software which allows computer users to send short messages in real time which appear on another user's screen

instant replay /ˌɪnstənt riː'pleɪ/ *noun* an immediate playback of a videotape, usually in slow motion and to show a particular moment in a sporting event on television

institution /ˌɪnstɪ'tjuːʃ(ə)n/ *noun* the cultural and political conventions within which media products are constructed and disseminated

institutional advertising /ˌɪnstɪtˈjuːʃ(ə)n(ə)l ˌædvətaɪzɪŋ/ *noun* advertising an organisation rather than a product

institutional documentary /ˌɪnstɪtjuːʃ(ə)n(ə)l ˌdɒkjʊ'ment(ə)ri/ *noun* a documentary based in and around a place of work such as a hospital

instrument patch /'ɪnstrəmənt pætʃ/ *noun* on a synthesizer, a 'voice' that recreates the sound of an instrument playing, for example a piano, a flute etc

insulating tape /'ɪnsjʊleɪtɪŋ ˌteɪp/ *noun* special tape that is used to make electrical wiring safe to touch

intaglio /ɪn'tɑːliəʊ/ *noun* 1. any printing technique in which the design is cut into the plate, such as engraving or etching. Also called **gravure 2.** a printing block into which a design is cut

integrated information response model /ˌɪntɪɡreɪtɪd ˌɪnfəmeɪʃ(ə)n rɪ'spɒns ˌmɒd(ə)l/ *noun* a model showing the response process to an advertising message which suggests that advertising leads to a low acceptance rate of information, but that after trials of the product the acceptance rate increases and this in turn leads to brand loyalty

integrated marketing /ˌɪntɪɡreɪtɪd 'mɑːkɪtɪŋ/ *noun* co-ordination of all of a company's marketing activities in establishing marketing strategies such as packaging, media promotion or after-sales service

Integrated Services Digital Network /ˌɪntɪɡreɪtɪd ˌsɜːvɪsɪz ˌdɪdʒɪt(ə)l 'net,wɜːk/ *noun* an adaptor that uses digital technology to increase the bandwidth of a telephone line. Abbreviation **ISDN**

integration /ˌɪntɪ'ɡreɪʃ(ə)n/ *noun* the way in which new ideas and values become part of the established social system

Intel Indeo /ˌɪntel 'ɪndiəʊ/ a trade name for software technology developed by Intel that allows a computer to store and play back compressed video sequences

intellectual /ˌɪntɪ'lektʃuəl/ *noun* a person who has expertise and education in some field and so can speak with authority

intellectual property /ˌɪntəlektʃuəl 'prɒpəti/ *noun* ideas, designs and creative material that are deemed to 'belong' to a person and should be protected from theft or use by others

COMMENT: Among the things which can be considered intellectual property are: inventions, trade names, pieces of literature, plays, musical works, pictures, photographs, designs, performances and broadcasts.

Intelsat /'ɪntelsæt/ *noun* an international organisation that owns and operates the communications satellites that orbit Earth

intensity /ɪn'tensɪti/ *noun* the amount of coverage and attention given to a particular news story, often at the expense of other stories

interabang /ɪn'terəbæŋ/ *noun* PRINTING another spelling of **interrobang**

interactive /ˌɪntər'æktɪv/ *adjective* referring to a system or piece of software that allows communication between the user and the computer in conversational mode

interactive advertising /ˌɪntər'æktɪv ˌædvətaɪzɪŋ/ *noun* advertising that requires some input from its audience, usually found on the Internet or through other new technology forms

interactive media /ˌɪntəræktɪv 'miːdiə/ *plural noun* media that provide two-way communications between users and their machines or systems and enable users to control their systems and obtain responses from them in real time

interactive multimedia /ˌɪntəræktɪv ˌmʌlti'miːdiə/ *noun* a multimedia system in which users can issue commands to which the program responds, or control actions and control the way the program works

interactive television /ˌɪntəræktɪv 'telɪvɪʒ(ə)n/ *noun* television which allows the user to take part in quizzes, vote in competitions, access more infor-

mation etc. through their remote control. Abbreviation **iTV**

interconnect /ˌɪntəkə'nekt/ *noun* two or more cable systems joined together for advertising purposes so as to give a wider geographical spread

intercultural communication /ˌɪntəkʌltʃ(ə)rəl kə,mjuːnɪ'keɪʃ(ə)n/ *noun* communication between people who are from different cultural or social backgrounds

intercut /ˌɪntə'kʌt/ *verb* to cut back and forth between filmed scenes or shots of different events or time periods to give the impression that they are taking place at the same time

interference /ˌɪntə'fɪərəns/ *noun* unwanted signals from other sources that disrupt radio, telephone or television reception

interframe coding /ˌɪntəfreɪm 'kəʊdɪŋ/ *noun* a system for compressing video images, in which only the differences between each frame are recorded

interior /ɪn'tɪəriə/ *noun* **1.** the inside of a building, a film set designed to look like the inside of a building or a scene filmed inside a building **2.** a painting or photograph of the inside of a building

interlace /ˌɪntə'leɪs/ *verb* to build up an image on a television screen using two passes to create two picture fields. One displays all the odd-numbered lines, the other all the even-numbered lines. The aim is to reduce the flicker effects on the television picture.

interlaced scanning /ˌɪntəleɪsd 'skænɪŋ/ *noun* a technique for producing an image on a television or computer screen that is clear and correctly aligned in the vertical plane. It involves scanning first all the odd numbered and then all the even numbered lines in the screen image.

intermedia comparison /ˌɪntəmiːdiə kəm'pærɪs(ə)n/ *noun* a comparison of different media to decide how suitable they are for advertising

international direct dial /ˌɪntənæʃ(ə)nəl daɪ,rekt 'daɪəl/ *noun* full form of **IDD**

International Federation of Journalists /ˌɪntənæʃ(ə)nəl ˌfedəʃeɪʃ(ə)n əv 'dʒɜːnəlɪsts/ *noun* an organisation formed to campaign for freedom of the press across the globe. Abbreviation **IFJ**

International Federation of News-paper Publishers /ˌɪntənæʃ(ə)nəl ˌfedərəɪʃ(ə)n əv ˈnjuːz‚peɪpə/ *noun* ♦ World Association of Newspapers

international media /ˌɪntənæʃ(ə)nəl ˈmiːdiə/ *plural noun* advertising media that cover several countries and can be used to reach audiences in them

International News Service /ˌɪntənæʃ(ə)nəl ˈnjuːz ‚sɜːvɪs/ *noun* a news agency that was the subject of controversy in 1918 when it was accused of 'lifting' stories from a rival agency, Associated Press. Abbreviation **INS**. ◊ Doctrine of Misappropriation

international roaming /ˌɪntənæʃ(ə)nəl ˈrəʊmɪŋ/ *noun* the facility to use a mobile phone outside the country in which the user have a contract

International Telecommunication Union /ˌɪntənæʃ(ə)nəl ‚telikəˌmjuːnɪ ˈkeɪʃ(ə)n ‚juːniən/ *noun* an organisation that promotes international cooperation in telecommunications and allots radio frequencies for various purposes. It was founded in 1865 and affiliated with the United Nations in 1947. Abbreviation **ITU**

internaut /ˈɪntənɔːt/ *noun* an Internet user, especially a habitual one

'To some analysts, Netbridge's greatest weakness is the lack of a coherent portal that would draw sufficiently large volumes of traffic – and notably internauts willing to spend money or draw advertisers.' [Andrew Jack, *The Financial Times*]

Internet phenomenon /ˈɪntənet fə ˈnɒmɪnən/, **Internet meme** *noun* something such as a person, site or image that captures the attention of multiple Internet users and becomes a fad that quickly spreads. Viral advertising tries to take advantage of this.

Internet protocol /ˈɪntənet ‚prəʊtəkɒl/ *noun* the standard that controls the addressing and format of data transmitted over the Internet

Internet Relay Chat /ˌɪntənet ˈriːleɪ ‚tʃæt/ *noun* software that allows users to join chat rooms and post instant messages that other users can read and reply to in real time. Abbreviation **IRC**

Internet service provider /ˌɪntənet ˈsɜːvɪs prəˌvaɪdə/ *noun* a company that sells connections providing access to the Internet. Abbreviation **ISP**. Also called **access provider**

Internet telephony /ˌɪntənet tə ˈlefəni/ *noun* a system that allows users to make telephone calls using the Internet to carry the voice signals. To make a call, users need a computer with a sound card fitted and a microphone and loudspeaker plugged in, and special software that manages the connection and transfers the voice data over the Internet.

internship /ɪnˈtɜːnʃɪp/ *noun* same as **work experience**

interpellation /ˌɪntəpəˈleɪʃ(ə)n/ *noun* in Marxist theory, the way in which people are addressed and how this relates to their position in society

interpersonal communication /ˌɪntəpɜːs(ə)n(ə)l kəˌmjuːnɪˈkeɪʃ(ə)n/ *noun* any communication between two people, whether verbal or non-verbal

interpersonal framing /ˌɪntəpɜːs(ə)n(ə)l ˈfreɪmɪŋ/ *noun* in interpersonal communication, the signals by which two people talking let each other know whether the conversation is serious or not, what purpose it has, whether it has to end soon etc.

interpersonal function of language /ˌɪntəpɜːs(ə)n(ə)l ‚fʌŋkʃən əv ˈlæŋgwɪdʒ/ *noun* the use of language to bond with other people, as opposed to its use for exchanging information. Compare **ideational function of language**

interpretant /ɪnˈtɜːprətənt/ *noun* the set of associations that are raised in the mind of a person on seeing a particular sign

interpretive community /ɪn ‚tɜːrprɪtɪv kəˈmjuːnɪti/ *noun* in aesthetic theory, the idea that a text's meaning is not an essential part of it, but comes from the shared ideology of the 'community' reading it

interrobang /ɪnˈterəbæŋ/ *noun* a punctuation mark in the form of a combined question mark and exclamation mark. It is used at the end of, or sometimes in place of, an utterance that is both question and exclamation, especially to indicate disbelief.

interrogate /ɪnˈterəgeɪt/ *verb* **1.** to question someone thoroughly, often in an aggressive or threatening manner and especially as part of a formal enquiry, for

example in a police station or courtroom
2. to send a request for information to a computer device or program

interruptible fold back /ˌɪntərʌptɪb(ə)l ˈfəʊld ˌbæk/ *noun* same as **clean feed**

interstitial /ˌɪntəˈstɪʃ(ə)l/ *noun* an advertisement on the World Wide Web that is shown briefly before a selected page

intertextuality /ˌɪntətekstjuˈælɪti/ *noun* the theory that all media texts are interrelated, and can only be defined by their relations with others

intervalometer /ˌɪntəvəˈlɒmɪtə/ *noun* a device that is designed to activate a mechanism automatically at regular intervals, especially one that operates a camera shutter

interval signal /ˈɪntəv(ə)l ˌsɪgn(ə)l/ *noun* a phrase of music, a jingle or other sound that a radio station uses to identify itself, broadcasting it between and sometimes during programmes

intervening variables /ˌɪntəviːnɪŋ ˈveəriəb(ə)lz/ *plural noun* any factors that influence how a message is finally interpreted, on the part of the sender, the receiver and the form of transmission

intervention /ˌɪntəˈvenʃən/ *noun* the ability of governments and those in power to intervene in the transmission of information through the media

interview /ˈɪntəvjuː/ *noun* a meeting during which a person is asked questions, for example by a journalist or a researcher

intimisation /ˌɪntɪmaɪˈzeɪʃ(ə)n/ *noun* the practice of making a news story more interesting or a message more convincing by appealing to the viewer's own values and beliefs

intramedia comparison /ˌɪntrəmiːdiə kəmˈpærɪs(ə)n/ *noun* a comparison of different advertising options within the same medium

intransient advertisement /ɪn ˌtrænziənt ədˈvɜːtaɪzɪŋ/ *noun* an advertisement that the target audience can keep and look at again, for example in a newspaper or magazine. Compare **transient advertisement**

intrapersonal communication /ˌɪntrəpɜːsən(ə)l kəˌmjuːnɪˈkeɪʃ(ə)n/ *noun* internal conversation, thoughts

intro /ˈɪntrəʊ/ *noun* the opening paragraph or paragraphs of a story that introduce it and its main angle

inventory /ˈɪnvənt(ə)ri/ *noun* advertising time or space that is not used and is available

inverse video /ˌɪnvɜːs ˈvɪdiəʊ/ *noun* a television effect created by swapping the background and foreground text display colours

inverted pyramid /ɪnˌvɜːtɪd ˈpɪrəmɪd/ *noun* the way in which news stories are generally structured, starting with the most important news at the beginning, continuing with less important pieces of information and finishing with a short background piece

investigative reporting /ɪnˈvestɪgətɪv rɪˈpɔːtɪŋ/, **investigative journalism** /ɪnˌvestɪgətɪv ˈdʒɜːnəlɪz(ə)m/ *noun* the type of reporting that involves the journalist having to do a lot of research to discover more detail, often an exposé of something that somebody is trying to cover up

investment advertising /ɪnˈvestmənt ˌædvətaɪzɪŋ/ *noun* large expenditure on advertising to achieve long-term objectives

investment spending /ɪnˈvestmənt ˌspendɪŋ/ *noun* the policy of spending more than normal on advertising with the expectation of increased sales and profits

invisibility /ɪnˌvɪzɪˈbɪlɪti/ *noun* the idea that particular minority groups are under-represented in the mainstream media and are as such 'invisible' to the majority of viewers

in-vision /ˌɪn ˈvɪʒ(ə)n/ *adjective* referring to subjects that are on camera, within the shot

iPod /ˈaɪpɒd/ a trade name for a portable electronic device onto which users can download music, radio programmes etc from their home computer

IPPV *abbreviation* **Impulse Pay-Per-View**

ips /ˌaɪ piː ˈes/ *noun* inches per second – a measurement of the speed of magnetic tape running over a head

IP terminal /ˌaɪ ˈpiː ˌtɜːmɪn(ə)l/ *noun* a special visual display unit that allows users to create and edit videotext pages before sending them to the main videotext page database

IR /ˌaɪ ˈɑː/ noun Independent Radio – in the UK, all non-BBC stations

IRC abbreviation **Internet Relay Chat**

iris diaphragm /ˈaɪrɪs ˈdaɪəfræm/, **iris** /ˈaɪrɪs/ noun a diaphragm consisting of thin overlapping plates that control the size of a hole, especially one controlling the amount of light allowed to enter a camera lens

iris in /ˌaɪrɪs ˈɪn/ verb to open up the iris diaphragm of a camera gradually in order to take in more of a subject or scene

iris out /ˌaɪrɪs ˈaʊt/ verb to close the iris diaphragm of a camera gradually in order to shrink the picture area until it disappears completely. Irising out was formerly a common way to end a film or sequence.

irony /ˈaɪrəni/ noun **1.** humour based on using words to suggest the opposite of their literal meaning **2.** something said or written that uses humour based on words suggesting the opposite of their literal meaning **3.** incongruity between what actually happens and what might be expected to happen, especially when this disparity seems absurd or laughable

ISDN abbreviation **Integrated Services Digital Network**

island position /ˈaɪlənd pəˌzɪʃ(ə)n/ noun advertising space separated from other advertising space in a newspaper or magazine

iso /ˈaɪsəʊ/ noun an 'isolated' television camera, the output from which is recorded separately to those of other cameras on the shoot

iSociety /ˌaɪsəˈsaɪəti/ noun the lifestyle choices characteristic of the late 1990s, with greater gender equality and less of a competitive focus

'"I became disenchanted with the corporate culture", says the 44-year-old. "It did not offer me the personal rewards or camaraderie I wanted". A quintessential member of the iSociety, he eschewed financial reward, tore up traditional family roles and risked his career setting up his own firm.' [The Observer]

isolation booth /ˌaɪsəˈleɪʃ(ə)n buːð/ noun in a recording studio, a small soundproof booth in which individual instruments, vocals etc can be recorded for mixing later

ISO rating /ˌaɪ es ˈəʊ ˌreɪtɪŋ/ noun a measure of film speed, where a doubling of the number represents twice as much sensitivity to light

ISP abbreviation **Internet service provider**

issue /ˈɪʃuː/ noun a copy of a regularly published magazine or newspaper that was put out on a particular date ∎ verb to produce and distribute a product such as a book, magazine or newspaper

issues /ˈɪʃuːz/ noun those ideas that are the source of controversy and debate in a society at any given time

'He described his new National Responsibility Party, which he hopes to steer to victory in next spring's election, as a "national liberal movement"… After decades of violence and two intifadas when security issues dominated most elections, the issue of poverty is likely to play a leading role this time round.' [Tim Butcher, The Daily Telegraph]

ITA abbreviation **Independent Television Authority**

ital. abbreviation PUBLISHING **italics**

italic /ɪˈtælɪk/ noun a style of printed letter that slopes to the right ∎ adjective referring to printed text using letters that slope to the right. Italic letters are often used to show emphasis in text. Abbreviation **ital.**

italicise /ɪˈtælɪsaɪz/ verb to print text in italics

Itar Tass /ˌɪtɑː ˈtæs/ noun a Russian news agency that replaced Tass, the news agency of the former Soviet Union, in 1992

ITC abbreviation **Independent Television Commission**

ITC Programme Code /ˌaɪ tiː siː ˈprəʊɡræm ˌkəʊd/ noun the code of broadcasting practice in the UK which rules that material not suitable for children must be shown after the watershed, that offensive (for example racist) jokes are subject to regulation, and other considerations about suitability of content

item /ˈaɪtəm/ noun a piece of reported news, for example in a newspaper or on television

ITU abbreviation TELECOMS **International Telecommunication Union**

iTV abbreviation **interactive television**

ITV *abbreviation* **Independent Television**

ITVA *abbreviation* **Independent Television Association**

IV /ˌaɪ ˈviː/ *noun* a system that uses a computer linked to a video disk player to provide processing power and real images or moving pictures

J

jack /dʒæk/ *noun* a female socket designed to receive a jack plug in order to complete a circuit

jack plug /'dʒæk plʌg/ *noun* a plug with a single pin, often used to connect items of audio equipment

jam /dʒæm/ *noun* **1.** a device for preventing a pre-recorded videotape from being copied **2.** a situation where radio or television signals are blocked ■ *verb* **1.** to prevent the reception of a radio or television signal by broadcasting other signals on the same frequency **2.** to adjust or adapt something such as a pre-recorded videotape, to prevent it from being copied

JANET /'dʒænɪt/ *noun* a computer network that is government-funded and used by academics and researchers, linking all British institutions of higher and further education to each other and to the Internet

jargon /'dʒɑːgən/ *noun* terms that are only used in one specialist area such as a profession, and are not widely understood outside that

'…business communication really does have too much jargon and obfuscation. Such vocabulary betrays a lack of clarity and lazy thinking. What do the following actually mean: "granular"; "traction"; "thoughtware"; "matrix"; "paradigm"; "disintermediate"?' [Luke Johnson, *The Daily Telegraph*]

jazz /dʒæz/ *noun* popular music that originated among black people in New Orleans in the late 19th century and is characterized by syncopated rhythms and improvisation

J-curve /'dʒeɪ kɜːv/ *noun* the correlation between the number of people who have heard about an event and the number that heard about it from non-media sources

jib /dʒɪb/ *noun* a swinging arm on a camera mounting, allowing the camera to move freely

JICNARS /'dʒɪknɑːz/ *abbreviation* **Joint Industrial Committee for National Readerships Surveys**

JICNARS scale /'dʒɪknɑːz ˌskeɪl/ *noun* one of six social groups into which consumers are divided for advertising purposes

COMMENT: The group categories are A – high managerial leaders, B – middle management, C1 – lower management and administrative workers, C2 – skilled manual workers, D – unskilled manual workers, and E – low waged or unwaged.

JICREG /'dʒɪkreg/ *abbreviation* **Joint Industry Committee of Regional Newspapers**

jihad /dʒɪ'hæd/ *noun* the idea of a culture which is homogenous, dominated by big corporations

Jim Henson Pictures /ˌdʒɪm ˌhens(ə)n 'pɪktʃəz/ *noun* a film production studio best-known for its Muppets feature films

jimmy-jib /'dʒɪmi dʒɪb/ *noun* a type of hoist which allows for smooth movement of a remote-controlled camera

jingle /'dʒɪŋg(ə)l/ *noun* a short musical piece identifying a station or presenter

jingoism /'dʒɪŋgəʊɪz(ə)m/ *noun* extreme national pride

jive /dʒaɪv/ *noun* jazz or swing dance music, especially that of the 1940s

JNRS *abbreviation* **Joint National Readership Survey**

jock /dʒɒk/ *noun* RADIO same as **DJ**

jog/shuttle /ˌdʒɒg 'ʃʌt(ə)l/, **jog/shuttle control** /ˌdʒɒg 'ʃʌt(ə)l kən

ˌtrəʊl/ *noun* a manual control on a video player or camera that allows a user to edit a sequence

Joint Industrial Committee for National Readerships Surveys /ˌdʒɔɪnt ɪnˌdʌstriəl kəˌmɪti fə ˌnæʃ(ə)nəl ˈriːdəʃɪps ˌsɜːveɪz/ *noun* previously, the body that carried out readership surveys in the UK, replaced in 1992 by the National Readership Survey. Abbreviation **JICNARS**

Joint Industry Committee of Regional Newspapers /ˌdʒɔɪnt ˌɪndəstri kəˌmɪti əv ˌriːdʒ(ə)nəl ˈnjuːzpeɪpəz/ *noun* a non-commercial organisation that provides readership statistics for regional newspapers in the UK. Abbreviation **JICREG**

Joint National Readership Survey /ˌdʒɔɪnt ˌnæʃ(ə)nəl ˈriːdəʃɪp ˌsɜːveɪ/ *noun* a commercial organisation that provides readership statistics for several major publications in the Republic of Ireland, using random probability testing. Abbreviation **JNRS**

jouissance /ˈʒuːɪsɒns/ *noun* in feminist theory, an extreme instance of intense joy, bliss or jubilation

journal /ˈdʒɜːn(ə)l/ *noun* a magazine or periodical that deals with an area of special interest or is produced by a professional body for its members, containing articles and papers relevant to their area of activity

journalese /ˌdʒɜːnəˈliːz/ *noun* the particular type of language used by journalists

journalism /ˈdʒɜːn(ə)lɪz(ə)m/ *noun* the act of reporting, writing or editing for a newspaper or magazine or for television or radio

journalist /ˈdʒɜːn(ə)lɪst/ *noun* a person whose job is to write for a newspaper or magazine or to prepare news for television or radio broadcasting

journalistic /ˌdʒɜːnəˈlɪstɪk/ *adjective* relating to journalism or resembling the style of journalism

journalistic standards /ˌdʒɜːnəlɪstɪk ˈstændədz/ *plural noun* the code of ethics which a journalist should observe, such as objectivity, honesty, accuracy and fairness

'..."there's no question that PR standards have risen, while arguably a lot of journalistic standards have declined", she says. She is not trying to "bash journalism", but adds: "I think that the economics of it, principally the rush to publish before facts can be checked or context can be gained, has impacted on accuracy".' [Vincent Graff, *The Guardian*]

journo /ˈdʒɜːnəʊ/ *noun* same as **journalist** (*informal*)

joypad /ˈdʒɔɪpæd/ *noun* same as **gamepad**

joystick /ˈdʒɔɪstɪk/ *noun* a hand-held game controller usually consisting of an upright stick which pivots on its base to control directions and additional buttons to control other actions

.jpeg *noun* a computer format for images, that compresses data with some loss of quality in the image

Juliet /ˌdʒuːliˈet/ *noun* an internationally recognised code word for the letter J, used in radio communications

jump cut /ˈdʒʌmp kʌt/ *noun* a cut from one shot in a film to another very similar frame within the same piece of footage, without the camera having changed position. It gives the impression that the subject has 'jumped' within the shot.

jumpstation /ˈdʒʌmpˌsteɪʃ(ə)n/ *noun* a website that simply provides links to other websites

junction /ˈdʒʌŋkʃən/ *noun* the point at which a radio or television programme or item has to end in order for the next to start on time

jungle /ˈdʒʌŋɡəl/ *noun* a rhythmically complex form of electronic dance music also known as 'drum and bass' that is largely instrumental with heavy beats and bass lines and shows the influence of jazz and techno

junk mail /ˈdʒʌŋk meɪl/ *noun* unsolicited advertising and promotional material that arrives through the post

justification /ˌdʒʌstɪfɪˈkeɪʃ(ə)n/ *noun* the adjustment of the spaces between words in text in order to make each line the same width

justified /ˈdʒʌstɪfaɪd/ *adjective* referring to printed text that has both left and right margins aligned

justify /ˈdʒʌstɪfaɪ/ *verb* to set text so that it begins and ends at a given point on the page

K

karaoke /ˌkæri'əʊki/ *noun* a form of entertainment in which amateur singers sing popular songs accompanied by prerecorded music from a machine that may also display the words on a video screen

Kelvin scale /'kelvɪn skeɪl/ *noun* the scale used in measuring colour temperature

Kepplinger and Habermeier's model of media events 1995 /ˌkeplɪŋgə ənd 'hɑːbəmeɪə/ *noun* a model predicting that coverage of a particular news event will increase interest in similar events

kern /kɜːn/, **kerne** *noun* the part of a printed character that extends beyond its body ■ *verb* **1.** to join or overlap printed characters **2.** to close or reduce the white space between printed letters

kerning /'kɜːnɪŋ/ *noun* the adjustment of the space between individual printed characters to improve the appearance of the text or alter its fit

kestrel /'kestrəl/ *noun* a large camera mounting with a jib arm on which the camera operator can sit

key /kiː/ *noun* the strength of tone of an image, especially with regard to its colour intensity ■ *verb* to mark symbols on the layout of artwork, or anything to be reproduced, to show the correct locations of its different parts

key account /'kiː əˌkaʊnt/ *noun* an important account or client, for example of an advertising agency

keyboarder /'kiːbɔːdə/ *noun* a person whose job is to input data using a computer keyboard or typesetting machine

keyed advertisement /ˌkiːd əd'vɜːtɪsmənt/ *noun* an advertisement that asks people to write to a specially coded address which will indicate where they saw it, thus helping the advertisers to evaluate the effectiveness of advertising in that particular newspaper or magazine

key frame /ˌkiː 'freɪm/ *noun* a frame that is recorded in full rather than being compressed or otherwise reduced in size to save storage space

key grip /ˌkiː 'grɪp/ *noun* the member of a television or film production team who is responsible for moving set equipment, especially cameras

key light /'kiː laɪt/ *noun* **1.** the main light source on a film set, used in conjunction with the fill light and the backlight to form a complete lighting set-up **2.** the main light source for a particular filmed scene or shot

key out /ˌkiː 'aʊt/ *verb* to select a particular colour or colour range in an image or piece of footage and digitally overlay it with some other colour or image. ◊ **chromakey**

keyword /'kiːwɜːd/ *noun* a term which is placed in the metadata of a webpage to attract search engines

kidult /'kɪdʌlt/ *noun* an adult who enjoys entertainment such as films or computer games intended mainly for children

kidvid /'kɪdvɪd/ *noun* a video aimed at children

kill /kɪl/ *verb* to decide not to use a story or feature that is already being written or has been written

killer application /'kɪlə ˌæplɪ'keɪʃ(ə)n/, **killer app** *noun* a piece of software that is so useful that a person will invest in the relevant hardware, operating system etc., just to use it

'More worryingly, [Microsoft] has missed the boat in search technology, the killer application on the internet that has catapulted Google into a position where senior Microsoft staff are left spluttering pathetically about their upstart competitor.' [*The Daily Telegraph*]

kill fee /'kɪl fiː/ *noun* money that is paid to a writer, photographer, artist or illustrator when a publisher decides not to publish the contracted work

kill off /ˌkɪl 'ɒf/ *verb* to end the fictional life of a serial or soap opera character by writing their death into the script

Kilo /'kiːləʊ/ *noun* an internationally recognised code word for the letter K, used in radio communications

kilowatt /'kɪləwɒt/ *noun* one thousand watts. Abbreviation **kW**

kinescope /'kɪnɪskəʊp/ *noun* **1.** a film of a television broadcast **2.** a television tube ■ *verb* TV to make a film of a television broadcast

kinesics /kɪ'niːsɪks/ *noun* the study of the way people communicate though movements of the body and gestures

kinetheodolite /ˌkɪnɪθi'ɒdəlaɪt/ *noun* an optical instrument use for tracking missiles or satellites, that contains a cine camera that follows the moving target while recording its altitude and trajectory

kinetoscope /kaɪ'netəskəʊp/ *noun* an early method of film projection, involving a wooden cabinet with a passing roll of film that could be viewed through a slit

Kinoflo /'kaɪnəʊfləʊ/ a trade name for a type of fluorescent light used on film shoots

kiosk /'kiːɒsk/ *noun* **1.** a small permanent or temporary structure in the street that sells items such as newspapers, travel and entertainment tickets and sweets **2.** the site of a phone or Internet access point that is used by the public

Kirlian photography /ˌkɪrliən fə'tɒgrəfi/ *noun* a photographic process that records the radiation emitted by, or the aura surrounding, an object to which an electric charge has been applied

KISS /kɪs/ *noun* the need to make sure your advertising is clear and concise so as to improve its chances of getting a response. Full form **keep it short and simple**

kiss and tell /ˌkɪs ən 'tel/ *noun* a record, often published in the tabloid press, of a person's past sexual experience, especially with a celebrity

kiss-and-tell /ˌkɪs ən 'tel/ *adjective* referring to revelations about an earlier sexual experience with somebody else

kitchen sink drama /ˌkɪtʃɪn 'sɪŋk ˌdrɑːmə/ *noun* a genre of film that became popular in the late 1950s and throughout the 1960s, focusing on the gritty reality of working-class life

kitsch /kɪtʃ/ *adjective* of poor taste, but used or displayed intentionally to imply a light-hearted lack of regard for considerations of high art, good taste etc.

klieg light /'kliːg laɪt/ *noun* an intense carbon-arc light formerly used in film-making

knock down /ˌnɒk 'daʊn/ *verb* to write a story challenging another story, usually one featured in a rival newspaper, and disproving its claims

knocking copy /'nɒkɪŋ ˌkɒpi/ *noun* advertising material aimed at showing the inferiority of a competing product

knowns and unknowns /ˌnəʊnz ənd 'ʌnnəʊnz/ *noun* the theory that people and things that are already famous are more likely to be given attention and coverage than those which are not

Kuleshov effect /'kuːləʃɒv ɪˌfekt/ *noun* the theory that a single shot or piece of film can be given a different significance when shown next to another

kuuki /'kuːki/ *noun* an environment in which agreement with social norms of opinion is more important than nurturing independence of thought

COMMENT: The word **kuuki** comes from the Japanese meaning 'mood' or 'atmosphere', referring to the idea of values, perceptions etc existing 'in the air around us', rather than in individual minds.

kW *abbreviation* **kilowatt**

kwaito /'kwaɪtəʊ/ *noun* a South African style of house music combining African samples and male vocals, usually shouted or chanted in African languages, English or a mixture, although more recently, artists are rapping rather than shouting their lyrics

kwela /'kweɪlə/ *noun* a style of South African street music with influences from jazz and originally played on the penny whistle

L

L/A *abbreviation* **low-angle**

label /'leɪb(ə)l/ *noun* **1.** a simple headline giving straight details of what a story contains, for example 'interview with…' **2.** a stereotype that is applied to a person, often offensively

label libel /'leɪb(ə)l ˌlaɪb(ə)l/ *noun* the idea that creating stereotypes with which to 'label' people can attach unwanted values, ideas etc. to them, which could be viewed as a form of libel

laboratories /lə'bɒrət(ə)riz/ *plural noun* the place in which film is developed and printed

laboratory test /lə'bɒrət(ə)ri test/ *noun* a test carried out under controlled conditions, for example of the reactions of consumers to advertising

LAD *abbreviation* **language acquisition device**

laddette /læ'det/ *noun* a young woman with a lifestyle that is more characteristic of that of some young men, usually involving heavy drinking and boisterous behaviour

lad mag /'læd mæg/ *noun* a magazine aimed at young men who are chiefly interested in sport, alcohol and sex

'What a difference a decade makes. The rise of lad mags and the post-irony, have-your-cake-and-eat-it anti-PC backlash have restored the swimsuit, evening gown, and perma-smile [Miss World] parade to something like centre stage.' [Stuart Husband, *The Independent on Sunday*]

LAN /læn/ *abbreviation* **local area network**

land-based /'lænd beɪst/ *adjective* referring to a business that exists in a physical location rather than as a website

landing page /'lændɪŋ peɪdʒ/ *noun* the page on a website where the user arrives, in particular the page arrived at when directed by a hyperlink

landline /'læn(d)ˌlaɪn/ *noun* a cable for carrying high-quality signals, especially before IDSN

landscape /'lændskeɪp/ *adjective* referring to the orientation of a piece of paper whose long sides are at the top and bottom of the page

language acquisition device /ˌlæŋgwɪdʒ ˌækwɪ'zɪʃ(ə)n dɪˌvaɪs/ *noun* the linguistic theory that parts of our brain are specifically hard-wired to receive and construct languages, a skill which is particularly sharp before the age of 5. Abbreviation **LAD**

language laboratory /'læŋgwɪdʒ lə ˌbɒrət(ə)ri/ *noun* a room equipped with audio recording and playback equipment for use by students learning languages

language pollution /'læŋgwɪdʒ pə ˌluːʃ(ə)n/ *noun* the use of language to confuse or mislead, such as to tell a lie

lantern slide /'læntən slaɪd/ *noun* a piece of transparent glass or plastic with an image on it that can be projected onto a screen by a slide projector or magic lantern

large-print /'lɑːdʒ prɪnt/ *adjective* referring to type that is bigger than normal so that partially-sighted readers can see it easily

Lasswell's model of communication 1948 /'læswel/ *noun* a model of lines of enquiry which can be followed when analysing a piece of communication, namely to look at who is speaking and to whom, through which channels they are speaking, what is said and what effect it has

latency /'leɪt(ə)nsi/ *noun* **1.** the state or condition of being latent **2.** the amount of time it takes data to move across an Internet connection

latent /'leɪt(ə)nt/ *noun* of thoughts, feelings or desires, present or existing but in an underdeveloped or unexpressed form ■ *adjective* of thoughts, feelings or desires, dormant or undeveloped but able to develop normally under suitable conditions

latent image /ˌleɪt(ə)nt 'ɪmɪdʒ/ *noun* the image that is recorded on light-sensitive materials such as photographic film or paper but that cannot be seen until it is developed

latitude /'lætɪtjuːd/ *noun* **1.** the degree of flexibility regarding how much light photographic paper can be exposed to while still providing an acceptable image **2.** the idea of three strata into which a new idea suggested to a person falls – that of acceptance (where it is close to the ideas that they already hold), non-commitment (where they are concerned either way) and rejection (where the new idea is too far removed from what is already thought)

laugh track /'lɑːf træk/ *noun* a recording of laughter that is added to a comedy programme in appropriate places

launch /lɔːntʃ/ *verb* to put a new product on the market, usually spending money on advertising it ■ *noun* an occasion such as a party at which a product is launched

lavaliere microphone /lə,væli'eə ˌmaɪkrəfəʊn/ *noun* a small microphone that is worn on a cord around a speaker's neck

law of primacy /ˌlɔː əv 'praɪməsi/ *noun* the theory that the argument that is presented first to an audience will stand a better chance of persuading them than subsequent ones

layback /'leɪbæk/ *noun* the process of laying together a finished audio track with the filmed sequence it accompanies

layer /'leɪə/ *noun* an audio track that can be played 'on top of' another, such as a spoken piece played over background music, to create a complete soundtrack ■ *verb* to put together different audio tracks to create a complete soundtrack

layout /'leɪaʊt/ *noun* the way in which the page is designed showing the position of text, graphics and photographs

lc, l.c. *abbreviation* PRINTING **lowercase**

LCD *abbreviation* **liquid crystal display**

ld *abbreviation* PRINTING **lead**

lead /led/ *noun* **1.** the main story on the front page of a newspaper. Abbreviation **ld 2.** the first and most important piece of news in a bulletin **3.** an electrical cable connecting pieces of equipment

leader /'liːdə/ *noun* **1.** same as **editorial 2.** coloured, non-recordable tape used on reel-to-reel tape to indicate the beginning (green) and end (red) of a piece of audio

leadership /'liːdəʃɪp/ *noun* the fact of being a leader, or the guidance provided by a leader to a group

lead-in /'liːd ɪn/ *noun* **1.** an introduction before an item on television or a topic for discussion **2.** a cable connecting an aerial with a transmitter or receiver

leading /'liːdɪŋ/ *noun* the blank spaces separating lines of text, originally created using strips of lead to separate the lines

leading article /ˌliːdɪŋ 'ɑːtɪk(ə)l/ *noun* PRESS same as **editorial**

lead out /ˌliːd 'aʊt/ *verb* to increase the amount of white space between lines of type in order to make the article fit the space allocated to it

leaflet /'liːflət/ *noun* a sheet of printed paper that is given out as part of an advertising or information campaign ■ *verb* to distribute leaflets in a particular place or to a particular group of people

leaf through /ˌliːf 'θruː/ *verb* to turn the pages of a book or magazine without reading much

leak /liːk/ *noun* an occasion when confidential information is given to the media, or the information itself ■ *verb* to give confidential information to the media unofficially, or become known unofficially

'Matters deteriorated further when she found Caithness's heir, Alexander, Lord Berridale, had a CD of their wedding photos. A friend said: "She was concerned he would leak them to the Press, which of course he would never do".'

[Louisa Pritchard, *The Mail on Sunday*]

leakage /'liːkɪdʒ/ *noun* the way in which confidential information reaches the media through unofficial channels

leakproof /'liːkpruːf/ *adjective* referring to a system of confidentiality that is guaranteed to work

leaky /'liːki/ *adjective* prone to allowing breaches in secrecy or confidentiality

LED *abbreviation* **light emitting diode**

legal /'liːg(ə)l/ *verb* to send a story to a lawyer to check that it is safe to publish it

legend /'ledʒənd/ *noun* **1.** a story that has been passed down for generations, especially one that is presented as history but is unlikely to be true **2.** a popular myth that has arisen in modern times **3.** somebody famous admired for a particular skill or talent **4.** an inscription, such as a title or motto, on an object

legitimation /lɪˌdʒɪtɪ'meɪʃ(ə)n/ *noun* the process by which certain values, ideas, beliefs etc. are introduced, preferred and considered to be 'mainstream' by the society in which they are found. Compare **delegitimation**

legman /'legmən/ *noun* a reporter who researches a story, especially from firsthand sources

legs /legz/ *plural noun* the ability of an advertising campaign, a film, a book or other usually short-lived product to interest people for a much longer time than normal ◼ *noun* an informal term for tripod

lemma /'lemə/ *noun* a heading that indicates the topic of a work or passage

lens /lenz/ *noun* a curved piece of glass or plastic that bends (refracts) light when filming or taking a photograph. Different types of curve produce different focal lengths, fields of view and distortion effects. ◊ **fisheye lens**, **telephoto lens**, **prime lens**, **zoom lens**

letter /'letə/ *noun* a style of typeface

letterbox /'letəbɒks/ *noun* **1.** a film format for television that shows a wider and shorter picture than usual to allow the complete frame of cinema films to be shown on television **2.** the appearance of a 4:3 screen on which a 16:9 picture is being shown, with black bars at the top and bottom

letterform /'letəfɔːm/ *noun* the shape of a letter of the alphabet

letterhead /'letəhed/ *noun* a printed heading for paper that a company uses for official letters and documents

lettering /'letərɪŋ/ *noun* writing that is printed, inscribed or painted on something

letterpress /'letəpres/ *noun* **1.** material that is printed using the letterpress technique **2.** a printing technique that works by covering raised type with ink and pressing it onto a surface such as paper

level /'lev(ə)l/ *noun* the volume of a speaker's voice or audio piece, recorded by a meter

lexis /'leksɪs/ *noun* the words that make up a language or the language of a particular person

lf *abbreviation* PRINTING **lightface**

libel /'laɪb(ə)l/ *noun* writing or recording in some permanent form, things that are not true about another person. Compare **slander**

library music /'laɪbrəri ˌmjuːzɪk/ *noun* music used in films or television shows, not recorded for the specific show but available from a specialist library for a fee

licence fee /'laɪs(ə)ns fiː/ *noun* the annual fee that must be paid by each household with a television set in return for BBC programming. A colour licence costs over £120 per year (the price being set by the government), a black-and-white set around £45. There is no fee for radio services.

life /laɪf/ *noun* an account of somebody's life, usually in writing

'life in the day' feature /ˌlaɪf ɪn ðə 'deɪ ˌfiːtʃə/ *noun* a feature that describes a typical day in the life of a subject. Compare **'day in the life' feature**

lifestyle /'laɪfstaɪl/ *noun* a way of classifying and grouping an audience according to the way in which they live, their possessions, living arrangements, beliefs etc.

lift /lɪft/ *verb* to re-use material from your own or another publication, changing very little

ligature /'lɪgətʃə/ *noun* a character that consists of two or more letters joined together, for example 'æ'

light emitting diode /ˌlaɪt ɪˌmɪtɪŋ 'daɪəʊd/ *noun* a series of blinking lights that indicates for example volume. Abbreviation **LED**

lightface /'laɪtfeɪs/ *adjective* referring to printed characters with relatively narrow lines. Abbreviation **lf**

lighting /'laɪtɪŋ/ *noun* **1.** the equipment used for lighting a theatre stage or a television or film set **2.** the overall effect produced by the lights used on a theatre stage or a television or film set

lighting cameraman /'laɪtɪŋ ˌkæm(ə)rəmæn/ *noun* a member of a film production team who is responsible for lighting and camerawork

lighting plot /'laɪtɪŋ plɒt/ *noun* a plan of where the lighting will be on a film set

light meter /'laɪt ˌmiːtə/ *noun* PHOTOGRAPHY same as **exposure meter**

light-struck /'laɪt strʌk/ *adjective* referring to photographic material that has a foggy appearance because it has been accidentally exposed to light

light viewer /ˌlaɪt 'vjuːə/ *noun* a person who watches very little television

Lightworks /'laɪtwɜːks/ a trade name for a non-linear editing system

Lima /'liːmə/ *noun* an internationally recognised code word for the letter L, used in radio communications

liminality /ˌlɪmɪ'næliti/ *noun* in sociology, a state of moving between social roles, such as between an adult and a child

linage /'laɪnɪdʒ/, **lineage** *noun* the number of lines of copy produced by a freelancer (used to calculate how much they are paid)

line /laɪn/ *noun* **1.** a sentence or short piece of dialogue which an actor has to deliver **2.** one of the horizontal scans that forms the picture on a television screen **3.** a horizontal row of words or numbers

linear perspective /'lɪniə pə ˌspektɪv/ *noun* a form of perspective in which depth and distance is shown in drawings or paintings by showing parallel lines as coming together on the horizon

line cut /'laɪn kʌt/ *noun* a printing plate made from a line drawing

line drawing /'laɪn ˌdrɔːɪŋ/ *noun* a simple black and white drawing or diagram

line in /ˌlaɪn 'ɪn/ *noun* an input connection to audio equipment such as an amplifier that accepts a low voltage audio signal

line noise /'laɪn nɔɪz/ *noun* unwanted interference on a telephone or communi-

cations line that causes errors in a data transmission

line of sight /ˌlaɪn əv 'saɪt/ *noun* a straight path, not passing over the horizon, between a transmitting and receiving aerial. Abbreviation **LOS**

line producer /'laɪn prəˌdjuːsə/ *noun* the member of a film production team who is responsible for the day-to-day practical considerations such as budgeting, technology hire and maintenance and scheduling

liner /'laɪnə/ *noun* RECORDING same as **sleeve**

line rate /'laɪn reɪt/ *noun* the rate charged for advertising space, based on the line space used in a newspaper or magazine

lines /laɪnz/ *noun* the dialogue which an actor has to deliver

lineup /'laɪnʌp/ *noun* the preparation and checking of electrical equipment at a shoot to make sure that it is ready to use

line-up /'laɪn ʌp/ *noun* TV a programming schedule of a television network

linguistic determinism /lɪŋˌgwɪstɪk dɪ'tɜːmɪnɪz(ə)m/ *noun* the theory that a person's language affects how they shape and understand the world

linguistics /lɪŋ'gwɪstɪks/ *noun* the scientific study of language

link /lɪŋk/ *noun* a piece of speech that introduces the next item in television or radio broadcasting ■ *verb* to make a linking piece of speech to the next broadcast item ■ *noun* a satellite dish

linkman /'lɪŋkmæn/ *noun* somebody who introduces the next item on radio or television

linocut /'laɪnəʊkʌt/ *noun* a print made from a design that has been cut into a piece of linoleum or the design itself

lip microphone /'lɪp ˌmaɪkrəfəʊn/ *noun* a microphone designed to be held close to the user's mouth so that background noise does not interfere with the recorded sound

lipstick camera /'lɪpstɪk 'kæm(ə)rə/ *noun* a small cylindrical digital camera that can be mounted on a military helmet, motor vehicle or fighter aircraft and used to make visual records of operations or targets etc.

lip-sync /'lɪp sɪŋk/ *verb* **1.** to make sure that the speech heard fits the mouth movements of the actor on film perfectly **2.** to mouth along to a recorded track as though performing it live

liquid crystal display /ˌlɪkwɪd ˌkrɪst(ə)l dɪsˈpleɪ/ *noun* a thin display screen for a computer or television which uses little power and gives superior picture resolution. Abbreviation **LCD**

listener /ˈlɪs(ə)nə/ *noun* somebody who listens, especially to a radio broadcast

listenership /ˈlɪs(ə)nəʃɪp/ *noun* the number or type of people who listen to a radio broadcast, programme or station

'MacKenzie's great achievement has been in taking a failing talk radio station, deliberately getting rid of its ageing, largely female listenership ("the old bags") and, amid considerable scepticism, turning it into a sports station aimed squarely at young men.' [Raymond Snoddy, *The Independent*]

listen in /ˌlɪs(ə)n ˈɪn/ *verb* **1.** to listen to a radio broadcast **2.** to listen to other people's radio or telephone communications

listening area /ˈlɪs(ə)nɪŋ ˌeəriə/ *noun* the area covered by a radio station's signal

listening share /ˈlɪs(ə)nɪŋ ˌʃeə/ *noun* the share of the total audience enjoyed by a radio station

listings /ˈlɪstɪŋz/ *plural noun* the details of future events such as concerts, plays, special events etc., usually including their venues, times, prices and contact details. Also can refer to cinema and television schedules.

lit. *abbreviation* PRINTING **literal**

literal /ˈlɪt(ə)rəl/ *noun* a printing error that is either a misspelling or the accidental swapping of two letters. Abbreviation **lit.**

literature /ˈlɪt(ə)rətʃə/ *noun* **1.** written works, for example fiction, poetry, drama and criticism, that are recognised as having important or permanent artistic value **2.** the body of written works of a culture, language, people, or period of time, or on a particular subject **3.** the body of musical compositions for a particular instrument or group of instruments **4.** printed material that gives information **5.** the creation of literary work, especially as an art or occupation

lithography /lɪˈθɒɡrəfi/ *noun* a method of printing using a plate of aluminium or

zinc, treated to attract or repel oily ink in the appropriate places

little magazine /ˌlɪt(ə)l ˌmæɡəˈziːn/ *noun* a magazine of literary work by writers who are not yet well known, usually having a limited circulation and a small format

live /laɪv/ *adjective* referring to the broadcasting of an event while it is happening ■ *adverb* so as to be broadcast at exactly the same time as a performance or event happens

live room /ˈlaɪv ruːm/ *noun* in a recording studio, a large room in which a band can play their instruments together and be recorded

live shot /ˈlaɪv ʃɒt/ *noun* a filmed incident that is broadcast live without a presenter at the scene

live voiceover /ˌlaɪv ˈvɔɪsˌəʊvə/ *noun* a voiceover for a pre-recorded piece of video often used in news reporting. Abbreviation **LVO**. Also called **underlay**

Lloyd's List /ˌlɔɪdz ˈlɪst/ *noun* one of the world's oldest international newspapers, first published in the City of London in 1734

load /ləʊd/ *verb* to put a film, plate or tape in a camera, or take one in

lobby /ˈlɒbi/ *noun* **1.** the small group of journalists that report from the House of Commons **2.** a group of supporters and representatives of particular interests who try to influence political policy on a particular issue ■ *verb* to campaign for or against a particular piece of legislation by attempting to influence politicians

lobby practice /ˈlɒbi ˌpræktɪs/ *noun* rules that lobby journalists must observe when reporting

lobster shift /ˈlɒbstə ʃɪft/ *noun* the night shift in a newspaper or other workplace

local advertising /ˌləʊk(ə)l ˈædvətaɪzɪŋ/ *noun* advertising in the area where a company is based

local area network /ˌləʊk(ə)l ˌeəriə ˈnetwɜːk/ *noun* a group of computers using the same communications link-up and server. Abbreviation **LAN**

localisation /ˌɡləʊkəlaɪˈzeɪʃ(ə)n/ *noun* the process of making national or international media products more suitable for a smaller local market

'According to a spokesman, the best-selling items in UK stores this season – skinny jeans, capelets and cashmere jumpers – have all been sourced out of London, rather than out of the US "That's given us confidence that the localisation strategy is working".'
[Harry Wallop, *The Daily Telegraph*]

localised advertising strategy /ˌləʊkəlaɪzd ˈædvətaɪzɪŋ ˌstrætədʒi/ *noun* an advertising campaign aimed at a particular country or area of a market rather than a global campaign

local media /ˌləʊk(ə)l ˈmiːdiə/ *plural noun* newspapers and radio and television stations in a small area of the country

local radio station /ˌləʊk(ə)l ˈreɪdiəʊ ˌsteɪʃ(ə)n/ *noun* a radio station that broadcasts over a small area of the country

location /ləʊˈkeɪʃ(ə)n/ *noun* a place away from a studio where filming takes place

location coordinating /ləʊˈkeɪʃ(ə)n kəʊˌɔːdɪneɪtɪŋ/ *noun* the organisation of things such as transport for crew and equipment, accommodation, catering etc., that are necessary for filming on location

location filming /ləʊˈkeɪʃ(ə)n ˌfɪlmɪŋ/ *noun* filming that takes place away from a studio and without a specially-built set, in a real-life place

location scout /ləʊˈkeɪʃ(ə)n skaʊt/ *noun* a member of a film and television production team who is responsible for finding suitable shooting locations

lock /lɒk/ *verb* to fix metal type in a printing press

locked-off camera /ˌlɒkt ɒf ˈkæm(ə)rə/ *noun* a camera that cannot be moved, whose shot has been fixed for filming

log /lɒg/ *noun* **1.** a recording of all a radio station's output, in case of legal disputes. Also called **programme as broadcast 2.** a note of all pieces of music broadcast so that royalties can be paid

log file /ˈlɒg faɪl/ *noun* a record of how many people have visited a website and how they have navigated through it, what links were followed etc.

'Gavin Hyde-Blake, a computer security expert with Carratu International, a corporate investigations firm, says there are two principal ways companies detect inappropriate web use. They can either examine the temporary files on an individual PC, or they can look at log files stored on a main server.'
[Stephen Overell, *The Financial Times*]

logging /ˈlɒgɪŋ/ *noun* the process of making a official record of each shot taken when filming

Logie /ˈləʊgiː/ *noun* in Australia, a statuette awarded annually for outstanding work or performance in the television industry

logo /ˈləʊgəʊ/ *noun* a design used by an organisation as an emblem by which it can easily be recognised

logocentricism /ˌlɒgəʊ ˈsentrɪsɪz(ə)m/ *noun* in cultural theory, belief in a central meaning, law, cause, reason etc.

logotype /ˈlɒgəʊtaɪp/ *noun* a single piece of type that has different unconnected characters on it

longitudinal timecode /ˌlɒŋgɪtjuːdɪn(ə)l ˈtaɪmkəʊd/ *noun* a method of recording a timecode signal on a linear audio track along a videotape. The disadvantage of this method is that the code is not readable at slow speeds or when the tape has stopped. Abbreviation **LTC**

long persistence phosphor /ˌlɒŋ pəˌsɪstəns ˈfɒsfə/ *noun* a television screen coating that retains the displayed image for a period of time longer than the refresh rate, so reducing flicker effects

long shot /ˈlɒŋ ʃɒt/ *noun* a camera shot that is taken from some distance away from the subject, showing for example the whole of a person's body. Abbreviation **LS**

long take /ˈlɒŋ teɪk/ *noun* a filmed take that lasts for more than 20 seconds

long wave /ˈlɒŋ weɪv/ *noun* the broadcasting or receiving of radio waves of 1,000m or more in length

look and feel /ˌlʊk ən ˈfiːl/ *noun* the appeal of the design, layout and ease of use of a website to potential customers and the way the site fits the image the company is trying to put across

lookism /ˈlʊkɪz(ə)m/ *noun* the idea that good-looking people are unconsciously preferred by most observers and have greater success in life

'…it's not only recruitment and promotion that is affected by lookism. A report last year by the University of

Helsinki showed that overweight women earned up to 30% less than their more slender colleagues.' [Kate Hilpern, *The Guardian*]

loony leftism /ˌluːni 'leftɪz(ə)m/ *noun* a largely journalistic term meaning 'political correctness gone mad', i.e. taking socialist principles to ridiculous extremes

loop /luːp/ *noun* a piece of film, video or music that repeats itself over and over, starting again as soon as it has finished

loose insert /ˌluːs 'ɪnsɜːt/ *noun* a sheet of advertising material slipped between the pages of a publication

Lord Chamberlain /ˌlɔːd 'tʃeɪmbəlɪn/ *noun* the official censor of all plays shown in the UK until 1967

LOS *abbreviation* BROADCAST **line of sight**

lot /lɒt/ *noun* a film studio and the land that belongs to it

loudspeaker /ˌlaʊd'spiːkə/ *noun* a device used to convert electrical energy into sound energy, producing the sound in equipment such as televisions, radios, CD players and public-address systems. Also called **speaker**

low-angle /ˌləʊ 'æŋgəl/ *adjective* referring to a camera shot taken from below the action being filmed. Abbreviation **L/A**

lowercase /ˌləʊə'keɪs/ *adjective* referring to characters that are written or printed in small rather than capital form ■ *noun* the small rather than capital form of letters. Abbreviation **l.c.**, **lc** ■ *verb* to put typescript or written material in lowercase form

low frequency /ˌləʊ 'friːkwənsi/ *noun* a radio frequency ranging from 30 to 300 kilohertz

low-involvement hierarchy /ˌləʊ ɪn 'vɒlvmənt ˌhaɪrɑːki/ *noun* a model of response to advertising where the customer is relatively indifferent to the product or service and only responds to repeated marketing

low-key /ˌləʊ 'kiː/ *adjective* referring to a style of lighting in which deep shadows and contrast are accentuated, creating a dark, dramatic effect. Compare **high-key**

LS *abbreviation* **long shot**

LTC /ˌel tiː 'siː/ *abbreviation* **longitudinal timecode**

luma /'luːmə/ *noun* the black and white parts of an image or video signal, represented by the symbol Y and controlling the brightness of an image. Compare **chroma**

luminance /'luːmɪn(ə)ns/ *noun* the part of a video signal or image that defines the brightness at each point. Compare **chrominance**

LVO *abbreviation* **live voiceover**

M

m, M *symbol* PRINTING em dash

M.A. *noun* a rating indicating that a film is not to be seen by anyone under fifteen unless they are accompanied by an adult

Mac /mæk/ *noun* same as **Apple Macintosh**

MAC /ˌem eɪ ˈsiː/ *noun* a system for transmitting pictures to colour televisions using satellites

macaronic /ˌmækəˈrɒnɪk/ *adjective* referring to verse containing words and phrases from everyday language mixed with Latin, other foreign words and phrases, or everyday words with Latinate endings, usually for comic effect

MacBride Commission /məkˈbraɪd kəˌmɪʃ(ə)n/ *noun* a commission set up by UNESCO in 1978 to investigate the effects of Western technology on developing countries, especially with regard to media and communications

machinery of representation /məˌʃiːnəri əv ˌreprɪzenˈteɪʃ(ə)n/ *noun* a view that the mass media is a machine which processes reality and produces a representation of it

mackle /ˈmæk(ə)l/ *noun* a blurred or double impression caused by the movement of paper or type during the printing process ■ *verb* to cause a printed impression to blur, or appear blurred ▶ also called (all senses) **macule**

Mac OS Z /ˌmæk əʊ es ˈzed/ a trade name for a user-friendly operating system developed by Apple, used in personal computers as a rival to the more widespread Microsoft Windows system. ◊ **Microsoft Windows, Unix**

macro lens /ˈmækrəʊ lenz/ *noun* a lens used for close-up photography that produces a life-size or larger image on film, with a minimum of 1:1 object-to-image ratio

macrophotography /ˌmækrəʊfəˈtɒɡrəfi/ *noun* close-up photography that produces images on the film that are life-size or larger than life

macule /ˈmækjuːl/ *noun* PRINTING same as **mackle**

mag. *abbreviation* PUBLISHING magazine

magalogue /ˈmæɡəlɒɡ/ *noun* a catalogue presented to look like a magazine and used for marketing

magazine /ˌmæɡəˈziːn/ *noun* **1.** a publication issued at regular intervals, usually weekly or monthly, containing articles, stories, photographs, advertisements and other features, with a page size that is usually smaller than that of a newspaper but larger than that of a book **2.** a space or compartment in a camera from which film is loaded without exposing it to light. Abbreviation **mag 3.** a container designed to hold a number of photographic slides and feed them automatically through a projector

magazine programme /ˌmæɡəˈziːn ˈprəʊɡræm/, **magazine** /ˌmæɡəˈziːn/ *noun* a television programme that has lots of entertaining features, reports, music spots etc. linked by a presenter

magic bullet /ˌmædʒɪk ˈbʊlɪt/ *noun* **1.** a quick and easy solution for a difficult problem, or a means of accomplishing the impossible **2.** same as **hypodermic model**

magic realism /ˌmædʒɪk ˈrɪəlɪz(ə)m/ *noun* a style of art or literature that depicts fantastic or mythological subjects in a realistic manner

magnate /ˈmæɡneɪt/ *noun* same as **baron**

magnetic tape /mæg,netɪk 'teɪp/ *noun* a thin strip of material, usually plastic, coated with iron oxide and used to record sounds, images or data

magnification /,mægnɪfɪ'keɪʃ(ə)n/ *noun* a copy of a map, photograph or other image that has been made larger than the original

Magnum /'mægnəm/ *noun* a cooperative of photojournalists with offices in London, New York, Paris and Tokyo, promoting independence and professional quality

maildrop /'meɪldrɒp/ *noun* the practice of sending unsolicited promotional material to potential customers as a way of advertising, or the material that is mailed

mailer /'meɪlə/ *noun* an advertising leaflet sent with a letter

mail form /'meɪl fɔːm/ *noun* a webpage designed to be used as an online order form

mailing /'meɪlɪŋ/ *noun* something sent through the post, especially as part of a mass advertising campaign

mailing list /'meɪlɪŋ lɪst/ *noun* a list, usually computerised, of names and addresses to which advertising material or information can be posted

'The trick, of course, is to add your name now to the online mailing list of every happening venue from the Almeida to the Young Vic, and to become a "friend" at the Tates and the National, buying yourself that one-hour slot on a Tuesday morning.' [Paul Vallely, *The Independent*]

mail shot /'meɪl ʃɒt/ *noun* a single mailing of direct-mail advertising

mainstream /'meɪnstriːm/ *adjective* referring to something that most people approve of. The term is often used in a derogatory way to suggest that a product is not new or imaginative.

mainstreamer /'meɪnstriːmə/ *noun* in advertising audience classifications, a person who wants products that are reliable and from a trusted brand. ◊ **aspirer**, **succeeder**, **reformer**

mainstreaming /'meɪnstriːmɪŋ/ *noun* the process by which the opinions of a group of television viewers from different backgrounds move together after they have watched the same broadcasts for a long time

mainstream media /,meɪnstriːm 'miːdiə/ *noun* same as **mass media**

maintain /meɪn'teɪn/ *verb* to make sure that something such as a website or a piece of software is kept up to date and in good order for the benefit of users

major /'meɪdʒə/ *noun* a media company that is powerful, important or very productive

major selling idea /,meɪdʒə 'selɪŋ aɪ ,diə/ *noun* the central theme in an advertising campaign

majuscule /'mædʒəskjuːl/ *noun* a large letter used in writing or printing, for example a capital letter or any of the large rounded letters (uncial) used in ancient manuscripts

make up /,meɪk 'ʌp/ *verb* to arrange columns of text and illustrations on a page

makeup /'meɪkʌp/ *noun* the arrangement of printed elements on a page

makeup artist /'meɪkʌp ,ɑːtɪst/ *noun* the member of a television and film production team who is responsible for the actors' make-up and hair

male /meɪl/ *adjective* **1.** relating or belonging to men or boys **2.** describes a projecting part such as a bolt or plug that is designed to fit into a hollow part or socket that is the female counterpart

male-as-norm /,meɪl əz 'nɔːm/ *noun* in feminist theory, the idea that female suffixes in language such as 'ess' and 'ette', as well as common uses such as 'man' to mean 'human', strengthen the idea that the male version is the normal one and that the female version is a special category within that, and therefore less important

male gaze /,meɪl 'geɪz/ *noun* in feminist theory, the idea that a man gains power through being able to view a woman without her looking back at him

Maletzke's model of the mass communication process 1963 /mæ 'letskə/ *noun* a complicated model of the factors influencing communication, such as the self-image of the sender and receiver, the organisations and social environments that they are in and other pressures and limitations caused by the medium and content of the message

Malvern screen /'mɔːlvən skriːn/ *noun* a thin, flexible television screen using LCD display, which can be rolled up for storage. Also called **flat-screen technology**

managing editor /ˌmænɪdʒɪŋ ˈedɪtə/ *noun* an editor of books, newspapers or other publications who is responsible for the editorial process, budget and schedules

M and E *abbreviation* **music and effects**

manga /ˈmæŋgə/ *noun* a Japanese style of comic-book fantasy drawing, characterised by over-large eyes and a layout in which the panels run right to left. ◊ **anime**

manifold /ˈmænɪˌfəʊld/ *verb* to make several copies of a book or page

manipulate /məˈnɪpjʊleɪt/ *verb* **1.** to control, influence or present somebody or something in a clever or devious way which distorts the truth **2.** to digitally alter a photograph by moving, adding, removing, shading, colouring etc any part of it

manual data processing /ˌmænjuəl ˈdeɪtə ˌprəʊsesɪŋ/ *noun* the process of sorting information without the help of a computer

manual handling /ˌmænjuəl ˈhændlɪŋ/ *noun* carrying or moving things by hand

manufacture of consent /ˌmænjʊfæktʃər əv kənˈsent/ *noun* the practice of controlling or manipulating the norms, values etc. held by an audience by controlling what they are exposed to in the media. This could be done by a government or other institution in authority.

manuscript /ˈmænjʊskrɪpt/ *noun* an author's text for a book, article or other piece of written work as it is given to a publisher

Marantz /məˈrænts/ *noun* a portable tape recorder

March of Time /ˌmɑːtʃ əv ˈtaɪm/ *noun* a US newsreel programme of the 1930s, which became a radio series and then a film

margin /ˈmɑːdʒɪn/ *noun* **1.** a blank space on the left or right edge, or at the top or bottom, of a written or printed page **2.** a straight line drawn down the left- or right-hand side of a page to separate a narrow section from the main part

marginality /ˌmɑːdʒɪˈnælɪti/ *noun* the feeling of minority groups that they are ignored or considered unimportant by mainstream society

margin of understanding /ˌmɑːdʒɪn əv ˌʌndəˈstændɪŋ/ *noun* the degree to which a message has 'lost something' in being encoded by the transmitter and decoded slightly differently by the receiver

market /ˈmɑːkɪt/ *noun* the number of potential buyers for a particular product

market area /ˈmɑːkɪt ˌeəriə/ *noun* a geographical area that represents a particular market, for example a television viewing area or a sales representative's territory

marketer /ˈmɑːkɪtə/ *noun* a person or company that carries out marketing activities

market forces /ˌmɑːkɪt ˈfɔːsɪz/ *noun* the relationship between supply of and demand for a product which dictates its market price

marketing /ˈmɑːkɪtɪŋ/ *noun* the process of transferring goods from buyer to seller, including advertising, distribution and product placement

marketing budget /ˈmɑːkɪtɪŋ ˌbʌdʒɪt/ *noun* money set aside by an organisation for its marketing activities

marketing communications /ˌmɑːkɪtɪŋ kəˌmjuːnɪˈkeɪʃ(ə)nz/ *plural noun* all methods of communicating used in marketing, for example television, radio and sales literature

marketing department /ˈmɑːkɪtɪŋ dɪˌpɑːtmənt/ *noun* the section of a company dealing with marketing and sales

marketing intelligence /ˈmɑːkɪtɪŋ ɪnˌtelɪdʒəns/ *noun* information about a market that can help a marketing campaign

marketing manager /ˈmɑːkɪtɪŋ ˌmænɪdʒə/ *noun* a person in charge of a marketing department

marketing mix /ˈmɑːkɪtɪŋ mɪks/ *noun* a mixture of marketing techniques such as pricing, packaging and advertising used to promote the sale of a product

'…draws on a database containing more than 75,000 new product marketing plans across 60 countries and more than 200 product categories. It provides database-based perspective for eight key marketing plan metrics covering the full marketing mix, including media,

promotion, and distribution.'
[*Business Wire*]

marketing model /'mɑːkɪtɪŋ ˌmɒd(ə)l/ *noun* an overview of the whole marketing process which can be shown graphically, often using a computer, and used to solve problems

marketing research /ˌmɑːkɪtɪŋ rɪ'sɜːtʃ/ *noun* all research carried out in order to improve marketing, including market research, media research and product research

marketing services /'mɑːkɪtɪŋ ˌsɜːvɪsɪz/ *plural noun* marketing functions other than selling, for example market research and advertising

marketing strategy /'mɑːkɪtɪŋ ˌstrætədʒi/ *noun* a plan for marketing activities

market intelligence /'mɑːkɪt ɪnˌtelɪdʒəns/ *noun* information about a market that can help a marketing campaign

market liberalism /ˌmɑːkɪt 'lɪb(ə)rəlɪz(ə)m/ *noun* an ideology similar to capitalism, in which market forces are allowed to develop without outside interference

market penetration /ˌmɑːkɪt ˌpenɪ'treɪʃ(ə)n/ *noun* the extent to which a product reaches the potential buyers in its market

market potential /ˌmɑːkɪt pə'tenʃəl/ *noun* the sales of a product that should be achieved with the right kind of marketing campaign

market research /ˌmɑːkɪt rɪ'sɜːtʃ/ *noun* investigating the potential consumers for a product and gathering data about their needs, lifestyle, habits etc which can be used for development and marketing purposes

market specialist /ˌmɑːkɪt 'speʃəlɪst/ *noun* a person who concentrates on a few markets, and is an expert on the media industry in these markets

marquee /mɑː'kiː/ *noun* **1.** a very large tent with straight sides that can be rolled up or removed, used for large gatherings such as parties, product launches, sales, and exhibitions **2.** a piece of text that scrolls across a screen horizontally or vertically in a highlighted band

Martindale /'mɑːtɪndeɪl/ *noun* a device the checks the electrical supply from a

socket is safe before any equipment is plugged in

Marxism /'mɑːksˌɪz(ə)m/ *noun* a philosophy that social inequality is caused by those people who are in power (the higher classes) being more represented in terms of their norms, values etc. than the working classes

COMMENT: The theory of Marxism was created by highly-influential philosopher Karl Marx (1818–83), who was concerned with social conflict and class struggle throughout history and the effect it has had on social development. He was particularly concerned with labour and the means of production of goods within a society, thinking it to be one of the major causes of social conflict.

Marxist /'mɑːksɪst/ *adjective* based on the values of Marxism

Marxist mode /'mɑːksɪst məʊd/ *noun* a mode of media analysis which emphasises the role of the media in reinforcing the norms, values etc. of the powerful members of society and presenting these as representative of the general population. Compare **functionalist mode**

Mary Whitehouse /ˌmeəri 'waɪthaʊs/ an important campaigner against falling moral standards in broadcasting. She formed the Clean Up TV Movement (later the National Viewers' and Listeners' Association) in 1963 and contributed to the banning of the film *A Clockwork Orange* on British TV as well as many other acts of censorship.

masala /mə'sɑːlə/ *adjective* referring to typical form of Hindi filmmaking which combines many different genres (action, romance, comedy etc.) in a single film. The term is Hindi for 'spices' or 'flavours'.

'Gurinder Chadha's follow-up to Bend It Like Beckham gives Jane Austen the masala treatment, with Bollywood song-and-dance routines pepping up the action.' [Sukhdev Sandhu, *The Daily Telegraph*]

mash-up /'mæʃ ʌp/ *noun* a song in digital format created by combining parts of different songs, for example the music track of one song and the vocal track of another

mask /mɑːsk/ *noun* a shield, often a sheet of paper, placed over areas of unexposed photographic film to stop light hitting it ■ *verb* to prevent unwanted light from reaching areas of unexposed photographic film, either using hands or a special shield

Maslow's hierarchy of needs /ˌmæzləʊz ˌheɪərɑːki əv 'niːdz/ *noun* the idea that when a person has pressing needs for essentials such as for food, rest, water etc., no other needs matter, and that other needs only begin to matter when these first are satisfied

masquerade /ˌmæskə'reɪd/ *noun* in feminist theory, the idea of a mask of 'womanliness' which women wear to satisfy the typical image of a woman in a male dominated society

mass /mæs/ *adjective* large-scale, involving large numbers (of people, products etc.)

mass communication /ˌmæs kəˌmjuːnɪ'keɪʃ(ə)n/ *noun* communication by means of broadcasting and newspapers, which reaches all or most people in society

massification /ˌmæsɪfɪ'keɪʃ(ə)n/ *noun* the act of taking all people in a group together as a whole, without reference to their individual characteristics or needs

mass manipulative model of media communication /ˌmæs məˌnɪpjʊlətɪv ˌmɒd(ə)l əv ˌmiːdiə kəˌmjuːnɪ'keɪʃ(ə)n/ *noun* a model that states that consumers passively receive communication that is fed to them by an all-powerful media, and that they can be influenced by it. Compare **commercial laissez-faire model of media communication**

mass-market /ˌmæs 'mɑːkɪt/ *adjective* having wide, popular appeal to large numbers of people, often used in a derogatory way to indicate a preference for sales over artistic integrity ■ *verb* to sell something to as many people as possible by advertising and promoting it widely

mass marketing /ˌmæs 'mɑːkɪtɪŋ/ *noun* marketing that aims at reaching large numbers of people

'The Office of Fair Trading is to assemble a new "scambusting" team, dedicated to stamping out the growing number of mass-marketing scams targeting UK consumers. The OFT estimates that Britons lose £1bn a year on various scams, which exploit low-cost marketing techniques to ensnare as

many victims as possible.' [James Daley, *The Independent*]

mass media /ˌmæs 'miːdiə/ *noun* all of the communications media that reach a large audience, especially television, radio and newspapers

mass observation /ˌmæs ˌɒbzə'veɪʃ(ə)n/ *noun* a technique of taking surveys by asking questions of very large groups of people

mast /mɑːst/ *noun* a tall broadcasting aerial

master /ˌmæs prə'djuːs/ *noun* an original copy of something, for example a recording tape from which other copies can be made ■ *verb* to produce a master recording of something ■ *adjective* original, not a copy

master antenna television /ˌmɑːstə ænˌtenə 'telɪvɪʒ(ə)n/ *noun* television signals that are received through an aerial or cable that serves several televisions, such as in a block of flats. Abbreviation **MATV**

master control room /ˌmɑːstə kən 'trəʊl ˌruːm/ *noun* the part of a studio that controls output to the transmitter. Abbreviation **MCR**

mastering /'mɑːstərɪŋ/ *noun* the act of recording data onto a master disk which can be copied from many times without loss of quality

master of ceremonies /ˌmɑːstə əv 'serɪməniːz/ *noun* full form of **MC**

Master of Fine Arts /ˌmɑːstə əv faɪn 'ɑːts/ *noun* a qualification in theatre and drama for people with a first degree, often held by set designers. Abbreviation **MFA**

master shot /'mɑːstə ʃɒt/ *noun* a wide camera shot in which all the action in a film scene is visible

masthead /'mɑːsthed/ *noun* the main headline on a newspaper's front page. Also called **flag**

materialism /mə'tɪəriəlɪz(ə)m/ *noun* in cultural theory, the idea that culture exists purely through its products such as texts, art, media products etc., and is not an independent concept

matinée /'mætɪneɪ/ *noun* a performance of a play, concert or film that is given during the day, especially in the afternoon, often with cheaper seats than the evening performance

matrix /'meɪtrɪks/ *noun* **1.** a metal mould from which type is made in the hot-metal process **2.** a mould made by pressing a raised surface in a substance such as plastic, used in stereotyping or electrotyping **3.** a mould used in the production of gramophone records

matt /mæt/ *noun* a dull finish, for example on paintwork or photographic prints ■ *adjective* referring to a matt finish

matte /mæt/ *noun* **1.** a mask used for covering part of an image so that another image can be put on top of the original **2.** a cover for a camera lens with a cut-out shape such as a key-hole, to give a particular effect when filming **3.** a post-production technique in which objects can be separated from their background, and moved around ■ *adjective* of a photographic print, not made on shiny paper. Compare **gloss**

matte artist /'mæt ˌɑːtɪst/ *noun* the member of a film and television production team who has responsibility for creating background sets and paintings to create a 'real' background image, such as the fantasy scenes in 'The Wizard of Oz' (1939)

matte shot /'mæt ʃɒt/ *noun* in film-making, a visual effect that is achieved by masking part of an image using a matte and replacing it with another image so that it combines with the rest of the original

MATV *abbreviation* TV **master antenna television**

maximal awareness /ˌmæksɪməl ə'weənəs/ *noun* the point at which a consumer is convinced enough by a product's advertising to buy the product

mbaqanga /ˌʊmbɑː'kæŋgə/ *noun* a rhythmic form of South African popular music

MC /ˌem 'siː/ *noun* **1.** someone who makes the opening speech and introduces speakers or performers at a formal event. Full form **master of ceremonies 2.** a performer who acts as the host of a variety show performed in front of an audience. Full form **master of ceremonies 3.** a rapper whose role is to excite a crowd at a party or in a club and involve them in the music ■ *verb* to speak rhythmically and often in rhyme over music

McComb and Shaw's agenda-setting model of media effects

1976 /məˌkuːm ənd 'ʃɔː/ *noun* a model to show the way in which the media present events as important or not, and how this affects the impression that the general public has of how important they are

McDonaldisation /məkˌdɒnəldaɪ'zeɪʃ(ə)n/ *noun* the process by which large corporations are coming to take over more and more sections of society

'In Italy, 42 towns now belong to the Slow Cities Association. To belong, they must limit pollution especially from noise… encourage environmentally-friendly local produce and preserve local cuisine, culture and traditions. In short, they must do everything in their power to combat McDonaldisation and promote the good life.' [Sebastian Cresswell-Turner, *The Daily Mail*]

McGregor Commission Report on the Press 1977 /mə'gregə/ *noun* a report that was largely ignored, recommending that newspapers should be excused from paying interest on loans so that they could modernise their equipment and methods

McGuffin /mə'gʌfɪn/ *noun* in a film, play or book, something that starts or drives the action of the plot but later turns out to be unimportant

MCI /ˌem si: 'aɪ/ *noun* an computer interface that allows any program to control a multimedia device such as a sound card or video clip

McLurg's Law /mə'klɜːgz lɔː/ *noun* the journalistic idea that events have less news value, the further away they are from the place where they are being reported. For example, the theory suggests that a single casualty in one's home country is as newsworthy as 1,000 casualties on the other side of the world

McNelly's model of news flow 1959 /mək'neli/ *noun* a model in which a report of a news event passes through several intermediary stages between the original reporter and publication, and the effect that this has

MCPS *abbreviation* **Mechanical Copyright Protection Society**

McQuail's accountability of media model 1997 /mək'weɪl/ *noun* a model of the responsibilities that the media have and the ways in which they are accountable

McQuail's four stages of audience fragmentation *noun* a model of the way in which the audience for television broadcasts has changed from 100%, totally mainstream to a large number of smaller, specialised groups, due to the greater choice available

MCR *abbreviation* **master control room**

MCU *abbreviation* **medium close-up**

McWorld /məkˈwɜːld/ *noun* the idea of a culture which is a single unit dominated by big corporations

MDK /ˌem diː ˈkeɪ/ *noun* a product developed by Microsoft that allows developers to produce multimedia applications more easily using ready-made routines to control video playback, process images and display text

mean world syndrome /ˌmiːn ˈwɜːld ˌsɪndrəʊm/ *noun* the idea that the media give their audience the impression that crimes such as violent attacks or rape etc. occur more frequently than they really do and that viewers therefore think it is a 'mean world'

measure /ˈmeʒə/ *noun* the width of the type area on a page or in a column

mechanical /mɪˈkænɪk(ə)l/ *noun* copy consisting of type proofs and artwork that is laid out and ready to be photographed or electronically scanned for the purpose of preparing printing plates

Mechanical Copyright Protection Society /mɪˌkænɪk(ə)l ˌkɒpiraɪt prə ˈtekʃ(ə)n səˌsaɪəti/ *noun* the body that arranges rights to use or sample recorded performances. Abbreviation **MCPS**

mechanical data /mɪˌkænɪk(ə)l ˈdeɪtə/ *noun* information relating to the printing of newspapers or magazines, for example format or column width

media /ˈmiːdiə/ *noun* the various means of mass communication considered as a whole, including television, radio, magazines and newspapers, together with the people involved in their production

media analysis /ˈmiːdiə əˌnæləsɪs/ *noun* the act of studying the media, in particular its role in society, how it has evolved, its effect on its audience, trends, its reliability when reporting news etc

media broker /ˈmiːdiə ˌbrəʊkə/ *noun* a business that offers organisations a media-buying service and possibly other services such as media planning

media buyer /ˈmiːdiə ˌbaɪə/ *noun* a person in an advertising agency who places advertisements in the media for their clients

media buying /ˈmiːdiə ˌbaɪɪŋ/ *noun* the process of buying space in a media product, for example a slot in a magazine, radio time etc., in which to place an advertisement

media centre /ˈmiːdiə ˌsentə/ *noun* **1.** the part of an organisation which releases information to journalists and the public, looks after promotions and public image etc **2.** a personal computer which, in addition to its usual functions, also provides access to digital television and radio, displays photographs, plays music etc

media circus /ˌmiːdiə ˈsɜːkəs/ *noun* a situation in which there is so much activity by the news media around an event that the coverage distorts the event's significance

media class /ˈmiːdiə klɑːs/ *noun* a basic type of medium, for example television, radio or the press

media control /ˌmiːdiə kənˈtrəʊl/ *noun* the amount of control that is placed on the media of a country by its government

"'Effective measures must be taken to prevent any invasion by harmful programming", the rules said. The tightening of media controls [in China] goes beyond foreign companies. Over the last year, the space granted to domestic newspapers, magazines and internet websites to report on politically sensitive topics has been noticeably reduced.'
[Mure Dickie, *The Financial Times*]

media coverage /ˈmiːdiə ˌkʌv(ə)rɪdʒ/ *noun* reports about something in the media

mediacy /ˈmiːdiəsi/ *noun* the ability to use and understand media texts, both new and traditional. The word has developed by analogy with 'literacy' and 'numeracy'.

media data form /ˌmiːdiə ˈdeɪtə ˌfɔːm/ *noun* a document giving basic data or information about a publication such as circulation, readership and geographical distribution

media event /ˌmiːdiə ɪˈvent/ *noun* an event that attracts a great deal of attention from the news media, often arranged specifically for that purpose

media images /ˈmiːdiə ˌɪmɪdʒɪz/ *plural noun* the stereotypes, reference points and conventions created by the media

media imperialism /ˌmiːdiə ɪmˈpɪəriəlɪz(ə)m/ *noun* same as **cultural imperialism**

media independent /ˌmiːdiə ˌɪndɪˈpendənt/, **media shop** /ˈmiːdiə ʃɒp/ *noun* a business that offers organisations a media-buying service, but without the creative services usually offered by advertising agencies

media messaging /ˌmiːdiə ˈmesɪdʒɪŋ/ *noun* the sending of images, sound, and text from one mobile phone to another

Media Monitoring Unit /ˌmiːdiə ˈmɒnɪt(ə)rɪŋ ˌjuːnɪt/ *noun* a subscription service for government ministers to keep them up to date with all the latest news developments, 24 hours a day. Abbreviation **MMU**

media objectives /ˌmiːdiə əbˈdʒektɪvz/ *plural noun* aims that an advertiser has in advertising through the media

media option /ˈmiːdiə ˌɒpʃən/ *noun* a single unit of advertising space or time

media organisations /ˈmiːdiə ˌɔːɡənaɪzeɪʃ(ə)nz/ *plural noun* organisations whose aim is to provide information or entertainment to their customers while at the same offering marketers a way of reaching audiences with advertising messages

media owner /ˈmiːdiə ˌəʊnə/ *noun* a person or company that owns a magazine or newspaper or a radio or TV station

media plan /ˈmiːdiə plæn/ *noun* a plan of an advertising campaign that shows which advertisements are to appear where and on which dates

media planner /ˈmiːdiə ˌplænə/ *noun* a person who deals with media planning

media planning /ˈmiːdiə ˌplænɪŋ/ *noun* a strategy concerned with what type of media should be used and how much advertising should be done and when

Media Research Group /ˌmiːdiə rɪˈsɜːtʃ ˌɡruːp/ *noun* a group at the London School of Economics who carried out an investigation into children, culture and the media during 1997–8

media schedule /ˈmiːdiə ˌʃedʒuːl/ *noun* same as **media plan**

media selection /ˈmiːdiə sɪˌlekʃən/ *noun* the process of choosing the right type of media for an advertising campaign

media service /ˈmiːdiə ˌsɜːvɪs/ *noun* an organisation that provides the full range of media functions to its clients

MediaSpan Selector /ˌmiːdiəspæn sɪˈlektə/ *noun* a questionnaire by TNS done every six months to examine the lifestyle and shopping habits of panel members

media species /ˈmiːdiə ˌspiːʃiːz/ *noun* a classification of audiences according to their attitude to advertising. ◊ **acquiescent**, **ambivalent**, **cynic**, **enthusiast**

mediasphere /ˈmiːdiəsfɪə/ *noun* the range of available media, its influence and structure, in relation to the public sphere

media strategy /ˈmiːdiə ˌstrætədʒi/ *noun* action plans for achieving media objectives

mediate /ˈmiːdieɪt/ *verb* to act as a medium that processes and transfers something such as information from one place to another

media text /ˈmiːdiə tekst/ *noun* any product related to media, for example a film, a television programme, a book, a magazine, a newspaper, an advertisement, a CD etc

mediation /ˌmiːdɪˈeɪʃ(ə)n/ *noun* **1.** in cultural theory, the process by which texts and media products are analysed through an intermediary 'structure', for example conventions of genre, form of production **2.** in cultural theory, the idea that texts interpret and hide meaning, and present it in a 'mediated' state, ie. one that is not to be trusted.

mediatisation /ˌmiːdiətaɪˈzeɪʃ(ə)n/ *noun* the process by which political activity and awareness raising has become more focused on media presentation, for example through the use of sound bites

media vehicle /ˈmiːdiə ˌviːɪk(ə)l/ *noun* the specific programme or publication used to carry an advertising message

Mediawatch-uk /ˌmiːdiəˌwɒtʃ juː'keɪ/ *noun* a pressure group (formerly the National Viewers' and Listeners' Association) that campaigns for high moral standards in programming and was formed in 1965 by Mary Whitehouse. In recent years it has also monitored Internet content.

medium /'miːdiəm/ *noun* **1.** a means of mass communication, for example television, radio or newspapers **2.** the physical means of transmitting a message through a channel of communication

medium close-up /ˌmiːdiəm 'kləʊs ˌʌp/ *noun* a camera shot that shows the head, shoulders and upper chest of a person. Abbreviation **MCU**

medium frequency /ˌmiːdiəm 'friːkwənsi/ *noun* a radio frequency lying between 300 and 3,000 kilohertz

medium long shot /ˌmiːdiəm 'lɒŋ ˌʃɒt/ *noun* a camera shot that shows a person from their head to just below the knee. Abbreviation **MLS**

medium shot /'miːdiəm ʃɒt/ *noun* **1.** a camera shot that shows the upper half of a person to about the waist. Abbreviation **MS 2.** a filmed view, midway between long shot and close-up, that shows a standing person from the waist up or the full body of a sitting person

medium wave /'miːdiəm weɪv/ *noun* a radio wave with a wavelength that lies between 100 and 1,000m

megaplex /'megəpleks/ *noun* a large cinema complex with at least fifteen screens, often with the same film playing at the same time in three or four of the theatres

melodrama /'melaʊdrɑːmə/ *noun* drama with exaggerated acting, extreme emotions and often comic overreaction

'The two hour-plus epic stars a Mexico City security guard in crisis, includes long, 360-degree pans of the megalopolis and unprecedented eroticism. Some critics herald the work as refreshingly original, breaking from the melodrama that has been a traditional staple of Latin American work.' [Monica Campbell, *The Times*]

Memory Stick /'mem(ə)ri stɪk/ a trade name for a small flash drive that can store data for use in portable electronic devices such as hand-held computers, digital cameras and mobile phones

merchandise /'mɜːtʃəndaɪz/ *noun* goods bought and sold for profit ■ *verb* to sell goods in a variety of ways, such as display, advertising or sending samples

merchandising /'mɜːtʃ(ə)n,daɪzɪŋ/ *noun* the creation of branded non-media products such as toys, food, posters etc., which take advantage of the success of something such as a popular film. ◊ **tie-in**

Mersey beat, Mersey sound *noun* pop music of the 1960s that originated in the Merseyside area, especially Liverpool, and was performed by groups such as the Beatles

message /'mesɪdʒ/ *noun* **1.** the informational content of a piece of communication **2.** a lesson, moral, or important idea communicated, for example in a work of art

messageboard /'mesɪdʒbɔːd/ *noun* a page or group of pages on the Internet which allows visitors to read and respond to messages posted by other users, usually on a specific topic

messaging /'mesɪdʒɪŋ/ *noun* sending short instant messages by mobile phone or computer

metadata /'metədeɪtə/ *noun* essential information contained in a document or webpage, for example its publication date, author, keywords, title, and summary, which is used by search engines to find relevant websites when a user requests a search

metafiction /'metəfɪkʃ(ə)n/ *noun* in aesthetic theory, a fictional text that talks about the structures and conventions of fiction writing – essentially talking about itself

metal /'met(ə)l/ *noun* **1.** printer's type made of metal **2.** MUSIC same as **heavy metal**

metalanguage /'metə,læŋgwɪdʒ/ *noun* language that describes language, such as the language of linguistics

metalingual /ˌmetə'lɪŋgwəl/ *adjective* of a message or piece of communication, referring to the language code in which is is transmitted. ◊ **conative**, **emotive**, **phatic**, **poetic**

metamessage /'metə,mesɪdʒ/ *noun* the 'real' message sent by a piece of communication, for example through tone of voice, which may be different or even contradictory to the content

metanarrative /ˈmetəˌnærətɪv/ *noun* in the theories of structuralism and discourse, a narrative that describes or includes other narratives

metaphor /ˈmetəfə/ *noun* the application of a word or phrase to somebody or something that is not meant literally but to make a helpful comparison

metasignals /ˈmetəˌsɪgn(ə)lz/ *plural noun* signals such as body language that show the metamessage in an encounter or piece of communication

meter /ˈmiːtə/ *noun* a device for measuring something such as audio levels

metonymy /meˈtɒnɪmi/ *noun* a figure of speech in which an attribute of something is used to stand for the thing itself, for example 'the press' to stand for 'journalists, newpapers etc'.

Metro-Goldwyn-Meyer /ˌmetrəʊ ˌgɒldwɪn ˈmaɪə/ *noun* a major Hollywood film studio formed in 1924, most notable for its 'golden age' in the 1930s when it produced stars such as Clark Gable and Jean Harlow. Abbreviation **MGM**

metropolitan bias /ˌmetrəpɒlɪt(ə)n ˈbaɪəs/ *noun* the argument that most media industries focus on London in their products because they are based there

MFA *abbreviation* **Master of Fine Arts**

MHP *abbreviation* **multimedia home platform**

mic /maɪk/ *noun* same as **microphone**

micro- /maɪkrəʊ/ *prefix* involving microfilm or microphotography

microcassette /ˈmaɪkrəʊkəˌset/ *noun* a small audiotape cassette designed to fit into a pocket-size tape recorder or dictation machine

microdot /ˈmaɪkrəʊdɒt/ *noun* a tiny photographic reproduction of something, about the size of a dot or a pinhead

microfiche /ˈmaɪkrəʊˌfiːʃ/ *noun* a sheet of microfilm containing information laid out in a grid pattern

microfilm /ˈmaɪkrəʊfɪlm/ *noun* a strip of photographic film on which tiny reproductions have been recorded ■ *verb* to photograph something on microfilm

micropayment /ˈmaɪkrəʊˌpeɪmənt/ *noun* a small charge made to users in return for Internet content, usually per page downloaded, on sites which are not sponsored by advertisers

'…the big newspaper and magazine publishers will quickly realise that the bulk of their readers are switching from paper to e-paper (which they eventually will)… it's a doddle to charge users for downloading a virtual copy – either as a one-off micropayment or as part of a longer term subscription.' [Paul Carr, *The Guardian*]

microphone /ˈmaɪkrəfəʊn/ *noun* a device that converts sounds to electrical signals which can then be amplified, transmitted for broadcasting or recorded

microphotograph /ˈmaɪkrəʊ ˌfəʊtəgrɑːf/ *noun* **1.** a photographic image, for example on microfilm, so small that it has to be magnified in order to be viewed **2.** a photograph of an object viewed through a microscope

microprint /ˈmaɪkrəʊˌprɪnt/ *noun* printed text, for example on microfilm, so small that it has to be magnified in order to be viewed

microprism /ˈmaɪkrəʊˌprɪz(ə)m/ *noun* a small prism that is part of the viewfinder of many single-lens reflex cameras

microreader /ˈmaɪkrəʊˌriːdə/ *noun* a device that projects enlarged images and text from microfilm and microfiche onto a screen for easy reading

Microsoft /ˈmaɪkrəsɒft/ *noun* the world's largest software corporation, based in Washington, USA

Microsoft Office /ˌmaɪkrəsɒft ˈɒfɪs/ a trade name for a software package developed by Microsoft, which allows the user to carry out desktop publishing and produce spreadsheets, presentations and databases

Microsoft Windows /ˌmaɪkrəsɒft ˈwɪndəʊz/ a trade name for the most popular operating system used in personal computers, developed by Microsoft. ◊ **Mac OS Z**, **Unix**

microwave link /ˈmaɪkrəweɪv lɪŋk/ *noun* a type of terrestrial link, different from a satellite link, in which there must be a clear line of sight between the transmitter and the receiver

middle-market /ˌmɪd(ə)l ˈmɑːkɪt/, **mid-market** *adjective* in format and style, somewhere between a broadsheet and a tabloid, for example the Daily Mail

MIDI /ˈmɪdi/ *abbreviation* the interface between an electronic musical instrument and a computer, used in composing and editing music to allow the computer to control an instrument or one instrument to control others. Full form of **Musical Instrument Digital Interface**

MIDI control-change message /ˌmɪdi kənˌtrəʊl ˈtʃeɪndʒ ˌmesɪdʒ/ *noun* a message sent to a synthesiser to control the volume or pitch of a sound or to change the instrument patch used to generate a sound

mike /maɪk/ *noun* same as **microphone** ■ *verb* to supply somebody with, or transmit something through, a microphone

Mike /maɪk/ *noun* an internationally recognised code word for the letter M, used in radio communications

mike cable /ˈmaɪk ˌkeɪb(ə)l/ *noun* the cable connecting a microphone to a speaker or piece of recording equipment

mike rattle /ˈmaɪk ˌræt(ə)l/ *noun* interference caused by moving the mike cable during recording

milline /ˈmɪlaɪn/ *noun* a unit of advertising copy equal to one column line in agate type in one million copies of a newspaper or magazine

milline rate /ˈmɪlaɪn/, **milline** *noun* the cost per unit of advertising copy

Milton's paradox /ˌmɪltənz ˈpærədɒks/ *noun* the idea that theory and practice may not correspond, as illustrated by Milton's work as a censor during Cromwell's reign despite the fact that he claimed to support freedom of the press. ◊ **Areopagitica**

mimetic plane /mɪˈmetɪk pleɪn/ *noun* in semiology, the parts of signs which represent something (their signifiers), as contrasted with the objects or meanings which they represent (their referents). Compare **semiosic plane**

mimic /ˈmɪmɪk/ *noun* somebody who imitates others, especially for comic effect

mimicry /ˈmɪmɪkri/ *noun* the practice of imitating other people's voices, gestures or appearance, often for comic effect

Minicam /ˈmɪnikæm/ a trade name for a portable, shoulder-mounted television camera used in outside broadcasts

MiniDisc /ˈmɪnidɪsk/ a trade name for a data storage facility like a small CD, with a different compression system for audio files

MiniDisk recorder /ˈmɪnidɪsk rɪˌkɔːdə/ *noun* a digital recording machine which uses MiniDiscs

Mini-DV /ˌmɪni diː ˈviː/ a trade name for a videotape format

miniseries /ˈmɪniˌsɪəriːz/ *noun* a short series of television programmes, often a serialised fictional story, usually broadcast on consecutive nights

Minority Report of Mr Selwyn Lloyd /maɪˌnɒrəti rɪˌpɔːt əv ˌmɪstə ˌselwɪn ˈlɔɪd/ *noun* an appendix to the Beveridge Committee Report 1950, which stated that the introduction of greater competition for the BBC would not lead to poorer quality broadcasting

minuscule /ˈmɪnɪskjuːl/ *noun* **1.** a small flowing style of writing used in medieval manuscripts **2.** a letter of the alphabet written in minuscule style **3.** a lower case letter ■ *adjective* in lower case letters

MIPCOM /ˈmɪpkɒm/ *noun* a 'marketplace' which organises conferences and functions for media content providers, so that they can network and reach new markets

MipTV /ˌmɪptiːˈviː/ *noun* the branch of MIPCOM dealing specifically with the television industry

Miramax /ˈmɪrəmæks/ *noun* a major Hollywood studio formed by brothers Bob and Harvey Weinstein in 1979, responsible for hits such as Pulp Fiction (1994), The Talented Mr Ripley (1999) and Sin City (2005)

mirror /ˈmɪrə/ *verb* to maintain an exact copy of a program, data, or website, usually on another file server ■ *noun* same as **mirror site**

mirror-phase /ˈmɪrə feɪz/ *noun* in psychology, the stage at which a child begins to recognise that it is independent from its parents and is a separate being, observed by others

mirror site /ˈmɪrə saɪt/ *noun* a copy of a website maintained on a different file server so as to spread the distribution load or to back up data

'The most that authorities can do is to try to shut down the website. That happened after the video footage of the beheading of Nick Berg, the US hostage, in May. But even with one website shut down,

several "mirror" sites are likely to appear, making it almost impossible to close down the terrorists' method of communicating.'
[Nicholas Rufford and Uzi Mahnaimi, *The Sunday Times*]

mise en abyme /ˌmiːz ɒn æ'biːm/ *noun* in the theories of structuralism and discourse, the technique of 'bottomless' reduplication, as when an image contains a smaller version of itself, which contains an even smaller version, and so on endlessly. Literally 'to put into the abyss'.

mise en scène /ˌmiːz ɒn 'sen/ *noun* **1.** a style of film directing characterised by long scenes, little camera movement and few changes of camera position **2.** the overall 'look' of a filmed scene, including such things as lighting, costume design, period detail etc, and the positioning of actors, scenery and props

misinformed society /ˌmɪsɪnfɔːmd sə'saɪəti/ *noun* a view that increased communications systems do not necessarily lead to better spread of information, because the information is often false or mistaken

misprint /'mɪsprɪnt/ *noun* an error in the printed copy of a text ■ *verb* to print something wrongly

misrecognition /ˌmɪsrekəg'nɪʃ(ə)n/ *noun* in psychoanalysis, the tendency of a person to look for a rational explanation for something that they cannot otherwise explain

mix /mɪks/ *verb* to put together various different audio feeds, for example music and the input from a microphone, or from several microphones

mix down /ˌmɪks 'daʊn/ *verb* to put together parts that have been recorded separately to create a final finished sound recording

mixdown /'mɪksdaʊn/ *noun* **1.** the process of converting a multitrack recording, usually a master tape recorded in a studio, into a stereo recording, usually for public release **2.** a new recording produced by a mixdown

mixed /mɪkst/ *adjective* referring to a feed on which the different audio and video components have been digitally combined to be transmitted as one. Compare **split track**

mixed light /ˌmɪkst 'laɪt/ *noun* different colour temperature light sources on the same film set

mixed media /ˌmɪkst 'miːdiə/ *noun* **1.** the use of different artistic media, for example painting, photography and collage, in a single composition or work **2.** the use of different advertising media together, for example billboards, television and radio

mixer /'mɪksə/ *noun* **1.** an electronic device used to adjust and combine various inputs, for example performed or broadcast sounds, to create a single output **2.** somebody who combines various sound recordings to create the final soundtrack of a film

mixing /'mɪksɪŋ/ *noun* the practice of putting together different pieces of audio, for example interview, music, effects etc., to make a complete piece for broadcasting

mixing desk /'mɪksɪŋ desk/ *noun* a piece of equipment for receiving, checking, adjusting the levels of etc incoming audio feeds and creating a blended audio output

mix minus /ˌmɪks 'maɪnəs/ *noun* same as **clean feed**

MLS *abbreviation* **medium long shot**

MMS /ˌem em 'es/ *noun* a system that allows sounds, images or animations to be included in text messages sent, usually, from mobile phones. Full form **multimedia messaging service**

MMU *abbreviation* **Media Monitoring Unit**

mobile control room /ˌməʊbaɪl kən'trəʊl ˌruːm/ *noun* a truck with production equipment inside, used for coordinating outside broadcasts

mobile phone /ˌməʊbaɪl 'fəʊn/ *noun* a portable telephone that works using a series of locally based cellular radio networks

mobilisation /ˌməʊbɪlaɪ'zeɪ(ə)n/ *noun* the ability of the media to stir up public feeling and encourage its audience or those in authority to take some action

moblogging /'mɒblɒgɪŋ/ *noun* the use of a mobile phone or other hand-held digital device to post text and images to a weblog

modality /məʊ'dælɪti/ *noun* in literary theory, the function of some words or phrases, such as 'might' or 'I suppose' etc. in a statement, that define levels of certainty or agreement

model /'mɒd(ə)l/ *noun* a way of explaining how something works

COMMENT: In media studies, a model is an illustration of the way in which something such as communication works, showing the inputs, outputs and processes and naming the factors which affect the process. It presents an idea or working theory in a clear, visual way.

modem /'məʊdem/ *noun* a device linking a computer to a telephone line so that the Internet can be accessed

mode of address /ˌməʊd əv ə'dres/ *noun* the way that a media product 'speaks' to its audience

modern /'mɒd(ə)n/ *noun* a typeface with heavy vertical strokes and straight serifs

modernisation /ˌmɒdənaɪ'zeɪʃ(ə)n/ *noun* the scientific and technological advances during the period of modernity which led to social, economic and political development, for example improved healthcare, more efficient transport and communications links

modernism /'mɒd(ə)nɪz(ə)m/ *noun* 1. various artistic movements involving a high level of innovation that developed during the 20th century 2. in aesthetic theory, the development in literature and the arts specifically between 1880 and 1940

modernity /mɒ'dɜːnəti/ *noun* in postmodernist theory, the social, economic and political development that took place in the period between the 18th century 'enlightenment' and the post-war period of the 20th century

modify /'mɒdɪfaɪ/ *verb* to make a minor change or alteration to something, or change slightly, especially in order to improve

modulate /'mɒdjʊˌleɪt/ *verb* to change the tone, pitch, or volume of sound, for example of a musical instrument or the human voice

mogul /'məʊg(ə)l/ *noun* same as **baron**

mole /məʊl/ *noun* a journalist's source who is secretly reporting on the activities of an organisation

MOMI /'məʊmi/ *abbreviation* **Museum of the Moving Image**

monitor /'mɒnɪtə/ *noun* 1. a receiving device used to show video or closed-circuit television pictures 2. somebody who listens to and checks broadcasts for a client or employer, for example to learn foreign news or discover secret plans 3. a receiver in a television studio that allows the audience to watch the recorded sections of a show or performers to view parts of the programme ■ *verb* to use an electronic receiver to check the quality of transmitted audio or visual signals

monochromatic /ˌmɒnəʊkrə'mætɪk/ *adjective* painted or printed in a single colour

monochrome /'mɒnəkrəʊm/ *noun* 1. a painting, drawing or print in shades of a single colour 2. the art of painting, drawing or printing in shades of a single colour 3. the condition of being only in black and white 4. the condition of being painted, drawn or printed in shades of a single colour 5. a black-and-white photograph or transparency ■ *adjective* 1. painted or drawn in shades of a single colour 2. using or displaying only shades of one colour or black and white

monochronic time /ˌmɒnəʊkrɒnɪk 'taɪm/ *noun* an image of the perception of time in some cultures in which it is strictly linear and deadlines etc. are taken very seriously. Abbreviation **M-time**. Compare **polychronic time**

monofunctional /ˌmɒnəʊ'fʌŋkʃ(ə)nəl/ *adjective* fulfilling only one function; in the case of the media this is often entertainment

monologue /'mɒnəlɒg/ *noun* 1. a play or film in which only one actor appears and speaks 2. a long passage in a play or film spoken by one actor

monopod /'mɒnəʊpɒd/ *noun* a camera stand like a tripod, but with a single leg. It is less stable but easier to set up.

monopoly /mə'nɒpəli/ *noun* a situation in which one seller holds a large share of the market and effectively controls prices and product supply

Monroe motivated sequence /mən 'rəʊ/ *noun* five steps for creating a persuasive speech which achieves its aim of making the audience take action

COMMENT: The five steps are 1) to capture the attention of the audience, 2) to outline a problem which is relevant to them, 3) to discuss various solutions to this problem, 4) to lead them to your 'preferred' conclusion, and, finally, 5) to encourage them to take some sort of action to achieve your aims.

montage /'mɒntɑːʒ/ *noun* a sequence of images and/or sounds edited together to stimulate a particular emotional or intellectual response

MOO /muː/ *noun* the next generation of MUD, which allows users to create a virtual reality in which they can interact with each other and the environment. Full form **MUD object-oriented**

mood music /'muːd ˌmjuːzɪk/ *noun* same as **library music**

moonlighter /'muːnlaɪtə/ *noun* a person who works as a journalist during the evenings and has another full-time job during the day

moral entrepreneur /ˌmɒrəl ˌɒntrəprəˈnɜː/ *noun* a person who decides to act as a moral watchdog for the media, expressing themselves most usually in letters of complaint but sometimes forming organisations in protest and trying to affect change. ◊ **Mary Whitehouse**

moral panic /ˌmɒrəl ˈpænɪk/ *noun* a sudden increase in public anxiety about the possible effects of media products on consumers for example music that encourages sexism, violent video games, etc.

'With 33% of British teenagers now classified as binge drinkers, alcohol abuse among the young is a rising problem, often overshadowed by moral panics over illegal, harder but less universally harmful drugs.' [Joss Hutton, *The Guardian*]

mores /'mɔːreɪz/ *plural noun* rules about acceptable social behaviour according to customs, morals etc.

morgue /mɔːg/ *noun* a room or file in a newspaper office containing various pieces of information that are kept for future reference, for example for writing obituaries

morphing /'mɔːfɪŋ/ *noun* in film, a change in an object from one form to another, presented as one continuous movement

morphology /mɔːˈfɒlədʒi/ *noun* the study of the structure of words in terms of combinations of meaningful units

morse code /ˌmɔːs ˈkəʊd/ *noun* a system for representing letters and numbers by using combinations of long or short beats, taps or beeps

mortise /'mɔːtɪs/ *noun* a hole cut in a printing plate to receive type or another plate ■ *verb* to cut a hole in a printing plate to receive type or another plate

mosaic /məʊˈzeɪɪk/ *noun* a light-sensitive surface on a television camera tube, consisting of a thin sheet covered by particles that convert incoming light into an electric charge for scanning by an electron beam

mosquito newspaper /mɒˈskiːtəʊ ˌnjuːzpeɪpə/ *noun* a short-lived, cheaply produced newspaper, often satirical in content

motif /məʊˈtiːf/ *noun* same as **super**

motion picture /ˌməʊʃ(ə)n ˈpɪktʃə/ *noun* a film

Motion Picture Association /'məʊʃ(ə)n ˌpɪktʃə əˌsəʊsieɪʃ(ə)n/ *noun* the international arm of the MPAA which protects the rights of Hollywood Studios to free trade and involvement in international markets. Abbreviation **MPA**

Motion Picture Association of America /ˌməʊʃ(ə)n ˌpɪktʃə ə ˌsəʊsieɪʃ(ə)n əv əˈmerɪkə/ *noun* the trade association in America which protects the interests of major Hollywood studios. Abbreviation **MPAA**

motivated /'məʊtɪˌveɪtɪd/ *adjective* referring to a camera shot that follows a particular piece of action or is prompted by some action within a scene. Compare **unmotivated**

motivation /ˌməʊtɪˈveɪʃ(ə)n/ *noun* a reason for doing something

motivational research /ˌməʊtɪveɪʃ(ə)nəl rɪˈsɜːtʃ/ *noun* the study of why people do things, specifically in media why they watch, listen, read, consume a product or respond to an advertisement

motor drive /'məʊtə draɪv/ *noun* a motorised mechanism to move film through a camera

Motown /'məʊtaʊn/ a trade name for a music company based in Detroit whose music, consisting of pop, soul and gospel, was especially popular during the 1960s and 1970s

mount /maʊnt/ *verb* to attach something securely to something else, such as a camera to a dolly

mounting /'maʊntɪŋ/ *noun* something on which something else is mounted, such as a tripod for a camera, which makes it easier to hold steady and adjust its position between shots

mouseover /'maʊsəʊvə/ *noun* a feature on a webpage, for example a pop-up menu or graphic image, that is activated when a user moves the cursor over a contact point on the page. The feature is designed to encourage the user to select it.

movie file /'muːvi faɪl/ *noun* a file stored on disk that contains a series of images that make up an animation or video clip

moviemaker /'muːviːˌmeɪkə/ *noun* same as **filmmaker**

MP3 /ˌem piː 'θriː/ *noun* a format for compressing music files to approximately one tenth of their original size, while losing little quality

MPA *abbreviation* **Motion Picture Association**

MPAA *abbreviation* **Motion Picture Association of America**

.mpeg *noun* a computer format for video data

MS *abbreviation* **medium shot**

M-time /em taɪm/ *abbreviation* **monochronic time**

MTV /ˌem tiː 'viː/ *noun* a global television service that broadcasts music videos and related programming such as celebrity interviews, award shows etc. It is extremely popular and has a great deal of influence in the music world

muckraking /'mʌkˌreɪkɪŋ/ *noun* journalism that tries to uncover scandal, corruption, crime, fraud etc. which is of interest to the public

'The press is also increasingly carrying such stories. The once staid but now transformed China Daily carries frequent articles on corruption, often in copious detail and with a muckraking tone.' [Martin Jacques, *The Guardian*]

MUD /ˌem tiː 'eɪ/ *noun* a piece of software usually used for gaming, which allows many different users to interact in the same environment. Full form **multi-user domain**

MUD object-oriented /ˌem ʌd ˌɒbjekt 'ɔːriənteɪtɪd/ *noun* full form of **MOO**

mug /mʌg/ *verb* to make exaggerated facial expressions in front of a camera

mug shot /'mʌg ʃɒt/ *noun* a head-and-shoulders shot

multi-actuality /ˌmʌlti ˌæktʃuˈælɪti/ *noun* the existence of many different and often contradictory meanings attached to any given sign or symbol

multiband /'mʌltibænd/ *adjective* referring to the separate processing of more than one bandwidth of a signal in order to achieve higher fidelity

multi-camera /ˌmʌlt 'kæm(ə)rə/ *adjective* using more than one camera

multi-channel home /ˌmʌlti ˌtʃæn(ə)l 'həʊm/ *noun* a household that can receive cable or satellite television as well as terrestrial channels

multicoloured *US* /ˌmʌlti'kʌləd/ *noun* of more than one colour ■ *adjective* able to print more than one colour at once

multiculturalism /ˌmʌlti 'kʌltʃ(ə)rəlɪz(ə)m/ *noun* in sociology, the different belief systems, customs and cultural products of different communities, brought together in a single society

multimedia /ˌmʌlti'miːdiə/ *noun* the combination of different media, for example sound, video, images or computer technology, in one package such as a CD-ROM ■ *adjective* using more than one media, as with an advertising campaign

multimedia document /ˌmʌlti 'miːdiə ˌdɒkjʊmənt/ *noun* an electronic document that contains interactive material from a range of different media such as text, video, sound, graphics and animation

multimedia home platform /ˌmʌltimiːdiə həʊm 'plætfɔːm/ *noun* a digital broadcasting standard that combines Internet and television broadcasting to create interactive television. Abbreviation **MHP**

multimedia messaging service /ˌmʌltimiːdiə 'mesɪdʒɪŋ ˌsɜːvɪs/ *noun* TELECOMS full form of **MMS**

multimodal /ˌmʌlti'məʊd(ə)l/ *adjective* using several different channels to access the same information, for example, cinema listings which are available in the press, by phone and on the Internet

multipath /'mʌltipaːθ/ *adjective* relating to television or radio signals that use more than one route from the transmitter to the receiver, causing picture or sound distortion

multiplane /ˈmʌltɪpleɪn/ noun the illusion of depth created by laying animation cells not directly on top of each other but with a tiny space between them

multiplayer /ˈmʌltiˌpleɪə/ adjective referring to a computer game that is played with other players, typically over a local area network or the Internet

multiple /ˈmʌltɪp(ə)l/ noun a system of wiring arranged so that a group of communication lines are accessible at a number of points

multiplex adjective with the digital technology to broadcast several different channels using a single wavelength ■ noun a large cinema with many screens

multiplexer /ˈmʌltiˌpleksə/ noun 1. a device for sending several data streams down a communications line and for splitting a received multiple stream into components 2. a device for transferring projected film to video

multiplexing /ˈmʌltɪpleksɪŋ/ noun the sending of two or more signals along one communication channel

multiplex provider /ˈmʌltɪpleks prəˌvaɪdə/ noun a service that carries several separate digital channels

multiplier effect /ˈmʌltɪplaɪə ɪˌfekt/ noun the effect by which the successful export of one product, such as a piece of technology, a popular television show etc., opens up the market for others

multiscreen /ˈmʌltiskriːn/ adjective with several screens for showing films, videos or slides

multistart /ˈmʌltistɑːt/ adjective beginning at several different times so that the viewer can select the most convenient start time. ◊ Near Video On Demand

multitrack /ˈmʌltitræk/ adjective using, capable of or produced by the separate recording of several different tracks

multi-user domain /ˌmʌlti ˌjuːzə dəˈmeɪn/ noun full form of MUD

Murdoch effect /ˈmɜːdɒk ɪˌfekt/ noun the process by which journalism is seen to have become more and more obsessed about money and big business

COMMENT: The term is named after Rupert Murdoch, who is said to exert an influence over the news that is reported in his media empire so that it doesn't conflict with his interests as a businessman.

Museum of Brands, Packaging and Advertising /mjuːˌziːəm əv ˌbrændz ˌpækɪdʒɪŋ ənd ˈædvətaɪzɪŋ/ noun a museum in London which displays advertising and branding on product packaging from the 19th century to the present day

Museum of the Moving Image /mjuːˌziːəm əv ðə ˌmuːvɪŋ ˈɪmɪdʒ/ noun formerly, an interactive museum of film and television culture on London's South Bank, closed in 1999 in favour of new BFI projects. Abbreviation MOMI

mush /mʌʃ/ noun radio interference, especially a hissing noise

mush area /ˈmʌʃ ˌeəriə/ noun a region where two or more radio signals overlap so that interference results

musical /ˈmjuːzɪk(ə)l/ noun, adjective a genre of film or stage production that features a lot of songs and musical numbers

Musical Instrument Digital Interface /ˌmjuːzɪk(ə)l ˌɪnstrəmənt ˌdɪdʒɪt(ə)l ˈɪntəfeɪs/ noun full form of MIDI

music and effects /ˌmjuːzɪk ən ɪˈfekts/ noun audio track used in dubbing stage. Abbreviation M and E

music centre /ˈmjuːzɪk ˌsentə/ noun a one-piece hi-fi unit that has a turntable, amplifier, cassette deck, radio and speakers

music hall /ˈmjuːzɪk hɔːl/ noun a type of entertainment, popular in the late 19th and early 20th centuries, that consisted of a variety of singing, dancing and comic acts

music reporting form /ˈmjuːzɪk rɪˌpɔːtɪŋ ˌfɔːm/ noun one of the four forms which must be submitted when delivering a programme to the BBC, giving details of all music used in the programme. ◊ billing form, transmission form, Programme as Completed form

music video /ˈmjuːzɪk ˌvɪdiəʊ/ noun a short video or film made to accompany a song or piece of popular music

musique concrète /mjuːˌziːk kɒnˈkret/ noun recorded music composed by electronically combining natural and musical sounds

must /məst, mʌst/ noun a piece of copy which cannot be dropped from an edition of a newspaper or magazine, for example an apology or correction

mute /mjuːt/ *adjective* with no sound

Mylar /ˈmaɪlaː/ a trade name for a thin strong polyester film used in recording tapes and photography

myth /mɪθ/ *noun* **1.** a traditional story about heroes or supernatural beings, often attempting to explain the origins of natural phenomena or aspects of human behaviour **2.** a set of often idealised or glamorised ideas and stories surrounding a particular phenomenon, concept or famous person **3.** a widely held mistaken belief

mythology /mɪˈθɒlədʒi/ *noun* **1.** a group of myths that belong to a particular people or culture and tell about their ancestors, heroes, gods and other supernatural beings, and history **2.** the study of myths, or the branch of knowledge that deals with myths **3.** a body of stories ideas, or beliefs that are not necessarily true about a particular place or person

N

n, N *symbol* PRINTING en dash

nabe /neɪb/ *noun* a local cinema

Nachträglichkeit /næxˈtreglɪxˌkeɪt/ *noun* literally 'deferred action'. The idea that dealing with a traumatic event may be deferred in a person's mind until a later time when they are mature enough to process it.

Nagra /ˈnægrə/ *noun* a Swiss company who make standard sound recording equipment

name super /ˈneɪm ˌsuːpə/ *noun* same as **super**

Napster /ˈnæpstə/ a trade name for software that allows users to share files, normally MP3-format music files, over the Internet

narcotising   dysfunction /ˌnɑːkətaɪzɪŋ dɪsˈfʌŋkʃ(ə)n/ *noun* the social consequence of the mass media overloading audiences with so much information that they are reduced to apathy

narrate /nəˈreɪt/ *verb* to tell the story or provide a commentary for a film or television programme

narration /nəˈreɪʃ(ə)n/ *noun* the process of explaining what is happening as a story or event progresses

narrative /ˈnærətɪv/ *noun* the way in which a story is told

    COMMENT: Considerations in a narrative are: the chronological order of events, the person who is telling the story, the ways in which themes and motives are represented, the way in which secrets are revealed, characterisation and role fulfilment, values and importance attached to events, and more.

narrative   paradigm /ˈnærətɪv ˌpærədaɪm/ *noun* the theory that part of what defines us as humans is our tendency to tell stories

narrator /nəˈreɪtə/ *noun* the person who tells the story in a film or book, not necessarily a character in the story themselves

narrowcast /ˈnærəʊkɑːst/ *verb* to aim a radio or television broadcast at a limited audience, defined by considerations such as geography or special interests

narrowcasting /ˈnærəʊkɑːstɪŋ/ *noun* a term formed by analogy with broadcasting, in which programming and advertisements are aimed at a narrow, specialist audience

national /ˈnæʃ(ə)nəl/ *noun* PRESS same as **national newspaper**

National Association of Television Program Executives /ˌnæʃ(ə)nəl əˌsəʊsieɪʃ(ə)n əv ˈtelɪvɪʒ(ə)n ˌprəʊgræm orəˌdjuːsəz/ *noun* an organisation which offers its members information on creative development in the US television industry. Abbreviation **NATPE**

National Broadcasting Company /ˌnæʃ(ə)nəl ˈbrɔːdkɑːstɪŋ ˌkɔːpəreɪʃ(ə)n/ *noun* an international media company based in the USA that operates terrestrial and cable broadcasting and Internet news provision. Abbreviation **NBC**

nationalism /ˈnæʃ(ə)nəˌlɪz(ə)m/ *noun* pride in a particular nation's cultural identity

    'Extremism in nationalism, like anything else, is ugly. But it is more than time that we learned to celebrate British history rather than forever abusing it, and encourage newcomers to Britain to do likewise. If we do not seem to believe in our own heritage, why should anyone else?' [Max Hastings, *The Daily Mail*]

national media /ˈnæʃ(ə)nəl ˌmiːdiə/ *noun* the broadcast and print products of a country that get nation-wide distribution, for example major newspapers and television programming

national newspaper /ˌnæʃ(ə)nəl ˈnjuːzpeɪpə/ *noun* a newspaper that is available and read in every part of a country. Also called **national**

National Readership Survey /ˌnæʃ(ə)nəl ˈriːdəʃɪp ˌsɜːveɪ/ *noun* a commercial organisation which provides readership statistics for 250 major publications in the UK, using random probability testing. Abbreviation **NRS**

National Television Systems Committee /ˌnæʃ(ə)nəl ˈtelɪvɪʒ(ə)n ˌsɪstəmz kəˌmɪti/ *noun* full form of **NTSC**

National Union of Journalists /ˌnæʃ(ə)nəl ˌjuːnjən əv ˈdʒɜːnəlɪsts/ *noun* the trade union for journalists in the UK and Ireland. Abbreviation **NUJ**

National Viewers and Listeners Association /ˌnæʃ(ə)nəl ˌvjuəz ənd ˈlɪs(ə)nəz əˌsəʊsieɪʃ(ə)n/ *noun* ♦ **Mediawatch-uk**

National Vocational Qualification /ˌnæʃ(ə)nəl vəʊˌkeɪʃ(ə)n(ə)l ˌkwɒlɪfɪˈkeɪʃ(ə)n/ *noun* a vocational qualification which measures standards of competence in a particular occupation such as journalism. Abbreviation **NVQ**

NATPE /ˈnætpi/ *abbreviation* **National Association of Television Program Executives**

natural break /ˌnætʃ(ə)rəl ˈbreɪk/ *noun* a convenient or reasonable point in a television programme for a commercial break

naturalism /ˈnætʃ(ə)rəlɪz(ə)m/ *noun* a method of filmmaking that represents characters and locations as they actually would be, as opposed to trying to create artificial drama and effects

naturalistic illusion of television /ˌnætʃ(ə)rəlɪstɪk ɪˌluːʒ(ə)n əv ˈtelɪvɪʒ(ə)n/ *noun* the impression given by some television programmes that what they are showing is real life when it is not

nature /ˈneɪtʃə/ *noun* **1.** the countryside or the environment in a condition relatively unaffected by human activity or as the home of living things other than human beings **2.** the intrinsic or essential qualities of a person or thing

navigable /ˈnævɪɡəb(ə)l/ *adjective* referring to a website that the user can move through by clicking on highlighted computer links

navigate /ˈnævɪɡeɪt/ *verb* to move about a website by using the links provided in it

NBC *abbreviation* BROADCAST, US **National Broadcasting Company**

NC-17 /ˌen siː ˌsev(ə)nˈtiːn/ *noun* a censorship classification in the United States indicating that a film should not be seen by children under the age of 17 because of its adult content

Near Instantaneous Amplitude Companding And Modulation *noun* full form of **NICAM**

Near Video On Demand /ˌnɪə ˌvɪdiəʊ ɒn dɪˈmɑːnd/ *noun* a situation in which the same programme or film is transmitted on several different sister channels at a short interval on each, so that the viewer can choose to start watching at the most convenient time for them. Abbreviation **NVOD**

needle /ˈniːd(ə)l/ *noun* the tone arm on the pickup of a record player

needle time /ˈniːd(ə)l taɪm/ *noun* the agreed maximum amount of time that a radio station can spend playing recorded music

'In fact Peel's role as the impresario and talent-broker of a certain kind of alternative contemporary music can hardly be overstated… he was practically the only national DJ prepared to give needle-time to the raucous DIY offerings of bands such as the Damned and the Buzzcocks.' [Spencer Leig, *The Independent*]

negative /ˈnegətɪv/ *noun* a photographic image that has been developed but not printed and shows black and white tones reversed and colours as complementary ■ *adjective* referring to photographic film that has been exposed to light and developed, used as a basis for preparing final prints

negative cutter /ˈnegətɪv ˌkʌtə/ *noun* the member of a film and television production team who is responsible for conforming negatives so that they match the director's view of what should be seen on screen

negotiated commission /nɪ ˌɡəʊʃieɪtɪd kəˈmɪʃ(ə)n/ *noun* a commission agreed with an advertising agency before work starts, and which may be different from standard commissions

negotiated meaning /nɪˌɡəʊʃiˈeɪtɪd 'miːnɪŋ/ *noun* the 'compromise' that is reached between the preferred reading offered by a text and the reader's own assumptions and interpretations

negotiation /nɪˌɡəʊʃiˈeɪʃ(ə)n/ *noun* the process of arriving at a compromise between the preferred reading offered by a text and the reader's own assumptions and interpretations

neo-noir /ˌniəʊ ˈnwɑː/ *adjective* relating to or reminiscent of the style of film noir

neorealism /ˌniəʊˈrɪəlɪz(ə)m/ *noun* a style of cinema focusing on issues of ordinary working-class life that began in Italy in the 1940s with the work of directors such as Roberto Rossellini

net /net/ *noun* a broadcasting network

net audience /ˈnet ˌɔːdiəns/ *noun* the total number of people reached by an advertising campaign, excluding duplications. According to this method, a person will be counted once whether they have seen an advertisement once or twenty times. Compare **advertising impression**

Net imperative /ˌnet ɪmˈperətɪv/ *noun* the idea that it is vital for organisations to use the Internet for business purposes if they are to be successful in the future

netiquette /ˈnetɪket/ *noun* an informal set of standard rules for how to use the Internet

'However familiar many parents are with the wonders, as well as the wiles, of the web, they still find the "netiquette" of chat rooms a mystery. "It's the language and syntax", says Fiona Derbyshire, mother of two teenage girls. "It's even more impenetrable than texting".'
[Martin Wroe, *The Sunday Times*]

netphone /ˈnetfəʊn/ *noun* a phone that makes connections via the Internet

NetShow /ˈnetʃəʊ/ a trade name for a system developed by Microsoft to provide audio and video delivery over the Internet without interruptions in the video sequence

Net surfing /ˈnet ˌsɜːfɪŋ/ *noun* the activity of moving through sites on the Internet out of interest

network /ˈnetwɜːk/ *noun* 1. an interconnected system of communications channels 2. a group of communication channels, for example television or radio stations, owned by a single company

networking /ˈnetwɜːkɪŋ/ *noun* 1. the process or practice of building up or maintaining informal relationships, especially with people whose friendship could bring advantages such as job or business opportunities 2. the process of interconnecting two or more computers either in the same room or different buildings, in the same town or different towns, allowing them to exchange information

network marketing /ˈnetwɜːk ˌmɑːkɪtɪŋ/ *noun* a marketing campaign carried out through a complete magazine network

network programming /ˌnetwɜːk ˈprəʊɡræmɪŋ/ *noun* the practice of scheduling television programmes over the whole network

network society /ˈnetwɜːk səˌsaɪəti/ *noun* a society that regularly uses global networks for the purposes of work, communication and government

neutral density filter /ˌnjuːtrəl ˌdensɪti ˈfɪltə/ *noun* a filter used on a camera lens to prevent overexposure in strong lighting conditions

Newcomb's ABX model of communication 1953 /ˈnjuːkəm/ *noun* a communication model in which there are three points of reference – the sender (A), the receiver (B) and the social situation in which the communication takes place (X)

new journalism /ˈnjuː ˌdʒɜːn(ə)lɪz(ə)m/ *noun* a type of reporting similar to gonzo journalism, in which the reporter records a stream of consciousness

New Line Cinema /ˌnjuː laɪn ˈsɪnɪmə/ *noun* a major film studio, a subsidiary of Time Warner, formed in 1967. It has produced such blockbusters as the Austin Powers series of films and the Lord of the Rings trilogy.

news /njuːz/ *noun* 1. a broadcast report on important events or developments that are taking place 2. information about current events and developments as it is reported in the mass media

news agency /'njuːz ˌeɪdʒənsi/ *noun* an organisation that provides accurate information on the news to other media such as newspapers and radio so that they can report it, and also to online subscribers. They are often global, operating in several languages. Examples of major news agencies are Reuters and Associated Press (AP). Also called **news service**, **press agency**

newsagent /'njuːzeɪdʒənt/ *noun* a person whose job is to sell newspapers and magazines, often together with confectionery, tobacco and other items

news aid /'njuːz eɪd/ *noun* the idea that news coverage that is aimed at alerting people to suffering, distress, victims of disasters etc. often gives a simplistic view of the reasons behind what has happened

newsboy /'njuːzbɔɪ/ *noun* a boy who sells or delivers newspapers

newsbreak /'njuːzbreɪk/ *noun* **1.** a short news bulletin during a radio or television programme **2.** something that is newsworthy

newscast /'njuːzkɑːst/ *noun* a programme of news reports on the television or radio

newscaster /'njuːzkɑːstə/ *noun* a person whose job is to read the news on television or the radio

news conference /'njuːz ˌkɒnf(ə)rəns/ *noun* BROADCAST, PRESS same as **press conference**

News Corporation /'njuːz ˌkɔːpəreɪʃ(ə)n/ *noun* one of the world's largest media conglomerates which owns book publishers, magazines, film studios and cable and satellite television channels across Australia, the UK and the US The majority shareholder is mogul Rupert Murdoch

newsdealer /'njuːzˌdiːlə/ *noun* a person who keeps a shop or stall selling mainly newspapers, magazines and often paperback books and confectionery

newsdesk /'njuːzdesk/ *noun* the place where a news editor prepares news for publication or broadcasting

new season /ˌnjuː 'siːz(ə)n/ *noun* the start of the television year, usually taken to be the autumn and winter programming season

news flash /'njuːz flæʃ/ *noun* a short report about an important piece of news, that interrupts a scheduled programme

'Last month the Broadcasting Complaints Commission (BCC) upheld a religious complaint against Eamon Dunphy's show on NewsTalk 106 which broadcast a spoof newsflash in December last year saying that Pope John Paul II had died.' [Dearbhail McDonald, *The Sunday Times*]

news frameworks /'njuːz ˌfreɪmwɜːks/ *plural noun* a shared set of rules or guidelines by a group of editors and journalists about what counts as 'newsworthy'

newsgathering /'njuːzˌɡæʃ(ə)rɪŋ/ *noun* the system by which news is obtained from sources, interviewees, observation, news agencies etc.

newsgirl /'njuːzɡɜːl/ *noun* a girl who sells or delivers newspapers

newsgroup /'njuːzˌɡruːp/ *noun* a news discussion group on the Internet

newshound /'njuːzhaʊnd/ *noun* a newspaper reporter

newsletter /'njuːzletə/ *noun* a report that contains matters of interest to a specific group such as the members of a society or employees of an organisation, and is regularly sent to them

news-literate /ˌnjuːz 'lɪt(ə)rət/ *adjective* referring to somebody who has the ability to 'read' the news intelligently taking into consideration its conventions, codes, norms etc.

news magazine /'njuːz ˌmæɡəziːn/ *noun* **1.** a radio or television programme consisting of news commentary, interviews, investigative reporting and features **2.** a magazine, often published weekly, that contains reports and analysis of the previous week's news

newsman /'njuːzmæn/ *noun* a male journalist or newsreader

newspaper /'njuːzpeɪpə/ *noun* **1.** a daily or weekly publication containing news reports and commentary, features and advertisements, and is printed on large folded sheets of paper. Also called **paper 2.** an organisation that publishes a newspaper **3.** a sheet or sheets of a newsprint

newspaperman /'nju:speɪpəmæn/ *noun* **1.** a male newspaper reporter or editor **2.** a man who owns a newspaper

newspaperperson /'nju:zpeɪpə ˌpɜːs(ə)n/ *noun* **1.** a newspaper reporter or editor **2.** somebody who owns a newspaper

newspaperwoman /'nju:zpeɪpə ˌwʊmən/ *noun* **1.** a female newspaper reporter or editor **2.** a woman who owns a newspaper

newspeak /'nju:spi:k/ *noun* an imaginary form of language in George Orwell's 1984, in which the size of vocabulary and ranges of meaning were so restricted that this in itself restricted the concepts and thoughts that a person was capable of formulating

newsperson /'nju:zˌpɜːs(ə)n/ *noun* a journalist or newsreader

newsprint /'nju:zprɪnt/ *noun* the cheap, low-quality paper that newspapers are printed on

news professional /'nju:z prə ˌfeʃ(ə)n(ə)l/ *noun* a person whose job it is to process and supply news according to the format of the institution or publication

newsreader /'nju:zri:də/ *noun* somebody who presents the news, especially the headlines, on a television or radio news broadcast

newsreel /'nju:zri:l/ *noun* news reports on film, often shown at the cinema before the main feature, which were popular from World War I until the advent of television

news release /'nju:z rɪˌliːs/ *noun* same as **press release**

newsroom /'nju:zru:m/ *noun* the office in which journalists, researchers, editors etc. gather to put news stories together

news service /'nju:z ˌsɜːvɪs/ *noun* BROADCAST, PRESS same as **news agency**

newsstand /'nju:zstænd/ *noun* a stall for selling newspapers and magazines

news values /'nju:z ˌvæljuːz/ *noun* the criteria applied to news stories and employed when gatekeeping

COMMENT: Examples of typical news values would be: the event's impact on the public (the number of people affected, its unexpectedness), the human interest (the involvement of a famous person or powerful nation, the relevance of the topic to the audience) and the pragmatics of news reporting (the existence of similar stories in the news, the time of the event taking place, etc).

newsvendor /'nju:zˌvendə/ *noun* a person who sells newspapers

newsweekly /nju:z'wi:kli/ *noun* a newspaper or news magazine that is published weekly

newswoman /'nju:zˌwʊmən/ *noun* a female journalist or newsreader

newsworthy /'nju:zwɜːði/ *adjective* referring to stories or issues that are interesting or important enough to be reported in the media

'For all the empowerment of women, though, violence by men against women is still far more serious than vice versa. Serious cases of women as the aggressors are newsworthy exceptions which prove the rule.' [Peter McKay, *The Daily Mail*]

newswriting /'nju:zˌraɪtɪŋ/ *noun* the process of writing news stories

new wave /ˌnju: 'weɪv/ *noun* **1.** a style of film-making that developed in France during the late 1950s and 1960s that was a reaction against established French cinema, emphasising unconventionality and the individual styles of directors **2.** a type of rock music in the late 1970s that developed from the punk rock era

New World Information and Communication Order /ˌnju: wɜːld ˌɪnfəmeɪʃ(ə)n ən kəˌmju:nɪ'keɪʃ(ə)n ˌɔːdə/ *noun* a UNESCO concept from the 1970s and 80s with the aim of making media representation of developing countries more equitable across the globe. It was unpopular with the United States who withdrew their membership from UNESCO in response.

next matter /'nekst ˌmætə/, **next-to-reading matter** /ˌnekst tə 'riːdɪŋ ˌmætə/ *noun* advertising material placed next to editorial matter in a publication

N-Gen /'en dʒen/ *noun* the Net Generation, referring to young people who have grown up with the Internet from an early age

nib /nɪb/ *noun* same as **brief**

NICAM /'naɪkæm/ *noun* a system in which digital quality audio can be transmitted through an analogue signal and decoded by compatible viewing equipment. Full form of **Near Instantaneous Amplitude Companding And Modulation**

niche /niːʃ/ *noun* an area of the market specialising in one type of product or service ■ *adjective* referring to something highly specific, that is relevant to only a small section of the population

niche audience /ˌniːʃ ˈɔːdiəns/ *noun* a small target audience that is highly specific

niche marketing /ˌniːʃ ˈmɑːkɪtɪŋ/ *noun* the process of marketing to small but potentially highly profitable specialist markets

nick /nɪk/ *noun* PRINTING a groove in the side of a piece of metal printing type, used to align and often, identify it

nickelodeon /ˌnɪk(ə)lˈəʊdiən/ *noun* an early 20th-century cinema where a ticket cost five cents

Nielsen Media Research /ˌniːlsən ˈmiːdiə rɪˌsɜːtʃ/ *noun* a multinational media company that provides television and audience viewing figures, information about print readership and information for the purposes of marketing and advertising

Nielsen Television Index /ˌniːls(ə)n ˈtelɪvɪʒ(ə)n ˌɪndeks/ *noun* the most-used television audience ratings in the USA, produced by media research company A. C. Nielsen. Abbreviation **NTI**

nl *abbreviation* a proofreading mark on a text that means 'new line'

NLE *abbreviation* non-linear editing

noddy /ˈnɒdi/ *noun* a cutaway shot of an interviewer nodding, looking interested etc., used to disguise editing, avoid jump cuts or simply break up a long speech by the interviewee

Noelle-Neumann's spiral of silence model of public opinion 1974 /ˌnəʊel ˈnɔɪmən/ *noun* a model of the way in which a person is less likely to voice their opinion if they think there is little support for it, meaning that it appears even less popular

noir /nwɑː/ *adjective* relating to or reminiscent of the style of film noir

noise /nɔɪz/ *noun* **1.** interference either visually or on the soundtrack when using magnetic tape **2.** any sort of interference affecting a channel of communication **3.** unwanted or meaningless data intermixed with the relevant information in the output from a computer

noise level /ˈnɔɪz ˌlev(ə)l/ *noun* the amount of unwanted information found when searching the Internet

nomadism /ˈnəʊmæˌdɪzm/ *noun* in feminist theory, the practice of rejecting mainstream cultural forms and territorialisation in order to undermine the theory that humans instinctively create an inclusive, unifying culture

non-aligned news pool /ˌnɒn ə ˌlaɪnd ˈnjuːz ˌpuːl/ *noun* a news agency formed by 85 countries, agreeing to share news gathered by their domestic agencies with each other

nonbroadcast /nɒnˈbrɔːdkɑːst/ *adjective* referring to material that is not suitable for, or transmitted by, radio or television

non-diegetic sound /ˌnɒn ˌdaɪəgetɪk ˈsaʊnd/ *noun* sound that is not coming from a recognisable source in a piece of film but has been added to the soundtrack, for example a voiceover or a piece of music. Compare **diegetic sound**

nonimpact /nɒnˈɪmpækt/ *adjective* referring to a printing method that does not involve pressing ink onto a surface, but uses laser or ink-jet technologies

non-linear editing /ˌnɒn ˌlɪniə ˈedɪtɪŋ/ *noun* film and video editing that is performed on a computer, in which the shots may be handled separately and digitally reassembled in any order. Also called **random-access editing**. Abbreviation **NLE**

non-media /ˌnɒn ˈmiːdiə/ *adjective* unconnected to the media

nonpareil /ˌnɒnpəˈreɪ(ə)l/ *noun* a size of printers' type equal to six points

nonprinted /nɒnˈprɪntɪd/ *adjective* referring to material that has not been printed

nonprinting /nɒnˈprɪntɪŋ/ *adjective* referring to characters not used or intended for printing

nonsexist /nɒnˈseksɪst/ *adjective* avoiding or not involving discrimination based on sex

non-sync /ˌnɒn ˈsɪŋ/ *noun* non-synchronised sound, i.e. a soundtrack that is produced separately from the picture. Compare **sync**

non-synchronised /ˌnɒn
ˈsɪŋkrənaɪzd/ *adjective* of sound, not
matching up exactly with the pictures
because for example the soundtrack was
recorded separately

non-verbal communication /ˌnɒn
ˌvɜːb(ə)l kəˌmjuːnɪˈkeɪʃ(ə)n/ *noun* any
communication that is not performed with
words, for example facial expression,
gesture, touch, tone, posture etc. Abbreviation **NVC**

non-verbal vocalisation /ˌnɒn
ˌvɜːbəl ˌvəʊkəlaɪˈzeɪʃ(ə)n/ *noun* a
sound or quality of sound made by a
person that is not language but communicates something about the speaker, for
example a laugh, a stutter, a change of
pitch

norm /nɔːm/ *noun* something which is
normal, usual, expected; a convention or
standard

normative /ˈnɔːmətɪv/ *adjective*
according to norms, what is expected as
opposed to what happens in reality

Northcliffe revolution /ˈnɔːθklɪf
ˌrevəluːʃ(ə)n/ *noun* a shift in the
economic basis of newspaper publication
in the late 19th and early 20th century, as
they became dependent on advertisement
revenue and therefore on grabbing attention and attracting more readers

COMMENT: The term is named after
newspaper baron Lord Northcliffe, who
founded the *Daily Mail* and the *Daily
Mirror* as well as turning around the
fortunes of other dailies by making their
content more sensational and populist in
deference to his advertisers. The Daily
Mail held the highest circulation of any
newspaper in the UK from its inception in
1896 until his death in 1922.

nostalgia /nɒˈstældʒə/ *noun* a mixed
feeling of happiness, sadness and longing
when recalling a person, place or event
from the past, or the past in general

'...the publication of The Best Of
Jackie, a book which celebrates the top-
selling teenage magazine of bygone
years, is a portal into another era. I sat on
the floor, pages spread around me,
swamped in nostalgia, instantly
transported back to another life, another
time...'
[Nina Myskow, *The Daily Mail*]

note /nəʊt/ *noun* an extra piece of information often given at the bottom of a
printed page or at the very end of a text

notice /ˈnəʊtɪs/ *noun* a written statement of information, often displayed on a
board or wall, or published in a newspaper
or magazine

noting scores /ˈnəʊtɪŋ skɔːz/ *plural
noun* the percentage of a publication's
readers who report having seen a particular article, advertisement etc.

November /nəʊˈvembə/ *noun* an internationally recognised code word for the
letter N, used in radio communications

n.p., NP *abbreviation* a proofreading
mark on a text that means 'new paragraph'

NRS *abbreviation* **National Readership Survey**

NTI *abbreviation* TV, US **Nielsen Television Index**

NTSC /ˌen tiː es ˈsiː/ *noun* the standard
television system in many countries
including the USA, Canada and Japan.
Full form **National Television Systems
Committee**

nudie /ˈnjuːdi/ *noun* a product such as a
film or magazine that features unclothed
performers or models

NUJ *abbreviation* UK, PRESS **National
Union of Journalists**

number /ˈnʌmbə/ *noun* one of a series
of things, especially a single issue of a
magazine

nut /nʌt/ *noun* PRINTING same as **en**

NVC *abbreviation* **non-verbal communication**

NVOD *abbreviation* **Near Video On
Demand**

NVQ *abbreviation* **National Vocational
Qualification**

O

OB, o.b. *abbreviation* **outside broadcast**

obeli PRINTING plural of **obelus**

obelise /ˈɒbəlaɪz/ *verb* to insert a dagger or obelus into a printed text

obelisk /ˈɒbəlɪsk/ *noun* PRINTING same as **dagger**

obelus /ˈɒbələs/ *noun* **1.** a symbol (†) used in modern printed editions of ancient manuscripts to show that a particular section is possibly not genuine **2.** PRINTING same as **dagger**

obit /ˈəʊbɪt/ *abbreviation* **obituary**

obituary /əˈbɪtʃuəri/ *noun* an account of a prominent person's life, published in a newspaper shortly after they have died. Abbreviation **obit**

object /ˈɒbdʒekt/ *noun* **1.** something that can be seen or touched, or something that is perceived as an entity and given a name **2.** a focus of somebody's attention or emotion **3.** a collection of variables, data structures, and procedures stored as an entity and forming a basic building block of object-oriented programming

object database /ˈɒbdʒekt ˌdeɪtəbeɪs/ *noun* a database that has the capacity to deal with audio and video files. Abbreviation **ODB**

object-image ratio /ˌɒbdʒekt ˈɪmɪdʒ ˌreɪʃəʊ/ *noun* the difference between the actual size of an object being photographed or filmed and the size of the final image produced

objective and task method /əb ˌdʒektɪv ən ˈtɑːsk ˌmeθəd/ *noun* a method of calculating an advertising budget by setting objectives, deciding what tasks are needed to achieve them and then calculating the actual costs involved

objectivity /ˌɒbdʒekˈtɪvɪti/ *noun* the idea that news can and should be reported without opinion or bias. Compare **subjectivity**

'A month ago, some of American television's most recognisable news reporters took on the unlikely role of conscience of the nation as they howled with indignation about the poor and dispossessed of New Orleans… They lost all pretence of detached objectivity and instead gave full vent to their frustration and anger.' [Michael Ainsworth, *The Independent on Sunday*]

object language /ˌɒbdʒekt ˈlæŋgwɪdʒ/ *noun* the meanings and symbolic values that a person attaches to objects around them

obl. *abbreviation* PRINTING **oblique**

oblique /əˈbliːk/ *noun* PRINTING same as **slash**

obscenity /əbˈsenɪti/ *noun* a word, phrase or statement that is offensive, especially because of being sexually explicit, and may be subject to legal restraints regarding broadcast or publication

obsolescence /ˌɒbsəˈles(ə)ns/ *noun* the state of becoming obsolete by being replaced by something new

obsolete /ˈɒbsəliːt/ *noun* no longer in use, usually because of having been replaced by something new and more interesting or efficient

occupational soap /ˌɒkjuˈpeɪʃ(ə)nəl ˌsəʊp/ *noun* a soap opera that is based around a place of work, rather than a street or other place where people live. An example of this is *The Bill.*

OCR *abbreviation* **optical character recognition**

octavo /ɒkˈtɑːvəʊ/ *noun* **1.** a book with 8 leaves and 16 pages resulting from the folding in half of a single sheet of standard-sized printing paper three times.

Also called **eightvo 2.** the size of one page of an octavo book

octodecimo /ˌɒktəʊˈdesiməʊ/ *noun* a book that measures about 10 by 16 cm/4 by 4 ¼ in, or this size of book. Also called **eighteenmo**

ODB *abbreviation* **object database**

oedipal complex /ˈiːdəp(ə)l ˌkɒmpleks/ *noun* according to Freudian psychology, the desire of every male child to sleep with his mother and kill his father

COMMENT: The term **oedipal complex** comes from the Greek myth of Oedipus, who marries his own mother Jocasta after murdering his father Laius, without knowing the identity of either.

oeuvre /ˈɜːvrə/ *noun* the creative work of a person

OFCOM /ˈɒfkɒm/ *noun* the telecommunications regulator in the UK Formed in 2003, it took over the licensing and regulatory duties formerly undertaken by the Radio Authority, The Broadcasting Standards Commission, the Independent Television Commission, the Office of Telecommunications and the Radiocommunications Agency. Full form **Office of Communications**

off-air /ˌɒf ˈeə/ *adjective* referring to events, speech or action taking place in broadcasting studios but not used during a broadcast

off-beat /ˌɒf ˈbiːt/ *adjective* slightly unexpected or humorous

off-camera /ˌɒf ˈkæm(ə)rə/ *adjective* referring to action that takes place out of range of a film or television camera that is recording. Compare **on-camera**

off-card rate /ˌɒf ˈkɑːd ˌreɪt/ *noun* a specially arranged price, lower than that on the rate card, for advertising space or time

off-diary piece /ˌɒf ˈdaɪəri ˌpiːs/ *noun* an article that was not scheduled to be covered but that a journalist writes on his or her own initiative. Compare **diary piece**

offensive spending /əˌfensɪv ˈspendɪŋ/ *noun* the practice of spending on advertising which aims to attract users of a rival brand or to attack the competition

Office of Communications /ˌɒfɪs əv kəˌmjuːnɪˈkeɪʃ(ə)nz/ *noun* full form of **OFCOM**

Office of Telecommunications /ˌɒfɪs əv ˌtelikəˌmjuːnɪˈkeɪʃ(ə)nz/ *noun* the body formerly responsible for regulating the non-military radio spectrum in the UK, issuing licences and protecting it from unauthorised use. It was replaced by OFCOM under the 2003 Communications Act. ◊ **OFCOM**

Official Secrets Act /əˌfɪʃ(ə)l ˈsiːkrəts ˌækt/ *noun* an act of Parliament that allows some censorship of the media, on the grounds that the information might be of use to the country's enemies

offline /ɒfˈlaɪn/ *adjective* **1.** referring to a computer not connected to the Internet **2.** referring to a printer that is not connected to or receiving data from a computer **3.** referring to people or processes involved in preparing but not transmitting material for broadcasting

off-line editing /ˌɒf laɪn ˈedɪtɪŋ/ *noun* the process of editing a film using a copy rather than the original recording. It does not result in a final copy for broadcast but uses cheaper equipment and so editors can take more time to decide how the final online edit should be done. Compare **online editing**

off-line newsreader /ˌɒf laɪn ˈnjuːzriːdə/ *noun* computer software that allows users to read newsgroup articles without being online at the same time

off-mike /ˌɒf ˈmaɪk/ *adjective* referring to noise that is audible in the background of a broadcast

offprint /ˈɒfprɪnt/ *noun* a separately printed article taken from a larger publication and often given to the contributor

off-screen image /ˌɒf skriːn ˈɪmɪdʒ/ *noun* an image that is first drawn in memory and then is transferred to the display memory to give the impression of fast display action

offset *noun* /ˈɒfset/ **1.** a method of printing in which inked impressions are transferred onto paper via an intermediate surface made of rubber. Also called **set-off 2.** the accidental transfer of ink, usually from one piece of paper to another ■ *verb* /ɒfˈset/ to print something by offset printing

off the record /ˌɒf ðə ˈrekɔːd/ *adjective* comments made off the record are not intended to be published or used by a journalist but only for background or further investigation, protecting the source

'Gloria Macapagal Arroyo, Philippine president… revealed during lunch with a columnist last week that military intelligence suspected a popular television reporter of coddling a suspected Islamic terrorist. While the information was "off the record", it proved too tempting for the columnist's newspaper not to publish.' [*The Financial Times*]

off-tube /ˌɒf 'tjuːb/ *adjective* referring to a commentary made without being physically present at the event but by watching a video feed

000 *noun* a list of items for sale with prices and product details and often, illustrations

Old English /ˌəʊld 'ɪŋglɪʃ/ *noun* a form of black-letter typeface used by English printers up to the 18th century

old face /'əʊld feɪs/ *noun* a typeface originating in the 18th century that shows little difference between light and heavy strokes and has slanting serifs

old style /'əʊld staɪl/ *noun* a modern typeface that imitates the characteristics of old face

oligopoly /ˌɒlɪ'gɒpəli/ *noun* an industry that is monopolised by a small number of producers

OMB *abbreviation* one-man-band

omnibus /'ɒmnɪbəs/ *noun* a radio or television programme that brings together all the instalments of a serial or soap opera that have been broadcast since the previous omnibus edition

omnibus survey /'ɒmnɪbəs ˌsɜːveɪ/ *noun* a survey carried out once a month by the Office for National Statistics, using a range of simple questions on all topics from contraception to media use

omnidirectional antenna /ˌɒmnɪdaɪrekʃ(ə)nəl æn'tenə/ *noun* an antenna which sends and receives signals equally effectively in all directions. Compare **directional antenna**

omnidirectional microphone /ˌɒmnɪdaɪrekʃ(ə)nəl 'maɪkrəfəʊn/ *noun* a general purpose microphone that picks up all sound in an area. Compare **gun mike**

omnimax /'ɒmnimæks/ *noun* a system of film projection that surrounds the viewer in a semi-circle, occupying the entire field of vision

on-camera /ˌɒn 'kæm(ə)rə/ *adjective* referring to action that takes place within range of a film or television camera that is recording. Compare **off-camera**

on demand /ˌɒn dɪ'mɑːnd/ *adjective* referring to a service whereby the user can select the start time of a particular programme rather than it being broadcast at a scheduled time

180º rule /ˌwʌn ˌeɪti dɪ'griː ˌruːl/ *noun* the idea that in filming, the camera should be placed behind a line and should not cross that 180º field of potential vision. Doing so is called 'crossing the line'.

one-man-band /ˌwʌn mæn 'bænd/ *noun* a camera operator who also deals with lighting and sound set-ups. Abbreviation **OMB**

one-plus-one /ˌwʌn plʌs 'wʌn/ *noun* an interview set-up in which there is one interviewer and one interviewee

one-step approach /ˌwʌn 'step ə ˌprəʊtʃ/ *noun* a form of direct marketing where advertisements are used to obtain orders directly

one-time order /ˌwʌn taɪm 'ɔːdə/ *noun* an order for an advertising spot for a particular time that is not scheduled to be repeated

one-to-one marketing /ˌwʌn tə wʌn 'mɑːkɪtɪŋ/ *noun* a method of marketing through a website which aims to establish a personal relationship with a customer, selling to each customer as an individual and trying to differentiate between customers

on-hold advertising /ˌɒn 'həʊld ˌædvətaɪzɪŋ/ *noun* a method of advertising to telephone callers while they are waiting to be connected to the person they want to speak to, usually involving voice messages about the firm and its products

online /ɒn'laɪn/ *adjective* **1.** referring to a printer that is connected to or receiving data from a computer **2.** referring to a computer that is connected to the Internet

on-line editing /ˌɒn laɪn 'edɪtɪŋ/ *noun* the practice of editing a film using the original recording to make the final edit for broadcast. It follows the decisions made in off-line editing. Compare **off-line editing**

onomatopoeia /ˌɒnəmætə'piːə/ *noun* the formation or use of words that imitate the sound associated with something, for example 'hiss' and 'buzz'

on-pack promotion /ˌɒn ˈpæk prəˌməʊʃ(ə)n/ *noun* the practice of placing advertising material on the outside of packaged goods

on-screen /ˌɒn ˈskriːn/ *adjective, adverb* referring to an event or action that can be seen by the audience during a television programme or film

on spec /ˌɒn ˈspek/ *adjective* referring to an article or piece that is submitted without having being commissioned by the newspaper

on the record /ˌɒn ðə rɪˈkɔːd/ *adjective* referring to comments that may be freely reported, quoted etc.

on-the-spot editing /ˌɒn ðə ˌspɒt ˈedɪtɪŋ/ *noun* editing together of footage from an outside broadcast straight away 'on site', using an edit caravelle or similar

OOV *abbreviation* **out of vision**

opacity /əʊˈpæsɪti/ *noun* the degree to which a material such as photographic film is able to stop light

opaque /əʊˈpeɪk/ *noun* a photographic pigment that can block out areas of a negative

op ed /ˈɒp ed/ *noun* **1.** an article expressing a personal viewpoint written for the op-ed section of a newspaper **2.** opposite editorial, i.e. on the facing page to that on which the editorial article appears

open /ˈəʊpən/ *adjective* referring to a narrative without a definite conclusion or resolution at the end. Compare **closed**

open access television /ˌəʊpən ˌækses ˈtelɪvɪʒ(ə)n/ *noun* same as **public access television**

open-ender /ˌəʊpənˈendə/ *noun* a continuous broadcast on a major event or piece of breaking news, which overrides all other scheduled broadcasts until further notice. Also called **rolling news**

open-face lamp /ˌəʊpən feɪs ˈlæmp/ *noun* same as **flood**

open letter /ˌəʊpən ˈletə/ *noun* a letter that is published in a newspaper or magazine but addressed to an individual or organisation

open rate /ˈəʊpən reɪt/ *noun* an advertising rate where discounts are available for frequent or bulk orders

open source creed /ˌəʊpən ˈsɔːs ˌkriːd/ *noun* the policy of making technology, data etc. freely available without charging a fee

open talkback /ˌəʊpən ˈtɔːkbæk/ *noun* talkback from the production gallery of a recording studio that can be heard continuously and by everybody. Compare **switched talkback**

open text /ˌəʊpən ˈtekst/ *noun* a text that allows plenty of scope for free interpretation. Compare **closed text**

Open University /ˌəʊpən ˌjuːnɪˈvɜːsɪti/ *noun* a British university founded in 1969 that offers degree courses that are mostly taken by mature students studying part-time and by correspondence, many classes being broadcast on television and radio

opera /ˈɒp(ə)rə/ *noun* **1.** a dramatic work where music is a dominant part of the performance, with the actors often singing rather than reciting their lines **2.** operas thought of collectively or as an art form

opéra bouffe /ˌɒp(ə)rə ˈbuːf/ *noun* a French opera with a comic or farcical theme

opera buffa /ˌɒp(ə)rə ˈbuːfə/ *noun* a comic opera, usually in Italian, using themes or characters from everyday life and usually having a happy ending. Mozart's *The Marriage of Figaro* is an example.

operetta /ˌɒpəˈretə/ *noun* a type of opera, usually with a comic theme, but with much spoken dialogue and usually some dancing. Gilbert and Sullivan wrote many operettas.

opinion leader /əˈpɪnjən ˌliːdə/ *noun* somebody who influences the values, beliefs etc. of others

opinion piece /əˈpɪnjən piːs/ *noun* an article in which the journalist expresses their own opinion on some topic, rather than reporting the facts

opinion poll /əˈpɪnjən pəʊl/ *noun* a poll that questions a sample of people about their opinion on an issue and makes generalisations about the whole nation from those answers. Findings may tend to 'dumb down' issues, as the questions have simple, yes-or-no answers and offer little background or analysis.

Opportunity To See /ˌɒpətjuːnəti tə ˈsiː/ *noun* the number of times it is theoretically possible to see or hear an advertisement. Abbreviation **OTS**

oppositional /ˌɒpəˈzɪʃ(ə)nəl/ *noun* referring to anything or person that rejects or disagrees with what is expected, preferred or in authority

oppositional reading /ˌɒpəˈzɪʃ(ə)nəl ˌriːdɪŋ/ *noun* an interpretation of a text by a reader whose social position puts them into direct conflict with its preferred reading

oppositions /ˌɒpəˈzɪʃ(ə)nz/ *plural noun* pairs of concepts which are diametrically opposed to each other or complement each other

optical character recognition /ˌɒptɪk(ə)l ˈkærɪktə ˌrekəgnɪʃ(ə)n/ *noun* a scanner which can 'recognise' text characters and save them as a text document. Abbreviation **OCR**

optical sound /ˌɒptɪk(ə)l ˈsaʊnd/ *noun* a form of sound reproduction in films where a photographed pattern of light on the film is read by a lamp in the projector. It has now largely been superseded by digital sound.

optical zoom /ˌɒptɪk(ə)l ˈzuːm/ *noun* a zoom facility on a camera that zooms using the lens itself, without losing quality. Compare **digital zoom**

optimal balance /ˌɒptɪm(ə)l ˈbæləns/ *noun* the best combination of elements or activities that can be achieved when a marketing strategy is being planned

optimisation /ˌɒptɪmaɪˈzeɪʃ(ə)n/ *noun* a computer package that automatically devises a media schedule for an advertising campaign

option /ˈɒpʃən/ *verb* to buy the right to make a film from something such as a book or script

opt out /ˌɒpt ˈaʊt/ *noun* the action of asking not to receive advertising e-mail messages and being removed from an e-mail list

'The catch? You'll have to spend a few seconds registering your home address and email. But don't worry about endless marketing emails as a result – tick the small opt-out box and you'll get the free money without the spam.' [Patrick Collinson, *The Guardian*]

oral culture /ˈɔːrəl ˌkʌltʃə/ *noun* a society in which most communication is by word of mouth, with little emphasis on written texts

orality /ɔːˈrælɪti/ *noun* oral communication through speech, often contrasted with literacy. Some cultures value oral communication as more authentic and immediate than text.

orbit /ˈɔːbɪt/ *noun* the practice of rotating advertisements among different programmes on a television station

organ /ˈɔːgən/ *noun* a newspaper or magazine regarded as a means of communicating the views of a particular group such as a political party

organisation culture /ˌɔːrgənaɪˈzeɪʃ(ə)n ˌkʌltʃə/ *noun* the way in which the power structure in an organisation is constructed. ◊ **person culture**, **power culture**, **role culture**, **task culture**

orientalism /ˌɔːriˈentəlɪz(ə)m/ *noun* in cultural theory, the misrepresentation and stereotyping of the culture of Asia and the characteristics of its people, as described by writers and artists of the West

orientation /ˌɔːriənˈteɪʃ(ə)n/ *noun* **1.** the way in which people stand or hold themselves in relation to each other when they meet, an element of non-verbal communication **2.** in typography, the position of a piece of paper in relation to the text that runs across it. ◊ **landscape**, **portrait**

originate /əˈrɪdʒɪneɪt/ *verb* to copy an image onto film from which printing plates will be made

orphan /ˈɔːf(ə)n/ *noun* the last line of a paragraph, placed at the top of a column or page while the rest is at the end of the last one. This is poor layout and to be avoided. Compare **widow**

orthochromatic /ˌɔːθəʊkrəˈmætɪk/ *adjective* referring to film that is sensitive to all the same colours as the human eye, except red

OS *abbreviation* **outside source**

Oscar /ˈɒskə/ a trade name for the golden statuette awarded annually by the Academy of Motion Picture Arts and Sciences to people in the film industry for achievement in the making of films

other /ˈʌðə/ *noun* social and cultural groups that are different from our own, whom we think about simply as being different

OTS *abbreviation* **Opportunity To See**

out /aʊt/ *noun* the last three words on a piece of audio, given to presenters and technicians as a cue that the piece is about to end

outdoor advertising /ˈaʊtdɔːr ˌædvətaɪzɪŋ/ *noun* **1.** advertising in the open air, including advertising in public transport, on roadsides, at bus stops, skywriting, etc. **2.** advertising on the outside of a building or in the open air, using posters on hoardings or neon signs

outline /ˈaʊtlaɪn/ *noun* **1.** a general, preliminary or rough plan or account of something, that concentrates on the main features and ignores detail **2.** the most prominent or important aspects of something **3.** a drawing which only describes the shape of something

out-of-home advertising /ˌaʊt əv ˈhəʊm ˌædvətaɪzɪŋ/ *noun* outdoor advertising including transport, skywriting, etc.

out-of-home viewing /ˌaʊt əv ˈhəʊm ˌvjuːɪŋ/ *noun* television viewers who are watching in public places such as bars. Compare **in-home viewing**

out of sync /ˌaʊt əv ˈsɪŋk/ *adjective* having the sound incorrectly synchronised with the pictures

out of vision /ˌaʊt əv ˈvɪʒ(ə)n/ *noun* an instruction on scripts to show that the person talking will not be shown on screen, but heard as a voiceover. Abbreviation **OOV**

out-point /ˈaʊt pɔɪnt/ *noun* the point at which a piece in an edited sequence should finish

output /ˈaʊtpʊt/ *noun* the audio that is actually broadcast

outside broadcast /ˌaʊtsaɪd ˈbrɔːdkɑːst/ *noun* a broadcast, often live, which is made from outside a studio using mobile equipment. Outside broadcasts are used, for example, for reporting from a sports game or other public event. Abbreviation **OB, o.b.**

outside source /ˌaʊtsaɪd ˈsɔːs/ *noun* a feed coming into a studio from an outside broadcast or other place. Abbreviation **OS**

outtake /ˈaʊtteɪk/ *noun* a scene or sequence that is left out of the final edit of a film or television programme, usually because it contains mistakes

overclaim /ˌəʊvəˈkleɪm/ *verb* in a survey, to exaggerate in your replies and say that you have had more opportunities to see or hear advertisements than you really have. Compare **underclaim**

overdetermination /ˌəʊvədɪˌtɜːmɪˈneɪʃ(ə)n/ *noun* the process of understanding all the different meanings and images that have been combined into a single, simple image during the dream process of condensation

overdevelop /ˌəʊvədɪˈveləp/ *verb* to produce too much contrast in a photographic image by exceeding the amount of time, temperature or strength of solution required to develop the film

overdub /ˌəʊvəˈdʌb/ *noun* an extra layer of sound or music added to a recording ■ *verb* to add another layer of sound or music to a recording

overexpose /ˌəʊvərɪkˈspəʊz/ *verb* to expose a film to too much light or for too long a time, so that the colours or tones in the resulting photograph are too light

overexposure /ˌəʊvərɪksˈpəʊʒə/ *noun* an act or incident of overexposing photographic film to light

overhearing /ˌəʊvəˈhɪərɪŋ/ *noun* the act of ignoring or altering those parts of a message we have received, but do not wish to process, often unconsciously

overkill /ˈəʊvəkɪl/ *noun* a very intensive and expensive marketing campaign that has the effect of putting customers off

'…political advertising is about to reach overkill proportions… The truth is that politicians' blind faith in the power of advertising is based on the myth that success is directly proportional to the size of the budget.' [*Campaign*]

overkill signal /ˈəʊvəkɪl ˌsɪgn(ə)l/ *noun* a gesture or facial expression which is too large or loud to be judged sincere, for example a smile which is too wide or bright

overlay *noun* /ˈəʊvəleɪ/ in traditional methods of printing, a piece of paper used to add more pressure on a forme or printing plate where the type is not printing evenly ■ *verb* /ˌəʊvəˈleɪ/ to attach a piece of paper to parts of the surface of an old-fasioned printing press to help make a uniform impression on a forme or plate

overline /ˈəʊvəlaɪn/ *noun* same as **strapline**

overmatter /ˈəʊvəmætə/ *noun* copy that has been typeset but exceeds the space available and cannot be included in the final version. Also called **overset**

overmiked /ˌəʊvəˈmaɪkd/ *adjective* referring to amplified or recorded sound that is too loud because a microphone has been positioned or adjusted incorrectly

overprint /ˌəʊvəˈprɪnt/ *noun* a further printing on a surface, especially text, numbers or another colour ■ *verb* to print additional material onto a printed surface, especially text, numbers or another colour ▶ also called (all senses) **surprint**

overrun *verb* /ˌəʊvəˈrʌn/ **1.** to print more copies than expected of a publication **2.** to transfer set type or illustrated material from one column, page or line to the next **3.** of a broadcast, to take more time than the allotted slot ■ *noun* /ˈəʊvərʌn/ an incident of a broadcast overrunning

overset /ˈəʊvəset/ *verb* to set too much type or copy for the available space ■ *noun* PRINTING same as **overmatter**

over-the-air /ˌəʊvə ðə ˈeə/ *adjective* referring to material transmitted by radio or television

over-the-shoulder shot /ˌəʊvə ðə ˈʃəʊldə ˌʃɒt/ *noun* a camera shot taken from over the shoulder of a character whose back can be seen at the side of the frame

over-the-transom /ˌəʊvə ðə ˈtræns(ə)m/ *adjective* referring to material that is submitted to a publisher in the hope that it will be accepted for publication

COMMENT: The phrase possibly comes from the US term **transom** meaning 'window over a door', conjuring up the image of an author throwing his manuscript onto a publisher's desk through a window left open.

Oz trial /ˈɒz ˌtraɪəl/ *noun* a 1971 obscenity trial in the UK against 'Oz' magazine, on the grounds of their having published a pornographic cartoon strip (produced by a 15-year-old) in an issue aimed at under-18s. The three editors were jailed for terms from 9 to 15 months.

P

P4A *abbreviation* **pre- and post-production paperwork automation**

PA *abbreviation* **1. Press Association 2. production assistant**

package /'pækɪdʒ/ *noun* **1.** a complete piece of audio, fully mixed and ready for broadcasting **2.** a series of interview clips linked together by a presenter or reporter ■ *verb* to create suitable or attractive packaging in which to sell a product

packager model /'pækɪdʒə ,mɒd(ə)l/ *noun* a group of themed channels provided by a broadcaster, usually on satellite or cable

package unit system /,pækɪdʒ 'juːnɪt ,sɪstəm/ *noun* the system of Hollywood film production in which each film is treated as a separate project with a separate team of director, actors and crew. It replaced the studio system in the 1950s and allows easier access to the industry for independent film-makers.

packaging /'pækɪdʒɪŋ/ *noun* **1.** the process of creating a slick and appealing image for a media product **2.** the design or style of the wrapping or container in which something is offered for sale, especially from the point of view of its appeal to buyers

'Investment in new print facilities means that our readers are being offered livelier, more colourful, more accessible packaging for a newspaper that has lost none of its gravitas, authority, breadth and fun.' [Martin Newland, *The Daily Telegraph*]

pack shot /'pæk ʃɒt/ *noun* a close-up shot in a commercial of the product itself

PACT /pækt/ *abbreviation* **Producers' Alliance for Cinema and Television**

paddle /'pæd(ə)l/ *noun* an device for operating early video games with a dial

that allowed the user to move an on-screen object up and down or from side to side

page /peɪdʒ/ *noun* **1.** a single sheet of paper, especially one bound into a book, newspaper or magazine **2.** one side of a single sheet of paper, especially one bound into a book, newspaper or magazine

page impression /'peɪdʒ ɪm,preʃ(ə)n/ *noun* a measure used to count how many times a webpage has been displayed to a visitor to a website

PageMaker /'peɪdʒ,meɪkə/ a trade name for an alternative page layout software to Quark Xpress

pager /'peɪdʒə/ *noun* a small electronic device, often with a small screen, that beeps, flashes or vibrates to let the user know that somebody is trying to contact him or her

page rate /'peɪdʒ reɪt/ *noun* the cost of a whole page of advertising space

page reader /'peɪdʒ ,riːdə/ *noun* a device which converts written or typed information to a form that a computer can understand and process

page requests /'peɪdʒ rɪ,kwests/ *plural noun* a measure of the number of webpages viewed in a day, providing an indication of the popularity of a website

Page Three /,peɪdʒ 'θriː/ a trade name for the page on which the *Sun* newspaper prints a large photograph of a nearly-naked woman

page view /'peɪdʒ vjuː/ *noun* **1.** an incident of one person looking at one webpage **2.** the number of times a webpage has been requested, assumed to be the number of responses there have been to a particular advertisement

pagination /ˌpædʒɪˈneɪʃ(ə)n/ *noun* the sequence of numbers given to pages in a book or document

painting /ˈpeɪntɪŋ/ *noun* a picture made using paint, or the art of creating pictures using paint

PAL /ˌpiː eɪ ˈel/ *noun* the system used for broadcasting television programmes in the UK, most of Europe, China and India. Full form **phased alternation line**

palmcorder /ˈpɑːmˌkɔːdə/ *noun* a small video recorder that fits into the palm of the hand

Palme d'Or /ˌpɑːm ˈdɔː/ *noun* the prestigious top prize awarded for Best Film at the Cannes Film Festival

pamphlet /ˈpæmflət/ *noun* a folded sheet or paper booklet that gives information or supports a position

pamphleteer /ˌpæmfləˈtɪə/ *verb* to write and distribute material for pamphlets, especially political ones ■ *noun* a writer or distributor of pamphlets, especially campaigning ones

pan /pæn/ *verb* to turn a camera smoothly and slowly on its axis, moving horizontally across the action being filmed without moving the base on which it is mounted. Compare **tilt** ■ *noun* a sound effect whereby sound appears to move around from one side to the other when listening using stereo speakers

panchromatic /ˌpænkrəˈmætɪk/ *adjective* referring to photographic film that is sensitive to the same colours as the human eye and some ultraviolet light

panel /ˈpæn(ə)l/ *noun* **1.** a piece of text that is separated from the main body of text by lines above and below, also usually printed in a larger size font **2.** same as **access panel 3.** a poster for advertising purposes

panorama /ˌpænəˈrɑːmə/ *noun* a picture or photograph that has a wide view, especially one that is unrolled gradually in front of the spectator

pantomime /ˈpæntəmaɪm/ *noun* a style of theatre, or a play in this style, traditionally performed at Christmas, in which a folktale or children's story is told with jokes songs, and dancing

pantomime dame /ˌpæntəmaɪm ˈdeɪm/ *noun* the comic role in a British pantomime of an ill-tempered elderly woman, traditionally played by a male actor

pantomime horse /ˌpæntəmaɪm ˈhɔːs/ *noun* a comic character in a British pantomime played by two actors in a horse costume, with one occupying the front half of the horse and the other the back half

Papa /ˈpɑːpə/ *noun* an internationally recognised code word for the letter P, used in radio communications

paparazzi /ˌpæpəˈrætsi/ *noun* persistent freelance photographers who aggressively shadow celebrities in order to take pictures of them, for example waiting outside their house or following their car

'In Los Angeles celebrities have found so few refuges from prying lenses that new laws have been brought in to protect them from the paparazzi.' [Damian Whitworth, *The Times*]

paper /ˈpeɪpə/ *noun* PRESS same as **newspaper**

paperback /ˈpeɪpəbæk/ *noun* a book with a soft flexible cover, often cheaper and in a smaller format than a hardback. Also called **soft cover**

paper edit /ˈpeɪpə ˌedɪt/ *noun* a preliminary edit of filmed material made using typed transcripts of the shots, before moving on to the recorded material

Paper Tiger TV /ˌpeɪpə ˌtaɪgə tiː ˈviː/ *noun* an alternative media organisation based in New York, which is dedicated to promoting free access and distribution for independent producers

Paperwork Reduction Act /ˌpeɪpəwɜːk rɪˈdʌkʃ(ə)n ˌækt/ *noun* an Act in the United States that aims to reduce the amount of bureaucracy and unnecessary government paperwork that is criticised for putting much information beyond the reach of ordinary citizens

par. *abbreviation* a journalistic abbreviation for 'paragraph'

parabolic reflector /ˌpærəbɒlɪk rɪˈflektə/ *noun* **1.** a curved reflector used to focus a beam of light **2.** a large disc, usually made of metal, used to funnel sound waves into a microphone placed at its centre

paradigm /ˈpærədaɪm/ *noun* **1.** a standard or typical example of a genre **2.** a set of concepts, assumptions, values or practices

paragraph /'pærəgrɑːf/ *noun* a short item in a newspaper ■ *verb* to report a news item in a short paragraph

parajournalism /ˌpærə'dʒɜːnəlɪz(ə)m/ *noun* PRESS same as **new journalism**

parallel broadcast /ˌpærəlel 'brɔːdkɑːst/ *noun* a broadcast that is transmitted by radio and on television or over the Internet at the same time

Paramount /'pærəmaʊnt/ *noun* a major film studio based in Hollywood and formed in 1914. Among the many blockbusters it has produced are Grease, Mission: Impossible, Titanic (jointly with 20th Century Fox) and War of the Worlds.

paraproxemics /ˌpærəprɒk'siːmɪks/ *noun* the creation of the viewer's perception of space in film and television, for example by the use of close-ups

parasocial interaction /ˌpærəsəʊʃ(ə)l ˌɪntər'ækʃən/ *noun* the 'relationship' between the viewer and an on-screen character

parchment /'pɑːtʃmənt/ *noun* strong, stiff, usually off-white paper used for special documents

parenthesis /pə'renθəsɪs/ *noun* PRINTING same as **bracket**

parody /'pærədi/ *noun* **1.** the humorous imitation of another object or text or style **2.** same as **spoof**

parole /pə'rəʊl/ *noun* the spoken or written word

participant observation /pɑːˌtɪsɪpənt ˌɒbzə'veɪʃ(ə)n/ *noun* a method of researching societies and culture in which the researcher becomes an accepted member of the community they are observing in order to get an 'inside' point of view

participation /pɑːˌtɪsɪ'peɪʃ(ə)n/ *noun* the practice of taking part in something, for example when advertisers buy advertising time on television

partisan /'pɑːtɪz(ə)n, ˌpɑːtɪ'zæn/ *noun* showing a bias or allegiance, as in news coverage of party politics

'In the US, the birthplace of blog culture, it was easy to see how almost any viewpoints expressed online were going to count as a breath of fresh air…. Britain's press, by contrast, has long been more politically diverse and unashamedly partisan, which may explain the blogs' lesser impact here.' [Oliver Burkeman, *The Guardian*]

partwork /'pɑːtwɜːk/ *noun* a series of magazines published over a period of time and intended to be collected to form a complete volume

party political broadcast /ˌpɑːti pə ˌlɪtɪk(ə)l 'brɔːdkɑːst/ *noun* a short television or radio programme in which representatives from a political party can comment on political issues or can campaign, especially during an election

p as b /ˌpiː əz 'biː/ *abbreviation* **programme as broadcast**

passage /'pæsɪdʒ/ *noun* a person passing the site of an outdoor advertisement such as a poster

passivity /pæ'sɪvɪti/ *noun* a view that the attitude of a typical audience is entirely passive and accepts all 'ideas' sold to them

pass-on reader /'pɑːs ɒn ˌriːdə/ *noun* same as **secondary reader**

paste up /ˌpeɪst 'ʌp/ *verb* to take printed pages or proofs and stick them onto separate sheets of paper so that they can be read and amended

paste-up /ˌpeɪst 'ʌp/ *noun* **1.** cards on which pieces of typesetting or artwork have been placed to be photographed for making printing plates **2.** a number of sheets of paper onto which printed pages or proofs have been pasted for checking

pastiche /pæ'stiːʃ/ *noun* a media product that mimics another maker, for example a film made in the style of a famous director. Compare **spoof**

patch /pætʃ/ *verb* to connect one telephone or radio caller with another or transfer a call

patriarchy /'peɪtriɑːki/ *noun* a view of society as a hierarchy dominated by the older male

Patriot Act 2001 /'peɪtriət ækt/ *noun* an Act in the United States rushed out in response to the September 11th terrorist attacks, designed to give authorities the 'tools' to prevent terrorism, mainly by allowing much greater access to personal information of suspects

pattern advertising /'pæt(ə)n ˌædvətaɪzɪŋ/ *noun* an advertising campaign that follows a global approach

patter song /'pætə sɒŋ/ *noun* a long song, especially in the works of Gilbert and Sullivan, that consists of a simple melody and very fast, usually comic, lyrics

pay cable /'peɪ ˌkeɪb(ə)l/ *noun* cable television that viewers who want to watch it have to pay for

pay-off /'peɪ ɒf/ *noun* the last sentence of a news report, often incorporating a sign-off

pay-per-play /ˌpeɪ pɜː 'pleɪ/ *noun* a website where the user has to pay to play an interactive game over the Internet

pay-per-view /ˌpeɪ pɜː 'vjuː/ *noun* a subscription system in which viewers pay for each television programme they wish to receive, which will then be decoded for them. Abbreviation **PPV**. Also called **encrypted service**

pay television /'peɪ telɪˌvɪʒ(ə)n/, **pay TV** /'peɪ tiː viː/ *noun* a system in which television programmes are transmitted in a scrambled form that can be decoded by viewers who have paid for the appropriate equipment. Abbreviation **PTV**

PBS *abbreviation* BROADCAST, US **Public Broadcasting Service**

PCC *abbreviation* **Press Complaints Commission**

PC/TV /ˌpiː siː tiː 'viː/ *noun* a personal computer that can receive, decode and display standard television images

.pdf *noun* a format that allows different types of documents to be viewed and printed using Adobe's Acrobat

pe, p.e. *abbreviation* PRINTING **printer's error**

peak performance meter /ˌpiːk pə 'fɔːməns ˌmiːtə/ *noun* a meter measuring the volume peaks of a broadcast. Compare **volume unit meter**

ped /ped/ *abbreviation* **pedestal**

pedestal /'pedɪst(ə)l/ *noun* a wheeled mounting for a studio camera. Abbreviation **ped**

Peewee /'piːwiː/ a trade name for a small wheeled camera dolly

penetrated market /ˌpenɪtreɪtɪd 'mɑːkɪt/ *noun* a market where more of a company's products are sold, shown as a percentage of the total market

penetration /ˌpenɪ'treɪʃ(ə)n/ *noun* the amount to which a given media has 'penetrated' the market, i.e. the number of people that use it or are able to use it

penetration strategy /penɪ'treɪʃ(ə)n ˌstrætədʒi/ *noun* a plan for selling a company's products to a particular section of a market, shown as a percentage of the total market

penny dreadful /ˌpeni 'dredf(ə)l/ *noun* a cheap book or comic containing sensational stories of adventure, crime or passion

pentaprism /'pentəˌprɪz(ə)m/ *noun* a prism with five faces that deviates light at a 90° angle, making it useful in presenting an image in the viewfinder of a single-lens reflex camera correctly

Peoplemeter /ˌpiːpəl'ɒmɪtə/ *noun* the method used by TNS to carry out their audience measurement surveys, using a remote control to register what they are viewing

People's Communication Charter /ˌpiːp(ə)lz kəˌmjuːnɪ'keɪʃ(ə)n ˌtʃɑːtə/ *noun* a proposal to protect every person's right to unrestricted and undistorted information and communication channels

perception /pə'sepʃən/ *noun* the process of using the senses to acquire information about the surrounding environment or situation

'The Prime Minister, for his part, understands no less keenly that the public's perception of crime has changed fundamentally. "I think most people would say that in virtually every aspect of their life things are better than they were 30 or 40 years ago".' [Matthew D'Ancona, *The Daily Telegraph*]

per diem /ˌpɜː 'diːem/ *noun* money that is given as an allowance for daily expenses

perfect /pə'fekt/ *verb* to print the second side of a page

perfect competition /ˌpɜːfɪkt ˌkɒmpə'tɪʃ(ə)n/ *noun* the ideal market, where all products are equal in price and all customers are provided with all information about the products

performance art /pə'fɔːməns ɑːt/ *noun* a form of art that combines two or more artistic media such as a traditionally static medium such as sculpture or photography, and a dramatic medium such as recitation or improvisation

performative /pə'fɔːmətɪv/ *noun* a verb which carries added information about the way in which an action is carried out, for example 'heave', which means 'lift or pull with effort'

performativity /pəˌfɔːməˈtɪvɪti/ *noun* in feminist theory, the way in which identity is constructed around expected social norms, which are 'performed' or acted out

Performing Rights Society /pə ˌfɔːmɪŋ ˈraɪts səˌsaɪəti/ *noun* a body that represents the rights of composers and performers and controls the payment of royalties to artists and publishers. Abbreviation **PRS**

period drama /ˌpɪəriəd ˈdrɑːmə/ *noun* same as **costume drama**

periodical /ˌpɪəriˈɒdɪk(ə)l/ *noun* a magazine or journal published regularly, especially weekly, monthly or quarterly ▪ *adjective* referring to something published at regular intervals

periodicity /ˌpɪəriəˈdɪsɪti/ *noun* the time period during which a news media text is on release and the news within it is considered to be current, for example 24 hours for a daily newspaper

peripheral /pəˈrɪf(ə)rəl/ *noun* a device that plugs into a computer, such as a printer, modem etc.

peripheral nations /pəˌrɪfərəl ˈneɪʃ(ə)nz/ *plural noun* countries that have restricted access to information, generally those whose communications systems are less developed. Compare **core nations**

permission /pəˈmɪʃ(ə)n/ *noun* a formal agreement that filming can be carried out in a particular location, or that images, sound or text may be used by somebody who does not hold the rights

personal ad /ˈpɜːs(ə)n(ə)l æd/ *noun* a usually classified newspaper or magazine advertisement in which somebody expresses interest in meeting others or sends a message of a personal nature to somebody else

personal column /ˈpɜːs(ə)n(ə)l ˌkɒləm/ *noun* a section of a newspaper or magazine in which personal ads are printed

personal content /ˌpɜːs(ə)n(ə)l ˈkɒntent/ *noun* content on a personal webpage such as home photographs

personal idiom /ˌpɜːs(ə)n(ə)l ˈɪdiəm/ *noun* an 'in-joke', a word or phrase that has a special meaning within a particular group or relationship

personalisation /ˌpɜːs(ə)nəlaɪˈzeɪʃ(ə)n/ *noun* the use of human interest to capture audience attention when reporting a news story, for example using tales of individual suffering to illustrate a large-scale disaster

personalising transformation /ˌpɜːs(ə)nəlaɪzɪŋ ˌtrænsfəˈmeɪʃ(ə)n/ *noun* the use of available news footage to capture audience attention by putting together emotive images and an emotive commentary, even if these are not directly related to the news item being covered

personality /ˌpɜːsəˈnælɪti/ *noun* **1.** a famous person, usually connected with television or sport **2.** the character, especially the tone, of an advertising e-mail, for example serious or cheerful

personal mic /ˌpɜːs(ə)nəl ˈmaɪk/ *noun* a small radio microphone clipped to a person's clothing so that they can move around

personal space /ˌpɜːs(ə)nəl ˈspeɪs/ *noun* the space around a person's body, possessions etc which it feels uncomfortable or stressful for another person (especially a stranger) to move into

person culture /ˈpɜːs(ə)n ˌkʌltʃə/ *noun* an organisational structure in a business which is constantly shifting and has no fixed power base or roles. Compare **power culture, role culture, task culture**

perspective /pəˈspektɪv/ *noun* **1.** the idea of seeing an object or scene from a particular point of view, by suggesting depth in something like a flat drawing **2.** seeing something from another person's mental 'point of view', by recreating their understanding of a situation

perspective correction /pəˈspektɪv kəˌrekʃ(ə)n/ *noun* in a three-dimensional scene, a method that is used to change the size and shape of an object to give the impression of depth and distance in an image

persuasibility /pəˌsweɪzɪˈbɪlɪti/ *noun* the degree to which a target audience can be persuaded through advertising that a product has good qualities

persuasion matrix /pəˈsweɪʒ(ə)n ˌmeɪtrɪks/ *noun* a planning model that shows how responses are affected by the communications they receive

pester power /ˈpestə ˌpaʊə/ *noun* the technique of selling to adults (who have the money) by appealing to children (who do not) and relying on them to pester their parents into buying the item for them

'David Beckham was accused of exposing parents to pester power yesterday as he prepared to launch his sixth pair of Adidas football boots in just 18 months. It means a £1,100 bill for any parent forced to fork out for all six pairs.' [Henry Mellor, *The Daily Mail*]

PG /ˌpiːˈdʒiː/ a trade name for a film classification indicating that a film may be seen by anyone, but that parents should decide on its suitability for their own children

PG-13 /ˌpiː dziː θɜːˈtiːn/ a trade name for a film classification indicating that a film may be seen by anyone, but that parents should decide on its suitability for their own children if they are under the age of 13

phallocentric /ˌfæləʊˈsentrɪk/ *adjective* according to feminist theory, centred on the view of the male (symbolised by the penis) as dominant in society, and psychological development according to this view

phallus /ˈfæləs/ *noun* the penis, as a symbol of male power and authority

phased alternation line /ˌfeɪzd ˌɔːltəˈreɪʃ(ə)n ˌlaɪn/ *noun* TV full form of **PAL**

phatic /ˈfætɪk/ *adjective* of a message or piece of communication, having the function of maintaining open channels of communication. ◊ **conative**, **emotive**, **metalingual**, **poetic**

phatic language /ˌfætɪk ˈlæŋgwɪdʒ/ *noun* language such as greetings, that is used primarily for maintaining social contact and interpersonal relationships, rather than for exchanging information

phenotypical /ˌfiːnəʊˈtɪpɪk(ə)l/ *adjective* of a person's appearance, characteristic of their genetic make-up which can be loosely linked to an originating area of the world

phish /fɪʃ/ *verb* to trick somebody into providing personal financial details by sending an e-mail that is supposed to be from a bank, Internet provider, etc. asking them to verify an account number or password on a (fake) website

'Over the past two weeks, [my laptop] has developed the habit of groaning and blinking and then launching all sorts of pop-up adverts… If you're surfing on eBay, up pops a suspicious eBay login screen, via Aurora, that may well be a so-called "phish" – an attempt to heist your password and personal information.' [Richard Siklos, *The Daily Telegraph*]

Phoenix log /ˈfiːnɪks lɒg/ a trade name for an automated computer program that picks up all timecodes, scene descriptions etc. from pieces of film ready to be edited, which can then be slotted into editing programs

phone-in /ˈfəʊn ɪn/ *noun* a radio or television programme in which the audience can call the host and any guests and ask questions, make comments or take part in discussions

phoneme /ˈfəʊniːm/ *noun* a basic unit of sound within a language, usually represented by a single letter in languages using the Roman alphabet

phoner /ˈfəʊnə/ *noun* an interview that takes place over the telephone, especially on a radio or television programme

phones /fəʊnz/ *plural noun* a set of earphones or headphones

phonetics /fəˈnetɪks/ *noun* the study of language sounds, how they are produced, understood and represented by symbols

phono /ˈfɒnəʊ/ *adjective* referring to signals transmitted over a telephone line

phono connector /ˈfəʊnəʊ kəˌnektə/ *noun* a standard plug and socket system used to connect audio and video devices

phonodisc /ˈfɒnəʊdɪsk/ *noun* an early method of video recording using a 10-inch record, which never caught on commercially

Phonographic Performance Ltd /ˌfɒnəʊgræfɪk pəˈfɔːməns ˌlɪmɪtɪd/ *noun* a licensing body for the broadcasting of music, representing record companies and collecting royalties for them. Abbreviation **PPL**

phonology /fəˈnɒlədʒi/ *noun* the study of the set and patterns of language sounds that make up a language

phosphor /ˈfɒsfə/ *noun* a substance that can emit light when irradiated with particles of electromagnetic radiation, used in television sets

photo /ˈfəʊtəʊ/ *noun* same as **photograph** ■ *verb* same as **photograph**

photocall /'fəʊtəʊkɔːl/ *noun* **1.** an occasion when celebrities pose for photographers, usually for publicity purposes **2.** MEDIA same as **photo opportunity**

photoconductive /ˌfəʊtəʊkən'dʌktɪv/ *adjective* electrically conductive in varying amounts according to exposure to light

photocopy /'fəʊtəʊkɒpi/ *noun* a copy of something printed, written or drawn that is produced almost instantly by a photographic process in a machine designed for this purpose

photodigital memory /ˌfəʊtəʊdɪdʒɪt(ə)l 'mem(ə)ri/ *noun* a computer memory system that uses a laser to write data onto a piece of film which can then be read many times but not be written to again

photoessay /'fəʊtəʊˌeseɪ/ *noun* MEDIA same as **photo story**

photoflash /'fəʊtəʊflæʃ/ *noun* PHOTOGRAPHY same as **flashbulb**

photoflood /'fəʊtəʊflʌd/ *noun* a very bright incandescent lamp used in photography and filming

photogram /'fəʊtəʊgræm/ *noun* a photographic image produced without a camera, usually by placing an object on or near a piece of film or light-sensitive paper and exposing it to light

photogrammetry /ˌfəʊtəʊ'græmətri/ *noun* the technique of making scale drawings from photographs, especially in the construction of maps, using aerial photography

photograph /'fəʊtəgrɑːf/ *noun* an image produced on light-sensitive film inside a camera, especially a print or slide made from the processed image, or a reproduction in a newspaper, magazine or book. Also called **picture** ■ *verb* **1.** to produce an image of something or somebody using a camera **2.** to be able to be photographed, or to have a particular quality or appearance in a photograph

photographic /ˌfəʊtə'græfɪk/ *adjective* relating to, used in or produced by photography

photographic truth /ˌfəʊtəgræfɪk 'truːθ/ *noun* the belief that photographs do not lie, i.e. that they cannot be altered and can be used as documentary proof. This is now not the case, with digital manipulation of images being readily available.

photography /fə'tɒgrəfi/ *noun* **1.** the process of recording images by exposing light-sensitive film to light or other forms of radiation **2.** the art, hobby or profession of taking photographs, and developing and printing the film or processing the digitised image

photogravure /ˌfəʊtəʊgrə'vjʊə/ *noun* an early process of reprinting in large quantities from a photographic image, using an engraved plate

photojournalism /'fəʊtəʊˌdʒɜːnəlɪz(ə)m/ *noun* a form of journalism in which photographs play a more important role than the accompanying text

photomap /'fəʊtəʊmæp/ *noun* a map created from an aerial photograph with added placenames, grid lines and other information ■ *verb* to make a photomap of an area

photomechanical /ˌfəʊtəʊmə'kænɪk(ə)l/ *adjective* referring to a method of producing printed text or images that uses photography

photo messaging /'fəʊtəʊ ˌmesɪdʒɪŋ/ *noun* TELECOMS same as **picture messaging**

photomicrograph /ˌfəʊtəʊ'maɪkrəgrɑːf/ *noun* a photograph made of something seen through a microscope

photomontage /'fəʊtəʊˌmɒntɑːʒ/ *noun* the art of combining different photographic images to create a single image

photomosaic /'fəʊtəʊməˌzeɪɪk/ *noun* a large picture made up of many photographs, for example a combination of aerial photographs to produce a detailed picture of an area

photo-offset /ˌfəʊtəʊ 'ɒfset/ *noun* a method of offset printing in which plates are created using photographic methods

photo opportunity /'fəʊtəʊ ˌɒpətjuːnɪti/ *noun* an opportunity for the media to photograph a politician or other public figure, especially when it is likely to produce favourable publicity because of the particular event or activity. Also called **photocall**

'[Davis] threw himself into a series of bizarre and perhaps unwise photo opportunities… At the Gloucestershire County Association for the Blind, he… nonchalantly tried out several vision inhibitors – black visors that would not have looked out of place on a Marvel superhero. This delighted the photographers, which is always a bad sign.' [Sam Coates, *The Times*]

Photoshop /'fəʊtəʊʃɒp/ a trade name for software that allows images to be manipulated

photo story /'fəʊtəʊ ˌstɔːri/ *noun* a series of photographs telling a story in a magazine or book. Also called **photoessay**

phototypeset /ˌfəʊtəʊ'taɪpset/ *verb* to prepare text for printing by the use of filmsetting

phototypesetter /ˌfəʊtəʊ'taɪpsetə/ *noun* a device that can make high-quality reproductions of text on photosensitive paper or film

pi /paɪ/ *noun* a pile of printing type that has been mixed up together ■ *verb* to mix printing type up together

pic /pɪk/ *noun* picture, photograph

pica /'paɪkə/, **pica em** *noun* a unit of measurement for printing type, equal to 12 points or 0.422 cm/0.166 in. Also called **em**

pick up /ˌpɪk 'ʌp/ *verb* to successfully receive something such as a radio or television signal or a radar image on a piece of equipment

pick-up /'pɪk ʌp/ *noun* **1.** a pick-up job is one in which the journalist collects news or photographs of an event from the organisers after it has happened **2.** RECORDING same as **tone arm**

pick-up pattern /'pɪk ʌp ˌpætən/ *noun* the sensitivity of a microphone to sounds from different directions

pictorial /pɪk'tɔːriəl/ *noun* a newspaper or magazine that has many pictures in it, especially one with far more pictures than text

pictorialism /pɪk'tɔːriəlɪz(ə)m/ *noun* a style of photography, popular at the beginning of the 20th century, which used soft-focus techniques to imitate academic painting

picture /'pɪktʃə/ *noun* **1.** a cinema film or motion picture **2.** the image on a television screen **3.** PHOTOGRAPHY same as **photograph** ■ *verb* to feature a picture, especially a photograph, of somebody or something in a newspaper, magazine or book

picture beam /'pɪktʃə biːm/ *noun* a moving electron beam in a television that produces an image on the screen by illuminating the phosphor coating and by varying its intensity according to the received signal

picture-grabber /'pɪktʃə ˌgræbə/ *noun* a device for capturing still pictures from a moving piece of video

picture-in-picture /ˌpɪktʃə ɪn 'pɪktʃə/ *noun* a facility on some televisions for showing a small screen view of another channel over the top of the main picture. Abbreviation **PiP**

picture library /'pɪktʃə ˌlaɪbr(ə)ri/ *noun* a photograph store, from which images may be borrowed for use in books, magazines and newspapers

picture messaging /'pɪktʃə ˌmesɪdʒɪŋ/ *noun* the practice of sending images and photographs from one mobile phone to another. Also called **photo messaging**

picture postcard /'pɪktʃə ˌpəʊstkɑːd/ *noun* a small card for sending through the post, which has a picture on one side and is left blank on the other side for the sender's message

picture researcher /'pɪktʃə rɪ ˌsɜːtʃə/ *noun* somebody whose job is to find the photographs, drawings and other illustrative material for a book or magazine, using picture libraries and other sources

pictures /'pɪktʃəz/ *plural noun* the cinema, as a place of entertainment, or a cinema show

pie /paɪ/ *noun* another spelling of **pi**

piece /piːs/ *noun* an article in a newspaper or magazine or an item on a television or radio programme

piece-to-camera /ˌpiːs tə 'kæm(ə)rə/ *noun* a shot in which a presenter or reporter speaks directly to the camera, usually used in news reporting. Abbreviation **PTC**. Also called **stand-up**

Pilkington Committee Report on Broadcasting 1962 /'pɪlkɪŋtən/ *noun* a report on the standards and effects of broadcasting after the introduction of ITV. It largely praised the BBC but strongly criticised ITV and recommended that it be externally regulated and planned, a proposal that was never taken up.

pilot /'paɪlət/ *noun* a television or radio programme made as an experiment, to test audience reaction to an idea for a possible new series

pilot study /ˈpaɪlət ˌstʌdi/ *noun* a study that is preliminary to an intended full study, to see whether it will be feasible and gives the intended results

pinch roller /ˈpɪntʃ ˌrəʊlə/ *noun* part of a device for playing back tape (such as a reel-to-reel machine) which holds the tape in place while it travels between reels

pinhole camera /ˈpɪnhəʊl ˌkæm(ə)rə/ *noun* a basic form of camera with a tiny hole for the aperture, and no lens. Light passes through the hole to form an inverted image on the film.

pink advertising /ˈpɪŋk ˌædvətaɪzɪŋ/ *noun* advertising aimed specifically at the gay and lesbian market

pip /pɪp/ *noun* a short, usually high-pitched sound, especially of the kind used in broadcasting as a time signal

PiP *abbreviation* **picture-in-picture**

piracy /ˈpaɪrəsi/ *noun* the illegal copying, distribution or broadcasting of copyright-protected media texts such as films, programmes, CDs etc

'The US movie industry won an important symbolic breakthrough in its fight against online piracy yesterday as it announced an accord with the creator of a technology that is widely used for copying movies and TV shows illegally over the internet.' [Richard Waters, *The Financial Times*]

pirate /ˈpaɪrət/ *noun* somebody who broadcasts television or radio programmes illegally

pirate radio /ˌpaɪrət ˈreɪdiəʊ/ *noun* radio stations that broadcast illegally (without a licence) and often do not pay royalties or other fees, but can attract huge numbers of listeners

pitch /pɪtʃ/ *noun* a presentation by an advertising agency to a potential customer

pitchman /ˈpɪtʃmæn/ *noun* somebody show presents commercials on television or radio, especially a man

pitchperson /ˈpɪtʃˌpɜːs(ə)n/ *noun* somebody who presents commercials on television or radio

pitchwoman /ˈpɪtʃˌwʊmən/ *noun* a woman who presents commercials on television or radio

pix /pɪks/ CINEMA, PHOTOGRAPHY, ARTS plural of **pic**

Pixar /ˈpɪksɑː/ *noun* a major animation studio which develops computer graphics technology and also has produced feature films such as Monsters Inc (2001) and The Incredibles (2004)

pixel /ˈpɪksəl/ *noun* a single dot on a computer screen which forms part of what is seen. The more pixels that a screen has, the sharper the image resolution.

pixelated /ˈpɪksəleɪtɪd/ *adjective* referring to an image on a computer or television screen that is made up of pixels, especially one that is unclear or distorted

plagiarism /ˈpleɪdʒərɪz(ə)m/ *noun* the process of copying another person's idea or written work and claiming it as original

plaintext /ˌpleɪnˈtekst/ *noun* text or information that has not been encrypted or coded

planer /ˈpleɪnə/ *noun* a flat block of wood used to hold printing type level in a chase

planned obsolescence /ˌplænd ˌɒbsəˈles(ə)ns/ *noun* the theory that certain manufacturers do not design their products to last as long as they could, so that consumers will be forced to buy more

planted news /ˌplɑːntɪd ˈnjuːz/ *noun* propaganda in the form of inaccurate 'news', reported as real and accurate, which discredits an enemy or presents the propagandist in a good light

plasma /ˈplæzmə/ *noun* a screen that displays pictures through a live camera to the rest of the studio

plasma screen /ˈplæzmə skriːn/ *noun* a type of flat display screen for computers and televisions, which gives clearer pictures than the older cathode ray tube technology

plate /pleɪt/ *noun* **1.** a template for printing, either an engraved metal sheet or a phototypeset page **2.** a full-page illustration or photograph in a book, especially on glossy paper **3.** a sheet of glass or other material coated with a light-sensitive film to receive a photographic image **4.** a print made from a printing plate, especially one inserted into a book on paper different from that on which the text is printed **5.** part of a tripod set-up that fixes the camera securely to the tripod ■ *verb* to set up movable printing type into page form ready for printing

platemaker /'pleɪt,meɪkə/ *noun* a person or machine that prepares plates for printing

platen /'pleɪt(ə)n/ *noun* a flat metal plate in a printing press that holds the paper against the inked type

platform /'plætfɔːm/ *noun* a purpose-built scaffolding platform that cameras can be mounted on for a good view of events

play /pleɪ/ *noun* a dramatic work written to be performed by actors on the stage, television or radio

playback /'pleɪbæk/ *noun* **1.** the replay of a sound or video recording after it has been made, often as a check for quality or accuracy **2.** the facility in a recording device for replaying recordings

playback rate scale factor /ˌpleɪbæk reɪt 'skeɪl ˌfæktə/ *noun* the point at which video playback is no longer smooth and appears jerky because of missed frames

playback singer /'pleɪbæk ˌsɪŋə/ *noun* a singer who sings songs that film actors are then able to mime to

playbill /'pleɪbɪl/ *noun* a poster advertising a play or other theatrical performance

play-by-play /ˌpleɪ baɪ 'pleɪ/ *noun* a spoken description of an event as it happens, especially of a sporting event being broadcast on radio or television (*informal*)

playlist /'pleɪlɪst/ *noun* a list of musical recordings that are to be played on a radio programme or by a radio station

play theory of mass communication /ˌpleɪ ˌθɪəri əv mæs kəˌmjuːnɪ'keɪʃ(ə)n/ *noun* the idea that media communications cannot have harmful effects because the audience uses them primarily for entertainment, rather than as serious sources of information

pleasure /'pleʒə/ *noun* in feminist theory, the desire for fulfilment of natural urges such as the sexual urge, ignoring social or moral considerations

plot /plɒt/ *noun* the story or sequence of events in something such as a novel, play or film ■ *verb* to plan the sequence of events in a story or script

plug /plʌg/ *noun* **1.** a mention given to something in order to advertise it, for example in a published article or on the radio. It is often given as a favour or in exchange for another service, for example plugging an artist's album in return for an exclusive interview. **2.** a line on the cover of a publication that boasts an interesting article inside

'When viewers settled down to watch Channel 4's blockbuster drama Lost, they were anticipating an hour of action and intrigue. What they got instead was almost 30 minutes of advertising, sponsor plugs, programme trailers and plot reminders.' [Ciar Byrne, *The Independent*]

pluralism /'plʊərəlɪz(ə)m/ *noun* the idea that there are many different ideas and value systems that make up a society, and that each are equal and should be allowed to thrive

podcasting /'pɒd,kɑːstɪŋ/ *noun* the act of offering audio or video files over the Internet to subscribing users

podding /'pɒdɪŋ/ *noun* the practice of having small groups of multi-skilled reporters and photographers work together

poetic /pəʊ'etɪk/ *adjective* of a message or piece of communication, referring to its own form or the context in which it is transmitted. ◊ **conative, emotive, metalingual, phatic**

Pogle /'pəʊg(ə)l/ a trade name for a grading system for use in post-production

point /pɔɪnt/ *noun* **1.** in printing or writing, a punctuation mark, especially a full stop **2.** a unit of measurement in printing equal to one twelfth of a pica or approximately 0.03515 cm/0.01384 in

point-and-shoot /ˌpɔɪnt ən 'ʃuːt/ *adjective* referring to a camera that requires no adjustment by the user before taking a photograph, because the focus and exposure are adjusted automatically or are fixed

point-of-purchase advertising /ˌpɔɪnt əv 'pɜːtʃɪs ˌædvətaɪzɪŋ/, **point-of-sale advertising** *noun* advertising at the place where the products are bought, for example posters or dump bins

point-of-view shot /ˌpɔɪnt əv 'vjuː ˌʃɒt/ *noun* full form of **POV shot**

point size /'pɔɪnt saɪz/ *noun* the unit of measurement of the font size in typesetting and on computers, generally ranging from 8 to 72

Point-to-Point Protocol /ˌpɔɪnt tə pɔɪnt 'prəʊtəʊkɒl/ *noun* a protocol for dial-up access to the Internet using a modem

polar diagram /'pəʊlə ˌdaɪəgræm/ *noun* a diagram showing the pick-up pattern of a microphone

polarisation /ˌpəʊləraɪ'zeɪʃ(ə)n/ *noun* the tendency to think and speak using oppositions, i.e. forming definitions by comparing something to something which it is not

Polaroid /'pəʊlərɔɪd/ a trade name for a camera that produces pictures that develop inside it within seconds of being taken, or the film used in such a camera

polecam /'pəʊlkæm/ *noun* a camera mounted on a pole and operated by remote control

police procedural /pə'liːs prə ˌsiːdʒərəl/ *noun* a crime novel or drama in which a crime is investigated by police officers rather than amateur detectives

police reporter /pə'liːs rɪˌpɔːtə/ *noun* a journalist who is assigned to cover news about crime and police work

politically correct /pəˌlɪtɪkli kə'rekt/ *adjective* marked by language or conduct that deliberately avoids giving offence, for example on the basis of ethnic origin or sexual orientation

polychronic time /ˌpɒlikrɒnɪk 'taɪm/ *noun* an image of the perception of time in some cultures in which it is flexible and fluid, deadlines etc are not adhered to and many things can be done at the same time, picked up and left off etc. Abbreviation **P-time**. Compare **monochronic time**

polysemic /ˌpɒli'siːmɪk/ *adjective* in semiology, referring to a combination of symbols that can be interpreted in many different ways

polysemy /pə'lɪsəmi/ *noun* the theory that an image can be interpreted in many different ways by different observers, and may need to be accompanied by text or sound to restrict the way it is interpreted

pool /puːl/, **pool arrangement** *noun* a small group of reporters who have personal access to an event or source, who distribute their reports to the wider media. Also called **pool system**

pool feed /'puːl fiːd/ *noun* a feed from a pool arrangement which is made available in full and without delay

pool system /'puːl ˌsɪstəm/ *noun* PRESS same as **pool**

pop /pɒp/ *adjective* referring to popular music

pop art /'pɒp ɑːt/ *noun* a post-modern form of art that makes use of graphic styles from the mass media, such as advertising, comic strips and science fiction, thereby attempting to comment on modern cultural values and society

popcorn movie /'pɒpkɔːn ˌmuːvi/ *noun* a popular and highly entertaining film

pop group /'pɒp gruːp/ *noun* a small musical band who play pop music together as a unit

pop music /'pɒp ˌmjuːzɪk/ *noun* modern commercial music, usually tuneful, up-tempo and repetitive, that is aimed at the general public and the youth market in particular

popping /'pɒpɪŋ/ *noun* distortion caused by a person speaking too close to a microphone

popular /'pɒpjʊlə/ *adjective* referring to anything that is widely liked, with a large appreciative audience, although this may be used in a derogatory way to imply a lack of artistic merit

popular culture /ˌpɒpjʊlə 'kʌltʃə/ *noun* the tastes, habits and values of the majority of people in society, that are not considered elite or 'highbrow'

populars /'pɒpjələz/ *plural noun* an old term for tabloid newspapers

populism /'pɒlɪtɪkz(ə)m/ *noun* the philosophical belief that the needs and desires of the masses should be promoted over and above those of the elite

populist /'pɒpjʊlɪst/ *noun* appealing to the masses, used in a derogatory way

'Under its new director of television, Simon Shaps, ITV is falling back on the staples of populist drama and brassy entertainment shows, following a disastrous summer with flops including Celebrity Wrestling and the critically panned Celebrity Love Island.' [Ciar Byrne, *The Independent*]

pop-under ad /'pɒp ʌndər ˌæd/ *noun* an Internet advertisement that appears in a separate browser window from the rest of a website

pop-up /'pɒp ʌp/ *noun* an advertisement which is activated when a user visits a particular webpage and launches itself in its own window

pornographic /ˌpɔːnəˈgræfɪk/ *adjective* **1.** sexually explicit and intended to cause sexual arousal **2.** producing or selling sexually explicit magazines, films or other materials

pornography /pɔːˈnɒgrəfi/ *noun* films, magazines, writings, photographs or other materials that are sexually explicit and intended to cause sexual arousal

portable single camera /ˌpɔːtəb(ə)l ˌsɪŋg(ə)l ˈkæm(ə)rə/ *noun* a small portable camera which uses video instead of film. Abbreviation **PSC**

portapak /ˈpɔːtəpæk/ *noun* a small portable video camera

Portaprompt /ˈpɔːtəprɒmt/ a trade name for a type of television prompting system

portrait /ˈpɔːtrɪt/ *noun* **1.** a painting, photograph or drawing of someone, especially just the face **2.** a description of something such as a person, place or period, which aims to give a rough overall picture ■ *adjective* referring to a piece of paper, illustration, book or page that is taller than it is wide

portraiture /ˈpɔːtreɪtʃə/ *noun* a picture of a person, especially of their face

positive /ˈpɒzɪtɪv/ *noun* a photographic image in which the light and dark tones and colours correspond to those of the original subject ■ *adjective* referring to photographic images that have colours or values of dark and light corresponding to the subject

positive appeal /ˌpɒzɪtɪv əˈpiːl/ *noun* advertising that is designed to show why a product is attractive

post /pəʊst/ *verb* **1.** to place or send a message on a newsgroup or bulletin board on the Internet or some other electronic network **2.** to update a database record by entering or transferring information **3.** to make text appear online or at an Internet location

postal sales /ˈpəʊst(ə)l seɪlz/ *plural noun* sales of products by post, through advertisements in the press

postbag /ˈpəʊstbæg/ *noun* the letters and messages received by an MP, famous person or television or radio programme

postcolonialism /ˌpəʊstkəˈləʊniəlɪz(ə)m/ *noun* the study of the effects of colonialism on the ideologies and cultures of the countries involved

poster /ˈpəʊstə/ *noun* **1.** a printed picture, often a reproduction of a photograph or artwork, used for decoration **2.** a bill or placard in a public place advertising something **3.** somebody who places a message on a website

poster specialist /ˈpəʊstə ˌspeʃəlɪst/ *noun* a company that organises an outdoor poster campaign for an advertising agency. Their job is to deal with considerations such as obtaining the rights to use each site and organising contractors to put them up.

post-feminist /ˌpəʊst ˈfemɪnɪst/ *adjective* **1.** differing from or showing a re-evaluation of the principles of feminism **2.** developing out of or including the principles of feminism ■ *noun* somebody who supports or believes in post-feminist ideas

post-Fordism /ˌpəʊst ˈfɔːdɪz(ə)m/ *noun* the process in which mass production has moved away from traditional industries such as ship-building, towards the service and technological industries

posthumanist /pəʊstˈhjuːmənɪst/ *adjective* referring to the idea that one day there will be such technological advances as can prolong human life, perhaps indefinitely, as well as improving its quality

posthumous /ˈpɒstjʊməs/ *adjective* referring to a work published or printed after the author's death

posting /ˈpəʊstɪŋ/ *noun* a message sent to and displayed on an online facility such as an Internet newsgroup or bulletin board

'London-based foreign extremists are using websites to post video footage of suicide operations and attacks by insurgents against coalition forces in Iraq. There are also postings of the execution of Russian soldiers by mujaheddin rebels in Chechnya.' [Abul Taher, *The Sunday Times*]

post-Marxism /ˌpəʊst ˈmɑːksɪz(ə)m/ *noun* a development of Marxist theories on the inequality of power in society, moving the focus away from upper/lower class-based distinctions and towards the power associated with access to technologies, education etc.

postmaster /'pəʊstmɑːstə/ *noun* **1.** a computer program that distributes, forwards and receives electronic mail **2.** the person responsible for the maintenance of a website and for being the contact point for information and complaints

postmodernism /pəʊst'mɒdənɪz(ə)m/ *noun* a concept in the arts referring to the way in which new products can be constructed with reference to existing ones

post-production /'pəʊst prə,dʌkʃ(ə)n/ *noun* the final stage in making a recording, film or television programme that includes editing, sound dubbing and adding special effects

post-purchase advertising /,pəʊst 'pɜːtʃɪs ,ædvətaɪzɪŋ/ *noun* advertising designed to minimise the possibility that a customer will regret making their purchase

PostScript /'pəʊstskrɪpt/ a trade name for a computer language that allows page layout to be described

post-synch /,pəʊst 'sɪŋk/ *verb* to add sound or music to a film after shooting

post-synchronisation /,pəʊst ,sɪŋkrənaɪ'zeɪʃ(ə)n/ *noun* same as **dubbing**

post-testing /'pəʊst ,testɪŋ/ *noun* the evaluation of an advertising campaign after it has been run, or of a product after it has been launched

postural echo /'pɒstʃərəl ,ekəʊ/ *noun* the practice of unconsciously mimicking another person's posture, gestures, facial expressions etc., as a sign of unity and closeness when interacting with them

posture /'pɒstʃə/ *noun* the way in which a person holds themselves as a means of communicating in addition to speech and gestures

pot /pɒt/ *verb* to perform a pot cut

pot cut /'pɒt kʌt/ *noun* a quick fade-out of the sound on an audio feed already being broadcast, because of overrun or to make room for another piece

POV shot /,pi: əʊ 'vi: ,ʃɒt/ *noun* a scene that is filmed from the point of view that a character would see it from. Especially effective in horror films where the character cannot see a lurking danger and the audience is waiting for them to see it,

heightening the drama. Full form **point-of-view shot**

power /'paʊə/ *noun* the idea of having a voice, being represented, having a positive and truthful image constructed of you and the groups to which you belong, etc.

PowerCD /'paʊə si: ,di:/ a trade name for a CD-ROM player produced by Apple that can connect to a television to display photo images, or to a Macintosh as a standard CD-ROM drive, or to play back music CDs

power culture /'paʊə ,kʌltʃə/ *noun* an organisational structure in a business which is based around a 'god-like' single power source. Compare **person culture**, **role culture**, **task culture**

power elite /'paʊə ɪ,liːt/ *noun* in Marxist theory, the members of a society who hold both political power and educational and financial privilege

PPL *abbreviation* **Phonographic Performance Ltd**

PPV *abbreviation* **pay-per-view**

pragmatics /præg'mætɪks/ *noun* consideration of what is sensible and will work, without reference to aesthetic values

preamplifier /pri'æmplɪfaɪə/ *noun* an amplifying circuit, for example in a radio or television, that is designed to strengthen very weak signals and then transmit them to a more powerful amplifier

pre- and post-production paperwork automation /,pri: ənd ,pəʊst prə,dʌkʃ(ə)n 'peɪpəwɜːk ,ɔːtəmeɪʃ(ə)n/ *noun* a computer program that automates all the paperwork associated with submitting a programme to the BBC, namely the billing form, the transmission form, the music reporting form and the Programme as Completed form. Abbreviation **P4A**

pre-comms /,pri: 'kɒmz/ *noun* a teaser that appears just before the commercials

predatory pricing /,pred(ə)t̬ɔːri 'praɪsɪŋ/ *noun* the practice of pricing a product in order to undercut the competition and make them unable to continue while still making a profit

'…the OFT has uncharacteristically backed down over its refusal to investigate the convenience store sector, in which independent traders claim they are being forced out by predatory

pricing from large supermarket groups.'
[Bob Sherwood, *The Financial Times*]

pre-emptive   censorship /ˌpri
ˌemptɪv ˈsensəʃip/ *noun* censorship that
takes place before the work in question is
released to the public, by editors or officials. Compare **punitive censorship**

pre-empt selling /ˌpri ˈempt ˌselɪŋ/
noun the practice of selling television
advertising time at a lower rate on condition that if another advertiser offers the
full rate, they will be able to take it over

pre-fade /ˌpriː ˈfeɪd/ *noun* RADIO a
facility on a studio desk that allows a
presenter to listen to an audio source and
adjust the level before it is recorded ■
verb to set a guest's microphone in a
broadcasting studio so that the feed can be
heard by all but the audience, so that he or
she can be briefed etc. before starting their
interview

preferred reading /prɪˈfɜːd ˌriːdɪŋ/
noun the interpretation of a media product
that was intended by the maker or which is
dictated by the ideology of the society in
which it is viewed

prejudice /ˈpredʒʊdɪs/ *noun* a pre-
formed opinion, usually an unfavourable
one, based on insufficient knowledge,
irrational feelings, or inaccurate stereotypes

pre-press /ˌpriː ˈpres/ *adjective* before
going to press

preprint /ˈpriːprɪnt/ *verb* **1.** to print
something in advance of its being used or
before the full print run **2.** to issue something, especially an article or other piece
of writing, in draft form before its official
publication ■ *noun* **1.** something that is
printed in advance, especially before
being published in full **2.** a piece of
writing, especially a contribution to an
academic journal, that is printed and often
distributed in a preliminary form before
its official publication

pre-production /ˌpriː prəˈdʌkʃ(ə)n/
noun the work done to a programme
before the filming stage, for example
script redrafting, budgeting and scheduling

prequel /ˈpriːkwəl/ *noun* a film or novel
set at a time before the action of an
existing work, especially one that has
achieved commercial success. Also called
back-story

pre-record /ˌpriː rɪˈkɔːd/ *verb* to record
something, for example a message or television or radio programme, for later use or
broadcasting

pre-roll /ˈpriː rəʊl/ *noun* leader tape or a
few seconds of blank tape at the start of a
section of film for editing

pre-sale /ˌpriː ˈseɪl/ *noun* the act of
selling distribution rights to a media
product before that product is completed,
so as to get more money for its production

pre-score /ˌpriː ˈskɔː/ *verb* to compose
or record the music or other sound for a
film or television programme before the
dialogue and picture have been produced

pre-sell /ˌpriː ˈsel/ *verb* to promote a
product or entertainment before it is
generally available to the public, by
means of advertising and publicity

present /prɪˈzent/ *verb* to introduce, or
act as the host of, a television or radio
programme or an infomercial

presentation   /ˌprez(ə)nˈteɪʃ(ə)n/
noun the department at a television station
responsible   for   links   between
programmes and trailers for future
programmes

pre-shoot /ˌpriː ˈʃuːt/ *noun* material
filmed in advance of an event

press /pres/ *noun* **1.** the news-gathering
business generally, or all the people
involved in gathering and reporting on the
news, especially journalists working on
newspapers **2.** a company that publishes
books **3.** same as **printing press**

press   advertising   /ˈpres
ˌædvətaɪzɪŋ/ *noun* advertising in newspapers and magazines

press agency /ˈpres ˌeɪdʒənsi/ *noun*
PRESS, BUSINESS same as **news agency**

press agent /ˈpres ˌeɪdʒənt/ *noun* a
promoter who deals with the press on
behalf of a client

Press   Association   /ˈpres   ə
ˌsəʊsieɪʃ(ə)n/ *noun* **1.** a national news
agency founded in 1868. Abbreviation **PA**
2. in the United States, a national, state or
local organisation of media companies
and their representatives

press clipping /ˈpres ˌklɪpɪŋ/ *noun* a
copy of a news item kept by a company
because it contains important business
information   or   is   a   record   of   news
published about the company

press communications /'pres kə
,mjuːnɪkeɪʃ(ə)nz/ *plural noun* communications that increase the awareness of journalists of a product or firm, for example press releases or news flashes

Press Complaints Commission /,pres kəm'pleɪnts kə,mɪʃ(ə)n/ *noun* the body that oversees the press in the UK, monitoring the newspapers for inappropriate content and investigating complaints. Abbreviation **PCC**

Press Complaints Commission Code of Practice 1977 *noun* the five guidelines by which the PCC operates, concerning the treatment of sensitive issues, the correction of mistakes, privacy matters, the conduct of journalists and subjects' right to reply

press conference /'pres ,kɒnf(ə)rəns/ *noun* a meeting where newspaper and television reporters are invited to hear news of something such as a new product or a takeover bid. Also called **news conference**

Press Council /'pres ,kaʊns(ə)l/ *noun* a self-regulatory governing body for the print media in many countries including Australia, New Zealand, India and the Netherlands

presser /'presə/ *noun* same as **press conference**

press freedom /'pres ,friːdəm/ *noun* ♦ **freedom of the press**

press gallery /'pres ,gæləri/ *noun* a raised gallery with seating at the back of a courtroom or legislative assembly room, where newspaper reporters and other members of the press can sit

press kit /'pres kɪt/ *noun* a package of background and promotional material relating to a product, distributed to the media by a press agent or publicity department

pressman /'presmæn/ *noun* **1.** a man working as a newspaper reporter **2.** somebody, especially a man, who operates a printing press

press officer /'pres ,ɒfɪsə/ *noun* somebody employed by an organisation or government department to provide the news media with information about the organisation or department

pressperson /'pres,pɜːs(ə)n/ *noun* **1.** a newspaper reporter **2.** somebody who operates a printing press

press relations /'pres rɪ,leɪʃ(ə)nz/ *plural noun* part of the public relations activity of an organisation, aimed at building up good relations with the press

press release /'pres rɪ,liːs/ *noun* an announcement usually in the form of a written piece, giving facts to be reported in the media. Also called **news release**

pressroom /'presruːm/ *noun* **1.** an enclosed area in a newspaper plant or printing works where the printing presses are located **2.** same as **media centre**

pressrun /'presrʌn/ *noun* **1.** the number of copies that are run off in one continuous printing operation **2.** the continuous running of a printing press until a set number of copies is printed

press secretary /'pres ,sekrət(ə)ri/ *noun* an employee who is responsible for dealing with the news media on behalf of an organisation or a prominent person

pressure group /'preʃə gruːp/ *noun* a number of people who work together to make their concerns known to those in government and to influence lawmaking

'Environmental pressure groups are divided on the best tactics to oppose moves to revive nuclear power. Some environmentalists are wary of campaigning on a negative anti-nuclear message, preferring to present the public with a more positive choice of combating climate change through renewable energy.' [Fiona Harvey, *The Financial Times*]

presswoman /'pres,wʊmən/ *noun* a woman working as a newspaper reporter

presswork /'preswɜːk/ *noun* the operation or management of a printing press, or the work done by it

prestige advertising /pre'stiːʒ ,ædvətaɪzɪŋ/ *noun* advertising in high-quality magazines to increase a company's reputation

pre-striping /,priː 'straɪpɪŋ/ *noun* the process of laying a timecode on a piece of film before filming starts

pre-testing /,priː 'testɪŋ/, **pre-test** *noun* the testing or evaluation of a product or advertising campaign before it is launched or run

preview /'priːˌvjuː/ *noun* **1.** a piece printed in a paper or magazine or broadcast on radio or television describing and commenting on something that is soon to be broadcast or presented to the public **2.** a short film shown on television or at the cinema promoting a forthcoming film or programme ■ *verb* to write, print or broadcast a short piece that describes and comments on something that is soon to be broadcast or presented to the public

price-fixing /'praɪs ˌfɪksɪŋ/ *noun* the practice, often illegal, of competing companies agreeing to set their prices at the same artificially high rate, rather than dropping them to compete with each other. ◊ **anti-trust laws**

'The threat of an inquiry into alleged price-fixing involving digital music services has emerged in New York state. Eliot Spitzer, the hawkish attorney general, has subpoenaed major companies in a preliminary investigation aimed at discovering whether they have been involved in illegal arrangements.' [Roland Gribben, *The Daily Telegraph*]

price mechanism /'praɪs ˌmekənɪz(ə)m/ *noun* the shifting of prices in a market according to, and affecting, supply and demand

primacy effect theory /'praɪməsi ɪ ˌfekt ˌθɪəri/ *noun* the theory that the first information in a message is most likely to be remembered

primary data /ˌpraɪməri 'deɪtə/ *noun* data or information which has not yet been published and must therefore be found by field research. Also called **primary information**

primary definers /ˌpraɪməri dɪ 'faɪnəz/ *plural noun* when commenting officially on events, the police, government officials and others who are in a position to speak on such matters. Compare **secondary definers**

primary demand advertising /ˌpraɪməri dɪ'mɑːnd ˌædvətaɪzɪŋ/ *noun* adevertising that increases demand for a generic product, rather than for a specific brand within that product category. Compare **selective demand advertising**

primary information /ˌpraɪməri ˌɪnfə 'meɪʃ(ə)n/ *noun* same as **primary data**

primary reader /'praɪməri ˌriːdə/ *noun* a person who buys and reads a publication themselves. Compare **secondary reader**

primary research /'praɪməri rɪˌsɜːtʃ/ *noun* information that is collected firsthand, for example an interview, original photographs or diagrams, etc. Compare **secondary research**

primary source /ˌpraɪməri 'sɔːs/ *noun* a news reporter's source (for example an eyewitness who gives an account) which provides them with primary research

primary text /'praɪməri tekst/ *noun* in textual theory, the media text which is created and transmitted, before reception. Compare **secondary text**, **tertiary text**

prime /praɪm/ *noun* a mark added to a number, character, or expression in order to distinguish it from another

prime lens /'praɪm lenz/ *noun* a lens that cannot have its focal length adjusted. Compare **zoom lens**

prime time /'praɪm taɪm/ *noun* the period in a radio or television schedule when there is the largest audience, for example weekday evenings

priming /'praɪmɪŋ/ *noun* the process of agenda-setting by giving certain news stories more prominence, airtime, attention etc

principal photography /ˌprɪnsɪp(ə)l fə'tɒɡrəfi/ *noun* same as **production period**

print /prɪnt/ *verb* **1.** to publish information or a publication **2.** to make a positive image or copy of a photograph or film from a negative **3.** to make a copy, document, or publication using a printing press or a computer printer ■ *noun* **1.** the state of being in a printed form or being published **2.** a copy of a film **3.** a photograph, usually on paper, made from a negative ■ *adjective* produced by or relating to the published media

printable /'prɪntəb(ə)l/ *adjective* sufficiently inoffensive, correct or well-written as to be fit to be printed in a publication

printed matter /'prɪntɪd ˌmætə/ *noun* published material, for example books, newspapers, magazines or catalogues

printed word /ˌprɪntɪd 'wɜːd/ *noun* written language as used in books, magazines, newspapers and other literature

printer /'prɪntə/ *noun* **1.** a machine that makes duplicates of film, normally a positive from a negative **2.** a machine that prints books, newspapers or magazines **3.**

a person or company in the business of printing books, newspapers or magazines

printer's devil /ˌprɪntəz 'devɪl/ *noun* an apprentice or young assistant to a printer

printer's error /'prɪntəz ˌerə/ *noun* a spelling error in a printed document made during typesetting

print farming /'prɪnt ˌfɑːmɪŋ/ *noun* the process in which an organisation sends out material such as advertising leaflets, catalogues, letterheads, etc. to be printed by outside printers

printhead /'prɪnthed/ *noun* the metal form of a character that is pressed onto an inked ribbon to print the character on paper

printing /'prɪntɪŋ/ *noun* the process or business of producing copies of documents, publications or images

printing press /'prɪntɪŋ pres/ *noun* a machine that presses inked type or etched plates onto paper or textiles that are fed through it

print media /'prɪnt ˌmiːdiə/ *plural noun* advertising media, for example magazines and newspapers

print run /'prɪnt rʌn/ *noun* the number of copies of a publication, document or artwork that are printed in a single batch

prior restraint /ˌpraɪə rɪ'streɪnt/ *noun* same as **pre-emptive censorship**

prism /'prɪz(ə)m/ *noun* a device used to bend and concentrate light, used in the workings of some types of camera

privacy /'prɪvəsi/ *noun* freedom from the observation, interference or attention of other people, sometimes protected by law

'Other aspects of press freedom assessments are more difficult to quantify. Would the privacy laws limiting the activities of paparazzi who pursue celebrities, as are currently being proposed in California, be a serious violation of press freedom?' [Duncan Campbell, *The Guardian*]

Privacy and Electronic Communications Directive /ˌprɪvəsi ənd ˌelektrɒnɪk kəˌmjuːnɪ'keɪʃ(ə)nz daɪ ˌrektɪv/ *noun* a European Union directive that limits the type of unsolicited direct marketing that is allowed to be sent through e-mail or text according to their content and the circumstances under which the contact details had been obtained

privatisation /ˌpraɪvətaɪ'zeɪʃ(ə)n/ *noun* the transferring of services in the public sector to private ownership

probe /prəʊb/ *noun* an investigation

problematic /ˌprɒblə'mætɪk/ *noun* a set of problems or questions that are answered by a theory, and those that are raised by it

process /prəʊ'ses/ *verb* to treat light-sensitive film or paper with chemicals so that an image that is held there becomes visible

process printing /'prəʊses ˌprɪntɪŋ/ *noun* a method of full-colour printing using multiple images from plates printed in yellow, magenta, blue and cyan

producer /prə'djuːsə/ *noun* **1.** the member of a television production team who is responsible for hiring the rest of the crew and generally overseeing the project **2.** the member of a film production team who is responsible for crew hire, general supervision and also financing of the project

producer choice /prəˌdjuːsə 'tʃɔɪs/ *noun* the ability of producers for the BBC either to use BBC facilities or less expensive independent facilities

Producers' Alliance for Cinema and Television /prəˌdjuːsəz əˌlaɪəns fə ˌsɪnɪmə ən ˌtelɪ'vɪʒ(ə)n/ *noun* the organisation that represents the interests of independent producers in the UK. Abbreviation **PACT**

Producers Guild of America /prə ˌdjuːsəz gɪld əv ə'merɪkə/ *noun* a trade union representing screen and television producers in the USA, formed in 1962

product /'prɒdʌkt/ *noun* a commodity that is produced by manufacture or by a natural process and is offered for sale

product advertising /'prɒdʌkt ˌædvətaɪzɪŋ/ *noun* the practice of advertising a particular named product, not the company that makes it

product endorsement /'prɒdʌkt ɪn ˌdɔːsmənt/ *noun* advertising that makes use of famous or qualified people to recommend a product

production /prə'dʌkʃən/ *noun* **1.** the way in which a society's economy runs, dependent on how efficiently goods are produced in relation to the demand for them **2.** a film, play, broadcast or recording that has been produced for the public **3.** the work of making a media text, especially something filmed

production assistant /prə'dʌkʃən ə ˌsɪst(ə)nt/ *noun* in live television production, the crew member who is responsible for planning the timing of the script in advance, monitoring timing of each segment during broadcast, prompts and communication between the studio and the broadcasting channel. Abbreviation **PA**

Production Code /prə'dʌkʃən kəʊd/ *noun* same as **Hays code**

production crew /prə'dʌkʃən kruː/ *noun* all members of a film or television crew responsible for filming, editing, organising and financing a production

production designer /prə'dʌkʃən dɪ ˌzaɪnə/ *noun* in film production, the crew member with overall responsibility for choosing locations, sets and costumes

production gallery /prə'dʌkʃ(ə)n ˌgæləri/ *noun* same as **gallery**

production manager /prə'dʌkʃən ˌmænɪdʒə/ *noun* the member of a film or television production team who is responsible for booking rehearsal and filming space and liaising between lighting, sound, set design etc.

production number /prə'dʌkʃən ˌnʌmbə/ *noun* a piece of music in a musical that is sung and danced by starring actors supported by the chorus

production period /prə'dʌkʃən ˌpɪəriəd/ *noun* the work done to a programme during the filming stage, for example rehearsals, costume fittings, location filming etc. Also called **principal photography**

product manager /'prɒdʌkt ˌmænɪdʒə/ *noun* the manager or executive who is responsible for marketing a particular product

product placement /'prɒdʌkt ˌpleɪsmənt/ *noun* a form of marketing in which a branded product is prominently featured in something such as a film or television show. Some consider this to be underhand practice as the audience are being subjected to advertisements without their consent.

prof ◊ **in prof** an abbreviation for 'in profanity', used to refer to a slight delay,

for example during a phone-in, to allow any profane language to be bleeped out

profane language /prə,feɪn 'læŋgwɪdʒ/ *noun* language showing disrespect for God, any deity or religion

profile /'prəʊfaɪl/ *noun* **1.** a description of a person or organisation giving a short history, key facts etc. **2.** the way that the total audience for a broadcast can be broken down according to such factors as age, gender, income etc.

profiling /'prəʊfaɪlɪŋ/ *noun* the analysis and classification of somebody based on personal information such as ethnicity, shopping habits, or behavioural patterns, used for example for advertising research

pro-filmic event /ˌprəʊ ˌfɪlmɪk ɪ 'vent/ *noun* the scene that the camera is recording

prog /prɒg/ *noun* a television or radio programme

program director /'prəʊgræm daɪ ˌrektə/ *noun* an executive who is responsible for the selection and scheduling of television or radio programmes for broadcast

programme /'prəʊgræm/ *noun* a television or radio broadcast

programme as broadcast /ˌprəʊgræm əz 'brɔːdkɑːst/ *noun* RADIO same as **log 1**

Programme as Completed form /ˌprəʊgræm əz kəm'pliːtɪd ˌfɔːm/ *noun* one of the four forms which must be submitted when delivering a programme to the BBC, giving all the contractual and rights information. ◊ **billing form**, **transmission form**, **music reporting form**

programme flow /'prəʊgræm fləʊ/ *noun* same as **flow**

programming /'prəʊgræmɪŋ/ *noun* the selection and scheduling of television or radio programmes, or the programmes themselves

Progressive Rock /prə'gresɪv rɒk/ *noun* a type of rock music originating in the early 1970s and characterised by technically complicated and sometimes experimental arrangements, often drawing on jazz or classical music influences

projection /prə'dʒekʃən/ *noun* **1.** the process of unconsciously attributing a personal thought, feeling or impulse, especially one considered undesirable, to somebody else **2.** the projecting of an image or picture on a surface

projectionist /prə'dʒekʃənɪst/ *noun* somebody whose job is to operate the projector and screen the film in a cinema and take responsibility for the quality of the image and sound

projection rate /prə'dʒekʃ(ə)n reɪt/ *noun* the rate at which filmed frames are shown, typically 24 per second for normal speed viewing

projection room /prə'dʒekʃən ruːm/ *noun* **1.** a private room with a projector and screen in which films are viewed **2.** an enclosed compartment in a cinema or theatre from where films, slides or lights are projected onto a screen or stage

projection television /prə'dʒekʃən ˌtelɪvɪʒ(ə)n/ *noun* a television picture display system in which an enlarged picture is projected onto a screen

projector /prə'dʒektə/ *noun* a piece of equipment for projecting the image from film onto a screen and for playing back recorded sound from tracks on the film

promo /'prəʊməʊ/ *noun* **1.** an advertisement for another programme or feature. Also called **trail 2.** same as **promotional material**

promotion /prə'məʊʃ(ə)n/ *noun* something such as an advertising campaign that is designed to promote a product, cause or organisation

promotional /prə'məʊʃ(ə)n(ə)l/ *adjective* used in an advertising campaign

promotional material /prə ˌməʊʃ(ə)nəl mə'tɪəriəl/ *noun* material used to advertise a film, such as trailers and television spots, printed flyers, free gifts etc

prompting system /'prɒmptɪŋ ˌsɪstəm/ *noun* a screen mounted by a camera which provides a rolling script for a presenter to read

proof /pruːf/ *noun* a printout of the page layout of material to be printed, including copy, pictures, advertisements etc., made available for checking and correction before final printing

proofing /'pruːfɪŋ/ *noun* **1.** the process of checking a text just before publication for spelling errors, problems with layout etc. **2.** the process of printing out an image as a test to check colour resolution away from the computer screen

proofread /'pruːfriːd/ *verb* to read the proofs of a text and mark corrections to be made

proof sheet /'pruːf ʃiːt/ *noun* a sheet of paper that has a printer's proof on it, usually with wide margins so that corrections can be marked up easily

propaganda /ˌprɒpə'gændə/ *noun* media text that is designed to persuade its audience of a particular belief or idea

'However, rather then allow epidemiologists free access to its H5N1 hotspots, the government in Hanoi balked at sharing biological samples with foreign scientists and instead went on a propaganda offensive.' [Adrian Levy and Cathy Scott-Clark, *The Guardian*]

propaganda model /ˌprɒpə'gændə ˌmɒd(ə)l/ *noun* a model of gatekeeping that outlines the forces such as funding and ownership, that determine how the media select and structure their news, making it in essence a form of propaganda, putting forward only one point of view

propagandist /ˌprɒpə'gændɪst/ *noun* an individual or organisation that distributes propaganda

properties /'prɒpətiz/ *plural noun* full form of **props**

property /'prɒpəti/ *noun* an original story that a film production company has bought the rights for

proposal /prə'pəʊz(ə)l/ *noun* an idea for development that is formally presented to a production company

Propp's people /'prɒps ˌpiːp(ə)l/ *noun* a set of basic characters who, it is argued, are vital components of every folk tale and narrative, including the hero, the villain, the object of the quest and the hero's helper

COMMENT: The idea comes from the research of Vladimir **Propp** (1895–1970), a Russian formalist, who analysed folktales and developed a list of basic characters and plot developments which he believed were present in almost all stories.

props /prɒps/ *plural noun* objects on a set that are small or light enough to be carried by the actors. These are distinct from larger pieces of furniture or décor which merely form the background of the set. Full form **properties**

prospects /ˈprɒspekts/ *plural noun* a list of news stories to be covered

protagonist /prəʊˈtægənɪst/ *noun* the most important character in a novel, play, story or other literary work

protocol /ˈprəʊtəkɒl/ *noun* software that controls the relationships between networked computers, such as on the Internet

prove /pruːv/ *verb* to make a test impression of a negative, etching or type

proxemics /prɒkˈsiːmɪks/ *noun* the study of personal space and how it is used in the interaction between ourselves and others, another form of body language

proximity /prɒkˈsɪmɪti/ *noun* in terms of news values, geographical closeness or ideological similarity of a country in which news has occurred to the one reporting it

PRS *abbreviation* **Performing Rights Society**

psa *abbreviation* **public service announcement**

PSC *abbreviation* **portable single camera**

pseudo-context /ˈsjuːdəʊ ˌkɒntekst/ *noun* the structure of information presented through the media, which is thought by some to be fragmented and useless

psychogalvanometer /ˌsaɪkəʊgælvəˈnɒmɪtə/ *noun* an instrument used to measure emotional reactions to advertising by checking the degree of sweating on the palms of the hands

psychogeography /ˌsaɪkəʊdʒiˈɒgrəfi/ *noun* in postmodernist theory, the analysis of the influence of a person's environment on their mental processes

psychographics /ˌsaɪkəʊˈgræfɪks/ *noun* the study of the lifestyle of different sectors of society for marketing purposes

PTC *abbreviation* **piece-to-camera**

P-time /ˈpiː taɪm/ *abbreviation* **polychronic time**

PTV *abbreviation* **1.** TV **pay television 2.** TV **public television**

pub. *abbreviation* **1. publisher 2. publication 3. publishing**

publ. *abbreviation* **1. publisher 2. publication**

public access television /ˌpʌblɪk ˌækses ˈtelɪvɪʒ(ə)n/ *noun* in the US, cable broadcasting facilities for the transmission of programmes produced by members of the public. Also called **open access television**

publication /ˌpʌblɪˈkeɪʃ(ə)n/ *noun* **1.** an item that has been published, especially in printed form. Abbreviation **pub.**, **publ. 2.** the act of making printed material, especially books, available for sale to the public

Public Broadcasting Service /ˌpʌblɪk ˈbrɔːdkɑːstɪŋ ˌsɜːvɪs/ *noun* a not-for-profit corporation in the US which oversees public service television broadcasting by more than 300 member stations. Abbreviation **PBS**

public domain /ˌpʌblɪk dəʊˈmeɪn/ *noun* any uncopyrighted work is considered to be in the public domain, ie. that can be rereleased by any company without having to pay for rights. The period for copyright expiration in the EU is 70 years after the death of the author.

publicise /ˈpʌblɪsaɪz/ *verb* to make something generally known or known to a group, typically by advertising

publicist /ˈpʌblɪsɪst/ *noun* a person whose job it is to raise awareness of, and get press coverage of, a production such as a film

publicity /pʌˈblɪsɪti/ *noun* activity, especially advertising and the publishing or broadcasting of information, designed to increase public interest in or awareness of something or somebody

public opinion /ˌpʌblɪk əˈpɪnjən/ *noun* the values, ideas, political beliefs etc. held by the general public

public relations /ˌpʌblɪk rɪˈleɪʃ(ə)nz/ *noun* the work of promoting a product by arranging for it to be featured in the media as opposed to paying for an advertisement

public sector /ˈpʌblɪk ˌsektə/ *noun* organisations that are funded by local or national government

public service /ˌpʌblɪk ˈsɜːvɪs/ *noun* a service that is run for the benefit of the general public, for example the emergency services, transport and broadcasting

public service advertising /ˌpʌblɪk ˈsɜːvɪs ˌædvətaɪzɪŋ/ *noun* the advertising of a public service or cause such as a disaster relief fund

public service announcement /ˌpʌblɪk ˈsɜːvɪs əˌnaʊnsmənt/ *noun* any announcement of information relevant to the public for example a police appeal. Abbreviation **psa**

public service broadcasting /ˌpʌblɪk ˈsɜːvɪs ˈbrɔːdkɑːstɪŋ/ *noun* non-commercial broadcasting sponsored by the state, for example programmes broadcast by the BBC

public sphere /ˌpʌblɪk ˈsfɪə/ *noun* the section of society that a person is likely to come into contact with, who they are aware of and who is aware of them

public television /ˌpʌblɪk ˈtelɪvɪʒ(ə)n/ *noun* television that is funded by the government, viewers and corporate sponsorship. Abbreviation **PTV**

publish /ˈpʌblɪʃ/ *verb* **1.** to prepare and produce material in printed or electronic form for distribution and, usually, sale **2.** to make the work of a particular author available in printed or other form

publisher /ˈpʌblɪʃə/ *noun* **1.** a company or person that publishes products such as books, journals or software **2.** the owner or representative of the owner of a newspaper, periodical or publishing house ▶ abbreviation **pub., publ.**

publisher's statement /ˈpʌblɪʃəz ˌsteɪtmənt/ *noun* a statement of circulation issued by a publisher, which may not have been independently verified

publishing /ˈpʌblɪʃɪŋ/ *noun* the trade, profession, or activity of preparing and producing material in printed or electronic form for distribution to the public. Abbreviation **pub.**

publishing house /ˈpʌblɪʃɪŋ haʊs/ *noun* an established publishing company that prepares and produces material in printed or electronic form for distribution and, usually, sale

puffery /ˈpʌfəri/ *noun* advertising that praises the product or service being sold in an exaggerated way, without any specific factual data

puff piece /ˈpʌf piːs/ *noun* an article giving publicity or uncritical support for an event, person, organisation etc.

'You have critics…who almost act as personal publicists for certain artists. There's no way they can have any critical detachment. We're a newspaper. It's not our job to write puff pieces, it's our job to break news.' [Stephen Armstrong, *The Guardian*]

Pulitzer Prize /ˈpʊlɪtsə praɪz/ *noun* an annual prize offered in the US for excellence in journalism and fiction writing

pull /pʊl/ *noun* a printing proof made for correction ■ *verb* **1.** to make a printing proof **2.** to remove something from circulation, or prevent it from ever getting into circulation

pullout /ˈpʊlaʊt/ *noun* part of a publication that can be pulled out, for example a removable section of a magazine or a part of a book that folds out

pull strategy /ˈpʊl ˌstrætədʒi/ *noun* an attempt by a producer to use heavy advertising to persuade final users to buy a product, so 'pulling' the product through the distribution process to the point of sale

pulp /pʌlp/ *noun* novels or magazines produced on cheap paper, especially crime, horror or science fiction stories

Punch and Judy /ˌpʌntʃ ən ˈdʒuːdi/ *noun* a children's comic puppet show featuring Punch and Judy, a quarrelsome couple, together with a number of other standard characters

punchline /ˈpʌntʃlaɪn/ *noun* the news angle of a piece

punchy /ˈpʌntʃi/ *adjective* having a strong news angle

pundit /ˈpʌndɪt/ *noun* an expert in a particular field who is frequently interviewed

punitive censorship /ˌpjuːnɪtɪv ˈsensəʃɪp/ *noun* censorship that takes place after the work in question is released to the public, in response to public protest. Compare **pre-emptive censorship**

punk rock /pʌŋk ˈrɒk/, **punk** /pʌŋk/ *noun* a type of fast loud rock music often with irreverent, aggressive lyrics and a lack of skilled instrumental playing

put out /ˌpʊt ˈaʊt/ *verb* to make something widely known, for example by announcing or broadcasting it

pyrotechnics /ˌpaɪrəʊˈtekniks/ *plural noun* explosive devices used in filmmaking and theatre, to imitate for example the effects of a gunshot or a fire, or to create a dramatic effect on stage

Pythonesque /ˌpaɪθənˈesk/ *adjective* absurdly or surreally comical in a way that is reminiscent of the 1970s British television comedy show *Monty Python's Flying Circus*

Q

Q and A /ˌkjuː ənd ˈeɪ/ *noun* a way of presenting news in which the presenter asks a correspondent questions about a story that they have been following

qr. *abbreviation* PRINTING **quire**

QRS *abbreviation* quality of reading survey

qto *abbreviation* PRINTING **quarto**

quadraphonic /ˌkwɒdrəˈfɒnɪk/, **quadriphonic, quadrophonic** *adjective* referring to the use of a four-channel system to record and reproduce sound. The four separate signals may be fed to individual loudspeakers placed in the corners of a room. Abbreviation **quad**

quadrat, quad *noun* /ˈkwɒdrət/; /kwɒd/ PRINTING in traditional hot-metal printing, a piece of blank type metal used for spacing ■ *adjective* RECORDING same as **quadraphonic**

qualitative audit /ˈkwɒlɪtətɪv ˌɔːdɪt/ *noun* the practice of examining an advertising agency's work in planning and developing a client's advertising programme

qualitative research /ˈkwɒlɪtətɪv rɪˌsɜːtʃ/ *noun* research that is not simply the collecting of statistics, but which focuses on reasoning and cultural and social factors, which are researched and then analysed. Compare **quantitative research**

quality /ˈkwɒlɪti/ *adjective* referring to certain media works such as television and radio broadcasts and the press which have high production values

quality document /ˈkwɒlɪti ˌdɒkjʊmənt/ *noun* an official report on the administrative systems of an organisation

quality of reading survey /ˌkwɒlɪti əv ˈriːdɪŋ ˌsɜːveɪ/ *noun* a survey into individual reading habits and attitudes towards the printed word. Abbreviation **QRS**

quality press /ˈkwɒlɪti pres/, **quality** /ˈkwɒlɪti/ *noun* same as **broadsheet**

quantitative research /ˈkwɒntɪtətɪv rɪˌsɜːtʃ/ *noun* the process of collecting information based on statistics. Compare **qualitative research**

Quark Xpress /ˌkwɑːk ɪkˈspres/ a trade name for standard software used for page layout throughout the media

quarterly /ˈk(w)ɔːtəli/ *noun* a magazine or journal published four times a year, at three-month intervals

quarto /ˈkwɔːtəʊ/ *noun* **1.** a book with pages of a size traditionally created by folding a single sheet of standard-sized printing paper in half twice, giving four leaves or eight pages **2.** the page size of a quarto book ▶ abbreviation **qto**

Quebec /kwɪˈbek/ *noun* an internationally recognised code word for the letter Q, used in radio communications

queercore /ˈkwɪəkɔː/ *noun* a style of music similar to punk rock with lyrics that proclaim homosexuality confidently and assertively

queer theory /ˈkwɪə ˌθɪəri/ *noun* in feminist theory, the idea that sexuality is not a set of a few rigidly-defined categories, but that it is variable and a choice which can be remade or put off

quest /kwest/ *noun* in a narrative, the 'journey' undertaken by the hero to achieve something or find some object or person, which provides an opportunity for action and narrative progression

QuickTime /ˈkwɪktaɪm/ a trade name for the graphics routines built into the Macintosh's operating system that allow windows, boxes and graphic objects, including animation and video files, to be displayed

quire /'kwaɪə/ *noun* a bundle of sheets of paper folded together for binding into a book, especially a four-sheet bundle, folded once to make eight leaves or sixteen pages. Abbreviation **qr.**

quizmaster /'kwɪzmɑːstə/ *noun* somebody who presents a quiz show and puts the questions to the contestants

quiz show /'kwɪz ʃəʊ/ *noun* a television or radio programme in the form of a game in which contestants compete against each other for prizes by answering questions that test their general or specialist knowledge

quota /'kwəʊtə/ *noun* a restriction on the amount of a particular media product that may be broadcast in order to ease competition. For example, in France at least 40% of the music broadcast by any radio station must be French-language.

quotable /'kwəʊtəb(ə)l/ *noun* of a person, easily quoted because their speech lends itself to snappy sound bites ■ *adjective* able to be quoted in a publication such as a newspaper because the person speaking or writing has given permission

quotation /kwəʊ'teɪʃ(ə)n/ *noun* a piece of speech or writing quoted somewhere, for example in a book or magazine

quote /kwəʊt/ *noun* something that somebody has said, word for word, reported in quotemarks ■ *verb* to repeat or publish what somebody has said, word for word

'Mr Blair's oft-quoted claim that he will "serve a full third term" and quit before Britain next goes to the polls has always been viewed sceptically, even by some of his closest allies.' [James Blitz, *The Financial Times*]

quotemarks /kwəʊ'teɪʃ(ə)n mɑːks/, **quotation marks** *plural noun* either of a pair of punctuation marks, either in single (' ') or double (" ") form, used around direct speech, quotations, and titles, or to give special emphasis to a word or phrase

R

r *abbreviation* PRINTING **recto**

R /ɑː/ in the United States, a trade name for a rating indicating that a film can be seen by children under the age of 17 only if accompanied by an adult ■ *noun* in Australia, a rating indicating that a film may not be seen by anyone under 18

rabbit ears /ˈræbɪt ˌɪəz/ *plural noun* a V-shaped aerial made up of two metal rods on a base, designed to sit on top of a television set

race /reɪs/ *noun* in postmodernist theory, the idea of a category to which a person belongs, based on phenotypical or ethnic distinctions between people. ◊ **phenotypical**

race reading /ˈreɪs ˌriːdɪŋ/ *noun* a commentary given by the production assistant via talkback about what is coming up next, for example to camera operators and presenters

racism /ˈreɪsɪz(ə)m/ *noun* **1.** prejudice against people who belong to other races **2.** the belief that people of different races have different qualities and abilities, and that some races are inherently superior or inferior

racks /ræks/ *plural noun* the area of the studio where cameras are controlled

radar antenna /ˈreɪdɑː ænˌtenə/ *noun* a device for sending and receiving radio waves

radical media /ˌrædɪk(ə)l ˈmiːdiə/ *noun* same as **alternative media**

radical response /ˌrædɪk(ə)l rɪ ˈspɒns/ *noun* one of three supposed responses to receiving a message, the radical response involves total rejection of whatever messages, values, ideas etc. are being received. ◊ **dominant response**, **subordinate response**

radio /ˈreɪdiəʊ/ *noun* **1.** radio broadcasting as an industry or profession **2.** sound broadcasts transmitted by means of radio waves **3.** the broadcasting by radio of programmes for the public **4.** a station which transmits radio broadcasts, or an organisation involved in radio broadcasting **5.** an electronic device for receiving sound broadcasts transmitted via radio signals

Radio Authority /ˈreɪdiəʊ ɔːˌθɒrəti/ *noun* formerly, the body that regulated independent radio in the UK It was replaced by OFCOM under the 2003 Communications Act. ◊ **OFCOM**

Radio Authority Programme Codes /ˌreɪdiəʊ ɔːˌθɒrəti ˈprəʊɡræm ˌkəʊdz/ *noun* two sets of guidelines concerning radio broadcasting covering such issues as bad language, sex and violence, bad taste humour and politically-biased programming

radio backpack /ˈreɪdiəʊ ˌbækpæk/ *noun* portable radio broadcast equipment

radio beam /ˈreɪdiəʊ biːm/ *noun* a beam of radio signals transmitted by a radio or radar beacon for communications and navigation purposes

radio cam /ˈreɪdiəʊ kæm/ *noun* a camera that transmits a signal to a nearby receiver without the need for cabling

radio car /ˈreɪdiəʊ kɑː/ *noun* a large van containing all the equipment needed for an outside radio broadcast

radio cassette /ˈreɪdiəʊ kəˌset/ *noun* a radio and a cassette player combined in a single, usually portable machine

Radiocommunications Agency /ˌreɪdiəkəˌmjuːnɪˈkeɪʃ(ə)nz ˌeɪdʒənsi/ *noun* the body formerly responsible for regulating telecommunications in the UK

It was replaced by OFCOM under the 2003 Communications Act. ◊ **OFCOM**

Radio Death /ˌreɪdiəʊ 'deθ/ *noun* the nickname given to Rwanda's main radio station after it was found to be broadcasting messages of racial hatred and incitement to violence against the country's minority Tutsi population

radio frequency /'reɪdiəʊ ˌfriːkwənsi/ *noun* **1.** a frequency on which a radio station broadcasts its programmes **2.** any of the frequencies of electromagnetic radiation in the range between 10kHz and 300MHz, including those used for radio and television transmission

radio-frequency device /ˌreɪdiəʊ 'friːkwənsi dɪˌvaɪs/ *noun* a measuring device such as a meter that transmits its reading by radio waves, which can then be picked up remotely

radiogram /'reɪdiəʊgræm/ *noun* **1.** a radio and a record player combined in a single cabinet **2.** a telegram sent by radio

Radio Joint Audience Research /ˌreɪdiəʊ dʒɔɪnt ˌɔːdiəns rɪˈsɜːtʃ/ *noun* the official body that measures audience figures for radio stations. Abbreviation **RAJAR**

Radio Luxembourg /ˌreɪdiəʊ 'lʌksəmbɜːg/ *noun* a seminal radio station operating out of Luxembourg (to avoid licensing restrictions), which served much of Northern Europe with broadcasts in English and German between 1933 and 1992

radio mic /'reɪdiəʊ maɪk/ *noun* a microphone that is not connected by wires but has its own radio transmitter, so that the user can move around freely

Radio Northsea /ˌreɪdiəʊ 'nɔːθsiː/ *noun* a pirate radio station operating in the Northsea area of Essex, which broadcast a heavy anti-Labour campaign during the 1970 general election and was found to have had a sigificant effect on voting patterns in that area

radio spectrum /'reɪdiəʊ ˌspektrəm/ *noun* the range of radio frequencies used for radio and television, between 10kHz and 300MHz

Radio Telefis Éireann *noun* the Republic of Ireland's public service broadcaster, which provides two television stations, four radio stations and an online news service. Abbreviation **RTE**

radio telegraph /'reɪdiəʊ ˌtelɪgrɑːf/ *noun* a telegram that is transmitted via radio signals rather than by wire. Abbreviation **RT**

radiotelephone, radiophone *noun* a telephone that transmits sound signals by radio waves rather than through wires. Abbreviation **RT**

radioteletype /ˌreɪdiəʊ'telɪtaɪp/ *noun* **1.** a teleprinter that transmits and receives by radio rather than along a cable **2.** a receiving and transmitting system that uses radioteletypes

radio waves /'reɪdiəʊ weɪvz/ *noun* a form of electromagnetic radiation sent in modulated waves which can transmit signals

radome /'reɪdəʊm/ *noun* a dome-shaped protective enclosure for a radar antenna, made from materials that do not interfere with the transmission and reception of radio waves

rag /ræg/ *noun* a newspaper with low journalistic standards, or any newspaper regarded with contempt

ragga, raggamuffin *noun* a style of reggae music characterised by long rap monologues and repetitive beats

ragtime /'rægtaɪm/ *noun* a style of popular music in the US in the late 19th and early 20th centuries characterised by distinctive syncopated right-hand rhythms against a regular left-hand beat. Ragtime was widely popularised by the pianist and composer Scott Joplin.

RAJAR /'reɪdʒɑː/ *abbreviation* **Radio Joint Audience Research**

r&b *abbreviation* MUSIC **rhythm and blues**

random-access editing /'ˌrændəm ˌækses 'edɪtɪŋ/ *noun* same as **non-linear editing**

random probability testing /ˌrændəm ˌprɒbəˈbɪlɪti ˌtestɪŋ/ *noun* the practice of carrying out a survey on a test group which is representative of the entire population, without any restrictions on type of person surveyed

rap /ræp/ *noun* a vocal style in which performers use rhythm and rhyme to speak in verse over music with a strong beat, usually hip-hop. Rap developed from African American hip-hop music and culture in the 1970s. ■ *verb* to speak in verse using rhythm and rhyme over music with a strong beat, usually hip-hop

rapper /'ræpə/ *noun* somebody who raps

rapport /ræ'pɔː/ *noun* good communication and understanding between two people

'He is quick to admit he was not "best friends" with the Princess. "We met three times, exchanged a few letters, phone calls. We had one portrait session". But the rapport they established shines through the photographs.' [Hermione Eyre, *The Independent on Sunday*]

rapport-talk /ræ'pɔː tɔːk/ *noun* the style of speech more common among women, according to some theorists, which is aimed more at establishing intimacy than exchanging information. Compare **report-talk**

rate card /'reɪt kɑːd/ *noun* a list of charges for advertising issued by a newspaper or magazine, excluding discounts

ratings /'reɪtɪŋz/ *plural noun* **1.** audience figures that are presented in the form of a league table of programmes achieving the highest numbers **2.** the estimated number of people who tuned in to a television or radio programme, used as an indication of its relative popularity

ratings point /'reɪtɪŋz pɔɪnt/ *noun* one percentage point of a television audience in a given area

rational appeal /'ræʃ(ə)n(ə)l ə,piːl/ *noun* the technique of designing advertising to appeal to a prospective customer using logical arguments to show that the product satisfies the customer's practical needs (as opposed to an emotional appeal). Compare **emotional appeal**

rave /reɪv/ *noun* **1.** a large party or club event at which dance music is played, sometimes lasting all night **2.** a very enthusiastic review ■ *verb* of a critic, to give a very enthusiastic review of something such as a film

RCD *abbreviation* **residual current device**

RDS /ˌɑː di 'es/ *noun* a system for tuning radio receivers automatically by sending digital signals with normal radio programmes

reach /riːtʃ/ *noun* **1.** the percentage of listeners in a station's TSA who are tuned in during a particular period **2.** the percentage of viewers, readers etc. who saw a particular publication, programme or advertisement

reaction shot /ri'ækʃən ʃɒt/ *noun* same as **noddy**

read /riːd/ *verb* **1.** to identify and understand the meaning of the characters and words in written or printed material **2.** to interpret the information carried by movements, signs or signals **3.** to say the words of written or printed material aloud

readerly /'riːdəli/ *adjective* in the theories of structuralism and discourse, referring to a text that conforms to various expected patterns of construction, style etc. in order to satisfy the reader. Compare **writerly**

reader panel /'riːdə ˌpæn(ə)l/ *noun* a small group who are questioned about their responses to any media product (not just a text)

reader research /'riːdə rɪ,sɜːtʃ/ *noun* research into the potential audience for a media product

readership /'riːdəʃɪp/ *noun* the number of people that actually read a publication (as opposed to the number of copies sold). Compare **circulation**

reader's inquiry card /ˌriːdəz ɪn 'kwaɪəri kɑːd/, **reader's service card** /ˌriːdəz 'sɜːvɪs kɑːd/ *noun* a card bound into a magazine that contains a matrix of numbers and letters on which readers can mark codes for products they wish to have further information about. The card is returned to the publisher, who gets the advertiser to send the relevant information to the reader.

readers per copy /ˌriːdəz pə 'kɒpi/ *noun* the number of people who have had access to a single copy of a magazine, ie. its primary and secondary readers. Abbreviation **RPC**

reading /'riːdɪŋ/ *noun* in aesthetic theory, a wide-ranging term roughly meaning 'the reception and interpretation of a text or sign'

read/write head /ˌriːd 'raɪt ˌhed/ *noun* the part of a disk drive mechanism in a computer which reads data from, or writes data onto, the disk

Real /rɪəl/ a trade name for a system used to transmit sound and video over the Internet, normally used to transmit live sound, for example from a radio station, over the Internet

RealAudio /ˌrɪəlˈɔːdiəʊ/ a trade name for a system used to transmit sound, usually live, over the Internet

real image /ˌrɪəl ˈɪmɪdʒ/ *noun* an optical image of something that is produced by reflection or refraction and can be transferred onto a surface such as the film inside a camera

realism /ˈrɪəlɪz(ə)m/ *noun* the concept that filmmaking and television reproduce a realistic situation, one which could occur in our world under all the given conditions. It is distinct, for example, from fantasy, which does not imply reality.

reality TV /rɪˈælɪti ˌtiː ˈviː/, **reality television, reality show** *noun* documentary-style programmes that use fly-on-the-wall footage of real people, not actors, either going about their everyday life or put into an unfamiliar situation to which they are reacting

Really Simple Syndication /ˌrɪəli ˌsɪmpəl ˌsɪndɪˈkeɪʃ(ə)n/ *noun* a type of XML file format which allows news websites to update regularly using a tagged-up source feed. Abbreviation **RSS**

real time /ˈrɪəl taɪm/ *noun* the recreation of an event in a piece of film or audio in exactly the same period of time that it would take for the same event to unfold in the real world. The drama series '24' is filmed entirely using this device.

ream /riːm/ *noun* the standard measure used in paper orders, which is 500 sheets

rebadged /riˈbædʒd/ *adjective* referring to an existing product that is being marketed in a different way to appeal to a different group of consumers. ◊ **badged**

rebroadcast /riːˈbrɔːdkɑːst/ *noun* something that is broadcast again, especially a radio or television programme ■ *verb* to broadcast something again, especially a radio or television programme

recall test /ˈriːkɔːl test/ *noun* in advertising, a research test that checks how well someone can remember an advertisement

recce /ˈreki/ *noun* a visit to a potential location for filming to assess its suitability

receive /rɪˈsiːv/ *verb* **1.** to pick up electronic signals and convert them into sound or pictures **2.** in interpersonal communication, to pick up signals and interpret them so that the message is understood

received pronunciation /rɪˌsiːvd prəˌnʌnsiˈeɪʃ(ə)n/ *noun* the accent generally accepted as the standard for broadcasters in the UK

COMMENT: Received pronunciation is often used by newsreaders, presenters etc as it is clear, easily understood, presents an air of authority and education, but is not connected with a geographical region. However, regional accents such as Scottish or Irish are sometimes used as well, as it is felt that they seem more friendly and 'down-to-earth'.

receiver /rɪˈsiːvə/ *noun* **1.** an electrical device that receives and converts electronic signals into sound or pictures **2.** the part of a telephone that contains the earpiece and mouthpiece and receives and converts electronic signals into sound **3.** in a piece of communication, the person who is receiving the transmitted message

recency /ˈriːsənsi/ *noun* the amount of time in between a person reading a particular publication or seeing a broadcast, and being interviewed about it for the purposes of a survey

reception /rɪˈsepʃən/ *noun* **1.** the quality of the signal received by a radio or television set, or by a mobile phone **2.** the process of receiving and converting electronic signals **3.** in interpersonal communication, the process of receiving signals containing a message

reception studies /rɪˈsepʃən ˌstʌdiz/ *noun* the study of how people receive media messages, how they interpret them and what they do with the meanings and impressions that they take away

reception theory /rɪˈsepʃən ˌθɪəri/ *noun* **1.** the idea that a person reading a text will have basic pre-conceived ideas and expectations which may shift over time, which they apply to their understanding of the text **2.** the idea that a person reading a text will anticipate and fill in meanings, scan and rescan it and arrive at a final understanding

reciprocal link /rɪˌsɪprək(ə)l ˈlɪŋk/ *noun* a link in both directions from one website to another

reciprocity failure /ˌresɪˈprɒsɪti ˌfeɪljə/ *noun* in photography, the failure of light intensity and exposure time to act together as expected, which may happen when their values are extremely high or low. This can affect the colour characteristics of the resulting photograph.

recital /rɪ'saɪt(ə)l/ *noun* **1.** a musical or dance performance given by a soloist or small group **2.** a performance given by music or dance students to demonstrate the progress they have made **3.** the reading aloud or reciting from memory of something such as a poem

recitation /ˌresɪ'teɪʃ(ə)n/ *noun* **1.** the public reading aloud of something or reciting of something from memory, especially poetry **2.** material read aloud or recited from memory in public, especially poetry

recitative /ˌresɪtə'tiːv/ *noun* **1.** a style of singing that is close to the rhythm of natural speech, used in opera for dialogue and narration **2.** a passage in a musical composition that is sung in the form of recitative

recite /rɪ'saɪt/ *verb* to read something aloud or repeat something from memory, either for an audience or in a class

recognition test /ˌrekəg'nɪʃ(ə)n ˌtest/ *noun* a research test in advertising that checks to see how well someone can remember an advertisement either with or without prompting

reconstruct /ˌriːkən'strʌkt/ *verb* to fundamentally change something such as a theory, concept, image or media text, by adding or removing elements or changing the relationship between them

record /'rekɔːd/ *noun* **1.** a piece of music in a format that can be listened to repeatedly **2.** something on which sound is copied, especially a plastic disc with a groove that can be played using a gramophone

recording /rɪ'kɔːdɪŋ/ *noun* a broadcast that is not live but has been recorded on an earlier occasion

recording off transmission /rɪ'kɔːdɪŋ ɒf trænz'mɪʃ(ə)n/ *noun* a copy of a programme or piece as it was broadcast. Abbreviation **ROT**

recording studio /rɪ'kɔːdɪŋ ˌstjuːdiəʊ/ *noun* a room or suite of rooms with facilities for recording professional-quality music, including a gallery, live room and isolation booth(s)

recordist /rɪ'kɔːdɪst/ *noun* somebody who records sound during the making of a film or broadcast

record player /'rekɔːd ˌpleɪə/ *noun* a machine for reproducing the sounds recorded on records, consisting of a turn-table on which the disc revolves and a needle that follows the groove to pick up sound

recto /'rektəʊ/ *noun* the right-hand page of a two-page spread. Abbreviation **r**. Compare **verso**

red, green, blue /ˌred griːn 'bluː/ *noun* the three colour picture beams used in a colour television

redeye /'redaɪ/ *noun* red pupils in the eyes of a subject in flash photography

redhead /'redhed/ *noun* an 800 watt halogen spotlight

red-top /'red tɒp/ *noun* same as **tabloid**

reduce /rɪ'djuːs/ *verb* to lessen the density of a photographic negative or print using a chemical substance

reducer /rɪ'djuːsə/ *noun* a chemical solution that lessens the density of a photographic negative by oxidising it

redundancy /rɪ'dʌndənsi/ *noun* the proportion of words in a piece of communication that are not meaningful. Compare **entropy**

reel /riːl/ *noun* **1.** the amount of cinema film stored on one reel **2.** a revolving device around which something such as thread, film or wire can be wound for storage

reel-to-reel /ˌriːl tə 'riːl/ *noun* a tape recorder that uses quarter-inch magnetic tape, wound onto and held between two reels

reference /'ref(ə)rəns/ *noun* **1.** a note directing a reader's attention to another source of information **2.** a source of information referred to by a footnote or citation

reference mark /'ref(ə)rəns mɑːk/ *noun* a printed symbol used to draw the attention of a reader to a note or bibliographical entry, for example an asterisk or number

referent /'ref(ə)rənt/ *noun* in semiology, the thing referred to by a symbol. Also called **signified**

referential code /ˌrefərenʃ(ə)l 'kəʊd/ *noun* one of five codes used in the analysis and deconstruction of texts, describing science and knowledge referred to in a narrative. ◊ **action code**, **enigma code**, **semantic code**, **symbolic code**

reflect /rɪ'flekt/ *verb* **1.** to redirect something that strikes a surface, especially light, sound, or heat, usually back towards its point of origin **2.** to show a reverse image of somebody or something on a mirror or other reflective surface

reflection /rɪˈflekʃən/ *noun* **1.** the image of somebody or something that appears in a mirror or other reflecting surface **2.** the process or act of reflecting something, especially light, sound, or heat

reflection theory /rɪˈflekʃən ˌθɪəri/ *noun* the idea that language 'mirrors' the objects around us, that its meaning is derived from what each word denotes in real life and the relationships between those objects

reflector /rɪˈflektə/ *noun* a reflective board used to direct light onto a subject during filming

reflector board /rɪˈflektə bɔːd/ *noun* a board that reflects and softens light onto a subject for photographing, filming etc.

reflector spotlight /rɪˈflektə ˌspɒtlaɪt/ *noun* a spotlight which uses internal reflectors to concentrate and intensify the pool of light it produces

reflex camera /ˈriːfleks ˌkæm(ə)rə/ *noun* a camera with an internal mirror that reflects the actual image from the lens into the viewfinder so that the photographer can check the composition and focus exactly

reflexive modernisation /rɪˌfleksɪv ˌmɒdənaɪˈzeɪʃ(ə)n/ *noun* in sociology, the idea that a modernised society could modernise itself further by eliminating the social problems caused by modern advances, for example global warming, genetic engineering etc.

reflexivity /ˌriːflekˈsɪvɪti/ *noun* in cultural theory, the process of recognising one's own values, beliefs etc. and comparing them to those held by other people

refocus /riˈfəʊkəs/ *verb* to change or adjust the focus of something such as a camera or telescope

reformer /rɪˈfɔːmə/ *noun* in advertising audience classifications, a person who wants products that will improve the quality of their lives rather than appealing to a sense of fashion or style. ◊ **aspirer, mainstreamer, succeeder**

refract /rɪˈfrækt/ *verb* **1.** to alter the course of a wave of energy that passes into something from another medium, such as light through a refracting lens **2.** to

measure the degree of refraction in a lens or eye

refraction /rɪˈfrækʃən/ *noun* **1.** the change in direction that occurs when a wave of energy such as light passes from one medium to another of a different density, for example through a lens **2.** the ability of the eye or a lens to change the direction of light in order to focus it

refresh /rɪˈfreʃ/ *verb* to update the information on a website, or to be updated

refresh rate /rɪˈfreʃ reɪt/ *noun* the number of times that an image on a television or computer screen is repainted, typically 60 times per second

refutation /ˌrefjuːˈteɪʃ(ə)n/ *noun* the act of arguing against or disproving a theory or allegation

'More recent history is scrutinised in Robert Greenwald's documentary Uncovered: the War on Iraq. The film consists of a point-by-point refutation of the charges made by President Bush in his State of the Union speech and Colin Powell in his address to the United Nations concerning the alleged threat posed by Saddam Hussein.' [Ian Johns, *The Times*]

reggae /ˈregeɪ/ *noun* a type of popular music, originally from Jamaica, that combines rock, calypso and soul and is characterised by heavy accentuation of the second and fourth beats of a four-beat bar

regional press /ˈriːdʒ(ə)nəl pres/ *noun* newspapers published and distributed in defined areas outside London, either in a region or in a town or a few neighbouring towns

regional production /ˈriːdʒ(ə)nəl prəˌdʌkʃən/ *noun* the BBC's policy not to restrict production to London but to spread it around the UK

register /ˈredʒɪstə/ *noun* **1.** language that is appropriate to a social situation or used for communicating with a particular set of people **2.** a range of sounds, such as of a voice or instrument, or part of this range

reglet /ˈreglət/ *noun* in traditional hot-metal printing, a piece of wood used to separate lines of type

regular readership /ˌregjʊlə ˈriːdəʃɪp/ *noun* the number of people who read all or most issues of a publication

regulation /ˌregjʊˈleɪʃ(ə)n/ *noun* the activity of controlling what happens in an industry and taking action when unfair or unreasonable practices occur. OFCOM is the body which regulates the media in the UK.

Regulation of Investigatory Powers Act 2000 /ˌregjʊleɪʃ(ə)n ən ɪnˈvestɪɡət(ə)ri ˌpaʊəz/ *noun* an act of Parliament that allows authorities to access and monitor personal e-mails and telephone communications, and forbids encryption which makes this difficult

regulatory favours /ˈrejələt(ə)ri ˌfeɪvəz/ *plural noun* the act of ignoring governmental regulations on the media in return for favourable coverage or suppression of unwanted coverage against the interests of large corporations

rehearsal /rɪˈhɜːs(ə)l/ *noun* a practice session or series of sessions for a production that is going to be filmed or performed live later

rehearse /rɪˈhɜːs/ *noun* to practise a performance, lines, blocking, a stunt etc., before filming or performing it live

reification /ˌraɪɪfɪˈkeɪʃ(ə)n/ *noun* in Marxist theory, the identification of a person with a commodity, such as of a worker with the products they produce

reimpression /ˌriːɪmˈpreʃ(ə)n/ *noun* a reprint of a book without any changes in the text

reinforcement /ˌriːɪnˈfɔːsmənt/ *noun* the theory that showing certain acts, such as violence, in the media, may not persuade viewers to commit the same acts if they had not considered them before, but may 'reinforce' tendencies that were already present

reinforcement advertising /ˌriːɪn ˈfɔːsmənt ˈædvətaɪzɪŋ/ *noun* advertising aimed at emphasising the positive features of a product in order to reassure people who have already purchased it

Reithian /ˈriːθiən/ *adjective* referring to the philosophies of Sir John Reith, the first Director General of the BBC. He believed that broadcasting should be free of commercial considerations and should be committed to producing high-quality, informative media products, not less 'worthy' products with popular appeal.

rejig /riːˈdʒɪɡ/ *verb* to rearrange a piece of writing to improve the structure

relative autonomy /ˌrelətɪv ɔː ˈtɒnəmi/ *noun* in Marxist theory, the idea that 'realms', or apparatuses of society such as art, culture, the economy etc., are more or less linked to and dependent on each other

relative cost /ˌrelətɪv ˈkɒst/ *noun* the relationship between the cost of advertising space and the size of the audience

relay /ˈriːleɪ/ *noun* **1.** an apparatus consisting of a receiver and a transmitter, used to receive and retransmit signals **2.** a message or broadcast passed on by an apparatus that receives and retransmits signals ■ *verb* TV to transmit a broadcast through a transmitting station

release pattern /rɪˈliːs ˌpætən/ *noun* the schedule of release for a media product across the world. A film may be released at different times in different regions to make promotion easier, or it may go on simultaneous release.

release print /rɪˈliːs prɪnt/ *noun* the version of a film released for distribution to commercial cinemas

relief /rɪˈliːf/ *noun* a printing process that uses raised surfaces to apply ink to the paper, for example engraving

reload /riːˈləʊd/ *verb* to put a new load into something, for example film into a camera or fresh ammunition into a gun

remake /ˈriːmeɪk/ *noun* something that has been made again or differently, especially a new version of an old film

remaster /riːˈmɑːstə/ *verb* to make a new master copy of an earlier audio recording or film to improve its quality of reproduction

reminder advertising /rɪˈmaɪndər ˌædvətaɪzɪŋ/ *noun* advertising designed to remind consumers of a product already advertised

reminder line /rɪˈmaɪndə laɪn/ *noun* a little advertising gimmick, for example a giveaway pen with the company's name on it

remnant space /ˈremnənt speɪs/ *noun* unsold advertising space that is usually available at a discount

remote /rɪˈməʊt/ *noun* a radio or television broadcast transmitted from outside the studio

remote control /rɪˌməʊt kənˈtrəʊl/, **remote** /rɪˈməʊt/ *noun* **1.** a hand-held device used to operate a television set, video cassette recorder or other electronic device from a distance **2.** the control of a device, system, or activity from a distance, usually by radio signals

rendering /'rend(ə)rɪŋ/ *noun* in software, the process of generating pixels in order to create an image or visual effect

renter /'rentə/ *noun* a film distributor renting films to cinemas

repeat /rɪ'piːt/ *verb* to broadcast a television or radio programme again, or be broadcast again ■ *noun* something that is broadcast, shown, or performed again

repeat sound /rɪ'piːt saʊnd/ *noun* a situation in which a presenter is not given a clean feed and can hear their own commentary with a slight delay, which is disorientating

repertoire /'repətwɑː/ *noun* the size and range of some resource that a person has at their disposal, for example gestures, expressions, jokes

repertoire of elements /ˌrepətwɑː əv 'elɪmənts/ *noun* the set of conventions associated with a genre

repetition and difference /ˌrepɪtɪʃ(ə)n ən 'dɪf(ə)rəns/ *noun* the combination of both expected and unexpected elements in a media product which attract and entertain the reader

repetitive strain injury /rɪˌpetɪtɪv 'streɪn ˌɪndʒəri/ *noun* pain caused by repeating the same physical action over and over, for example by using a keyboard and mouse continually. Abbreviation **RSI**

replay /'riːpleɪ/ *noun* something recorded on tape, video or film that is played again ■ *verb* to play again something that has been recorded on tape, video or film

replicability /ˌreplɪkə'bɪlɪti/ *noun* the idea that research findings should be so clear that the same research done by a different researcher or at a different time would give exactly the same results

report /rɪ'pɔːt/ *noun* an account of news presented by a journalist, in a print or broadcast medium ■ *verb* to find out facts and tell people about them in print or a broadcast

reportage /'repɔːtɑːʒ/ *noun* **1.** the use of print and electronic media to inform people about news and current events **2.** a body of reported news **3.** a particular way of gathering and presenting news

reporter /rɪ'pɔːtə/ *noun* somebody whose job is to find out facts and use the print or broadcast media to tell people about them

Reporters Sans Frontières /rɪ ˌpɔːtəz sɒn 'frɒntieɪ/ *noun* an international organisation of journalists who actively promote freedom of the press in countries where this is not enforced by law, and defend journalists who have been silenced or punished for reporting in these countries

report-talk /rɪ'pɔːt tɔːk/ *noun* the style of speech more common to men, according to some theorists, in which the the exchange of useful information is more important than establishing an interpersonal relationship with the other party. Compare **rapport-talk**

reposition /ˌriːpə'zɪʃ(ə)n/ *verb* to change the marketing strategy of a company or product in order to have a wider or different appeal

repositioning /ˌriːpə'zɪʃ(ə)nɪŋ/ *noun* a shift in the position of a product in the market, or the consumers' idea of it, by changing its design or by different advertising

representation /ˌreprɪzen'teɪʃ(ə)n/ *noun* the way in which a particular group or section of society is presented on screen or the image that is created of them

'Are they "old codgers" or vigorous protectors of civil liberties? Asking young people what they think judges are and what they do may throw up some interesting observations. It is likely that most students' ideas will be derived from TV and film representations.' [Jerome Monahan, *The Guardian*]

representative /ˌreprɪ'zentətɪv/ *adjective* referring to words in a language which are directly connected to the features of the object they name, for example onomatopoeic words such as 'buzz', 'snap' etc., which represent the sound itself. Compare **arbitrary**

re-press /ˌriː 'pres/ *verb* to press something again, especially to manufacture another issue of a recording

reprint /'riːprɪnt/ *noun* a printed copy of something that has already been in print ■ *verb* to print something again, especially with few or no changes

reproduction /ˌriːprə'dʌkʃ(ə)n/ *noun* in feminist theory, the way in which the dominant ideology of a society is represented and spread

reproduction proof /ˌriːprə
ˈdʌkʃ(ə)n pruːf/, **repro** /ˈriːprəʊ/ *noun* a
printed proof, usually on glossy paper, of
such high quality that it can be photographed for making a printing plate

reprography /rɪˈprɒɡrəfi/ *noun* the
reproduction of something printed, for
example by offset printing, microfilming,
photography or xerography

republication /riːˌpʌblɪˈkeɪʃ(ə)n/
noun **1.** something published again, especially in an unchanged form **2.** the act or
process of publishing something again

republish /riːˈpʌblɪʃ/ *verb* to reissue a
publication, especially in an unchanged
form

request /rɪˈkwest/ *noun* a piece of
music played on a radio programme, at a
live performance or at a disco because
somebody asks for it

rerecord /ˌriːrɪˈkɔːd/ *verb* to record
something again

rerecording /ˌriːrɪˈkɔːdɪŋ/ *noun* a
further recording of something

re-regulation /ˌriː ˌreɡjʊˈleɪʃ(ə)n/
noun the theory that deregulation of
media companies has merely led to regulation in a different form, which does not
give more freedom

rerelease /ˈriːrɪliːs/ *noun* a music
recording or a film that has been released
again to the public ■ *verb* to release a
music recording or a film again for distribution to the public

rerun /riːˈrʌn/ *noun* a repeat showing of
recorded entertainment, especially a television series

re-run /ˌriː ˈrʌn/ *verb* to show or broadcast a television series, video or film again

research /rɪˈsɜːtʃ/ *noun* methodical
investigation into a subject in order to
discover facts, to establish or revise a
theory or to develop a plan of action based
on the facts discovered ■ *verb* to carry out
research

researcher /rɪˈsɜːtʃə/ *noun* the
member of a film and television production team who is responsible for putting
together material for a project

residual /rɪˈzɪdjuəl/ *noun* a payment to
performers, directors or writers when
their filmed work is shown again, especially on television

residual current device /rɪˌzɪdjuəl
ˌkʌrənt dɪˈvaɪs/ *noun* a piece of equip-

ment that checks the electrical supply
from a socket and trips a switch if any
changes in the flow are detected,
protecting people and equipment. Abbreviation **RCD**

resistive reading /rɪˈzɪstɪv ˌriːdɪŋ/
noun the act of reading while actively
resisting taking in the preferred meaning

resolution /ˌrezəˈluːʃ(ə)n/ *noun* the
quality of detail offered by a TV or
computer screen or a photographic image,
expressed usually as the number of dots of
colour or pixels per inch

resonance /ˈrez(ə)nəns/ *noun* a situation in which what a viewer sees corre-
sponds closely to their own experiences or
expectations, so reinforcing them

respondent /rɪˈspɒndənt/ *noun* a
person who has taken part in a survey.
Also called **informant**

response function /rɪˈspɒns
ˌfʌŋkʃən/ *noun* a figure that represents
the value of a particular quantity of advertising impressions on a person

response mechanism /rɪˈspɒns
ˌmekənɪz(ə)m/ *noun* a method of
showing a response to an Internet advertisement, or the way in which a customer
can reply to an advertisement or direct
mailshot, such as sending back a coupon
or a faxback sheet

restricted code /rɪˈstrɪktɪd kəʊd/
noun the speech patterns thought to be
more common among working-class, less
educated people, using a smaller vocabulary, simpler grammatical structure and a
greater assumption of shared understanding. Compare **elaborated code**

Restricted Service Licence /rɪ
ˌstrɪktɪd ˈsɜːvɪs ˌlaɪs(ə)ns/ *noun* a
licence to broadcast granted by OFCOM.
These licences are valid either for a period
of a month, such as a licence to trial a new
radio station or serve a special event, or
for longer period, such as for hospital and
schools radio. Abbreviation **RSL**

retail media /ˈriːteɪl ˌmiːdiə/ *noun*
advertising media in retail outlets, for
example ads on supermarket trolleys

retake /ˈriːteɪk/ *noun* an instance of
recording, photographing or filming
something again, or the product that
results from this ■ *verb* to record, photograph or film something again in order to
get it right

'Musicians working with the demanding star have become used to endless retakes and reworking of the tracks that have resulted in some songs taking up to four years to complete.' [Paul Scott, *The Daily Mail*]

retention /rɪ'tenʃ(ə)n/ *noun* the act of keeping the loyalty of existing customers, one possible aim of an advertising campaign. Compare **acquisition**

reterritorialisation /ˌriˌterɪtɔːriəlaɪ'zeɪʃ(ə)n/ *noun* the process of reclaiming cultural 'territory' by interpreting cultural meanings and artifacts in new and different ways

retouch /riː'tʌtʃ/ *noun* something that has been retouched, especially a photograph ■ *verb* to alter a photographic negative or print by removing imperfections or adding details

retransmit /ˌriːtrænz'mɪt/ *verb* to transmit a television broadcast by cable

retrospective /ˌretrəʊ'spektɪv/ *noun* an article looking back at recent events

retune /riː'tjuːn/ *verb* to readjust a radio or television set to a different station or channel

Reuters /'rɔɪtəz/ a trade name for a London news agency providing international news reports

revamp /riː'væmp/ *verb* to update an article or page because new material has emerged

reverb, reverberation *noun* a musical effect that gives the impression of depth in the sound

reverse /rɪ'vɜːs/ *verb* to print text or graphics in white against a dark or colour background

reversion /rɪ'vɜːʃ(ə)n/ *verb* to make a new or different version of an existing thing, especially a radio or television programme or a piece of software

review /rɪ'vjuː/ *noun* **1.** a journalistic article giving an assessment of a book, play, film, concert or other public performance **2.** a magazine or journal that publishes reviews ■ *verb* **1.** to examine something to make sure that it is adequate, accurate, or correct **2.** to write a journalistic report on the quality of a new play, book, film, concert or other public performance

revise /rɪ'vaɪz/ *noun* the final page ready for printing after a proof has been checked and amended

revision /rɪ'vɪʒ(ə)n/ *noun* a revised and republished version of a text

revolutions per minute /ˌrevəluːʃ(ə)nz pə 'mɪnɪt/ *noun* a measurement of how fast something turns, usually used to describe the speed that a gramophone record plays at. Abbreviation **rpm**

rewind /ˌriː'waɪnd/ *noun* a function that quickly winds a film or tape backwards, for example on a camera or video recorder ■ *verb* to wind something such as video or audio tape back onto its original spool or back to an earlier point

rewrite /riː'raɪt/ *verb* to reword an article using the same information (not updating it)

RFD *abbreviation* RADIO **radio-frequency device**

RF shielding /ˌɑː 'ef ˌʃiːldɪŋ/ *noun* thin metal foil wrapped around a cable that prevents the transmission of radio frequency interference signals

rhetoric /'retərɪk/ *noun* speech or writing that communicates its point persuasively

'On the advice of their spin-doctors, the rhetoric of politicians will become more and more tabloid in its vehemence. Home secretaries, and even perhaps prime ministers, will attend funerals and utter profound words of condemnation.' [Simon Heffer, *The Daily Telegraph*]

rhetorical /rɪ'tɒrɪk(ə)l/ *adjective* **1.** relating to or using language that is elaborate or fine-sounding but insincere **2.** relating to the skill of using language effectively and persuasively

rhetorician /ˌretə'rɪʃ(ə)n/ *noun* **1.** a speaker or writer of elaborate or fine-sounding but insincere language **2.** a teacher of the effective and persuasive use of language **3.** a skilled and effective speaker or writer

rhetoric of image /ˌretərɪk əv 'ɪmɪdʒ/ *noun* the way in which pictures are used to persuade the viewer of a message or reinforce it

rhizome /'raɪzəʊm/ *noun* in the theories of structuralism and discourse, a structure which grows and evolves simultaneously in many different directions and has no defined centre, as with a language

rhyme /raɪm/ *noun* a similarity in the sound of word endings, especially in poetry

rhythm /ˈrɪð(ə)m/ *noun* **1.** the regular pattern of beats and emphasis in a piece of music **2.** in poetry, the pattern formed by stressed and unstressed syllables **3.** a pattern suggesting movement or pace in something such as a work of art **4.** a mood or effect in a book, play or film created from repetition

rhythm and blues /ˌrɪð(ə)m ən ˈbluːz/ *noun* a style of music combining blues and jazz, originally developed by African American musicians. Abbreviation **r&b, R'n'B**

rich e-mail /ˌrɪtʃ ˈiː ˌmeɪl/ *noun* an e-mail that has a voice message attached to it

riffle /ˈrɪf(ə)l/ *noun* a quick flick through the pages of a book, magazine or newspaper ■ *verb* to flick through the pages of a book, magazine or newspaper, glancing casually at the contents

rifle mike /ˈraɪf(ə)l maɪk/ *noun* same as **gun mike**

right of reply /ˌraɪt əv rɪˈplaɪ/ *noun* the right of persons represented in the media to 'answer back' to the media if they are dissatisfied

'The last time I happened to discuss astrology in a newspaper article, some years ago, Professor Richard Dawkins was so enraged that he demanded an immediate and lengthy right of reply, in which he denounced my "frivolous tolerance".'
[Justine Picardie, *The Daily Telegraph*]

rim light /ˈrɪm laɪt/ *noun* same as **backlight**

ring-around /ˈrɪŋ əˌraʊnd/ *noun* the act of calling lots of people to gather material for an article

ringtone /ˈrɪŋtəʊn/ *noun* the sound that indicates the arrival of an incoming call on a mobile phone, for example, a series of beeps or a musical tune

COMMENT: Ringtone companies often involve themselves in large, persistent advertising campaigns which tap into the large youth market for these. The Advertising Standards Authority ruled in September 2005 that one such company be largely banned from advertising before 9pm, on the grounds that their advertisements were targeting young people who would be unlikely to read their **small print**.

risk assessment /ˈrɪsk əˌsesmənt/ *noun* the process of working out what potential dangers there are in a situation (for example, on a set) and taking steps to avoid them

risk society /ˈrɪsk səˌsaɪəti/ *noun* a community which is preoccupied with the increasing risks created by modernisation and how to prevent or circumvent these

R'n'B *abbreviation* MUSIC **rhythm and blues**

road blocking /ˈrəʊd ˌblɒkɪŋ/ *noun* the practice of placing an advertisement on different television channels or in different publications at the same time, so as to maximise the number of people who will see it

road movie /ˈrəʊd ˌmuːvi/ *noun* a film that depicts the adventures of a person or people who leave home and travel from place to place by road, often to find or escape from something

roadshow /ˈrəʊdʃəʊ/ *noun* a live open-air radio or television show that travels to a series of locations, usually during the summer months

rock /rɒk/ *noun* a style of popular music, derived from rock and roll, usually played on electric or electronic instruments and equipment ■ *verb* **1.** to sing, play or dance to music, especially to rock music **2.** to have or play music with a strong solid beat

rockabilly /ˈrɒkəbɪli/ *noun* a style of popular music originating in the late 1950s, that combines rock and roll with country music

rock and roll /ˌrɒk ən ˈrəʊl/, **rock'n'roll** *noun* popular music derived from blues music that has heavily stressed beats. It is usually played on electric instruments and has simple, often repetitive, lyrics.

rocker /ˈrɒkə/ *noun* **1.** a fan of rock music or rock and roll **2.** a rock singer or musician **3.** a rock music song

rock steady /ˌrɒk ˈstedi/ *noun* Jamaican reggae of the early 1960s, popular as dance music

rockumentary /ˌrɒkjʊˈment(ə)ri/ *noun* a film documentary about rock music in general or a particular rock band or musician, containing film footage of relevant performances

role /rəʊl/ *noun* **1.** a person's social position in relation to others **2.** an individual part in a play, film, opera or other performance

role culture /ˈrəʊl ˌkʌltʃə/ *noun* an organisational structure in a business which is based around a hierarchy of roles with diminishing power and influence. Compare **person culture, power culture, task culture**

role fulfilment /ˈrəʊl fʌlˌfɪlmənt/ *noun* in a narrative, the way in which characters fulfil or subvert the expectations attached to the traditional roles they are playing, for example hero or villain, and the effect that this has

roll /rəʊl/ *verb* **1.** to cause credits, titles or other captions to move in a continuous upwards direction on a cinema or television screen, or move in this way **2.** to apply to type or a plate with a roller **3.** to function, or cause something to function, especially a cine camera or printing press

roller /ˈrəʊlə/ *noun* a hard tube, usually of compressed rubber, on which ink is spread and rolled over type or an engraved plate before printing

rolling credits /ˌrəʊlɪŋ ˈkredɪts/ *plural noun* credits at the end of a broadcast programme that gradually roll up the screen in a continuous list

rolling news /ˌrəʊlɪŋ ˈnjuːz/ *noun* same as **open-ender**

rolling spider /ˌrəʊlɪŋ ˈspaɪdə/ *noun* a spreader mounted on wheels, so that the camera and tripod can be moved around

rom. *abbreviation* PRINTING **roman**

roman /ˈrəʊmən/ *noun* normal typeface that is not bold or italic. Abbreviation **rom.**

romance /rəʊˈmæns/ *noun* a novel, film or play with a love story as its main theme

romantic comedy /rəʊˌmæntɪk ˈkɒmədi/ *noun* a humorous film, play or novel about a love story that ends happily. Abbreviation **romcom**

romcom /ˈrɒmkɒm/ *abbreviation* CINEMA, TV **romantic comedy**

Romeo /ˈrəʊmiəʊ/ *noun* an internationally recognised code word for the letter R, used in radio communications

roof rig /ˈruːf rɪg/ *noun* a terrestrial transmitter attached to the roof of a building, used where outside broadcasting will take place over a long period (such as at a court during a lengthy trial) and parking for a satellite truck is not available

rostrum /ˈrɒstrəm/ *noun* **1.** a bench used for filming an object such as a map, on which it can be held securely and lit evenly **2.** a platform, stand or raised area supporting a film or television camera

rostrum camera /ˈrɒstrəm ˌkæm(ə)rə/ *noun* a camera that is set up to face an evenly-lit surface so that drawings or other still images can be filmed, photographed or exposed for a single frame to create animation

ROT *abbreviation* **recording off transmission**

rotary press /ˈrəʊtəri pres/ *noun* a printing press that prints from curved plates mounted on a revolving cylinder, often onto a continuous roll of paper

rotogravure /ˌrəʊtəʊɡrəˈvjʊə/ *noun* **1.** a printing process in which images are etched onto copper cylinders mounted in a rotary press, from which they are printed onto moving paper **2.** something printed using rotogravure, for example a magazine or a photographic section of a newspaper

rough cut /ˈrʌf kʌt/ *noun* **1.** the first stage of editing in which all the pieces are put in the correct order **2.** the preliminary version of a cinema film, with only basic editing done to put the scenes together in sequence

round bracket /ˈraʊnd ˌbrækɪt/ *noun* PRINTING same as **bracket**

roundsman /ˈraʊndzmən/ *noun* a journalist, especially a man, employed to cover stories on a specific topic or field of interest

roundsperson /ˈraʊnzˌpɜːs(ə)n/ *noun* a journalist employed to cover stories on a specific topic or field of interest

round-up /ˈraʊnd ʌp/ *noun* an article composed of different small pieces of news

roving camera /ˈrəʊvɪŋ ˌkæm(ə)rə/ *noun* a camera that is not fixed

roving reporter /ˌrəʊvɪŋ rɪˈpɔːtə/ *noun* a journalist who travels around to get stories from different places

royal /ˈrɔɪəl/ *noun* a size of paper, especially a British size of writing paper 483 x

610 mm/19 x 24 in or a size of printing paper 508 x 635 mm/20 x 25 in

Royal Photographic Society /ˌrɔɪəl ˌfəʊtəˈgræfɪk səˌsaɪəti/ *noun* an organisation in the UK that promotes photography as an art and science, with an open membership policy. Abbreviation **RPS**

Royal Television Society /ˌrɔɪəl ˈtelɪvɪʒ(ə)n səˌsaɪəti/ *noun* an organisation in the UK which provides a forum for the discussion of television standards and reform

royalties /ˈrɔɪəltiz/ *plural noun* **1.** a fee paid for the right to play commercially-produced music on a radio station **2.** money payable when an artist's work is used, according to copyright

'Little-known indie outfit Looper have earned about £500,000 in royalties – despite having no record deal and giving their music away free on the internet. Mondo 77 is now heard each day by millions of Americans on national television after Xerox snapped it up [for an advertisement] three years ago.' [Elaine Reid, *The Daily Star*]

RPC *abbreviation* readers per copy

rpm *abbreviation* revolutions per minute

RPS *abbreviation* Royal Photographic Society

RSI *abbreviation* repetitive strain injury

RSL *abbreviation* Restricted Service Licence

RSS *abbreviation* Really Simple Syndication

RT *abbreviation* **1.** radio telegraph **2.** radiotelephone **3.** radio telegraphy

RTE *abbreviation* Radio Telefis Éireann

RTS *abbreviation* Royal Television Society

ruffle /ˈrʌf(ə)l/ *verb* to flick rapidly through the pages of a book or magazine

rule /ruːl/ *noun* a thin printed line or design used for borders or for separating columns of type

rule of thirds /ˌruːl əv ˈθɜːdz/ *noun* the technique of mentally dividing a scene or frame into three sections horizontally and vertically, so as to create a balanced composition

run /rʌn/ *noun* the length of time taken to print an edition

runaround /ˈrʌnəˌraʊnd/ *noun* an arrangement of printed type where lines are shortened to leave room for an illustration or symbol

run in /ˌrʌn ˈɪn/ *verb* to insert additional text in printed matter

run-in /ˈrʌn ɪn/ *noun* a section of text added to a page that has already been typeset or printed

runner /ˈrʌnə/ *noun* a general helper on a film shoot or at an editing session, who makes coffees, goes out for food, relays messages etc.

running head /ˈrʌnɪŋ hed/ *noun* a heading printed on every page or every other page of a book. Also called **running title**

running order /ˈrʌnɪŋ ˌɔːdə/ *noun* **1.** the order in which the items on a magazine show will appear, and their duration **2.** the order of items in a broadcast programme

'The 7 O'Clock News, presented by Paddy O'Connell and Sevan Lawson and produced by a team of 24 staff, attempted to put a different spin on the day's news and often featured an alternative running order to the evening bulletins on BBC1.' [Owen Gibson, *The Guardian*]

running story /ˌrʌnɪŋ ˈstɔːri/ *noun* a story that is followed in a series of articles over a number of editions of the same publication

running title /ˌrʌnɪŋ ˈtaɪt(ə)l/ *noun* PUBLISHING same as **running head**

run of book /rʌn əv bʊk/, **run of paper** *noun* advertising space bought at the basic rate, but not in a specific position in the publication

run of network /ˌrʌn əv ˈnetwɜːk/ *noun* banner advertising that runs across a network of websites

run of site /ˌrʌn əv ˈsaɪt/ *noun* banner advertising that runs on one single website

run of station /ˌrʌn əv ˈsteɪʃ(ə)n/ *noun* television advertising for which a particular time period has not been requested

run of week /ˌrʌn əv ˈwiːk/ *noun* advertising space bought at the basic rate, but not in a specific issue of the publication

run on /ˌrʌn ˈɒn/ *verb* of text, to continue to the next line, column or page

run-on /ˌrʌn ˈɒn/ *adjective* referring to material that is added to an existing line of text without a line break ■ *noun* an added section of text that continues a line, without a line break

Rupert Murdoch /ˌruːpət ˈmɜːdɒk/ one of the most influential media moguls in the world, majority shareholder of News Corporation with holdings in Australia, the UK and the US

rushes /ˈrʌʃɪz/ *plural noun* an early print of all material filmed on a particular day, used to check progress and whether reshooting of any scenes is required

S

SABC *abbreviation* BROADCAST **South African Broadcasting Corporation**

safelight /'seɪflaɪt/ *noun* a light used in darkrooms that filters out the rays that are harmful to sensitive film and photographic paper

safety film /'seɪfti fɪlm/ *noun* nonflammable cinema film made with a cellulose acetate or polyester base. Formerly, film was made with cellulose nitrate and often caught fire as it aged.

sales house /'seɪlz haʊs/ *noun* a company that specialises in selling advertising space in the media

sales literature /'seɪlz ˌlɪt(ə)rətʃə/ *noun* printed information such as leaflets or brochures about a product that salespeople and customers can use

salience /'seɪliəns/ *noun* the degree to which something stands out among other things

salutation display /ˌsæljʊ'teɪʃ(ə)n dɪˌspleɪ/ *noun* elements of language and non-verbal communication such as gestures, which reveal that a person is pleased to enter into communication with another person and feels friendly towards them

samizdat /'sæmɪzdæt/ *noun* an underground publication by dissident writers, circulated at great risk of punishment during the Soviet Communist era

sample /'sɑːmpəl/ *noun* **1.** a representative group of people chosen for larger audience research **2.** a piece of recorded sound or a musical phrase taken from an existing recording, especially in digital form, and used as part of a new recording ■ *verb* to take a sample of recorded music, especially in order to use it in another recording

sampler /'sɑːmplə/ *noun* **1.** an electronic device that can record sounds or take short musical phrases from an existing recording and alter them digitally before they are used to make a new recording **2.** an electronic device that converts sound to digital information for electronic storage

sample survey /'sɑːmpəl ˌsɜːveɪ/ *noun* a statistical study of a selected group of individuals designed to collect information on specific subjects such as their buying habits or voting behaviour

sampling /'sɑːmplɪŋ/ *noun* the process of selecting a sample from the larger population for the purposes of a survey or experiment

sandbag /'sændbæg/ *noun* a weight (literally a bag full of sand) used to hold equipment firmly in place, such as a lighting stand

sandwich /'sænwɪdʒ/ *noun* a piece-to-camera followed by a video insert, and finished with a second piece-to-camera. Also called **top and tail**

sans serif /ˌsænz 'serɪf/, **sanserif** *noun* a typeface in which there are no angled lines (serifs) at the ends of the main strokes of the characters. ◊ **serif**

Sapir-Whorf linguistic relativity hypothesis /sə'pɪə 'wɔːf/ *noun* the theory that a person's ability to form original thoughts is limited by the way they can express those thoughts, ie. by the structure of the language that they use and the size of their vocabulary.

Sarah's Law /'seɪrəz lɔː/ *noun* a campaign by The News of the World newspaper in the UK, proposing changes to privacy laws which would allow public access to records of registered sex offenders. It argues that the rights of parents to protect their children from convicted paedophiles are more important than the rights of the offenders to privacy.

satellite /'sætəlaɪt/ *noun* an object that orbits Earth or another planet in order to relay communications signals or transmit scientific data

satellite broadcasting /ˌsætəlaɪt 'brɔːdkɑːstɪŋ/ *noun* broadcasting using satellites in space to receive and send material back to Earth

satellite dish /'sætəlaɪt dɪʃ/ *noun* a bowl-shaped aerial for receiving television signals broadcast via satellite

satellite link /'sætəlaɪt lɪŋk/ *noun* a communications signal or link from a transmitting Earth station to a satellite and back to a receiving Earth station

satellite master antenna television /ˌsætəlaɪt ˌmɑːstə ænˈtenə ˌtelɪvɪʒ(ə)n/ *noun* satellite television signals that are received through a shared dish, such as in a block of flats. Abbreviation **SMATV**

satellite phone /'sætəlaɪt fəʊn/ *noun* a wireless phone that connects callers via a communications satellite that receives transmissions, then relays them back to Earth

satellite station /'sætəlaɪt ˌsteɪʃ(ə)n/ *noun* a radio or television station that receives programmes from another station and rebroadcasts them immediately on a different wavelength

satellite telephone /ˌsætəlaɪt 'telɪfəʊn/ *noun* a mobile phone that can send voice messages over extremely long distances via links with communications satellites

satellite television /ˌsæt(ə)laɪt 'telɪvɪʒ(ə)n/ *noun* a television service for which the signal is relayed via satellite to be broadcast to customers who have suitable receiving equipment

satellite transmission /ˌsætəlaɪt trænzˈmɪʃ(ə)n/ *noun* transmission of communication signals using satellite technology

satellite truck /'sætəlaɪt trʌk/ *noun* a truck with portable satellite broadcasting equipment, used for outside broadcasts. Also called **satvan**, **scanner**

satire /'sætaɪə/ *noun* the use of wit, especially irony, sarcasm and ridicule, to criticise faults

'Ali G star Sacha Baron Cohen has been forgiven for taking the mick out of Kazakhstan. [An official said] "We understand that it is satire and it appears his target is not the Kazakh people but foreigners stupid enough to believe all this rubbish about our country".' [Andy Lea, *The Daily Star*]

satirical /səˈtɪrɪk(ə)l/ *adjective* referring to speech or writing which uses satire to make a person or thing look ridiculous

saturated colour /ˌsætʃəreɪtɪd 'kʌlə/ *noun* colour that is rich and intense, supposedly with a high concentration (saturation) of pigments. Compare **desaturated colour**

saturation /ˌsætʃəˈreɪʃ(ə)n/ *noun* the intensity of a colour

saturation advertising /ˌsætʃə 'reɪʃ(ə)n ˌædvətaɪzɪŋ/ *noun* a highly intensive advertising campaign

saturation testing /ˌsætʃəˈreɪʃ(ə)n ˌtestɪŋ/ *noun* the process of testing a communications network by transmitting large quantities of data and messages over it

satvan /'sætvæn/ *noun* same as **satellite truck**

satyr play /'sætə pleɪ/ *noun* in ancient Greece, a comic play that made fun of a mythological subject and included a chorus of satyrs

SB *abbreviation* **simultaneous broadcast**

S band /'es bænd/ *noun* a microwave band in the 2655–3353 MHz range, used in radio astronomy and satellite communications

SBS *abbreviation* **Special Broadcasting Service**

sc *abbreviation* PRINTING **small capital**

scaleboard /'skeɪlbɔːd/ *noun* very thin wood used when hand-setting type, in bookbinding and picture-framing

scandal sheet /'skænd(ə)l ʃiːt/ *noun* a magazine that features scandalous stories about people's private lives

scanner /'skænə/ *noun* **1.** a receiver that continuously broadcasts radio signals it picks up from specific frequencies **2.** any mobile control room at an outside broadcast

scatter /'skætə/ *noun* a strategy by which an advertising message is put out through several different channels at the same time

scenario /sɪˈnɑːriəʊ/ *noun* a screenplay for a film

scenarist /ˈsiːnərɪst/ *noun* same as **scriptwriter**

scene /siːn/ *noun* a division of an act of a play or opera, presenting continuous action in one place

scenery /ˈsiːnəri/ *noun* the set or decorated background for a play, film or opera

scenic designer /ˈsiːnɪk dɪˌzaɪnə/ *noun* same as **set designer**

scenography /siːˈnɒɡrəfi/ *noun* the process of painting of theatrical scenery

schedule /ˈʃedjuːl/ *noun* **1.** the planned order of programmes on a broadcasting station during one day or week **2.** the planned order of activities when starting on a major project, for example filming ■ *verb* to decide which programmes should be shown at which times and in what order

schedule evaluation /ˈʃedjuːl ɪˌvæljueɪʃ(ə)n/ *noun* an analysis of how a particular media plan has performed in relation to its target audience

schema /ˈskiːmə/ *noun* a mental framework of some concept, based on previous experience, which affects and is affected by further relevant information

schizoanalysis /ˌskɪtsəʊəˈnælɪsɪs/ *noun* in psychoanalysis, a theory which focuses on the conflict between the suppressed libido (the id) and the constraints of society (the super-ego)

Schramm's models of communication 1954 /ʃræm/ *noun* an expansion of Shannon and Weaver's model of communication 1949, which emphasises how the roles of the sender and receiver (the 'encoder' and 'decoder') overlap

sci *abbreviation* PRINTING **single column inch**

science fiction /ˌsaɪəns ˈfɪkʃən/ *noun, adjective* a form of fiction, usually set in the future, that deals with imaginary scientific and technological developments and contact with other worlds

scissor /ˈsɪzə/ *verb* to define an area of an image and delete any information that is outside this area

scissor lift /ˈsɪzə lɪft/ *noun* a large platform for cameras that can be hydraulically raised and lowered

scoop /skuːp/ *noun* a story that appears in only one newspaper

'US politicians have made no secret of their deep hostility to the TV station [Al-Jazeera], whose scoops have included exclusive interviews with Osama bin Laden and other al-Qaida leaders as well as videos showing masked terrorists beheading western hostages.' [*The Guardian*]

scopophilia /ˌskɒpəˈfɪliə/ *noun* a term, from the Greek word meaning 'the pleasure of looking', used when considering the relationship between a film unfolding and the audience who is watching it

score /skɔː/ *noun* the music that has been composed for a film, play or musical

Scottish Television /ˌskɒtɪʃ ˈtelɪvɪʒ(ə)n/ *noun* the ITV franchise operating in Scotland, which features original Scottish and regional programming

Scottish Vocational Qualification /ˌskɒtɪʃ vəʊˌkeɪʃ(ə)nəl ˌkwɒlɪfɪˈkeɪʃ(ə)n/ *noun* a National Vocational Qualification issued in Scotland. Abbreviation **SVQ**

scramble /ˈskræmb(ə)l/ *verb* to make a telecommunications or broadcast signal unintelligible by means of an electronic device

scrambler /ˈskræmblə/ *noun* an electronic device that makes telecommunications or broadcast signals unintelligible without a special receiver

screamer /ˈskriːmə/ *noun* **1.** an exclamation mark, especially as part of a newspaper headline **2.** same as **flash prank**

screen /skriːn/ *noun* **1.** a large flat white or silver surface onto which a film or slide is projected **2.** the broad flat end of a cathode-ray tube or liquid crystal display on which images are displayed, for example in a television set or computer monitor **3.** the film industry **4.** a glass plate marked with very fine lines used in producing half-tone reproductions **5.** a glass plate in a camera that is used in focusing an image before photographing it ■ *verb* **1.** to broadcast a film, programme or other item on television, or be broadcast on television **2.** to project a film onto a screen in a cinema, or be projected in a cinema **3.** to photograph something through a glass plate to make a half-tone reproduction

screen editor /'skriːn ˌedɪtə/ *noun* software that allows the user to edit text on-screen, with one complete screen of information being displayed at a time

screen grab /'skriːn græb/ *noun* the process of digitising a single frame from a display or television

screening /'skriːnɪŋ/ *noun* **1.** the projection of a film on a screen in a cinema **2.** a showing of a film, programme or other item on television

screenplay /'skriːnpleɪ/ *noun* the script and acting directions for a film production

screen quota /'skriːn ˌkwəʊtə/ *noun* a national law that a particular country must screen a certain proportion of 'home-grown' cinema compared to the amount of imported film

'Korean movies accounted for almost 50 per cent of domestic screenings last year, whereas Hollywood dominates 85 per cent of the global market. This success has been boosted by a screen quota system, adopted by Seoul in 1966, which works on the principle that 40 per cent of the films projected should be domestically produced.' [James Pringle, *The Times*]

screen test /'skriːn test/ *noun* an audition for a film role in which an actor is filmed, or the film made of the audition

screenwriter /'skriːnraɪtə/ *noun* same as **scriptwriter**

screwball comedy /ˌskruːbɔːl 'kɒmədi/ *noun* a film, especially a Hollywood comedy of the 1930s, featuring the comic adventures of appealing characters in a glamorous world

scrim /skrɪm/ *noun* a wire mesh used over a lamp to soften the light

script /skrɪpt/ *noun* **1.** the planned dialogue for a filmed or recorded piece, together with camera and production instructions **2.** in psychoanalytical theory, a set of preconceptions about life which are applied to all interaction and can be changed or strengthened by experience

script doctor /'skrɪpt ˌdɒktə/ *noun* a scriptwriter who is employed to improve another writer's script, for example to tighten up the dialogue

scriptwriter /'skrɪptraɪtə/ *noun* a person who writes and prepares a screenplay for filming. Also called **screenwriter**, **scenarist**

ScriptX /ˌskrɪpt'eks/ *noun* software that allows a developer to write multimedia applications that can be played on a range of different platforms

scrub /skrʌb/ *verb* to wipe information off a disk or remove data from store

sculpture /'skʌlptʃə/ *noun* **1.** the process of creating a three-dimensional work of art, especially by carving, modelling or casting **2.** a work of art created by sculpture, or such works collectively

SDI *noun* a standard in digital video equipment, allowing different pieces to be connected easily. Full form **Serial Digital Interface**

search directory /'sɜːtʃ daɪ ˌrekt(ə)ri/ *noun* a website in which links to information are organised alphabetically and in categories to provide the widest response to a query

search engine /'sɜːtʃ ˌendʒɪn/ *noun* a facility on the Internet that searches webpages for a particular word or phrase, then provides the user with quick links to each one

'The web is a network of interlinked pages and search engines use robot "spiders" to crawl it. Any website will be found if it has incoming links. The more incoming links there are, the sooner a site will be noticed and indexed, so get people to link to your site.' [Jack Schofield, *The Guardian*]

season /'siːz(ə)n/ *noun* a 'package' of episodes of a television show, for example 8 or 12 episodes, which are scripted, filmed and released together and form a coherent set. A television show may run for several seasons, with large breaks in between each being broadcast.

seasonal discount /ˌsiːz(ə)n(ə)l 'dɪskaʊnt/ *noun* a discount offered at specific times of the year during periods of slow sales, such as by media owners to advertisers

season finale /ˌsiːz(ə)n fɪ'nɑːleɪ/ *noun* the last episode in a season, which usually contains dramatic plot revelations and a cliffhanger

SECAM /ˌes iː siː eɪ 'em/ *noun* the standard television system used in France and much of eastern Europe. Full form **Sequential Couleur à Memoire**

secondary data /'sekənd(ə)ri ˌdeɪtə/ *noun* data or information that has already been compiled and is therefore found through desk research

secondary definers /ˌsek(ə)ndəri dɪ'faɪnəz/ *plural noun* when speaking authoritatively about events, the media, who interpret what the primary definers say. Compare **primary definers**

secondary reader /'sekənd(ə)ri ˌriːdə/ *noun* a person who does not buy a publication themselves but reads somebody else's copy. Also called **pass-on reader**. Compare **primary reader**

secondary research /'sekənd(ə)ri rɪˌsɜːtʃ/ *noun* information that is collected from secondary sources, for example a news agency, an report from an eye-witness, other media sources. Compare **primary research**

secondary source /ˌsek(ə)ndəri 'sɔːs/ *noun* a news reporter's source (for example library resources, other news articles) which provides them with secondary research

secondary text /'sekənd(ə)ri tekst/ *noun* in textual theory, the media text as it is received by the audience for the first time. Compare **primary text**, **tertiary text**

secondary viewing /'sekənd(ə)ri ˌvjuːɪŋ/ *noun* the act of watching television while doing other things, such as housework

second assistant director /ˌsekənd əˌsɪst(ə)nt daɪ'rektə/ *noun* the person whose job it is to look after the cast and supporting actors, mark changes to call times and the shooting schedule and generally assist the director and first assistant director of a film

second class /ˌsekənd 'klɑːs/ *noun* a mail delivery service for newspapers and periodicals

second-generation /ˌsek(ə)nd ˌdʒenə'reɪʃ(ə)n/ *adjective* referring to a wireless communications technology which is designed to transmit digital signals, as opposed to the earliest technologies which used analogue only. Abbreviation **2G**. ◊ **third-generation**

second season /ˌsekənd 'siːz(ə)n/ *noun* the period when a second series of a network television programme is shown

section /'sekʃən/ *noun* a separate part of a paper on some topic such as money, culture etc., often included with weekend editions of newspapers

section mark /'sekʃən mɑːk/ *noun* a printed symbol (§) sometimes used to mark the beginning of a section of a book or one of a series of footnotes

secure server /sɪˌkjʊə 'sɜːvə/ *noun* an Internet server that allows data encryption and is therefore suitable for use in e-commerce

'...each user is supplied with a token that displays the constantly changing number. When logging on to the secure server, user names and secret Pin codes have to be keyed in along with the current passcode on the token. This system provides much stronger authentication than the standard username and password.' [Eric Doyle, *The Guardian*]

secure website /sɪˌkjʊə 'websaɪt/ *noun* a website on the Internet that encrypts the messages between the visitor and the site to ensure that nobody else can get access to the information

seg, segue *noun* the continuation from one piece of music to another without a link or commercial in between

segment /seg'ment/ *verb* to divide a target audience into smaller, more special-ised groups for advertising purposes

segmentation /ˌsegmən'teɪʃ(ə)n/ *noun* **1.** the way in which television schedules are divided into sections by genre of programme, or the way in which multi-channel providers may broadcast specific genres only on separate channels **2.** the process of dividing audiences into categories according to their lifestyle choices for advertising purposes

segment producer /'segmənt prəˌdjuːsə/ *noun* a film or television producer who is responsible for only one part of a multi-part production

selective demand advertising /sɪˌlektɪv dɪ'maːnd ˌædvətaɪzɪŋ/ *noun* advertising that increases demand for a specific brand, rather than for a generic product. Compare **primary demand advertising**

selective exposure /sɪˌlektɪv ɪk'spəʊʒə/ *noun* same as **overhearing**

selective retention /sɪˌlektɪv rɪ'tenʃən/ *noun* the process by which people remember some information but not everything they hear

selectivity /sɪˌlekˈtɪvɪti/ *noun* the degree to which an electronic device or circuit can distinguish one frequency from other adjacent frequencies, as in the tuning circuits in radio or television receivers

selector /sɪˈlektə/ *noun* a computer program that selects a sequence of records for a playlist, appropriate for the time of day and audience, based on pre-programmed information such as the track's chart position, mood, tempo etc.

self-censorship /ˌself ˈsensəʃɪp/ *noun* a situation in which journalists fail to question aggressively on a sensitive issue because they are under pressure from the institution or government that they work under

'French broadcasters have been criticised for self-censorship in covering the country's worst unrest since the student riots of May 1968. Jean-Claude Dassier, director general of the rolling news channel LCI, admitted censoring coverage of the riots for fear of encouraging support for far-right politicians.'
[Kim Willsher, *The Guardian*]

self-concept /ˌself ˈkɒnsept/ *noun* a person's perception of how they appear to others (their self-image) and how they feel about that image (their self-esteem)

self-disclosure /ˌself dɪsˈkləʊʒə/ *noun* the way in which people reveal pieces of information about themselves to others and the effect that this has on interpersonal relationships

self-focusing /ˌself ˈfəʊkəsɪŋ/ *adjective* referring to a camera lens that is focused automatically rather than manually

self-fulfilling prophecy /ˌself fʊlˌfɪlɪŋ ˈprɒfəsi/ *noun* an event about which expectations are so strong that they have the effect of making those expectations come true

self-identity /ˌself aɪˈdentɪti/ *noun* a person's concept of who they are in relation to the world, how they fit in

self-justifying /ˌself ˈdʒʌstɪfaɪɪŋ/ *adjective* PRINTING automatically providing an even right or left margin for text printed on a page

self-monitoring /ˌself ˈmɒnɪt(ə)rɪŋ/ *noun* the degree to which a person is aware of social demands on and expectations of their behaviour, and is able to modify it accordingly

self-presentation /ˌself ˌprez(ə)nˈteɪʃ(ə)n/ *noun* the way in which a person behaves in a given social situation

self-published /ˌslef ˈpʌblɪʃd/ *adjective* referring to a text that is published without a publisher, and therefore at the author's own expense

self-reflexive /ˌself rɪˈfleksɪv/ *adjective* referring to a media product which is 'self-aware', i.e. makes reference to its own status as a media product

self-regulation /ˌself ˌregjʊˈleɪʃ(ə)n/ *noun* the practice of some industries who set up their own regulatory agencies

selling costs /ˈselɪŋ kɒsts/**, selling overheads** /ˌselɪŋ ˈəʊvəhed/ *plural noun* the amount of money that has to be paid for the advertising, representatives' commissions and other expenses involved in selling something

Selsdon Committee Report on Television 1935 /ˈselzdən/ *noun* the report on television development and financing that recommended that the BBC should continue to be paid for by the licence fee system

semantic code /səˈmæntɪk kəʊd/ *noun* one of five codes used in the analysis and deconstruction of texts, describing the 'human voice' portrayed in a narrative. ◊ **action code, enigma code, referential code, symbolic code**

semantic differential /səˌmæntɪk ˌdɪfəˈren ʃ(ə)l/ *noun* a research method that asks audiences to grade their reactions on a scale, for example 'offensive' – 'mildly offensive' – 'not offensive'

semantics /sɪˈmæntɪks/ *noun* the study of meaning in language

semibold /ˌsemiˈbɒld/ *adjective* PRINTING darker than ordinary type but not as dark as bold type

semidocumentary /ˌsemiːdɒkjʊˈment(ə)ri/ *noun* a film or TV programme that is fictional but makes use of or is based on factual details or events

semimonthly /ˌsemiˈmɒnθli/ *noun* a publication that appears twice each month, usually at equal intervals

semiology /ˌsemiˈɒlədʒi/ *noun* the study of signs and symbols and how they affect society

semiosic plane /ˌsemiɒzik ˈpleɪn/ *noun* in semiology, the objects or meanings which are represented by signs (their referents), as contrasted with the symbols which represent them (their signifiers). Compare **mimetic plane**

semiotic power /ˌsemiɒtik ˈpaʊə/ *noun* the ability of an audience to attach meanings to a sign or symbol which were not originally intended

semiotics /ˌsemiˈɒtiks/ *noun* the study of the way in which signs and symbols are used to create systems of social meaning

'A classic example of a semiotics-driven campaign is the TV advertisements for Pot Noodle, which show the fast-food snack as a sinful indulgence and a lapse of taste. Pot Noodle was difficult to justify on a nutritional basis, so semioticians turned the idea on its head.' [Maija Pesola, *The Financial Times*]

COMMENT: Semiotics is an important part of media analysis, and is especially used to deconstruct promotional tools such as package design, logos and slogans in marketing. It explores both the signifier and the signified in any given sign as part of a media product.

sender /ˈsendə/ *noun* in a piece of communication, the person who is transmitting the message

sensitisation /ˌsensɪtaɪˈzeɪʃ(ə)n/ *noun* the way in which media coverage can create a moral panic amongst the public by drawing attention to a social issue

sensitise /ˈsensɪtaɪz/ *verb* to make a photographic film, plate or other medium sensitive to light by coating it with an emulsion

sensitive /ˈsensɪtɪv/ *adjective* 1. of a radio or other receiver, able to respond to transmitted signals 2. PHOTOGRAPHY extremely responsive to radiation, especially to light of a specific wavelength

sensitivity /ˌsensɪˈtɪvɪti/ *noun* 1. the ability of a radio or other receiver to respond to transmitted signals 2. the capacity to respond to radiation, especially light, as of photographic paper

sensitometer /ˌsensɪˈtɒmɪtə/ *noun* an instrument for measuring degrees of sensitivity, especially one used on photographic materials

sentence meaning /ˈsentəns ˌmiːnɪŋ/ *noun* the 'absolute' meaning of a set of words put together in a grammatical structure, without any considerations of context, tone, gestures etc. Compare **utterance meaning**

separate channel signalling /ˌsep(ə)rət ˌtʃæn(ə)l ˈsɪgn(ə)lɪŋ/ *noun* the process of using independent communications channels or bands in a multichannel system to send the control data and messages

sepia /ˈsiːpiə/ *noun* 1. a brownish tone produced by some photographic processes, especially seen in early photographs 2. a drawing done in sepia, or a photograph with a brownish tone

sequel /ˈsiːkwəl/ *noun* a film, novel or play that continues a story begun in a previous film, novel or play

sequelitis /ˌsiːkwəlˈaɪtɪs/ *noun* the tendency of authors and film-makers to continue to produce sequels to their works as long as they are financially successful

sequence /ˈsiːkwəns/ *noun* a section of a film showing a single incident or set of related actions or events

Sequential Couleur à Memoire /sɪ ˌkwenʃɑːl kuˌlɜː æ meˈmwɑː/ *noun* full form of **SECAM**

sequential sampling /sɪˌkwenʃ(ə)l ˈsɑːmplɪŋ/ *noun* the process of continuing sampling until enough people have been interviewed to provide the necessary information

sequential scanning /sɪˌkwenʃ(ə)l ˈskænɪŋ/ *noun* a system that scans a television picture using lines in a numerical sequence

serial /ˈsɪəriəl/ *noun* a story that is split into a number of episodes and shown on television at a particular time each day or week ■ *adjective* published or broadcast in parts, usually at regular intervals

Serial Digital Interface /ˌsɪəriəl ˌdɪdʒɪt(ə)l ˈɪntəfeɪs/ *noun* full form of **SDI**

serialisation /ˌsɪəriəlaɪˈzeɪʃ(ə)n/ *noun* a story which has been divided into parts suitable for publishing or broadcasting

serialise /ˈsɪəriəlaɪz/ *verb* 1. to adapt a work so that it can be published or broadcast as a serial 2. to publish or broadcast a story in parts at intervals

serial rights /ˈsɪərɪəl raɪts/ *plural noun* the right to publish a story or book in parts as a serial

series /ˈsɪəriːz/ *noun* **1.** a set of regularly broadcast programmes, each of which is complete in itself **2.** same as **season 3.** a television programme that is shown at the same time each day or week, keeps the same actors and situation but tells a different, self-contained story in each episode **4.** a number of books, pamphlets or periodicals published by one company or organisation on the same topic or in the same format

serif /ˈserɪf/ *noun* **1.** a small line on a text character at the end of the main strokes **2.** text with these serifs. ◊ **sans serif**

seriocomic /ˌsɪəriəʊˈkɒmɪk/ *adjective* with both serious and comic aspects

server /ˈsɜːvə/ *noun* a computer that controls network services available on other computers

service area /ˈsɜːvɪs ˌeərɪə/ *noun* the area over which a radio or television broadcasting station can transmit a satisfactory signal for reception

service provider /ˈsɜːvɪs prəˌvaɪdə/ *noun* a company that provides people and businesses with access to the Internet, usually charging a monthly fee

set /set/ *noun* an artificially-created location in which a play is performed for filming in or outside a studio, for example the inside of a room. This means that only the part of the room to be filmed needs to be created, with plenty of space in front for the cameras and crew.

set and hold /ˌset ən ˈhəʊld/ *noun* same as **hold**

set designer /ˈset dɪˌzaɪnə/ *noun* the member of a film, television or theatre production team who is responsible for designing the scenery and props for a set or stage. Also called **scenic designer**

set meter /ˈset ˌmiːtə/ *noun* a device in a television that records which channels are being shown and for how long, used in television audience research

set-off /ˈset ɒf/ *noun* PRINTING same as **offset**

set-top box /ˌset tɒp ˈbɒks/ *noun* a device that enables digital and/or cable television signals to be received, and for subscription services to be decoded using a special card

setup /ˈsetʌp/ *noun* the position of a camera at the beginning of a film scene

set-up /ˈset ʌp/ *noun* the three main light sources on a film set, consisting of the key light, the fill light and the backlight

sexism /ˈseksɪz(ə)m/ *noun* discrimination against or stereotyping of a person on the grounds of their sex

sexploitation /ˌseksplɔɪˈteɪʃ(ə)n/ *noun* the deliberate use of sexual material to make a product, especially a film, commercially successful

'…in the case of Channel 4, it is demonstrably true that a decade ago, an evening spent watching the channel would have harvested rather more than repeats, imported sitcoms and sexploitation masquerading as factual television.' [Alasdair Palmer and Chris Hastings, *The Sunday Telegraph*]

sextodecimo /ˌsekstəʊˈdesɪməʊ/ *noun* a size of book page traditionally created by folding a single sheet of standard-sized printing paper four times, giving 16 leaves or 32 pages. Also called **sixteenmo**

sexual difference /ˌsekʃuəl ˈdɪf(ə)rəns/ *noun* in feminist theory, the idea of the difference between the sexes being biological and ideological, and how the media expresses and encourages this

sexuality /ˌsekʃuˈælɪti/ *noun* part of a person's identity related to their sexual activities or preferences

sexy /ˈseksi/ *adjective* referring to an article that has popular appeal (*informal*)

sh. *abbreviation* PRINTING **sheet**

shadow mask /ˈʃædəʊ mɑːsk/ *noun* a metal sheet with very small holes in it that is situated close to the back of the phosphor screen of some types of colour television tubes. The shadow mask is used to direct the electron beam to the correct phosphor colour element.

shank /ʃæŋk/ *noun* PRINTING the body of a piece of type, between the foot and shoulder

Shannon and Weaver's model of communication 1949 /ˌʃænən ənd ˈwiːvə/ *noun* one of the earliest models of the communicative process, which describes it as a linear series of events transmitting information from A to B

share /ʃeə/ *noun* the total percentage of potential audience in a radio station's TSA listening during a particular period of time

share of voice /ˌʃeə əv ˈvɔɪs/ *noun* the way that one advertiser's activities compare to those of another at any given time

Shawcross Commission report on the Press 1962 /ˈʃɔːkrɒs/ *noun* a report that first suggested that monopolies held by large successful newspapers could be bad for other publications and should possibly be regulated externally

sheet /ʃiːt/ *noun* **1.** a single piece of paper. Abbreviation **sh.**, **sht 2.** a newspaper or periodical, especially one dismissed as trivial

shellac /ˈʃelæk/ *noun* an old type of gramophone record originally made from a material containing purified lac, played at 78 rpm

shield law /ˈʃiːld lɔː/ *noun* in North America, a law that protects a journalist from being forced to reveal the name of a source who provided information confidentially

shipping forecast /ˈʃɪpɪŋ ˌfɔːkɑːst/ *noun* a weather forecast for ships and sailors around the UK coast that is broadcast at regular times by the BBC

shirt-tail /ˈʃɜːt teɪl/ *noun* a short additional and related piece of writing at the end of a newspaper article

shock jock /ˈʃɒk dʒɒk/ *noun* a DJ or radio host who uses provocative language and broadcasts his or her extreme views

shock site /ˈʃɒk saɪt/ *noun* a website with content which is designed to shock and offend most viewers, usually distasteful images

Shockwave /ˈʃɒkweɪv/ a trade name for a system developed by Macromedia that allows web browsers to display complex multimedia effects

shoegazing /ˈʃuːˌɡeɪzɪŋ/ *noun* a style of early 1990s guitar music characterised by relaxing sounds and static performances

shoot /ʃuːt/ *noun* an occasion when a professional photographer or film-maker is photographing or filming something ■ *verb* to record a shot, scene, film or programme on film with a camera

shoot-'em-up /ˈʃuːt əm ˌʌp/ *noun* a film, television programme or video game featuring a large amount of shooting and personal violence

shooting ratio /ˈʃuːtɪŋ ˌreɪʃiəʊ/ *noun* the ratio between the amount of material that is filmed and the amount used in the finished television programme

shooting script /ˈʃuːtɪŋ skrɪpt/ *noun* the final screenplay for a cinema or television film that includes directions for shooting and is divided into scenes with the shots numbered consecutively

shop /ʃɒp/ *noun* an advertising agency

shopper /ˈʃɒpə/ *noun* a usually free newspaper that carries advertising and some local news

shopping channel /ˈʃɒpɪŋ ˌtʃæn(ə)l/ *noun* a television channel dedicated to advertising products, usually with one or more presenters talking about and demonstrating them. The products can then be bought by dialling a telephone number shown on screen.

short /ʃɔːt/ *noun* a film whose running time is approximately 30 minutes or less

short end /ˈʃɔːt end/ *noun* the unused film left over when a shoot is finished

shortfall signal /ˈʃɔːtfɔːl ˌsɪɡn(ə)l/ *noun* a gesture or facial expression that seems insincere or shows some hidden emotion, for example a smile that appears unnatural

short message service /ˌʃɔːt ˈmesɪdʒ ˌsɜːvɪs/ *noun* full form of **SMS**

short subject /ˌʃɔːt ˈsʌbdʒɪkt/ *noun* a short film of approximately 30 minutes or less, sometimes a documentary, shown before a full-length feature film

short wave /ˈʃɔːt weɪv/ *noun* **1.** a radio wave with a wavelength between 10 and 100m **2.** a radio capable of transmitting or receiving short waves

shot /ʃɒt/ *noun* a piece of filming, measured from the moment that the camera is turned on until the moment it is turned off

shot list /ˈʃɒt lɪst/ *noun* a list of the shots that have been taken in a period of filming

shot-reverse-shot /ˌʃɒt rɪˈvɜːs ˌʃɒt/ *noun* a method of filming a conversation in which scenes are first shown from one character's point of view, then the other's

shoulder /'ʃəʊldə/ *noun* a flat surface of printers' type below the raised letter or character

show /ʃəʊ/ *noun* a public entertainment, for example a theatre performance, film or radio or television programme

show bill /'ʃəʊ bɪl/ *noun* a poster advertising or publicising something

show business /'ʃəʊ ˌbɪznəs/ *noun* the entertainment industry, including films, radio, television, theatre and music recording

'Funnyman Jasper Carrott has quit television. In fact, he's quit show-business. The ginger haired comic – real name Bob Davis – is stepping down after three decades of entertaining.' [Nicola Methvyn, *The Mirror*]

showcard /'ʃəʊkɑːd/ *noun* a piece of cardboard with advertising material, put near an item for sale

showing /'ʃəʊɪŋ/ *noun* a measurement of an audience's exposure to outdoor advertising

show print /'ʃəʊ prɪnt/ *noun* the final print of a film that will be broadcast

show reel /'ʃəʊ riːl/ *noun* a compilation of a film-maker's work made in order to demonstrate their skills

showtime /'ʃəʊtaɪm/ *noun* the scheduled time for an entertainment such as a film or play to begin

sht *abbreviation* PRINTING **sheet**

shutter /'ʃʌtə/ *noun* a mechanical part of a camera that opens and closes the lens aperture to expose the film or plate to light

shutterbug /'ʃʌtəbʌg/ *noun* a keen amateur photographer (*informal*)

shutter speed /'ʃʌtə spiːd/ *noun* the length of time the shutter remains open when a photograph is taken

S/I *abbreviation* **superimpose**

side /saɪd/ *noun* a television channel

sideband /'saɪdbænd/ *noun* in telecommunications, the band of frequencies on either side of the carrier frequency, produced by modulation of a carrier wave

sidebar /'saɪdbɑː/ *noun* **1.** a short news story containing additional relevant information that is printed beside a featured story **2.** a block of text set beside the main text in a web document

Sierra /si'erə/ *noun* an internationally recognised code word for the letter S, used in radio communications

sight gag /'saɪt gæg/ *noun* a joke that has to be seen, to be appreciated

'Knowing nothing of the practicalities she hires a general manager, Vivian Van Damm (Bob Hoskins), to run the place, and then can't keep from interfering in it…. paving the way for a couple of lame sight gags as she disguises herself, first as a Chinese matron, then as a polar bear, to spy on him.' [Anthony Quinn, *The Independent*]

sign /saɪn/ *noun* **1.** in semiology, a term used to express the existence of a symbol (a signifier) and the existence of an object or concept which it represents (the referent or signified) **2.** a publicly displayed structure carrying lettering or designs intended to advertise a business or product, for example a painted board or neon lights

signal /'sɪgn(ə)l/ *noun* information transmitted by means of a modulated current or an electromagnetic wave and received by telephone, telegraph, radio or television

signature /'sɪgnɪtʃə/ *noun* **1.** a letter or mark printed on the first page of a section of a book, indicating its order in binding **2.** a sheet of paper with several pages printed on it that, when folded and cut, makes up a section of a book

signature tune /'sɪgnətʃə tjuːn/ *noun* a piece of music used to introduce or identify a performer, group or television or radio programme

significant symboliser /sɪg ˌnɪfɪkənt 'sɪmbəlaɪzə/ *noun* a sign that is common to all members of a community, for example clapping the hands together to indicate praise, bowing to show respect etc.

signification /ˌsɪgnɪfɪ'keɪʃ(ə)n/ *noun* the existence of and relationship between a physical sign and the mental concept it represents

signification spiral /ˌsɪgnɪfɪ 'keɪʃ(ə)n ˌspaɪrəl/ *noun* a situation in which media coverage of separate events implies a link between them, suggesting a more widespread problem

signified /'sɪgnɪfaɪd/ *noun* same as **referent**

signifier /'sɪgnɪfaɪə/ *noun* in semiology, the symbol that represents some other meaning

sign language /'saɪn ˌlæŋgwɪdʒ/ *noun* communication, or a system of communication, by gestures as opposed to written or spoken language, especially the highly developed system of hand signs used by or to people who are hearing-impaired

sign off /ˌsaɪn 'ɒf/ *verb* to bring to an end a communication or transmission such as a radio or television programme or an e-mail message

sign-off /'saɪn ɒf/ *noun* **1.** same as **byline 2.** a straight-to-camera piece by a television reporter at the end of a report, in which they give their name and location

sign painting /'saɪn ˌpeɪntɪŋ/ *noun* in the US, the activity or profession of designing and painting signs, especially for advertising

silence /'saɪləns/ *noun* not speaking, an element of non-verbal communication

silent /'saɪlənt/ *noun* a film made without sound ■ *adjective* referring to films made without sound, especially those made before 1927

silent majority /ˌsaɪlənt mə'dʒɒrɪti/ *noun* the idea that there is a large section of society who agree with a particular point of view, but that they have not yet spoken up to confirm this

silly season /'sɪli ˌsiːz(ə)n/ *noun* a period during which there is little hard news to report, and papers and broadcasters cover a lot of trivial stories

'Victoria Beckham squeezed yet another headline out of the silly season with the announcement that she is to give up her musical career (I know, it's tempting – but let's not) in favour of staying home to look after her children.' [Carol Sarler, *The Guardian*]

Silver Lion /ˌsɪlvə 'laɪən/ *noun* an award given at the Cannes International Advertising Festival

silver screen /ˌsɪlvə 'skriːn/ *noun* films or the cinema industry in general

sim card /'sɪm kɑːd/ *noun* a smart card inside a mobile phone that stores user information

simple device /ˌsɪmp(ə)l dɪ'vaɪs/ *noun* a multimedia device that does not require a data file for playback, such as a CD drive used to play audio CDs

simulation /ˌsɪmjʊ'leɪʃ(ə)n/ *noun* in cultural theory, the way in which a sign or signifier represents some version of reality

simulcast /'sɪməlkɑːst/ *noun* a situation in which a programme is broadcast on two channels at the same time, for example analogue and digital, or a television channel and a radio station. Also called **simultaneous broadcast**

simulcasting /'sɪm(ə)lkɑːstɪŋ/ *noun* broadcasting the same transmission on different frequencies, for example on both analogue and digital

simultaneous broadcast /ˌsɪm(ə)lteɪniəs 'brɔːdkɑːst/ *noun* same as **simulcast**

simultaneous release /ˌsɪm(ə)lteɪniəs rɪ'liːs/ *noun* the practice of releasing a media product at the same time across the world. This usually implies a major, popular product which may be leaked if it becomes available in one place before another.

sincerity test /sɪn'serɪti test/ *noun* the ability of an audience to assess every implication, tone, gesture etc. of a politician on a television broadcast and decide whether he/she is sincere and trustworthy

single column inch /ˌsɪŋg(ə)l ˌkɒləm 'ɪntʃ/ *noun* same as **column inch**

single-lens reflex /ˌsɪŋg(ə)l 'lenz ˌriːfleks/ *noun* a camera in which the light passes through one lens to the film and, by means of a mirror and prism system, to the viewfinder. Abbreviation **SLR**

single-space /'sɪŋg(ə)l speɪs/ *verb* to type or print text without a blank space between the lines

sisterhood /'sɪstəhʊd/ *noun* GENDER ISSUES the empathy and loyalty that women feel for other women who have similar goals, experiences or points of view

sister paper /'sɪstə ˌpeɪpə/ *noun* a paper that is owned by the same company as another

sit /sɪt/ *verb* to pose for a portrait or picture

sit-com /'sɪt kɒm/ *noun* a television or radio comedy series in which a regular cast of characters, usually working or living together, experience everyday situations in a humorous way. Full form **situation comedy**

sitter /'sɪtə/ *noun* an artist's or photographer's model, especially for a portrait

sitting /'sɪtɪŋ/ *noun* a period of time during which somebody is posing for a portrait

situational **attribution** /ˌsɪtʃueɪʃ(ə)nəl ˌætrɪ'bjuːʃ(ə)n/ *noun* the tendency to analyse a person's actions according to the situation they are in, rather than their innate characteristics. Compare **dispositional attribution**

situation comedy /ˌsɪtʃueɪʃ(ə)n 'kɒmədi/ *noun* full form of **sit-com**

sixteenmo /'sɪkstiːnməʊ/ *noun* PRINTING same as **sextodecimo**

sixteen nine /ˌsɪkstiːn 'naɪn/ *adjective* referring to the normal aspect ratio of widescreen broadcasts (often written 16:9). ◊ **four-by-three**

sixty-fourmo /ˌsɪksti 'fɔːməʊ/ *noun* a size of book page traditionally created by folding a single sheet of standard-sized printing paper 6 times, giving 64 leaves or 128 pages

skeletonised copy /'skelɪtənaɪzd ˌkɒpi/ *noun* a shortened copy of a publication consisting of the front page and a few key articles, used by researchers for evaluating people's reactions to, and experience of, different publications

sketch /sketʃ/ *noun* a flippant article describing an event, usually used in relation to happenings at the House of Commons

skiffle /'skɪf(ə)l/ *noun* a type of popular music in the 1950s, usually played by a small group on guitars with improvised instruments such as a washboard used as percussion

skill /skɪl/ *noun* the ability to do something that you have learned

Skillset /'skɪlset/ *noun* the organisation responsible for training and qualifications within the film and broadcasting industries

skin flick /'skɪn flɪk/ *noun* a pornographic film

skip /skɪp/ *verb* to fail to play properly by jumping from one place to another

skip distance /'skɪp ˌdɪstəns/ *noun* the shortest distance between a radio transmitter and receiver that permits

waves of a specific frequency to be sent and received by reflection from the ionosphere

skit /skɪt/ *noun* **1.** a short piece of comic writing that satirises somebody or something **2.** a short comic sketch

skylight filter /'skaɪlaɪt ˌfɪltə/ *noun* a photographic filter that is slightly pink and is used to filter out ultraviolet light and reduce blueness

Skype /skaɪp/ a trade name for a piece of downloadable software that allows free phone calls to be made over the Internet, using a standard computer headset and speakers

skywriting /'skaɪraɪtɪŋ/ *noun* **1.** the use of an aircraft releasing coloured smoke to form letters in the sky, often for advertising purposes **2.** letters or a message formed in the sky by coloured smoke released from an aircraft

slander /'slɑːndə/ *noun* an untrue spoken statement which damages somebody's reputation. Compare **libel**

'Such wild, malicious and deeply personal allegations are far too grave to be dealt with by the FA. Slander is a matter for the civil courts only.' [*The Daily Telegraph*]

slang /slæŋ/ *noun* words, expressions and usages that are casual replacements for standard ones, are often short-lived and are usually considered unsuitable for formal contexts

SLAPP /slæp/ *noun* the practice of companies taking out large, expensive lawsuits against their critics, who cannot possibly compete and are forced to back down. Full form **Strategic Lawsuits Against Public Participation**

slash /slæʃ/ *noun* a punctuation mark (/) that is used to separate optional items in a list or to express fractions or division, and that has various uses in computer programming. Also called **diagonal**, **forward slash**, **oblique**, **solidus**

slash-and-burn /ˌslæʃ ən 'bɜːn/ *noun* rapid editing in order to get a piece to air

slate /sleɪt/ *noun* **1.** the list of major films that are to be produced during a single production period **2.** same as **clapper board**

sleeper effect /'sliːpər ɪˌfekt/ *noun* a response in an audience to a message that is not immediately apparent, only surfacing after some time

sleeve /sliːv/ *noun* a decorated protective cover for a record or CD that usually lists the performers and contents. Also called **liner**

sleeve notes /'sliːv nəʊts/ *plural noun* information about a record, printed on its cover

slide /slaɪd/ *noun* a small piece of film that carries a positive photograph that can be viewed by projection on a screen or through a magnifying device

slidefile /'slaɪdfaɪl/ *noun* same as **stills store**

slider /'slaɪdə/ *noun* a control knob or lever on a piece of equipment that moves horizontally or vertically, for example to change the volume of a radio or CD player

slip /slɪp/ *noun* a special pull-out section covering a particular event

slipsheet /'slɪpʃiːt/ *noun* a sheet of blank paper placed between newly printed sheets to prevent wet ink on the printed sheets from rubbing off or smearing ■ *verb* to place a blank sheet of paper between newly printed papers on which the ink is still wet

slogan /'sləʊgən/ *noun* a short catchy phrase used in advertising to promote something

slomo /'sləʊməʊ/ *abbreviation* **slow-motion**

slot /slɒt/ *noun* the allocated place in a schedule for a particular programme

slow drip /,sləʊ 'drɪp/ *noun* regular, 'low-dose' exposure to some idea or view that gradually persuades its audience over time

slow motion /,sləʊ 'məʊʃ(ə)n/ *noun* a method of filming action at a rate faster than the normal projection rate, so that it appears on the screen at a slower than normal rate

slow-motion /,sləʊ 'məʊʃ(ə)n/ *adjective* referring to film that is shot or shown in slow motion. Abbreviation **slomo**

SLR *abbreviation* PHOTOGRAPHY **single-lens reflex**

slug /slʌg/ *noun* same as **catchline**

slur /slɜː/ *noun* an image that is smeared or blurred ■ *verb* to blur or smear wet ink on a page, or be blurred or smeared

small capital /,smɔːl 'kæpɪt(ə)l/ *noun* a capital letter that is the same height as a lowercase letter. Abbreviation **sc**

small print /'smɔːl prɪnt/ *noun* items printed at the end of an official document such as a contract in smaller letters than the rest of the text

COMMENT: People sometimes do not pay attention to the small print in a contract, but it can contain important information, and unscrupulous operators may deliberately try to hide things such as additional charges or unfavourable terms in it because they know that people are unlikely to read it before signing up.

small screen /'smɔːl skriːn/ *noun* the medium of television, especially as distinct from the cinema

Small World Media /,smɔːl wɜːld 'miːdiə/ *noun* a UK-based alternative media company that is dedicated to covering overlooked or buried news through video and Internet broadcasts

SMATV *abbreviation* TV **satellite master antenna television**

smiling professions /'smaɪlɪŋ prə,feʃ(ə)nz/ *plural noun* the media, seen as dedicated to portraying a happy image of events and providing entertainment

SMPTE *abbreviation* **Society of Motion Picture and Television Engineers**

SMS *noun* same as **text message**

snail mail /'sneɪl meɪl/ *noun* mail sent through the postal service, as distinct from the faster electronic mail

'Digital photography… has revolutionised the way travellers communicate. Forget writing picture postcards to send by snail mail, now you can be in the world's remotest internet cafe and upload photos of where you are to send instantly to the folks back home.'
[Charlotte Hindle, *The Independent*]

snap /snæp/ *noun* a brief summary of a story provided by a news agency

snapper /'snæpə/ *noun* a photographer

snapshot /'snæpʃɒt/ *noun* a photograph, especially one taken by an amateur with simple equipment

sneak preview /,sniːk 'priːvjuː/ *noun* a public screening of a film before to its general release, in order to test public reaction to it

sniffer /'snɪfə/ *noun* a program on a computer system designed legitimately or illegitimately to capture data being transmitted on a network, often used by hackers to discover passwords and user names

snuff film /'snʌf fɪlm/ *noun* a pornographic film or video that is supposed to end with the real-life murder of one of the actors on film

soap /səʊp/, **soap opera** /'səʊp ˌɒp(ə)rə/ *noun* a serial drama that is broadcast at the same time and at regular intervals (ie. every day or every weekday)

COMMENT: Soap operas have their own format which features long-running, open-ended storylines, often with several stories taking place at the same time which may or may not affect each other. The plots tend to be based around a set of friends or families or around a place of work, and characters are able to enter and exit the soap easily (for example by moving to the street, taking a new job etc)

sob stuff /'sɒb stʌf/ *noun* something such as a film, intended to provoke feelings of sadness

soc *abbreviation* **standard out cue**

social action mode of media analysis /ˌsəʊʃ(ə)l 'ækʃən məʊd əv ˌmiːdiə əˌnæləsɪs/ *noun* a view of the media as being instrumental in documenting social conflict and the processes that bring about change

socialisation /ˌsəʊʃ(ə)laɪ'zeɪʃ(ə)n/ *noun* the process by which a person comes to understand the beliefs, conventions etc. of a society, by living in it

'Children frequently converse about a video or a computer game or a television programme. Heated exchange of views on such topics is part of their experience of socialisation. However, they rarely have such conversations about books.' [Frank Furedi, *The Daily Telegraph*]

socialism /'səʊʃəlɪz(ə)m/ *noun* **1.** a political theory or system in which the means of production and distribution are controlled by the people and operated according to equity and fairness rather than market principles **2.** in Marxist theory, the stage after the proletarian revolution when a society is changing from capitalism to communism, marked by pay distributed according to work done rather than according to need

social psychology /ˌsəʊʃ(ə)l saɪ'kɒlədʒi/ *noun* the study of human behaviour, taken as a product of both mental processes and social pressures

social space /ˌsəʊʃ(ə)l 'speɪs/ *noun* in the theories of structuralism and discourse, an environment in which a social group such as a family, a group of friends or workmates exists and operates

Society of Motion Picture and Television Engineers /sə,saɪəti əv ˌməʊʃ(ə)n ˌpɪktʃə ən ˌ'telɪvɪʒ(ə)n ˌendʒɪ'nɪəz/ *noun* a union for technicians working in the film and television industries in the US. Abbreviation **SMPTE**

sociology /ˌsəʊsi'ɒlədʒi/ *noun* the study of human social interactions. Compare **anthropology**

COMMENT: The study of sociology encompasses such areas as economic, political and religious behaviours, and examines prevailing social structures and problems such as violent crime, divorce and substance addiction.

sociometrics /ˌsəʊʃiə'metrɪks/ *noun* the study of small groups and the power structures and interpersonal relationships within them

SOF *abbreviation* **sound on film**

soft /sɒft/ *adjective* dealing with other than serious issues or facts

soft core /'sɒft kɔː/ *noun* films, photographs or publications which are provocative but not sexually explicit

soft-core /'sɒft kɔː/ *adjective* sexually suggestive or provocative without being explicit

soft cover /'sɒft ˌkʌvə/ *noun* same as **paperback**

soft focus /ˌsɒft 'fəʊkəs/ *noun* a deliberate slight blurring of a photograph or a filmed image, giving it a hazy appearance, in order to achieve a special effect such as romance or nostalgia

soft news /ˌsɒft 'njuːz/ *noun* news reported in a chatty, colourful style with less emphasis on straight facts and quotes. Compare **hard news**

soft rock /'sɒft rɒk/ *noun* rock music that tends to be slower and more melodic than hard rock, often influenced by folk or country and western music

soft sell /ˌsɒft 'sel/ *noun* a method of selling or advertising goods and services that uses subtlety and persuasion, rather than aggressive insistence

software /'sɒftweə/ *noun* in computer science, the programs, procedures, rules and languages which are installed onto the hardware and enable it to run. Compare **hardware**

solarise /'səʊləraɪz/ *verb* to overexpose photographic materials to light for deliberate effect, usually in order to exaggerate highlights

solid /'sɒlɪd/ *adjective* without spaces between lines of type in printing

solidus /'sɒlɪdəs/ *noun* PRINTING same as **slash**

sophism /'sɒfɪz(ə)m/ *noun* an argument or explanation that seems very clever or subtle on the surface but is in fact misleading or intended to deceive

sort /sɔːt/ *noun* PRINTING a character in a font of type

SOT *abbreviation* **sound on tape**

soul music /'səʊl ,mjuːzɪk/, **soul** /səʊl/ *noun* a style of African American popular music with a strong emotional quality, related to gospel music and rhythm and blues

sound /saʊnd/ *noun* **1.** the music, speech or other sounds heard through an electronic device such as a television, radio or loudspeaker, especially with regard to volume or quality **2.** the recording, editing and replaying of music, speech or sound effects in the broadcast or entertainment industry

sound bite /'saʊnd baɪt/ *noun* **1.** a short extract from an interview or speech **2.** a short, succinct quote

Sound Blaster /'saʊnd ,blɑːstə/ a trade name for a type of sound card for personal computers developed by Creative Labs that allows sounds to be recorded to disk (using a microphone) and played back

Sound Broadcasting Act 1972 *noun* the act of Parliament that allowed the setup of commercial radio stations

sound capture /'saʊnd ,kæptʃə/ *noun* the conversion of an analogue sound into a digital form that can be used by a computer

sound card /'saʊnd kɑːd/ *noun* an expansion card that produces analogue sound signals under the control of a computer

sound chip /'saʊnd tʃɪp/ *noun* a device that will generate a sound or tune

sound crew /'saʊnd kruː/ *noun* all the members of a film or television crew who are responsible for recording, editing and mixing sound

sound effect /'saʊnd ɪ,fekt/ *noun* a recording or imitation of a sound used in a film, radio or television programme, play or other theatrical performance

sound file /'saʊnd faɪl/ *noun* a computer file that contains sound data

sound image /'saʊnd ,ɪmɪdʒ/ *noun* a term used to refer to the action of 'reading' a sound in the same way as a picture can be read

sound mixer /'saʊnd ,mɪksə/ *noun* a person or machine that combines or balances sounds for a recording, broadcast or film soundtrack

sound on film /,saʊnd ɒn 'fɪlm/ *noun* the background sounds recorded with a piece of video, not those edited on afterwards. Abbreviation **SOF**

sound on tape /,saʊnd ɒn 'teɪp/ *abbreviation* SOT. Same as **sound on film**

sound on videotape /,saʊnd ɒn 'vɪdiəʊteɪp/ *noun* a mark on a script indicating that the sound accompanying a piece of video should be the sound already on it, not from a voiceover or other track. Abbreviation **SOVT**

Sound Recorder /'saʊnd rɪ,kɔːdə/ a utility included with Microsoft Windows that allows a user to play back digitised sound files or record sound onto disk and carry out very basic editing

sound stage /'saʊnd steɪdʒ/ *noun* a large room or studio, usually soundproof, where film scenes are shot. Also called **stage**

soundtrack /'saʊndtræk/ *noun* **1.** the recorded music, dialogue and sound effects in a film or video production. Also called **track 2.** a commercially released recording of the music that has been used in a film

sound waves /'saʊnd weɪvz/ *plural noun* pressure waves produced by vibrations, which are transmitted through air (or a solid) and detected by the human ear or a microphone (in which they are converted to electrical signals)

source /sɔːs/ *noun* a person, organisation, book or other text that supplies information or evidence for someone such as a journalist

source feed /'sɔːs fiːd/ *noun* content provided for a website using Really Simple Syndication technology, which is submitted directly to the system in a form which it can automatically process

SOVT *abbreviation* **sound on videotape**

spaceband /'speɪsbænd/ *noun* a device used in printing to provide even spacing between words in a justified line of text

spacebridge /'speɪsbrɪdʒ/ *noun* a way of communicating internationally by television, using transmissions from orbiting satellites

space buyer /'speɪs ˌbaɪə/ *noun* a person who buys advertising space in magazines and newspapers

space segment /'speɪs ˌsegmənt/ *noun* a period of time which a broadcaster books in advance for the use of a satellite

spaghetti western /spəˌgeti 'westən/ *noun* a film in the style of the cowboy epics set in the Wild West, but actually filmed in Italy or Spain during the 1960s and 70s

spam /spæm/ *verb* **1.** to send an unsolicited e-mail message, often an advertisement, to many people **2.** to post a message many times to a newsgroup, or an inappropriate message to multiple newsgroups ■ *noun* an unsolicited, often commercial, message transmitted through the Internet as a mass mailing

'When police first took him in for questioning, Francis-Macrae asked officers for the name of their chief constable. A bogus spam e-mail suddenly appeared around the world threatening to remove £400 from people's bank accounts to pay for an iPod. The name and telephone number given for the "customer services manager" was the Chief Constable.' [Dominic Kennedy, *The Times*]

spam killer /'spæm ˌkɪlə/ *noun* a piece of software that automatically identifies and deals with spam in incoming e-mail

spamming /'spæmɪŋ/ *noun* the sending of unsolicited electronic messages through the Internet to a large number of recipients

spark /spɑːk/ *noun* an electrician responsible for lighting on a film shoot (*informal*)

spatial zone /'speɪʃ(ə)l zəʊn/ *noun* the physical space maintained between people in communication, according to the nature of their relationship

speaker /'spiːkə/ *noun* same as **loudspeaker**

special /'speʃ(ə)l/ *noun* a television programme that is not part of a network's normal schedule

Special Broadcasting Service /ˌspeʃ(ə)l 'brɔːdkɑːstɪŋ ˌsɜːvɪs/ *noun* a broadcasting corporation in Australia that is dedicated to representing and reaching a multicultural, multilingual audience. Abbreviation **SBS**

special effects /ˌspeʃ(ə)l ɪ'fekts/ *plural noun* effects that are planned, constructed and filmed as though they were real, for example explosions, fires etc.

'[in Harry Potter and the Goblet of Fire] Ralph Fiennes does a great job as Lord Voldemort, helped by some brilliant effects used to keep his character just as dark and dangerous as it is on the printed page – the film's budget was £80 million and required 1,600 special effects shots.' [Emma Urquhart, *The Sunday Telegraph*]

specialist editor /'speʃəlɪst ˌedɪtə/ *noun* a film editor with specialist knowledge, such as of special effects or a particular piece of technology used in production

special position /ˌspeʃ(ə)l pə'zɪʃ(ə)n/ *noun* an especially good place in a publication for advertising

special sort /'speʃ(ə)l sɔːt/ *noun* a character that is not on the usual printing font, for example an accented or Greek letter

specification /ˌspesɪfɪ'keɪʃ(ə)n/ *noun* detailed instructions regarding information such as font, point size and layout that are sent with material to be typeset and printed

spectacle /'spektək(ə)l/ *noun* in cultural theory, something that people want to look at, which attracts attention

spectrum scarcity /'spektrəm ˌskeəsɪti/ *noun* a situation in which there are not enough wavelengths to match the number of channels which wish to broadcast. This situation no longer arises since the advent of digital broadcasting.

speech bubble /'spiːtʃ ˌbʌb(ə)l/ *noun* same as **balloon**

speech chip /'spiːtʃ tʃɪp/ *noun* an integrated circuit that generates sounds (usually phonemes) which when played together sound like human speech

speech-recognition technology /ˌspiːtʃ ˌrekəg'nɪʃ(ə)n tekˌnɒlədʒi/ *noun* a system of computer input and control in which the computer can recognise spoken words and transform them into digitised commands or text

speed /spiːd/ *noun* a measure of the sensitivity of photographic film to light, expressed according to any of various numerical rating systems

spider /'spaɪdə/ *noun* a piece of equipment for locking the three legs of a tripod in place. Also called **spreader**

spike /spaɪk/ *verb* to reject a piece of copy

spin /spɪn/ *noun* the act of interpreting and presenting news according to a particular point of view

spin doctor /'spɪn ˌdɒktə/ *noun* a person working in public relations, whose job is to influence the way in which news is interpreted and presented to protect somebody's public image, for example a politician

spine /spaɪn/ *noun* the back of a book cover to which the pages are fixed

splash /splæʃ/ *noun* the front page, most important story

splash page /'splæʃ peɪdʒ/ *noun* a webpage, usually containing advertisements, that is displayed to visitors to a website before they reach the homepage

splatterpunk /'splætəpʌŋk/ *noun* a form of narrative, for example a story, film or comic strip, that contains a large amount of bloody violence

splice /splaɪs/ *verb* to join the ends of two pieces of film or magnetic tape, for example in editing

splicing tape /'splaɪsɪŋ teɪp/ *noun* adhesive tape used for connecting pieces of magnetic tape edited by hand

split run /'splɪt rʌn/ *noun* the printing of the same issue of a publication in several production runs, so that different advertisements may be placed in different printings, allowing the effects of the advertising to be compared

split screen /'splɪt skriːn/ *noun* a cinema or television screen frame divided into more than one image

split track /'splɪt træk/ *adjective* referring to a feed in which the different audio and video components are transmitted separately so that they may be used independently later. Compare **mixed**

spoiler /'spɔɪlə/ *noun* a newspaper or magazine that is deliberately released at the same time as a rival publication in order to divert interest in it and reduce its sales

'[Hello! magazine] provoked an expensive legal battle five years ago when it ran a set of snatched "spoiler" photographs of the marriage of the actors Catherine Zeta-Jones and Michael Douglas. The couple, who had sold the rights to their wedding to the rival magazine OK! for £1 million, sued Hello! at the High Court.' [Richard Eden, *The Sunday Telegraph*]

sponsor /'spɒnsə/ *noun* a person or a business that pays for radio or television programming by buying advertising time

sponsorship /'spɒnsəʃɪp/ *noun* the act of paying full or part costs towards the production of something such as a television show, in return for a regular advertising slot on it

spoof /spuːf/ *noun* a media product that mimics a more serious product and ridicules it with humour. For example, the Hot Shots! films (1991 and 1993) mimic Top Gun, a hugely-popular film of 1986 starring Tom Cruise. Same as **parody**. Compare **pastiche**

sportscast /'spɔːtskɑːst/ *noun* a radio or television broadcast of a sports event or of sports news

sportswriter /'spɔːtsˌraɪtə/ *noun* somebody who writes about sport, especially for a newspaper or magazine

spot /spɒt/ *adjective* referring to a news report that is broadcast from the place where it happens ■ *noun* **1.** a brief announcement or advertisement inserted between regular radio or television programmes **2.** a lamp with a narrow, focused beam, concentrating the light on one spot. Also called **closed-face lamp**. Compare **flood**

spot news /'spɒt njuːz/ *noun* news coverage that is not planned, because it is covering an event which is still unfolding or has only very recently happened. Also called **breaking news**. Compare **diary piece**

spotter /'spɒtə/ *noun* an assistant to a sports commentator who identifies the players in a game

spread /spred/ *noun* **1.** an advertisement or story that occupies two or more columns in a newspaper or magazine **2.** two facing pages in a newspaper, magazine or book, often with material printed across the fold

spreader /'spredə/ *noun* same as **spider**

sprocket holes /'sprɒkɪt həʊlz/ *plural noun* the holes that run down the side of a piece of film, allowing it to be held steady and wound on by the mechanism of a camera

spun /spʌn/ *noun* a flameproof sheet made from fibreglass that is used to diffuse lights

Spycatcher case /'spaɪkætʃə ˌkeɪs/ *noun* the attempted censorship by the British government of revelations made by a former MI5 intelligence officer in his book 'Spycatcher', published in 1987. Despite arguments that he had signed the Official Secrets Act, the courts held that the book should be published in full and the press could publish excerpts, as the information was in the public interest.

spyware /'spaɪweə/ *noun* software that is secretly installed on a hard disk without the user's knowledge and collects encoded information on his or her identity and Internet use via an Internet connection

'Nilay Patel, director of engineering at MailFrontier, the internet security company… gives warning of the risks of e-mail Christmas cards. "These could look pretty on your screen, but behind the flickering Christmas lights could be spyware installing itself on your PC, which can filter all your internet password and card details to fraudsters", he says.' [Joe Morgan, *The Times*]

square bracket /ˌskweə 'brækɪt/ *noun* either of a pair of symbols, [ ], used in keying, printing or writing to indicate some kind of special comment, for example that made by an editor

squeegee /'skwiːdʒiː/ *noun* an implement, usually a rubber roller, that is used in printing and photography to remove excess water or ink

squib /skwɪb/ *noun* a short humorous piece that acts as a filler in a newspaper

st. *abbreviation* PRINTING **stet**

stab /stæb/ *noun* a short piece of music such as a jingle

stage /steɪdʒ/ *noun* CINEMA, RECORDING same as **sound stage**

stage left /ˌsteɪdʒ 'left/ *noun* the left-hand side of a stage or set from the actor's point of view, facing towards the audience or camera. Compare **cam L**

stage right /ˌsteɪdʒ 'raɪt/ *noun* the right-hand side of a stage or set from the actor's point of view, facing towards the audience or camera. Compare **cam R**

stage window /'steɪdʒ ˌwɪndəʊ/ *noun* a window in which a video or animation sequence is viewed on a computer

stamp /stæmp/ *noun* a small block with a raised design or lettering that can be printed onto paper by inking the block and pressing it to the paper

stamp duty /'stæmp ˌdjuːti/ *noun* a tax on newspapers in the late 18th and early 19th century, which pushed the prices of publications up to damaging levels

stamper /'stæmpə/ *noun* a mould from which disc recordings are pressed

standard error /ˌstændəd 'erə/ *noun* an estimate of possible errors when calculating the results of a particular survey. A large standard error leads to lowered confidence limits.

standardisation /ˌstændədaɪ'zeɪʃ(ə)n/ *noun* the process of making or becoming standard

standard out cue /ˌstændəd 'aʊt ˌkjuː/ *noun* same as **sign-off**

Standard Rate & Data Service /ˌstændəd reɪt ənd 'deɪtə ˌsɜːvɪs/ *noun* an American publication listing advertising rates, circulation and other details of major American magazines, newspapers and other advertising media

standards conversion /'stændədz kən'vɜːʃ(ə)n/ *noun* the process of converting a television picture from one standard to another, for example from PAL to SECAM

standfirst /'stændfɜːst/ *noun* a short introductory few lines between the headline and the body of text in a longer article or feature

stand-in /'stænd ɪn/ noun a replacement for an actor in a film, for example when preparing scenes or during dangerous action

stand-up /'stænd ʌp/ noun same as **piece-to-camera**

stand-up position /'stænd ʌp pə ˌzɪʃ(ə)n/ noun a spot at an incident or event where pieces-to-camera can be filmed, usually with some sort of view of events in the background

star /stɑː/ noun a person in the public eye because of a particular achievement or talent of theirs, for example a sports star, a film star. Compare **celebrity**

starch ratings /'stɑːtʃ ˌreɪtɪŋz/ plural noun a method of assessing the effectiveness of an organisation's advertising

star image /'stɑː ˌɪmɪdʒ/ noun the reputation of a star, used as an additional way of marketing a film

starlet /'stɑːlət/ noun a young female actor seen as a possible major film star of the future

star system /'stɑː ˌsɪstəm/ noun the system of deliberately exploiting an individual performer by creating an appealing off-screen persona for them, in order to sell films

start page /'stɑːt peɪdʒ/ noun the webpage to which a visitor to a website is automatically taken first, or the page to which a user is automatically taken first whenever he or she goes online

startup screen /'stɑːtʌp skriːn/ noun text or graphics displayed when a computer application or multimedia book is run

statement /'steɪtmənt/ noun 1. the expression in spoken or written words of something such as a fact, intention or policy, or an instance of this 2. a specially prepared announcement or reply that is made public, such as by a politician

statement of circulation /ˌsteɪtmənt əv ˌsɜːkjʊ'leɪʃ(ə)n/ noun a report prepared by a magazine or newspaper publisher giving their own circulation figures

static /'stætɪk/ noun electrical interference in a radio or television broadcast, causing a crackling noise or disruption of a picture ■ adjective 1. not moving 2. referring to a medium in art which does not involve drama and movement, such as sculpture, photography or painting.

Compare **dramatic 3.** relating to or caused by electrical interference in a radio or television broadcast

static object /ˌstætɪk 'ɒbdʒekt/ noun an object in an animation or video that does not move within the frame

station /'steɪʃ(ə)n/ noun 1. a place equipped to make and broadcast radio or television programmes 2. a television or radio channel

station break /'steɪʃ(ə)n breɪk/ noun a time when a radio or television programme is interrupted by an announcement giving the name, and sometimes other details, of the company that is broadcasting the programme

statistics /stə'tɪstɪks/ plural noun facts or information in the form of numbers

status quo /ˌsteɪtəs 'kwəʊ/ noun the way that things are, i.e. the current ideology, social system etc.

statutory regulation /ˌstætʃʊt(ə)ri ˌregjʊ'leɪʃ(ə)n/ noun regulatory powers that have been established by law, for example those conferred by the 2003 Broadcasting Act on OFCOM

Steadicam /'stedikæm/ a trade name for a type of camera that can be strapped to the body of the operator and contains technology to keep an image steady artificially

Steenbeck /'stiːnbek/ noun a flatbed editing table for film

stem /stem/ noun an upright stroke, especially the main one, in a letter or character

stenotype /'stenətaɪp/ noun a machine whose keyboard is used to record speech by means of phonetic shorthand

step frame /'step freɪm/ verb to capture a video sequence one frame at a time, used when the computer is not powerful or fast enough to capture real-time full-motion video

stereo /'steriəʊ/ adjective same as **stereophonic** ■ noun 1. an audio system or device that reproduces stereophonic sound 2. photography using stereoscopy

stereogram /'steriəgræm/ noun a radiogram that gives stereo sound reproduction

stereograph noun a picture with two superimposed images or two almost identical pictures placed side by side which, when viewed through special glasses or a stereoscope, produce a three-dimensional image

stereophonic /ˌsteriəˈfɒnɪk/ *adjective* referring to an audio system based on two or more soundtracks to make recorded sound seem more natural when reproduced. Also called **stereo**

stereopticon /ˌsteriˈɒptɪkɒn/ *noun* a slide projector able to allow one image to gradually replace another

stereoscope /ˈsteriəskəʊp/ *noun* a device resembling a pair of binoculars in which two-dimensional pictures of a scene taken at slightly different angles are viewed concurrently, one with each eye, creating the illusion of three dimensions

stereoscopy /ˌsteriˈɒskəpi/ *noun* the creation of a 3D illusion in photography and film, using two images taken from slightly different angles which mimic those seen by each eye

stereotype /ˈsteriətaɪp/ *noun* a way of classifying people which is over-simplified, based on a narrow set of attributes and assuming others, which may be offensive to the person in question

COMMENT: The creation and perpetuation of stereotypes is something for which the media are often blamed. Care must be taken in the representation of any group or individual in the media, and particularly those which are less often represented, to avoid unfair and lasting attributions.

stet /stet/ *noun* PRESS a proofreading mark meaning 'ignore marked deletion'. Abbreviation **st.**

stickiness /ˈstɪkinəs/ *noun* the extent to which a website attracts, and especially keeps, visitors

'Wimbledon claims to have been the first big sports event in the UK to use its website as a promotional and marketing tool… The site claims 2.8m unique users, each spending an average of two hours nine minutes on the site, a degree of "stickiness" that most commercial organisations would kill for.' [Alan Cane, *The Financial Times*]

sticky /ˈstɪki/ *adjective* referring to an Internet site that attracts, and especially keeps, visitors

still /stɪl/ *noun* a photographic print, either made from a single frame of a film or shot independently with a still camera during production ■ *adjective* designed for, or relating to the process of, taking photographs as opposed to making films

still frame /ˈstɪl freɪm/ *noun* a single frame from a film or television programme displayed as a photograph

still photography /ˈstɪl fəˌtɒɡrəfi/ *noun* photography of objects or people that are not moving

stills /stɪlz/ *plural noun* photographs or still images taken from a film

stills store /ˈstɪlz stɔː/ *noun* an electronic file of still shots that can be easily located for use in a production. Also called **slidefile**

stimulus-response model /ˈstɪmjʊləs rɪˌspɒns ˌmɒd(ə)l/ *noun* an attempt to describe the relationship between the stimulus provided by advertisers and the audience reaction in terms of actually buying the advertised product

sting /stɪŋ/ *noun* same as **stab**

stitch /stɪtʃ/ *verb* to bind the pages of a book, pamphlet or other publication with thread or staples

stock /stɒk/ *noun* unused film

stock shot /ˈstɒk ʃɒt/ *noun* a general piece of footage of an area, object or person that is stored in a library for later use

stone /stəʊn/ *noun* a very smooth flat table used for arranging printing type

stooge /stuːdʒ/ *noun* a comic actor, usually part of a double act, who acts as the butt of most of the jokes

stop /stɒp/ *noun* one of the graded settings for the size of the aperture of a camera lens

stop bath /ˈstɒp bɑːθ/ *noun* an acid solution in which a negative or print is dipped in order to stop the developing process

stop down /ˌstɒp ˈdaʊn/ *verb* to make the aperture of a camera lens smaller

stop-motion /ˌstɒp ˈməʊʃ(ə)n/ *noun* a filming technique in which filming is stopped, something about the scene changed (an object added or removed, for example) and filming resumed, giving the impression that something has changed 'by magic'

stop press /ˈstɒp pres/ *noun* a blank column on the back page of a newspaper allowing space for a last-minute addition of breaking news

story /ˈstɔːri/ *noun* **1.** a report in the news of something that has happened **2.** a subject or material for a news report

storyboard /'stɔ:ribɔ:d/ *noun* a written plan for the filming of a sequence with drawings of how the scenes should appear and camera and lighting instructions, timings etc.

STR *abbreviation* BROADCAST **synchronous transmitter receiver**

straight-to-camera /ˌstreɪt tʊ 'kæm(ə)rə/ *adjective* referring to speech that delivered straight into the camera as though talking directly to the viewer

straight-to-video /ˌstreɪt tə 'vɪdiəʊ/ *adjective* referring to a film that is released only in video format rather than shown in cinemas

stranding /'strændɪŋ/ *noun* same as **stripping**

strap /stræp/ *noun* a blocked-out strip, usually at the bottom of a picture, over which text can be placed and easily read

strapline /'stræplaɪn/ *noun* a smaller headline summing up the article in a neat accessible way. Also called **overline**

strap titles /'stræp ˌtaɪt(ə)lz/ *plural noun* a caption that appears at the bottom of a television screen, for example giving the name of a person being interviewed

strategic bargaining /strəˌtiːdʒɪk 'bɑːɡɪnɪŋ/ *noun* the practice in which public figures feed news items to the press in return for exposure or favourable coverage

Strategic Lawsuits Against Public Participation *noun* full form of **SLAPP**

strategic marketing /strəˌtiːdʒɪk 'mɑːkɪtɪŋ/ *noun* marketing according to a plan that is developed after analysing the market, designing the advertising messages and launching the product

strategic silence /strəˌtiːdʒɪk 'saɪləns/ *noun* the act of leaving something out, as with news selection and coverage

strategy /'strætədʒi/ *noun* a communicative act that has a clear purpose and has been pre-planned, for example to persuade or make a sale

strays /streɪz/ *plural noun* electrical interference in a radio or television broadcast, causing disruption of a signal

stream /striːm/ *verb* to broadcast video, audio etc. material via the Internet or a computer network in real time ■ *noun* a video or audio broadcast made via the Internet or a computer network in real time

'...Sling Media. This US-based company has developed a television set-top box, decorously called the "Slingbox", which connects to the internet allowing the consumer to watch the live video stream from his or her television over a broadband link on a personal computer anywhere in the world.'
[Alan Cane, *The Financial Times*]

streamer /'striːmə/ *noun* a large headline that extends the entire width of a newspaper page

streaming video /ˌstriːmɪŋ 'vɪdiəʊ/ *noun* video data that is continuously transmitted (normally over the Internet) using a streaming protocol to provide smooth moving images

stream of consciousness /ˌstriːm əv 'kɒnʃəsnəs/ *noun* **1.** a literary style that presents a character's continuous random flow of thoughts as they arise **2.** the continuous uninterrupted flow of thoughts and feelings through somebody's mind

street furniture /'striːt ˌfɜːnɪtʃə/ *noun* lamps, litter bins, bus shelters etc., on which advertising can be placed

strike /straɪk/ *verb* to take a film set apart or remove an unwanted prop from a set

strike off /ˌstraɪk 'ɒf/ *verb* to print a copy, document or publication

strikeover /'straɪkˌəʊvə/ *noun* **1.** a character or word that has been typed over by something else **2.** the typing of one character over another already typed without erasing the first one

stringer /'strɪŋə/ *noun* PRESS, RADIO same as **freelancer**

strip /strɪp/ *verb* to put pieces of photographic film or paper together to make a plate for printing

strip cartoon /'strɪp kɑːˌtuːn/ *noun* same as **comic strip**

stripping /'strɪpɪŋ/ *noun* in scheduling, showing the same programme or genre of programme at the same time each day. Also called **stranding**

stroke /strəʊk/ *noun* a short diagonal line (/) used to separate groups of numbers or in written text to mean 'and' or 'or'

structuralism /'strʌktʃərəlɪz(ə)m/ *noun* a technique of critical analysis that focuses on the basic structures of media products and how meanings are created through the interrelation of existing structures

COMMENT: According to structuralist analysis, meaning can only be interpreted in terms of the constructed system that the sign fits into, such as the other things with which it is associated or which it is opposite to.

structure of reassurance /ˌstrʌktʃə əv ˌriːəˈʃʊərəns/ *noun* the way in which news is presented in a familiar, trustworthy manner in which in order to make the audience believe it

studio /'stjuːdiəʊ/ *noun* **1.** a commercial film production company **2.** a room or building equipped for making films, television or radio productions or musical recordings **3.** all the buildings connected with a film production company, used for shooting and producing films

studio system /'stjuːdiəʊ ˌsɪstəm/ *noun* the system of Hollywood film production from the 1930s-1950s in which the major studios controlled the production of each film with their own strict management style, allowing little opportunities for independent film companies to break into the industry

stunt double /stʌnt ˌdʌb(ə)l/ *noun* a person who replaces a film actor in scenes involving dangerous action sequences. Also called **stuntperson**

stuntman /'stʌntmæn/ *noun* a man whose job is to take the place of a screen actor in a scene involving danger or requiring acrobatic skill

stuntperson /'stʌntˌpɜːs(ə)n/ *noun* same as **stunt double**

stuntwoman /'stʌntˌwʊmən/ *noun* a woman whose job is to take the place of a screen actor in a scene involving danger or requiring acrobatic skill

STV *abbreviation* **Scottish Television**

style /staɪl/ *noun* a set of guidelines for a particular publication regarding 'house rules' on punctuation, grammar and spelling

stylist /'staɪlɪst/ *noun* somebody employed to set up scenes to be photographed in a magazine, including supplying any accessories or decorative objects required

stylus /'staɪləs/ *noun* the jewel-tipped needle of a record player that rests in the grooves of a record as it revolves and transmits vibrations to the cartridge

sub /sʌb/ *noun* **1.** a subtitle to a document or printed matter **2.** same as **subeditor** ■ *verb* to add subtitles to something

subconscious /sʌbˈkɒnʃəs/ *adjective* below the level of conscious realisation

subculture /'sʌbkʌltʃə/ *noun* in sociology, a smaller, 'breakaway' cultural group characterised by non-mainstream activities, interests, styles of dress, religion etc.

subedit /sʌbˈedɪt/ *verb* to read and correct written material before it is published, particularly for newspapers and magazines, under the general supervision of an editor

subeditor /'sʌbedɪtə/ *noun* **1.** an assistant editor helping to prepare material for publication **2.** somebody whose job is to read and correct written material before it is published, particularly for newspapers and magazines, under the general supervision of an editor ▶ also called **sub**

subhead /'sʌbhed/ *noun* a secondary heading or title

subject /'sʌbdʒɪkt/ *noun* the person or thing that a camera is looking at, or who is being interviewed or having a programme made about them

subjectivity /ˌsʌbdʒekˈtɪvɪti/ *noun* the practice of allowing personal opinion to affect news reporting, a situation which should be avoided, unless it is made obvious that this is the case. Compare **objectivity**

subliminal /sʌbˈlɪmɪn(ə)l/ *adjective* below the level of conscious realisation, especially of some stimulus that provokes a reaction

subliminal advertising /sʌb ˌlɪmɪn(ə)l ˈædvətaɪzɪŋ/ *noun* a technique that supposedly puts an idea into a viewer's head by flashing barely-perceptible images between frames in a filmed piece

'Deploying the music from a successful older film to advertise a new one must be about as close to subliminal advertising as it's legally possible to get: the makers of the trailers for the recent movie Lemony Snicket's A Series of

Unfortunate Events... knew the movie they wanted viewers to be reminded of... and so they bought the rights to its score.'
[Oliver Burkeman, *The Guardian*]

submaster /'sʌbmɑːstə/ *noun* a copy from an original video cassette, made as a backup in case the master tape is damaged or lost

subminiature /sʌb'mɪnɪtʃə/ *adjective* referring to a camera that is smaller than a compact camera, using film smaller than the 35mm miniature format ■ *noun* a subminiature camera

subordinate response /sə,bɔːdɪnət rɪ'spɒns/ *noun* one of three supposed responses to receiving a message, the subordinate response involves general acceptance of whatever messages, values, ideas etc are being received, with slight questioning of or disagreement with them. ◊ **dominant response, radical response**

subplot /'sʌbplɒt/ *noun* a second and less important story within a book, play or film

subscribe /səb'skraɪb/ *verb* 1. to pay money for a service such as cable or satellite television, Internet access, a series of issues of magazines etc 2. to add your name and e-mail address to a mailing list in order to receive messages from a website automatically, with or without charge

subscriber /səb'skraɪbə/ *noun* a user who chooses to receive information, content or services regularly from a service provider such as a cable or satellite television company

subscript /'sʌbskrɪpt/ *adjective* referring to characters that are printed on a lower level than other characters in a line of type ■ *noun* a character that is printed on a level lower than the rest of the characters on the line, for example the '2' in the chemical formula 'H_2O'

subscription /səb'skrɪpʃən/ *noun* money that is paid in advance for a series of issues of a magazine, for membership of a society or for access to information on a website or cable or satellite television services

subscription-based publishing /səb,skrɪpʃən beɪst 'pʌblɪʃɪŋ/ *noun* a form of publishing in which content from a website, magazine, book or other publi-

cation is delivered regularly by e-mail or other means to a group of subscribers

subscription channel /səb'skrɪpʃən ,tʃæn(ə)l/ *noun* a cable or satellite channel that is only available on payment of a subscription

subscription process /səb'skrɪpʃən ,prəʊses/ *noun* the process by which users register and pay to receive information, content or services, from a website or cable or satellite television service

substratum /'sʌbstrɑːtəm/ *noun* a layer of a substance placed on a photographic film or plate as a foundation for an emulsion

subtext /'sʌbtekst/ *noun* an underlying meaning or message in something such as a piece of literature

subtitle /'sʌbtaɪt(ə)l/ *noun* 1. a printed translation of the dialogue in a foreign-language film, usually appearing at the bottom of the screen 2. a caption for the action or dialogue of a silent film, appearing at intervals as a full-screen panel 3. the printed text of what is being said in a television programme, provided for the hearing-impaired and usually at the bottom of the screen

sub-woofer /'sʌb ,wʊfə/ *noun* a large loudspeaker that can reproduce very low frequency sounds, normally with frequencies between 20 to 100Hz, used with normal loudspeakers to enhance the overall sound quality

succeeder /sək'siːdə/ *noun* in advertising audience classifications, a person who wants products that increase their power and control in life. ◊ **aspirer, mainstreamer, reformer**

succès de scandale /sək,seɪ de skɒn'dɑːl/ *noun* something that is successful because it is controversial, for example a book, film or play, or the success that is gained as a result of controversy

succès d'estime /sək,seɪ des'tiːm/ *noun* a book, film or play that is successful with critics but not with the public, or the success that is gained because of this

suggestion /sə'dʒestʃən/ *noun* the deliberate introduction into somebody's mind of an opinion, belief or instruction, for example through hypnosis or advertising, so that it is accepted or acted on as that person's own idea

Sundance Film Festival /ˌsʌndəːns ˈfɪlm ˌfestɪvəl/ *noun* a major film festival for independent film producers, held annually in Utah, USA

Sundays /ˈsʌndeɪz/ *plural noun* special format newspapers published every Sunday

sungun /ˈsʌngʌn/ *noun* an unmounted light that runs on batteries, useful when other types of light sources are impossible to set up on location

sunlamp /ˈsʌnlæmp/ *noun* a lamp with parabolic mirrors that are directed to focus light, used in cinema photography

super /ˈsuːpə/ *noun* **1.** something superimposed onto a picture **2.** a starched cotton gauze fabric that is used to strengthen the bindings of books **3.** a character generator such as an Aston. Also called **name super, motif**

super 16 /ˌsuːpə sɪkˈstiːn/ *noun* a professional film format used for widescreen pictures

super-cardioid microphone /ˌsuːpə ˌkɑːdiɔɪd ˈmaɪkrəfəʊn/ *noun* TV same as **gun mike**

superhero /ˈsuːpəhɪərəʊ/ *noun* a fictional character, for example from a cartoon, who has superhuman powers and uses them to fight crime or evil

superhigh frequency /ˌsuːpəhaɪ ˈfriːkwənsi/ *noun* a radio frequency between 3,000 and 30,000 megahertz

superimpose /ˌsuːpərɪmˈpəʊz/ *verb* to lay an image on top of another image so that both are visible. Abbreviation **S/I**

superimposition /ˌsuːpəɪmpə ˈzɪʃ(ə)n/ *noun* an image which has been superimposed on another

superior /sʊˈpɪəriə/ *adjective* placed above a main line of print ■ *noun* a character placed above a main line of print

superstation /ˈsuːpəˌsteɪʃ(ə)n/ *noun* a television channel broadcast nationally or internationally through satellite and cable

superstitial /ˌsuːpəˈstɪʃ(ə)l/ *noun* an animated advertisement that pops up on a viewer's screen between page views on the Internet

superstructure /ˈsuːpəˌstrʌktʃə/ *noun* ♦ **base and superstructure**

supervening social necessity /ˌsuːpəviːnɪŋ ˌsəʊʃ(ə)l nɪˈsesɪti/ *noun* a requirement from society that motivates the development of technology, for example to be informed, to be entertained, to have household tasks simplified etc.

super video graphics array /ˌsuːpə ˌvɪdiəʊ ˈɡræfɪks əˌreɪ/ *noun* a standard of video adapter developed by IBM that can support a display with a resolution up to 800 x 600 pixels in up to 16 million colours. Abbreviation **SVGA**

supervising producer /ˌsuːpəvaɪzɪŋ prəˈdjuːsə/ *noun* the member of a film or television production team who is responsible for supervising one or more producers in some aspects of their work

support advertising /səˈpɔːt ˌædvətaɪzɪŋ/ *noun* advertising that is designed to back up a campaign which is being primarily conducted in other media

supporting /səˈpɔːtɪŋ/ *adjective* referring to an actor or other entertainer who appears in the same film, play or programme as the main star or attraction

supporting artist /səˌpɔːtɪŋ ˈɑːtɪst/ *noun* same as **extra**

support media /səˈpɔːt ˌmiːdiə/ *plural noun* non-traditional media that are used to reinforce messages sent to target markets through other more traditional media

surf /sɜːf/ *verb* **1.** to go on the Internet and look at a variety of different websites for recreation, education or entertainment **2.** same as **channel-hop**

surprint /ˈsɜːprɪnt/ PRINTING *verb* same as **overprint** ■ *noun* same as **overprint**

surround sound /səˈraʊnd saʊnd/ *noun* a system of recording and reproducing sound that uses three or more channels and speakers in order to create the effect of the listener being surrounded by sound sources. ◊ **ambisonics**

surveillance society /səˈveɪləns səˌsaɪəti/ *noun* the idea that increased use of technology such as credit cards, mobile phones etc. means that people can be tracked and traced more easily by the authorities

suspension of disbelief /səˌspenʃən əv ˌdɪsbɪˈliːf/ *noun* the need to accept unlikely situations and plot developments (for example in fantasies and science fiction) for the purposes of enjoying the film or programme

suspension point /səˈspenʃən pɔɪnt/ *noun* each of a series of dots, usually three, used in printed and written material to indicate an omission or an incomplete phrase

sustaining program /sə'steɪnɪŋ ˌprəʊgræm/ *noun* a US radio or television programme that does not have commercials because the station or network on which it is broadcast supports it

suture /'suːtʃə/ *noun* an edit that makes two filmed shots appear continuous, 'stitching up' the gap between them

SVGA *abbreviation* **super graphics video array**

S-VHS /ˌes viː eɪtʃ 'es/ *noun* an enhanced version of VHS videotape

S-Video /ˌes 'vɪdiəʊ/ *noun* a method of transmitting a video signal in which the luminance and colour components (the luma, Y, and chroma, C) are transmitted over separate wires to improve the quality of the video. It is used in Hi8, S-VHS and other video formats to provide better quality than composite video.

SVQ *abbreviation* **Scottish Vocational Qualification**

swashbuckler /'swɒʃbʌklə/ *noun* a play, novel or film about a swordsman or adventurer

swash letter /'swɒʃ ˌletə/ *noun* an italic letter with elaborate flourishes and tails

sweeps /swiːps/ *plural noun* a survey of television ratings that is used to fix advertising prices or the period when these ratings are taken

sweetheart deal /'swiːthɑːt diːl/ *noun* the practice of employing known and favoured staff, such as ex-employees, when commissioning independent productions

switched talkback /ˌswɪtʃd 'tɔːkbæk/ *noun* talkback in a broadcasting studio from the production gallery that is activated by a button or switch, so that a presenter hears only the instructions intended for them and not a continuous feed. Compare **open talkback**

switcher /'swɪtʃə/ *noun* same as **vision mixer**

swivel /'swɪv(ə)l/ *noun* a pivoting support that allows something such as a camera to turn from side to side or up and down, sometimes in a full circle

swung dash /ˌswʌŋ 'dæʃ/ *noun* a character (~) used in printing to represent all or part of a word previously spelt out

Sykes Committee Report 1923 /saɪks/ *noun* an investigation into the future of BBC radio, which recommended that the company as a whole should be considered a public service and put into public administration

symbol /'sɪmbəl/ *noun* in semiology, an image which represents some object or concept

symbolic /sɪm'bɒlɪk/ *adjective* in semiology, something symbolic is not a sign or symbol itself but represents a set of ideas and values outside itself, for example a flag which represents a country

symbolic code /sɪmˌbɒlɪk 'kəʊd/ *noun* one of five codes used in the analysis and deconstruction of texts, describing symbols used in a narrative. ◊ **action code, enigma code, referential code, semantic code**

symbolic convergence theory /sɪmˌbɒlɪk kən'vɜːdʒəns ˌθɪəri/ *noun* the theory that in order to fulfil the psychological needs of a group, events must be interpreted as a group, even though the resulting shared interpretations may be inaccurate and fantastical

symbolic interactionalism /sɪmˌbɒlɪk ˌɪntər'ækʃənəlɪz(ə)m/ *noun* the theory that a person assigns a meaning and symbolic value to an object as a result of other people's reactions to it

symbolic violence /sɪmˌbɒlɪk 'vaɪələns/ *noun* in sociology, the repression that the non-dominant classes experience, having been designated 'wrong' and a 'minority'

symbolism /'sɪmbəlɪz(ə)m/ *noun* the use of symbols to invest things with a representative meaning or to represent something abstract

sync /sɪŋk/ *noun* synchronised sound, i.e. sound that is recorded simultaneously with the picture. Compare **non-sync**

syncbite /'sɪŋkbaɪt/ *noun* same as **sound bite**

synchroflash /'sɪŋkrəʊflæʃ/ *noun* a mechanism in a camera that opens the shutter at the moment when the light from the flashbulb or electronic flash is brightest

synchronic /sɪŋ'krɒnɪk/ *adjective* in the theories of structuralism and discourse, current, referring to the study of something as it currently is. Compare **diachronic**

synchronic linguistics /sɪŋˌkrɒnɪk lɪŋˈgwɪstɪks/ *noun* the study of language focusing on its qualities at one particular point in its development. Compare **diachronic linguistics**

synchronise /ˈsɪŋkrənaɪz/ *verb* to make the soundtrack of a film match up with the action

synchroniser /ˈsɪŋkrənaɪzə/ *noun* a piece of film editing equipment that allows the picture and the sound to be matched up

synchronous transmitter receiver /ˌsɪŋkrənəs trænzˌmɪtə rɪˈsiːvə/ *noun* a communications device that is able to both send and receive signals at the same time. Abbreviation **STR**

syncopate /ˈsɪŋkəpeɪt/ *verb* to modify a musical rhythm by shifting the stress to a weak beat of the bar

syncopation /ˌsɪŋkəˈpeɪʃ(ə)n/ *noun* a rhythmic technique in music in which the accent is shifted to a weak beat of the bar

syncretism /ˈsɪŋkrətɪz(ə)m/ *noun* in cultural theory, the combination in harmony of supposedly opposite things such as cultural forms

syndicate *noun* /ˈsɪndɪkət/ **1.** a group of newspapers that have the same owner **2.** a business or agency that sells news stories or photographs to the media ■ *verb* /ˈsɪndɪkeɪt/ **1.** to sell something such as an article or a comic strip for publication in a number of newspapers or magazines simultaneously **2.** to sell television or radio programmes directly to independent stations

syndication /ˌsɪndɪˈkeɪʃ(ə)n/ *noun* the act of packaging a programme for sale to other, international networks, or something such as a news column or cartoon for publication elsewhere

synergy /ˈsɪnədʒi/ *noun* the relationship between different media products in which one is used to improve the exposure of another

COMMENT: Examples of synergy in products would be the soundtrack from a film that is released on CD, further advertising the film while making money as a product in its own right, or a newspaper that carries an advertisement for a sister paper in its pages.

syntactics /sɪnˈtæktɪks/ *noun* in semiology, the study of signs and sign systems without reference to their meanings

syntax /ˈsɪntæks/ *noun* the study of grammatical structure in language

synthesis /ˈsɪnθəsɪs/ *noun* **1.** a new unified whole resulting from the combination of different ideas, influences or objects **2.** the production of music or speech using an electronic synthesiser

synthesise /ˈsɪnθəsaɪz/ *verb* **1.** to combine different ideas, influences, or objects into a new whole, or be combined in this way **2.** to produce music using an electronic synthesiser

synthesiser /ˈsɪnθəsaɪzə/ *noun* a device that generates and modifies sounds electronically, especially a musical instrument

synthespian /sɪnˈθespiən/ *noun* a digital image of a person created by a precise full-body scan and used by animators to produce animated characters or films

T

T1 /ˌtiː ˈwʌn/ *noun* a high-capacity telephone line suitable for high-speed digital access to the Internet and able to handle 24 voice or data channels simultaneously

T3 /ˌtiː ˈθriː/ *noun* a high-capacity telephone line capable of transferring data at speeds great enough to provide full-screen full-motion video and able to handle 672 voice or data channels simultaneously

tablet /ˈtæblət/ *noun* a flat device that allows a user to input graphical information into a computer by drawing on its surface

tabloid /ˈtæblɔɪd/ *noun* a smaller-sized format of newspaper such as the Sun, The Daily Mirror etc., with the added implication that it covers the news in a light-hearted, entertaining and less serious manner than a broadsheet. Also called **red-top**. Compare **broadsheet** ■ *adjective* light and entertainment-based. This term is often used pejoratively.

tabloidese /ˌtæblɔɪˈdiːz/ *noun* a style of reporting associated with the tabloids that is sensational and uses a lot of clichés and emotive language

COMMENT: Tabloidese is overly sensational, clichéd and characterised by snappy phrases and emotive language. It also uses indirect, coded language and ambiguous statements which discourage accusations of libel, such as the often-cited use of 'romp' to imply a sexual encounter.

tabloidisation /ˌtæblɔɪdaɪˈzeɪʃ(ə)n/ *noun* a change towards the style of news coverage commonly associated with the tabloid press

'He has made the headlines bigger and more catchy, used populist design gimmicks, run more human interest stories on the front page, created a quirky centre spread and reduced foreign coverage... How does he respond to charges of tabloidisation? "I suppose I plead guilty".' [Roy Greenslade, *The Guardian*]

tabloid TV /ˌtæblɔɪd tiː ˈviː/ *noun* television programming that combines gossip, scandal and news about media celebrities in the style associated with tabloid journalism

tachistoscope /təˈkɪstəskəʊp/ *noun* a device used to measure the recognition level when a customer is exposed to a brand package or advertising material. Also called **T-scope**

tag /tæg/ *noun* a label that describes a piece of data, for example to facilitate later retrieval or text formatting ■ *verb* to mark a piece of data with tags so that it can be formatted or retrieved

tagline /ˈtæglaɪn/ *noun* a short secondary phrase attached to the title of a film that expands on its nature and helps to capture audience attention

tag question /ˈtæg ˌkwest(ə)n/ *noun* a short phrase at the end of a statement that is intended to elicit a response, for example '..., isn't it?'

tail /teɪl/ *noun* the bottom of a printed page, or the margin between the bottom of the page and the lowest line of type

tailpiece /ˈteɪlpiːs/ *noun* a decoration at the bottom of a page, for example at the end of a chapter

take /teɪk/ *noun* **1.** a repetition of the same shot when filming, because the previous one was not satisfactory for some reason **2.** a single uninterrupted session in which a work or section of a work is recorded by audio recording equipment **3.** a page or number of pages that are part of a larger article

take back /ˌteɪk 'bæk/ *verb* to move a portion of text back to the previous line

takeoff /'teɪkɒf/ *noun* an imitation of somebody or something, especially for comic effect

take-ones /'teɪk wʌnz/ *plural noun* advertising leaflets or promotional cards that are delivered to shops where they are displayed in racks

take over /ˌteɪk 'əʊvə/ *verb* to move a section of text forward to the next line

take-up /'teɪk ʌp/ *noun* **1.** the degree to which something made available is accepted or used by people **2.** part of a mechanism onto which something such as tape is wound

talent /'tælənt/ *noun* the performer, actor, presenter, singer etc. appearing in front of the camera

talk /tɔːk/ *adjective* involving mainly interviews, discussions and telephone calls from viewers or listeners

talkback /'tɔːkbæk/ *noun* **1.** an off-air communication system used for example to link a studio with the control room **2.** a communications system allowing for example the production gallery to speak to presenters or camera operators on the studio floor, via an earpiece

talkboard /'tɔːkbɔːd/ *noun* an online discussion group on a specific topic, sometimes involving experts who will answer questions

talkie /'tɔːki/ *noun* an early film with a soundtrack

talking heads /ˌtɔːkɪŋ 'hedz/ *plural noun* head-and-shoulder shots of people talking to camera or to an interviewer

talk show /'tɔːk ʃəʊ/ *noun* **1.** a television or radio programme in which ordinary people discuss aspects of their lives or current social issues **2.** a television or radio programme made up mainly of interviews with guests, especially famous people

Talloires Declaration 1981 /'tælwɑː/ *noun* a response from representatives of 20 countries to the UNESCO plans for creating a New World Order giving journalists a special protected status, asserting that such measures were unnecessary. ◊ **New World Information and Communication Order**

tally light /'tæli laɪt/ *noun* same as **cue light**

TAM *abbreviation* TV **television audience measurement**

Tango /'tæŋgəʊ/ *noun* an internationally recognised code word for the letter T, used in radio communications

tank /tæŋk/ *noun* **1.** a large tray or container for processing a number of sheets of film together **2.** a lightproof container for developing film, designed so that processing chemicals can be poured in and out without light entering

tap-dance /'tæp dɑːns/ *verb* to engage in complicated evasion or hesitation in order to avoid making a commitment or a definitive statement

'Is Tony Blair finally losing his precious ability to tapdance his way out of a hole? His latest stumble came after a lacklustre performance in the Commons during which his former flatmate, Lord Chancellor Charlie Falconer, was forced to come to his rescue much to his embarrassment.' [Hickey, *The Express*]

tape /teɪp/ *noun* **1.** magnetic tape used in cassettes **2.** a cassette used for audio or video recording or playback ■ *verb* to record something, especially music or a television programme, on magnetic tape

tape deck /'teɪp dek/ *noun* a piece of electrical equipment that plays and records tapes, especially audio cassettes

tape header /'teɪp ˌhedə/ *noun* identification information at the beginning of a tape

tape recorder /'teɪp rɪˌkɔːdə/ *noun* a machine that can record and play audio tapes, especially one with its own speaker

tape recording /'teɪp rɪˌkɔːdɪŋ/ *noun* a recording made on magnetic tape, especially an audio recording

target /'tɑːgɪt/ *noun* a surface or electrode, often luminescent, that is hit by an electron beam to produce an output signal, for example in a television camera tube

target audience /'tɑːgɪt ˌɔːdiəns/ *noun* the group of society at whom a media product is specifically aimed, for example young couples, 30-something males, teenagers etc.

Target Group Index /ˌtɑːgɪt 'gruːp ˌɪndeks/ *noun* a large annual consumer survey into purchasing habits and lifestyle. Abbreviation **TGI**

Target Group Rating /ˌtɑːgɪt 'gruːp ˌreɪtɪŋ/ *noun* an analysis of TGI demographic data side-by-side with BARB audience research. Abbreviation **TGR**

target marketing /'tɑːɡɪt ˌmɑːkɪtɪŋ/ *noun* the process in which advertising or selling is aimed a particular group of consumers who all have similar characteristics

task culture /'tɑːsk ˌkʌltʃə/ *noun* an organisational structure in a business that is based around the particular skills and expertise of each employee. Compare **person culture**, **power culture**, **role culture**

task method /'tɑːsk ˌmeθəd/ *noun* the way of calculating an advertising budget by basing it on the actual amount needed to achieve the objectives

Tass /tæs/ *noun* the official news agency of the former Soviet Union

taste /teɪst/ *noun* the subjective judgement of individuals on such matters as dress, music, film etc.

tasting /'teɪstɪŋ/ *noun* same as **copy tasting**

Taylor Nelson Sofres plc /ˌteɪlə ˌnelsən 'sɒfrəz/ *noun* full form of **TNS**

tbu *abbreviation* **telephone balancing unit**

t-commerce /ˌtiː 'kɒmɜːs/ *noun* a business conducted by means of interactive television

team approach /'tiːm əˌprəʊtʃ/ *noun* a method of measuring the effectiveness of an advertising campaign when the evaluators are actually involved in the campaign

tear sheet /'teə ʃiːt/ *noun* a single page taken from a magazine or other periodical, often used to prove to an advertiser that an advertisement has been published

tease /tiːz/ *noun* a short advertisement for something coming up later on in the programme or item, for example a news story

teaser /'tiːzə/ *noun* **1.** a preview intended to interest the audience in a forthcoming broadcast or publication **2.** an advertisement that gives a little information about a product in order to attract customers by making them curious to know more

teasers /'tiːzəz/ *plural noun* same as **cover lines**

technical director /'teknɪk(ə)l daɪˌrektə/ *noun* the member of a film or tele-

vision production team who has responsibility for overseeing technical operations, maintenance of camera equipment etc.

Technicolor /'teknɪkʌlə/ a trade name for a method of colour film production developed in the 1930s, in which three different pieces of film are developed for each primary colour and then layered together

techno /'teknəʊ/ *noun* electronic dance music characterised by its quick tempo and use of digitally synthesised instruments

technological determinism /ˌteknəlɒdʒɪk(ə)l dɪ'tɜːmɪˌnɪz(ə)m/ *noun* the idea that all technology that can be feasibly produced is desirable and is likely to be developed and become available

technophobia /ˌteknəʊ'fəʊbiə/ *noun* fear of technology or machines

   '...it is not all IT's fault. Users who wear their technophobia as a badge of honour similarly need to be smoked out. Users do not need to become technology experts at the bits and bytes level, but they do need to understand how IT can be used to deliver business value...'
[Ade McCormick, *The Financial Times*]

tech review /'tek rɪˌvjuː/ *noun* the process of checking that a finished filmed piece is of a suitable technical standard, that the levels are correct and it is correctly marked with the timecode and ident clock

tech run /'tek rʌn/ *noun* a rehearsal in which the lighting, camera angles, sound etc. for a television broadcast are practised

tec. op. *noun* a person who does technical work outside the studio, for example on an outside broadcast

telco /'telkəʊ/ *noun* a telecommunications company

telecamera /'telikæm(ə)rə/ *noun* a television camera

telecast /'telikɑːst/ *noun* a television broadcast ■ *verb* to broadcast a programme on television

telecommunication /ˌtelikəˌmjuːnɪ'keɪʃ(ə)n/ *noun* the transmission of encoded sound, pictures or data over significant distances, using radio signals or electrical or optical lines

telecommunications /ˌtelikə
ˌmjuːnɪˈkeɪʃ(ə)nz/ *noun* the science and technology of transmitting information electronically by wires or radio signals with encoding and decoding equipment

teleconferencing /ˈteli
ˌkɒnf(ə)rənsɪŋ/ *noun* a system of video conferencing that uses a restricted band of frequencies and allows participants to be connected by telephone lines

teledemocracy /ˌtelidəˈmɒkrəsi/ *noun* the idea that democracy is served by telecommunications systems, because these help to disseminate information to everybody so that they can make free choices

teledrama /ˈtelidrɑːmə/ *noun* a drama filmed to be broadcast on television

telefilm /ˈtelifɪlm/ *noun* a film made for television

telegenic /ˌteliˈdʒenɪk/ *adjective* appearing attractive on television, a quality prized by politicians as it helps to hold an audience

'[Matt] Skinner sets off for America today on a book tour with [Jamie] Oliver. They make a veritable dream team: telegenic, articulate and youthfully evangelical as they broadcast their epicurean message to the masses.' [Judith Woods, *The Daily Telegraph*]

telegram /ˈtelɪɡræm/ *noun* a printed message sent by telegraphy

telegraph /ˈtelɪɡrɑːf/ *noun* same as **telegram** ■ *verb* to send a message to somebody by telegraph

telegraphic /ˌtelɪˈɡræfɪk/ *adjective* relating to telegraphy or telegrams

telegraphy /təˈleɡrəfi/ *noun* a method of long-distance communication by coded electrical impulses transmitted through wires

teleimmersion /ˌteliɪˈmɜːʃ(ə)n/ *noun* a teleconferencing technology that uses banks of video cameras linked to computers to allow users in remote locations to communicate as if they were in the same room

telematics /ˌtelɪˈmætɪks/ *noun* the technology that allows computer data to be sent from one terminal to another via a telephone line

telemeter /ˈtelimiːtə/ *verb* to collect and transmit data about a remote object, especially using a satellite

telenovela /ˈtelinɒˌvelə/ *noun* a melodramatic type of soap opera popular in South America, usually made in Portuguese or Spanish

telephone /ˈtelɪfəʊn/ *noun* **1.** an electronic apparatus containing a receiver and transmitter that is connected to a telecommunications system, enabling the user to speak to and hear others with similar equipment **2.** a system of communication using telephones ■ *verb* to contact and speak to somebody using the telephone

telephone balancing unit /ˌtelɪfəʊn ˈbælənsɪŋ ˌjuːnɪt/ *noun* a device used to balance the level of a broadcast telephone call with the standard level of the output. Abbreviation **tbu**

telephoto /ˈteliˌfəʊtəʊ/ *adjective* producing a large image of a distant object ■ *noun* a photograph taken using a telephoto lens

telephotography /ˌtelifəˈtɒɡrəfi/ *noun* the photographing of distant objects with the use of special lenses or electronic equipment

telephoto lens /ˌtelifəʊtəʊ ˈlenz/ *noun* a camera lens with a narrow field of view, capable of sharply focusing on objects a long way away

teleplay /ˈtelipleɪ/ *noun* a treatment or script for a play written for presentation on television

teleprinter /ˈteliˌprɪntə/ *noun* a piece of equipment for telegraphic communication that uses a device like a typewriter for data input and output

teleprompt /ˈteliprɒmpt/ *noun* same as **Autocue**

TelePrompTer /ˈteliprɒmptə/ a US trade name for a device showing text for somebody speaking on television to read

telerecording /ˌtelirɪˈkɔːdɪŋ/ *noun* the process of recording television or computer screens on film by adjusting the flicker rate of the film camera so that there is no distortion

telescoping /ˈteliskəʊpɪŋ/ *noun* the process that occurs when a respondent exaggerates what they remember seeing

teletext /ˈtelitekst/ *noun* a system of broadcasting news and other information in written form that can be viewed on specially equipped television sets

teletheatre /ˈteliθɪətə/ *noun* a viewing area where horse races are broadcast live on video screens, for example in a betting shop

telethon /ˈtelɪθɒn/ *noun* a lengthy television broadcast that combines entertainment with appeals to donate to a charity

teletranscription /ˌtelɪtrænsˈkrɪpʃ(ə)n/ *noun* the transcription of a television programme using videotape

televise /ˈtelɪvaɪz/ *verb* to broadcast something on television

television /ˌtelɪˈvɪʒ(ə)n/ *noun* **1.** an electronic device for receiving and reproducing the images and sounds of a combined audio and video signal. Also called **television set**, **tv**, **telly 2.** a system of capturing images and sounds, broadcasting them via a combined electronic audio and video signal, and reproducing them to be viewed and listened to. Also called **tv 3.** the image, sound or content of a combined audio and video broadcast **4.** the industry concerned with making and broadcasting programmes combining images and sounds

television audience measurement /ˌtelɪvɪʒ(ə)n ˈɔːdiəns ˌmeʒəmənt/ *noun* ♦ **audience measurement**

television consumer audit /ˌtelɪvɪʒ(ə)n kənˈsjuːmə ˌɔːdɪt/ *noun* a survey carried out on a sample of television viewers about their viewing habits and impressions

television network /ˌtelɪvɪʒ(ə)n ˈnetwɜːk/ *noun* a system of linked television stations covering the whole country

television ratings /ˈtelɪvɪʒ(ə)n ˌreɪtɪŋz/ *plural noun* statistics showing the size and type of television audiences at different times of day for various channels and programmes. Abbreviation **TVR**

Television Receive Only /ˌtelɪvɪʒ(ə)n rɪˌsiːv ˈəʊnli/ *noun* full form of **TVRO**

television receiver/monitor /ˌtelɪvɪʒ(ə)n rɪˌsiːvə ˈmɒnɪtə/ *noun* a device able to receive or relay television pictures and sound

television set /ˌtelɪˈvɪʒ(ə)n ˌset/ *noun* same as **television**

television spot /ˈtelɪvɪʒ(ə)n spɒt/, **tv spot** *noun* an advert or short promotional feature such as an interview, broadcast on television

television tube /ˌtelɪˈvɪʒ(ə)n ˌtjuːb/ *noun* a cathode ray tube used to reproduce television images

teleworker /ˈteliwɜːkə/ *noun* an employee that works from home, using communication systems such as e-mail to stay in touch with co-workers

telex /ˈteleks/ *noun* a communications system using teleprinters that communicate via telephone lines

telly /ˈteli/ *noun* same as **television** (*informal*)

Telstar /ˈtelstɑː/ *noun* a low-orbiting satellite used by the BBC and other broadcasters

temporary studio /ˌtemp(ə)rəri ˈstjuːdiəʊ/ *noun* a compromise between a permanent studio and an outside broadcast with movable equipment, usually built in advance for some large event

tentpole movie /ˈtentpəʊl ˌmuːvi/ *noun* a film that 'supports' the other films on a studio's slate financially and will be an almost guaranteed success

terminal poster /ˈtɜːmɪn(ə)l ˌpəʊstə/ *noun* an advertising display in stations or airline terminals etc.

terms of trade /ˌtɜːmz əv ˈtreɪd/ *noun* the rate of exchange for goods or services being imported and exported between two countries

ternion /ˈtɜːniən/ *noun* a set of three sheets of paper folded once to make 12 pages

terrestrial /təˈrestriəl/ *adjective* not broadcast using satellite but by land-based transmitters

territorialisation /ˌterɪtɔːriəlaɪˈzeɪʃ(ə)n/ *noun* the tendency of humans to divide the world up into ever smaller territories and groups, to which an individual either belongs or is excluded from

territoriality /ˌterɪtɔːriˈælɪti/ *noun* the desire to establish and guard personal space, a factor in creating spatial zones

territory /ˈterɪt(ə)ri/ *noun* **1.** the geographical area for which rights are bought (not necessarily a country) **2.** a field of knowledge, investigation or experience

terrorism /ˈterərɪz(ə)m/ *noun* the threatening of or carrying out of major destructive incidents, usually involving human casualties, as a means of attracting publicity for a cause

tertiary text /'tɜːʃəri tekst/ *noun* in textual theory, the media text after reception by an audience as it is analysed and different readings discussed. Compare **primary text, secondary text**

test card /'test kɑːd/ *noun* a geometric pattern with areas of different colours, transmitted by a television broadcasting organisation to help viewers to tune in their television sets for optimum reception

testimonial advertising /ˌtestɪ'məʊniəl ˌædvətaɪzɪŋ/ *noun* advertising that uses statements from famous or qualified people, or from satisfied customers, to endorse a product

test impression /'test ɪmˌpreʃ(ə)n/ *noun* a print of a work made to see how the final printed version will appear

test marketing /'test ˌmɑːkɪtɪŋ/ *noun* the use of a sample of a larger market to try out a marketing strategy or product

test pattern /'test ˌpæt(ə)n/ *noun* a pattern of colours, shapes etc. that is used in setting up and calibrating video equipment

test-screening /'test ˌskriːnɪŋ/ *noun* a screening of a provisional version of a film to test audience reaction

'Sutherland said that it was decided that US audiences needed a "sweeter film"'. The romantic ending was chosen for release after a test screening in a US cinema. Audiences reportedly "swooned"' as Elizabeth and Darcy kissed on a terrace, as he cooed: "Mrs Darcy… Mrs Darcy".'' [Hugh Davies, *The Daily Telegraph*]

tête-à-tête /ˌtet æ 'tet/ *adjective* of a conversation, private and between two people only

text /tekst/ *noun* **1.** a style of type that is suitable for printing running text **2.** the main body of a book or other printed material, as distinct from the introduction, index, illustrations and headings **3.** same as **text message** ■ *verb* to send a text message to somebody

text box /'tekst bɒks/ *noun* a box within a computer dialog box in which characters such as text, dates or numbers can be typed and edited

text chat /'tekst tʃæt/ *noun* a real-time communication between Internet users in which messages are typed via a keyboard

text edition /'tekst ɪˌdɪʃ(ə)n/ *noun* the printed version of something that is published in some other form such as a CD-ROM or on the Internet

text message /'tekst ˌmesɪdʒ/ *noun* a short message written and sent from one mobile phone to another. Also called **SMS**

textuality /ˌtekstju'ælɪti/ *noun* in aesthetic theory, the 'essence' of a text, that which makes it a text and reveals knowledge about it

textual theory /'tekstjuəl ˌθɪəri/ *noun* the study of the construction of literature and related topics such as editing strategies, structures, symbolism, etc

TGI *abbreviation* **Target Group Index**

TGR *abbreviation* **Target Group Rating**

theatre /'θɪətə/ *noun* **1.** a building, room or other setting where plays are put on for an audience **2.** the industry of preparing for and putting on plays

The Future of the BBC: Serving the Nation, Competing Worldwide *noun* a government white paper that reviewed the status of the BBC as the UK's major public service broadcaster. ◊ **BBC**

thin /θɪn/ *adjective* referring to a photographic negative that lacks density or contrast

think piece /'θɪŋk piːs/ *noun* an article that analyses a topic currently in the media

think tank /'θɪŋk tæŋk/ *noun* a committee of experts that undertakes research or gives advice, especially to a government

third assistant director /ˌθɜːd ə ˌsɪst(ə)nt daɪ'rektə/ *noun* the person whose job it is to assist the first assistant director

third-generation /ˌθɜːd ˌdʒenə'reɪʃ(ə)n/ *adjective* referring to the latest specification for mobile communication systems, including mobile telephones. ◊ **second-generation**

'Vodafone has also to persuade its customers to switch…to third generation (3G), where video and high quality sound services mean average revenues per subscriber can be more than double those for 2G services.' [Alan Cane, *The Financial Times*]

thirty-twomo /ˌθɜːti 'tuːməʊ/ *noun* a size of book page traditionally created by folding a single sheet of standard-sized printing paper 5 times, giving 32 leaves or 64 pages

three-colour /ˌθriː ˈkʌlə/ *adjective* using, produced by or relating to a colour printing process in which the print is produced by superimposing separate plates for the colours yellow, magenta and cyan

3D /ˌθriː ˈdiː/ *abbreviation* **three-dimensional**

3D gaming /ˌθriː ˈdiː ˈgeɪmɪŋ/ *noun* computer games that create the illusion of a three-dimensional universe in which a character can move around

three-dimensional /ˌθriː daɪ ˈmenʃ(ə)nəl/ *adjective* possessing or appearing to possess the dimensions of height, width and depth. Abbreviation **3D**

3G /ˌθriː ˈdʒiː/ *abbreviation* **third-generation**

three-quarter binding /ˌθriː ˈkwɔːtə ˌbaɪndɪŋ/ *noun* bookbinding in which the spine and most of the sides of a book are covered in the same material

throat microphone /ˈθrəʊt ˌmaɪkrəfəʊn/ *noun* a microphone that is placed in contact with a person's throat to pick up the vibrations produced by speech

through-the-lens /ˌθruː ðə ˈlenz/ *adjective* as a scene would appear through a camera lens, with the framing. Abbreviation **TTL**

throw /θrəʊ/ *verb* to hand over to another presenter

throwaway /ˈθrəʊəˌweɪ/ *noun* an advertising leaflet or handbill that is discarded after being read

thumb /θʌm/ *verb* to glance through the pages of a book or magazine

thumb index /ˈθʌm ˌɪndeks/ *noun* a series of labelled indentations cut into the pages of a book down the edge opposite the binding to allow a particular section to be located quickly

ticker /ˈtɪkə/ *noun* a service from news agencies in which a toolbar-sized scrolling band on a computer screen delivers constantly-updated headlines

tie-in /ˈtaɪ ɪn/ *noun* merchandise attached to a film or other media product. ◊ **merchandising**

tie line /ˈtaɪ laɪn/ *noun* the cables etc. which physical connect a recording studio to the gallery

tilt /tɪlt/ *verb* **1.** to move a camera up or down vertically from a fixed point **2.** to turn a camera smoothly and slowly on its axis in a vertical direction (from up to down, or vice versa). Compare **pan**

time buyer /ˈtaɪm ˌbaɪə/ *noun* a person who buys advertising time on radio or television

timecode /ˈtaɪmkəʊd/ *noun* **1.** a system in which each piece of film is digitally identified, frame by frame, using criteria such as time and frame number **2.** an electronic signal that is added to a piece of video to identify it, consisting of tape number, minutes, seconds, frames since the start of filming

time exposure /ˈtaɪm ɪkˌspəʊʒə/ *noun* **1.** the exposure of photographic film for an unusually long time to achieve a desired effect **2.** a photograph taken by time exposure

time-lapse photography /ˌtaɪm læps fəˈtɒɡrəfi/ *noun* a method of filming a slow process such as the opening of a flower by taking a series of single exposures, then showing them at higher speed to simulate continuous action

timelength /ˈtaɪmleŋkθ/ *noun* the length of a cinema, television or radio advertisement

time segment /ˈtaɪm ˌsegmənt/ *noun* a period set aside for advertisements on television

time-shift viewing /ˌtaɪm ʃɪft ˈvjuːɪŋ/ *noun* the act of watching recorded television programmes on video up to 7 days after they were originally shown

Tin Pan Alley /ˈtɪn pæn ˌæli/ *noun* **1.** a city district in which the business of composing and publishing popular music is carried on **2.** popular music composers and publishers considered collectively

COMMENT: The phrase comes from a street in New York (West 28th) formerly known as **Tin Pan Alley** in which many musicians and composers set up home in the late 19th and early 10th century. The name evokes the sound that could be heard when walking past, of different music playing from every house creating a cacophonous noise like pans clattering together.

tint /tɪnt/ *noun* a pale colour printed as a background onto which another colour is printed

tip-off /'ˈtɪp ɒf/ *noun* information given to a journalist to follow up

'Zardad was traced to south London after the BBC's John Simpson received a tip-off in Afghanistan that he was living in Britain.' [Sandra Laville, *The Guardian*]

tip sheet /'tɪp ʃiːt/ *noun* a newspaper that gives information about shares which should be bought or sold

title /'taɪt(ə)l/ *noun* 1. a name that identifies a book, film, play, painting, musical composition or other literary or artistic work 2. a descriptive heading for something such as a book chapter, a magazine article or a speech 3. a work published or recorded by a company

title role /'taɪt(ə)l rəʊl/ *noun* the role of the character in a play or film whose name appears in the work's title

title sequence /'taɪt(ə)l ˌsiːkwəns/ *noun* the series of pictures, on-screen graphics, credits and music that are shown as the introduction to a television programme

title sequence designer /'taɪt(ə)l ˌsiːkwəns dɪˌzaɪnə/ *noun* in television production, the person responsible for designing and editing the title sequence

title track /'taɪt(ə)l træk/ *noun* the song or piece of music whose name is used as the title of a particular recording

tittle /'tɪt(ə)l/ *noun* a small mark used in printing and writing, for example an accent, punctuation mark or diacritical mark

TiVo /'tiːvəʊ/ *noun* a digital box attached to a television, that automatically records programming based on the viewer's personal taste and also allows programmes being watched 'live' to be paused, rewound etc.

TNC *abbreviation* transnational corporation

TNS *noun* a market research company that carries out audience measurement surveys. Full form **Taylor Nelson Sofres plc**

tonality /təʊ'næliti/ *noun* the scheme connecting the colour tones in a work of art such as a painting

tone /təʊn/ *noun* 1. the impression given by a text or media product of its creator's attitude, for example serious, humorous etc. 2. the quality of a sound that makes it distinctive, for example in a voice or musical instrument 3. a signal sent before an audio feed for technicians so that they can set levels

tone arm /'təʊn ɑːm/ *noun* a record player's arm with a stylus on its end

tone control /'təʊn kənˌtrəʊl/ *noun* a control on a radio, record player or other piece of audio equipment that adjusts the tone of the sound reproduction, accentuating the higher or lower sound frequencies

toner /'təʊnə/ *noun* 1. a chemical solution used in photograph development 2. ink in powder or liquid form for a photocopier or computer printer

toon /tuːn/ *noun* 1. a character in a cartoon 2. same as **cartoon**

top /tɒp/ *noun* an article at the top of a page

Top 10 /ˌtɒp 'ten/ *noun* a list of the ten best-selling pop records in the previous week

Top 40 /ˌtɒp 'fɔːti/ *noun* a list of the 40 best-selling pop records in the previous week, usually announced on the radio on a Sunday

top and tail /ˌtɒp ən 'teɪl/ *noun* 1. to edit a piece of audio cleanly at the beginning and end 2. same as **sandwich**

top-shelf /ˌtɒp 'ʃelf/ *adjective* referring to pornographic magazines that are very sexually explicit and are therefore displayed on the top shelf in a shop, out of direct view

top shot /'tɒp ʃɒt/ *noun* a camera shot of an incident or event, taken from a crane or something such as a helicopter or balloon

tormentor /tɔː'mentə/, **tormenter** *noun* a panel of sound-absorbent material used to eliminate echo on a film set

Toronto International Film Festival /təˌrɒntəʊ 'fɪlm ˌfestɪvəl/ *noun* a prestigious film festival considered second only to Cannes in terms of importance. It is held annually in September and is often used as an opportunity to create publicity for the Oscars.

total audience package /ˌtəʊt(ə)l 'ɔːdiəns ˌpækɪdʒ/ *noun* a media owner's arrangement or scheduling of advertisements across time segments on television and radio, so as to reach the widest range of viewers or listeners

totality /təʊ'tælɪti/ *noun* in cultural theory, everything, ie. all the people, all the products and means of production, everything in every possible world.

total service area /ˌtəʊt(ə)l 'sɜːvɪs ˌeəriə/ *noun* the geographical area that is served by a radio station, used by RAJAR to determine audience figures

tots /tɒts/ *noun* 'triumph over tragedy story', a human interest piece

touch /tʌtʃ/ *noun* an element of non-verbal communication, transmitting messages of comfort, solidarity, sexual interest etc.

touchdown /'tʌtʃdaʊn/ *adjective* offering computer and telephone connections and Internet access to visitors and business travellers

touchscreen /'tʌtʃskriːn/ *adjective* referring to a kiosk or public access computer that has a screen that responds to touch (either pressure or heat) so that it can be operated without a keyboard or mouse

Touchstone /'tʌtʃstəʊn/ *noun* a major film studio, a subsidiary of the Walt Disney Company, created to handle slightly more adult content films than is possible under the Disney label. It also has a television arm that produces the hit series Lost and Desperate Housewives.

town meeting /ˌtaʊn 'miːtɪŋ/ *noun* a television programme centring on an issue of national interest, in which people from a town or region ask questions of debaters or speakers

townscape /'taʊnskeɪp/ *noun* a painting or photograph of an urban scene

tr. *abbreviation* PRINTING **1.** transpose **2.** transposition

track /træk/ *noun* **1.** a physical movement by a camera (on its guiding rails or movable mounting), following action or movement in the scene **2.** a guiding rail along which a camera moves when taking a tracking shot. The rail allows a smooth, gliding movement. **3.** same as **soundtrack 4.** a component of the finished soundtrack, prepared in the editing suite and layered together with others, for example the dialogue track and the music track

tracking /'trækɪŋ/ *noun* a function on a video player that adjusts the quality of the picture

tracking shot /'trækɪŋ ʃɒt/ *noun* a camera shot filmed from a moving dolly, following the movement of somebody or something

track laying /'træk ˌleɪɪŋ/ *noun* the process of layering tracks together to produce a complete soundtrack

tract /trækt/ *noun* a pamphlet that sets out a position or an analysis, especially one dealing with a political or religious issue

trade /treɪd/ *noun* a publication meant for people in a specific line of business

trade advertising /'treɪd ˌædvətaɪzɪŋ/ *noun* advertising to trade customers and not to the general public

trade journal /'treɪd ˌdʒɜːn(ə)l/ *noun* a periodical devoted to news and features relating to a specific trade or profession

traditional transmission /trəˌdɪʃ(ə)n(ə)l trænz'mɪʃ(ə)n/ *noun* the way a language is passed from one generation to the next through immersion and formal teaching

traffic /'træfɪk/ *noun* **1.** the number of visitors to a website **2.** a department at a radio station that decides where commercials should be placed

'Once material [content] on the web becomes paid for, a number of things happen. First, your traffic drops dramatically, so if you do have advertising its value will fall. Second, you stop being something stumbled on by Google or linked to by blogs, and potentially your growth stagnates.' [Emily Bell, *The Guardian*]

traffic data /'træfɪk ˌdeɪtə/ *noun* statistical information about messages sent and received on a network without reference to their content

tragedy /'trædʒədi/ *noun* **1.** an event in life that evokes feelings of sorrow or grief **2.** a serious play with a tragic theme, often involving a heroic struggle and the downfall of the main character **3.** a literary work that deals with a tragic theme **4.** the genre of plays or other literary works that deal with tragic themes

tragicomedy /'trædʒiˌkɒmədi/ *noun* **1.** tragicomic plays or literary works considered as a genre **2.** an event or situation that has both tragic and comical aspects

trail /treɪl/ *noun* same as **promo**

trailer /'treɪlə/ *noun* **1.** an advertisement for a film consisting of extracts from it, shown on television or in a cinema **2.** a blank piece of film at the end of a reel ■ *verb* to advertise a film with extracts from it

train on /'treɪn ɒn/ *verb* to aim something such as a camera at somebody or something

trance /trɑːns/ *noun* electronic dance music with a repetitive hypnotic beat

transactional analysis /træn ˌzækʃ(ə)nəl ə'næləsɪs/ *noun* the investigation of motives behind interpersonal exchanges and what is given and taken away by each participant

transactional television /trænz ˌækʃənəl 'telɪvɪʒ(ə)n/ *noun* services available to viewers through a television channel, such as home shopping

transcribe /træn'skraɪb/ *verb* **1.** to record something so that it can be broadcast at a later time **2.** to broadcast something that has been transcribed earlier

transculturation /ˌtrænzkʌltʃə 'reɪʃ(ə)n/ *noun* the exchange of cultural artefacts across borders, where they are assimilated and modified

transference /'trænsf(ə)rəns/ *noun* **1.** in psychoanalytical theory, a patient's projection of deeply-hidden desires onto their analyst **2.** the attachment of meanings to signs

transformational advertising /ˌtrænsfə'meɪʃ(ə)nəl ˌædvətaɪzɪŋ/ *noun* a form of emotional advertising that aims to relate emotional experiences to the product or service being advertised, and then tries to change these emotions into an active interest in purchasing

transgender /trænz'dʒendə/ *adjective* relating to transsexuals or transvestites

transgressive /trænz'gresɪv/ *adjective* in feminist theory, referring to somebody or something that goes against social norms

transient advertisement /ˌtrænziənt əd'vɜːtɪsmənt/ *noun* an advertisement that the target audience cannot keep to look at again, for example a cinema advertisement. Compare **intransient advertisement**

transistor radio /trænˌzɪstə 'reɪdiəʊ/ *noun* a small portable radio that uses transistors in its circuits

translation /træns'leɪʃ(ə)n/ *noun* in the theories of structuralism and discourse, the process of transferring a message from one semiotic system (language) to another

translator /træns'leɪtə/ *noun* a radio transmitter that receives a signal on one frequency and retransmits it on another

transmission /trænz'mɪʃ(ə)n/ *noun* **1.** a radio or television broadcast. Abbreviation **TX 2.** something transmitted, for example a radio signal **3.** the act or process of transmitting something, especially radio signals, radio or television broadcasts or data

transmission area /trænz'mɪʃ(ə)n ˌeəriə/ *noun* same as **total service area**

transmission form /trænz'mɪʃ(ə)n fɔːm/ *noun* one of the four forms that must be submitted when delivering a programme to the BBC, giving information to the presentation department. ◊ **billing form**, **music reporting form**, **Programme as Completed form**

transmission medium /trænz 'mɪʃ(ə)n ˌmiːdiəm/ *noun* a means by which data can be transmitted, for example radio or light

transmit /trænz'mɪt/ *verb* **1.** to broadcast a radio or television programme **2.** to send a signal by radio waves, satellite or wire

transmitter /trænz'mɪtə/ *noun* **1.** a piece of broadcasting equipment that generates a radio-frequency wave, modulates it so that it carries a meaningful signal and sends it out from an antenna **2.** in a piece of communication, the person who is receiving the transmitted message

transnational corporation /trænz ˌnæʃ(ə)nəl ˌkɔːpə'reɪʃ(ə)n/ *noun* a giant corporation that produces and distributes products in more than one country, such as Coca Cola, Microsoft, HSBC, Sony etc. Abbreviation **TNC**

transparency /træns'pærənsi/ *noun* the way in which the structure of a media text should be invisible to the casual reader

transponder /træn'spɒndə/ *noun* **1.** a receiving and transmitting device in a communication or broadcast satellite that relays the signals it receives back to Earth **2.** a channel system on a satellite that allows it to send and receive many different signals simultaneously

transport advertising /'trænspɔːt ˌædvətaɪzɪŋ/ *noun* advertising appearing on or in forms of transport such as buses or trains

transpose /træns'pəʊz/ *verb* to make two things change places or reverse their usual order, for example two letters in a word. Abbreviation **tr., trs.**

transposition /ˌtrænspə'zɪʃ(ə)n/ *noun* a reversal or alteration of the positions or order in which things stand. Abbreviation **tr.**

travel /'træv(ə)l/ *verb* to scan an object or scene in the process of observing or filming it

travelogue /'trævəlɒg/ *noun* a film, video or piece of writing about travel, especially to interesting or remote places, or about one person's travels

'A gentle culture-clash comedy from those pre-Eurostar days when France seemed a whole exotic continent away from stuffy olde England, Gordon Parry's amiable period piece works better nowadays as a handsome travelogue of 1950s Paris than as a true snapshot of Brits abroad.' [Stephen Dalton, *The Times*]

treatment /'triːtmənt/ *noun* a document that expands the ideas in a proposal, describing how the idea will be developed into a film or programme

treble /'treb(ə)l/ *noun* **1.** the higher audio frequencies electronically reproduced by a radio, recording or sound system **2.** a control for increasing or decreasing the high-frequency output of a radio or audio amplifier

treeware /'triːweə/ *noun* books and other material printed on paper

trial by media /ˌtraɪəl baɪ 'miːdiə/ *noun* the idea that the media can make judgments about a person's actions and deliver punishment in the form of shame, ridicule, loss of career and reputation etc.

trichromatic /ˌtraɪkrəʊ'mætɪk/ *adjective* **1.** relating to, involving or using three colours **2.** involving the combination of the three primary colours to produce the other colours

trim /trɪm/ *noun* a piece of film eliminated from a shot during editing ■ *verb* to cut pieces from a film during editing

trimetrogon /traɪ'metrəgɒn/ *noun* a technique in which three aerial photographs are taken at the same time, one vertical and two at oblique angles, in order to obtain more topographical detail

trims /trɪmz/ *plural noun* the sections of footage which are removed in editing, both before and after the selected frames. They are filed away in case they are needed for later use.

trip hazard /'trɪp ˌhæzəd/ *noun* something such as a wire that people might catch their feet on and trip over

trip hop /'trɪp hɒp/ *noun* a rhythmic dance music that developed from hip-hop in the 1990s. It uses electronic sampling to create a psychedelic effect.

tripod /'traɪpɒd/ *noun* a frame or stand with three legs that are usually collapsible, used for supporting something such as a camera or other piece of equipment

TRIPS agreement /'trɪps əˌgriːmənt/ *noun* a paper released by the WTO in 1995 covering aspects of intellectual property protection across the world, such as what should be protected, how long for, how to resolve disputes etc. Full form **Agreement on Trade-Related Aspects of Intellectual Property Rights**

tripwire /'trɪpwaɪə/ *noun* a wire that activates a device such as a camera when it is pulled or disturbed

trs. *abbreviation* PRINTING **transpose**

trunking /'trʌŋkɪŋ/ *noun* same as **elephant trunking**

TSA *abbreviation* **total service area**

T-scope /'tiː skəʊp/ *noun* same as **tachistoscope**

T-square /'tiː skweə/ *noun* a drawing-board ruler consisting of a rectangular handle with a straight-sided wooden or plastic blade attached to it, to form a T shape, used in animation and story-boarding

TTL *abbreviation* PHOTOGRAPHY **through-the-lens**

tube /tjuːb/ *noun* **1.** a cathode ray tube used to reproduce television images **2.** same as **television**

tune /tjuːn/ *verb* to adjust a radio or television set to a station or channel

tune in /ˌtjuːn 'ɪn/ *verb* to adjust a radio or television to receive a signal, programme or channel

tune out /ˌtjuːn 'aʊt/ *verb* to adjust a radio or television set to prevent the reception of something undesired such as interference

tuner /ˈtjuːnə/ *noun* a device used for accepting a desired signal from a mixture of signals, for example in a radio or television set containing one or more resonant circuits

tunesmith /ˈtjuːnsmɪθ/ *noun* a composer of popular songs or music (*informal*)

tungsten /ˈtʌŋstən/ *noun* the glowing metal filament used in artificial studio lighting, which has an orange tone

tungsten lamp /ˈtʌŋstən læmp/ *noun* professional-grade lighting equipment with a tungsten filament, similar to a normal household lightbulb

turn-around /ˌtɜːn əˈraʊnd/ *noun* a script that has been purchased but discontinued by a studio (due to, for example, lack of funds), which can be repurchased by another studio

turnover /ˈtɜːnəʊvə/ *noun* the number of times something is used or sold in a period, usually one year, expressed as a percentage of a total

"'In terms of staff morale, extensive monitoring of productivity is demoralising for staff and part of the reason why burn-out and staff turnover in the UK is so high", Fleming says. "Call centre employers need to rethink their approach to getting staff to be more productive".'
[Vicky Frost, *The Guardian*]

turntable /ˈtɜːnteɪb(ə)l/ *noun* the flat round revolving plate on which the record rests on a record player

turntables /ˈtɜːnteɪb(ə)lz/ *noun* a piece of equipment used by a DJ for playing and mixing music, consisting of two or more circular rotating platforms on which records are played, usually with controls to create audio effects. Also called **decks**

TV /ˌtiː ˈviː/ *noun* same as **television**

TVCR *noun* a television set with a built-in video recorder

TV Licensing /ˌtiː viː ˈlaɪs(ə)nsɪŋ/ *noun* the company responsible for collecting the BBC licence fee

TV-out /ˌtiː ˈviː ˌaʊt/ *noun* a connector on a computer or graphics adapter that provides a modulated signal that can be

displayed on a standard television or recorded on a video recorder

TVR *abbreviation* **television ratings**

TVRO /ˌtiː viː ɑːr ˈəʊ/ *noun* an aerial used for receiving television signals from a broadcasting satellite. Full form **Television Receive Only**

TV spot /ˌtiː ˈviː ˌspɒt/ *noun* a short period on television that is used for commercials. Same as **television spot**

tweeter /ˈtwiːtə/ *noun* a loudspeaker used to reproduce high-frequency sounds, for example in a hi-fi system

12 /twelv/ *noun* in the United Kingdom, a rating given to films and videos considered unsuitable for children under the age of twelve

12A /ˌtwelv ˈeɪ/ *noun* in the United Kingdom, a rating given to films and videos which children under the age of twelve may only watch in the cinema if accompanied by an adult

twelve-inch /ˈtwelv ɪntʃ/ *noun* a record that is 30.5 cm/12 in in diameter and played at 45rpm, usually containing a single, often extended track

twelvemo /ˈtwelvməʊ/ *noun* PRINTING same as **duodecimo**

25% production quota /ˌtwenti faɪv pəˌsent prəˈdʌkʃ(ə)n ˌkwəʊtə/ *noun* in British broadcasting, the requirement that 25% of programmes should be commissioned from independent programme makers

24/96 /ˌtwenti fɔː ˌnaɪnti ˈsɪks/ a popular standard for high-performance digital audio equipment that provides 24-bit samples and a sample rate of 96KHz

20th Century Fox /ˌtwentiəθ ˌsentʃəri ˈfɒks/ *noun* a major film studio formed in 1935 by the merger of two smaller studios, Fox Film Corporation and Twentieth Century Pictures, based in California and responsible for many big-budget blockbusters including the Star Wars series of films. It also has a television syndication arm, 20th Century Fox Television.

twin bill /ˈtwɪn bɪl/ *noun* CINEMA same as **double feature**

twin-lens reflex /ˌtwɪn lenz ˈriːfleks/ *noun* a camera that has two forward-facing lenses, one for focusing through and one for taking pictures

2G /ˌtuː ˈdʒiː/ *abbreviation* **second-generation**

two-shot /ˈtuː ʃɒt/ *noun* a camera shot with two people in a single frame

two-step flow model /ˌtuː step ˈfləʊ ˌmɒd(ə)l/ *noun* a model of mass media influence as being shaped and modified by interactions with social groups, particularly with opinion leaders

two-way /ˈtuː weɪ/ *noun* RADIO same as **Q and A**

TX *abbreviation* **transmission**

tympan /ˈtɪmpæn/ *noun* a piece of padding that fits between the impression cylinder of a printing press and the paper to be printed, ensuring an even image

typ. *abbreviation* PRINTING **1. typographical 2. typography**

type /taɪp/ *noun* **1.** printed words, letters or symbols as they appear on a page **2.** an individual piece of type bearing a single character **3.** the set of small metal blocks used in printing, especially formerly, each of which has a raised figure that is the mirror image of a number or letter on one of its sides

typeface /ˈtaɪpfeɪs/ *noun* a set of text characters, numbers and punctuation marks in a consistent design. Also called **type style**

type founder /ˈtaɪp ˌfaʊndə/ *noun* a manufacturer of metal printing type

type-high /ˈtaɪp haɪ/ *adjective* as high as the standard height of a block of printer's type, 23.3 mm/0.9186 in

typeset /ˈtaɪpset/ *verb* to prepare text for printing, either by the use of computers or by arranging blocks of type manually

typesetter /ˈtaɪpsetə/ *noun* a mechanical or electronic device that prepares text for printing

typesetting /ˈtaɪpsetɪŋ/ *noun* the process of arranging text on a page, now almost always done using computer software

type style /ˈtaɪp staɪl/ *noun* same as **typeface**

typewriter /ˈtaɪpraɪtə/ *noun* an electrical or mechanical device with keys that are pressed to print letters or other characters one by one on a sheet of paper inserted into the machine

typo /ˈtaɪpəʊ/ *noun* a typographical error

typo. *abbreviation* PRINTING **1. typographical 2. typography**

typographical /ˌtaɪpəˈɡræfɪk(ə)l/ *adjective* to do with the appearance of printed characters on the page. Abbreviation **typ., typo.**

typography /taɪˈpɒɡrəfi/ *noun* the appearance of printed characters on the page. Abbreviation **typ., typo.**

U

U *noun* in the UK, a film classification for films that can be seen by everybody, regardless of age

u.c. *abbreviation* PRINTING uppercase

Ullswater Committee Report on Broadcasting 1936 /ˈʌlzwɔːtə/ *noun* a report on the performance of the BBC after its first term of office, which largely praised its programming, but suggested that a greater range of political viewpoints could be broadcast and power decentralised

Ultimatte /ˈʌltɪmæt/ a trade name for a system for producing chromakey effects

Ultimedia /ˌʌltiˈmidiə/ a trade name for a multimedia concept developed by IBM that combines sound, video, images and text, and defines the hardware required to run it

U-Matic /ˌjuː ˈmætɪk/ *noun* an old video cassette format using 3/4 inch tape

umbrella advertising /ʌmˈbrelə ˌædvətaɪzɪŋ/ *noun* the advertising of an organisation or an association of companies rather than a single product

UMTS /ˌjuː em tiː ˈes/ *noun* a third-generation mobile communication system that supports voice data and video signals to the handset. Full form **universal mobile telecommunications system**

unaided recall /ʌnˌeɪdɪd ˈriːkɔːl/ *noun* same as **unprompted recall** (a)

unaired /ʌnˈeəd/ *adjective* not broadcast on radio or television

uncensored /ʌnˈsensəd/ *adjective* published, reported or broadcast without being subject to censorship

uncial /ˈʌnkiəl/ *noun* a letter of the kind used in Greek and Latin manuscripts written between the 3rd and 9th centuries that resembles a modern capital letter but is more rounded

unconscious /ʌnˈkɒnʃəs/ *noun* in psychoanalysis, the workings of the mind that we are unaware of but which reveal themselves through dreams, actions etc.

uncut /ʌnˈkʌt/ *adjective* with the edges of the pages not yet trimmed to separate them

underclaim /ˌʌndəˈkleɪm/ *verb* in a survey, to deny that you have had exposure to media vehicles for advertising when you have. Compare **overclaim**

underdeveloped /ˌʌndədɪˈveləpt/ *adjective* referring to a photograph, negative or film that was inadequately developed during processing, usually through being taken out of the developer too soon, and lacks contrast as a result

underexpose /ˌʌndərɪkˈspəʊs/ *verb* to expose photographic film to light for too short a time, or expose it to inadequate light

underground /ˈʌndəɡraʊnd/ *noun* a movement or group that is separate from the prevailing social or artistic environment and often exerts a subversive influence ■ *adjective* separate from a prevailing social or artistic environment, and often exercising a subversive influence

underground press /ˈʌndəɡraʊnd ˌpres/ *noun* newspapers that are anti-establishment and likely to attract censorship

underlay /ˈʌndəleɪ/ *noun* same as **live voiceover**

underline /ˈʌndəlaɪn/ *noun* a line underneath a headline or crosshead

underplay /ˌʌndəˈpleɪ/ *verb* to act a role in a deliberately restrained or subtle way

undeveloped /ˌʌndɪˈveləpt/ *adjective* referring to film which has not yet chemically treated to produce a negative or print

unexposed /ˌʌnɪkˈspəʊzd/ *adjective* referring to a film that has not been exposed to light

unexpurgated /ʌnˈekspəgeɪtɪd/ *adjective* not edited to remove words or passages considered offensive or unsuitable

'Nor has she [Sharon Osborne] refrained from telling the unexpurgated story of her life. Those years of betrayal in her marriage, tormented relationships with her parents and battle against cancer have been documented in her ballsy autobiography My Life Of Extremes.' [Sue Carroll, *The Mirror*]

Uniform /ˈjuːnɪfɔːm/ *noun* an internationally recognised code word for the letter U, used in radio communications

unilateral /ˌjuːniˈlæt(ə)rəl/ *noun* a war correspondent who chooses to work independently rather than being attached officially to a military unit ■ *adjective* referring to something such as a feed or journalist's report which may only be used by one organisation, as opposed to a pool arrangement

unindented /ˌʌnɪnˈdentɪd/ *adjective* printed without a space set in from the margin

uninterruptible power supply /ˌʌnɪntərʌptɪb(ə)l ˈpaʊə səˌplaɪ/ *noun* a safety system of supplying power to equipment, which has a back-up source if the main source should fail. Abbreviation **UPS**

unipod /ˈjuːnɪpɒd/ *noun* a one-legged stand, for example for a camera

unique selling point /juːˌniːk ˈselɪŋ pɔɪnt/, **unique selling proposition** /juːˌniːk ˈselɪŋ ˌprɒpəzɪʃ(ə)n/ *noun* a special quality of a product that makes it different from other goods and is used as a key theme in advertising. Abbreviation **USP**

United Press International /juːˌnaɪtɪd ˌpres ˌɪntəˈnæʃ(ə)nəl/ *noun* an international news agency set up in 1907, which delivers content in English, Spanish and Arabic. Abbreviation **UPI**

universality /ˌjuːnɪvɜːˈsælɪti/ *noun* the theory that some services such as healthcare and access to information should be freely available to everyone

universal remote control /ˌjuːnɪvɜːs(ə)l rɪˌməʊt kənˈtrəʊl/ *noun* a remote control that works with any television set

universal service /ˌjuːnɪvɜːs(ə)l ˈsɜːvɪs/ *noun* a broadcasting service that is available to everybody at the same price

Universal Studios /ˌjuːnɪvɜːs(ə)l ˈstjuːdiəʊz/ *noun* a major film studio and television production company based in Hollywood and formed in 1912. Although not as prolific as other studios it has produced such popular films as Spartacus (1960), E. T. the Extra-Terrestrial (1982) and the Back to the Future trilogy (from 1985).

universe /ˈjuːnɪvɜːs/ *noun* the total number of people / homes / television-owning homes etc. in the UK, taken for statistical purposes

Univision /ˈjuːniˌvɪʒ(ə)n/ *noun* a Spanish language television network that broadcasts in the US

Unix /ˈjuːnɪks/ a trade name for a family of operating systems, commonly used for business technical servers and desktop computers in more technical professions. ◊ **Mac OS Z**, **Microsoft Windows**

unjustified /ʌnˈdʒʌstɪfaɪd/ *adjective* referring to text that is not arranged evenly in such a way that the ends of the lines on a page form a straight vertical line parallel to the margin

unlead /ʌnˈled/ *verb* in traditional hot-metal printing, to take out the leading or leads separating lines of type

unleaded /ʌnˈledɪd/ *adjective* referring to lines of type that are not separated by leads

unload /ʌnˈləʊd/ *verb* to remove a roll of film from a camera

unmetered /ʌnˈmiːtəd/ *adjective* referring to an Internet service that is available at a flat rate, typically by the month, rather than by connection time

unmotivated /ʌnˈməʊtɪveɪtɪd/ *adjective* referring to a camera shot that moves without being prompted by the action on screen, for example panning across the scene. Compare **motivated**

unposed /ʌnˈpəʊzd/ *adjective* referring to a camera shot with subjects who have not been arranged in a special position or who are not adopting a special pose or facial expression

unprinted /ʌn'prɪntɪd/ *adjective* not printed or published

unprompted recall /ʌn,prɒmptɪd 'riːkɔːl/, **unprompted awareness test** /ʌn,prɒmptɪd ə'weənəs test/ *noun* an advertising research test to see how well a respondent can remember an advertisement when he or she is given no help in remembering it. Compare **aided recall**. Also called **unaided recall**

unsubscribe /,ʌnsəb'skraɪb/ *verb* to end a subscription to or registration with something, especially an e-mail mailing list

UPI *abbreviation* **United Press International**

uplink /'ʌplɪŋk/ *noun* the transmission of data upwards to a satellite, from where it will be beamed back down to receivers. Compare **downlink**

uppercase /,ʌpə'keɪs/ *adjective* relating to or written or printed in capital letters. Abbreviation **u.c.** ∎ *verb* to write, type, typeset or print something in capital letters ∎ *noun* capital letters used in writing, typing, typesetting or printing. Abbreviation **u.c.**

UPS *abbreviation* **uninterruptible power supply**

urban blues /,ɜːbən 'bluːz/ *noun* a type of blues music that has a stronger beat than country blues, often played with electric instruments and featuring songs about life in the city

urban legend /,ɜːbən 'ledʒənd/ *noun* a popular myth that is quickly spread, especially via the Internet, and is widely believed to be true

urban music /,ɜːbən 'mjuːzɪk/ *noun* a genre of music covering such styles as hip-hop, drum and bass, R'n'B and garage

URL /,juː ɑː 'el/ *noun* a string of characters that identify the location of a webpage or set of webpages. Full form **Uniform Resource Locator**

uses and gratifications theory /,juːsɪz ənd ,grætɪfɪ'keɪʃ(ə)nz ,θɪəri/ *noun* the idea that audiences of mass media texts actively use these to fulfil a complex set of needs – for example to gain information, to be entertained, to discuss with others as a 'social facilitator', to explore the ideas and values of others

USP *abbreviation* **unique selling point**

utopia /juː'təupiə/ *noun* a representation of a 'perfect' society, in which all citizens are happy and no social problems exist. Compare **dystopia**

COMMENT: Examples of works of literature which describe a utopian world are 'News from Nowhere' (William Morris, 1890) and the work which coined the term, 'Utopia' (Sir Thomas More, 1891).

utter /'ʌtə/ *verb* to publish something, for example in a book or newspaper

utterance meaning /'ʌt(ə)rəns ,miːnɪŋ/ *noun* the meaning of something that is said, including the words used, the speaker's tone and posture and other contextual considerations. Compare **sentence meaning**

V

v *abbreviation* **1.** PRINTING **verso 2. volt**

validity effect /vəˌlɪdɪti ɪ'fekt/ *noun* the tendency of people to believe in the truth of a statement if it is repeated often enough, for example in the press

VALS typology /'vælz taɪˌpɒlədʒi/ *noun* a classification of people according to their values and lifestyle choices, based on a research project carried out in the USA in 1980. It describes categories of people by needs, aspirations etc., and also how changing economies might affect these over time. Full form **Values and Lifestyles**

value /'væljuː/ *noun* **1.** what an item is worth, how much money it would cost if it were to be sold **2.** the 'worth' of an idea, belief, way of behaving etc. to a person or society

valued impression per pound /ˌvæljuːd ɪmˌpreʃ(ə)n pɔː 'paʊnd/ *noun* a method of showing how many readers are reached by advertising for a given sum of money

vamp /væmp/ *noun* in the early days of Hollywood, a seductive and glamorous female film star

variety show /və'raɪəti ʃəʊ/ *noun* a theatrical show made up of a number of short performances of different kinds, such as singing, comedy sketches, dancing and magic acts

vaudeville /'vɔːdəvɪl/ *noun* **1.** a type of entertainment popular in the late 19th and early 20th centuries consisting of singing, dancing and comedy acts **2.** a comic play with songs and dances

Vbox /'viːbɒks/ a trade name for a device that allows several VCRs, video-discs and camcorders to be attached and controlled by one unit, developed by Sony

V-chip /'viː tʃɪp/ *noun* an electronic chip in a television that enables parents to block programmes with sexual or violent content

'Watchdogs … rejected high-technology "electronic gate-keeping devices" such as the V -chip, which block material unsuitable for some viewers. They offered an "inadequate, quick-fix solution" which could lead in future to broadcasters relaxing their standards.'
[Stuart Millar, *The Guardian*]

VCR *abbreviation* **video cassette recorder**

VDA *abbreviation* **video distribution amplifier**

V disc /'viː dɪsk/ *noun* musical recordings made available at reduced cost to the British Army during the World War II as an attempt to boost morale

Venice film festival /ˌvenɪs 'fɪlm ˌfestɪvəl/ *noun* an international film festival held annually in Venice, Italy in late August/early September

verso /'vɜːsəʊ/ *noun* the left-hand page of a two-page spread. Abbreviation **v, vo.**. Compare **recto**

vertical integration /ˌvɜːtɪk(ə)l ˌɪntɪ 'greɪʃ(ə)n/ *noun* the acquisition of companies at all levels of production in the same market sector as each other – for example, a single company owning the newspaper offices, the printers that produce the papers and the chain of news-agents that sell them. Compare **horizontal integration**

vertical interval timecode /ˌvɜːtɪk(ə)l ˌɪntəv(ə)l 'taɪmkəʊd/ *noun* a system of recording timecode by marking it on the vertical spaces between the frames of a film. Abbreviation **VITC**

very high frequency /ˌveri haɪ ˈfriːkwənsi/ *noun* the radio frequency band between 30 and 300 MHz, reserved for the transmission of television and FM radio signals

very long shot /ˌveri ˈlɒŋ ˌʃɒt/ *noun* a camera shot that shows its subject from a distance, so that it does not fill the whole frame. Abbreviation **VLS**

VF *abbreviation* TV **video frequency**

VGA *abbreviation* **video graphics array**

VHS /ˌviː eɪtʃ ˈes/ *noun* a videotape for use in domestic video recorders rather than for professional recording

victim funds /ˈvɪktɪm fʌndz/ *plural noun* money raised by the underground press to help pay governmental fines imposed on papers that could not afford to pay stamp duty

vidclip /ˈvɪdklɪp/ *noun* a short excerpt from a film or television production, used for news or promotion

video /ˈvɪdiəʊ/ *noun* 1. the visual part of a television broadcast 2. something that has been recorded on videotape, especially a feature film or a short promotional film made to accompany a newly issued pop record 3. the industry of recording and broadcasting visual information and entertainment, especially that which can be viewed on a television 4. videotape, or a video cassette

video blog /ˈvɪdiəʊ blɒg/ *noun* a weblog that uses video as a means of communication, for example to conduct an interview or illustrate a story

video camera /ˈvɪdiəʊ ˌkæm(ə)rə/ *noun* a camera that records onto videotape

video cassette /ˈvɪdiəʊ kəˌset/ *noun* a flat rectangular plastic cassette containing two tape reels and a magnetic videotape

video clip /ˈvɪdiəʊ ˌklɪp/ *noun* a short video sequence

video conferencing /ˈvɪdiəʊ ˌkɒnf(ə)rənsɪŋ/ *noun* the holding of meetings in which the participants are in different places but are connected by audio and video links. Also called **video-teleconferencing**

videodisc /ˈvɪdiəʊdɪsk/ *noun* a read-only disc that can store up to two hours of video data, usually used either to store a complete film, as a rival to video cassette, or to use in an interactive system with text, video and still images

video display terminal /ˈvɪdiəʊ dɪ ˈspleɪ ˈtɜːmɪn(ə)l/, **video terminal** /ˈvɪdiəʊ ˌtɜːmɪn(ə)l/ *noun* same as **visual display terminal**

video distribution amplifier /ˌvɪdiəʊ ˌdɪstrɪˈbjuːʃ(ə)n ˌæmplɪfaɪə/ *abbreviation* VDA. ◊ **distribution amplifier**

video editing /ˈvɪdiəʊ ˌedɪtɪŋ/ *noun* a method of editing a video sequence in which the video is digitised and stored in a computer

video editor /ˈvɪdiəʊ ˌedɪtə/ *noun* a computer that controls two videotape recorders to allow an operator to play back sequences from one and record these on the second machine

video EDL /ˌvɪdiəʊ ˌiː diː ˈel/ *noun* ♦ **editing decision list**

video feed /ˈvɪdiəʊ fiːd/ *noun* recorded video sent from one place to another where it can be used

video frequency /ˈvɪdiəʊ ˌfriːkwənsi/ *noun* a frequency in the range of signals used to carry the image and synchronising pulses in a television broadcasting system. Video frequencies range from the very high to the ultra high in the US and are found in two ultra high bands in Europe. Abbreviation **VF**

video game /ˈvɪdiəʊ geɪm/ *noun* an electronic or computerized game, usually controlled by a microprocessor, played by making images move on a computer or television screen or, for hand-held games, on a liquid-crystal display

video graphics array /ˌvɪdiəʊ ˈgræfɪks əˌreɪ/ *noun* a standard of graphics display software developed by IBM that can support a display with a resolution up to 640 x 480 pixels in up to 256 colours, superseded by SVGA. Abbreviation **VGA**

video graphics card /ˌvɪdiəʊ ˈgræfɪks ˌkɑːd/ *noun* an expansion card that fits into an expansion slot inside a PC and allows a computer to display both generated text and graphics and moving video images from an external camera or VCR

videography /ˌvɪdiˈɒgrəfi/ *noun* the art or practice of using a video camera to make films or programmes

video insert /'vɪdiəʊ ˌɪnsɜːt/ *noun* a piece of pre-recorded footage which is cued and played at the appropriate point in a news or magazine show by the VT operator. Also called **VT**

video interface chip /ˌvɪdiəʊ 'ɪntəfeɪs ˌtʃɪp/ *noun* a chip that controls a video display allowing information such as text or graphics stored in a computer to be displayed

video jockey /'vɪdiəʊ ˌdʒɒki/ *noun* somebody who plays videos, especially music videos, on television. Abbreviation **VJ**

video monitor /'vɪdiəʊ ˌmɒnɪtə/ *noun* **1.** a device able to display, without sound, video signals from a computer **2.** a television-like screen which only plays back a video feed, sometimes without sound

video nasty /ˌvɪdiəʊ 'nɑːsti/ *noun* a film on videotape that contains explicitly violent or pornographic scenes

'…here's a great chance to judge for yourselves if the fear stories about "video nasties" have any validity. [Six famous horror movies] are all collected here and none make pleasant viewing. But are they a fascinating product of their time, or merely slices of sick self-indulgence?' [Iain Miller, *The Independent on Sunday*]

video news release /ˌvɪdiəʊ 'njuːz rɪˌliːs/ *noun* video shots released to illustrate a news story. Abbreviation **VNR**

video on demand /ˌvɪdiəʊ ɒn dɪ 'mɑːnd/ *noun* a pay-per-view facility in which a subscriber can order a film or programme and it will be broadcast to them at the most convenient time for them. Abbreviation **VOD**

videophile /'vɪdiəfaɪl/ *noun* somebody who enjoys watching or making video recordings

videophone /'vɪdiəʊˌfəʊn/ *noun* a communications device that can transmit and receive both video and audio signals using a camera, receiver and screen

video recorder /'vɪdiəʊ rɪˌkɔːdə/ *noun* a tape recorder that can record and play video cassettes through a standard television receiver

Video Recording Act 1984 /ˌvɪdiəʊ rɪ'kɔːdɪŋ ˌækt/ *noun* the act of Parliament that designated a body to classify videos for home viewing according to the

adult nature of their content, in the same way that films are classified

videotape /'vɪdiəʊteɪp/ *noun* magnetic tape on which pictures and sound can be recorded. Abbreviation **VT**

videotape recording report /ˌvɪdiəʊteɪp rɪ'kɔːdɪŋ rɪˌpɔːt/ *noun* a report that must be delivered with a recording to the BBC giving its technical details. Abbreviation **VTRR**

video teleconferencing /ˌvɪdiəʊ 'teliˌkɒnf(ə)rənsɪŋ/ *noun* same as **video conferencing**

videotext /'vɪdiəʊtekst/ *noun* a communications service linked to an adapted television receiver by telephone or cable television lines to allow access to pages of information. Systems can be one-way, allowing only for the display of selected information, or on-line or interactive, allowing for two-way communication.

video vérité /ˌvɪdiəʊ 'verɪteɪ/ *noun* the use in video documentaries of the realistic unrehearsed portrayal of people and situations

videowall /'vɪdiəʊwɔːl/ *noun* a bank of monitors or video screens arranged so that several different pictures can be viewed at once (such as the feeds from separate cameras), or displaying one single large image

vidicon /'vɪdɪkɒn/ *noun* a light-sensitive television camera tube in which an image is stored on a photoconductive plate as an electric charge pattern that is scanned by an electron beam and transmitted

view /vjuː/ *verb* to watch a television programme

viewdata /'vjuːdeɪtə/ *noun* an interactive system for transmitting text or graphics from a database to a user's terminal by telephone lines, providing facilities for information retrieval, transactions, education, games and recreation

viewer /'vjuːə/ *noun* a person who watches television

viewfinder /'vjuːfaɪndə/ *noun* **1.** a device on a camera that lets the user see what is being photographed **2.** the part of a camera through which the operator can see the framing and focus which will be recorded by the lens

viewing /'vjuːɪŋ/ *noun* **1.** the act of watching television programmes **2.** television programmes considered collectively or with respect to their nature or quality

viewing figures /'vju:ɪŋ ˌfɪgəz/ *plural noun* figures showing the numbers of people watching a television programme

viewscreen /'vju:skri:n/ *noun* the screen on a digital camera on which the user can view the image he or she has just recorded

vignette /vɪn'jet/ *noun* **1.** a brief scene from a film or play **2.** a painting, drawing or photograph that has no border but is gradually faded into its background at the edges **3.** a small decorative design printed at the beginning or end of a book or chapter of a book, or in the margin of a page ■ *verb* to finish a painting, drawing or photograph by gradually fading it into its background at the edges rather than giving it a border

villain /'vɪlən/ *noun* in a narrative, the character who represents 'bad', whom the hero (representing 'good') has to defeat

vinyl /'vaɪn(ə)l/ *noun* gramophone records made of a vinyl polymer, as opposed to compact discs

violence /'vaɪələns/ *noun* the use of physical force to injure somebody or damage something

violence debate /'vaɪələns dɪˌbeɪt/ *noun* a moral panic that recurs frequently, based on the supposed effects of violence in films and on television on the audience

Violent and Sex Offenders Register /ˌvaɪələnt ənd 'seks əˌfendəz ˌredʒɪstə/ *noun* a database of registered sex offenders, people who have served more than one year in prison for violent assaults and, controversially, people who have not offended but are thought likely to. The information is available only to the police and probation services. Abbreviation **ViSOR**

VIPer /'vaɪpə/ *noun* a continuous consumer and lifestyle panel survey of 1,000 people in the highest socio-economic group, AB, run jointly by Channel 4, Classic FM and The Times Newspaper Group

viral advertising /'vaɪrəl ˌædvətaɪzɪŋ/ *noun* an advertisement posted on the Internet that tries to capture people's attention and encourage them to 'pass it on' (like a virus) to their friends

'…there's been a boom in making ads specifically for e-mail. It's called viral advertising… These short films are electronic word-of-mouth. Once they're made they cost nothing to place, as media space is free. Some are sexy or violent. Others are funny, or just weird. The best virals go round the world in moments.'
[John Carver, *The Independent*]

viral marketing /'vaɪrəl ˌmɑːkɪtɪŋ/ *noun* **1.** the distribution over the Internet of a service that becomes so immediately desirable that it leads to an enormous growth in traffic **2.** a form of marketing in which an organisation's customers, intentionally or not, act as advertisers for its products by spreading knowledge of them by word of mouth

virtual /'vɜːtʃuəl/ *adjective* representative, not the real thing

virtual community /ˌvɜːtʃuəl kə'mjuːnɪti/ *noun* a group of people who 'meet' and interact on the Internet, for example on a messageboard or discussion page

Virtual Private Network /ˌvɜːtʃuəl ˌpraɪvət 'netwɜːk/ *noun* full form of **VPN**

virtual reality /ˌvɜːtʃuəl ri'ælɪti/ *noun* the use of multimedia technology for example headsets, video displays, body tracking motion sensors etc., to create the illusion of a three-dimensional alternate universe

virtual studio /ˌvɜːtʃuəl 'stjuːdiəu/ *noun* an entirely computer-generated set in which a presenter or actor is present, using a blue screen

virus /'vaɪrəs/ *noun* a short computer program, hidden within another, that makes copies of itself and spreads them, disrupting the operation of a computer that receives one. A virus may be transmitted through networks, on-line services and the Internet.

vis FX *abbreviation* **visual effects**

vision /'vɪʒ(ə)n/ *noun* the picture on a television screen

vision mixer /'vɪʒ(ə)n ˌmɪksə/ *noun* **1.** the member of a television production team who is responsible for switching between feeds and pre-recorded video sources. Also called **switcher 2.** the piece of studio equipment used to switch between feeds and video sources

vision mixing /'vɪʒ(ə)n ˌmɪksɪŋ/ *noun* in a live broadcast, the work of editing and switching between the inputs from different cameras, putting captions on screen etc.

visit /'vɪzɪt/ *verb* to view a website

visitor /'vɪzɪtə/ *noun* an Internet user who views a website

ViSOR /'vaɪzə/ *abbreviation* **Violent and Sex Offenders Register**

Vistavision /'vɪstə,vɪʒ(ə)n/ *noun* the brand name for the process resulting in widescreen pictures developed by Paramount in the 1950s

visual aid /'vɪʒʊəl eɪd/ *noun* something that is looked at as a complement to a lesson or presentation, for example a model, chart or film

visual display terminal /,vɪzjʊəl dɪ 'spleɪ ,tɜːmɪnəl/, **visual display unit** /,vɪʒʊəl dɪ'spleɪ ,juːnɪt/ *noun* a screen attached to a computer that shows the information stored in the computer

visual effects /,vɪʒʊəl ɪ'fekts/ *plural noun* effects created in an editing suite on a piece of filmed footage, such as distorting or moving an image, superimposition etc. Abbreviation **vis FX**

visual effects director /,vɪʒʊəl ɪ 'fekts daɪ,rektə/ *noun* the member of a film or television production team who has responsibility for supervising visual effects production staff

visualiser /'vɪʒʊəlaɪzə/ *noun* a person who produces visual ideas for advertisements or advertising campaigns

vitaphone /'vaɪtəfəʊn/ *noun* the first film soundtrack process that made use of a synchronised audio disc, first played in 1926 to a showing of 'Don Juan' by the Warner Brothers studio

VITC *abbreviation* **vertical interval timecode**

Vivo /'viːvəʊ/ a trade name for a data format used to deliver video over the Internet

VJ *abbreviation* **video jockey**

VLS *abbreviation* CINEMA, TV **very long shot**

VNR *abbreviation* **video news release**

VO *abbreviation* **voiceover**

vo. *abbreviation* PRINTING **verso**

VOA *abbreviation* BROADCAST, US **Voice of America**

vocal cues /'vəʊkəl kjuːz/ *plural noun* aspects of speech other than the words

themselves, for example tone, pitch, speed, pronunciation etc.

VOD *abbreviation* **video on demand**

voice /vɔɪs/ *noun* **1.** the sound produced by using the vocal organs, especially the sound used in speech **2.** a right to express an opinion ■ *verb* to provide the voiceover for a character in a cartoon or a radio or television advertisement

voicebank /'vɔɪsbæŋk/ *noun* a system used for recording information that journalists can access, for example by the emergency services

voice data entry /,vɔɪs ,deɪtə 'entri/, **voice data input** /,vɔɪs ,deɪtə 'ɪnpʊt/ *noun* the input of information into a computer using a speech recognition system and the user's voice

voicemail /'vɔɪsmeɪl/ *noun* an electronic communications system that stores digitised recordings of telephone messages for later playback

Voice of America /,vɔɪs əv ə'merɪkə/ *noun* a US government-funded international multimedia broadcasting company that provides radio, television and Internet news and cultural programming in 44 languages. Abbreviation **VOA**

voice output /'vɔɪs ,aʊtpʊt/ *noun* the production of sounds that sound like human speech, made as a result of voice synthesis

voiceover /'vɔɪs,əʊvə/ *noun* **1.** a voice track added to a piece of film from someone who is not seen to be speaking in the footage, such as a commentator or one of the participants speaking later. Abbreviation **VO 2.** the voice of, or the words spoken by, an unseen narrator, commentator or character in a film or television programme

Voice-over-Internet Protocol /,vɔɪs ,əʊvə 'ɪntənet ,prəʊtəkɒl/ *noun* full form of **VoIP**

voice piece /'vɔɪs piːs/ *noun* a scripted report of a story read by a reporter

voicer /'vɔɪsə/ *noun* a report that has a voiced-over section by a different reporter from the one presenting the report

voice synthesiser /'vɔɪs ,sɪnθəsaɪzə/ *noun* a device that generates sounds that are similar to the human voice

VoIP /vɔɪp/ *noun* a technology that enables voice messages to be sent via the Internet, often simultaneously with data in text or other forms. Full form **Voice over Internet Protocol**

volt /vəʊlt/ *noun* a measure of potential electrical force. Abbreviation **V**

volume /'vɒljuːm/ *noun* **1.** the loudness of a sound **2.** a set of issues of a periodical spanning one calendar year **3.** a bound collection of printed or written pages **4.** the knob or button on a radio, television or audio player that controls loudness

volume level /'vɒljuːm ˌlev(ə)l/ *noun* the volume of a sound, expressed as a reading on a scaled meter

volume peak /'vɒljuːm piːk/ *noun* the highest volume level of a broadcast reached during the observation period

volumetrics /ˌvɒljuː'metrɪks/ *noun* analysis of the relative influence of various media by considering the number of people who are exposed to them, and their importance as buyers

volume unit meter /ˌvɒljuːm 'juːnɪt ˌmiːtə/ *noun* a meter measuring the average volume level of a broadcast. Abbreviation **VU**. Compare **peak performance meter**

voluntary control /ˌvɒlənt(ə)ri kən'trəʊl/ *noun* a system adopted by the advertising industry for maintaining standards, which involves following guidelines laid down for the industry as a whole

vortal /'vɔːtəl/ *noun* a web portal devoted to one specific industry which enables business-to-business e-commerce transactions by bringing together busi-

nesses at different points in the supply chain

vox pop /'vɒks pɒp/ *noun* a series of replies to a question posed to 'people in the street', used to give a popular response to an issue

voyeurism /'vwaɪɜːrɪz(ə)m/ *noun* the pleasure of looking at something or somebody without being seen yourself

'Few films deal more fascinatingly and uncomfortably with voyeurism than Hitchcock's gorgeously designed masterpiece. James Stewart… serves as our eyes in the story, a temporarily wheelchair-bound photographer who amuses himself by spying on people in the apartment block opposite.' [*The Financial Times*]

VPN /ˌviː piː 'en/ *noun* a network that provides remote offices or users with secure access to their organisation's network using the Internet or other public telecommunications system. Full form **Virtual Private Network**

VT *abbreviation* **videotape** ■ *noun* same as **video insert**

VT operator /ˌviː 'tiː ˌɒpəreɪtə/ *noun* the member of a television production team who is responsible for cueing video inserts and also for preparing replays and highlights during a live-action broadcast

VTRR *abbreviation* **videotape recording report**

VU *abbreviation* BROADCAST **volume unit meter**

W

W *abbreviation* **watt**

W3C /ˌdʌb(ə)l juː θriː 'siː/ *noun* a consortium of organisations, programmers, developers, industry executives and users that seeks to guide the future development of the World Wide Web and ensure that all web technologies are compatible with one another. Full form **World Wide Web Consortium**

W/A *abbreviation* **wide-angle**

walkie-talkie /ˌwɔːki 'tɔːki/ *noun* a hand-held battery-operated radio transmitter and receiver often used by emergency personnel to communicate with one another

Walkman /'wɔːkmən/ a trade name for a small portable cassette player with earphones

walk-on /'wɔːk ɒn/ *noun* **1.** an actor who has a small part, usually a nonspeaking one, in a stage or film production **2.** an extra at a film shoot who has to perform some specific action (without speaking), rather than generally being in the background, walking by etc. **3.** a small part, usually a nonspeaking one, in a stage or film production

walk through /'wɔːk θruː/ *verb* **1.** to rehearse something in a simple way, without props or costumes, mainly practising basic moves and positions **2.** to rehearse a television programme without cameras

walk-through /'wɔːk θruː/ *noun* an early play rehearsal without props or costumes, or a television rehearsal without cameras, usually held to practise basic moves and positions

walled garden /ˌwɔːld 'gɑːd(ə)n/ *noun* a browsing environment for viewing websites that provides a means of controlling the information and websites that a user is able to access. It may either protect users such as children from unsuitable information or direct users to specific, often paid content supported by an Internet service provider.

'But for large media owners, fear of the poorly lit, sinister back alleys of the web is useful. It drives people into "walled gardens", safe havens of manicured web content, provided on subscription; guaranteed free of bad guys; well stocked with familiar brands.' [Rafael Behr, *The Observer*]

wall of sound /ˌwɔːl əv 'saʊnd/ *noun* a recorded musical effect on pop records achieved by overdubbing or layering many different instruments around a pop tune

wallpaper /'wɔːlpeɪpə/ *noun* **1.** a soundless video picture used in news bulletins to illustrate a story coming up, over which the presenter reads a short commentary **2.** background shots which are necessary and unavoidable, but dull **3.** the background pattern for a computer screen, composed of graphics

Walt Disney Pictures /ˌwɔːlt ˌdɪzni 'pɪktʃəz/ *noun* a Hollywood film studio producing hundreds of well-known, family-friendly films, both animated and live-action, starting with Snow White and the Seven Dwarves in 1937

WAN /wæn/ *abbreviation* **World Association of Newspapers**

want ad /'wɒnt æd/ *noun* a classified advertisement in a newspaper or magazine

WAP /wæp/ *noun* a standard protocol for the transmission of electronic data between hand-held narrowband devices such as mobile phones and pagers and other sources of digital information such as the Internet. Full form **Wireless Application Protocol**

WAP browser /'wæp ˌbraʊzə/ *noun* a simple web browser that works on a hand-held WAP device

war correspondent /'wɔː ˌkɒrɪspɒndənt/ *noun* a journalist reporting from a war

wardrobe mistress /'wɔːdrəʊb ˌmɪstrəs/ *noun* the woman in charge of the costumes in a theatre or on a film set

warmth /wɔːmθ/ *noun* the effect created by using colours such as red, orange and yellow, which suggest heat and are soft and flattering

warm-up /'wɔːm ʌp/ *noun* the act of preparing an audience before a show is filmed by telling jokes, breaking the ice and coaching them in any specific reactions they will have to make

Warner Bros /'wɔːnə brɒs/ *noun* one of the world's largest producers of family film and television entertainment, based in Hollywood. It is responsible for the Looney Tunes cartoon series and the Superman, Batman and Harry Potter films, among many other family favourites.

War of the Worlds /ˌwɔː əv ðə 'wɜːldz/ *noun* a radio adaptation of H G Wells' 1938 novel about interplanetary invasion, delivered in the style of an actual radio news broadcast, which caused many listeners to believe the 'reports' were real

waste coverage /'weɪst ˌkʌv(ə)rɪdʒ/ *noun* media coverage that goes beyond the target audience

watchdog /'wɒtʃdɒg/ *noun* a person or organisation guarding against illegal practices, unacceptable standards or inefficiency

'The Channel Five daytime talkshow [Trisha] hosted by Trisha Goddard is known for its unsavoury subject matter. Three years ago the 47-year-old presenter was criticised by TV watchdogs after featuring "love rat" specials straight after children's programmes.'
[Matt Born, *The Daily Mail*]

watchdog journalism /'wɒtʃdɒg ˌdʒɜːn(ə)lɪz(ə)m/ *noun* a type of journalism that monitors reports from other sources, exposing news reports that are inaccurate or 'yellow'

Watergate /'wɔːtəgeɪt/ *noun* the scandal that forced US President Nixon to resign in 1972, in which journalists were responsible for uncovering hidden evidence and pushing the trial forward

COMMENT: Investigative journalists Bob Woodward and Carl Bernstein and their anonymous source Deep Throat were responsible for exposing the Watergate scandal and uncovering hidden evidence which was crucial to the later trial. The suffix '…gate' is often used to jokily name other political scandals, such as 'Monicagate'/ 'Sexgate', the alleged affair between US president Bill Clinton and White House aide Monica Lewinsky.

watershed /'wɔːtəʃed/ *noun* the time before which programmes unsuitable for children (featuring strong language or inappropriate content) may not be broadcast. Currently in the UK this is 9pm.

watt /wɒt/ *noun* a measure of the amount of power used by an appliance. Abbreviation **W**

waveband /'weɪvbænd/ *noun* a range of radio frequencies within which transmissions occur

waveform /'weɪvfɔːm/ *noun* a visual representation of sound in the form of a computer-generated 'wave'

waveform editor /'weɪvfɔːm ˌedɪtə/ *noun* a software program that displays a graphical representation of a sound wave and allows a user to edit, adjust levels and frequencies or add special effects

waveform monitor /'weɪvfɔːm ˌmɒnɪtə/ *noun* a device that measures the output of a video signal with respect to luminance and chrominance, used for checking that different cameras are in line with each other

waveform synthesiser /'weɪvfɔːm ˌsɪnθəsaɪzə/ *noun* a musical device that creates sounds of an instrument by using recorded samples of the original waveform produced by the instrument

wavelength /'weɪvleŋθ/ *noun* **1.** a measurement of radio waves, describing the distance between the peak of one wave and the peak of the next. ◊ **amplitude, frequency 2.** in broadcasting, the wavelength of the fundamental radio wave used by a broadcasting station

wax /wæks/ *noun* a gramophone record (*informal*)

weak /wiːk/ *adjective* PHOTOGRAPHY not having much contrast between tones

weather forecast /'weðə ˌfɔːkɑːst/ *noun* a radio or television broadcast predicting weather conditions

web /web/ PRINTING *noun* a roll of paper that is used on a rotary printing press ■ *verb* to form or produce a web

web browser /'web ˌbraʊzə/ *noun* a computer program used for displaying and viewing pages on the World Wide Web

Webby /'webi/ *noun* an annual award made by the International Academy of Digital Arts and Sciences for the best website

webcam /'webkæm/ *noun* a digital camera connected to the Internet which can transmit moving images live

webcast /'webkɑːst/ *noun* a piece of video filmed with a webcam, that can be viewed live or downloaded from an archive for later viewing

webcasting /'webkɑːstɪŋ/ *noun* the use of the World Wide Web as a medium for broadcasting information

web crawler /'web ˌkrɔːlə/ *noun* a computer program used to search through pages on the World Wide Web for documents containing a specific word, phrase or topic

web-enabled /'web ɪnˌeɪb(ə)ld/ *adjective* referring to the ability of mobile phones and other hand-held devices to access the Internet

web form /'web fɔːm/ *noun* an electronic document similar to a printed form, that can be used to collect information from a visitor to a website. When the form has been filled in, it is usually returned to the owner of the website by e-mail.

webhead /'webhed/ *noun* a frequent user of the World Wide Web (*informal*)

web hosting /'web ˌhəʊstɪŋ/ *noun* the business of supplying server space for storage of websites on the Internet, and sometimes the provision of other services such as website creation

webisode /'webɪsəʊd/ *noun* an episode, preview or promotion of a film, television programme or music video on a website

weblish /'weblɪʃ/ *noun* the form of English used globally online, with characteristic features such as the omission of apostrophes and capital letters, the use of

abbreviations and the rapid absorption of new words

'Weblish is having a profound effect on written English: the informality and speed of e-mail especially are eroding capital letters, punctuation and the importance of perfect spelling, as well as making Mr, Mrs, Miss, Yours faithfully and Yours sincerely seem impossibly dusty.' [Barry Collins, *The Sunday Times*]

weblog /'weblɒg/ *noun* a frequently updated personal journal on a website, intended for public viewing

COMMENT: Weblogs are usually updated regularly and feature short posts with opinions, information etc, as well as images and links to other webpages. They are usually in a chatty, personal style and may take the form of a personal diary, a round-up of news on a particular topic, a way of sharing information on something such as science, politics etc, and can be written by one person or many collaborators.

web marketing /'web ˌmɑːkɪtɪŋ/ *noun* marketing that uses websites to advertise products and services and to reach potential customers

webmaster /'webmɑːstə/ *noun* somebody who creates, organises or updates information on a website

web offset /'web ˌɒfset/ *noun* PRINTING offset printing carried out on a web press

webpage /'webpeɪdʒ/ *noun* a computer file, encoded in HTML and containing text, graphics files, and sound files, that is accessible through the World Wide Web

webpage design software /ˌwebpeɪdʒ dɪ'zaɪn ˌsɒftweə/ *noun* software that provides features that make it easier for a user to create webpages

webphone /'webfəʊn/ *noun* a phone that uses the Internet to make connections and carry voice messages

web portal /'web ˌpɔːt(ə)l/ *noun* a webpage on a particular topic which provides links to many other relevant webpages, services etc

web press /'web pres/ *noun* a printing press that is fed paper from a large roll

web server farm /ˌweb 'sɜːvə ˌfɑːm/ *noun* a business with a group of interconnected servers engaged in web hosting

website /'websaɪt/ *noun* an interconnected group of webpages, available through computers over the Internet

WebTV /,web tiː 'viː/ a trade name for a television that also lets a user view webpages

'Wedom' and 'Theydom' /,wːdən ənd 'ðeɪdəm/ *noun* the division of the world into two groups for the purposes of persuasion and journalistic colour: 'us' and 'them', friends and enemies

weekly /'wiːkli/ *noun* a newspaper or magazine published once a week

weepie, weepy, weeper *noun* a film, play or book that tends to move people to tears, especially one that is blatantly sentimental in tone

weight /weɪt/ *noun* PRINTING the heaviness or thickness of a typeface ■ *verb* to multiply results in a survey group according greater significance to the results of one section than to another

well-made /,wel 'meɪd/ *adjective* referring to a film or programme that is skilfully plotted or structured, though often considered to be unadventurous in subject matter or treatment

western /'westən/ *noun* a film, novel or radio or television programme set in the western US, usually during the late 19th century

Westerstähl and Johansson's model of news factors in foreign news 1994 /,vestəʃtel ənd jəʊ 'hænsən/ *noun* a model of news values relating to foreign news, in which its 'proximity' to the ideology of the reporting country is key along with access to information, importance of the originating country and drama of the event

Westminster view /'westmɪnstə vjuː/ *noun* the idea that political news reporters in the United Kingdom are more concerned with the activities of Parliament than with political events elsewhere

wf *abbreviation* a proofreading mark meaning 'wrong font'

WGA *abbreviation* **Writers Guild of America**

Whisky /'wɪski/ *noun* an internationally recognised code word for the letter W, used in radio communications

whisper microphone /'wɪspə ,maɪkrəfəʊn/ *noun* a small highly sensitive microphone with headphones, used especially by military or security personnel

whistleblower /'wɪs(ə)l,bləʊə/ *noun* a person who reveals information to the media about a scandal or other newsworthy secret

whistler /'wɪslə/ *noun* an interference signal in a radio receiver, resembling a whistling sound of decreasing pitch and caused by lightning or other electromagnetic disturbance

white /waɪt/ *verb* to put or leave blank spaces in something, especially something printed

white balancing /'waɪt ,bælənsɪŋ/ *noun* the process of balancing a camera to combine the three primary colours in the correct proportions, so that white always appears neutral

white coat rule /,waɪt 'kəʊt ,ruːl/ *noun* a rule for advertising on television stating that doctors or actors in white coats cannot promote medical products

white list /'waɪt lɪst/ *noun* a list of e-mail addresses, for example from friends or customers, to which somebody wants to permit access

white noise /'waɪt nɔɪz/ *noun* low-volume electrical or radio noise of equal intensity over a wide range of frequencies

white space /'waɪt speɪs/ *noun* an area of a page or other printed surface where no text or pictures appear

whizz-pan /'wɪz pæn/ *noun* a very fast panning camera movement that has the effect of blurring the frames

wide-angle /'waɪd ,æŋgəl/ *adjective* **1.** relating to or using a camera lens with an unusually wide field of view **2.** a wide-angle shot is one that shows a wider than usual view. Abbreviation **W/A**

wide screen /'waɪd skriːn/ *adjective* **1.** referring to a type of film projection in which the image is substantially wider than it is tall **2.** referring to a television whose screen is noticeably wider than average ■ *noun* an image that is substantially wider than it is tall, at a ratio of 16–9 rather than the usual 4–3

wide shot /'waɪd ʃɒt/ *noun* **1.** a camera shot that takes in a panoramic view of the set or an outside scene. Abbreviation **WS** **2.** a shot taken with a wide-angled lens, with a field of view of more than 60°

widow /'wɪdəʊ/ *noun* the first line of a paragraph, stranded at the bottom of a column or page while the rest of the paragraph is at the top of the next one. This is poor layout and to be avoided. Compare **orphan**

Wi-Fi /'waɪ faɪ/ *noun* technology in newer computers, mostly laptops, that allows them to connect to a wireless local area network or Internet connection. Also called **wireless Internet**

'Life, on the whole, is better without cables. So we should welcome cameras with wireless capabilities, like this one from Nikon. Exclusive to Jessops, this camera has wi-fi… if you're in an area with a wireless network, you can transmit images from your camera to your computer.' [Daniel Paddington, *The Independent*]

wild shooting /ˌwaɪld 'ʃuːtɪŋ/ *noun* shooting either picture or sound without synchronising the other to it

wild track /'waɪld træk/ *noun* same as **atmosphere**

Williams Committee Report on Obscenity and Film Censorship /'wɪljəmz/ *noun* a report on the state of laws concerning obscenity in the UK, especially on film censorship, which suggested that pornography does not have too great an effect on the values of society

wind machine /'wɪnd məˌʃiːn/ *noun* a device used to simulate the sound or effects of wind, for example a machine used backstage in a theatre

windshield /'wɪndʃiːld/ *noun* a protector used on a microphone to prevent wind noise

wind up /ˌwaɪnd 'ʌp/ *verb* to bring something such as an interview to a close

wipe /waɪp/ *noun* a way of mixing from one image to another in which neither fades, but the incoming image replaces the second in any of a variety of ways, such as 'opening up' from the centre or rushing in from the side. Compare **cross fade**

wipeout /'waɪpaʊt/ *noun* the receiving of a radio signal that is so strong it makes receiving other signals impossible

WIPO /'waɪpəʊ/ *abbreviation* **World Intellectual Property Organisation**

wired world /ˌwaɪəd 'wɜːld/ *noun* a view of communities and societies being globally interconnected by multiple telecommunications links

wireless /'waɪələs/ *adjective* using radio signals rather than wires ■ *noun* a radio or a radio set

Wireless Application Protocol /ˌwaɪələs ˌæplɪˈkeɪʃ(ə)n ˌprəʊtəʊkɒl/ *noun* full form of **WAP**

wireless Internet /ˌwaɪələs 'ɪntənet/ *noun* same as **Wi-Fi**

wireless local area network /ˌwaɪələs ˌləʊk(ə)l ˌeərɪə 'netwɜːk/ *noun* a local area network that uses high-frequency radio signals to connect computers within its range without the need for cables. Abbreviation **WLAN**

wireless telegraphy /ˌwaɪələs tə 'legrəfi/ *noun* early methods of sending messages to and from ships using radio waves, before the arrival of radio broadcasting into the home

wire recorder /'waɪə rɪˌkɔːdə/ *noun* an early type of magnetic recorder that used stainless steel wire instead of magnetic tape to record sound

wire service /'waɪə ˌsɜːvɪs/ *noun* news stories sent by computer from national and international news agencies

wiring /'waɪərɪŋ/ *noun* **1.** a network of electrical wires **2.** the act or process of installing a system of electrical wires

WLAN *abbreviation* **wireless local area network**

woman suffrage /ˌwʊmən 'sʌfrɪdʒ/ *noun* same as **women's suffrage**

women's liberation /ˌwɪmɪnz ˌlɪbə 'reɪʃ(ə)n/ *noun* a political movement intended to free women from oppression

women's movement /'wɪmɪnz ˌmuːvmənt/ *noun* a movement seeking to promote and improve the position of women in society

women's studies /'wɪmɪnz ˌstʌdiz/ *noun* a course of study examining the historical, economic and cultural roles and achievements of women

women's suffrage /ˌwɪmɪnz 'sʌfrɪdʒ/ *noun* the extension of equal rights to women with regard to voting, owning property etc. Also called **female suffrage**, **woman suffrage**

wordbreak /'wɜːdbreɪk/ *noun* the point in a word where it can be divided if there is not enough space at the end of a line for the entire word

word of mouth /ˌwɜːd əv 'maʊθ/ *noun* the way that cult media products become known, by people recommending them to their friends and through webpages etc., instead of through mainstream advertising

'At first, the reputation of Antony and the Johnsons was a slow-burning, word-of-mouth thing. For myself, it was a chance meeting with Andres Lokko (effectively Sweden's John Peel) at a pop singer's wedding, who said "I think you'd like this". It was a self-selecting thing: people recommended A&TJ to people who would "understand".'
[Simon Price, *The Independent on Sunday*]

work experience /'wɜːk ɪkˌspɪəriəns/ *noun* a period of time spent in a place of work such as a newspaper office or television studio, observing how others carry out their jobs and sometimes undertaking small tasks. It is usually unpaid, but provides valuable experience of the workplace, and can often be a stepping stone to a permanent position. Also called **attachment**, **internship**

workie /'wɜːki/ *noun* a person doing work experience (*informal*)

work print /'wɜːk prɪnt/ *noun* a print of a film used in various stages of editing and as a guide in cutting the original negative from which the final commercial prints are made

World Association of Newspapers /ˌwɜːld əˌsəʊsieɪʃ(ə)n əv 'njuːzpeɪpəz/ *noun* a non-profit international association based in Paris, protecting the rights of newspaper agencies and publications and promoting press freedom and communication (formerly the Fédération Internationale des Editeurs de Journaux et Publications). Abbreviation **WAN**

World Intellectual Property Organisation /ˌwɜːld ˌɪntələktʃuəl 'prɒpəti ˌɔːgənaɪzeɪʃ(ə)n/ *noun* a global organisation that is dedicated to protecting intellectual property rights in its 182 member states. Abbreviation **WIPO**

World Press Freedom Committee /ˌwɜːld 'pres ˌfriːdəm kəˌmɪti/ *noun* an alliance of more than 30 international press and news publishing agencies in defence of journalistic freedom

World Trade Organisation /ˌwɜːld 'treɪd ˌɔːgənaɪzeɪʃ(ə)n/ *noun* an organisation that deals with trade disputes between countries and seeks to establish free and fair trade. Abbreviation **WTO**

World Wide Web /ˌwɜːld ˌwaɪd 'web/ *noun* the entire array of websites available through computers over the Internet

World Wide Web Consortium /ˌwɜːld waɪd 'web kənˌsɔːtiəm/ *noun* ONLINE full form of **W3C**

wow /waʊ/ *noun* a distortion in recorded sound in the form of slow fluctuations in the pitch of long notes, caused by variations in the speed of the reproducing or recording equipment

wow factor /'waʊ ˌfæktə/ *noun* the ability of a advertisement to impress its audience and remain in the memory

wrap /ræp/ *noun* **1.** the conclusion of a piece of filming, either for the end of the day or for the end of the entire production **2.** a news item consisting of a short interview or sound bite with the presenter giving a link before and after

wraparound /'ræpəˌraʊnd/, **wrapround** *noun* a plate of flexible material that can be attached to the cylinder of a rotary press

wrapper /'ræpə/ *noun* a piece of paper wrapped around a magazine or newspaper sent by post

write /raɪt/ *verb* to create books, poems or newspaper articles for publication, often as part of a job

write head /'raɪt hed/ *noun* part of a disk drive or other recording mechanism which can write data onto a tape or disk

write out /ˌraɪt 'aʊt/ *verb* to remove a regular character from a radio or television series

writer /'raɪtə/ *noun* a person who creates an original story or adapts another story for the purposes of making a script

writerly /'raɪtəli/ *adjective* referring to a text that moves away from the expected norms of structure, character, plot development etc. in a way that may be confusing to the reader. Compare **readerly**

Writers Guild of America /ˌraɪtəz ˌgɪld əv ə'merɪkə/ *noun* the trade union which represents scriptwriters in the US, protecting their rights to a fair wage and to be properly credited for their work. Abbreviation **WGA**

write-up /'raɪt ʌp/ *noun* a written account of material, especially a published review of a new play, book, or film

WS *abbreviation* **wide shot**

WTO *abbreviation* **World Trade Organisation**

www *abbreviation* **World Wide Web**

XYZ

X /eks/ *noun* a censorship classification used in the UK until 1982 for films that could not be shown publicly to anyone under 18 and until 1990 in the United States for films considered unsuitable for under-17s

xerography /zɪəˈrɒgrəfi/ *noun* photocopying using an electrically-charged plate to transfer ink powder to paper

x-height /ˈeks haɪt/ *noun* the height of the lowercase letter 'x' in a typeface, used as a measure of the height of the main body of all lowercase letters in that typeface

Xinhua news agency /ʃɪnˌwɑː ˈnjuːz ˌeɪdʒənsi/ *noun* the major national and international news agency in China, which releases news in seven languages

X-rated /ˈeks ˌreɪtɪd/ *adjective* referring to something that has a high level of sexual or violent content. ◊ **X**

X-ray /ˈeks ˌreɪ/ *noun* an internationally recognised code word for the letter X, used in radio communications

yagi /ˈjɑːgi/ *noun US* a directional radio or television aerial consisting of several components arranged in line

Yahoo! /jɑːˈhuː/ *noun* a computer services company that offers free e-mail and is the most-visited web portal on the Internet

Yankee /ˈjæŋki/ *noun* an internationally recognised code word for the letter Y, used in radio communications

Y/C /ˌwaɪ ˈsiː/ *noun* two parts of a video signal representing the luminance (Y) and the chrominance (C) parts of the image

Y/C delay /ˌwaɪ ˈsiː dɪˌleɪ/ *noun* an error caused by wrong synchronisation between the luma and chroma signals in a video transmission, seen as a colour halo around objects on the screen

yearly /ˈjɪəli/ *noun* something that happens or appears once a year, especially an annual publication

yellow /ˈjeləʊ/ *adjective* using scandalous or sensational material, often greatly exaggerating or distorting the truth

yellow journalism /ˈjeləʊ ˌdʒɜːn(ə)lɪz(ə)m/ *noun* a style of journalism that makes unscrupulous use of scandalous or sensationalised stories to attract readers

'[Actress] Karki took her life after the weekly tabloid Jana Aastha published what it said was a picture of her in the nude. King Gyanendra wrote to Lokendra Bahadur Chand, the prime minister, asking him to change the law to control "yellow journalism".' [Michael Sheridan, *The Sunday Times*]

yellow press /ˈjeləʊ pres/ *noun* collectively, the newspapers that make unscrupulous use of scandalous or sensationalised stories to attract readers

yoke /jəʊk/ *noun* equipment for recording or reproducing sounds or music on more than one track simultaneously, by joining together two or more magnetic recording heads

youth market /ˈjuːθ ˌmɑːkɪt/ *noun* the potential market for a product which is specifically aimed at (usually) 18–35 year olds

YUV encoding /ˌwaɪ juː ˈviː ɪn ˌkəʊdɪŋ/ *noun* a video encoding system in which the video luminance (Y) signal is recorded at full bandwidth but the chrominance signals (U&V) are recorded at half their bandwidth

zap /zæp/ *verb* to change channels on a television set using a remote control device, especially to change channels rapidly ■ *interjection* used especially in comic books to indicate sudden and violent force

zapping /'zæpɪŋ/ *noun* **1.** flicking between television channels using a remote control, looking for something interesting **2.** changing channels during commercial breaks to avoid watching the advertisements

'...we would be far less likely to reach for the remote control if we were watching people we could imagine sleeping with... aware that people are never more than a hair's breadth from zapping channels, [producers] exploit our weakness. So it was goodbye Noel Edmonds and Mike Read and hello Cat Deeley and Gail Porter.' [David Hepworth, *The Mail on Sunday*]

zarzuela /ˌzɑːzuˈelə/ *noun* Spanish musical theatre, usually comic, combining dialogue, music and dance

zine /ziːn/ *noun* a self-published paper, Internet magazine or other periodical, issued at irregular intervals with and usually appealing to a specialist readership

Zinoviev letter 1924 /zɪ'nɒviev/ *noun* a forged letter that was leaked to the UK government in 1924 before the general election, discrediting the socialists by alleging communist links and plans for military action

zipping /'zɪpɪŋ/ *noun* fast-forwarding through commercial breaks on recorded programmes during playback, thereby avoiding the advertising

Zircon affair /'zɜːkɒn əˌfeə/ *noun* an incident of attempted censorship by the UK government of a television programme about the proposed launch of a spy satellite, Zircon, in 1987. The police raided the programme makers' offices and seized tapes, although the programme was later proven not to actually reveal any state secrets.

zoetrope /'zəʊətrəʊp/ *noun* an early method of simulating moving pictures by mounting them on the inside of a spinning wheel, with slots for viewing

zoom /zuːm/ *noun* **1.** same as **zoom lens 2.** a shot in which a zoom lens is used to make the object in focus appear to move closer or farther away while the camera itself stays still

zoom in /ˌzuːm 'ɪn/ *verb* to make an object appear bigger or closer, or to decrease the area in view, by use of a zoom lens or a graphic imaging device

zoom lens /'zuːm lenz/ *noun* a lens that can be adjusted to have a longer or shorter focal length. Also called **zoom**. Compare **prime lens**

zoom out /ˌzuːm 'aʊt/ *verb* to make an object appear smaller or farther away, or to increase the area in view, by use of a zoom lens or a graphic imaging device

zouk /zuːk/ *noun* a style of dance music originating in Guadeloupe and Martinique and played with guitars and synthesisers, combining a strong fast disco beat and Caribbean rhythms

Zulu /'zuːluː/ *noun* an internationally recognised code word for the letter Z, used in radio communications

zydeco /'zaɪdekəʊ/ *noun* a style of dance music originating in Louisiana that is usually played on accordion, guitar and violin and combines traditional French melodies with Caribbean and blues influences

SUPPLEMENTS

Communications Theorists
Media Resources on the Web
Media Law in the UK
National Daily Newspapers in the UK
Major Magazines in the UK

Communications Theorists

Name	Specialisations	Major Works
Louis Althusser	Marxism, ideological state apparatuses	*Ideology and Ideological State Apparatuses* (1977); *Marxism and Humanism* (1969); *Contradiction and Overdetermination* (1962)
Ien Ang	media audiences, identity politics, globalisation, ethnicity and representation	*On Not Speaking Chinese: Living Between Asia and the West* (2001); *Desperately Seeking the Audience* (1991); *Living Room Wars: Rethinking Media Audiences for a Postmodern World* (1996)
Roland Barthes	effects of the mass media, creation of meaning; the pleasure of reading	*Mythologies* (1957); *The Pleasure of the Text* (1973)
Daniel Bell	effects of the mass media, modernity	*Cultural Contradictions of Capitalism* (1996); *The End of Ideology* (2000)
Daniel Biltereyst	controversial media works, censorship, film classification, reality television	published widely in journals such as *European Journal of Communication*, *Media, Culture & Society*, *Journal of International Communication*, *Intercom* and *Cultural Policy*
J.G. Blumler	audience interaction with media texts – co-author of the uses and gratifications theory	*The Uses of Mass Communication* (with E. Katz) (1974); *Television In Politics* (with D. McQuail) (1979); *The Role of Theory in Uses and Gratifications Studies* (article in *Communication Research*, 6)
Pierre Bourdieu	cultural sociology, especially the notion of cultural capital	*La Distinction* (1979); *The Logic of Practice* (1990)
Manuel Castells	sociology of media, Marxist theory	*The Urban Question. A Marxist Approach* (1977); *City, Class and Power* (1978); *The Power of Identity*, *The Information Age: Economy, Society and Culture*, Vol. II. (2004)

Communications Theorists *continued*

Name	Specialisations	Major Works
Noam Chomsky	power structures of media institutions; mainstream mass media, globalisation	*Manufacturing Consent: The Political Economy of the Mass Media* (1988); *Media Control* (2002); *Hegemony or Survival: America's Quest for Global Dominance* (2003); *Understanding Power* (2002); *Necessary Illusions: Thought Control in Democratic Societies* (1989) and many others
James Curran	globalisation, mass communication	*Mass Media and Society* (2005); *Culture Wars: The Media and the British Left* (2005); *De-Westernising Media Studies* (ed.) (2000)
Jan A.G.M. van Dijk	new media; social and cultural effects of technology	*The Network Society* (1999); *Digital Democracy* (2000); *The Deepening Divide, Inequality in the Information Society* (2005)
Marjorie Ferguson	globalisation of media, media technologies; representation of women in the media	*Forever Feminine: Women's Magazines and the Cult of Femininity* (1983); *Cultural Studies in Question* (with P. Golding) (1997), editor of several journals including *Culture and Communication* and *Journal of Communication*
John Fiske	discourse surrounding media events, generation of meaning	*Media Matters* (1996); *Understanding Popular Culture* (1989); *Television Culture* (1987)
George Gerbner	media and culture – creator of cultivation theory	*The Global Media Debate* (1993), author and editor of many journal articles and collections
Peter Golding	media and European culture	*European Culture and the Media* (2004); editor of the *European Journal of Communication*

Communications Theorists *continued*

Name	Specialisations	Major Works
Antonio Gramsci	Marxism, hegemony, power struggle through ideas	various articles in Italian journals including *L'Ordine Nuovo* and *Avanti!*
Klaus Bruhn Jensen	research methodology in communications theory	*Handbook of Media and Communications Research* (2002); *A Handbook of Qualitative Methodologies for Mass Communication Research* (with N. Jankowski)
Elihu Katz	diffusion of ideas through mass media, globalisation, communication models – co-creator of the two-step flow model	*Media Events* (1992); *The Export of Meaning* (1990); *Personal Influence: The Part Played by People in the Flow of Mass Communications* (with Lazarsfeld) (1956)
Paul Lazarsfeld	communication models – co-creator of the two-step flow model; audience research methods	*The People's Choice* (1948); *Personal Influence: The Part Played by People in the Flow of Mass Communications* (with Katz) (1956)
Tamar Liebes	decoding media texts, perception, cultural anthropology	*The Export of Meaning* (with Katz) (1999); *Media, Ritual and Identity* (ed) (1998)
Denis McQuail	theories of mass media and communication, communication models, the effect of media texts on their audience	*Communication Models* (1981); *Mass Communication Theory* (1983); *Media Performance* (1992)
David Morley	audience research, communications technologies, cultural imperialism	*Home Territories: media, mobility and identity* (2000); *The Nationwide Television Studies* (with C. Brunsdon) (1999)
Kaarle Nordenstreng	theory of communication, international communication, media ethics	editor and author of many reports, papers and journal articles

Communications Theorists *continued*

Name	Specialisations	Major Works
Neil Postman	media technology (its limitations and dangers)	*Amusing Ourselves to Death* (1985); *Conscientious Objections* (1992); *The End of Education* (1996)
Philip Schlesinger	media and politics, media ethics	*Open Scotland?* (2001); *Women Viewing Violence* (2002); *Putting 'Reality' Together: BBC News* (2002)
W. Schramm	mass communications	*Process and Effects of Mass Communications* (ed. with D. F. Roberts) (1954)
Stuart Hall	Marxism, ideology and ideological state apparatuses, interpretation of texts	*Policing the Crisis* (1978); *Encoding/Decoding* (1980)
J. Tomlinson	globalisation of media	*Globalisation and Culture* (1999); *Media and Modernity* (1995); *Cultural Imperialism* (1991)
Jeremy Tunstall	the state of British national and regional media, power hierarchies in media organisations, the relationship between the British and American media	*The Anglo-American Media Connection* (with David Machin) (1999); *Newspaper Power: The New National Press in Britain* (1996); *Media Moguls* (1991)
Lisbeth van Zoonen	feminism and gender representation in the media	articles in collections including *Questioning The Media* (J. Downing et al) (1995)

Media Resources on the Web

Copyright and Intellectual Property

Information on protecting Intellectual Property:
www.intellectual-property.gov.uk

World Intellectual Property Organisation:
www.wipo.int

The UK Patent Office (information on copyrights, trademarks and patents):
www.patent.gov.uk

The European Patent Office:
www.european-patent-office.org

Alternative to patenting:
www.researchdisclosure.com

The Copyright Licensing Agency:
www.cla.co.uk

Mechanical Copyright Protection Agency AND the Performing Right Society:
www.mcps-prs-alliance.co.uk

Media Law

Office of Public Sector Information (the full texts of all statutes):
www.opsi.gov.uk

Overview of media laws and reports:
www.terramedia.co.uk/law

Media Training

Official guide to NVQs:
www.dfes.gov.uk/nvq

BBC online guide to media training, including free online courses:
www.bbctraining.com

Helpful guide to further education, choosing the right course etc:
www.aimhigher.ac.uk

Media Resources on the Web *continued*

International News Agencies

Agence France-Presse (France):
www.afp.com/english/home

All Headline News (web-based):
www.allheadlinenews.com

Associated Press (USA):
www.ap.org

Austral International (Australia):
www.australpress.com.au/home.html

Bloomberg L. P. (financial news)
www.bloomberg.com

British Broadcasting Corporation:
http://news.bbc.co.uk

Cable News Network:
www.cnn.com

Canadian Press:
www.cp.org

China News Service:
www.chinanews.cn

Deutsche Presse-Agentur (Germany):
www.dpa.de

EFE (Spain):
www.efenews.com

Inter Press Service:
www.ipsnews.net

ITAR-TASS (Russia):
www.itar-tass.com/eng

Kyodo News:
http://home.kyodo.co.jp

Pacific News Service (alternative news):
http://news.pacificnews.org/news

Press Association (UK):
www.pressassociation.co.uk

Press Trust of India:
www.ptinews.com

Reuters:
www.reuters.com

United Press International:
www.upi.com

Xinhua News Agency (China):
www.xinhuanet.com/english

Zenit (the news agency of the Roman Catholic Church):
www.zenit.org/english

Films and Festivals

Academy of Motion Picture Arts and Sciences:
www.oscars.org

British Academy of Film and Television Arts:
www.bafta.org

British Board of Film Classification:
www.bbfc.co.uk

British Film Institute:
www.bfi.org.uk

Cannes Film Festival:
www.festival-cannes.fr

Cannes International Advertising Festival:
www.canneslions.com

DreamWorks SKG:
www.dreamworks.com

Metro-Goldwyn-Meyer:
www.mgm.com

Motion Picture Association of America:
www.mpaa.org

New Line Cinema:
www.newline.com

Sony Pictures (formerly Columbia Pictures):
www.sonypictures.com

Sundance Film Festival:
www.sundance.org

Toronto International Film Festival:
www.e.bell.ca/filmfest

Touchstone Pictures:
http://touchstone.movies.go.com

20th Century Fox:
www.foxmovies.com

Universal Studios:
www.universalstudios.com

Walt Disney Pictures:
http://disney.go.com/disneypictures

Warner Bros:
www.warnerbros.com

Media Resources on the Web *continued*

Press Organisations

Audit Bureau of Circulations:
www.abc.co.uk

International Federation of Journalists:
www.ifj.org

Joint Industrial Committee of Regional Newspapers:
www.jicreg.co.uk

Joint National Readership Survey:
www.jnrs.ie

National Readership Survey:
www.nrs.co.uk

Press Complaints Commission:
www.pcc.org.uk

Reporters Sans Frontières:
www.rsf.org

Royal Photographic Society:
www.rps.org

World Association of Newspapers:
www.wan-press.org

Broadcasting

Advertising Standards Authority:
www.asa.org.uk/asa

Broadcasters' Audience Research Board (BARB):
www.barb.co.uk

CEEFAX:
www.ceefax.tv

Corporation for Public Broadcasting:
www.cpb.org

Office of Communications – OFCOM:
www.ofcom.org.uk

Paper Tiger TV:
www.papertiger.org

Radio Joint Audience Research – RAJAR:
www.rajar.co.uk

Taylor Nelson Sofres plc (TNS):
www.tnsofres.com

TiVo:
www.tivo.com

Telecommunications

Community Media Association:
www.commedia.org.uk

European Cable Communications Association:
www.ecca.be

Federal Communications Commission:
www.fcc.gov

Unions and Campaigns

American Federation of Television and Radio Artists:
www.aftra.com

Broadcasting Entertainment Cinematograph and Theatre Union:
www.bectu.org.uk

Campaign for Press and Broadcasting Freedom:
www.cpbf.org.uk

International Telecommunication Union:
www.itu.nit/home

Mediawatch-uk:
www.mediawatch.org

National Union of Journalists:
www.nuj.org.uk

Producers' Alliance for Cinema and Television:
www.pact.co.uk

Producers' Guild of America:
www.producersguild.org

Royal Television Society:
www.rts.org.uk

Society of Motion Picture and Television Engineers:
www.smpte.org

World Press Freedom Committee:
www.wpfc.org

World Trade Organisation:
www.wto.org

Writers' Guild of America:
www.wga.org

Media Law in the UK

Press

Criminal Justice Act 1925:
> made it illegal to take photographs or make sketches inside a court-room (although it is still legal to make later sketches from memory and publish them)

Race Relations Act 1976:
> made it an offence to discriminate against people on grounds of race, or to publish or distribute any material which does this

Contempt Of Court Act 1981:
> made it illegal to film court proceedings, or to report anything which may prejudice a trial

Public Order Act 1986:
> made it an offence to publish or distribute material intended to stir up 'racial hatred' against citizens of Great Britain

Criminal Justice Act (Section 11) 1988:
> gave leave to the press to officially appeal against reporting restrictions under the Contempt of Court Act 1981

Official Secrets Act 1989:
> made it an offence to disclose official information which may be damaging or against the public interest, such as military secrets

Sexual Offences (Amendment) Act 1992:
> made it illegal to publish anything which may reveal the identity of a victim of a sexual offence

Defamation Act 1996:
> stated that the author, editor or publisher of a work must take 'reasonable care' to avoid publishing defamatory statements, in print or on the Internet

Human Rights Act (article 8) 1998:
> protected the privacy of citizens from intrusion, surveillance, harassment etc by the press

Human Rights Act (article 10) 1998:
> defends the right to freedom of expression

Youth Justice And Criminal Evidence Act 1999:
> made it illegal to publish anything which may reveal the identity of an accused or convicted young offender

Anti-Terrorism, Crime and Security Act 2001:
> expanded the crime of 'racial hatred' in the Public Order Act 1986 to include that against citizens of other countries; introduced the offence of inciting hatred against those with different religious views

Radio / Television Broadcasting

Television Act 1954:
> established the Independent Television Authority to regulate television broadcasts

The Marine, etc, Broadcasting (Offences) Act 1967:
> made broadcasting from ships and off-shore equipment illegal

Sound Broadcasting Act 1972:
> renamed the Independent Television Authority the Independent Broadcasting Authority; established local commercial radio broadcasting to be licensed by the IBA

Media Law in the UK *continued*

Broadcasting Act 1980:
> allowed the IBA to set up Channel 4

Public Order Act 1986:
> made it an offence to broadcast or perform material intended to stir up 'racial hatred' against citizens of Great Britain

Consumer Protection Act 1987:
> banned the use of misleading wording in advertisements which encourages people to buy

EU Directive 89/552 1989:
> introduced rules governing international broadcasts and fair competition across the EU

Broadcasting Act 1990:
> introduced new licensing framework for broadcasters; set up two new regulatory bodies (Independent Television Commission and the Radio Authority); made provisions for greater quality control and more independent output on commercial television

EU Directive 93/83 1993:
> defined satellite transmission; set rules for cable retransmission of broadcasts

Criminal Justice and Public Order Act 1994:
> extended powers of censorship under the Protection of Children Act 1978 to include doctored images purporting to show indecent acts (even where none had taken place); introduced harsher penalties for unclassified videos; introduced the notion of 'harm' caused to the viewer by watching depictions of sex, violence, crime etc

Broadcasting Act 1996:
> paved the way for digital broadcasting and multiplex licenses; introduced rules on cross-media ownership; formed the Broadcasting Standards Commission

Communications Act 2003:
> formed OFCOM by merging 5 older regulatory bodies; relaxed rules on cross-media ownership

Film

Cinematograph Act 1909:
> introduced licensing and safety regulations for private cinemas

Cinematograph Film Act 1927:
> established a quota of British films which must be exhibited in UK cinemas, first 7.5%, later lifted to 20% (no longer in force)

Sunday Entertainments Act 1932
> established a fund to promote cinema as a means of entertainment, which originally funded the British Film Institute

Cinematograph Films (Animals) Act 1937:
> made it illegal to depict actual cruelty to animals in film

British Film Institute Act 1949:
> introduced government grants for the British Film Institute

Obscene Publications Act 1959:
> defined obscene works as any which 'tend to deprave or corrupt' and allowed for official censorship of these

Protection of Children Act 1978:
>made it illegal to own, broadcast or distribute indecent images of children (under 16 years of age)

Cinematograph (Amendment) Act 1982:
>covers regulations for the public exhibition of pornographic films

Video Recordings Act 1984:
>introduced compulsory age classifications for videos, administered by the British Board of Film Classification

Films Act 1985:
>introduced regulations for the designation of films as British and funding of these

Cinemas Act 1985:
>introduced the current regulations governing the exhibition of films and licensing of cinemas

Finance (No.2) Act 1997:
>made provision for tax breaks for British independent film makers on productions costing less than £15 million

Telecommunications

Wireless Telegraphy Act 1949:
>defined wireless broadcasting (the sending of electro-magnetic signals without the use of a dedicated communications line) and introduced the need to hold a licence to do this commercially

Wireless Telegraphy Act 1967:
>allowed information on the sale or hire of televisions to be made available to the Secretary of State

British Telecommunications Act 1981:
>separated British Telecom from the Post Office and made it a stand-alone telecommunications corporation; allowed competition to BT from other providers

Telecommunications Act 1984:
>introduced regulatory bodies for broadcast media; formed OFTEL

Cable And Broadcasting Act 1984:
>established the Cable Authority for regulation of cable transmission services

Telecommunications (Fraud) Act 1997:
>made it an offence to possess any equipment related to tele-communications systems which is intended to be used for fraud

Media Law in the UK *continued*

Data Protection

Data Protection Act 1984:
> introduced regulations on the storage, security and transferring of personal information of individuals held electronically by companies

Data Protection Act 1998:
> expanded the 1984 Act to cover manual as well as electronic records; introduced the notions of 'sensitive' data and accountability of directors for company transgressions

Freedom of Information Act 2000:
> allowed access by members of the public to any and all information held by public bodies

Regulation of Investigatory Powers Act 2000:
> allowed those in authority to access and monitor all personal e-mail and telephone communications; forbade encryption which makes this difficult

Anti-Terrorism, Crime and Security Act 2001:
> allowed authorities greater access to personal information about suspected terrorists

Copyright

Copyright Act 1956:
> set up copyright protection for all original literary, dramatic, musical or artistic works made in the UK under the control of the Government

Copyright, Designs And Patents Act 1988:
> introduced the rights for the author of a work to be identified as such, and to not suffer harm to their reputation through mistreatment of their works

EU Directive 92/100 1992:
> clarified intellectual property rights in relation to copying or distribution of a person's work

EU Directive 93/98 1993:
> made copyright periods uniform throughout the EU, extending post-mortem copyright protection of a work from 50 to 70 years in the UK

Trademarks Act 1994:
> made provision for registration of trademarks and sets out guidelines for what constitutes infringement

National Newspapers in the UK

Daily Newspapers

Daily Express   *Circulation: 810,827*
Northern & Shell Building, 10 Lower Thames Street,
London EC4R 6EN.
Tel. 0871-434 1010
www.express.co.uk

Daily Mail   *Circulation: 2,350,694*
Northcliffe House, 2 Derry Street,
London W8 5TT.
Tel. 020-7938 6000
www.dailymail.co.uk

Daily Mirror   *Circulation: 1,684,660*
1 Canada Square, Canary Wharf, London E14 5AP.
Tel. 020-7293 3000
www.mirror.co.uk

Daily Record   *Circulation: 454,247*
1 Central Quay, Glasgow G3 8DA.
Tel. 0141-309 3000
www.dailyrecord.co.uk

Daily Sport   *Circulation: no figures available*
19 Great Ancoats Street, Manchester M60 4BT.
Tel. 0161-236 4466
www.dailysport.co.uk

Daily Star   *Circulation: 820,028*
Ludgate House, 245 Blackfriars Road,
London SE1 9UX.
Tel. 020-7928 8000
www.dailystar.co.uk

The Daily Telegraph   *Circulation: 901,667*
1 Canada Square, Canary Wharf, London E14 5DT.
Tel. 020-7538 5000
www.telegraph.co.uk

Financial Times   *Circulation: 419,249*
1 Southwark Bridge, London SE1 9HL.
Tel. 020-7873 3000
www.ft.com

The Guardian   *Circulation: 403,297*
119 Farringdon Road, London EC1R 3ER.
Tel. 020-7278 2332
www.guardian.co.uk

The Herald   *Circulation: 75,541*
Newsquest Ltd, 200 Renfield Street, Glasgow G2 3PR.
Tel. 0141-302 7000
www.theherald.co.uk

The Independent   *Circulation: 267,037*
Independent House, 191 Marsh Wall,
London E14 9RS.
Tel. 020-7005 2000
www.independent.co.uk

Morning Star   *Circulation: no figures available*
People's Press Printing Society Ltd, William Rust House, 52 Beachy Road,
London E3 2NS.
Tel. 020-8510 0815
www.morningstaronline.co.uk

Racing Post   *Circulation: 74,552*
Trinity Mirror, Floor 23, One Canada Square, Canary Wharf,
London E14 5AP.
Tel. 020-7293 3291
www.racingpost.co.uk

The Scotsman   *Circulation: 65,194*
Barclay House, 108 Holyrood Road, Edinburgh EH8 8AS.
Tel. 0131-620 8620
www.scotsman.com

The Sun   *Circulation: 3,224,427*
News Group Newspapers Ltd, Virginia Street, London E1 9XP.
Tel. 020-7782 4000
www.the-sun.co.uk

The Times   *Circulation: 703,492*
1 Pennington Street, London E98 1TT.
Tel. 020-7782 5000
www.timesonline.co.uk

Weekly Newspapers

The Business   *Circulation: 178,528*
292 Vauxhall Bridge Road, London SW1V 1DE.
Tel. 020-7961 0000
www.thebusinessonline.com

Daily Star Sunday   *Circulation: 404,723*
Express Newspapers, Ludgate House, 245 Blackfriars Road, London SE1 9UX.
Tel. 020-7928 8000
www.megastar.co.uk

The Independent on Sunday   *Circulation: 230,053*
Independent House, 191 Marsh Wall, London E14 9RS.
Tel. 020-7005 2000
www.independent.co.uk

The Mail on Sunday   *Circulation: 2,292,258*
Northcliffe House, 2 Derry Street, London W8 5TS.
Tel. 020-7938 6000
www.mailonsunday.co.uk

News of the World   *Circulation: 3,773,705*
1 Virginia Street, London E98 1NW.
Tel. 020-7782 1000
www.newsoftheworld.co.uk

The Observer   *Circulation: 451,781*
3-7 Herbal Hill, London EC1R 5EJ.
Tel. 020-7278 2332
www.observer.co.uk

National Newspapers in the UK *continued*

The People   *Circulation: 905,494*
1 Canada Square, Canary Wharf, London E14 5AP. Tel. 020-7293 3000
www.people.co.uk

Scotland on Sunday   *Circulation: 84,192*
108 Holyrood Road, Edinburgh EH8 8AS. Tel. 0131-620 8620
www.scotlandonsunday.co.uk

Sunday Express   *Circulation: 829,064*
Northern & Shell Building, 10 Lower Thames Street, London EC4R 6EN.
Tel. 0871-434 1010
www.express.co.uk

Sunday Herald   *Circulation: 58,140*
200 Renfield Street, Glasgow G2 3QB.
Tel. 0141-302 7800
www.sundayherald.com

Sunday Mail   *Circulation: 549,129*
1 Central Quay, Glasgow G3 8DA.
Tel. 0141-309 3000
www.sundaymail.com

Sunday Mirror   *Circulation: 1,457,792*
1 Canada Square, Canary Wharf, London E14 5AP.
Tel. 020-7293 3000
www.sundaymirror.co.uk

The Sunday Post   *Circulation: no figures available*
D. C. Thomson & Co. Ltd, 144 Port Dundas Road, Glasgow G4 0HZ.
Tel. 0141-332 9933
www.sundaypost.com

Sunday Sport   *Circulation: 148,385*
840 Melton Road, Thurmaston, Leicester LE4 8BE.
Tel. 0116-269 4892
www.sundaysport.com

The Sunday Telegraph   *Circulation: 661,425*
1 Canada Square, Canary Wharf, London E14 5DT.
Tel. 020-7538 5000
www.telegraph.co.uk

The Sunday Times   *Circulation: 1,404,616*
1 Virginia Street, London E1 9BD.
Tel. 020-7782 4000
www.timesonline.co.uk

The Sunday Times Scotland   *Circulation: no figures available*
Times Newspapers Ltd, 124 Portman Street, Kinning Park, Glasgow G41 1EJ.
 Tel. 0141-420 5100
www.timesonline.co.uk

Wales on Sunday   *Circulation: no figures available*
Thomson House, Havelock Street, Cardiff CF10 1XR.
Tel. 029-2058 3583
www.icwales.co.uk

(circulation figures net average October 2005, courtesy of the Audit Bureau of
Circulations – see www.abc.org.uk for further details)